Bodies Politic

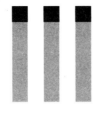

Bodies Politic

Negotiating Race in the American North, 1730–1830

John Wood Sweet

University of Pennsylvania Press

PHILADELPHIA

Originally published 2003 by The Johns Hopkins University Press
Copyright © 2003 John Wood Sweet

Printed in the United States of America on acid-free paper

10   9   8   7   6   5   4   3   2   1

Published 2006 by
University of Pennsylvania Press
Philadelphia, Pennsylvania 19104-4112

A Cataloging-in-Publication record is available from the Library of Congress

ISBN-13: 978-0-8122-1978-4
ISBN-10: 0-8122-1978-3

CONTENTS

ILLUSTRATIONS

ACKNOWLEDGMENTS

In many ways, I owe this project to the town where I grew up, Concord, Massachusetts—a community where everyone knows that ethnic identities are not simply black and white, where my brothers and I used to manufacture fake Indian artifacts for our parents to dig up in the garden, and where I spent many, many hours exploring the untold treasures of the Free Public Library. But it was only when I got to college and benefited from the tremendous generosity and enthusiasm of Bob Gross that I considered pursuing history as a profession.

It was at graduate school at Princeton that this book really began. The faculty and fellow students there—including Sharon Block, Natalie Zemon Davis, Jesús Escobar, Walter Johnson, Derek Krueger, Frank Ordiway, Nell Irvin Painter, and Moshe Sluhovsky—provided friendship, intellectual excitement, and models of professionalism. Nell Painter has consistently been a savvy advisor, an exemplar of professional courage, and an inspiring mentor. During my time at Princeton, I was supported by a generous university graduate fellowship and by grants from Amherst College, the Andrew W. Mellon Foundation, the Library Company of Philadelphia, and the Massachusetts Historical Society. Most of all, I am grateful to John M. Murrin, my advisor. His expansive vision of the field broadened my horizons, his confidence encouraged me to take on a challenging project, and his amazing ability to avoid the appearance of giving advice helped me to become more independent. In both public seminars and private conversations, I have always been inspired by his ability to focus on what is best in scholarship and his knack for suggesting new ways of putting it to use.

The research on which this project is based depended on the knowledge, patience, and resourcefulness of many archivists and librarians. Among those who were most crucial to my work was Phillip Lapsansky at the Library Company of Philadelphia, whose knowledge of African Americana is unparalleled. I also benefited from the help of Cynthia Bendroth and Rick Stadtler at the Rhode Island Historical Society; Carol Pace at the Providence City Archives; Elizabeth Bouvier at the Massachusetts Supreme Court Archives; Philip Budlong at Mystic Seaport; Nicholas Graham and Peter Drummey at the Massachusetts Historical Society; Bonnie Lillienfeld at the National Museum of American History; and Ray Rickman and Joaquina Bela Teixeria of the Rhode Island Black Heritage Society. All this research was made possible by financial support from a number of institutions, including Princeton University, the Catholic University of America, the Rhode Island Historical Society, the American Historical Association, the David Library of the American Revolution, the Library Company of Philadelphia, the Historical Society of Pennsylvania, and the American Philosophical Society. Most of all, this work is indebted to Stephen Grimes, archivist of the Rhode Island Supreme Court Judicial Records Center in Pawtucket. This facility had just opened when I began my research, and for the first time it brought together all the state's legal records in a professionally managed archive; but the records I most wanted to see were not readily accessible. In a terrific act of trust, Stephen allowed me to paw through hundreds of boxes of colonial file papers that had been damaged during the hurricane of 1938 and closed to public access ever since. The next several months were as exciting as they were dusty!

While finishing my dissertation and, later, while working to revise and expand the project, I was grateful for opportunities to work in a number of different academic communities. At the John Nicholas Brown Center for the Study of American Civilization, I enjoyed the savvy, good cheer, and friendship of executive director Joyce Botelho. I was also enriched by friendships with Matthew Bird, Peter Hocking, and Pierre Saint-Amand. During this time I met Ramón Gutiérrez, who has been a much valued mentor and friend over the years. And it was at the JNBC, years ago, that I first met Lucy Barber. When I have been faced with challenges finishing my dissertation, surviving the job market, learning how to teach, and writing this book, Lucy has always been an inspiring role model and a steadfast supporter. She read this entire manuscript—often in multiple drafts—and along the way taught me a great deal not only about structuring stories but also about the meaning of friendship, sanity, biking, dogs, and mud baths.

After receiving my degree, I spent a year at the Johns Hopkins Center for the Study of History, Culture, and Power, where I was challenged to refine my ways of thinking by historians, anthropologists, and literary critics—particularly Herman Bennet, Toby Ditz, Kirsten Fischer, Jack Greene, Michael Johnson, and my old college friend Maria Farland. It was also during that year that I met Henry Abelove, whose acuity I admire and whose friendship I enjoy but whose concision I suspect I may never successfully emulate. As I began a new life in Washington, D.C., it was my pleasure to meet John Guillory, a fellow commuter to Baltimore, and the ever fabulous Ann Little, who was teaching in D.C. that year. During my time in Washington, I happily renewed my old friendship with Kate Jansen—who has been a wonderful and generous colleague. Clarence Walker has also been a dear friend and an invigorating critic. I am also grateful to Ioulia Alechina, who not only helped me get on with my work but also has enriched my life in countless ways. For providing a little plot of earth in this lush city, I am grateful to the Temple Community Garden. From the very start, my time in Washington has been shaped by the friendship of Andre Spearman, whose style, good spirits, and companionship have helped make this strange place seem like home.

More recently, I enjoyed a year in Philadelphia as a fellow at the McNeil Center for Early American Studies at the University of Pennsylvania. Richard Dunn's leadership created an ideal atmosphere of intellectual exchange and camaraderie. Penn colleagues Bob Lockhart, Dan Richter, and Mike Zuckerman provided encouragement, support, and suggestions—and not a little good food. While at the McNeil Center, I had the good fortune to become friends with Stephanie Brooks, Eric Slauter, and Kirk Swinehart.

As this project has developed, it has benefited from the advice I've received and questions I've been asked at various conferences and seminars. I am grateful for invitations to present work in progress at the Early American Seminar at Columbia; the American Seminar at the John Nicholas Brown Center; the McNeil Center Seminar; the Institute for Global Studies at Johns Hopkins; the History Department at George Washington University; the Early American Seminar at the University of Maryland, College Park; and the Omohundro Institute for Early American History and Culture. Public lectures in the Queer Theory Series, American Studies Program, Wesleyan University, and at the Rhode Island Black Heritage Society also helped me refine my ideas.

When I was thinking about what kind of book I wanted this to be, I received generous advice from Harry Houghton Jr., Gerry McCauley, and Joyce Seltzer. At the Johns Hopkins University Press, Jack Greene and Jack Pole offered timely interest and encouragement. Bob Brugger, my editor, shared an ambitious vision of what this project could be and suggested important improvements. Ann Kraybill's acuity and hard work in copyediting a draft of the manuscript helped me tighten and clarify my thoughts. And Grace Buonocore copyedited the final manuscript with great care and precision. In addition to those mentioned above, this project has been enriched by the suggestions and questions of Kathy Brown, Nicole Eustace, Ruth Herndon, Daniel Mandell, Joanne Melish, Ann Plane, and John Saillant. Lázaro Lima, Jennifer Spear, Jerry Passanante, Tim Meagher, and Terry Murphy all read drafts of chapters and offered encouragement and ideas. Along the way—since we began cooking together in Princeton ten years ago—I have been grateful for the generosity, intelligence, and good humor of Joanna Dougherty. She has read more drafts than I care to remember and provided critiques and suggestions ranging from the placement of commas to the arrangement of chapters. And lastly, I thank Chloe Dougherty—for her unflagging energy, unflappable friendliness, and infectious *joie de vivre.*

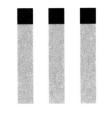

Bodies Politic

After Origins

America is a nation of new beginnings—and each new beginning provides an opportunity to revisit the past and reshape its legacy. When the bicentennial of the Landing of the Pilgrims came around on 22 December 1820, the town fathers of Plymouth seized the opportunity to celebrate their ancestors' voyage across the Atlantic as the true beginning of the great new American nation. On Landing Day, Plymouth hosted a large banquet, served on special commemorative plates, and invited the prominent orator Daniel Webster to speak. As the political storm clouds that ultimately foreshadowed the Civil War began to gather on the national scene, Webster extolled New England's colonial past, dwelling on the Pilgrims' flight from persecution, their courage in setting out into a forbidding New World, and their enduring love of liberty. As he told the story, New England's colonial past—distinguished by family values, religious liberty, and social equality—not only set New England apart from the rest of the country but also blazed the path the rest of the new nation was destined to follow. This mythic narrative was echoed by the commemorative plates used for the banquet. The dominant central image shows the Pilgrims arriving on a rocky, snow-covered shore as two almost naked Indians look on. Two large medallions in the border proclaim the greatness that grew from this inauspicious start: America, born on the Fourth of July in 1776 and brought into being by that greatest of all Founding Fathers, the Revolutionary hero George

FIGURE 1. "The Landing of the Fathers at Plymouth, Dec. 22 1620," Enoch Wood and Sons, Burslam, England, 1819–46. English white-glazed earthenware plate, 10½" diameter. Courtesy of the National Museum of American History, Mrs. Ellouise Baker Larson Collection.

Washington. After the festivities were over, one local later recalled, the plates underwent a new birth of their own—they were cleared from the tables, washed off, and sold as souvenirs. If America was a nation of heroic origins and high ideals, it was also a nation of commerce.[1]

The Founding Fathers liked to think of the Revolution as a new birth: the motto they chose for the Republic's great seal (still imprinted on our one-dollar bills) hails the inauguration of a "Novus Ordo Seculorum," a new order for the ages. In this sense there is a clean break with the colonial period, which is in turn defined as a kind of prehistory of political dependency that ended abruptly and forever with the Declaration of Independence. The idea that the revolutionaries were throwing off the "dead hand of the past" was appealing to many at the time in part because they were aware that, even though the nation was new, its various peoples had a long history—indeed, a number of more or less distinct histories. In addition, declaring the nation newly born was a defense against invidious comparisons with the great nations of the Old World—whose culture and learning, advances in manufacturing, and dominance in overseas trade were enough to make many in the former colonies continue to feel provincial. Given time, America would prove its worth. Meanwhile, the leaders of the new Republic faced the real challenge of uniting a disparate group of states with distinct regional cultures, political traditions, and economic interests. Obscuring these entrenched historical divisions was another benefit of imagining the nation to be new. Nonetheless, the new nation was shaped by its long colonial past. Indeed, in many ways the colonial past is still—as William Faulkner remarked about southern history—not even the past.

In this book, I explore the nature of colonial society and its relationship to the development of democracy in the antebellum North. To do so I investigate the lives of English settlers, native Indians, and enslaved Africans in mid-eighteenth-century New England and trace their interactions through the Revolutionary period and into the early decades of the nineteenth century. Historians have long imagined "colonial" New England—by which they mean the period from the beginning of English settlement to the Fourth of July, 1776—to be uniquely detached from the larger dynamics of colonialism. In recent years, historians of early America and other colonial societies have emphasized that colonialism involves encounters, exchanges, and conflicts among different groups of peoples—often with sweeping social, cultural, and political consequences. In the centuries since their first encounters, the interactions between native peoples, English settlers, and enslaved and free Africans in the American North resulted in what were truly new worlds: new cultures, new societies, even new peoples. These relationships did not end with the Declaration of Independence: indeed, they continued to shape the development of American society profoundly in the early years of the Republic.

This is true even in America's most homogeneous and most European region—New England. The same kind of colonial encounters that we associate with other regions occurred there: the mingling of settlers and Indians in borderland regions, the interactions of settlers and Africans as slavery became established, and the development of both self-conscious hierarchies and new lines of affinity around new racial identities. When the Pilgrims arrived in the winter of 1620, they soon recognized their dependence on local Wampanoag leaders for food, land, and military protection. Despite devastating epidemics and brutal wars, Indians continued to control the landscape of New England for many years. Not until 1675–76, during King Philip's War, did settlers establish their dominance along the entire New England seaboard by crushing the powerful Narragansett confederation.

Around the same time, New England's Indian population plummeted from about sixty thousand to about fifteen thousand: many died fighting; some were sold into slavery by the victors; others migrated beyond the reach of aggressive settlers. But those who remained became an integral part of New England society, either re-grouping in enclaves on their remaining territory or living as laborers among an expanding population of colonists. Meanwhile, the colonial economy had grown to depend on trade with the slave-dominated sugar islands of the West Indies. First through this coastal trade—and later through the triangle trade that joined New-port with the so-called Guinea Coast as well as the Caribbean—enslaved Africans were gradually introduced to New England. By the mid-eighteenth century, con-siderable numbers of slaves worked in the bustling port towns and on the most prosperous commercial farmland. Even the most remote rural villages included a scattering of slaves. By the time of the Revolution, almost a third of all New England households included at least one black member. In such a setting, the lives of con-quered Indians, enslaved Africans, and English settlers grew densely entwined.

In order to understand how the lives of these disparate individuals related to the development of the American body politic, I decided to focus on the theme of cit-izenship—particularly the often conflicted boundary that separated legally recog-nized citizens from those who lived among them but did not enjoy the same rights and privileges. Membership in early American communities was defined by legal formalities, but it was also expressed, enacted, and negotiated in encounters rang-ing from the everyday and habitual to the rare and ritualistic. These relationships of inclusion, exclusion, and hierarchy called on the agency of all involved, and out-comes were contingent and often surprising.

Because I was especially curious about how the legacy of colonialism shaped the emergence of a democratic nation, I decided to begin by exploring life in New England a hundred years after the landing of the Pilgrims at Plymouth. By the early eighteenth century, Indians, English settlers, and enslaved Africans had come together to form a distinctive colonial society. Their interactions shaped the po-litical status of Indian nations within colonial territory, the development of slavery throughout the region, and the symbolically charged and intensely personal mat-ter of conversion to Christianity. During the Revolutionary period, members of all three groups continued to live together. Their continuing negotiations are revealed in the intimate realms of family life and sexuality, in wartime decisions about po-litical allegiance and military service, and in the dramatic struggle to abolish slav-ery. During the early decades of the Republic, most slaves became free, and the na-

tion emerged as democratic. Yet in many ways whites, blacks, and Indians also
began to move apart.

Attempting to make sense of this apparent paradox required the exploration of
the new understandings of human nature and racial difference that emerged in the
late eighteenth century; the new political strategies pursued by Indians, African
Americans, and whites to define their respective places in the nation; and the enduring relationship between the colonial legacy of white supremacy and the emergence, in the early nineteenth century, of American democracy. Throughout, I emphasize that race acquires its power by exaggerating, extending, and transmuting
other social cleavages and modes of self-understanding. I conclude by reflecting on
how the conflicted national history of colonialism continued to bind the new nation together, even as the politics of slavery and continuing conquests began to split
northern and southern regions apart.

| | |

The complex interactions of settlers, Indians, and Africans are often revealed in
intimate and surprising detail by the rich sources documenting life in early New
England. In contrast to historians of the South, for whom records from the early
period are often sparse, and historians of western borderlands, for whom records
can be even more meager, historians of New England are blessed with a wealth of
documentation, which in many cases has been carefully preserved. This project
seeks to bring together many different kinds of sources—some of them familiar,
others often ignored—to develop a rich sense of life in early New England from
diverse points of view.

The breadth and complexity of these different perspectives emerged quite
vividly when I worked at the newly opened Rhode Island State Judicial Records
Center in the run-down mill town of Pawtucket. There, archivist Steve Grimes revealed hundreds of cartons of early file papers but explained that many of them had
been badly damaged during a severe hurricane in 1938 and in subsequent storage
in the attic of the state capitol. The folded packets of brittle paper had to be hu-
midified before they could be unfolded and then pressed flat. Often, mold covered the pages so thickly that it had to be brushed off to reveal the writing underneath. Yet what I found was an endless series of surprises: thick files from lawsuits
over the governance of the Narragansett tribe, including dozens of depositions from
both Indians and settlers about the tribe's most ancient customs and contemporary
practices. Another set chronicled lawsuits in which enslaved blacks and Indians

claimed that they were, by rights, free. Together, these papers opened up new insights into the nature of slavery in colonial society and the process by which slaves in New England ultimately gained their freedom. Like all court records, these files document conflicts—they often include evidence from a variety of witnesses, including ordinary and even illiterate people who left few other records, and they always present contested versions of events. Often the tangential details are the most tantalizing, such as the routine of breakfast on a farm described in a trespassing case. And, of course, all this evidence was to some extent shaped and selectively marshaled by attorneys, which reminds us not to take statements too literally and also opens up new avenues of exploration. The strategies attorneys pursued, the decisions judges made, and the verdicts arrived at by juries hint at how individual cases fit into broader social and cultural dynamics.

Rather different windows on the past are opened up by personal and government papers housed in a wealth of local and regional archives. Diaries, often kept by well-educated and relatively prosperous individuals, can illuminate not only their keepers' personal perspectives but also a wider range of interactions and interests. For instance, the Reverend Ezra Stiles, a longtime minister in Newport and later president of Yale, kept voluminous diaries. In the process of recording stories, observations, and dialogues, he preserved remarkably vivid evidence about Indian life in southern New England in the mid-eighteenth century, such as the unique sketch he drew while sitting at the tea table in Elizabeth Mohege's wigwam. Likewise, the Reverend James MacSparran's journals, letters, and sermons not only suggest how this Anglican clergyman thought of himself as a slave master and servant of God but also provide details about the lives of the men and women he enslaved and the complex relationships that developed among them—relationships marked by both harsh violence and deep affection. Other town, colony, and state records are full of references to blacks and Indians and document their place in the local politics of poor relief, public morality, and military service. More surprising is the volume of letters, petitions, and other records produced by Indians and Africans, both enslaved and free. During the 1760s in Newport, Caesar Lyndon kept what may be the only extant journal by an American slave; it details his family life, his relationship with his master's family, and a wide variety of small business ventures he developed with an expansive network of fellow slaves and free people of color. The Reverend Samson Occom, a Mohegan protégé of the widely known minister Eleazar Wheelock, maintained an extensive correspondence with a wide range of individuals; published sermons and collection of hymns; and kept a journal that chronicles his life for almost half a century. His writings document his evolving sense of himself as a Christian, an Indian, and an American. Finally, institutional records, such as the proceedings and minutes of the Free African Union Society of Newport in the 1790s and early 1800s, help explore the communal strategies that free black men and women pursued to define their place among often hostile neighbors.

At the same time these manuscripts were created, an immense variety of books, pamphlets, and other printed texts were published and circulated on both sides of the Atlantic. In some cases, manuscripts suggest new understandings of printed works. For instance, Phillis Wheatley's acerbic and politically pointed private correspondence helps illuminate the often coded racial meanings in her published poems. Often, printed sources were part of extended dialogues. The first American slave narrative, *The Life and Adventures of Venture* (1798), was written by an African-born Connecticut resident. His story not only contrasted with the views expressed in records produced by slaveholders but also used allusions to Benjamin Franklin's recently published autobiography to claim a role for free blacks as virtuous and productive citizens of the new Republic. Newspapers, broadsides, and almanacs—cheap, widely distributed, and usually ephemeral productions—can often be compared with less widely circulated and more intellectually refined tracts, novels, and monographs. Printed texts offer particularly useful perspectives on transatlantic interactions and the development of distinct regions in North America. Comparing published narratives helps evaluate how different the regions were and what common ground they shared. For instance, I use texts from a variety of distinct genres to explore the place of racial ideas and assumptions within broader intellectual currents. The natural history of racial bodies and character in the late eighteenth century, for instance, was part of a much broader set of intellectual concerns that involved the nature of human reproduction, the inheritance of physical and mental traits, the potential of education to shape character, and the extent to which physical bodies manifest inner qualities of mind. This larger mind-body question also had a complex relationship to policy debates and popular assumptions about public education, republican citizenship, and the potential of blacks and Indians for full inclusion in the emerging American body politic.

| | | |

As they emerge from these sources, the intersecting lives of English settlers, Native Americans, and African New Englanders suggest patterns and paradoxes that challenge several common assumptions—assumptions about the dynamics of cultural change in colonial societies, the role of the public in social life, and the formation of racial and national identities.

Nowadays, when thinking about the coming together of disparate groups of peoples, we often begin with culture. The early encounters of colonists and the colonized are frequently described as "cultural encounters"—and certainly settlers, Indians, and Africans came together in colonial New England from very different backgrounds. Yet we too often assume that the source of conflict between these groups lay in their lack of cultural understanding. For instance, it is tempting to imagine that English settlers and Native Americans fought over land because the two groups traditionally held such different assumptions about the nature of property ownership. This is true enough, but conflict over land also developed because members of both groups saw advantages to its exclusive ownership, occupation, and use. Contemporary assumptions about cultural conflict are in large part a legacy of the nineteenth-century theory that national peoples have intrinsic "folk" cultures—an idea that, despite its patent absurdity, continues to have currency in a variety of cultural nationalist guises. For example, we often think of missionaries as malevolent figures because they threatened to destroy native and African cultural traditions. Certainly, colonial propagandists could be quite arrogant in trumpeting the superiority of their culture and in their desire to convert and civilize the peoples they sought to dominate, displace, and exploit. Yet many settlers found missionaries dangerous for the opposite reason: because settlers used the difference between Christians and "strangers" to define racial hierarchies, the missionaries' erasure of this distinction threatened to disrupt the colonial social order. Indeed, those Indians and Africans who became most conspicuously anglicized, such as Phillis Wheatley, were often attacked as though they were just covering up their essentially inferior selves with a veneer of English civility. Consequently, I think we should be wary of taking out of context evidence—abundant as it is—of Indian and African cultural "survivals" and influences. The origin of a cultural feature is important and often interesting, but so too are its dynamic and often contested meanings over time. The cultural world of colonial America—and the nation that emerged after the Revolution—was marked by hybridity, paradox, and constantly shifting strategies for claiming respect, power, and citizenship.

The paradoxes of colonial culture stemmed in large part from fundamental conflicts over membership in a body politic. Almost all settlers tried to define citizenship in ways that were at once racially ranked and exclusively white, but their consensus about white preeminence ultimately foundered over the question of slavery. Perhaps no clearer example exists of the role of a broadly defined "public" in shaping the lives of ordinary individuals than the history of slavery. Masters in colonial New England liked to think of slavery as essentially private—as were domestic affairs generally. What they did to their slaves, they hoped, was of no concern to anyone else. This model is easy to take for granted if we think of slavery in terms of the colonial Caribbean and the antebellum South—where most slaves lived on large plantations and where there was comparatively little civil infrastructure. However, in colonial New England—where farms were smaller and more people lived in commercial seaports—slaves were intimately intertwined in the tangled web of household and community relations. In the mid-eighteenth century, a master could advertise for a runaway slave and expect that local legal officials and settlers would work together to identify, capture, and return the person. Masters seeking to enhance their authority could also turn to town governments, state officials, and the courts—as well as a more informal set of family members, neighbors, and other settlers. These dynamics gave masters tremendous power—but they changed over time. By the end of the century, masters had largely given up placing advertisements for runaway slaves. By then, local citizens, instead of helping to return a slave, were more likely to shelter, protect, and employ runaways. This shifted the balance of power between masters and slaves and allowed many of the latter to win their freedom. Public life—along with recognition as a member of the body social—was a constantly contested locus of power.

If defining who belonged and how perplexed many in the early days of the American nation, today we may find their understanding of identity equally confusing. Racial identity is particularly complicated because of the way the categories themselves shift over time. In early New England, settlers generally used different sets of racial labels during different periods: in the mid-eighteenth century legal records employed a wide range of labels including not only "white," "black" (largely synonymous with "Negro"), and "Indian" but also "mulatto" and "mustee." By the early nineteenth century, government records often collapsed these distinctions by lumping everyone who was not "white" into the catchall category "people of color." More complicated is the fact that not everyone saw either the categories or their meanings in the same way. It seemed obvious to many settlers that all "Indians" were essentially alike. It was more problematic for Algonquian-speaking Christians in New England to recognize any meaningful affinity or common cause with Iroquoian-speaking pagans living beyond the New York frontier. The alliances that

developed among these groups were rooted not so much in shared cultural traditions as in their common experiences of dealing with settlers who treated them as
though they all were simply Indians. Perhaps most fascinating are the ways in
which associations that came to be seen as racial were actually part of much broader
cultural and social dynamics. For instance, in the early years of the Republic a
stereotyped Negro dialect became a staple of popular humor. At the same time,
Noah Webster was leading an influential campaign to create a standard American
speech that would bridge regional and class differences and announce the nation's
cultural independence from England.[2] These two trends drew symbolic power from
each other: the "broken lingo" of fictional black speech was made meaningful because ordinary white Americans were self-conscious about the ways in which their
own speech betrayed their regional and social origins or signified their attainments
and ambitions. Throughout, the nexus between race and nationalism was crucial.
In many ways, America came to present itself as a white nation when it was, and
had been from the start, diverse, hybrid, and multiracial. Behind the fantasy of
America as a white nation is another set of agendas, assumptions, and struggles.

| | | |

When Alexis de Tocqueville reflected on the general character of the nation in
the 1830s, he was struck that Plymouth Rock had become such a hallowed historical relic: hauled up from the shore for display on the Plymouth common, it had
to be surrounded with a fence to keep souvenir hunters from chipping it apart.
"Does not that clearly prove that man's power and greatness resides entirely in his
soul?" he marveled. "A few poor souls trod for an instant on this rock, and it has
become famous; it is prized by a great nation; fragments are venerated, and tiny
pieces distributed far and wide." In such passages, Tocqueville wrote as though New
England typified the nation, and until recently many historians took this claim
for granted. But Tocqueville and the Pilgrims' bicentennial boosters were not really describing the nation as it was.[3] They were describing America as they wished
it to be—a utopian vision of public life, free commerce, and racial homogeneity.
Yet even if their utopian vision was distorted, their interest in the relationship between the story of New England and the story of the American nation remains
useful.

The American North emerged in the early years of the Republic as a region that
would be free but not equal. In large part, the North came together in opposition
to the South as the nation divided over the politics of slavery and western con-

quests. But this conflict has obscured underlying similarities that derive from a shared legacy of colonialism. True, New England and the Mid-Atlantic states developed more communitarian institutions and an economy that grew not so much extensively as intensively. These northern areas developed a more complex, independent economy, whereas the South remained essentially a colonial economy producing raw materials for metropolitan markets in both Europe and the North. Nevertheless, the everyday realities of race continued to unite the new nation long after the politics of slavery began to divide it.

Indeed, white claims to racial preeminence became more urgent, rigid, and consistent in the 1820s and 1830s, just as new democratic ideals were becoming established and new class divisions were becoming entrenched. Jim Crow, after all, began his long, strange career in the antebellum North. Only after the Civil War would the style of occupational, geographic, and symbolic segregation that developed in the North take hold in the New South.[4] The nation eventually settled with the northern model: universal freedom but racial inequality. Americans would always be split apart by race, but the story of the intertwined lives of New Englanders in the generations before and after the Revolution reveals how race would also always bring them together.

PART I

Coming Together

| Aaunchemókaw. | *Tell me your newes.* |
| Cuttauchemókous. | *I will tell you newes.* |

. . . .

| Awaun mesh aunchemókau. | *Who brought this newes?* |
| Awaun mesh kuppíttouwaw. | *Of whom did you heare it?* |

| Uppanáunchim. | *Your newes is true.* |
| Cowawwunnâunchim. | *He tells false newes.* |

ROGER WILLIAMS

A Key into the Language of America, 1643

Common Ground

||| Narragansett Country, 1744 |||

Travelers stopping at the tavern in Charlestown, Rhode Island, on their way along the post road that snaked up the seacoast from New York to Boston, were often regaled by their host with romantic stories about the region's Indian rulers in times past—and even more extraordinary accounts of the Narragansetts' current king, who lived a short ways down the road. One traveler whose curiosity was piqued was Dr. Alexander Hamilton, a Scottish-born physician who spent much of 1744 journeying up and down the eastern seaboard, filling his journal with sardonic accounts lampooning provincial pretensions. Yet when he presented himself at the door of the Indian king's fine stone house, he had to admit that he was impressed. He visited with the Narragansett ruler, George Augustus Ninigret, enjoyed a surprisingly good glass of wine, and afterwards wrote an uncharacteristically flattering description of his host: "He possesses twenty or thirty 1000 acres of very fine levell land round this house, upon which he has many tennants and has, of his own, a good stock of horses and other cattle. This King lives after the English mode. . . . His queen goes in a high modish dress in her silks, hoops, stays, and dresses like an English woman. He educates his children to the belles letters and is himself a very complaisant mannerly man."[1]

The snobbish Scot was hardly exaggerating. The Narragansetts' leading family was in the midst of a remarkable transformation. A century earlier, the Narragansett nation had indeed been a force to be reckoned with, but its crushing defeat in King Philip's War (1675–76) had cost the Narragansetts most of their territory and political clout. Yet, unlike most leading Indian families across New England, the Ninigrets retained control over enough land to produce substantial revenues and command the attention of the colony's ruling elite. During the early eighteenth century, they made a bid to reinvent themselves as colonial aristocrats. And they had been remarkably successful. Or so it seemed.

Across the post road from the Indian king's imposing house lived his putative subjects—mostly in small, domed wigwams. Their position was similar to that of most of the other ordinary Indians who had persevered in New England in the aftermath of King Philip's War. About a dozen Indian enclaves had emerged across southern New England as the survivors of the war abandoned smaller, isolated villages (map 1). Some migrated away from English settlements, but others went to work on colonists' farms and in their households. Many regrouped on larger, legally recognized reservations, transforming old alliances, confederations, and clans into new notions of tribal identity. The Narragansett enclave was, as late as 1745, about a dozen square miles of land, bounded by the ocean to the south and a great cedar swamp to the north. About five hundred men, women, and children lived there throughout the century. Another thousand or so Indians lived in Rhode Island towns—mainly as servants and laborers. For more than a century, Narragansett Indians and Rhode Island settlers had been living together intimately, if not always harmoniously. Like their ruling family, ordinary Indians were seeking to define new roles. Around 1740, many of them had converted to born-again Christianity, and many began to emulate English farming roles. Instead of remaining impoverished, indebted laborers, serving their prosperous English neighbors, many Narragansetts were developing new, independent lives.

The Narragansett Indians seemed poised to disrupt the division between natives and settlers that structured colonial society. Yet the closer they came to succeeding, the more apparent it became that they faced serious challenges. Over time, the Narragansett rulers and their people had developed two conflicting visions of Indian roles in colonial society. The members of the tribe's ruling family, the Ninigrets, saw themselves as colonial aristocrats and sold land in order to buy the other accoutrements of provincial gentility. Some settlers encouraged these aspirations but it remained uncertain whether the local gentry was really ready to accept them as peers. Many ordinary tribe members saw themselves more humbly, as yeomen,

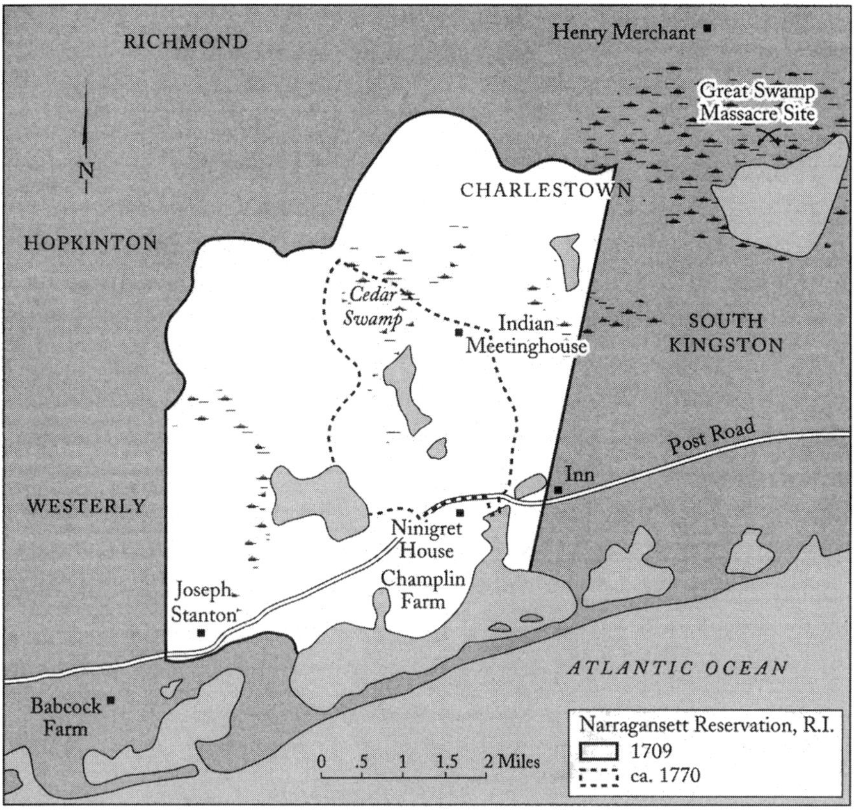

Map 1. The Narragansett Reservation (Rhode Island). In 1709, George Ninigret's grandfather, named Ninigret, granted most of his territory (150,000 acres/210 square miles) to the colony of Rhode Island; the remaining lands (16,000 acres/25 square miles) were regulated to prevent their dissipation. As the location of the Champlin and Babock farms indicate, the Ninigret family's colonial trustees and attorneys gained control of most of the best farmland by the middle of the century. By 1770, in the aftermath of Thomas Ninigret's death, only about 3,000 acres remained, mostly the Cedar Swamp to the north—tribe members were particularly concerned to retain the thin strip of land near the Ninigrets' house leading into the salt pond.

and devoted their lives to Christian piety and improving the very lands the sachem was selling out from under them. A few sympathetic settlers and missionaries fought to keep the Narragansetts' lands intact and help them become respectable members of colonial society. The essential problem was recognized early on by the Reverend Samuel Hopkins, who in his youth had labored as a missionary at the

Stockbridge Indian enclave in western Massachusetts. His goal was to educate his students in a way that would "tend to make them *the people*, and prevent their viewing themselves as *underlings*."[2]

For many of "the people" that was just the problem. Most English settlers were indifferent, or even hostile, to the aspirations of local Indians: they valued the Ninigret family largely as a source of cheap land and ordinary tribe members only as sources of cheap labor. Ultimately, the question was not whether native peoples would—or could—adapt to colonial life but whether they would be allowed to succeed. Today, we often take it for granted that settlers lied, cheated, and murdered their way across the continent. We often imagine that Indian peoples bravely fought to retain their traditions in the face of overwhelming cultural imperialism. And we all too often assume that Indians stopped playing an important role in American history after early moments of encounter or ultimate defeat. This was essentially the attitude adopted by the British government, particular after the Seven Years' War ended in 1763: the basic strategy of imperial officials was to balance the interests of settlers and Indians while keeping the two groups apart. When defeat of the French and their native allies seemed to open up a vast region of Indian country west of the Appalachians to land speculators and settlers, British officials attempted to prevent conflict between overweening settlers and the Iroquois confederacy by drawing the Proclamation Line of 1763 on their maps and sending thousands of soldiers to guard it. It was the cost of those troops that provoked the imperial crisis over colonial taxation.[3] But, in eighteenth-century New England, there was no way to draw a similar, geographic line between "savage" Indians and "civil" settlers.

By the time Dr. Hamilton passed through in 1744, a bitter dispute had broken out among members of the Ninigret family, their English supporters, and ordinary Narragansetts. The dispute dragged on for years, spawning a welter of petitions, lawsuits, and even two appeals to the king in council. These records bring to life a dramatic, complex story of the colonial encounters that continued in the wake of conquest, a story of ongoing efforts to establish a viable common ground. The conflict was always, at root, about political power and the control of land, but it turned on efforts to document and interpret the Indians' most solemn traditions. Dozens of Narragansetts and settlers gave long depositions, and many of them were subsequently cross-examined by two sets of attorneys. Elders reminisced about events dating from the seventeenth century and described their most solemn customs. Interpreters were engaged to translate; clerks often kept a verbatim record of what was said. Many times, individuals were given the chance to confirm or refine their testimony ten or more years later. Rich as they are, these efforts to establish the "truth" of tribal tradition cannot be taken at face value. For one thing, members of the tribe did not agree—on what had happened in the past or on what it implied for their future. The problem was deeper than the obvious biases and the inevitable tricks of memory. If legal testimony made anything clear, it was that for generations tribe members had been fostering fundamentally different views of tribal governance and ritual. As the tribe split into two factions, each developed its own version of "tradition" to lend authority to its claims for power and its vision of the tribe's future. Often common ground had been reached when both sides agreed to accept loose analogies and tolerate a degree of misunderstanding on crucial issues. Everyone knew, for instance, that the Narragansetts' traditional "sachems" were not precisely like European monarchs, but often individuals had good reason not to press the point.[4]

Nowadays, it is common to imagine that conflict between groups results from cultural differences, that the route to harmony is improved communication. The case of the Narragansetts offers an opportunity to explore some of the limits and dangers of this assumption. Certainly, relations between the Narragansetts and the Rhode Island governments *did* hinge on efforts to explain, understand, and translate their respective political traditions. Ever since the Narragansetts' crushing military defeat a century earlier, colonial officials had been involving themselves in the governance of the tribe and asserting their authority to adjudicate conflicts over the possession and transfer of land. At one level, this effort at communication was always doomed to failure. Even if Narragansetts could have reached agreement among themselves about the implications of their past customs, the attempt to resolve these issues in the colonial courts inevitably distorted the meanings of Indian traditions and their English analogues. Indeed, as the imperial crisis of the 1760s made clear, English customs of monarchy and representation were themselves in flux. At another level, we might ask why English arbiters focused on attempting to pin down the tribe's most ancient and authentic customs rather than on taking stock of practical problems and evaluating viable solutions. At one level this effort seems remarkably open-minded, but it also had the effect of extending colonial sovereignty over the internal politics of the tribe. Sometimes, efforts at cross-cultural understanding could also be part of a colonial scramble for wealth and power.

During their long struggle, the two Narragansett factions struggled over the invention of tribal tradition not so much to prevent change as to turn the process of anglicization to their advantage. The dispute began in the 1730s, when members of the ruling Ninigret family split over the choice of the next sachem: Should it be the previous sachem's younger brother, George, or his infant son, Charles? The dispute escalated into a bitter legal battle because both factions turned to powerful English allies for support and to the colonial legislature and courts for arbitration. There, the legal issues centered on attempts to document the tribe's ancient customs of royal marriage, tribal rituals, and rules of succession. Meanwhile, as these and other records reveal, ordinary Narragansetts were also remaking their roles—developing new identities as Christians and yeomen and seeking economic autonomy within colonial society. How these two trends came into conflict is revealed in the resurgence of open conflict within the tribe in the 1760s. By then, no one disputed that George Ninigret's son, Thomas, was the rightful sachem, but his conduct provoked new questions about who owned tribal lands and the limits of a sachem's power. In the end, the entire dispute became one about republican governance and constitutional monarchy and rebelling against a tyrant. Ironically, these were precisely the issues that were then beginning to inflame colonists' sentiments against their own monarch and that ultimately led to the war for American independence.

||| Becoming an Indian King |||

In the spring of 1736, George Ninigret's elder brother, Charles, languished in one of the spacious second-floor chambers of a fine new house that represented a series of tangled alliances and endangered aspirations. Facing death, he worried about the fate of his infant son. As chief sachem of the Narragansett tribe, Ninigret had long striven to exalt his office. Since the death of his father in 1723, he had presided as sovereign over his people, controlled large tracts of land, and enjoyed wide regard among local colonists as the "Indian King." Since the seventeenth century, the Ninigret family had found analogies between the role of sachem and that of king tremendously useful. Over the course of several generations, the Ninigrets pushed for more authority over their putative subjects, members of the tribe, and more respect from their putative peers, the colonial grandees. Charles Ninigret treated the Narragansett enclave as his own personal estate and emulated the genteel style of local colonial gentry. That winter, he had taken the dramatic step of moving out of his old wigwam into one of the few stone houses in the region, a residence so grand that it was called his "palace." Sachems had long been honored with larger and richer dwellings than those of ordinary tribe members, but this structure was more than that. Its construction had been financed by the sale of land to local settlers. In order to sell the land, Ninigret had been obliged to gain consent from the English trustees appointed by the colonial government to superintend his finances. Although appointed to prevent him from being cheated, they agreed to the sale of land only after receiving special sweetheart deals. After all that, the Indian king's achievement seemed on the verge of unraveling. A crucial aspect of his vision of Indian kingship was to pass his wealth and position on to his heir. Now, he feared, his only son, Charles, "would be wronged."[5]

The dying father was right to worry. After succeeding to the office of sachem in 1723, Charles Augustus Ninigret had grown keenly aware that even in the best of times the analogy between Narragansett sachem and British prince was weak: he did not really enjoy the authority of a prince within his tribe, and the local colonists did not really treat him like an aristocrat. Bridging this gap would require a wholesale reinvention of himself. To make his metamorphosis seem plausible, he had manipulated a loose set of analogies to disguise the depth and implications of his transformation of his office and himself. In claiming legitimacy as a king, Charles Augustus Ninigret had sought to conflate English regal authority with English material culture and kinship systems. However the Narragansett sachem went about asserting the prerogatives of kingship, he needed to maintain delicate balances of power. On the one hand, the Ninigrets remained beholden to their colonial trustees, who might never allow a complete transformation of sachem to king. In the end, the local gentry might decline to recognize Indian kings as peers. On the other hand, whatever the Ninigrets did to appease colonists risked alienating their support within the tribe. Tribe members could also reject the process of transforming the sachemdom and challenge the Ninigrets' authority and legitimacy. The analogy between sachem and king was loose enough to avoid open conflicts for decades, but—as became abundantly clear when the sachem fell ill— beneath this seeming consensus were enduring and deep divisions.

Even as Sachem Charles lay dying, his younger brother, George, began positioning himself as the rightful successor. Most of the tribe was convinced, but Charles's wife and his English guardians were alarmed. A fierce battle for power developed when the sachem died in April 1763, and the struggle dragged on in the colonial courts and legislature for the better part of two decades. In the process of legal wrangling, a rather simple question—who should be the next sachem?— mushroomed into a much more abstract and, in some ways, insoluble dispute. Tribe members might have long resented Charles Augustus Ninigret's self-serving land policies and arrogant style of governance, but they founded their opposition to his son's becoming sachem on Charles's disregard for tribal customs concerning their leaders of "high," or royal, rank. Although central issues at stake were clearly the centralization of power in the hands of the sachem-as-king and control over tribal lands, the fate of the Narragansett sachemdom came to rest on the memories of dozens of witnesses, Indian and English, who testified about the tribe's ancient customs of "high blood," its rituals of royal marriage, and the proper succession of the office of sachem. For both factions within the tribe, it was a major loss of power that the ultimate arbiters of tribal tradition and the succession of the office of sachem had become not tribe members but English courts and politicians. Worse still, many of these officials, particularly the sachem's trustees, had an interest in continuing, not resolving, the dispute. What this protracted dispute makes clear is that the analogy between the sachem as leader of the Narragansetts and the sachem as an "Indian King" was always a political strategy fraught with intersecting ambitions and risks. The evidence collected about the history of the Ninigret family and the Narragansetts' customs makes it possible to piece together how this process unfolded: how the analogy between sachem and king became useful for both the Ninigret family and colonial elites around the turn of the seventeenth century; how Charles Ninigret's flouting of tribal marriage customs provided unhappy tribe members with a means of expressing resistance to his policies; and how his younger brother, George, ultimately cobbled together a more effective amalgam of Narragansett and English notions of legitimacy.

"I have the honour to descend from a family of princes absolute," Charles Ninigret had declared in a letter to the British monarch George II—and by 1728, when the illiterate sachem dictated this epistle, the analogy between sachem and prince seemed true enough to most local settlers. Indeed, English settlers had been encouraging a monarchical view of native rulers since their earliest encounters in North America more than a century earlier. In the 1640s, Roger Williams, one of the most sensitive of all early observers of native culture, described the Narragansett sachemdom as "Monarchicall" despite obvious differences with the English model. As Williams noted, the office of sachem was held by two—not one—men with complementary roles. Nonetheless, the royal analogy helped settlers believe that the office of sachem followed rules analogous to their own customs of patrilineal inheritance. As an elderly settler declared in the Ninigret case, "I Never heard by White or Black but that the Sachems held their Right of being Sachem by Heirship."[6]

FIGURE 2. In the aftermath of King Philip's War, Ninigret emerged as the leader of the Indians from several local sachemdoms who regrouped in the Narragansett enclave. The anonymous painter emphasizes the Narragansett leader's exoticism while also placing him in the tradition of European aristocratic portraits. *Portrait of Ninigret II, Son of Ninigret I, Chief of the Niantic Indians,* ca. 1681. Oil on canvas, 33" × 30". Courtesy of the Museum of Art, Rhode Island School of Design, Gift of Mr. Robert Winthrop.

Rhode Island officials had good reason to encourage the Ninigret family to consider its role monarchical (fig. 2).[7] Treating local rulers like petty princes helped the colonists make sense of alien forms of governance and facilitated the making of treaties and the purchase of land. Even after King Philip's War, the Narragansett sachems retained title to some of the most fertile land in New England—an area that soon became well known for its large commercial farms or "plantations." As the chief power of the sachem became the authority to alienate tribal lands to English settlers, and as the position became increasingly hereditary, the English were able to exert more control over the legitimacy of individual sachems.

During old Ninigret's lifetime, the political and military dominance of the English undermined the traditional diplomatic functions of marriage among the leading Indian families. The most powerful sachems of southern New England had maintained their dominance partly by intermarrying with the families of minor local sachems and with the families of neighboring "great" sachems. These marriages were quite different from the Puritan norm. Multiple marriages, polygamy, and divorce were common. Typically, Ninigret himself married five times. As a young man in the late seventeenth century, he married first a Pequot woman of high rank; she bore him two children, who died young. His next wife was Mary Wamsitta, the daughter of the "Black Sachem" of nearby Kingstown; their son also died young. Then Ninigret married a woman from the Mohegan enclave in Connecticut. His fourth wife was a woman of royal status from Long Island, probably the squaw sachem of the Montauk. Ultimately, Ninigret's most important marriage was his fifth: to Oskoosooduck, also known as Mary, the daughter of the Pequot great sachem in Stonington, Connecticut, and a "sunks squaw" or "Queen" in her own right. She bore him two sons, Charles and George, but their marriage ended violently. One night around 1717, the sachem and his wife fell asleep with a group of people in front of a fire. When he woke up, she was lying suspiciously close to another man, and he suspected her of infidelity. He slashed three scars into her cheek and sent her back home in humiliation. Her people, the Pequots, were enraged and threatened to mount a military expedition to revenge themselves on Ninigret. But their days of military prowess were over, and the sachem's trustee, Colonel Joseph Stanton, intervened and kept the peace.[8]

Ninigret had been compelled to accept colonial trustees to supervise his finances at the end of a long struggle against rivals to his position and claims to his territory. The trouble began in 1679 when members of the related Garrett family began selling Narragansett land, claiming that they were the true sachems. Because the sale of land was controlled by the colonial courts, Ninigret's elder sister, Wuenquesh, had to turn to the colonial legislature for help.[9] After her death, Ninigret became sachem and faced a series of similar challenges. Meanwhile, around the turn of the century, the Connecticut-based Atherton Company renewed efforts to claim ownership of Narragansett country on the basis of a foreclosed mortgage dating from 1662. Colonial officials responded to these disputes by collecting genealogical evidence about the rival lineages and lines of inheritance. Rhode Island officials ruled in the Ninigret family's favor on the grounds that its members were the most direct descendants of the previous sachem. In each case, official support was followed by grants of land to influential settlers.[10] The legitimacy of the sachem no longer turned on who could persuade fellow tribe members to follow his or her leadership but on an "invented tradition" of heredity enforced by colonial officials. One consequence of this genealogical emphasis on heredity was that the older practices of multiple marriages became a serious liability: in English eyes, they confused the legitimate line of inheritance.

Another consequence was the high price Ninigret paid for the support of Rhode Island officials. Shortly after the most serious challenge to his authority, colonial officials convinced him to grant 135,000 acres of "vacant" lands to the colony. On 28 March 1709, Ninigret, his fifth wife, Oskoosooduck, and several counselors signed the deed. In return he received no payment, but he kept a twenty-five-square-mile tract of land that was to be reserved for the benefit of his heirs in perpetuity. This "reservation," as it came to be called, comprised most of present-day Charlestown. The legislature promised to protect this land from the claims of Connecticut and the Atherton Company. In next few years, powerful colonists managed to procure large grants of land and cheap timber rights from the sachem. These scandalous deals were quickly voided by the General Assembly, which in 1713 barred any sales of land or timber without its approval. Soon afterwards, Ninigret agreed to allow the colony to appoint trustees to oversee leases of land and timber rights to colonists and prevent his being "cheated." This move accorded with developing British understandings of monarchy: around the turn of the century the extravagant habits of William III prompted Parliament to prevent him from selling or wasting additional Crown properties. In part because it enhanced their own power, Ninigret's trustees encouraged the interpretation of the sachemdom as a monarchical office, inherited through the patrilineal rules of descent.[11]

When Ninigret fell ill for a time in 1717, his guardians saw to it that he didn't die without a will. English neighbor Samuel Clark recalled that in mid-March of that year he "was riding by the Wigwam of . . . Ninegret & seeing some Horses about the Door alighted and went in." Crowded inside were English and Indian men gathered to see Ninigret take up a pen and scratch his scraggy initials on the document. In it, he bequeathed the bulk of his estate to his elder son, Charles. Soon thereafter he faced a final challenge from members of the rival lineage, which again the colony rejected, leaving the sachem owing money to the colony for his legal expenses. Shortly afterwards the colony doubled the number of years for which his lands could be leased.[12]

When he died in 1723, the old king's funeral was attended not only by Narragansetts but also by leading colonists and was a complex mixture of native and English customs. The respectful obituary notice that appeared in the region's principal newspaper, published in Boston, was soon followed by a sarcastic letter from an anonymous Newporter. The corpse had been placed in an English-style coffin, but the grave was lined with woven mats in the local manner, and before the burial the widow opened the coffin and filled it with provisions, which included not only pipes of tobacco, pieces of bread, and a pot of cornmeal mush but also three bottles of rum—one of which she poured out over the corpse. The sachem, it was explained, had died from "drinking too largely of that Princely Liquor." After the body was buried, the seventeen-year-old "Prince" was "declar'd King" by one of his late father's colonial trustees. The estate he stood to inherit was reported to be worth as much as thirty thousand pounds. The Ninigrets' claims to regal decorum might invite mockery, but their estate was worth enough to be taken seriously.[13]

Soon thereafter, many of these individuals gathered again for the new sachem's first marriage. The occasion was full of good auspices. In accordance with Narragansett custom, young Charles Augustus Ninigret married a woman of royal rank from a nearby settlement—Mary Wamsitta, a close relative of his father's second wife—and the ceremony was large and public. Men, women, and children contributed wampum and money for the dowry. When Mary died a year or so later, Ninigret arranged another suitable marriage, to Betty Sachem. Among the Narragansetts, the Sachems were of impeccably high rank (chart 1). On her father's side, Betty was closely related to the Ninigrets; on her mother's side, she was descended from Pennewis, the Block Island sachem. Again, the ceremony was a large, public, event in which many Narragansetts participated. But, although Charles was following long-honored customs, the diplomatic importance of these royal marriages had by the 1720s been almost completely undermined by the impoverishment of other enclaves and the political isolation of the Narragansett reserve. By this time, Sachem Pennewis had lost his territory, fallen into debt, and been forced into servitude on the mainland. And perhaps it was a sense that he had little to gain by respecting outdated alliances and inconvenient customs that prompted the young sachem to begin acting increasingly cavalier. Less than a year after his marriage to Betty Sachem, Charles "cast her away" on the spurious grounds that she "would not breed"—she was then barely thirteen years old and probably had not even reached the age of menarche. After that, the sachem showed little regard for the conventions of royal marriage. His third marriage was to a woman of "low blood"—Betty Coheis, the daughter of a tribal counselor. This time, the ritual was a small, private matter in her father's wigwam. Later, witnesses could remember little about the ceremony except that the sachem sent someone off hurriedly to fetch rum.[14]

As construction began on his new house, it was pointed out to Sachem Charles Ninigret that a gentleman's country seat required more than classical design, an elevated site, and fine furnishings: he needed a proper housewife. The woman who proposed herself for this job was Handsome Hannah, another member of the Pennewis lineage; after leaving Block Island, she had worked in Newport, probably as a domestic servant, and arrived at the Narragansett enclave around 1730. She told the sachem that his wife was not keeping him "clean" like an English gentleman. Having lived in wigwams all her life, Betty Coheis simply "Did Not Under Stand how to Live in a English hous." Sachem Charles was convinced and cast aside his third wife. He and Handsome Hannah lived together, apparently without ceremony, and when their young son died in 1732, the gravestone they erected described them as man and wife. Meanwhile, the sachem's former wife Betty Coheis had also given birth to a son, whom she named Charles and claimed was the sachem's. By then, however, she was living with another man, and this complication was largely ignored. Shortly thereafter, the sachem put Handsome Hannah out and took up with her cousin Catherine "Kate" Harry.[15]

As the sachem's house neared completion, Kate grew "big with child." They moved in with an English neighbor for a few months to learn how to live in a house. It was only then that Charles grew aware of the problem he had been overlooking: the legitimacy of the unborn child he already envisioned as his heir. In the fall of 1735, one of the sachem's English friends alerted him to the problem. George Babcock warned Charles that the child "would be a bastard and would not have his estate after him." Under English law, legitimacy was an important part of inheritance customs, and many settlers presumed that the child of a sachem could not inherit if it was "counted a bastard." The ailing sachem accepted their concern but worried that the usual large, public, royal marriage ritual was out of the question because he would never gain his people's approval. As Charles sourly observed,

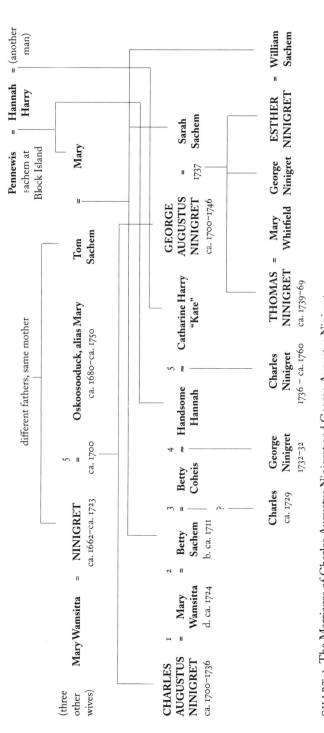

CHART 1. The Marriages of Charles Augustus Ninigret and George Augustus Ninigret

"almost all the Indians hated him & did not love him." Pretty much any ceremony would do, Babcock responded, even if it was attended by only "three four or five" of his friends.[16] All the sachem needed was a ritual that would appear plausible to English observers.

Before the child was born, Babcock and other allies helped the sachem stage a curious ceremony. A handful of English and Indian supporters gathered, and one tribe member presided. At one point the Indian ritual leader publicly announced, apparently for the benefit of English onlookers, that the ceremony was in accordance with Narragansett custom. This emphasis on authenticity is striking because under English law no ceremony at all was really necessary: until the law was changed in the 1750s, a marriage contract could be sealed simply by a man and woman saying "I do." In any case, after the makeshift ceremony, Charles and his wife moved into their new house, just in time for the child to be born there. The sachem named the child after himself and told anyone who would listen that the child was his true and only heir. When one pair of English neighbors failed to call and pay their respects, he brought the child to them. Perhaps, with more time, Charles would have been able to finish his project of establishing the legitimacy of his son. But then he fell sick and died.[17]

Meanwhile, Charles's brother, George Augustus Ninigret, attempted to push his infant nephew aside and claim the sachemdom for himself. The late sachem's English trustees, led by Colonel Joseph Stanton, and other colonial officials grew alarmed. They wished to see the child inherit his father's office and property but were aware that he was quite unpopular within the tribe. The strategy they devised was to establish, first, the general principle that the sachemdom should devolve by strict inheritance and, second, that the marriage in question was legitimate. Colonel Stanton scrambled to collect legal testimony from the late sachem's allies within the tribe and insinuated to colonial officials that George was trying to "cheat" his nephew.[18] But George Ninigret fought back skillfully and demonstrated that seeing the son recognized as his father's heir was not the only way for these settlers to pursue their interests. First, George made it clear that he could request the legislature to appoint a new set of trustees. Then, he dramatically demonstrated his authority within the tribe.

When Sachem Charles Augustus Ninigret died, members of the tribe honored him with elaborate rites of mourning. A New York newspaper described the funeral as "attended by many People, both English and Indian; a Sermon was preached by Mr. *Joseph Park*, Missionary." It concluded that the young sachem left "a very valuable Estate in lands, a Widow and one Son about 4 months old." Tribe members blackened their faces for three months. Then some fifteen hundred Indians from across southern New England gathered for a funeral dance that lasted a week.[19] Although the Narragansetts proudly affirmed their traditions in the face of English domination, most residents of the enclave were aware that Charles Augustus Ninigret had shown little respect for the most resonant rituals of his rank or the practical interests of his people. After tribe members honored his death, few were inclined to honor his wishes about his son. If for no other reason, a six-month-old infant was hardly a suitable leader, and few tribe members wanted to concede tribal governance completely to colonial guardians.

Soon after Sachem Charles's death, the tribe met to determine the succession. The late sachem's trustees—including Joseph Stanton—stayed away, presumably because they suspected the likely outcome, but many other prominent settlers were happy to take their places as participants and observers. George Augustus Ninigret joined the men, women, and children of the tribe who gathered near the late sachem's new house, in a meadow that ran down to a coastal salt pond.[20] An elaborate ceremony followed, which later became the center of legal disputes. By and large, settlers and Indians recalled congruent events, but they emphasized different details and drew very different conclusions.

Several powerful English settlers were actively involved in the ceremony. One settler proposed that the Indians leave the house and "Chose their King." George Ninigret sat down toward the east, and a man representing the child Charles sat toward the west. Supporters of each candidate drew off to the respective sides: not more than six toward the child, close to a hundred toward George. Although all members of the tribe participated in the ceremony, including Narragansett women and children, English observers counted only male voters. So far the ceremony resembled an election. But then it began to look more like a coronation. The local tavern keeper recalled: "They made Proclamation that George was their King and they brought out a Great Chair and placed George in it and an old Indian called Tobey Cawheese according to the best of my Memory made a Speech in Indian and put a Belt of Peege upon George's Head and a great Many of the sd Indians gave George Money which I understood was their Custom." The tavern keeper's son explained that the belt of wampumpeag was "in Lew of a Crouyn" (see fig. 2).[21]

Native descriptions of George Ninigret's succession emphasized the tribe members' role in choosing the sachem but differed from English notions of election. In fact, most remembered the decision as unanimous. All agreed that women and children as well as men participated. And all considered the center of the ritual the presentation of gifts or tribute. Old Indians testified that at the coronations of Wuenquesh, Ninigret, Charles, and George collective offerings of wampumpeag and money had been presented: it was by this act that the tribe "made" an individual sachem.[22]

For some time afterwards it seemed that George had won. In the end, the excluded trustees proved less concerned with cultural punctiliousness than with political expediency. True, when tracking down descriptions of George's investiture ceremony, they focused narrowly on acts and symbols such as the "crown" that reinforced royal analogies and, by inference, their position in favor of strict inheritance. Yet when threatened with the loss of their lucrative positions, the former trustees were ready enough to compromise. Appearing again before the colonial General Assembly, Colonel Stanton changed his tune. Now he argued that it was necessary to give George a hand in the tribal governance because there had developed "a Hatred or Variance subsisting between some of the old Indian Queens & the said Catharine" and that if it was not defused the "Infant Charles would be Murdered or made way with." Compromise was made possible by a deliberate ambiguity: the colonial government and the former sachem's trustees recognized George as a regent, but he and the tribe considered him to be sachem in his own right. Even the late sachem's widow seemed willing to accept defeat. When George Ninigret, as the new sachem, moved into his predecessor's house, the widow Kate and her infant son moved out. In an attempt to save face, she explained to a friend that it was because "it was Cold & her Child was Sick" that she "moved into a Wigwam that was warm."[23]

Open conflict resurfaced in 1740, when George Ninigret tried to cement his claim to the sachemdom outright. For years, he had been signing official documents jointly with Kate on behalf of her son, but in a 1740 petition seeking permission to sell land, he signed the document alone and claimed the rather awkward title "Proprietor of the Lands in the Narragansett Country undisposed of and Sachem." Many tribe members supported his claim. When the implications of this move became clear, Kate engaged an attorney and fought to protect her son's claims. In this legal tug of war, the figurative rope was the rent paid by individual English tenants. George would try to extract rents from "his" tenants; Kate would try to convince them to pay rents to her instead. Whatever tenants did, they might find themselves sued for the rent by the party they did not pay, their side in the suit taken up by the party they did pay. Whoever lost in the lower courts could then appeal to the superior court. Procedural matters could be appealed from the superior court to the General Assembly, and decisions of the superior court could be appealed to London. Significantly, the two sides specifically excluded any question of the sachem's right to transfer lands to the English, an issue that would later be raised by tribe members but which favored neither side of the Ninigret family. And settlers didn't want anything to do with it either: it threatened to call into question virtually all claims to land ownership by settlers throughout the region.[24]

In this context, perhaps the most striking aspect of the tangle of lawsuits that raged on intermittently between 1741 and 1755 was the relentless emphasis on testimony about the ancient customs of the tribe regarding "royal" marriages. In depositions and examinations, dozens of tribe members argued that the late sachem's son Charles was not the rightful sachem, in part because, according to Indian customs, he was illegitimate. Of course, the precise standing of the marriage of Charles Ninigret to Catherine Harry in 1735 was legally relevant only if it was assumed that the Narragansett sachemdom was a monarchy that devolved by heredity. Why did the courts insist on entertaining the notion that Narragansett succession was even more strictly hereditary than the British monarchy, to which they were constantly comparing it? Settlers, of course, had a strong practical interest in the notion that the sachemdom was strictly hereditary: it gave them power over the sachem. By the same token, tribe members also had a strategic interest in emphasizing their choice and the importance of tribal tradition. If the sachem ruled at their choice, *they* might be better able to influence his actions. At the same time, it may have been easier for them to try to influence the sachem's leadership through a protest about symbolic legitimacy than through a direct conflict with his policies.[25] Unfortunately for ordinary tribe members, English settlers also had another vested interest: keeping the legal dispute going so that the need for patronage and the expense of legal fees would keep both sides of the Ninigret family indebted and prompt them to sell land cheaply.

The legal testimony that was collected during these lawsuits shows how little the issues at stake really involved problems of communicating or understanding tribal custom. Virtually all members of the tribe agreed on basic rules about the marriages of sachems, the legitimacy of their children, and the succession of the sachemdom. The most authoritative account of Narragansett customs came from Oskoosooduck, sometimes called Mary, now a very old woman. Through a translator, the old queen described a series of rules that explained the events of the past century. First, a sachem could only marry a woman of "high" or royal blood, often a woman from another tribe in the region. Her son Charles had bowed to this custom in his first two marriages. Second, to be legitimate, even a marriage to a royal woman had to be witnessed and approved by the assembled tribe, and this approval had to be sealed by the presentation of gifts of money and wampum. Charles's first two marriages had been just such large public affairs. Third, royal rank figured significantly, though "high blood" was calculated not just according to the paternal line, as was usual among the English, but also along the maternal line. Historically, the tribe had generally preferred the eldest son of the sachem's most royal wife. Fourth, multiple marriages were common and divorce available at will. Charles Ninigret followed a typical pattern of serial monogamy: his first wife died, he "cast away" his second, and he married three times after that. Finally, sachems could also marry common women, in private ceremonies, but these were not royal marriages, and their offspring could not ascend to the sachemdom.[26]

Other testimony revealed that even Sachem Charles Ninigret had known, before his death, that staging a marriage to make his child with Kate legitimate in English eyes would not satisfy members of his tribe. He tried to control the public perception of reality by intimidation: when tribal elder Tobias Coheis suggested that Charles did have a child by his daughter Betty, the sachem physically assaulted him. Charles even encouraged the rumor that Kate was of high blood, but nobody within the tribe was fooled. Indeed, the purpose of George's trip to Block Island while Charles lay on his deathbed may have been to trace her background. Afterwards, Kate's own brother and sister testified that the family had only a remote connection to Pennewis, the last Block Island sachem. None of them were of "high blood."[27]

Despite the virtual unanimity of Narragansett witnesses and the clarity of their testimony, legal and political decisions went back and forth. George Ninigret generally prevailed, but he paid dearly for the continued support of his trustees. He needed their consent to sell land to finance his long legal battle and lavish mode of living, and they took every opportunity to fleece his estate. As George explained to an English neighbor, "In giving them Land they Allow me to Sell Land." In addition, he helped the colonial government raise troops for the expedition against Cape Breton in 1745 by offering to grant farms to any tribe members who enlisted.[28] Meanwhile, the sachem's tenants and buyers took advantage of his precarious position to underpay and otherwise cheat him, and his trustees did little to stop them.

At least one settler who cheated the sachem clearly enjoyed not just the bargain he got but also the racial dominance it represented. William Welch paid for forty acres but managed to expand the tract to sixty acres with a time-honored ruse. The survey of the boundaries was done by the metes and bounds method, in which a starting point was defined and then the perimeter of the tract was measured out with a sixty-six-foot chain. One man in front would walk until he ran out of chain and place a stake, and then the team would begin again from there. Various helpers along the way kept the chain free from obstructions. In this case, Welch carried the hind end of the chain himself and simply walked past many of the stakes the front man had placed. He later bragged that even though the Indian chain men knew his bounds were fraudulent, they were powerless to object: in court, "an Indian's Evidence was good for nothing against a white man."[29]

Indeed, there is reason to suspect that many local settlers were more interested in encouraging the Ninigret family to aspire to genteel status than in seeing them attain it. Buying fine wine, wearing silk clothes, and building elaborate houses cost money, which the Ninigrets acquired by selling land through their English trustees; their estate would hardly be so easy to plunder if the Ninigrets were to be treated as equals. One sign of respect accorded to the Ninigrets was the fact that by the mid-eighteenth century English legal documents consistently labeled them "gentlemen," a relatively rare distinction. At the same time, the notion of Indian "kings" had already entered into public discourse as exotic and uncanny—as a pale imitation of the standard of British royalty, at a time when settlers were increasingly aware of the inferiority of their own claims to gentility when compared with those of their metropolitan counterparts. "The Indian King" was becoming a common name for taverns in colonial towns and even in London. When Indian leaders traveled to London, they were regarded as exotic spectacles.[30] In managing the Ninigrets' finances, too, the trustees appointed to steward their estate entertained their wards as peers on certain ceremonial occasions, but they did not encourage them to capitalize on their assets. The trustees encouraged the sale of land over the improvement and cultivation of that land, so the Ninigrets never developed an English-style economic base to go along with their English-style habits of consumption. The result was both the legal consolidation of the sachem's new role and the land policies that would soon undermine it.

Ironically, George Augustus Ninigret, who succeeded to his late brother's office by arguing that the sachemdom was not like English kingship, would emerge from this dispute by virtue of his unprecedented skill in bridging the symbolic and practical distance between the customary role of sachem and the English office of kingship. Chastened by his brother's disastrous example, George found a way of satisfying and even reconciling the expectations of settlers and tribe members. He made the same loose analogies between sachem and king more plausible by limiting himself to actions appropriate under both ritual systems. Most obvious was his single marriage. He chose an unimpeachable woman, Sarah Sachem, who was from a closely interrelated family with well-established "high blood." Moreover, they were married in a hybrid ceremony that honored the salient aspects of both English law and Narragansett royal custom. The sachem's trustee, Colonel Joseph Stanton, who was also a justice of the peace, presided at the wedding, a large public event attended by hundreds of tribe members, who contributed coins and wampumpeag to the dowry.[31]

In addition to blurring potentially explosive cultural differences, George Ninigret helped maintain consensus by rewarding his supporters within the tribe. Roger Wappy, who had worked for the late Sachem Charles Ninigret as his "waiting man," readily admitted that when he renounced his support for the young Charles in the mid-1740s, George rewarded him by allocating to this family a particularly large tract of land. Consequently, when Sachem George Ninigret died in 1746, there was little question that his only son, Thomas, would succeed him. Young Thomas became sachem in another hybrid ceremony in which he sat in a thronelike chair and was crowned with a belt or cap of wampum. While attorney Christopher Champlin tallied a list of what he saw as "male voters," all of the tribe's men, women, and children sealed the ritual by presenting money and wampumpeag.[32]

After this second, decisive rejection by the tribe, the ten-year-old Charles Ninigret staged a strange ritual of his own. With a few bedraggled followers, Charles Ninigret erected an effigy of his cousin, the new sachem Thomas Ninigret, and fired guns at it. This seems like a vengeful variation of colonial Pope's Day festivities. Even more curiously, at the moment of crowning, the ritual leader proclaimed, "We crown this pretender king." The Pretender was what supporters of the British monarch called the current descendant of the Stuart family who had been excluded from the royal succession in 1688. In 1746, colonial newspapers breathlessly reported Bonnie Prince Charlie's attempt to claim his throne and his decisive defeat by the Crown. Like his Scottish namesake, Charles Ninigret was also a claimant who considered himself the true heir.[33] Not surprisingly, however, this clumsy combination of English ceremonies convinced no one of the young claimant's legitimacy.

In the end, by managing to get a minor son recognized as his successor, Sachem George Ninigret both thwarted his late brother's most cherished hope and consolidated his most ambitious vision of the family's place in colonial society.

||| Improving Indian Town |||

While the dynastic dispute wracked the Ninigret family, ordinary Narragansetts were also seeking to reinvent themselves. Across the colonial post road from Ninigret's grand house was a cluster of wigwams called "Indian Town," where most of the enclave's five or six hundred tribe members eked out a sparse subsistence. From the shores of the coastal salt pond, the lands of the Narragansett enclave stretched up into a large cedar swamp. The swamp provided wood for fencing; the soil, although stony, produced corn and vegetables; the pond provided the fish that had long been the mainstay of the Narragansetts' diet. But their old hunting grounds were now depleted of game, and their most fertile land had been acquired by settlers (see map 1). Another thousand Indians lived "scattered about where the English [would] employ them"—chiefly on the large, commercial farms settlers had built in the heart of the Narragansetts' former territory along Block Island Sound and in the bustling ports of Newport and Providence. In the aftermath of conquest, with their old ways of subsistence radically disrupted, ordinary Narragansetts, like their sachems, found themselves straddling cultural worlds. They had little choice but to reconcile themselves with the presence and dominance of the English.[34] What they could control was the strategy they pursued.

Unlike their sachems, ordinary Indians aspired not to be kings or gentlemen but to become more like independent yeomen. They did not control large tracts of land and had little to live on other than the fruits of their labor. The standard English view of the role of conquered Indians in colonial society was hardly encouraging. In 1739, the colony's first historian described Indians in Rhode Island like they were a group of people conquered by the biblical Israelites: the English conquerors had suffered them to live, but at the price of serving settlers as "hewers of wood and drawers of water."[35] Ordinary Indians resisting this kind of role and seeking better options would have to remake themselves, just as members of the Ninigret family had done. And like the Ninigrets, they depended for their success on both the reserve of ancestral territory many still lived on and the responses of local settlers and colonial officials.

The economic struggles of ordinary Indians in the early eighteenth century are well illustrated by the story of Betty Thompson. During the 1720s, Betty Thompson lived with "Long Peter" Coheis in a wigwam on the western outskirts of Indian Town, near the house of the prominent local settler Colonel Christopher Champlin. Champlin's accounts, preserved in the records of a subsequent legal

battle, vividly depict their struggle to escape from a cycle of poverty. Thompson
and Coheis farmed on a small scale: they bought hoes and scythes; occasionally
paid Champlin to plow new ground; and bought sheep from him in the spring.
They dressed largely in the English style, buying shoes, shirts, jackets, and cloth.
Coheis also probably hunted, for he bought a gun and several times returned for
more gunpowder. No doubt they also fished in the Great Salt Pond; probably for
this reason they hired Champlin's team to haul their canoe. In exchange, they intermittently worked for Champlin, but Thompson and Coheis never earned quite
enough to pay off their debt.[36] To reduce their expenses and avoid becoming even
more dependent on Champlin, they sent their two young boys to live with another
settler, George Babcock. A close associate of Sachem Charles Augustus Ninigret
and one of the few settlers who spoke the Narragansett language, Babcock would
prove a useful ally.

A crisis struck one summer in the late 1720s, when Peter Coheis fell sick. As
he lay ill, his creditors hovered anxiously—not by his sickbed but at Champlin's
purse strings. The ministrations of a local doctor only added to Coheis's debts and
to Champlin's anxiety. In early September, the ailing Coheis ate a bad bunch of
grapes and died. His brothers decided to bury him in a wooden coffin. From inside his old wigwam they scavenged the boards that he and Betty had used as a
sleeping platform. For nails and more boards, they knocked on Champlin's door.
Several months of mourning were observed, followed by a customary funeral dance.
Meanwhile, Champlin refused to settle with the doctor and Coheis's other creditors. He seized Coheis's most valuable belongings—the gun and a store of corn—
and grumbled to his neighbors that he had gotten nothing else for Coheis's debt.[37]
That was not quite true: he also got Betty Thompson.

Like many Indians working for settlers, Betty Thompson found that her relationship with Champlin devolved into a vicious cycle of dependency. For the next
five years, Thompson continued her previous arrangement with Champlin and
slowly slid deeper into debt. When Champlin began pressing her to settle their account in early 1732, she took action to get out from under his grasp. She asked the
man who was raising her boys, George Babcock, for help. Babcock agreed to pay
her debt to Champlin if she would formally indenture her boys to him. When
Champlin refused to abate what seemed excessive charges, Babcock refused to pay
any of the debt and instead promised to provide Thompson with legal protection
if Champlin tried to recover the money at law. When the seventy-six-year-old
Champlin died several weeks later, his son did take the matter to court. But Babcock succeeded in protecting Thompson by exploiting the legal technicalities for

which the Rhode Island legal system was notorious. He got the first suit tossed out of court because the opposing declaration confused the pronouns *he* and *she*. When these gambits succeeded, the younger Christopher Champlin gave up. Thompson was free.[38]

Betty Thompson's victory was unusual, but her experience suggests the special challenges New England Indians faced in trying to remake themselves as independent yeomen. Few Indians tried to challenge unfair treatment, and even fewer actually won at law. But a great many Indians were, like Betty Thompson, drawn into relationships of dependence, debt, and bound labor. Sometimes native men made arrangements as sharecroppers, working settlers' land "to the halves." More often, Indian men and women were sued for debt and bound by the courts to work for their creditors. Often, these relationships were servile. Whereas Thompson's native relatives tended to describe Peter Coheis as "living" with Champlin or working in his "Imploy," English neighbors described Peter in the possessive, as "Champlin's Indian." To his face, Betty called Champlin "master."[39]

Indians joined in the transatlantic explosion in demand for consumer goods, which were becoming available in an ever expanding array. Like many settlers, many Narragansetts found that consuming English goods led to debt. Even for those still living in traditional dwellings, the accumulation of English goods and furniture made wigwams increasingly like houses. We can glimpse inside one such dwelling because Ezra Stiles carefully sketched it—complete with chests and a dresser, a tea table and chair, pots hanging from hooks, dishes on shelves (fig. 3). Many of these objects improved on aboriginal ones: pots, hoes, and guns were more effective than carved soapstone vessels, quahog shells, and bows and arrows. Other goods supplied new needs; among these were farm tools, rum, clothing, and petty luxuries such as ribbons and handkerchiefs. Native New Englanders even participated in the international craze for tea imported from the East Indies. In an even more exaggerated way than settlers who resented imperial mercantilism, native people such as Betty Thompson found themselves on the wrong end of a structural trade imbalance. Before the arrival of the English, individual Narragansetts had enjoyed more reciprocal exchanges with one another and neighboring peoples, but with colonists bargains were almost always lopsided.[40]

What this Indian debt meant depended on whom you asked. Settlers were generally unsympathetic. When English settlers considered their own finances or the broader patterns of trade with Britain, they responded ambivalently: even deeply indebted individuals repeated homilies cautioning against credit and urging eco-

FIGURE 3. Wigwam of Phebe and Elizabeth Mohege in the Western Niantic enclave in Niantic, Connecticut, 1761. Ezra Stiles drew a plan of the wigwam and its furnishings while sitting at the tea table. The wigwam's domed frame, measuring about 17 by 12 feet, was covered with bark and woven mats to provide a warm shelter; the customary sleeping platform surrounds a fire. A variety of English furnishings fill the space: a tea table and chair, dressers, shelves with pottery. As late as the 1760s, most residents of New England enclaves lived in wigwams, but increasingly they were building frame houses out of milled timbers. Adapted by the author from a cutaway perspective view drawn by Edward G. Schumacher at the direction of William C. Sturtevant.

nomic independence, but they also recognized trade as a problem of policy. In the colonies, the lack of domestic manufactures, encouraged by parliamentary policies, created justifiable anxiety because this exploitation was at the heart of mercantilist economic theory. These structural dynamics were only exaggerated for native peoples living in colonial territory. Nonetheless, settlers persistently viewed native indebtedness not as a matter of policy or power, nor even as simple personal failing, but as characteristic of Indians as a group. English settlers tended to imagine Indians as irresponsible economic agents—consumers of nonproductive goods and makers of bad bargains. Symbolic of Indians' poor economic choices was their much vaunted weakness for rum, a staple of the Rhode Island economy and the transatlantic slave trade and the ordinary lubricant of settlers' working days. Typical of many such stories was an account in a Boston newspaper about an Indian woman who leaned up against a barn while tippling one cold evening and awoke to find herself frozen to the ground.[41] Whatever else it was, Indians' much touted affinity for alcohol soon became a symbol of their profligate consumption, their economic imprudence, even their self-destruction. Of course, this evaluation of Indians' behavior assumed that their motives were irrational responses to markets that were free and equal.

For their part, Indians tended to blame their economic misfortune on the unfair practices of English settlers. Indians were overcharged for goods and services and underpaid for their labor so blatantly and so routinely that the General Assembly enacted a series of statutes to prevent such abuses, beginning with "An Act, to prevent *Indians* being Sued for Debt," passed in 1718. Such statutes proved of little use because the legal system itself was hardly egalitarian. When Christopher Champlin locked horns with Betty Thompson, he had many advantages: he started out rich, and she started out poor; he was literate and legally savvy, and she needed an English patron to defend herself. Around this time a group of Nantucket Indians vividly expressed their view of colonial law: "If [we] sue the English, the Judges, Jury, Sheriff & Clerk are the Defendants." Indeed, trials were often colored by racial bias. Indians not only were excluded from the ranks of magistrates and attorneys and from service on juries but also formally excluded even from roles as translators (on the grounds, stated by an attorney in one of the Ninigret cases, that Indians were inherently untrustworthy).[42] As Indians and settlers became economically and culturally enmeshed, they increasingly thought of themselves as members of antagonistic groups.

Frustrated by often unfair treatment by their English neighbors, Indians trying to control the process of anglicization focused their energy on those aspects of the process over which they could exercise some influence. This is one way to understand their various attempts to establish continuity with familiar gender roles, to learn skilled trades, and to shape the use of land within the tribal enclave.

Indians responded to the limited economic opportunities available to them in colonial society in ways deeply influenced by their customary notions of the proper roles of men and women. But in colonial New England these roles were becoming outmoded. The transformation of the landscape and the economy affected men particularly, foreclosing most hunting and ending warfare among tribes. Men persevering as hunters were forced to range farther and farther in pursuit of less plentiful game; those dedicated to fighting had to turn to service in English armies. Symptomatic of the profound disruption of native customs in New England in the aftermath of King Philip's War, Betty Thompson and Peter Coheis likely were not married according to native tradition. They might have had an English ceremony. Probably they just lived together unceremoniously, as the then sachem Charles Ninigret and his fourth wife, Handsome Hannah, did.[43] In this time of transition, gender relations were changing in ways that may have seemed as uncertain then as they do to us now.

With a landscape changing around them, native men and women had little choice but to adapt to new work roles. Men, when they had a chance, tended to seek out employment outside the enclave in English analogues of traditional masculine domains: they went sailing; they fought in wars. For men mired in debt, one popular, if dangerous, option was military service; large numbers of native men from enclaves and towns across New England fought alongside settlers in colonial wars. But wars were both dangerous and sporadic, and sailing was notoriously dangerous to Indian men, who were thought to be particularly susceptible to ship-borne diseases. So most men ended up doing farmwork that was either entirely alien or traditionally feminine.[44]

Despite all these challenges, an increasing number of Narragansett people began to escape the cycle of servitude and poverty and to practice husbandry on the tribal reserve. By the middle years of the century, many men such as John Daniel could boast that they had been "bro't up with the best of Farmers." Some Indians disappointed English visitors with their dense hedgerows, irregular garden patches, and inattention to clear roads. Although their work looked sloppy to their English neighbors, families such as the Shattocks farmed in basically English styles. Indeed, Indians even adopted English methods for cultivating indigenous crops that the English had appropriated: potatoes, corn, beans, and squash. They also slowly embraced the keeping of livestock. Moreover, Indians also began to develop skills in trades and to perform specialized services for their English neighbors. When a new highway was built near the great salt pond, John Shattock seized the business opportunity to set up a market to peddle fish. In fact, by the 1750s, enough Indians had "farms" close enough to English models that the voters of Charlestown attempted to tax them. A group of Narragansetts protested to the colonial General Assembly, which ordered the town to rescind the tax. Although local settlers proved happy enough to add Indians to their tax lists—apparently assuming that it was Indian men who generally controlled land—the Narragansetts resisted such efforts, insisting on the autonomy of their tribal governance.[45]

The most visible sign of successful anglicization in enclaves across southern New England was the replacement of traditional wigwams with English-style frame houses. In the late 1750s several Narragansetts organized the construction of a sawmill and dam, moving simultaneously toward adoption of English economic methods and economic autonomy. Not only were Indians felling trees and milling lumber, but they were framing and finishing the structures without the help of their English neighbors. During the 1760s, John Shattock himself worked as a "House Carpenter." He built one house that his father later sold to a settler, and for himself he built not a wigwam but a little hut.[46]

Around the same time, a number of Narragansetts became interested in formal schooling for their children, but the missionaries who supported such efforts tended to have quite limited ambitions for their Indian protégés. By the 1750s, the sachem and a group of tribe members began seeking sponsorship for a school, and during the 1760s, they tested several schoolmasters and settled on one who stayed for more than a decade.[47]

A number of the most proficient and pious Narragansett boys and girls went off for advanced study with the Reverend Eleazar Wheelock, a Connecticut minister who had opened "Moor's Indian Charity School" in the late 1750s. In the 1760s, he expanded the school and moved it to a tract of land in New Hampshire donated by the earl of Dartmouth. There, his students were schooled not only in reading, writing, and Christian virtues but also in sharply differentiated gender roles: he set boys to farmwork, girls to spinning and weaving. At least some students and parents were resentful of his assumption that they came to him ignorant of such things and were offended by his practice of sending students off to work for long terms of manual labor to subsidize what was supposed to be a "Charity School." In part, this practice stemmed from Wheelock's assumption that Indians should be prepared for relatively humble walks of life—an assumption he shared with other contemporaries. The Reverend Gideon Hawley, the missionary at the Mashpee enclave on Cape Cod during the 1760s, believed that Indians should content themselves with the modest lot of "common people." It was best simply to "enable a young Indian and give him a will to attend an acre of corn or even a yard of potatoes" and to "teach a young female savage to spin a skaine of yarn, milk cows or even raise a brood of chickens."[48]

All these trends only emphasized the importance of a substantial reserve of tribal lands. Nowhere is this more evident than in the continuing migration of Indians across the New England countryside. Despite high mortality and constant movement away from the Narragansett reserve, immigration helped keep the tribe's population up. About half of Rhode Island's Indians at any time lived in English households in South County or in the town of Newport, and many crossed back and forth between English and native territory, but the population of the Narragansetts reserve remained stable at about five hundred for most of the century. Oftentimes, Indians isolated in smaller enclaves that were losing ground to local settlers moved onto the larger, legally established reservations. Native communities had long been fluid, and among the Narragansetts, people from other tribes had come and gone over the years. A multiplicity of small enclaves in southern New England quietly disappeared in the century after the war of 1675. English farming practices filled in and smoothed over Indian "barns" and Indian hills, erasing the traces of the aboriginal presence. Many settlers thought native New Englanders were themselves disappearing. Ezra Stiles was one: he kept meticulous track in his itineraries of the declining populations of numerous local enclaves, counting present numbers against the memories of local settlers. But, the Indians were not dying off. Often, they were moving away from the English onto their own territory.[49]

By the 1760s, Eleazar Wheelock could write of the Narragansett, "They have bid the fairest to be built up, and become a people, of any party of Indians I know of in New England." Ultimately, the process of becoming culturally more like the English made natives more conscious of themselves as members of a distinct group.[50] Tribe members adorned their bodies with manufactured textiles, worked on English farms, were sued in colonial courts, and filled their wigwams with English goods. But settlers did not consistently treat them equally. Thus, it was hard for any Indians to avoid feeling like underlings in colonial society. Gradually, many ordinary Narragansetts, feeling exploited and disrespected by individual settlers and colonial officials, turned to the economic development of their own resources and began to farm their land, build houses, and develop skilled trades and literacy. The result for the Narragansetts was not simple incorporation into colonial society but rather the reinforcement of a powerful sense of common cause with other enclave communities in the region.

||| Revolt |||

For a time it seemed that these roles—the Ninigrets living like aristocrats, and the common Indians living like yeomen—might be compatible. Young Thomas Ninigret encouraged this view when he returned to Narragansett country in 1756. He had spent his minority living in Stonington with his grandmother Oskoosooduck and in Newport at school. Now of age, he was determined to assume his office and establish his independence from the colonial guardians who had been supervising his affairs. They had allowed his father's house to fall into ruin, so he ordered its replacement with a new structure, fashionably designed and richly appointed. His cousin Charles had initiated a new flurry of lawsuits, and his English tenants were refusing to pay their rent, so he fought them in the courts and won. The young sachem ended the dynastic dispute once and for all by negotiating a financial settlement that included a payment of some five hundred pounds sterling.[51]

Both tribe members and colonial officials wanted to believe that the route to a better future lay in the sachem's independence. A fateful moment came in 1758, when Thomas Ninigret petitioned the colonial legislature to grant him authority to manage his estate free from the supervision of his guardian and trustees. Ordinary Narragansetts, with good reason to be suspicious of the sachem's trustees and struggling for their own autonomy from English settlers, briefly debated the implications of the move. Some tribe members later insisted that they had explained to Ninigret that in taking him "from under Gardeans" they did not mean "to vest the fee of any land" in him. They claimed that he agreed to treat the land as his own. In any case, tribe members signed the petition in large numbers. The General Assembly quickly complied, voiding all laws that restricted the "Native *Indians*" from "selling and disposing of their Estates."[52]

In the long run, the sachem, striving to become a gentleman, was bound to come into conflict with tribe members, who were striving to become yeomen. Each strategy for gaining Indian autonomy emulated different English roles and required mutually exclusive uses of limited resources. The Ninigret family's strategy of emulating the gentry depended on renting and selling large tracts of land to English settlers. The tribe members' strategy of emulating the yeomanry depended on directly improving myriad small, family tracts. Since the conquest of the Narragansetts by the English, depopulation, widespread servitude among colonists, and a relatively large tract of land had insulated the tribe from the effects of changing customs and compromises. There seemed to be plenty of land to go around. Later, in the 1760s, land became increasingly scarce, and therefore control over it became a more urgent concern. The sachem's tactics skillfully exploited lingering anxieties within the tribe about the benefits of anglicization and the role of Indians in colonial society. He succeeded in pitting a more conservative faction against the tribe's dynamic, progressive leaders. The controversy ultimately turned, through an extended series of legal and political appeals, into a debate about the tribe's ancient constitution that revealed longstanding and startling differences in understandings of past practices and their meanings. Was land within the enclave rented from the sachem? Or was it owned, collectively, by tribe members? Did the sachem have absolute authority? Or was he bound by the will of his counselors and his people? Once again, legal debates produced tangles of conflicting evidence about analogies between native roles and English concepts.

Trouble developed soon after the 1758 order freed Thomas Ninigret to sell land with impunity. Instead of husbanding his resources, curtailing the abuses of the past, and increasing the profits from the lands he managed, the sachem was selling off his assets at bargain prices, piling up new debts for luxuries such as his new house, fine wines, and a pleasure boat. He further flouted tribal sensibilities by marrying a "mulatto" woman named Moll Whitfield, who clearly was not of "high" blood; and he held the ceremony far off in the Anglican Church in Newport. But most important was his rapid sale of land. In the past, it may have seemed that there was plenty of land to go around, but by the 1760s land on the reserve had become critically short. When Ninigret returned in the mid-1750s, only about 5,000 acres remained. By 1764, he had sold as much as two-thirds of that amount, some 3,274¼ acres. Yet his debts—reckoned as high as twenty-five hundred pounds sterling—only continued to rise.[53]

Soon the residents of the Narragansett enclave, faced with the dissipation of the one inheritance that could ensure a viable future in colonial society, were plunged into an open controversy over the control of land and the customs of tribal governance. Some tribe members entreated the sachem to stop selling land and obey the advice of his counselors. Ninigret did little to quell their concerns. When some members of his council refused to go along with his dealings, Sachem Ninigret ignored them and went about his business with just the loyal remnants, who soon became known as the "King's Council." The insurgent leaders came to be known as the "Tribe's Council." Further antagonizing those who protested, Ninigret punished his opponents and rewarded his supporters by redistributing land.[54]

Although members of the Tribe's Party insisted that the tribe had always retained its sovereignty—the right not to be "dictated to by other nations"—they were forced to turn for resolution to colonial and, later, imperial officials. Soon, the Tribe's Party had secured the assistance of the prominent attorney Matthew Robinson, who had led young Charles Ninigret's final legal assault against his uncle Thomas. In 1763, they escalated the dispute by petitioning the General Assembly to curb the sachem's disastrous sales of land.[55]

The General Assembly managed to pressure the two parties into an agreement, in principle, to partition the enclave. Before the legislature Thomas Ninigret conceded, "The Tribe have some Right to such Lands as they for many Years have Improved." The Tribe's Party in turn admitted that the sachem deserved the land he had actually been using. Both parties agreed to divide the enclave: so much land for the sachem, so much land and rights of way to fishing grounds for the tribe. This latter portion of the enclave was to be granted to the "whole Tribe as a Joint Body" for their "sole Use and Maintenance and Support" in perpetuity. Legislators sent a surveying team out so the boundary lines could be drawn, but the surveyors delayed matters further with a report that land tenure was so complex and intermingled on the reserve that sorting it out would be a long and difficult process.[56] With the legislature stymied by the logistical difficulty of producing an accurate survey, Ninigret did his best to sabotage the agreement—and in fact was able to divide the tribe sufficiently to give the colonial government an excuse to delay any resolution to the conflict for years.

Ironically, Ninigret was able to do this by animating fears within the tribe about a more market-defined conception of land ownership. His success with this gambit suggests how threatening the process of anglicization was for many ordinary Indians. The land should remain under his stewardship, he argued, so that it could remain, in practice, collective. The sachem displaced attention from his own behavior that contradicted this fantasy by vigorously insisting that it was his opponents in the Tribe's Party who were trying to break up the enclave. He claimed they wanted to divide the available land up into individual tracts. His leading opponents, he asserted, were scheming to seize the best and biggest tracts for themselves. The truth behind these aspersions was that supporters of the Tribe's Party tended to be Christian, husbandmen, owners of the "best farms," those with skills in trades the English recognized—such as John Shattock, a carpenter, and Samuel Niles, a Baptist preacher. Those who led the charge for economic anglicization and "improvement" on the reserve, it seems, felt they had most to lose and were best able to organize supporters. Something of the anxiety such changes evoked within the enclave is clear from the fact that a considerable number of tribe members were not completely alienated by the sachem's stated belief that they were not capable of individualistic competition in a market economy. If ordinary tribe members were granted individual tracts, they would soon waste or sell it. After all, the sachem told Sir William Johnson, "they are but Indians."[57]

In the ensuing lawsuits and political challenges, a crucial question was, Who owned the Narragansett enclave? Both parties began with the mistaken assumption that this question was simple and easily resolved. Members of the Tribe's Party insisted that the tribe, as a body, owned the reserve—not the sachem, as an individual. At first, they insisted that the Ninigrets' 1709 deed proved their point: its purpose had been to preserve a corner of their ancestral territory on which the natives could pursue their livelihoods, to protect them from the incursions of settlers, "to prevent the Indians from coming to Poverty by means of Impositions from designing, ill minded People." The tribe's oral tradition, however, was contradicted both by the memories of the sachem's supporters and, devastatingly, by the written document itself. In one intemperate moment in 1764, Thomas Ninigret reportedly declared that all the lands in the country were his, that he would do with them as he pleased, and that there was no law to stop him. The sachem's opponents did not obtain a copy of the original deed until early 1767 and were distressed to find that it made no mention of the tribe's welfare or collective ownership of the reserved lands.[58] Apparently, until this point, members of the Ninigret family, their attorneys, and colonial officials had done their best to keep the implications of the 1709 deed obscure, at least on the reserve. In the 1740s, George Ninigret had been careful to stake his claim to a role as "proprietor" of Narragansett country only in written legal documents presented to colonial officials. In speaking to his council and tribe members, he emphasized that ownership of the enclave was common and that his administration was bound by the will of his council. The sachem and tribe members could sustain this ambiguity, or duplicity, only as long as there was plenty of land and as long as the two interpretations were not subjected to practical tests.

Failing to prove their case with the 1709 deed, members of the Tribe's Party emphasized the traditional ways in which land within the enclave had been allocated to individuals and families. Here again conflict developed, not so much about what actually had happened in the past as about what those customs implied about ownership.

All witnesses agreed that land was normally "set off" to individuals and their families by the sachem and his council. All householders in the enclave had received their land this way, some as much as a hundred acres, others somewhat less.

Requests for land were considered by the sachem and his council, and the formal laying off of tracts was a public event. The sachem, council members, and others walked the bounds and marked them. Grants were not permanent but rather for three generations—a time span that may well have derived from English land law. Residents of the enclave also adopted an old English ritual for transferring land. When John Shattock's sister Mary Sock sold land to a settler in the 1770s, she "took a Knife and Cut up a piece of Turf of the land & gave it to him." Subsequently, Narragansetts recalled that when the council allocated land a council member would place the piece of turf on the head of the person receiving the plot and then symbolically plant a twig in it. Traditionally, this symbolic "livery of seisin" represented the rights of the new owner to till the earth and to cut the timber on it. Ironically, by the mid-nineteenth century the ritual had fallen out of practice among most Americans and came to be seen as a distinctive, Narragansett custom.[59]

In the 1760s, the controversy centered on the question of whether ordinary tribe members paid rent for the land they occupied. Everyone agreed that tribe members annually performed labor services for the sachem. The fencing at Fort Neck had been erected with such labor for Charles Ninigret in 1733. But what exactly were these payments to the sachem? Thomas Ninigret, his supporters, and their attorneys argued that this annual labor service was like rent. This analogy supported the claim that the sachem owned the reserve and therefore had the right to sell land to English settlers or reallocate it among tribe members. His opponents, however, argued that these apparent payments were not rent and did not imply ownership— they were, in fact, tribute given to the sachem to honor him "as sachem."[60]

An early test of the sachem's ownership of tribal land came in a lawsuit that developed when he revoked a tract of land in the enclave from one of his opponents and gave it to his brother-in-law William Sachem, a strong supporter. One of many witnesses was Mary Sock. She disagreed with her brother, John Shattock, and testified in support of the sachem's position: "My Husband always paid a quit Rent to the Sachem or King for the Land by his Labour." Such descriptions suggested two broad similarities to English custom. Implicitly, Sock accepted the notion that men were the principal holders and managers of land and hence that Narragansett custom was like English custom. Explicitly, she declared that the Narragansett sachem, like an English manorial lord, owned his domain absolutely and granted only limited tenancy to his subjects. That is, instead of owning the land in fee simple as most settlers in New England did, ordinary Indians would always owe a special form of rent. Quit rents represented a more secure hold on the property than ordinary rents implied, since under this form of tenancy one could not be evicted for nonpayment. During much of the colonial period such "quit rents" had been on the books in the vast proprietary tracts granted by the Crown to individual families in the seventeenth century, but it was only the land shortages of the 1760s that allowed the Penn family and their peers to begin successfully extracting them on a large scale. Thus, the analogy makes sense, for that was precisely what the Ninigret family had been trying to accomplish: a feudal revival.[61]

The Tribe's Party insisted that these payments were not rent. "No," one Indian man testified, this custom was not rent, nor was it payment for land use: "not as I know of but I used to work for the Sachem at some times to acknowledge him to be my King." And the overwhelming majority of witnesses agreed that the "tribute" or "acknowledgement" was performed by women as well as men, by both adults and children. As one settler put it, "the Squaws and Children (as well as the men) met and paid money as an Acknowledgement." Attorneys cross-examining Mary Sock sought to undermine the plausibility of the analogy with rent:

Q1:   did you ever Know your husband pay any Money to the Sachem for
        the Rent of the Land now in Dispute—
Ansr   No
Q2:   did you Ever Know your Husband bargain with the King to pay
        him Rent for the Land now in Dispute the whole time he Lived on
        sd Land.
A.   No.

Money and bargaining were not, of course, legally essential to rent. But how else was the Tribe's Party to prove whether the analogy stuck? The broader point of the Tribe's Party was that the sachem's authority over land transactions was limited. Although in this case the representative of the Tribe's Party, James Niles, prevailed, the battle was far from over.[62]

Meanwhile, the two parties developed conflicting interpretations about the nature of tribal governance in general, with the sachem claiming authority as an absolute monarch and the Tribe's Party arguing that in fact the Narragansett polity was more like a representative republic. By the mid-1760s, such language powerfully evoked the contemporary imperial crisis, which brought to a head longstanding debates over a "country ideology" that sought to limit monarchical authority by emphasizing the rights of representatives, the advantages of mixed institutional structures, and the tendency of power to corrupt virtuous governance.[63]

Much of the debate centered on the role of the council, a group of elders that had existed as long as anyone could remember. Since old Ninigret's times, colonial officials had recognized the tribal council's authority by having its members sign their names, or marks, on important documents such as the 1709 deed. But the council's role had never been explicitly defined in the colonial legal record. Many tribe members recalled that in the mid-1740s George Ninigret had categorically stated, "It was a Law that the Sachem could not do anything of himself nor could the Tribe do any thing of themselves, but the Sachem & Tribe must Join in transacting their Business, for that a Deed given by the Sachem must be approved of by the Council & Tribe or it would be good for nothing." It may well be that the council had seen a temporary increase in its status during the legal disputes of the 1740s and 1750s, when George Ninigret needed its support in the fight against his rival nephew Charles. Presumably, the council largely ran tribal affairs during the decade or so that young Thomas Ninigret was away from the enclave. In the long run its authority was eroded by the explicit legal recognition of the sachem as the official head of the tribe and owner of the reserved lands. But the Tribe's Party nonetheless has had some basis for arguing that the sachem was by custom bound to respond to the needs and wishes of his people.[64]

Thomas Ninigret, for his part, was willing to make a show of popular or council support when it was to his advantage: when his opponents produced petitions with long lists of signatures, he replied with petitions with long lists of signatures. But he also insisted that his authority did not depend on their consent. In 1763, he told the General Assembly that he held his office, first, as "the legal heir, according to the course of descent" and, second, as "as one who had the voice of the tribe upon the decease of his father." Indeed, he claimed, his subjects were currently "enjoying greater Rights than ever they have done any time heretofore in any of the Sachim's Reigns."[65]

By 1765, the crisis in the Narragansett enclave reached a head. Personally, Thomas Ninigret seemed to be veering out of control. His unhappy marriage became a humiliating spectacle when it became public knowledge that he had been cuckolded by a neighboring settler. His wife moved out of his house and in with her lover. Thomas responded by publishing a notice that since she had eloped he would not pay her debts, and he then sued for divorce. During the divorce proceedings it was reported that her lover had bragged that he had carnal knowledge of the "Indian King's wife" more than a hundred times. Nonetheless, the court slapped Thomas with a restraining order, which suggests it may have sympathized with her and suspected him of beating her. Certainly, by this time he was widely rumored to be a drunkard. Shortly thereafter, Ninigret placed another advertisement for the return of a runaway Indian servant, whose broken jaw and knocked-out teeth he explained as the result of being kicked by a horse.[66]

Ninigret's domestic disarray reflected the ruinous state of his finances. After the General Assembly had abandoned the agreement of 1763 to divide the reserve, it had issued a series of stopgap measures that further escalated the crisis. The remaining tribal estate had seemingly been protected by an order barring the sachem from contracting any additional debts and declaring any such contracts void. Instead of learning to live within his means, he simply resorted to more desperate agreements for credit. In 1765 the General Assembly decided to protect the interests of his English creditors and ordered the sale of as much land from the enclave as necessary to pay these illegally contracted obligations. The Tribe's Party howled in protest that if this was done there would be nothing left.

Support for the Tribe's Party swelled, and in early in 1766 it took a drastic step. John Shattock and his brother Tobias were recalled from Eleazar Wheelock's school in New Hampshire to preside over the crisis. The Tribe's Party called a meeting in which a large portion of the residents of the enclave gathered and voted to depose the sachem. Subsequently, the tribe would be governed by the council. Careful to document its actions, the Tribe's Party crafted a formal declaration addressed to Thomas Ninigret; it was signed by some 157 men and women, including many of the sachem's longtime supporters.

The document recapitulated all the controversies over tribal governance of the previous three decades, beginning with a summary of customs and practices. The sachem, chosen by acclamation of the tribe, held his office legitimately only so long as he observed the customs of royal kinship, respected the will of the tribe, and promoted the common good of the tribe. Thomas Ninigret had violated each of these principles:

> In the first place ye marrying a mulatto woman without ye approbation of ye Tribe.
>
> Secondly in refusing to be advised by ye Tribe.
>
> Thirdly in extravagantly wasting, spending and making sale of ye lands appropriated to ye use and benefit of ye Indians when forbid by them.[67]

The first complaint recalls the earliest objections to the nonroyal marriages of Charles Augustus Ninigret in the 1730s. None of this family drama had appeared in the objections of the tribal party during the previous five years, so it seems to have been included here both to evoke a rather atavistic notion of royal comport-ment and to rub salt in the wounds of his public humiliation. The document closes by holding out the possibility that, if Ninigret returned to good behavior, the Tribe's Party might reinstate him.

As was the case so often before, the question became not what the will of the tribe was but whether tribe members could prevail upon colonial authorities to respect their wishes. The sachem, predictably, denied their right to take such action—a drastic step for which no member of the tribe could remember any precedent. The legislature dragged the tribe's dispute with the sachem on until there was little left to fight over. It imposed ineffective restraints on the sale of the tribal land, repeatedly postponed any resolution to the dispute, allowed Thomas Ninigret's debts to mount, and ultimately allowed him to sell more land.[68] Stymied by the colonial government, members of the tribe turned to the supervening power of the imperial government, from which they claimed protection as loyal subjects of the British monarch.

The letters the Tribe's Party sent soliciting patronage outside the colony show how sharply tribe members had come to view their victimization as a result of both ordinary kinds of corruption and a special colonial antipathy toward Indians. They understood that astonishing judicial decisions were possible because justices were sitting on cases involving their own loans to Ninigret. As one of the tribe's attor-neys sardonically put it, "Some how or other it so happens that the Delays, and continuances at our General Assembly, give *Tom* and his White Allies, and Friends much time to Serve themselves & Get good Estates." In 1767, Tobias Shattock bit-terly rebuked the chair of a committee established to settle the sachem's finances: "Certain Gentleman has endeavored to advance their Interest by the poor Indians, thinking (perhaps) their extream Poverty may prevent their being called into Ques-tion." These accusations fed a paranoid vision of the entire century of colonial in-teractions; as Shattock told Sir William Johnson, the tribe's genteel enemies had been plotting for sixty years to "rob us poor Indians of our Land."[69]

For the aggrieved faction, the process of rallying support and protesting tended to help the tribe members develop wider imperial networks. At each stage, they hoped that benevolence or impartiality would overcome local self-interest. But they were increasingly disillusioned with the British. As in other similar cases across contemporary New England, the tribe's early supporters were mainly those who sympathized with exploited people on the margins of colonial society (such as attorney Matthew Robinson) or who hoped that Indians would become civilized (such as clergymen Joseph Fish and Matthew Graves). It was during the 1760s that Narragansetts had developed ties with the Reverend Eleazar Wheelock; his school gave the Shattock brothers the polish they needed to represent the Tribe's Party before prominent English people. Yet Wheelock, whose attempts to educate Indians were controversial and who was struggling to develop his school in New Hampshire, had an interest in avoiding conflict. When his star student, the Reverend Samson Occom, set out on a tour of England to raise money for the school, Wheelock pressured him to suppress his outrage against Connecticut settlers in a widely publicized lawsuit over Mohegan land, which was similar to the case of the Narragansetts and currently under review in London. Sir William Johnson, imperial superintendent of Indian affairs, personally visited many tribes in southern New England in the spring of 1768 but declined decisive action: "I . . . really think their case very hard, tho' it is too common to be Extraordinary."[70]

Meanwhile, John Shattock took the case of the Narragansetts all the way to London. Like a host of colonial representatives who came to the center of imperial power to press home mounting concerns about taxation, representation, and the proper place of the colonies within the empire, Shattock, too, spoke the republican language of liberty, corruption, and tyranny. Shattock's petition on behalf of the "Indians of the Narragansett Nation" began with a story that was already becoming all too familiar. At the first arrival of the English 150 years earlier, the Narragansetts had been a "Numerous Body of People" who occupied an extensive territory, but colonial settlement had diminished their numbers to only about 315 adults who lived in a rapidly shrinking enclave. The matter at hand concerned the Indians' "ancient and established constitution" and the limits of their ruler's authority. Shattock used the language of constitutional monarchy to explain the problem the Narragansetts faced: their nation had always been governed by a sachem who was elected by a majority of the people and whose power was strictly limited. On assuming office, he was administered an oath: "You being chosen Sachem by these Men and Women now standing here, you shall no longer [be] Sachem than you obey the Council and the Tribe." Just such a crisis now faced the Indian nation. The current sachem, a young man named Thomas Ninigret, had been selling off large portions of the dwindling tribal enclave to finance extravagant expenditures. Impoverished tribe members had tried to stop him, but their petitions and lawsuits dragged on inconclusively, accumulating expenses. At length the Narragansetts held a meeting, declared Thomas Ninigret a tyrant, and voted to depose him. Colonial officials, however, refused to recognize the tribe's decision and continued to allow "King Tom" to sell land. Now, the British monarch was the tribe's final appeal.[71]

The British monarch declined to intervene on behalf of the Narragansetts—a case about sovereignty and tyranny that had remarkable parallels to the mounting imperial crisis. The Rhode Island government swung into action only late in 1769, when the sachem's spiral of self-destruction threatened to uproot the Narragansetts entirely. If colonial officials had little interest in seeing Indians prosper, the last thing they wanted to see was hundreds of Indians completely dispossessed, living in their towns, and burdening their public relief rolls. Sensing that the end of the crisis was near, the sachem's former allies turned against him. His creditors buried him in litigation and seized even the proverbial "clothes on his back." No sachem of the Narragansetts would ever again enjoy the financial wherewithal to claim the role of gentleman, and his former allies were quick to demote Thomas Ninigret, in their legal papers, to the status of "husbandman." That fall, the legislative committee appointed years earlier to settle his debts finally acted decisively, making it clear that it would ignore its previous orders and sell as much land as necessary to pay all settlers for all loans they had made him. Clearly, even if a scrap of tribal land was preserved, it would not be enough to enable the tribe to develop a prosperous subsistence as yeomen. Soon, the Tribe's Party saw public notices advertising for sale the crucial tracts of "Fort Neck, & Indian town."[72]

By this time, it was clear that neither faction of Indians was going to win: neither would be able to pursue its vision of a viable role in colonial society—not the sachem as gentleman, nor the tribe as yeomen. Eleazar Wheelock captured the pathos of their plight: "And now just as they have got engaged in cultivating their Lands, and begin to know the worth of them, by tasting the sweets of a civilized Life, the best farms are slipping from under them, one after another." Thomas Ninigret himself recognized as much. At one point, he declared that his creditors had seized all his land and that, as he had been ruined, he intended to "ruin the Indians."[73]

Late in 1769, as the Tribe's Party scrambled to prevent final critical parcels of land from being lost to the tribe, the tenure of the vengeful sachem ended. According to local lore, he was returning home from dinner one night with the colony's governor when he fell off his horse and died.[74] For the rest of the century the bitterly divided tribe would struggle to work out a new system of governance and land tenure, to piece together a viable life with the legacy of its colonial possessions.

||| Swords into Plowshares |||

The legacy of colonial encounters was on Ezra Stiles's mind one day in the spring of 1782, as his horse trotted along an ancient aboriginal path, now upgraded by the colonists into the post road from Newport to New London. Pausing in South Kingstown, Stiles searched out the site of the Great Swamp Massacre, the principal monument of the war that a century earlier had ended the power and autonomy of the Narragansett tribe. "The swamp Islet is surrounded every way with a hideous Swamp 40 Rds to one Mile wide & inaccessible but at a SW Entrance & there a deep Brook or Rivulet must be passed. All the Narrag. Indian Tribe with the Indians of Mt Haup or Bristol were assembled there in the Winter of 1675, when they were attacked by our Army of about a thousd men, who rushed over the only narrow passage of Entrance & set fire to the Wigwawms—a great Slaughter!" The earthen outlines of the fort were still visible, as were remnants of food stored in the hope of withstanding a long siege and evidence of its brutal end. "The burnt Corn remains to this day, & some of the Bones are yet above ground, as I saw at this time." Stiles wanted to see these things before they disappeared from view. The site of the ruined fort was occupied by an English settler who was preparing to transform the site, to "improve" it, to farm it. "Mr Clark is now clearing up the Land, has cut down the Timber & Brush, and will plough it up this Summer" (fig. 4).[75]

What did the imminent erasure of this macabre memorial mean to colonists in the age of imperial crisis? Anticipating the romantic tradition of a lost Indian past that still endures today, many New England settlers thought by the 1760s that Indians were disappearing from their midst. A century after King Philip's War had effectively ended forcible Indian resistance to English encroachment, the implication seemed often that Indians and settlers could never live together harmoniously because Indian nature was incompatible with civilization. The Indians, of course, were still there. And their view of why they were not better integrated into colonial society was quite different.

The Narragansetts and other native peoples in conquered territory across New England in the eighteenth century had proved that they could negotiate complex cultural worlds and dramatic changes in the ecological and political landscape. They embraced new identities and used English models to define viable roles in colonial society. They fought among themselves, not so much over whether there would be change but rather over the path of change. Faith in "improvement" fal-

FIGURE 4. When visiting the site of the Great Swamp Massacre, Ezra Stiles stayed at the Henry Marchant farm, the country residence of a Newport attorney. Its formal gardens and elegant house are typical of the genteel style of the region's prosperous commercial farmers. *S.W. View of the Seat of Henry Marchant in South Kingstown, R.I,* ca. 1785–90. Ink on paper. Courtesy of the Rhode Island Historical Society (RHi X3 3019).

tered only when their efforts began to seem futile, and no other strategy supplanted it. In the end, the problem was not disease, or incompatible cultures, or intransigent nativism, or poor communication. The problem the Narragansetts faced was that to succeed they needed the cooperation of local settlers and government officials. Indeed, few of the English were willing to facilitate viable roles for Indians as "a people."

In fact, during the spring of 1782, even as Mr. Clark prepared to plow, the leaders of the Narragansett tribe, among them John Shattock, were struggling to stop him. The site of the Great Swamp Massacre, with its haunting memories and mortal remains, lay as contested ground between English and Narragansett space. To the east were the imposing estates of the South Kingstown planters; to the west lay the humble homesteads of the Narragansett reserve. Much of the ground in between was claimed by both. Some of it, such the site of the Great Swamp Massacre, had simply been taken over by audacious settlers, often decades earlier. Now the tribe was trying to reestablish its ownership of such tracts. The dispute forcing Clark to relinquish that tract would drag through the legal system for another decade.

Decades of disputes with settlers left Indians both alienated from English settlers and increasingly identified with other Indians. The process of anglicization helped erase the differences between ethnic cultures but also prompted increasingly vital senses of racial identity. Ironically, the route to solidarity with other Indians was often through the bureaucracy of the British empire. For members of the aggrieved faction, contact with Sir William Johnson, the imperial superintendent of Indian affairs headquartered near Albany in Mohawk territory, expanded their sense of solidarity with other Indians, partly because he was the center of overlapping diplomatic and economic networks and partly because he often viewed the disparate native peoples of the American Northeast as members of a single group. Responding to an exhortation from Johnson, Sachem Thomas Ninigret haughtily disclaimed any sense of identity: he was not like those "savage" nations that Johnson had been authorized to superintend. For much of the Narragansett tribe, it became clear that whatever strategy they pursued, it would have to be far away from English-settled territory. By late 1768, leaders of the tribal faction were seriously entertaining the prospect of leaving their ancestral homeland.[76] The closer they got to English culture, the farther away from English people they wanted to get.

C H A P T E R   T W O

Negotiating Slavery

||| Boston, 1701 |||

When Adam bundled up his belongings and left his master's house, he set in motion a chain of events that produced a dramatic legal battle, eventually secured his freedom, and placed him at the center of colonial New England's most prominent public debate about African slavery. The trouble began when Adam realized that his master, the prominent merchant John Saffin, did not intend to honor an agreement they had made in 1694. At that time, Saffin had rented out a farm in Bristol complete with the livestock on it—and Adam to work it. In part out of "meer kindness" and in part to encourage Adam to serve his temporary master "chearfully," Saffin promised to free him at the end of a seven-year term. Over the years, Adam worked the farm, ate at table with the tenant and his family, and was allowed the use of a garden plot, which he used to earn money by growing and selling tobacco. But New Year's Day in 1701 came and went, and Saffin refused to free Adam; instead, he sent him back to Bristol to begin work for another farmer. So Adam took the document with him and headed across Boston to seek out the assistance of another, even more powerful magistrate, Samuel Sewall.[1]

Sewall is best known today as the judge in the Salem witch trials who first confessed his misgivings about those proceedings. He was also a major investor in land in Rhode Island's Narragansett country. But Adam likely turned to Sewall because he was developing a reputation as a friend of mistreated slaves. Sewall, who was probably a slaveholder himself, had first felt misgivings about the practice one day in June 1700, while reading a book of biblical exegesis that discussed servants in general and Blackamoors in particular. Already uneasy, he was interrupted by a friend seeking his support for a petition to the General Court "for the freeing of a Negro and his wife who were unjustly held in Bondage." Meanwhile, Cotton Mather was preparing a tract to urge masters to convert their slaves, and a bill was in the works to discourage the importation of slaves. In *The Selling of Joseph*, published that fall, Sewall argued that New Englanders would be better off without slavery. His views were controversial; but, as a justice of the superior court and a member of the governor's council, he wielded considerable power.[2]

Without such a staunch and well-connected ally, Adam didn't have a chance. After Sewall and another magistrate reviewed the original agreement and advised Saffin to free Adam, the recalcitrant master turned to the lieutenant governor for help. Saffin succeeded in having a legal complaint entered against Adam as a fugitive slave and in getting the matter referred to the next meeting of the state's highest court. At issue were two questions: whether the original agreement had been contingent on Adam's cheerful and faithful service to Saffin's tenant, and whether Adam had, in fact, behaved accordingly. A good deal of the evidence supported Adam's argument, and Saffin was not inclined to take any risks. In the weeks before the trial, Saffin managed to get himself appointed to the three-man court that heard the case. Sewall, also sitting on the court, further suspected Saffin of conniving to place on the jury one of his own tenants and of tampering with the jury's foreman. Given these egregious improprieties, it was no surprise that Saffin won that round. And he managed to drag the legal proceedings out for years: the case returned to the superior court twice more, went through the lower court four times, and was considered twice in petitions to the governor and his council. Meanwhile, Saffin published a scathing rebuttal to Sewall's antislavery tract, which anticipated many of the basic arguments used in later centuries to justify slavery on moral, religious, and legal grounds. *A Brief and Candid Answer to a Late Printed Sheet Entituled, The Selling of Joseph* . . . argued that biblical injunctions against slavery did not apply to African slavery in the English colonies and that there was nothing wrong with servitude in general or permanent enslavement in particular. It was indisputable that "God hath set different Orders of Degrees of men in the World" and obvious that Africans were inferior to Europeans. Saffin's poem "The Negroes

Character" speaks mostly to Saffin's own anger and vengefulness: "Cowardly and cruel are those *Blacks* Innate, / Prone to Revenge, Imp of inveterate hate."[3]

In the end, Adam won the battle for his freedom, but it was Saffin who won the broader argument about slavery. Around 1700, political leaders in New England, as well as in the Chesapeake Bay region, passed laws recognizing slavery as an accepted custom. Despite the continuing practice of selling Indian war captives into slavery (generally to faraway colonies), slavery in both regions became more closely and exclusively associated with Africans. New England settlers had always been proud to come from a society that had centuries earlier abolished permanent hereditary servitude and considered themselves fortunate to live in a society in which servitude was less a matter of class than of age: most people cycled into servitude as children and out as adults. Early on, although the region's economy depended on trade with the rich plantations of the West Indies, many New Englanders considered themselves better off without the social, spiritual, and cultural divisions they associated with African slavery. In 1659, as a scattering of Africans began to appear in New England towns and villages, the Rhode Island legislature flatly banned the importation of enslaved Negroes. In 1705, partly in response to Sewall's continued agitation, Massachusetts officials conceded that enslaving Negroes was undesirable and agreed that it would be better to encourage "the importing of white servants from Great Britain, &c." But European immigration to New England had virtually stopped in the 1640s and failed to revive. And the small duties Massachusetts imposed on imported slaves proved far less significant than the tacit acceptance of the legality of permanent, hereditary servitude for Africans. Around the same time, Rhode Island officials didn't even bother to revoke their forty-year-old prohibition against African slavery when they, too, imposed a tax on imported African slaves and prohibited the importation of Indian slaves, who were considered unruly and dangerous. In Boston, Sewall continued helping individual Negroes negotiate better arrangements with their masters, but never again did he bring a slave case to court or argue the matter in print. For more than half a century, public challenges to slavery per se virtually stopped.[4]

In the eighteenth century, enslaved Africans continued to arrive in New England on ships returning from the West Indies, either coastal trading vessels or larger ships that were part of the increasingly important triangle trade (fig. 5). The transatlantic triangle was dominated by Newport merchants: ships loaded with rum left New England and sailed to West Africa, where the rum was traded for slaves. All but a few of the slaves were then traded in the West Indies for molasses, which was

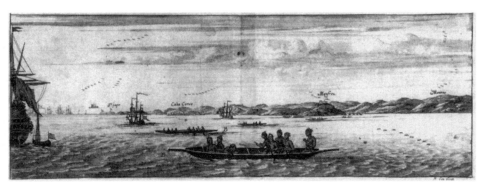

FIGURE 5. On the coast of West Africa, local slave traders paddle out to British ships. At midcentury, both provincial and metropolitan slavers were relatively small ships (about 100 tons), cramped and extremely unhealthy. Engraving by Johannes Kipps, in Awnsham and John Churchill, eds., *A Collection of Voyages and Travels* . . . (London, 1732), 156 (pl. 9, pt. b). Courtesy of the Library Company of Philadelphia.

brought back home to be manufactured into a rough, fiery rum. New England produced few valuable resources of its own, and this trading circuit helped solve this problem; it also allowed merchants to make profits at each step. Although never capturing more than 15 percent of the international slave trade, the triangle trade was crucial to the region's economy—and though few voyages brought more than a few slaves back home, a growing number of enslaved Africans were soon living in towns and villages across New England.

In coastal towns, Africans were soon a substantial part of the populace—men worked in dockyards, on ships, and in workshops, and women worked in urban households. In busy ports such as Newport and Philadelphia, fully one in five inhabitants was black. Some rural areas also developed large slave populations. In especially fertile areas such as the Connecticut and Hudson River valleys and Rhode Island's Narragansett country, large commercial farms employed thousands of African workers. By around 1730, South Kingstown, Rhode Island, was about a quarter black. In most of the New England countryside, on the other hand, there were fewer African faces. Poor soil and a short season provided little opportunity to profit from permanent workers. Nevertheless, some rural New Englanders— ships' officers, prosperous widows, and well-settled ministers—needed and could afford slaves. Overall, by 1750, about one in twenty New Englanders was enslaved.[5]

Today, in a few old New England houses one can visit the cramped garrets and dark cellar chambers where African slaves typically lived. Settlers in northern colonies often had more intimate relations with slaves than did inhabitants of the "big" and "little" houses of Chesapeake and West Indian plantations. Since few New Englanders could afford more than one or two slaves, slaves were diffused over a large number of households; at midcentury as many as a third of all households had at least one "Negro" member. Moreover, quarters were close: instead of living in outbuildings as they might have on a large plantation, enslaved New Englanders generally lived inside their masters' houses along with family members and other servants.[6]

With close quarters came close personal relations. The majority of northern slaves worked in conditions like those of antebellum southern house servants. Such servants, although often imagined as privileged, not only worked under close supervision but also had to negotiate personal relationships that were often tense. Indeed, archaeological evidence from the African Burial Ground in New York City reveals the grinding brutality of slavery in northern places: bones were enlarged and damaged by routine, heavy work, and there is evidence of more malnutrition, less cultural autonomy, and more surveillance than slaves experienced on contemporary plantations in the Chesapeake region. At the same time, the relatively small scale of slavery in New England meant that masters and slaves were densely enmeshed in the overlapping relationships that formed local communities. The everyday lives of masters and slaves were shaped by the thoughts, actions, and expectations of family members, gossiping neighbors, and legal authorities.[7] The real triangle of slavery in New England was not the transatlantic trade but the relationships that bound masters, servants, and members of a broad, if sometimes diffuse, public.

The Selling of Joseph offers an important insight into the nature of these triangular relationships. Despite his sympathy for enslaved individuals and his public attacks on slavery, Sewall was quite conventional in his views about race. He began with the assumption that the American polity was, ideally, pure white. Because Europeans shared a kinship, even poor immigrant servants could eventually be incorporated into the polity—if they were white. But strangers, such as Negroes, would always have to be excluded. Whether by nature or by happenstance—Sewall declined to say—Africans were simply too different. New England settlers, he argued, would never "embody" (or intermarry) with Africans or let them participate equally in "the Peopling of the Land." In Sewall's vision, the presence of this alien population weakened the body politic. Enslaved Africans were so degraded, so completely excluded from social recognition, that they were essentially non-persons—in other words, socially dead. In an image that hauntingly anticipates twentieth-century fantasies of zombies and body snatchers, Sewall argued that enslaved Africans took up the places of vital, free English people. Recognizing that black men were allowed neither to serve in colonial militias nor to marry white women, he wrote: "As many Negro men as there are among us, so many empty places there are" in our militia companies "and the places taken up of Men that might make Husbands for our Daughters." The children of Africa were like a dark, festering clot of blood under the fair, hale skin of New England. Once Africans were allowed to enter colonial society, Sewall warned, they were doomed to "remain in our Body Politick as a kind of extravasat Blood."[8]

In a way, Sewall was right. The fantasy of social death—that slaves existed outside the polity—was crucial to the network of relationships that enabled some New Englanders to enslave others. English settlers allowed their society to become increasingly multiracial, but they did not give up the notion that their polity was for whites only. Thinking of slaves as somehow outside the social order helped New Englanders to imagine slavery as a permanent, absolute, and essentially private relationship between masters and servants. Yet, as Sewall recognized, even this view could not obscure the fact that enslaved people remained part of the society. On one occasion, Sewall rubbed Cotton Mather the wrong way and earned the complaint that while he "pleaded much for Negroes" he was not above treating a settler "worse than a Negro."[9] Enslaved Africans were, on the one hand, excluded from social recognition and, on the other, a constant point of reference. Indeed, the presence of even a small number of enslaved Africans would transform the ways all New Englanders lived, how they thought about themselves, and the character of their body politic.

As Adam's story suggests, slavery in New England was never simply private, rarely absolute, and not always permanent. Enslaved New Englanders constantly negotiated two dynamic sets of relationships. Slaves did not simply resist or submit to their masters; their relationships were generally complex and ongoing negotiations. Perhaps less obviously, both slaves and masters had complex relationships with the members of a broad, if amorphous, public. The options of masters and slaves were constrained by their relationships with other family members and servants, with neighbors, with town officials, legal officials, politicians, and readers of newspapers, pamphlets, and books. Not only slaves and members of slaveholding households but also their nonslaveholding neighbors had to learn how to live with enslavement.

What a master could demand, and what a slave could get away with, depended on their access to the sympathy and protection of the public. Of course, as the extraordinary powers exercised by John Saffin suggest, these relationships were also always lopsided, in large part because masters enjoyed greater sympathy in the eyes of public opinion and greater access to the courts of law and the halls of politics. Nonetheless, the boundary between public and private was always contested, authority was always negotiated, and relationships were always potentially unstable.

III   Mastering Authority   III

As he mounted the gallows and allowed the hangman to place the noose around his neck, Arthur knew that, in the end, he was playing the role expected of him. A quick trial in early October 1768 had convicted him of raping a white woman; his execution soon thereafter in the rural town of Worcester had been orchestrated as a civic spectacle. Two ministers in town had preached sermons about his execution, and they had very likely visited him in prison to encourage him to confess his sins both in private and in public. As so often happened in such cases, they succeeded. As crowds gathered to witness his hanging, printers hawked hastily produced copies of Arthur's *Last and Dying Words*. As he had told the story at the local jail two days earlier, his life was a classic Puritan narrative of small sins leading progressively to major crimes. As a youth he should have been grateful for the indulgence he received from his master, but instead he grew proud and disobedient; soon he began a pattern of running away from masters. On the lam, he freely indulged his appetites for alcohol and sex. On one occasion he met an English woman at a late-night corn husking and was soon running from her angry husband and the posse he rallied. He had spent weeks on end living in Indian enclaves in idleness and debauchery and developed an enduring relationship with an Indian woman. Always, in the end, he would be caught and forcibly returned to his master. A series of exasperated masters gave up on reforming him and sold him. Thus, the rape he committed was only the culmination of a series of challenges he had offered to his master, to other English settlers, and to the basic structures of colonial society. But, in the end, the ritual of Arthur's execution turned his rebellion into an affirmation of the authority of masters, of the social order, and of God.[10]

Settlers in colonial New England faced a constant cultural struggle to domesticate slavery—to understand, explain, and rationalize their collaboration with this most extreme form of servitude. The role of the public is most clear in negotiations over who was liable to be enslaved and how masters were able to construct their

FIGURE 6. This domestic scene suggests the ambiguous position of slaves within English households. The affluent Connecticut woman who embroidered this picture showed her journey through life: beginning at birth, in the cradle; moving through middle age, sitting and sewing; and at death, in the coffin that bears her initials. The African servant, though prominently represented within the family circle, stands outside the cycle of life: eternally nurturing the baby, she herself never ages. In fact, the servant may be a young woman named Jenny who was enslaved by this family until the early nineteenth century and then married when living as a free woman. Prudence Pundersen, *The First, Second, and Last Scenes of Mortality*, Preston, Conn., ca. 1778–80. Embroidery on silk. Courtesy of the Connecticut Historical Society.

authority. Restricting slavery largely to Africans helped English settlers avoid thinking much about the process of enslavement. Market relations distanced people from the unpleasant consequences of their economic choices by attenuating agency: Africans arrived in New England already enslaved. To question the legality of that enslavement was beyond the jurisdiction of local courts; the community had only to accept the status quo. Not just anyone, or even any person of African descent, could be successfully enslaved in eighteenth-century New England. Disputes over the freedom of kidnapped individuals revealed how the options of masters and enslaved people were determined largely by the actions or inaction of the public. Meanwhile, the role of the public was also apparent in efforts to define the kinds of roles that were appropriate in slavery (fig. 6). Naturally, masters sought to control this process. With considerable success they attempted to convince the public to accept slavery as both a private relationship, within the domain of their households, and as a public institution, integral to the social order.

Much of the time, New England settlers looked the other way when the rights of free blacks and Indians were trampled on, but they did set some limits. Like other poor people in the eighteenth century, free blacks and Indians faced various forms of servitude. And all people of color were "socially dead" to a considerable extent. Town officials typically failed to provide free people of color the same protections they routinely granted to even the poorest whites. Town councils generally extended at least minimal paternalist protections even to the poorest English children: they routinely bound white children for limited terms of servitude and put provisions in their contracts for education in reading and writing and training in professional skills. One exceptional free mother did manage to get her mulatto child, Solomon Seasor, an indenture contract that required teaching the art of husbandry, reading, and writing. Even such modest benefits were rarely extended to other Indian and Negro children. The courts, too, acted unevenly when they resorted to selling debtors into indentured servitude to pay judgments. They routinely ordered blacks and Indians to be sold for periods of labor in order to satisfy legal judgments and sometimes sold white criminals and defendants as well. But people of color generally received longer and harsher terms—and were sometimes even sold into permanent slavery to pay small fines. Legal discrimination helped keep many Indians in southern New England in a state of virtual debt peonage. Acknowledging these "abuses," the Rhode Island legislature periodically passed laws to protect Indian debtors, none of which had much effect.[11]

On the other hand, free blacks and Indians could not be grabbed off the street and sold with impunity. Not that there weren't settlers willing to try. Some enterprising souls stole other people's slaves, and others claimed indentured children as permanent slaves and attempted to kidnap and sell free people.[12] These cases of *illegal* enslavement are documented because sometimes the victims managed to make their way into court. And, once in court, wrongfully enslaved people often won. Juries of local white men of property were hardly willing to treat blacks and Indians equally in most contexts, but they were not willing to collaborate with active, obvious, illegal enslavement.

Consider the legal tug-of-war waged over the servant girl Sarah Chauqum sometime after she was sold as a slave. She had grown up under indentured servitude in an English household and at age eight still had at least a decade left on her contract. She was separated from her parents; nothing is known of her father, but it seems her mother worked as a servant and was an Indian. To those contemplating Sarah's enslavement, she seemed a likely prospect, as she had no powerful kin to protect her, her freedom was already compromised, and she was not white. Her kidnappers' plan was simple: in January 1728 they bought her contract as an indentured servant from her Rhode Island master, sold her as a slave to a confederate just across the Connecticut border, and then sold her again to a possibly unsuspecting shopkeeper in New London. This strategy was designed both to make the paper trail more difficult to trace and to remove her further from her mother and away from possibly sympathetic locals. It was a well-known ploy. Kidnappers of all stripes enhanced their likelihood of success by choosing victims whose enslavement would not disrupt local sensibilities, by avoiding angering owners, by complicating the legal record, and by removing their victims from familiar communities where they might rally support. For several years, the young girl lived as a slave in the shopkeeper's house, working mostly at spinning wool.

After almost four years, Sarah managed to escape and make her way back to her mother in South Kingstown. The case made it into court because Sarah's mother managed to attract the sympathy of two prominent attorneys. Matthew Robinson, without charge, launched a vigorous legal defense of the girl's freedom—first before a local Justice's Court, where she was declared free, and then through a series of appeals to the Court of General Sessions of the Peace, the Court of Common Pleas, and finally the Superior Court. English settlers could occasionally defend their children through petitions or lawsuits, but "Negroes," "Indians," "mulattos," and "mustees" had to pin their hopes on assistance by a patron. Unlike Sewall, Robinson did not give up on such difficult and no doubt unpopular cases: this was the first of a long series of lawsuits he would see through court in the ensuing decades, attempting to secure the freedom of Indians and Negroes held in slavery illegally. Although kidnappers chose their victims from a rather wide and vaguely defined spectrum of the population, in court, racial identities had very specific symbolic meanings for both parties. Typically, those claiming Sarah as a slave described her as a Negro or "Molatto"; those claiming her to be free insisted she was an Indian. After securing her freedom, Sarah gained the assistance of a second lawyer, Daniel Updike—for many years the colony's attorney general—who helped her successfully sue her kidnappers for back wages. She was awarded some fifty-five pounds and court costs for three years and eight months of unpaid work.[13]

The role of the New England public in protecting the liberty of free people can be seen most clearly through its absence on the high seas. On ships in the Atlantic, normal community controls were suspended, and new opportunities for illegal enslavement appeared. The phenomenon of kidnapping men of color was widely enough known to appear in a fictional account of an Indian out in a small whaling vessel off Martha's Vineyard. Written in a satiric dialect, it appeared in the *Newport Mercury:* "I tak Vyage to ketch Vale, an Spanyad ketch me, make mee slave." In fact, it was hardly a Spanish specialty—and the perpetrators were typically not pirates but otherwise respectable merchant captains and privateers. On one occasion, Reuben Cognehew, the Indian delegate from the Mashpee tribe, was trying to get to London to present a petition to George III. The captain who provided his passage lied about his destination, sailed to the Caribbean, and sold him as a slave. Through an amazingly fortuitous series of events, Cognehew ended up free and in London. This kind of alchemy operated across the Atlantic, turning free people into slaves and sometimes back again. In 1746, for instance, a group of free prisoners of war were sold in the West Indies by the privateer Captain John Sweet Jr.[14]

The few cases that came to light generally involved foreign powers creating diplomatic waves to protect their subjects. In 1746, a Rhode Island privateer claimed as slaves twenty-two Spanish prisoners of war who had been legally free. Privateers were a kind of contract navy chartered by the government during the interminable wars fought in the Atlantic. When a privateer captured a ship, the crew and passengers became prisoners of war, but the cargo became prize money to be split among a hierarchy of officials, owners, officers, and crew members. Slaves counted not as passengers but as booty. So, even though many black or Indian crew members were actually free men working for wages, the privateer had a strong financial incentive to claim them as slaves. (The matter was further complicated by the fact that, anticipating this situation, the owners of slaves working on ships sometimes did their best to represent them as free, even issuing them false certificates of freedom.) The Rhode Island privateer sold most of the captured Spanish sailors on the voyage home; the nine who remained were formally condemned by an admiralty judge in Newport and sold at a public auction. The Spanish governor of Havana retaliated by taking nineteen English sailors hostage and directing pointed letters to the governors of the English colonies where the illegally enslaved men had ended up. Rhode Island's governor expressed his shock that such an outrage had taken place and acted swiftly: the captives were promptly declared free, and the four men still in the colony were taken up by a deputy sheriff, detained in jail for a while, and then returned to Havana with a letter explaining that the surviving others would soon follow. The Newport purchasers of the free Spaniards showed neither remorse nor shame but rather indignation. In fact, they successfully prosecuted the deputy sheriff for "stealing" their property.[15] In general, colonial privateers were much more likely to sell free prisoners than were British privateers, suggesting that colonists were, through experience, learning a kind of racial ruthlessness.

In a way, resistance to illegal kidnapping helped New Englanders make peace with slavery as an institution. Resisting dramatic, illegal changes of status allowed the community to view slavery as private, absolute, and permanent. Normally, the community did not need to enforce the status of slaves violently but only to be active in righting problems sufficiently grievous that they intruded into public consciousness. In general, the public was asked not to interfere in relations of mastery. Masters went to great lengths to encourage the public to think this way.

Masters maintained their status as patriarchs by keeping "domestic" matters private and outside public scrutiny and interference. In general, masters defined roles—and rules—that everyone acceded to in public. They defined flexible roles for themselves, hands-off or collaborative roles for the community, and deferential roles for slaves. This projected consensus shaped expectations and obligations for masters, slaves, and community members. Usually masters claimed a wide range of behavior as private, but sometimes it was to their advantage to have their slave relations become public and indeed to enlist the active assistance of the public.

Like the biblical Adam naming the creatures of the earth, or parents naming children, masters assigning new names to captive Africans symbolized their dominance, the totality of their possession, and their determination that a servant's identity could be reshaped at will. They chose names that set slaves apart from the polity. Like dogs, horses, and other animals, slaves received only first names, not family names: Boteer did not become "Venture Mumford," just "Venture." Since West Africans were often named after the day of the week on which they were born, variations of these names adapted to the ears of English-speaking masters became the most common slave names: Cuffee, Quash, Cudjo, and Phillis. Other times, slaves received quite ordinary names, such as Tom or Phoebe. As with "Venture," however, it was especially common to give slaves names not usually used for

English people, such as the geographic designations Boston or Newport. Like dogs, slaves often received exalted names that pointed up their degraded status: classical names such as Pompey, Venus, or Caesar, or aristocratic titles such as Duchess or Prince.[16] The English community generally accepted the master's authority in this regard by using not the names by which enslaved Africans had previously known themselves but the names by which masters wished them to be known.

To justify their authority, masters invoked a nostalgic tradition of paternalism. This notion was part of a broad worldview in which each person in a great chain of being had a hierarchical relationship with everyone else. Children and parents, wives and husbands, poor and rich, humans and the Lord—each had their own duties and obligations. The Reverend James MacSparran, an Anglican minister and the owner of a large South Kingstown estate worked by several enslaved men and women, was particularly explicit about characterizing servility as next to godliness. He recorded himself praying for consolation after suffering a social slight: "Dear Redeemer enable me to live like yr best Servants and wt I want in the world, will be made up in yr Rewards of the next." To be a master was to be allied with the eternal authority of the Lord: "Gracious God," he prayed, "give my Servants Grace to live in a holier manner, that my Peace & Property mayn't be invaded by their evil doings."[17] However appealing this kind of analogy was, the fit was not perfect. Slavery exaggerated and distorted the familiar model of patriarchal authority. The basic model of servitude in New England was as a temporary stage for juveniles, but slavery was permanent, the paternal role lasting forever.

As paternal figures, masters claimed the right to use violence to regulate their households. In an age when corporal punishment was common, masters resorted to various forms of violence to force their will on their slaves—whippings, beatings, and restraints such as shackles, handcuffs, or iron collars fitted with "pothooks." Neighbors, justices of the peace, judges, and juries all tended to accept the master's view that such violence against dependents was legitimate. In Boston, for a period, masters could send servants to the public House of Corrections for whipping.[18] Recourse to violence, of course, made it clear that a master's power was not absolute. There were limits to the violence individual slave owners could inflict: even if the public would look the other way, shackled servants could be controlled but were not very productive. Nevertheless, violence was an essential private and public part of slavery.

The Reverend MacSparran used violence when his slaves deviated too far from the roles he cast for them. His diary records battles of wills escalating into violence.

Whipping was a ritualized battle of wills, staged not just for the malefactor but as a semipublic performance for the entire farm community. Awaking early one August morning in 1751, MacSparran discovered that Hannibal had been out that night—up to something that led his master to pray that God would give his servants "the Gift of chastity." With the help of another slave, MacSparran stripped Hannibal to the waist, tied him up, and then "gave him a few Lashes till he begged." MacSparran was ready to relent, but his wife interrupted: "My poor passionate dear, saying I had not given him eno', gave him a lash or two, upon which he ran." After an extended chase, Hannibal was taken to a blacksmith and fitted with "pothooks" around his neck—a thick iron collar with long, unwieldy prongs. This extended performance dramatized MacSparran's dominance, served as a threat for other slaves, and affirmed his—and his wife's—authority to use violence against his dependents with impunity. Violence attracted public disapproval only when it seemed exceptionally brutal. Little more than a week later, Hannibal again disobeyed his mistress, was whipped, and ran off. This time, he was sent home by a neighbor with a note asking that he be spared further punishment. "I did," MacSparran concluded, "upon his Promise of better Behavior."[19]

In fact, the public gave masters wider latitude over slaves than they did over other members of a master's household, such as his wife and children. Courts rarely came to the aid of battered spouses in eighteenth-century New England, but husbands who killed their wives were prosecuted for murder and often convicted. In contrast, slaves had no way of divorcing themselves from abusing masters and were only on rare occasions vindicated by prosecutions for murder or attempted murder. In Rhode Island, the first case in which a man was prosecuted for the murder of a slave in his household came in 1733, and he was acquitted. The only other case was in 1771, when a master brutally beat a slave in the head with a pair of iron fire tongs until the man fell unconscious and was believed dead; the grand jury hearing the case declined to indict the master for the assault. The victim, in accordance with colonial custom that barred Indians and blacks from testifying against whites, was not permitted to testify against his assailant.[20] Even lethal force could be accepted as forms of "correction" properly within the purview of a master.

Masters turned to the wider community when they feared violence from slaves. Here, too, the public tended to adopt the master's point of view. In two early cases in which slaves tried to kill their masters, the Rhode Island courts and General Assembly found the customary punishments inadequate and invented even harsher ones. In 1727, a young indentured Indian named Peter fired a musket at his master, but the bullet passed through the master's hat without doing any harm. Not able to prosecute him for a capital crime, the Rhode Island General Assembly created a new punishment: it ordered the criminal to be branded on his forehead, whipped at public spots throughout the city of Newport, and sold outside the colony for as much time as would compensate his master for his remaining term of service and other charges. This was tantamount to a sentence of death by hard labor in the West Indies. In another case, a young enslaved man succeeded in killing his Kingstown mistress but then tried to cheat the hangman by jumping over a cliff. Death did not protect him from the wrath of the General Assembly, which ordered his corpse subjected to an elaborate ritual dismemberment: "that his head, legs, and arms be cut from his body, and hung up in some public place, near the town, to public view, and his body to be burnt to ashes." This action was intended not just as a particularly macabre punishment in an age when the integrity of the body after death was a matter of serious concern but also to send powerful messages. At one level, one might imagine, the execution calmed fears by reestablishing the social order. More explicitly, in the words of the judicial order, the public torture and display of the body were intended—"if it please God"—to serve as "terror to others."[21]

The newspapers that began to proliferate in the mid-eighteenth century lavished attention on slave violence as though it represented a public danger. Lurid narratives of murders, rapes, and arson committed by slaves implied that such violence was much more common than it was. Even relatively minor incidents were retold throughout a broad region, with the result that slave violence seemed more pervasive than it was in any locale. Moreover, newspaper accounts were written to interpret slave violence as not just illegitimate but also irrational, senseless, meaningless. In 1764, the *Newport Mercury* featured an elaborate story about a Connecticut man who attempted to blow up his master's house with gunpowder. Although his plot was detected and disrupted, the man did manage to ignite kegs of gunpowder stored in his garret room. The explosion blew the roof off the house and sent him flying. Even fatally wounded, burned, and with much of his skin torn off, the story continued, the crazed slave had to be physically restrained from going back up into the ruins of the garret to try again. By way of explanation, the article noted that he had been "irritated at some members of the family."[22] The public narrative served the symbolic needs of masters and erased any alternate view from the slave's perspective that might give meaning or legitimacy to his actions. In publishing such stories, newspapers allowed their readers a kind of voyeuristic role—

imagining, as victims of slave violence, their own mastery over other people's re-bellious slaves.

Settlers seeking to define the roles of master and slave often turned to the language of paternalism, which was always at some level a fantasy. Masters never actually enjoyed total domination; slaves never completely surrendered themselves to a master's will.[23] But paternalism helped masters extend their power. The public acceptance of a master's power as almost absolute—of a master's control over slaves as private and of a slave rebellion against masters as a social threat—endowed masters with an intangible force field of power. It helped masters limit the options of slaves and community members so that overt challenges to the status quo were discouraged and people could be controlled less directly, less explicitly, and less consciously.

Arthur's confession suggests both the power of this cultural authority and some of its limits. Although he showed that he could escape from any individual master almost at will, he also showed that he could never escape the system that ultimately punished his defiance with destruction. Pervasive and powerful as this language of public order was, however, it never achieved the ultimate goal of defining how Arthur saw himself. If Arthur could never entirely escape slavery in New England, his text suggests that he enjoyed the process of escape more than the prospect of remaining free. He seems to revel in telling his ribald tale of out-smarting people all his life and to have enjoyed life on the lam. The two-faced tone of Arthur's narrative foreshadowed a larger cultural shift. Soon other criminal narratives adopted a similar tone, supplanting the deferential, redemptive, hierarchical message of the Puritan confession with new narratives that capitalized instead on a growing market for sensation, titillation, and prurience.[24]

||| Negotiating Relationships |||

The Providence merchant Moses Brown liked to think of himself as a just, even benevolent, master: in the 1760s, he paid tutors to instruct his slaves in reading and writing, and he took them with him to church on Sundays. But his slaves did not always see things that way—at least if stories they passed down to their children and grandchildren are any indication. One story began with Mrs. Brown feeding the servants a turkey soup that was decidedly "musty." Noah, a young man at the time, screwed up the courage to complain. He avoided a direct confrontation and appealed to the master of the house, who asked his wife to improve the quality of their servants' food. This complaint was successful because it pointed to a set of ideals any master could be expected to embrace and suggested a relatively easy way to live up to them. But the strategy was not without danger. Brown and his wife were exposed to the charge that they had been failing to live up to their own ideals, and Mrs. Brown was dishonored by the ability of a slave to direct the management of her kitchen. She got her revenge quietly. Formerly, Noah had slept in an outbuilding with his brothers and family. Now, Mrs. Brown revoked this privilege and required him to sleep in a garret in the main house, under her constant watch.[25]

Although masters liked to think that their authority was absolute, in fact it was always subject to negotiation. Slaves seized opportunities to force masters to compromise, and their repertoire included sticks as well as the proverbial carrots. The same qualities that made slavery in New England so intimate and masters' control so pervasive provided people enslaved there with special flexibility to shape their lives.[26] On the one hand, slaves could harm masters by threatening violence, resisting their authority, or slacking off at work. Of course, these options were limited by the public's ready defense of the social order. Slave violence was always a threat, but in practice it was less about liberation than about desperation: it represented the failure of negotiations, the loss of hope, the breakdown of viable roles. Open conflict tended to emerge only when passive modes of resistance were discovered, in which case masters made the conflict open, or when circumstances changed to make a slave's accustomed role intolerable, in which case slaves lashed out with uncharacteristic recklessness. Generally, slaves focused on making the best of their roles within slavery, rather than trying to overturn their status completely. In a world in which open rebellion was generally fatal, they had to strive to bring their self-images and conditions of life together in more subtle and negotiated ways. On the other hand, slaves could also entice masters by working harder and more cheerfully—and even by earning their own income and giving their masters a cut. We have only recently begun to appreciate how actively slaves and masters used a broader network of market relations to reach agreements that met both of their needs. In practical ways, such bargains helped enslaved people accommodate or resist some of the more grating aspects of enslavement. In symbolic ways, slaves could realize alternative self-ideals for themselves, attempt to hold masters to community standards, and even seek to have their self-made identities honored by the public.

Naturally, slaves often avoided open conflict by doing what they could behind their masters' back. Since they kept few of their own records, we know mostly about what happened when they got caught. The Reverend James MacSparran constantly suspected his slaves of committing the "sins of uncleanness, stealing & lying." Their specific actions suggested some of what was important enough to how slaves viewed themselves to risk punishment: often these struggles were about food, as when Maroca stole sugar; or about sex and romance, as when Hank was caught out all night; or about difficulty suppressing anger and resentment, as when Peter got into trouble for being "malpert," or insolent, to Mrs. MacSparran. Such "sins" recurred year after year, suggesting a certain, probably necessary, toleration of the illicit activity on MacSparran's part and a certain toleration of punishment by his slaves. Even an act as simple as stealing sugar hardly had transparent meaning. Maybe Maroca didn't actually take it and MacSparran was overly suspicious. Maybe this time he punished pilfering he would otherwise have winked at because he was angry for some other reason. Maybe she took sugar just to please herself, maybe she used it to make a treat for her boyfriend, maybe she did it just to irritate her master. In any case, the battle of the sugar cake was embedded in a long, often painful struggle to establish the terms of their lives together.[27]

Slaves—like other household dependents such as apprentices, wives, and children—generally limited their resistance to deliberate and often symbolic actions such as theft. Like disempowered people everywhere, slaves recognized that the public saw them in a very different way than they saw themselves. Slaves did not enjoy the (relatively) integrated worldview of their masters but rather had a deeply split conception of themselves versus the body politic, a double consciousness of events and of themselves that required constant work to reconcile. Consider an investigation in the 1740s on the island of Jamestown, where a network of enslaved and indentured women were suspected of stealing, exchanging, and fencing various items of their mistresses' clothing and linens. The investigation did not reveal whether the servants were wearing these items, trading them to suit individual tastes or to avoid identification, or using them as a kind of currency to pursue other ends. The choice of items stolen—handkerchiefs and undergarments—seems to suggest that they were trying to avoid detection while also wearing intimate symbols of refinement and gentility. Perhaps, in effect, they were secretly dressing up as their mistresses.[28] If theft was always an act of resistance, it could express resentment as well as envy, mockery as well as emulation.

If masters did not like having their slaves act out behind their back, they were even more threatened by open confrontation. The memoirs of one former New England slave, Venture Smith, detailed a range of confrontational strategies. A number of his early conflicts arose when he was receiving contradictory instructions from more than one person. As a young man, for instance, he went through a difficult period when his master, Thomas Stanton, would give him instructions and then leave the farm for extended periods. Stanton's son, who was about Venture's age, would then interfere with his own demands. Venture was growing into a man of astonishing physical strength, and on one occasion he flatly refused to do what his master's son told him to do. It was intolerable, he explained in his *Narrative*, to serve two masters. Enraged, the son attacked him. But Venture was strong enough to fight him off. The son called other farmhands to help him subdue Venture, but they, too, failed. Soon, the putative master was reduced to tears and the comfort of his mother. Venture, of course, knew that he could not keep up this defiance forever. Eventually, he consented to be tied up in a cattle gallows to be whipped. But his master, on returning, pardoned him from that punishment. In retrospect, Venture presented this crisis as part of a process of negotiating relationships with his masters. Venture never described himself as crossing the line into illicit behavior, symbolic vengeance, or aggressive violence. But throughout his narrative, he defends acts of resistance as responses to abuse at the hands of his masters.[29]

On one occasion, Venture interposed in a violent dispute between his wife and his mistress. Mrs. Stanton raised a horsewhip against him; he snatched it from her hand and threw it into the fire. This was a more serious breach of her authority than simply evading or resisting punishment. Retribution came several days later when his master came up to him from behind and clubbed him on the head. Venture seized the club, averted a second blow, and left his master calling for help. Venture acted out of injured pride and a sense of masculine honor and because he was physically capable. A slave's open resistance to a master's authority raised the stakes: it threw their relations into crisis and was hard to resolve. If Venture's version of this story is complete and accurate, what is most striking is that in the heat of anger he limited his actions to defensive maneuvers. He blocked blows and disarmed his antagonists but refrained from using his own superior strength against them. But Venture, who now had a history of violent confrontations with two different masters, chose not to let this incident pass.

In an extraordinary move, Venture escalated the conflict with his master by seeking legal recourse: he marched over to a neighboring justice of the peace and lodged a complaint. Like Noah complaining to Moses Brown, Venture honored the structure of authority in colonial society by seeking protection from a higher power. Yet Venture's action was radical because it sought to move a previously private dispute into the public world of male honor. It was one thing for a slave to ask his mistress to submit to her husband's authority; it was quite another to ask the head of a household to submit his domestic affairs to his neighbor. The justice knew as much and declined to intervene. He told Venture to return to his master and to come back if he was beaten again. But when Stanton and his brother appeared to retrieve Venture, the justice reprimanded them. Stanton was momentarily mollified, but as soon as they were out sight of the justice, he and his brother attacked Venture and tried to beat him. They lost the fight when Venture ended up standing on their chests. But again, even when Venture won, he lost. He eventually had to submit to handcuffing by the local blacksmith. When Mrs. Stanton gloated on his return, Venture replied sardonically that he was delighted with his new "gold rings." Mr. Stanton retaliated by manacling Venture's legs with ox chains and padlocks.

If Venture's options were limited, so were his master's. Keeping Venture chained hand and foot was hardly a viable option. Stanton needed to establish his authority decisively enough to end the conflict and get Venture back to work. Stanton interrupted his own barrage of verbal abuse to ask whether Venture would prefer to go back to work and be rid of the chains. Venture refused. Stanton even threatened to sell him to the West Indies but was reluctant to try further restraint, punishment, or torture.[30] He needed to restore his honor while maintaining viable relationships with his slaves.

Of course, slaves could be worse than useless—they could be dangerous. Masters had a great deal to lose—their property, their public reputation, their lives. Violence against masters threatened to overturn the basic master-slave dyad, and it predictably produced drastic retribution. Arson was certainly in the social repertoire of New Englanders; it appears far more frequently in Rhode Island's higher-court records than assault or murder. One enslaved boy who had clearly burned down a neighboring farmer's barn was found not guilty because he had done so under orders from his master. An advantage of arson was that it did not require great physical force: late in the century a young boy repeatedly tried to burn down his master's home by holding a candle to a window curtain. It was also often difficult to detect or punish, as became clear in the wave of paranoia that befell New York City in 1741 after a series of suspicious fires.[31]

If sabotage revealed the slave's ability to inflict damage, it was risky, and the stakes could be deadly. Nonetheless, legal records of such acts often suggest that rebellious slaves were responding to specific, sometimes highly symbolic, ways in which their roles had come to seem intolerable. One of the most widely publicized slave acts of revenge in eighteenth-century New England occurred in Newport in 1762. Fortune, the slave of a Newport blacksmith, was one of the workers whom merchant Thomas Hazard hired to run a load of rum from his recently arrived brig to his warehouse—as usual, avoiding paying duties to the king by working quickly under the cover of darkness. Hazard evidently refused to pay what Fortune expected for his services and, in fact, whipped him. Fortune was incensed. Unable to get redress through other means, he took matters into his own hands. The next night between nine and ten o'clock, Fortune returned to the Long Wharf alone, got some "fire" from a house near the end of the wharf, put it through a hole in the side of Hazard's warehouse, and then left the building to burn. The rumor spread that gunpowder was in the warehouse, so the fire brigade stayed away. Hazard's warehouse, along with merchandise worth some fifty thousand pounds, was destroyed. But revenge, however sweet, did not materially improve Fortune's lot. He was soon arrested, confessed, and was sentenced to hang. His confession was published, and his execution was a major spectacle. But no public mention was made of his assertion that Hazard had made false promises and cheated him.[32]

The role of civil society in some ways served to limit the ability of slaves to resist their masters successfully, but the market economy opened up other options and incentives. In 1773, John Quamine—who had been illegally enslaved by a ship captain who had been hired to take him to Newport for an English education—and a friend split the price of a lottery ticket. They won almost enough money to buy their freedom. Many other slaves and servants also played the numbers, a fact much bemoaned by their masters. Years earlier, the town of Newport had threatened to crack down on the numerous small lotteries that poor townspeople favored. Its notice in the local newspaper turned on the notion that slaves and servants were incompetent and illegitimate actors in the world of the market. Unofficial lotteries were often fraudulent, town officials argued, offering as prizes only "refuse Goods and Trash." Even if their organizers were honest, lotteries—like drinking and other forms of gambling—inevitably tended "to excite Servants to defraud their Masters."[33] On the other hand, slaves naturally fantasized that they might receive a sum large enough to effect a dramatic reversal of fortunes. More than any other form of gambling, a lottery presented a model of economic success based on luck and fantasy, rather than industry and prudence. Enslaved New Englanders may have enjoyed the sheer random, arbitrary, and irrational nature of the investment: although lotteries were not fair, neither was any other aspect of their daily lives.

In their complaints about lotteries, masters and officials assumed that slaves controlled no money of their own and were entirely removed from the realm of market relations. In this vision of slavery, most powerfully promoted by nineteenth-century pro-slavery propagandists, the world of slavery was self-contained, and masters and slaves confronted each other alone. The master's authority was absolute, and to keep it that way, slaves were never permitted to do things such as grow their own food. If allowed any autonomy, they might get ideas. This was probably never true in the Old South and was certainly not true in other slave societies.[34]

In truth, slaves in eighteenth-century New England were intimately integrated into local economies. Many did have money, often obtained by working for wages. Masters knew this, because it was only with their permission that their slaves could enter into contracts, earn wages, or accumulate property. Masters benefited because market incentives helped discipline slaves into working hard. Recalcitrant or underemployed slaves could be managed by others: a widow could rent out a slave and live on the income, a small farmer could rent out part of the time of a slave who was not fully employed at home, a widow could send a difficult slave out to sea rather than try to manage him at home. Slaves benefited from such arrangements because being needed in this way gave them power. They could use that power to accumulate savings, gain autonomy, or negotiate better living conditions.

Venture, working in the Connecticut countryside, illuminated some of the possibilities, limits, and dilemmas that slaves faced as they negotiated the line between private servile relations and public economic relations. In a rural landscape dominated by farming and offshore fishing, Venture spent most of his life working at menial tasks and manual labor. As a young child, Venture, like other servants who typically received tips for serving guests in their masters' households, earned money for cleaning gentlemen's boots and drawing shoes. Soon, he was also earning rewards for catching muskrats and minks; at night and during "odd spells" he fished. By his early twenties, both Venture and the fellow slave he had married had accumulated some savings, she some five pounds and he some seventeen pounds in New York currency. He managed their money, loaning it at interest to his master's brother. In his thirties, he began to negotiate more lucrative and autonomous arrangements. He bought land next to his master's farm, which he cultivated "with the greatest diligence and economy" at times when his master did not require his labor. Next, Venture asked his master to let him hire himself out to work one winter; his master agreed on the condition that he receive a quarter of Venture's proceeds. Venture's size and stamina were perfect for the arduous winter task of chopping firewood, and this work netted him almost five pounds. Finally, Venture proposed that his master let him "go out to work" during the more lucrative summer months. After some haggling, he agreed. Venture stopped working on his master's farm and instead paid the equivalent of a rental for his time, saving his surplus. In winter, he continued to thresh grain and cord wood. When he was about thirty-seven, he had accumulated savings of more than fifty pounds.[35]

Venture got obvious personal satisfaction from working hard, overcoming obstacles, and accumulating savings—and came to define himself through his indefatigable industry. He proudly described his work as a child in Africa, shepherding the flock of a rich landowner at the age of six. He performed this duty conscientiously despite hardship and danger—such as the lion attack that left him scarred for life. Throughout his life, he retained both pride in his tremendous physical endurance and resentment against the unreasonable burdens he bore so triumphantly. On one occasion, Mumford ordered him to fetch a barrel of molasses from two miles away and to carry it back on his shoulders—and he did it. He went on to perform feats that he reported like badges of honor, such as the time in the winter of 1764 when he threshed seventy-five bushels of grain and chopped four hundred cords of wood: "Many other singular and wonderful labors I performed in cutting wood there." In rural society, such physical prowess was widely recognized and valued. Sometimes Venture performed feats of strength as public spectacles: one time—"only to try my strength"—he carried seven bushels of salt some twenty feet; and if there was any doubt about the truthfulness of this story, he assured his readers, eyewitnesses were still living. In fact, even after his death, he figured in local imaginations as a Paul Bunyanesque hero: old men disputed the heft of his axe, how much wood he could chop in a day, or just when he had carried all that salt.

Venture was also proud of his economic prudence, extreme frugality, and rational choices. "I bought nothing which I did not absolutely want. All fine clothes I despised in comparison with my interest. . . . Perhaps I would have a garment or two which I did not have on at all times, but as for superfluous finery, I never thought it to be compared with a decent homespun dress, a good supply of money and prudence." He continued: "Expensive gatherings of my mates I commonly shunned, and all kinds of luxuries I was a perfect stranger to." His narrative was no doubt editorially manipulated to echo Benjamin Franklin's own autobiography and emphasizes a narrative of getting ahead in the world through industry and thrift—and when it was published in 1790 it was no doubt intended to help promote the notion that freed blacks could be easily integrated into the free market.[36]

Many of the same themes, if differently inflected, appear in a private document written thirty years earlier—perhaps the only diary of a slave extant. Across Narragansett Bay amid the urban bustle of Newport, Cesar Lyndon would never have earned Venture's approval. He spent far too much money on things such as silver shoe buckles. The slave of Josias Lyndon, a rich merchant and future governor of the colony, Cesar Lyndon developed the specialized skills of eighteenth-century commerce by working as his master's clerk and secretary. During the 1760s, he also kept his own notebooks of accounts, copied letters, and wrote journal entries, which reveal how he capitalized on these skills to earn money, invest it, and spend it. Although not above manual labor, he specialized as a manager, organizer, and financier of petty entrepreneurial ventures. At a time when pigs proliferated in the city—they lived in pens or roamed free, ate garbage, and were butchered for meat—Cesar Lyndon owned many pigs, but he arranged with others, mainly other enslaved black men, to raise, butcher, and sell them. One morning, Prince Richards bought a sow from Mrs. Stoneman; that afternoon, Lyndon bought the sow from Richards; that evening he turned the sow over to Primas Searing to breed; months later, Lyndon arranged for someone else to sell the meat to English settlers and divide the profits. Similarly, he operated truck gardens: he rented small plots of land, purchased supplies from English settlers, and contracted with other black men first to tend the plants (peas and turnips in June, squashes in July, celery root, carrots, endive, cabbage, potatoes in the fall) and then to sell the produce, generally to their masters and other English settlers. Lyndon even entered the coastal maritime trade in a modest way, shipping a variety of goods to his New York–based friend Mr. Scipio Virgil Gray and ordering various goods in return, either for resale or for his own consumption.[37]

Unlike Venture, Cesar was not reluctant to spend money either unnecessarily or extravagantly. In the bustling town of Newport, Cesar Lyndon cut a figure of fashion and luxury. His knives had ivory handles, and he drank tea from red china; he wrote in a polished copperplate, and his diction expressed the intricate etiquette and refined tones of genteel correspondence. Since his master largely covered his necessary expenses, he was free to spend his own money. He supplemented clothing his master handed down to him, buying fancy buckles for his kneebands; for his wife, he bought luxuries such as a striped silk gown. In the summer of 1768, he sent a quarter of a hog off to Suriname with Boston Vose, who returned with a set of china teacups and saucers and a round looking glass in a yellow-painted frame. Cesar Lyndon's income financed an active social life. In August 1776, he hosted a picnic for eight friends: they "took a pleasant ride out to Portsmouth" and enjoyed a repast of roast pig, corn, wine, punch, and tea. Such extravagant generosity defined him in relation to other peers. In a rigidly hierarchical society in which public display accorded status, he asserted his ability to play the part of gentility with polite amusements, genteel accoutrements, and a gracious manner.

By working independently, slaves such as Venture and Cesar asserted their membership in a wider society, suggesting that they belonged to themselves, not to their masters. The two men faced very different options, however. In the countryside, Venture faced a limited range of public roles for working men; this constraint prompted him to develop a rather absolute sense of the opposition between slavery as private and freedom as public. Even after Venture managed to purchase his freedom, he continued to seek personal liberation by controlling money. In the city, enslaved people, especially men, had more choices about roles. So Cesar, rather than single-mindedly seeking to become free, developed a distinctive role within slavery. He enjoyed a kind of liberation—often through purchases—that gave him access to both a local community of fellow blacks and a public world of symbolic capital. In both cases, however, Venture and Cesar found that there was a big difference between acting out their own self-conceptions and getting others to honor them.

Venture's determination to trumpet the liberating potential of the market accompanied story after story of betrayal by the market. Although masters could entice slaves into mutually beneficial contracts and hold slaves to their end of such agreements, there was nothing to prevent masters from reneging on their own obligations. As in its regulation of violence, the public recognized a master's rights but not those of a slave. When one master feared that his slave, a skilled chimneysweep, was not bringing back a sufficient share of his earnings, he could advertise in the local newspaper, asking his fellow citizens to pay him directly.[38]

Slaves had no such recourse to public appeals. Venture reports that his masters repeatedly stole his savings and refused to honor promises. At one point his master's brother, who owed him money, attacked him, ripped up his note, and refused to make good on the loan. Disillusioned, Venture learned to take precautions: when arranging a deal with another master, he made sure to have a free black man to take his security for it: "as I was the property of my master, and therefore could not safely take his obligation myself." Slaves were well aware that prudence and industry were not always rewarded with the honesty and justice that economic bargains implied.[39] They could be admitted to the public world of honor and contracts at one moment and excluded the next. For Venture, this vulnerability represented a basic conflict between his self-definition and the social order.

Cesar's accounts and letters do not present him as cheated, at least financially, perhaps because his master honored him and manumitted him on his death. Yet the respect he sought was elusive. The most formulaic aspects of his correspondence suggest the ways in which he sought to be recognized. He quietly defied the convention that slaves did not have surnames and that black men and women did not merit titles of honor: he made a point of always dignifying men and women of African or native descent with their full names and the usually omitted titles "Mr." and "Mrs."[40] At the same time, he was punctilious about representing himself as a slave. Eighteenth-century business letters conventionally ended with a metaphoric invocation of a servile role: "your humble and obedient servant." Enslaved people, of course, did not have the luxury of offering their devotion either lightly or at will. Lyndon signed himself, literally, "a servant to Col. Lyndon." Cesar Lyndon had to walk a fine line between evading social death and flirting with social life.

Negotiations through the market helped both masters and slaves, but the ultimate bargain was with the public. In all negotiations between masters and slaves, a key point of contention was the ability of the master to control what passed for truth, to make one version of a story command public acceptance, and to hold his dependents to agreements while refusing to be bound by commitments he made to them.[41] Members of both groups likely felt betrayed. Masters felt betrayed when slaves tried to evade the absolute mastery they claimed. Slaves felt betrayed when masters reneged on agreements or violated accepted customs. In their different ways Venture and Cesar Lyndon, both committed to the notion that work could bring freedom, found themselves trying to hold the public to a bargain the public entertained but to which it never wholly bound itself. It was indeed a lottery: often you lost, and even when you won, the prizes were unpredictable.

||| Breaking Bonds |||

Venture Smith spent much of his life working out bargains to become free eventually, but only once did he actually try to escape. As he told the story, an Irish indentured servant named Heddy, who also worked for his master—at this point Robertson Mumford—organized the plan in 1751. Heddy, Venture, and another servant secretly stored up provisions (six huge wheels of cheese, two small barrels of butter, bread, clothes) and set out at night in Mumford's boat. The plan was to head for the Mississippi. But they had barely made it to the nearest tip of Long Island, Montauk Point, before fear and mistrust did them in. Was Heddy scheming to abandon the others? Would he row off in the boat with all their provisions? The thought was enough for Venture, so he collared his companions and rowed them all back to their master. Turning himself and the others in, Venture hoped, would mitigate his punishment for having run away and might even help him secure his freedom. If Mumford's anger was soothed a bit, he did not overlook the damage done to his relationships with his indentured and enslaved servants. He immediately sent the Irish man to jail and put him up for sale; several months later he sold Venture, too.[42]

If relationships between masters and slaves were constantly subject to negotiation, they were also fragile and vulnerable to disruption through sale or escape. But masters and slaves did not share this power to sever relations equally. In New England during the mid-eighteenth century it was easier for masters to sell slaves than for slaves to escape; masters could turn to the public marketplace with legal force and legitimacy, whereas runaway slaves succeeded only to the extent that they outran the law and evaded public recognition. This imbalance shaped ongoing negotiations: masters had less need to compromise to maintain good relations, but servants were more dependent on successful accommodations. Nevertheless, the rupture of relations between a master and slave suddenly shifted domestic relations into the domain of the public.

Transitions in ownership made the public complicit in sustaining the basic illusions that made slavery's double standards palatable: if slavery was not entirely private, or entirely unilateral, neither was it always permanent. Family members, neighbors, and the public at large found themselves called into negotiations. Under what conditions would they permit sales? How far would they go in detecting and turning in runaways? So, as they helped to reconstitute severed relations between individual masters and servants, members of the public also had to face their own disrupted relationships, expectations, and senses of self.

By running away the servant suspended relations with his or her master. More than a physical journey, running away was a wrenching attempt by slaves to assert an independent, even free, identity. Masters seeking to cut off avenues of escape enlisted the help of the public to prevent runaways from being able to pass themselves off as free. Family members, neighbors, and other settlers were actively hostile to slaves who tried to change their status suddenly, forcibly, and unilaterally.

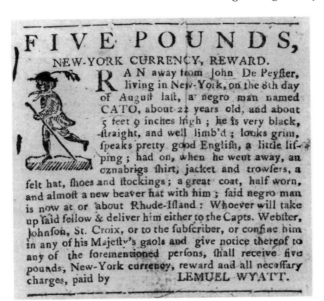

FIVE POUNDS,
NEW-YORK CURRENCY, REWARD.

RAN away from John De Peyfter, living in New-York, on the 8th day of Auguft laſt, a negro man named CATO, about 22 years old, and about 5 feet 9 inches high ; he is very black, -ſtraight, and well limb'd ; looks grim, ſpeaks pretty good Engliſh, a little liſ-ping ; had on, when he went away, an oznabrigs ſhirt, jacket and trowſers, a felt hat, ſhoes and ſtockings ; a great coat, half worn, and almoſt a new beaver hat with him ; ſaid negro man is now at or about Rhode-Iſland : Whoever will take up ſaid fellow & deliver him either to the Capts. Webſter, Johnſon, St. Croix, or to the ſubſcriber, or confine him in any of his Majeſtv's gaols and give notice thereof to any of the forementioned perſons, ſhall receive five pounds, New-York currency, reward and all neceſſary charges, paid by   LEMUEL WYATT.

FIGURE 7. The reader of this copy of the *Newport Mercury* paid at least some attention to this advertisement: he underlined key information and drew a jaunty feather in the iconic runaway's hat. The master, a New Yorker, relied on such advertisements to gain the help of people as far away as Newport in identifying, apprehending, and returning individuals trying to escape slavery. *Newport Mercury*, 25 Jan. 1773. Courtesy of the Rhode Island Historical Society (RHi X3 7461).

They placed advertisements and encouraged habits of surveillance that fixed the public eye on an escapee's prior identity as a slave. In this struggle over identity and truth, the public played a crucial role as the audience to be convinced and motivated to act one way or the other. Through the middle of the century, the New England public dedicated itself to preventing runaways from escaping their masters either literally or symbolically.

Early on, colonial and town governments passed laws establishing curfews and requiring slaves to present passes when boarding ferries or boats. Some constables and private citizens surpassed the requirements of these laws, taking up strange blacks "strolling" through town, remanding them to the local jail, and aggressively seeking out masters to claim them. Such practices soon became customary. A public composed of many who collaborated in this widespread surveillance and few, if any, who resisted it greatly extended the power of masters. Masters encouraged this public surveillance by offering private rewards and by advertising in newspapers the escape of servants, much the same way that military officials advertised deserters and legal officials advertised suspected criminals and escaped prisoners (fig. 7). Such advertisements described the absconded individual, offered rewards for recapture, and prohibited the provision of shelter or employment. Newspaper readers could vicariously participate in especially dramatic conflicts. The *Newport Mercury* reported the story of a New Hampshire man who attempted to take up two runaways who overpowered, beat, and robbed him and who remained on the loose for some time before being recaptured after a vigorous manhunt. On the same day, the *Mercury* also reported the fate of a Coventry man who, having escaped from slavery and being pursued for a few days, cut his own throat. Such publicity helped masters make slaves feel that there was no way out from slavery: escapees could not succeed in reinventing themselves as free because the community would never accept their new impostures but rather would relentlessly detect, reveal, and enforce their former slave selves.[43]

If successfully escaping from enslavement was extremely difficult, there were nonetheless other reasons to try. For a servant seeking to elude the way a master defined his or her identity, running away could take several forms. Running away even quite briefly could succeed as an expressive gesture, conveying impetuous emotions. When Harry ran away after an unusually severe whipping by the Reverend MacSparran, he made no plans to stay away, but he did dramatize his anger and wounded pride. Running away could allow a temporary respite from the loneliness of those separated from their families and friends: when Abigail stole away at night to visit her husband, everyone knew where to find her if she wasn't back by dawn. Running away could also be a more explicit tactic in ongoing negotiations. Indeed, probably only a minority of runaways actually envisioned permanent escape from slavery and were absent long enough to prompt masters to place newspaper advertisements. Runaways sought to modify their conditions or assert alternate aspects of identity, but escapees sought to re-create themselves radically— a formerly enslaved self in a new guise—against all odds.

Advertisements placed by masters in newspapers provide substantial, but incomplete, information. Not all runaways were advertised. Sheriff Beriah Brown drafted a notice for the return of his runaway slave Pomp but never published it; twenty-one months later he noted that the young man had "come home."[44] Masters placing advertisements rarely disclosed much about why the person ran away.

Jonathan Hazard, for instance, advertised the escape of his slave Ben in a notice that focused almost exclusively on physical description; the dramatic reasons for the escape are suggested only by records of a contemporary lawsuit in which his master was called to defend his actions. At his master's behest, Ben had illegally grazed sheep in another man's field. For him, nothing good could come out of the trial: whether he lied, testified against his master, or was scapegoated, the public, legal role of witness threatened to rupture his status.[45] Did he succeed in running away? Again, advertisements don't tell us. Nonetheless, taken together, advertisements do document some significant patterns.

The destinations of would-be escapees suggest how expectations about the public's behavior shaped their options and limited their horizons. When Venture and his comrades fled the coast of southern New England, their destination was clear: the Mississippi. They no doubt had some sense of the practical challenges they faced, taking a boat and loading it with food, but the fantasy of getting to French or Spanish territory—escaping out of their society altogether—was astoundingly impractical. What did they know of the tiny French outpost at New Orleans? Why did they think there would be roles for them there? Presumably, their choice of destination says less about where they wanted to go than about whence they originally came. African-born people, such as Venture, tended to run away in groups and to try to escape entirely the society that held them captive. In the Caribbean, these "new Africans" escaped to the mountains and formed self-governing and often longstanding maroon communities. The African-born participants in the Stono Rebellion in South Carolina were enticed by the presence of Spanish Florida, which offered freedom to escapees from the colonies. In Venture's case, the only comrade in escape he described at any length was not an African-born slave but a servant born in Ireland. Clearly, in addition to distinctively African sensibilities, one affinity that could bind together people from opposite ends of the Atlantic was that of arriving in America from abroad. In contrast, native-born slaves most often ran away singly, perhaps to avoid detection, and sought new, free lives by integrating themselves into colonial society. Most New England runaways fall into this pattern. Indeed, it may be that even people born abroad were more likely in New England to attempt "internal" rather than "external" escapes because of the intimacy and low density of slavery in the region.

The timing of escape attempts suggests that runaways acted strategically to increase their odds of success. Like Venture, most slaves and servants ran away in the spring and summer, when the weather was most hospitable to life on the lam and when farmwork was heaviest and thus employment most available. Other correlations are more ambiguous: several masters who advertised for the return of runaway servants also advertised the fact that their wives had abandoned them. Were these men generally abusive? Were they taking out anger at recalcitrant slaves on their wives, or vice versa? Did a runaway slave inspire a woman to elope?[46] In any case, the most striking pattern in advertisements for runaway slaves and other servants is that those who attempted to escape were overwhelmingly young and male. Why did the opportunities available to those running away and the senses of self prompting enslaved people to attempt escape so favor young men?

Certainly it was possible for New Englanders, whether enslaved or not, to develop networks and subcultures that did not uphold the values of the public order, and this was a serious weakness to the hegemony of the master class. Urban communities were sufficiently large to afford some anonymity and to allow these groups to develop some solidarity. Some urban slaves even enjoyed living arrangements autonomous enough that they could secretly house and feed friendly runaways. In 1716, Caesar ran away from his Boston master in the winter and lived throughout the winter and spring in the city in barns and stables, breaking into various houses, including that of his master, to steal food, clothes, and alcohol.[47] Caesar spent much of his time on the lam with another escaped servant who is described in legal records as "Indian," suggesting that common status and shared experiences helped Indians and blacks recognize common bonds. But both of them found that in colonial towns and cities clandestine shelter and stolen food often led to discovery and apprehension.

Another haven for escaped slaves and servants was Indian enclaves. Indians, who often had their own bitter experiences of servitude in English households, could feel solidarity with blacks, even at the expense of forgoing financial rewards from whites for helping to identify and return runaways. The elective affinities between enslaved Africans and Indians in New England are most richly evoked by the narrative of Arthur, a slave who ran away repeatedly before his execution in 1768. He describes Indians offering him shelter, protection, and even active collusion in his efforts to evade English searchers. He lived for months on end at the Natick and Sandwich enclaves and developed a strong friendship with an Indian woman whom he encountered in her extensive travels around the region. At one point she helped him evade a posse by dressing him up as an Indian woman, rolling his clothes up into a bundle like a papoose, and walking him right past a search party to the home of an Indian family.[48]

Such behavior suggests the advantages and limits of these ruptures in the New England public. Urban black communities could provide temporary shelter, but these arrangements seem unlikely to have provided sustainable solutions. Ultimately, some transition to a new, free identity was necessary. Indian enclaves were more like maroon communities of escaped slaves living outside the reach of colonial authority, offering an alternate community but one based on another cultural mode, which runaways such as Arthur often did not want to adopt permanently. When they did, native residents began to debate just how welcome they were. Advertisements rarely mentioned the possibility that slaves, free blacks, or Indians might harbor runaways.

Masters writing advertisements, however, were explicit about another, ultimately more crucial group of people that might harbor escaped runaways: English employers, especially ship captains. Just as husbands warned shopkeepers not to honor the credit of deserting or eloping wives, so masters forbade ships' captains to employ or transport runaway servants and slaves. English employers were potential allies for runaways. Cheap labor set the self-interest of individual employers against the public interest of refusing harbor to fugitive servants. For runaways, it was easiest to get work if their skills were marketable and relatively anonymous, and this helped favor the prospects of young men. Many male runaways, for instance, had previous experience as sailors—and employment on an outbound ship offered not only work and shelter but also transportation far away. Thus, master Joseph Underwood suspected that his runaway servant York had left Newport "to go to Nantucket, from thence to sail on a whaling voyage."[49] The public broadly enforced standard gender divisions in the labor market. Maritime and other important labor markets were by custom closed to women. Women were largely restricted to work in domestic service, which was more likely to be local, personal, and long term than was sailing or day labor. Thus, women may have experienced not only closer surveillance but also greater difficulty in securing new employment.[50]

Whether enslaved men and women ran away was determined not just by perceived opportunities but also by gendered reactions to dependence and subordination. It may be that women ran away in different ways than men—staying closer to home, perhaps, or staying away for shorter periods of time—so that their escapes were less likely to be documented by advertisements. It may be that many enslaved women had children and may have chosen not to run away because of their sense of the rewards and obligations of motherhood. Men seem to have felt less bound by family ties. Venture, for instance, ran away within months of marrying a fellow slave and did not appear to consider taking her with him. In any case, it seems clear that eighteenth-century gender ideologies encouraged women of all stations to reconcile themselves to dependency. Women's transition at adulthood conventionally moved them from under the paternal rule of father to under the manly coverture of husbands, so the contrast for women living as dependents in servitude was not so stark. In contrast, men were widely encouraged to associate masculinity with independence. Venture's narrative, for instance, appealed to widely resonant gender sensibilities when it recounted the story of his original enslavement: the conquering army killed his father, who is represented as proud and defiant, and enslaved his mother and him (at the age of six), who are depicted as passive and submissive.

In this respect, the behavior of enslaved African women and men was similar to the behavior of English settlers when they found themselves held captive. During recurrent colonial wars, hundreds of settlers—men, women, and children—were captured by Indians. Those who survived capture and endured captivity were almost always either children or adult women. Men were killed more often in combat, died more often in fights after capture, and tried more often to escape. Overall, English men proved so recalcitrant that tribes learned not to attempt adopting them, although they continued to adopt English women and children.[51] When advertisements for escapees described personal characteristics, they tended to focus on traits that signified either submission or rebellion. For instance, numerous advertisements described slaves as "flippant," suggesting a master's annoyance at disrespect. Clearly, notions of male and female honor and varied styles of reacting to domination were deeply embedded in the culture that enslaved Africans and English settlers shared. If African behavior seemed to fulfill English expectations, it may suggest not so much that enslaved Africans adopted English gender roles as congruence in their cultural values. Indeed, this may have been one area in which West African notions of dignity and selfhood were reinforced by English values.

Among both English captives and enslaved Africans, those most likely to die or try to escape were not just men but young men. Venture ran away at age twenty-two, and other runaways were most commonly in their late teens or early twenties; the pattern holds for women as well as men and for servants, slaves, and apprentices alike.[52] Was this because youths were spryer and had better reason to think they might succeed? Or was it because young men tended to have stronger emotional reasons to express resistance to domination? Certainly it would seem that for Venture running away was part of a difficult process of self-definition as a man coming of age. His recurrent conflicts with the young Robinson Mumford, for instance, suggest that he faced not so much practical problems as emotional conflicts reconciling his servile role with colonial norms of independent masculinity. Perhaps the transition to adult masculinity was a special spur to running away, one that was more expressive than instrumental. For many enslaved young men—like young English captives who tried to escape even though it was quite likely they would end up dead—getting away may not have been as important as trying.

In order to help identify runaways, town and colonial governments often required enslaved people and free blacks to carry written passes. Slaves needed passes from their masters; free people generally had to rely on former employers for such certificates. Since masters discouraged the education of slaves and free blacks, relatively few runaways had the wherewithal to forge their own passes. In early July 1729, two enslaved Newporters paid a literate acquaintance, the "mulatto" slave Isaac, to forge their freedom papers by giving him a Bible and a pair of striped breeches. He crafted two different identities for them: one of the forged passes was purportedly written by a former employer and certified that "this youngster" had lived and worked with him for three years at a coke furnace and had been born free; the other pass, written in a different hand and bearing a different address and date, was purportedly written by a former master, who had bought "this negro man" for a seven-year term at the expiration of which he had become free. Having obtained passes, the two men ran away from their masters, following the main road toward New York City. At New London, a suspicious ferryman ascertained that they did not have the type of pass required by Connecticut law and remanded them to a local justice of the peace. Confessing all, they were sent back into their masters in Newport. And Isaac faced both criminal prosecution and civil lawsuits for his part in the escape attempt.[53]

Even with carefully crafted passes, runaways needed to be able to tell a convincing story in order to pass for free. Where were they going? For whom had they worked in the past? Why were they dirty, why carrying so much stuff? Blacks, Indians, and even suspicious-looking whites on the road could be asked to identify and explain themselves. They could end up in serious trouble if their answers were not persuasive. A man in his mid-thirties named Sam Simons was traveling through South Kingstown when he attracted the attention of William Potter, Esq., who interrogated him. Simons said that he had been born among the Mohawks, had served his time with General Johnston, had sailed in the employ of Colonel Bowers of Swanzey, Massachusetts, and was well known there and in New London and Norwich, Connecticut. But "he had no pass and . . . behaved himself like a Rogue," so Potter had him jailed on suspicion of being a runaway. To test the man's story, Potter published an advertisement calling on his owner to identify and claim him.[54] This was a dangerous situation even for legally free people, for no equivalent procedure was used to test the stories of putative masters claiming people as their servants. Advertisements were always attempts by masters to control the public's image of the person they claimed was a slave, their property.

The other way master-slave relationships were ruptured was in the act of sale, when a master both renounced his authority and exercised his most absolute power. Sale was often the event that sealed the conversion of a person into property. Sales were thus routine and often not particularly personal, for the relationships they severed were often either brief or already disrupted. When slavers docked in harbor, they sold their cargoes; when a large farmer went bankrupt or died, his executors sold his slaves along with his other possessions. Traders advertising in newspapers described people for sale in terms of physique, sex, stamina, and geographic designations that suggested, at most, stereotyped assumptions about ethnic character types. Such notices gave little attention to personality, because these traders were introducing strangers into the local slave system. For people already enmeshed in domestic slavery, sale was often extremely personal, a crucial phase in ongoing negotiations between masters and servants.

The option of selling slaves gave masters the power to sever personal relationships unilaterally. Although Cesar Lyndon was able to keep his own family ties largely intact, his master was not above selling slaves: in 1771, Josias Lyndon sold a man named Prince for $150 in Spanish silver.[55] Masters had such latitude because the public granted them virtual carte blanche by refusing to intervene in any way that differentiated slaves from any other form of transferable property. Other than a small import duty, eighteenth-century New Englanders imposed no direct legal or customary restrictions on when, to whom, or under what conditions a master could sell a slave. Enslaved people might try to negotiate or resist to obtain a more satisfactory relationship, but their options were restricted by the simple fact that they needed a viable resolution much more than any master did. For masters, sale could be used as a threat, a punishment, or a last resort. Faced with slaves who refused to bend sufficiently to their will, masters always had the option of ending the relationship without losing their investment: they could cash in.

Even in sale masters found their power limited, however, at least if money was a priority. Despite the absence of such language from trader's advertisements, buyers assessed the value of slaves on their perceptions of the individual's personality and aspirations. Personality was important because of the intimacy of New England slavery and its informal regulation by the public. A buyer in New England knew that he or she would have to establish a working and living relationship with anyone purchased. Masters offering slaves for sale emphasized special skills and personal character. In newspaper notices, they would note that a slave was being sold for "no fault" in particular or would emphasize reliability, intelligence, and docility. In a private letter, one master described a slave for sale: "He is not so quick a Negro as some, has been faithful since he has lived with me, & is easy governed, & is careful, in short he has done more labour for me than any man I could hire." Personal relationships were so important that in this case the man was sent out on trial—to determine not whether his new buyer would like him but whether he would like his new buyer. "I have informed the Negro he might come back, if he did not like [to stay]."[56] Slaves gained such room for negotiation because masters needed their cooperation to maximize profits. And slaves used this power to make the best possible bargains for themselves.

Masters often began talking about sale when a slave pushed their relations to the breaking point. Venture's *Narrative* recounts a series of sales, each of them more or less explicitly negotiated. He was sold for the first time in New England after his failed escape attempt. He was next threatened with sale after a protracted violent struggle with his master and mistress that he had further escalated by appealing to the local justice of the peace. Even then, with Venture handcuffed and shackled, his master attempted to negotiate, threatening to sell him to the West Indies if he didn't behave. The notorious brutality of slavery in the West Indies made it both the most terrible threat available to New England masters and a relatively easy place to dispose of difficult slaves. When this threat failed to bring Venture around, Stanton decided to sell him locally. Ironically, at this point, Stanton again became dependent on Venture's cooperation. Slaves or other servants could influence their own selling prices. By modifying their attitude, they could present themselves as more or less attractive to potential buyers. New England slave owners respected this power and sought to use it by gaining the slave's assistance. They often encouraged slaves to go out and find their own buyers; some passes issued for this purpose survive.[57]

Slaves and other servants had an incentive to negotiate sales because so much

was at stake. One the one hand, they might be able to upgrade their current situation, an opportunity to start relations over. Indentured Indian servant Ruth Cockaway was able to get out from under a "very Difficult & hard" master by convincing another colonist to pay for her redemption. In exchange, she apprenticed herself
to him: the possibilities of a better master induced her to exchange a partially served
six-year indenture for a new ten-year one. On the other hand, slaves sold to the
wrong master, or sent to live in the wrong place, could be extremely unhappy. Sold
away from Boston into a rural country town in 1752, the slave Pompe grew de-
spondent. When he was not allowed to go out at night, Pompe's discontent became
sullen and menacing. His new mistress grew afraid of him. He threatened that if
she didn't sell him back to Boston he would sabotage the fall harvest. And indeed
he did, by running away—straight back to his old master. The ploy worked. His
country purchaser wrote a letter voiding the sale and demanding a refund of the
purchase price.[58]

Venture, too, drove the best bargains he could. When faced with sale by Stanton, he made an explicit bargain with a potential buyer, a local farmer who approached Venture and asked him if he would go live with him. Venture agreed to
open negotiations: "[The farmer asked me to] make myself discontented and to
appear as un-reconciled to my master as I could before . . . he bargained with him
for me and that in return he would give me a good chance to gain my freedom."
The sale soon went through, and his new buyer immediately removed Venture's
chains; but he did not give Venture a chance to earn his freedom. Instead, his new
owner put him up for sale to a man who wanted to take him to German Flats. Venture flatly refused to go. The potential buyer threatened to force him, tied down
in his sleigh if necessary. "I replied to him, that if he carried me in that manner no
person would purchase me, for it would be thought he had a murderer for sale."
The threat worked. The prospective buyer gave up, the man trying to sell Venture
reneged on his agreement with Stanton, and Venture was left to negotiate his own
sale. In the end, Venture got himself sold to a Colonel Oliver Smith of Stonington, Connecticut, near where his wife and children were living.[59]

At one level, such negotiations seemed to undermine the power of masters, since
they presented the spectacle of slaves choosing their own masters. At another level,
such autonomy emphasized the power of masters to control not so much individual
slaves as the system of slavery: they allowed slaves such room to negotiate at moments of transition because they could be confident that in the end even resource-
ful individuals such as Venture would have to remain within narrow parameters.

Indeed, masters retained the upper hand even in agreements that promised individuals escape from perpetual servitude. Sale was always a kind of reinvention—from the master's point of view by translating a person into cash value, from the slave's point of view by redefining the conditions of servitude.

What most enslaved people wanted was a chance to become free, and they expected to pay a price. Manumission was the process by which a master could legally free a slave. Characteristically, Venture convinced a series of masters to let him earn money to buy his freedom in return for good behavior, hard work, or a cut of his profits. Such agreements emphasized the dependence of masters on sustaining good working relations with their slaves and provided slaves with powerful incentives to work hard to please their masters.

Because masters held such disproportionate power, the sale of slaves to themselves held many advantages for masters and many dangers for slaves. To begin with, prices were likely to be high: few people were willing to pay more for freedom than the enslaved person. Moreover, many manumissions did not require any immediate sacrifice from masters at all: they were arranged in the form of a promised bequest. Cesar Lyndon, for instance, gained his freedom under the terms of his master's will. Most important, once slaves kept their part of the bargain, the master's obligation was largely voluntary. In general, the public refrained from enforcing unfulfilled manumission agreements. Naturally, this reticence gave masters the upper hand and allowed them to renege on agreements with impunity. In Venture's case, each of his masters—first Mumford, then Stanton, then Miner—agreed to let him purchase his manumission; each in the end reneged on his agreement, stole Venture's savings, or just sold him to someone else. No court would honor the notion that a master could steal money from a slave, who was, after all, property as well. Venture's only recourse was to try again with a new master.

Venture kept trying until he found a master who actually honored a manumission agreement. About 1764, when he was in his mid-thirties, Venture convinced Colonel Smith to let him earn independent money and purchase his freedom. Wary from past betrayals, he made sure that the agreement would be public rather than private by getting a free black man to hold his money for him. Venture's price was set at seventy pounds, which, despite some pride in his own financial value, he described as no bargain. But Colonel Smith kept his promise: Venture was grateful and free. His first act as a free man was to adopt the surname of this honorable master, becoming Venture Smith.[60]

The public responded to sales of slaves very differently depending on whether a slave was being sold to another master or buying his or her own freedom. The public treated most slave sales like other commercial contracts conveying property from one owner to another. The sale of slaves was a public event, commonly advertised in newspapers, sometimes conducted in public markets, and usually sealed by legal documents. The law imposed duties on imported slaves but otherwise imposed few restrictions other than to enforce agreements that came into dispute when property rights were at stake. In contrast, the government and the public in general were more likely to interfere in sales resulting in manumission and discouraged such transactions by direct and indirect means. Early in the century, the colonial assembly discouraged masters from agreeing to free their slaves by ordering that former masters would always remain liable should their former slaves ever become paupers or town charges. The public's failure to recognize the legal right of slaves to make contracts with their masters rendered these bargains very unequal. Many slaves may have found themselves cheated, but few such cases got into court.

The response of the public was more symbolic than practical. The sale of a slave from one master to another represented a momentary rupture in the ideological system of slavery. At a time when the public found it soothing to think of slavery as natural, inevitable, and beyond individual control, all sales emphasized that mastery was not permanent, not always private, and likely not absolute. Everybody knew that slaves used leverage to negotiate elbow room within a system that was stacked against them. Sales to other masters only reaffirmed the slave system, reinforcing the power of both the old and the new master and the illusion of slavery as private. But manumission was a more troubling threat to these sensibilities because it transformed a person who was socially dead into one who was socially alive. This asked the public to reverse the status quo and recognize the contractual rights of people who previously stood outside the civic order.

In the end, attempts by enslaved people to escape and by masters to stop them created an ambivalent public image of Africans in America. Running away was, at root, about the ability to control the publicly accepted identities of the individuals in question: Could the runaway get the public to treat him or her as free? Could the master expose the escapee's slave status and make it stick?[61] On the one hand, advertisements represent individuals with distinctive bodies, personal styles of self-presentation, special skills, and complex aspirations. On the other hand, the prevalence of slave advertisements in colonial newspapers reiterated a generic image of blacks as suspicious, rebellious, and duplicitous. White servants were about as likely to run away as enslaved blacks, but there were proportionately far fewer of them; whereas almost all blacks were enslaved, only a few whites were. Consequently, the figure of the white runaway did not become a powerful stereotype. Perhaps the constant and apparently necessary surveillance of slaves and strange black people created a public image of all blacks as potential runaways, as always suspect. At the same time, slave owners and their families promoted the image that enslaved people living with them in the intimacy of their households were like family members. These two modes of representation may help explain the emerging split in public images of blacks as docile, happy servants—and as dissimulating, vengeful rebels. The public needed both images: the first to imagine slavery as a private, absolute, permanent status beyond its intervention, and the second to justify collaborating in the myriad acts of omission and commission necessary to keep the institution functioning.

||| Buyer Beware |||

Samuel Sewall's attack on slavery in *The Selling of Joseph* included not only appeals to reason and piety but also a warning. In the "everlasting" law of equity, "Man Stealing" ranked among the most atrocious of all capital crimes: "What louder Cry can there be made of that Celebrated Warning, *Caveat Emptor!*"[62] Over the course of the century, not only slave owners themselves but members of a broad public learned to take this warning to heart.

Such fears were inflamed in a Newport tavern on May Day, 1750, when talk turned away from the rituals of spring to fantasies of violence. Cambridge, the slave of a local butcher, regaled a group of comrades with a scheme for revolt. As he saw it, "the best way for cutting off the White People was for Every negro to kill his own Master." Was this a real plot or just big talk? Probably Cambridge and his fellow slaves knew that any kind of successful revolt was impracticable. But he and his comrades enjoyed such talk almost as much as colonists feared it. One of those afraid, or at least acting concerned, was an Indian woman who overheard this conversation, perhaps while she was working as a barmaid: she quickly reported to legal authorities that Cambridge was conspiring to "murder and destroy" the town's "Inhabitants." Of course, a fifth of the city's inhabitants were black and enslaved, and it was this discrepancy between colonial fantasies and colonial realities that was at the root of the problem, both practical and symbolic.

The specter of slave rebellion confronted New Englanders with the instability not so much of their social structure as of the symbolic self-understanding that had developed to accommodate slavery. Slave revolt symbolized the return of repressed discrepancies between notions of slavery as social death and the facts of slavery as social life. Slaves were not separate from the public but were within it; they were not completely dominated by masters but only partially controlled by masters and the public; slavery was not a private relationship but an institution supported by the actions of a broad and unified public. For slaves, these discrepancies provided opportunities.

From the slave's point of view, the fantasy of revolt expressed—in a dangerous but provocative way—a need for self-assertion in the face of overwhelming force and symbolic annihilation. Cambridge himself had long enjoyed a reputation for menacing violence. Years earlier, he had attacked the house of a local weaver in the middle of the night; unable to break his way in, he terrorized the occupants from without for hours. For this bluster he paid a severe price: the local justices sentenced him to twenty-nine stripes on his naked back at the public whipping post.[63] This incident suggests the public determination to keep slaves in line and also that, in the end, Cambridge was more full of bluster than violence. Why revolt would be compelling to enslaved blacks seems obvious enough. Revolt meant freedom and revenge; revolt meant destroying the entire system of slavery. Slaves' enjoyment of the prospect of revolt suggests that they did not accept the basic parameters of the system under which they lived.

Yet, ironically, it would seem that the fantasy of overturning the system was fueled by rage generated by the constant self-abnegation, dissimulation, and compromise made necessary by efforts to work within it. The experience of enslavement in eighteenth-century New England fostered simultaneous and conflicting identities. Onstage, before masters or the public, slaves had good reason to act deferential and contented; offstage, that is, among their peers, they could express resentment and question the legitimacy of colonial authority. Slavery, as it was negotiated in practice, informally with masters, depended on slaves making bargains in the context of unequal power and without recourse to public authority. Manumissions could be promised but denied. Violence was treated by the public in keeping with a strict double standard. Negotiations generally depend on the hope that the other party will honor his or her end of the bargain, but for "socially dead" slaves this was always just a hope. Slaves could assert public roles: they could try to encourage masters to act in keeping with the public persona of the good master; they could engage in the market and define consumer identities; they could make bargains to improve their conditions. But they could rarely be confident that these roles were going to be honored. This vulnerability produced in slaves a sense of betrayed expectations. Slavery depended on agreements between masters and servants, which masters often casually abrogated. Such caprice has in other times and places also undergirded authoritarian power: here, the master gained cooperation by allowing latitude much of the time while inspiring terror by occasional, arbitrary punishments. Individual masters were not the only ones at fault: the people who let them get away with their brutality, cheating, and false promises were a broad and diffuse public.

In this sense, slaves' talk of revolt—talk not just of killing a master or two but of "cutting off the white people"—was a kind of revenge against the public. It was an ostentatious reversal of the proper public role of slave. Slaves, who were supposed to be contented, even grateful, suddenly appeared angry and betrayed. And such talk revealed a hidden aspect of the proper role of the public: master-slave relations that the public wanted to imagine as private were now suddenly revealed as public. Thus the fantasy of revolt was also, for the slave, a very real exercise of power, the power to make whites feel vulnerable, implicated, and guilty.

So when rumors of a slave revolt became public, the public seized on the news. Exaggerated reporting of rebellions real and imagined appeared in colonial newspapers. In 1741, a rash of arson in New York revived fears provoked by the Stono Rebellion in South Carolina several years earlier and gave rise to an exhaustive and bloody series of trials to rout out the presumed conspirators. Edgy New Englanders attended to the news: one newspaper reader wrote an ironic editorial letter in which he complained of the tedium of having each week to read yet more details of yet more executions.[64] Other readers, more self-righteous, sold their slaves overseas and admonished the public to take firm measures to suppress any such revolt in their city.[65] Why was slave revolt such a resonant fear and fantasy for whites? In part, presumably, because it reinforced an image of blacks as a menacing "other," an image that helped justify their collaboration with the institution of slavery.

The public had its own split self-images. New Englanders allowed slavery to develop without readjusting their self-conception as a homogeneous white society. To bridge this gap between structure and symbolic understanding they relied on the illusion of slavery as a kind of social death—that slave relations were private, absolute, and permanent. But daily experience confronted individuals with the fact

that slavery was public, negotiated, and fragile. Even nonslaveholders played a crucial role in empowering masters, limiting slave options, and reconciling ruptured
relations. In the end, the capriciousness of slavery may help explain colonists' exaggerated fears that the British Empire was attempting to "enslave" them when
imperial reforms in the 1760s began to infringe on customary notions of citizenship, privileges, and rights. They became especially obsessed with clear-cut rules,
suspicion of arbitrary power, and the danger of being enticed into sacrificing symbolic honor by the advantages of practical compromise.[66]

No public spectacle was staged to punish Cambridge. Within several days of
his bold talk in the tavern, he was arrested and arraigned before three justices. They
concluded that his talk tended to "raise fear & Terror to the Inhabitants of this
town, if not to raise a Sedition among the Negroes." He was tried in the lowest
possible jurisdiction, the Court of General Sessions of the Peace, found guilty of
drawing "the Slaves of sd. Town from the Duty & Fidelity they owe to their Masters," sentenced to be banished from the colony, and ordered sold to pay the costs
of his prosecution.[67] Why did officials want to whisk him away so quietly?
Unwilling to dismiss talk of slave revolt as idle banter, they were apparently also
unwilling to inflame it with unnecessary public attention.

The expulsion of Cambridge from their body politic did not, however, eradicate the fear, and fantasy, of slave revolt. On 10 May many Newporters traveled
across the bay to witness the execution of a celebrated murderer in South
Kingstown. This was a dramatic execution, partly because the murder had been
particularly shocking and the punishment was to be extremely brutal. Moreover,
the convict was refusing to play his allotted part in the spectacle of his death. The
ritual of execution was intended to reverse transgressions literally, by punishing the
evildoer and warning others, and symbolically, by featuring the criminal's confession, a confession that recognized and honored the authority that was about to destroy him. This murderer had been sentenced to be hanged until dead; then his
body was to be gibbeted, that is, suspended in an iron cage at the side of the busy
post road. The gibbet had its intended effect: steadfast and unrepentant in the face
of death, the convict, confronting this after-death horror, lost his self-possession.
He cried out for mercy, exclaiming that the gibbet was "too hard." The majesty of
the law triumphed over his individual will.

And yet it was at just this symbolic moment of public power affirmed that the
audience itself began to lose its nerve. It should have been clear to anyone in the
crowd that the town of Newport must have been largely depopulated by the mass

exodus to attend this spectacle. Anxious messengers began to arrive, calling the townspeople back: those few who had remained behind feared that the slaves would take the opportunity to revolt.[68] In this war of nerves, faith that public authority would remain supreme gave way to panic. The public rushed back to town. Living with slavery was changing New England—and not always in ways settlers anticipated or desired.

CHAPTER THREE

Strange Christians

||| Westerly, Rhode Island, about 1700 |||

When drought threatened their corn one summer, a group of Narragansetts performed an ancient rite to appease the malevolent spirit who withheld the rain. The ritual lasted for days, and kept them from their work on the colonial farms that were transforming their ancestral landscape and ensnaring many of them in cycles of debt and bound labor. At one point a young English settler approached on horseback, called off the Indians employed by his father, and rebuked them all for worshiping the Devil. In the early years of colonial encounters, such confrontations over spiritual authority were not uncommon: sometimes native spiritual leaders and colonial ministers faced off in explicit competitions. When Christians needed rain or were afflicted by disease, they prayed not to the Devil but to God. In this case the Indian spiritual leader, or powwow in the local language, rose to the challenge and rebuked the interloper: "You are proud, young Man." He went on to explain that they prayed to Chepi because he was the spirit afflicting them. "If I was to beat you, who would you pray to? To me or to your Father ten miles off?" It will rain, he predicted, before you get home—as though Chepi, who seemed impervious to his devotee's supplications, would be more responsive to this interloper's insults. Sure enough, the arrogant young settler arrived home drenched.

At least that's how the Reverend Ezra Stiles reported the story half a century later. As in many other stories told by colonists, the Christian challenger loses, and the pagan powwow holds his ground. To be sure, Stiles, a man of great scholarly erudition and wide-ranging curiosity, harbored little doubt that ultimately, among the local settlers and Indians alike, the ancient system of magic and superstition had largely fallen apart by the mid-eighteenth century. But he respected this quick-witted powwow's proud defense of his beliefs. In a way, this story evokes the nostalgia Stiles felt for what he saw as an Indian population on the verge of disappearance. On the other hand, the Indians who remained very much present in eighteenth-century New England seem to have told rather different stories about this kind of colonial religious confrontation. In the Indian stories passed down through oral tradition and recorded by anthropologists, the powwow very often loses.[1] Although this symbolic defeat may have been humiliating in some ways, it also emphasized the fact that by the eighteenth century many New England Indians were devout Christians. By midcentury most enclaves supported their own churches, often with Indian pastors. Stiles knew all this, but he was nonetheless drawn to a narrative that emphasized Indians' resistance to English settlers and their religion. These contrasting narratives of colonial conversion remind us that spiritual encounters in early America were often confrontational and competitive and that these struggles ramified long after the English had taken possession of the landscape.

For colonial New Englanders, the question was very often not whether Indians, or enslaved Africans, would be pagan or Christian but what the bonds of Christian fellowship would mean. In this sense, the story of the old powwow echoed a basic paradox of colonial culture: although cultural exchanges brought English settlers, Native Americans, and enslaved Africans onto common cultural ground, these exchanges also tended to drive them apart.

In their almanacs, newspapers, and joke books, eighteenth-century settlers in New England told and retold two common stories about colonial conversions: one for Indians, and another for Negroes. One of the "amusing anecdotes" that animated the popular press featured a missionary who had been catechizing an Indian maiden. He asks her to recite the Ten Commandments. She recites nine and stops. Don't you remember, he asks, I taught you ten? "Yes, Mr. Minister," she replies, "and last night you *taught me to break one.*" Other jokes of this genre modified stock English anti-Catholic jokes that mocked priests and nuns for sexual hypocrisy. Rather different jokes played on the popular perception that Indians generally dis-

dained to convert to Christianity. Benjamin Franklin enlivened his "Remarks on
the Savages of North America" by recasting an old story about Indians rebuffing
colonial missionary arrogance: in his version, an Iroquois chieftain was offered the
chance to send six boys to Wheelock's Indian charity school. The chief declined
but offered to allow six English boys to come for an education among his people.[2]
In both of these examples, the butt of the joke was a missionary, who appeared either arrogant or downright immoral, and the Indians were honored for their dignified independence and skepticism.

Negroes, on the other hand, appeared in this genre of jokes as nominally Christian but false or misguided. One joke featured a Negro man who went to hear the
evangelist George Whitefield; it was recorded at the time by the celebrated itinerant himself and was still being repeated by locals a century later. The Negro man,
caught up in the fervor of the gathering, gestured wildly until someone told him
that the preacher was not who he thought it was. "Not Massa Whitfield?" he exclaimed. "Den I hab made all dis *hubbabboo* for nothing?"[3] Many other jokes also
used Negroes and evangelicals to make fun of each other, suggesting that both were
superficial and prone to serious delusions. Despite the different narratives they implied, such stories about both Indians and Negroes consistently emphasized the
failures of colonial conversions. Why were these jokes so prevalent when settlers
were supposed to be in favor of conversion?

British settlers were indeed eager to talk about the barbarity of native peoples
and Africans and had made this distinction central to their view of the body politic
they created in North America. Early colonists used a conventional European distinction between "Christians" and "strangers" to justify their dispossession of indigenous peoples and their enslavement of Africans. This logic was as ancient as
the Old Testament curse: "Like as ye have forsaken me, and served strange gods in
your land, so ye shall serve strangers in a land *that is* not your's." Since the crusades
of the Middle Ages, most Europeans accepted that it was wrong to enslave fellow
Christians. English colonists, first in Ireland and later in North America and elsewhere, were thus inclined to emphasize the heathen or pagan character of local
religions. Yet they shied away from claiming that pagans could be treated with impunity. Rather, they argued that by enslaving or conquering these pagans Christians could better rescue them from their false beliefs and lead them to the true
faith. Characteristically, the seal of the Massachusetts Bay Colony featured the figure of a naked savage with a dialogue bubble coming out of his mouth: "Come over
and help us" (fig. 8).[4] In practice, however, even in New England, with its strong

FIGURE 8. On the seal of the Massachusetts Bay Company an
Indian begs, "Come over and help us." Among the first im-
prints of this woodcut by John Foster, this example is from a
triumphant colonial account of King Philip's War. Increase
Mather, *A Brief History of the War with the Indians in New-
England* (London, 1676), 15. Courtesy of the Library Company
of Philadelphia.

sense of religious mission, few settlers embraced the duty of proselytization. Rather,
most missionary efforts were sporadic, largely unsuccessful, and plagued by
controversy.

Resistance to missionary endeavors stemmed from one of the basic problems of
imperial ideology, a paradox familiar from other times and places: the danger of
the white man's burden, or the *mission civilatrice,* was that the process of civilizing
colonized peoples might, in the end, succeed. Colonized subjects might become
Christian and thus deserve rights as citizens. The most radical variants of missionary ideology included a progressive view of human development that discov-

ered, despite apparent differences, a potential and essential unity among humankind. Some of the earliest propagandists of English imperialism in North America went so far as to emphasize that the Britons themselves had experienced a similar transformation, by reminding their readers that their own ancestors had been uncivilized heathens who became civil and Christian only after the Roman conquest. In 1590, Thomas Hariot's *Briefe and True Report of the New Found Land of Virginia* used this parallel with the peoples of ancient Britons to show "that the Inhabitants of great Bretannie have bin in times past as sauvage as those of Virginia."[5] Nevertheless, the egalitarian promise of conversion also threatened colonists.

The importance of Christianity as a badge of citizenship was perhaps most apparent in the anxiety and ingenuity the threat of conversion inspired among slaveholders. Anxious about the longstanding convention against enslaving fellow Christians, slave owners resisted proselytization among their slaves even after colonial legislatures solved the legal problem by decreeing that conversion did not alter the status of those *descended* from pagan lands. This colonial opposition continually frustrated British missionary organizations. At midcentury, Swedish traveler Peter Kalm was also struck by colonial opposition to missionary efforts: "To this they are led partly by the conceit of its being shameful to have a spiritual brother or sister among so despicable a people; partly by thinking that they would not be able to keep their negroes so subjected afterwards; and partly through fear of the negroes growing too proud on seeing themselves on a level with their masters in religious matters."[6] Faced with the basic contradiction of their own imperial ideology of culture, colonizers took refuge in extending indefinitely the time required to complete the process of conversion. For their part, the colonized were left wondering when they would, as it were, stop becoming and start being.

When people of color did come to worship the Christian God, however, settlers in North America learned to draw new lines of difference. Ultimately, cultural convergence did tend to erase "ethnic" differences, but it also helped to invent "racial" identities. Stories of colonial conversions illustrate how settlers parlayed the alleged responses of Africans and Indians to Christianity into stereotypes about racial natures. Ideas about both cultural differences and racial characters served the same purpose of explaining why black people and Indians could never be incorporated as equals into American society. By the mid-nineteenth century this damned-if-you-do-damned-if-you-don't logic of cultural history and racial nature had become so commonplace that Alexis de Tocqueville could sum up in one sentence the seemingly obvious truth about blacks and Indians: "The servility of the former delivers him over into slavery; the pride of the latter leads him to death."[7]

Such exclusionary stereotypes, with their flat, inexorable logic of racial nature, cover up a complex history. Nowadays, as historians seek to rebut such interpretations and recapture this history, many suggest that colonized peoples did not really convert. Instead, they emphasize the perseverance of "traditional" native and African American cultures and their selective combination with Anglo-American ways. Many members of colonial society did adapt aspects of Christian belief and practice to suit their own needs, and various groups did develop distinctive styles of Christian worship. Cultural exchanges also went both ways: ephemeral cultural middle grounds developed between Anglo-Americans, natives, and Africans, as well as enduring transfers to the dominant culture. In this sense, we Americans are none of us converts; we are all of us converts. But such lines of argument imply assumptions about culture and conversion that bear an uncanny resemblance to the colonial ideologies they seek to rebut. By emphasizing continuity, such arguments imply, first of all, that there was something *wrong* with conversion—the process of exchanging one set of beliefs and practices for another. They suggest that conversion must imply mimicry and that mimicry must imply an apish character. It is as though the European, African, or American "origins" of each culture did determine its social meaning—as though races had inherent cultures. Certainly, propagandists of colonization in North America tried to convince themselves that race and culture were inextricable—they called themselves the "sons of God." But shouldn't we consider the alternate possibility that individuals and groups reproduce culture through more complex processes?

In colonial New England, conversion had two discrete meanings. On the one hand, it signified a more or less conscious change of affiliation from one system of belief to another. This collective sense of conversion was invoked when colonists emphasized the superiority of European culture, the inferiority of pagan beliefs and practices, and the analogy of cultural transformation and political subordination. On the other hand, conversion also referred to an individual's experience of spiritual rebirth, which was typically marked by baptism and the rite of communion. Because individual conversion experiences were evaluated by both ministers and current church members, conflicts sometimes developed. These battles became particularly heated when the evangelical revival of the 1740s, known as the Great Awakening, divided many towns, parishes, and families. Factional divisions split apart many of the old town churches and realigned denominational divisions: conservative Congregationalists, or Old Lights, suddenly found themselves in alliance with Anglicans; evangelical Congregationalists, or New Lights, forged new bonds with Baptists. Partly because of their divergent views of the process of spiritual rebirth, Old Light and New Light settlers faced very different challenges when confronted with the prospect of extending the bonds of Christian fellowship to Indians and Africans. These challenges help illuminate the process by which Christianity became, in colonial America, a ground for claiming and disputing citizenship.

The diverse and competitive religious culture of eighteenth-century New England presented native peoples and enslaved Africans with many choices. Of course some, like many settlers, never showed much interest in any form of Christianity. We often assume that Africans and Native Americans were drawn especially to evangelical styles of Christianity because of their more egalitarian character and because their emotional, oral, visionary style of worship echoed familiar customs. Indeed, many embraced New Light Christianity. Nonetheless, many Africans and some Indians, particularly those who lived in English towns, ignored the evangelicals and worshiped in the standing Congregational, Anglican, and Baptist churches. They apparently embraced the Old Lights' hierarchical rituals, literary styles, and authoritarian ideologies. At the same time, many Indians found that New Light faith offered them opportunities for spiritual and institutional autonomy, as well as repeated, unequal interactions with English religious authorities. Ironically, as native peoples, Africans, and English settlers increasingly came onto common cultural ground in eighteenth-century New England, they increasingly tended to think of themselves as members of different "races," with separate destinies. For members of all three groups the conversion of "strangers" into "Christians" supplanted a potentially *mutable* form of difference—culture—with the more stubborn, essentialist identities of race.

||| Colonial Conversions |||

In 1767, an aspiring young missionary on his way back to college in New Haven stopped at a tavern and entered an argument so disturbing that he sent a detailed account of it to his mentor, Eleazar Wheelock. The tavern was crowded, so he took his lunch at a table already occupied by two gentlemen. Embarrassed by his social inferiority, the young man concentrated on handling his knife and fork handsomely. But he was increasingly distracted. The gentlemen were joking about the conversion of Indians to Christianity. The best means of Christianizing or civilizing Indians, they jeered, was "powder and balls." Missionaries, they claimed, only pretended to love Indians: Wheelock's charity school in New Hampshire, for instance, was just a ploy to extort missionary money. For Wheelock's young protégé, this was too much. He interrupted, objecting that not all missionaries "despised" Indians. The gentlemen fixed him with a condescending gaze and challenged him with a simple question: "Would you permit your daughter to marry an Indian?" He could only stammer in protest. The gentlemen concluded that Indians would never be truly converted and civilized unless the English were willing to treat them as equals, and that would never happen. One of them observed pointedly that he "could never respect an Indian, Christian or no Christian so as to put him on a level with white people on any account especially to eat at the same Table." No, they declared, citing Wheelock's most celebrated protégé, a Mohegan-born minister, "not with Mr Ocham himself be he ever so much a Christian or ever so Learned."[8]

Like these gentlemen, many New England settlers regarded missionaries as threatening because they challenged the status quo. Today, we often think of these missionaries as having been threatening too, but in a different way. Nowadays, missionaries often appear as threats to the people they were trying to convert: we debate their intentions, the resistance they encountered, and the havoc they wrought in native or African economic systems, gender roles, and spiritual practices. True enough, missionaries who tried to civilize Indians or educate blacks often deferred or obscured the question of equality: they emphasized a basic, even atavistic, curriculum, intended to teach Indian men to be small-scale farmers, Indian women to be housewives, and slaves to be humble and obedient servants. Most taught their potential converts not to claim too much power or aspire to too much equality.[9] Still, the relationships between missionaries and their objects were only part of a broader struggle over the nature of Christian fellowship and the meaning of colonial citizenship.

The conversion of Indians and blacks threatened colonial New Englanders because they had made Christian fellowship a powerful symbol of membership in the body politic. The standing Congregational and Anglican religious societies typically upheld a hierarchical, patriarchal, even monarchical view of society as an organic structure. Their rituals, institutions, and theologies upheld the notion that Christian fellowship meant respect for the differences between young and old, men and women, rich and poor, humble and exalted. Typically, when Cotton Mather sought to encourage the conversion of slaves, he took pains to emphasize the obedience and deference slaves owed to their masters.[10] In the 1740s, the awakening of religious enthusiasm provoked public debates about the extent to which Christian fellowship should embody the social order or transcend it. Notably, New Light Congregationalists and Baptists challenged lines of age, gender, and class. These longstanding struggles of spiritual authority and the social order were exaggerated, extended, and distorted by the politics of race. For members of both groups, distinctive views about the experience of spiritual conversion shaped their response to the prospect of colonial conversions. The symbolic power of Christianity to represent citizenship helps explain the troubles that plagued Eleazar Wheelock's ill-fated Indian school. Ironically, the closer Indians and blacks came to converting and becoming civilized, the more adamant settlers grew about drawing new lines of exclusion.

As a young man, in 1742, Eleazar Wheelock helped bring the nightmare of the Great Awakening home to the pastor of the town church in Lebanon, Connecticut. The revival upset many ministers, divided congregations, and challenged assumptions about the relationships between men and women, young and old, genteel and humble. Lebanon's Congregational pastor, the Reverend Jacob Eliot, regarded the revival as a threat to the entire social order. Returning home from a two-month visit to Boston, where he found solace in the company of the Old Light advocate Charles Chauncey, Eliot caught up on local gossip by compiling a lurid list of "Remarkables in a Time of New Light"—mostly stories of converts, particularly slaves, who disrupted household governance. In one, an unregenerate settler attempted to punish his born-again slave only to have his brother and his maid cry out in protest: "What a vile thing it was for a Reprobate to correct a child of God." Eliot's mind filled with fantasies of slaves overthrowing all control: "What would they come to—what of Bristol's stealing—Flora's getting drunk[?]" And what of the born-again slave Caesar? Eliot wrote in horror about one night when Caesar exhorted at the home of a local settler and then tried to seduce an Indian woman who had come to hear him, telling her "that Hell was not so dreadful a place as had been described, neither was it so difficult to get to heaven as he had set forth."[11]

Despite the alarm of the standing clergy about the role of Negroes and Indians in the revivals, their very emphasis on order and decorum may have made it easier for the standing churches to incorporate enslaved Africans and conquered Indians into their circles of Christian fellowship. The standing churches had long embraced social difference and hierarchy, and the rituals they practiced and the ethics they propounded were grounded in their core convictions about the nature of spiritual conversion. Conservative Congregationalists and Anglicans looked for gradual and rational enlightenment over a lifetime, with grace manifesting itself in "steady habits." Old Lights tended to associate true Christianity with reverence for education, authority, morality, and virtue. To them, uneducated youths, emotional women, and unruly blacks and Indians seemed unsteady Christians. As such, members of these groups were excluded from the civil franchise—and symbolically subordinated in the rituals of Christian fellowship.

As members of Old Light congregations assembled for public worship each Sabbath, filing into their various meetinghouses and taking their seats, their arrangement in space represented their places in the body politic. In most Congregational meetinghouses, men and women sat on opposite sides of the aisle, those distinguished by age, status, and wealth up front, those of middling and humble status toward the back, children and servants on the stairs or high in the galleries. Segregating blacks and Indians merely required adding on another, even more humble division of space. By midcentury, the practice of seating Indians and blacks in separate pews and galleries was pervasive. When Juno Larcom, a slave, and her family first went to meetings in Beverly, Massachusetts, they sat with the congregation, though probably in the back, as servants; in 1738 the church had voted down a proposal to establish separate seats for blacks. When a new meetinghouse was built in 1769, however, the church fell into line with the custom across the region as seats for blacks were built in a separate section over the stairs. St. Paul's Church in South Kingstown was typical of New England's Anglican churches: families sat together in private pews, those who paid the most up front, those who paid the least down back. Blacks and Indians, outside this familial order, sat upstairs in a separate gallery. Even churches built by missionary organizations for the benefit of Indians were rigidly segregated. One town even boarded over the Negro pew so its occupants would be invisible to the other members of the congregation.[12]

Wherever they sat, those assembled for public worship in Old Light meetings heard ministers exhort them to respect authority and embrace their appointed roles. Parents and children had reciprocal duties and obligations, as did husbands and wives, masters and servants, rulers and the ruled. Servitude was a pervasive metaphor for social relations of all sorts, even the relationship between an individual and God. The Anglican minister in South Kingstown, James MacSparran, a slave owner himself, took to heart the notion that good servitude was being "more humble, useful and cheerful." Once, upset by a social slight, he prayed, "My dear Redeemer enable me to live like thy best Servants and what I want in this world, will be made up in the Rewards of the next." He also conspicuously directed this message to his slaves. Likewise, a Congregational minister in Newport told the slaves in his congregation to be grateful that they had been rescued from their "Native Superstition" and brought to a "Land of Light." If they would repent and convert, they could be saved just like any free Englishman. But such spiritual equality, the minister warned, did not free one from the duties of one's station, specifically obedience to masters. When the sermon was later published, this point was italicized for emphasis: "*He that is called in the Lord, being a Servant, is the Lord's freeman.*"[13]

Yet the closer Christian fellowship came to transcending social differences, the more Old Light churches had to distort their practices to maintain racial hierarchies. The Congregational churches faced special problems with baptism and communion. Congregationalists made a sharp distinction between members of the "church"—who had given public conversion narratives and were formally recognized as converted and therefore accepted into communion—and the "society," those who merely attended worship. Congregational ministers restricted baptism to only those children whose parents either were full members of the church or had signed a "halfway" covenant promising to raise their children under the inspection of the church. Here, slavery presented a problem. Should enslaved children be baptized according to the religious status of their parents or according to the religious status of their masters? Ezra Stiles, for one, sought an answer to this troubling questing by examining the practices of other ministers and searching for biblical precedents and theological guidance. Eventually, he followed the practice of having the slave's master stand in as surrogate parent, as head of household, regardless of the status of the enslaved child's parents. Less easily resolved were the implications of communion. Those admitted to communion constituted the "church" and conducted most of the business of admitting members, calling ministers, and administering discipline. When it came to business, admission to the "church" normally suspended worldly distinctions. Adult women as well as men without sufficient property did not have a civil franchise, but they did have an equal vote in important church business—if they were white. Black and Indian church members, on the other hand, frequently found their voting rights challenged or denied outright.[14] Evidently, Congregationalists preferred to compromise some of their core theological convictions rather than admit blacks and Indians on terms of equality.

Baptism and communion remained key symbols of racial hierarchy even in Anglican churches that did not share the same theological or institutional difficulties. Anglicans considered all children in the kingdom eligible for baptism into the

Church of England, and they did not distinguish between church and society members: in their institutions, power was brokered by committees of vestrymen, ministers, and a centralized church bureaucracy. Nonetheless, in Newport in 1772, several hundred Negroes attended public worship in the various religious societies—but only a handful were baptized, much less admitted to communion. One clergyman recognized the problem: "not one third" of the inhabitants of Rhode Island had been admitted to the church by baptism, and even unbaptized white churchgoers objected to the baptism of others, "more especially the blacks, whom they are disposed to consider as an inferiour or rather despicable race."[15]

Similar resistance to the conversion of Africans was reported by incredulous English ministers arriving in North American communities from Boston to Savannah. When the Reverend Thomas Pollen arrived in Newport in 1755, fresh off the boat from London, he knew that his principal duties were to care for the Anglican flock in Newport and to ward off the incursions and insinuations of Baptists, Quakers, and members of other sects; but he also eagerly looked around for pagans to convert. He was disappointed to find few Indians, but he was excited to find another group of people within the city who were "in the same state of Heathen Ignorance, as the Wild Indians"—namely, enslaved Negroes. Pollen blithely told a group of Negro parishioners, "I am ready to instruct any of them, in the Christian Religion" and "I shall make no scruple of baptizing them." He even obtained funding from the Associates of Dr. Bray, an English missionary organization dedicated to the conversion of Indians and Africans in the American colonies, to support a modest school for Negro children. He also armed himself with British missionary tracts exhorting "All Christian Masters" to recognize, as the title of one such tract put it, the *Indispensable Duty . . . to Bring Up Their Slaves in the Knowledge and Fear of God.* But masters met his efforts—and those of a long series of successors—with steady, if stealthy, opposition. Early on, Pollen sought out several church members. How was it, he asked, that "masters have taken no more care to see their Negroes baptized?" They told him that slaves "grow worse after Baptism." Surprised, Pollen asked several slaves if this was true. No, the slaves said. In fact, they could think of no reason that masters opposed their religious edification "unless The Masters thought that their Servants would by Baptism come too near Themselves."[16]

As the Great Awakening spread new modes of worship and conversion, the question of Christian fellowship between colonists and Indians and Negroes took on new meanings. During the revival he helped spearhead in 1741, the young

Eleazar Wheelock was proud that he could raise the spiritual pitch of a meeting so high that the general "outcry" would force him to break off his sermon, but he was especially pleased by the effect of his preaching on slaves. "I believe 30 cried out; almost all the negroes in town wounded, 3 or 4 converted . . . Col. Leonard's negro in such distress that it took 3 men to hold him." Evangelical leaders such as Jonathan Edwards and George Whitefield celebrated the effect of the Awakening on groups previously unmoved by Christianity. The conversion of blacks and Indians symbolized the power of New Light rebirth over the established order of the past. Evangelical publicists even found ways of defending secular reversals of power, recasting stories about the domestic upheavals wrought by awakened slaves. One evangelical periodical featured the story of a master who overheard his slave imitating Whitefield's preaching—and was so moved that he was immediately converted.[17]

Especially at the height of revivals, evangelicals tended to think of themselves not as reproducing civic hierarchies in their religious practices but rather as standing outside the "world." Overturning secular authority appealed to New Lights as a symbol of the process of conversion itself: grace was manifest not in the long practice of civic morality but in the ardent pitch of emotional conviction that signaled a "rebirth." But this rejection of the "world" could never be complete or stable. The Religious Society of Friends is often heralded as racially egalitarian because of its early witnessing against slavery, but the limits of its dedication to equality was revealed by another, more consistent and unchallenged practice: it kept its congregations homogeneous by excluding all blacks and Indians.[18] New Light Baptists and Congregationalists developed less consistent practices and faced recurrent tensions over racial hierarchy.

New Lights' rituals embodied their antiauthoritarian impulses. They tended to have plain meetinghouses or even meet outdoors; they had itinerant preachers or even lay exhorters. And they emphasized the distinction between baptism and communion much more than even the Congregationalists. For them baptism was appropriate only for those who showed clear signs of saving grace. But if the distinction between church members and non–church members was stronger, New Lights erased the lines between church members. They celebrated a fervent bond with fellow church members, rejecting titles such as "Mr.," "Mrs.," "Widow," and "Dr." and using instead terms that disregarded all social distinctions except gender, "Brother" and "Sister." Moreover, New Lights defied the convention that only ministers should lead public worship by allowing lay leaders to organize prayer groups and providing opportunities for exhorters to speak during public worship. As Old Lights complained, "Young *Persons,* sometimes *Lads,* or rather *Boys:* Nay *Women* and *Girls;* yes *Negroes,* have taken upon themselves to do the Business of Preachers." And it may well have been true that, as the *Boston Gazette* reported in 1765, one black man converted by Whitefield was preaching "to crowded audiences." But a more typical New Light record is the public confession of a black woman named Flora, who was strongly reprimanded for exhorting in her church.[19]

Ironically, the New Lights' radically egalitarian model of spiritual fellowship made it particularly difficult for white adherents to embrace their Negro and Indian brethren. They were particularly ambivalent about how to respond to Negro and Indian preachers. Consider the career of James Simon, a Pequot Indian from Groton, Connecticut. In the 1750s, he was living among the Narragansetts and struggling for control of their New Light church; he also developed an itinerant role. When he visited the Reverend Isaac Backus, they fell into a pattern of preaching before separate, segregated audiences. Brother Simon exhorted at the homes of local Indians, and Backus preached to English settlers. But, over time, Backus encouraged Simon to exhort before audiences including "all Sorts of people"—and even at predominantly white meetings. After a particularly powerful meeting, Backus reflected: "Now tho' some have quarreled against his improvements yet many I believe will bless God for his coming."[20] But the moment of integration was over, and Simon did not return.

New Lights even disagreed with one another about educating and baptizing blacks. While Anglican ministers struggled to establish a Negro school in Newport, an equally controversial venture flourished under the leadership of Sarah Osborne. Since her rebirth during the Great Awakening, Sarah Osborne had led a women's prayer group in the First Congregational Society. During a revival in the early 1760s, she added special meetings for children, for young men and women, for heads of households—and for blacks. Yet she worried about assuming too active a role and worried particularly about the black meeting. Even though Osborne may have harbored antislavery sympathies and even influenced the local newspaper to include pieces questioning the morality of the slave trade, in front of her black charges she toed a very conservative line. "I only read to them talk to them and sing a Psalm or Hymn with them . . . they call it school," she reported, somewhat defensively. "Ministers and Magistrates send their servants and approve." But many others criticized her in more or less subtle ways. Church members, she complained, shunned her for keeping a "Negro house."[21]

New Lights were, in fact, stung by critics associating them with the presumed ignorance, outlandishness, and subservience of Negroes. A particularly dramatic example unfolded when a defiant New Light exhorter tried to bring his message to Hingham, Massachusetts—a staunchly Old Light town that, since the Great Awakening, had officially banned itinerant preaching. When Brother Richard Lee arrived to speak at a private home, he was greeted by a large mob headed by Captain Theophilus Wilder, a prominent member of the established town church. When he refused to stop preaching, the mob hauled him clear out of town. At the town border, an eyewitness recalled, members of the mob knocked the Bible from his hand, and one of them threw soft cow dung in his face. Captain Wilder shook a long club over his head and threatened to whip him if he returned. Symbolically crowning his degradation, they staged a mock debate: "They presented Prince Wilder, a large negro man, and said, there is your disputer, and some said, here he is as black as hell!"[22] Brother Lee had no ready way of dismissing the insult of being paired with a black man. This vigilante action expressed a usually latent conflation of literal and metaphoric membership in the town's body politic and of religious orthodoxy and virtuous citizenship. At a time when citizenship and power were increasingly resting on the claims of white men to steady habits, Negroes, women, and children were all being depicted as unstable, excessively emotional, and inclined to the excesses of New Light enthusiasm.

In the face of such attacks, New England Baptists tended to adopt more conservative policies. By the 1770s, their radical upheavals of gender conventions were challenged by impulses to become more respectable and patriarchal. The growing discomfort of Baptists and other New Lights with racial equality in part reflected the tendency for sects to mature into more respectable institutions. By the time the imperial crisis developed into a war for colonial independence, Baptists were disfranchising or questioning the rights of black members to vote in church matters. And they began seating their meetinghouses in the same ways as Anglicans, with family pews and separate "Negro Boxes." Increasingly, the differences between New Lights and Old Lights narrowed to the question of formal rankings among white men.[23]

As the Reverend Eleazar Wheelock developed his role as the pastor of an evangelical congregation in Lebanon, Connecticut, he also began taking born-again Indian students under his wing. His star student, Samson Occom, was ordained in 1758 and went to work as a pastor and schoolteacher on a Long Island Indian reservation. By the mid-1760s, Wheelock decided to expand his school and dedicate himself to it full-time. In 1765, Occom embarked on a tour of Britain that, as anticipated, raised "bushels of money" for the school—some eleven thousand pounds sterling. Meanwhile, Wheelock persuaded the earl of Dartmouth to grant a tract of land in New Hampshire on which to build the new Indian Charity School. Students from native enclaves in New England came to study with him, and through the network of Sir William Johnson, the imperial superintendent of Indian affairs, others arrived from the far-flung Iroquois nations. Wheelock planned to educate young men to work as missionaries among other Indians, and young women to marry them and demonstrate the virtues of pious housewifery. Yet Wheelock and his school were plagued by contention and scandal. Perhaps no one in eighteenth-century North America worked as hard as Wheelock to educate and edify Indians; certainly, no one left students feeling more betrayed or critics of missionary work more relieved.

Because Wheelock shared a volatile New Light piety with his students and combined the roles of teacher, spiritual authority, and father to youngsters living far from their parents, it was perhaps inevitable that he would be the target of strong emotions. Students wrote Wheelock teary letters of contrition begging for forgiveness, angry letters in alienation, and desperate letters voicing their personal sense of abasing vileness. But recurrent in these letters is a more disturbing sense of betrayal—a suspicion that Wheelock, rather than helping to uplift his charges, was exploiting and degrading them.[24]

Wheelock raised the hackles of his students by frequently indenturing new students to work long stints in local English households. His rationale was that students needed to help pay their way and that they needed to learn the skills of civil life. But indentured labor raised the hackles of young Indians all too familiar with debt and servitude to English settlers. One student left the school complaining that Wheelock kept his students too hard at work; he reported to the Narragansetts that Wheelock was working young Mary Secutor and Sarah Simon as though they were "Slaves." Other students more explicitly rejected the notion that they had to work enough to pay their way. Otherwise, one asked, "what good will the Charity money do the Indians; which was given to them"? While Wheelock dismissed these complainers as lazy and ungrateful, students and parents also rejected his assumption that his charges needed to learn the rudiments of husbandry or housewifery. "I always tho't Your School was free to the Natives; not to learn them how to Farm it, but to advance in Christian Knowledge," wrote one father angry about his son's treatment. "I can as well learn him that myself and have the prophet of his Labour, being myself bro't up with the best of Farmers."[25]

Students also complained that Wheelock denied his students food and clothing he deemed "too good for Indians." Wheelock certainly did enforce sumptuary restrictions. One disgruntled student, Hezekiah Calvin, visited the Narragansett enclave and gave a very negative report about Wheelock's management of the school: for instance, a Scottish missionary organization sent large quantities of rice, flour, coffee, and sugar, as well as fine-quality cloth—all of which Wheelock sold. With the proceeds he clothed the students in cheap cloth and fed them a "mean" diet. And saving money was not Wheelock's only concern. He also confiscated Calvin's "Silver Watch & Shoe-buckles with other things his Father gave him." As Calvin reported, Wheelock refused to give Indians any "more learning than to Read, & Write"—because more than a rudimentary education "would make them Imprudent."[26]

Education was closely tied to notions about social rank. "The People ought to be ignorant," declared a prominent Boston attorney, to the amusement of young John Adams. "And our Free schools are the very bane of society. They make the lowest of the People infinitely conceited."[27] Wheelock explained the broader political context of his policies in an exchange that developed when one student purchased four pairs of shoes at his expense. Wheelock objected, calling the young David Fowler "Proude as the Devil" and implying that all the "Money and Pains" spent on his education were for naught. Fowler stormed out of the school—declaring, "I will ha' no shoes I'll wear Indian shoes"—but soon found himself "weeping in the Road homeward." He reminded Wheelock, "I have been so faithful to you as if I was your Negro." Clearly, his racial honor was at stake: "I can get Payment as well as white man." In response, Wheelock came close to apologizing but pointed out that his actions had had only their best interests at heart and that, politically, his hands were tied: "I was afraid that the Prid of your heart aspird after such Grandeur as was not for the Glory of God. . . . I begrutchd you nothing that was necessary for you.— That you shod affect to cloath yourself and Hannah like Courtiers & when you know that I had already been reproachd thro' the country . . . only for letting you Wear an old velvet Coat . . . I told you that the Eyes of all Europe & America were Upon you & me too."[28]

Wheelock's efforts to control his students failed to win over his critics. Like the gentlemen at the tavern, Wheelock's critics asserted that he did not really love Indians and was acting in bad faith. Part of the problem was that Wheelock's financial management left the school strapped despite the common knowledge that it was well endowed with funds from England. But critics—echoing earlier efforts to discredit George Whitefield—relentlessly accused Wheelock of extorting charitable contributions. Local critics even resorted to mailing around a moldy piece of bread they claimed had been served at the school: they insinuated that he profited personally by stinting his students.[29] Ironically, these critics attacked North America's most prominent missionary school by posing as champions of Indian students.

By the late 1760s, morale at the school was low, and enrollment fell. Samson Occom, who had many personal reasons for feeling betrayed by Wheelock, complained, "If you rightly managed the Indians, your Instruction would have flourished by this Time." "[But] your present Plan is not Calculated, to Benefit the poor Indians, it is in no ways winning to them." Frustrated by recurrent tensions with his Indian students and subject to continual attack, Wheelock opened his door to English students in 1771, a move that confirmed the suspicions of both former students and colonial observers. "I am very jealous," protested Occom, "that instead of your institution becoming Alma Mater to my brethren, she will be too Alba Mater to nourish tawnies."[30]

Occom was right. By 1776, the last Indians departed, driven out of the college by hostile white boys. The metamorphosis of Moor's Indian Charity School into Dartmouth College reinforced a quiet shift away from missionary efforts. During the early 1770s, the Narragansetts' English schoolteacher alienated his few loyal Indian students by admitting white boys, and soon the school was closed altogether. For Indians across New England, such betrayals confirmed a longstanding fear that English settlers pretending to help them were just trying to fleece them. And they were not entirely wrong. In Boston, the commissioners of the Society for the Propagation of the Gospel used Wheelock's renunciation of his Indian mission to justify their decision that it was futile to support further work in the "Indian service." As the trustees of a substantial fund endowed to support missionaries working with "such Pagans or blacks as lye neglected," they surreptitiously transferred the money to Harvard College, where they established a professorship of "Physick."[31] Focusing on Indians as objects of missions, settlers increasingly learned to think of themselves, and their culture, in the abstract, rigid terms of race—as "white." When settlers ignored the role their own racism played in causing Wheelock's school to fail and fantasized about Indian disappearance from New England, they confirmed a pervasive image of Indians as too proud and independent to live among the English. In fact, the school's closing came just as many of the Narragansetts and other New England natives had converted to Christianity, were embracing English styles of land tenure and farming, and had recognized their need for literacy and education that would prepare them for full integration into the colonial social order.

Despite all this, the benevolent message of the young missionary who so earnestly defended Wheelock in 1768 was not forgotten at Dartmouth College. Perhaps Wheelock displayed the letter to his English students; in any case, several years latter, its themes were reworked into a theatrical dialogue by John Smith, a professor at Dartmouth, and performed there sometime during the Revolutionary period. The part of the hostile gentlemen was cast as a generic Englishman, probably played by a student, and the part of the aspiring missionary as an Indian, reportedly played by "a real Aboriginal." The scene is set when an Englishman encounters a downcast Indian on the road, who explains that he is depressed by the negative "opinion the English entertain of us poor Indians!" "Are you not sensible," the gentleman asks, "[that] you are a savage, cruel race?" They go on to debate the relative cruelty of their two races. The Indian points out that the Spaniards had butchered some twenty million natives. After an exchange in which the Indian displays superior knowledge and logic, the frustrated Englishman erupts, "I wish you, and all the rest of Doctor Whee——ks Indians were sent to Guinea, or had your throats cut." His adversary gently upbraids him: "Have you one spark of that *generous benevolence* to mankind, which stamps a *dignity* on the human soul, when you regret, that endeavors should be used to civilize and christianize an unpolished and savage people; yet *capable* of improvement, and of being made *good members* of society?"[32] The chastened Englishman replies, "Perhaps I have been too much prejudiced against the Indians." It would seem that only after the specter of actual Indian conversion had been dismissed at Dartmouth—and from the minds of most settlers in the new war-torn confederacy—was it becoming safe for young white men to advocate Indian conversion publicly.

||| "Surrender All" |||

When the great evangelist George Whitefield died in a provincial Massachusetts seaport, no one mourned him more effectively than a young, enslaved girl in Boston. Whitefield's career had ridden the crest of two great waves of evangelical enthusiasm on both sides of the Atlantic, and he owed much of his success to his ability to reconcile seemingly opposed symbols of equality and hierarchy. His emotional revivals splintered congregations, upset the standing churches in many places, and encouraged the Baptists and other dissenting sects, but he never surrendered his role as a minister in the Church of England. He might preach in the open air in common fields, but he always wore his formal surplice and white wig.[33]

The young poet Phillis Wheatley also attracted attention for her combination of apparently opposed identities: born in the heathen ignorance of Africa, she rapidly became, while enslaved in Boston, the composer of polished Christian verses. Whitefield's death presented an opportunity that she seized with aplomb. Most of her previous poems had been pious elegies for local, bereaved families. Mourning Whitefield, she exalted his evangelical egalitarianism. At the poem's climax, she imagined him exhorting all humankind to accept God's embrace:

> Ye thirsty, come to this life-giving stream,
> Ye preachers, take him for your joyful theme;
> Take him my dear *Americans*, he said,
> Be your complaints on his kind bosom laid:
> Take him ye *Africans*, he longs for you,
> *Impartial Savior* is his title due.

This plea for the equal inclusion of Africans and Americans in Christian salvation provided Wheatley with an excuse to introduce herself and her poetry to a figure at the center of Britain's evangelical movement, Whitefield's own patroness, the countess of Huntington. The countess welcomed the poetic offering, brought Wheatley to London, and helped arrange the publication of a volume of her poetry. Yet Wheatley's integration into a transatlantic community of Christians did not entirely bridge the separation she always felt between "Americans" and "Africans." Instead, her growing celebrity as a prodigious convert to Christianity fostered a sense that she would always stand apart from Anglo-Americans, that she shared a common racial destiny with other children of Africa.[34]

Less prominent enslaved Africans also did their best to hold English settlers to the promise of Christian fellowship. English settlers in North America segregated their meetinghouses, emphasized pro-slavery messages, discouraged baptism, and forestalled the racial implications of church membership. Nonetheless, many black slaves and Indian servants turned to Christianity for spiritual salvation and public recognition. The attraction of Christianity is partly explained by their unique immigrant experience, which gave them powerful incentives to assimilate to English ways and negotiate their social identities within the hierarchies and constraints of Christian institutions. Enslaved New Englanders, unlike local Indians who lived in ancestral enclaves, lived far from the grounds of any common past that could offer a coherent system of meanings and rituals; and unlike slaves in the plantation regions of the South and the Caribbean, they were few enough in number and too dispersed among settler households to have much room or incentive to constitute new, Creole cultures. Celebrated converts such as Phillis Wheatley and Samson Occom emerged as public figures only in the northern colonies and in Britain, where English culture dominated. Despite the preoccupation of many observers then and now with the "problem" of African origins, this concern was largely focused in the public print culture on a relatively small number of celebrated individuals.

For many enslaved Africans, the choice was not so much whether to become Christian as which style of Christianity to favor. Many slaves and servants chose the type of worship of God through relationships with the people they lived with and worked alongside: masters, fellow servants, and family members. Many slaves likely attended public worship with their masters' families, some of them no doubt at their masters' behest, others voluntarily. Some went on to embrace their masters' religious styles. One pious Connecticut slave left a will that carefully distributed his religious books among his master's daughters. For these individuals, Christian community followed the lines of their patriarchal households and meshed with a "tribal" notion of Christian fellowship rooted in kinship and community.[35]

Other slaves chose styles of Christianity that conflicted with their masters' predilections, establishing more independent religious identities. One Connecticut woman joined an evangelical church even though her master belonged to the Old Light church. For many slaves, joining a church did not express an affinity with masters so much as strong ties with fellow servants. In Newport, Zingo Stevens "laboured greatly"—and successfully—to bring his Guinea-born wife Phillis into a "saving Acquaintance with her Redeemer." Existing networks of black Christians smoothed the way for later arrivals and contributed to the trend toward heavily concentrated clusters of admissions to churches. The first identifiable black members of the Providence First Baptist Church, sixteen total, all joined the church within a few months in the winter of 1774–75. At least three of them, Mary, Phillis, and Providence Brown, had lived in the household of Moses Brown, who had likely introduced them to the Baptist church a few years earlier when he had been a member.[36] The choices of these early black church members reflected their identities as Christians and African and Americans, their most private spiritual values, their relations to their masters, and their sense of themselves as members of the public order. And their choices reflected their sense of the distinct possibilities and limits of Christian fellowship in New Light and Old Light churches.

Despite contemporary stereotypes associating blacks with the egalitarianism and enthusiasm of evangelical religion, blacks were also attracted in large numbers to even the most hierarchical and staid Anglican, Congregational, and Presbyterian congregations. Around 1770, black men and women constituted as much as a third of all churchgoers in Newport—not only in Sarah Osborne's evangelical Second Congregational Society but also in the Anglican Trinity Church and in Ezra Stiles's conservative First Congregational Society.[37] At the same time, only about seven had been admitted to communion in any of these institutions. Clearly, Newport's blacks were seeking in Christianity something other than signs of social parity. To some extent, they responded to the spiritual outreach of individual ministers, such as Osborne or Stiles, who also organized a series of Negro meetings at his home and regularly attracted eighty or ninety people. His accounts of these meetings sometimes seem condescending—"Many of them came up to me and thanked me, as they said, for taking so much Care of their souls, and hoped they should remember my Counsels"—but at other times they attest to sincere spiritual fellowship—"We seemed to have the delightful presence of Jesus."[38]

The rigid physical segregation of black members of the congregation during public worship and in private prayer meetings may also have helped reinforce a sense of community, provided a measure of autonomy, and helped reconcile West African values with colonial conditions. It could help develop social networks among local servants, slaves, and free blacks. Chloe Spear recalled that the separate black seats in her church in Boston were so remote that she and her friends could not understand the preaching; instead they passed their time there playing games. The racially channeled practices of church leaders fostered the expansion of community networks and even the development of subsidiary leadership roles. Ezra Stiles, for instance, called pious blacks to witness the experiences of other blacks in the midst of spiritual crises and later started his own regular "Negro" prayer meetings. At the same time, the standing churches, with their strong claims to representing the secular society, may have been particularly useful venues for slaves seeking public recognition as members of the colonial body politic. Even though the public rituals of these churches consistently subordinated black people, there were also moments when they became the focus of public, positive attention. In the Anglican church in Newport during the 1760s, the Negro schoolchildren normally sat separately, but once a year during Lent they were publicly catechized and displayed their piety and education to the entire congregation.[39] In addition, although many aspects of New Light religion may have resonated with West

African cultures and styles, elements of Old Light emphasis on ranking, hierarchy, and ritual also resonated with behaviors and beliefs that enslaved Africans may have brought with them to America.

One of the many enslaved New Englanders who chose to embrace evangelical Christianity was Susanna Low. In the summer of 1764, she stood before the Chebacco parish in a small Massachusetts seaport town and publicly related the story of her "saving change." Her narrative of conversion focused on the problem of complacency: she had always taken Christian redemption either too lightly or for granted. "I saw when I was a Child that there was a heaven and a Hell," she confessed, "and . . . went about to build a righteousness of my own." But her focus on righteousness waned somewhat until 1755. Then, an earthquake devastated Lisbon and sent waves of news that shocked people on both sides of the Atlantic. "I was shaken much and set about making myself better"—for a while, but again she lapsed into a false confidence in the "sandy foundation" of her own righteousness. Only ten years later, during a revival that ranged up and down the New England seaboard, was she suddenly visited by God. She recognized that she was "the chief of Sinners" in a moment of transformation. "I was cast off wholly from myself" and "surrendered all unto God." She took consolation in his revealed Word, particularly touched by passages that emphasized the Lord's special mercy for those who are "weary and heavy-laden." Humbly, in 1764, she asked the church to pray for her and to recognize the stamp of the gospel on her spiritual rebirth. In addition to Low, four other black men and women were accepted into the church that summer.[40] Their public testimonials illuminate their religious convictions and testify to the attractions—and limits—of spiritual fellowship in evangelical churches.

Enslaved New Lights used their spiritual experiences to claim Christianity as their cultural birthright and to understand their lives as slaves. Sometimes they enjoyed the most egalitarian aspects of New Light religion—suspension of normal lines of racial, class, and gender hierarchy in ritual practice; opportunities for leadership and authority; and a legitimate mode of attacking their masters and the system of slavery. But at other times, they found spiritual consolation in the most authoritarian aspects of evangelical faith—their relationship to an often angry Lord from whom they could never expect mercy and whom they could only hope to appease through absolute surrender.

In their testimonials of spiritual rebirth, neither Susanna Low nor her peers mentioned Africa, paganism, or slavery; rather, these enslaved New Englanders emphasized that Christianity had always been part of their lives. "Being favoured

with a religious Education I began the practice of religion when I was young," related one convert who described New England as "a Land of Light." Their spiritual
narratives demonstrate just how thoroughly integrated enslaved New Englanders
were into the culture of colonial evangelicalism. Like those of their English neighbors, their accounts of conversion commonly emphasize fear of damnation, a period of anguishing uncertainty, the special role of the preacher in helping them feel
God's saving grace, and a powerful sense of transformation. For instance, Susanna
Low saw the Lisbon earthquake of 1755 as a transforming event—as did many
Anglo-Americans. Indeed, a long tradition of New England spiritual narratives
began by noting early education in morality and then emphasized sudden, fearful
events such as accidental deaths, natural disasters, and other "acts of God" that
jolted sinners out of their complacency by confronting them with the imminence
of damnation. More specific to New Light narratives was the intense, anguished
vacillation described by Low. In these, like other New Light narratives, the moment of conversion was often mediated by others, prompted by a preacher, or
inspired by passages in the Bible. Another black member of the Chebacco congregation, Mary Rust, finally converted in 1764 after pastor John Cleaveland
exhorted on the text "How shall we escape if we neglect so great a salvation?" And,
in true New Light style, these individuals described conversion as a radical, public break with their past lives. Like Susanna Low, Mary Rust publicly renounced
her old self of sin and embraced her "Saving Change" of heart.[41]

Some enslaved New Englanders used evangelical religion to challenge their oppression, though most often they did so privately. For instance, some simply relished portions of Scripture that questioned slavery or expressed the outrage they
felt. Chloe Spear later wrote that her favorite Scripture passage during her enslaved
life in Boston was Psalms 71:4, "Deliver me, oh my God, out of the hand of the
wicked, out of the hand of the unrighteous and cruel man." More publicly, when
word got around that a visiting Quaker was going to speak to the Negroes in Newport, in 1770, a huge crowd gathered—presumably because of the Friends' struggle to witness against slavery.[42]

One of the very few slaves who spoke out publicly against slavery in an evangelical church was a member of the evangelical Church of Christ in Canterbury,
Connecticut. After his baptism into the church in 1752, Greenwich devoted considerable effort to reading the Bible and questioning common justifications for
racism and slavery. "As I have ben Instructed by the Lord," he began an address to
his brethren in 1754. The Old Testament, he argued, permits enslaving people only

under specific conditions—conditions that the contemporary European pillaging of Africa did not meet. Those who argued that blacks were biblically cursed were unable even to develop a consistent interpretation, he observed: "Some say that we are the seed of Canaan and some say that we are the Tribe of Ham." Nor did biblical accounts of the enslavement of the native Canaanites by the children of Israel provide any appropriate analogy to contemporary slave trading in Africa. The emotional core of this passage is an exhortation to his mostly white audience: "Now bretherin suppose any nation shold have a continual war amongst themselves and any of you should supply them of ammonition and when you have don this you will steel as many of them and bring them over into your Contry to make slaves of them their soul and body." Others likely shared Greenwich's sense of outrage and his emphasis on the Bible as a source of legitimate authority, but few were so vocal. At the height of revolutionary fervor in 1776, Lemuel Haynes, a free man of color, wrote an essay called "Liberty Further Extended." Yet he left it unpublished.[43]

Indeed, many slaves used evangelical religion not so much to challenge their enslavement as to reconcile themselves to a conservative Christian ethos. Briton Hammon, a New Jersey slave who published a number of tracts after the Revolution, may have been more unusual by that time, but these earlier narratives also frequently emphasized the theme of acquiescence to slavery. Slaves such as Phillis Wheatley, who focused on solace and comfort rather than outrage and resistance, came very close to the old Puritan message of deference, humility, and faithful servitude. They tended to seek to conquer the pride and vanity that led them to resist current "afflictions" in the hope that they would be rewarded in the afterlife with far greater benefits than mere temporal comfort and secular freedom. This strain of piety is prominent in the Chebacco narratives. Although none of these make any explicit reference to their authors' slave status, the emotional centers of many of these narratives were passages that resonated with the experience of slavery. "Come unto me, all ye that labour and are heavey laden, and I will give you rest" was cited by Susanna Low and several of her enslaved peers. For Phillis Cogswell the passage took on special meaning one day when she was hard at work. "I tho't with myself, I am weary and heavy-laden, I have a burden of guilt lying on me, Christ is all-sufficient to give rest. . . . I will come to Christ for Rest." Another passage cited by two of these converts and by another slave elsewhere was Isaiah 55:1: "Ho, every one that thirsteth, come ye to the waters, and he that hath no money; come ye, buy and eat; yea, come, buy wine and milk without money and without price." This passage gives comfort to the poor, the humble, and those with low self-esteem, one of the consequences of being enslaved for many people. In this respect the tone of the correspondence between Phillis Wheatley and Obour Tanner, a slave in Newport, was quite typical. Resignation and suffering are some of their main themes: "Your reflections on the sufferings of the Son of God, & the inestimable price of our immortal souls, plainly demonstrate the sensations of a soul united in Jesus. What you observe of Esau is true of all mankind, who, (left to themselves) would sell their heavenly birth rights for a few moments of sensual pleasure, whose wages at last (dreadful wages!) is eternal condemnation. Dear Obour, let us not sell our birthright for a thousand worlds, which indeed would be as dust upon the balance." The letter closes with a prayer to be endowed with cheerfulness and filled with gratitude. Wheatley and Tanner took comfort from the Calvinist message of the utter unworthiness of humankind for salvation and their dependence on God's mercy.[44]

This emphasis on domination, fear, and the comfort of submission is every bit as much a part of evangelical experiences of conversion as their more widely noted emphasis on equality, self-assertion, and defiance. Many slaves interpreted their relations to God in ways that echo the conservative language of faithful servitude: respecting God was like respecting masters, father, elders, betters; submitting to divine will was like submitting to the hierarchies of the social order. Susanna Low spoke of the crucial moment at which she "surrendered all unto God to his divine dispose." Mary Rust spoke of herself as held by the "Bonds of Iniquity" until the moment of her salvation: "I was now made entirely to surrender all to God. I had done it divers Times before, but now I gave up all with my whole heart, my Body Soul and all to God."[45]

Unlike most slaves and Indians who practiced Christianity in relative obscurity, Phillis Wheatley quickly became an international celebrity. From the start, her poetry was always at one level a political symbol because it represented her mastery of Christian spirituality and polite letters—her integration into the highest levels of provincial British culture. Such evidence of black capacity for refinement posed a threat to defenders of the racial status quo. Ironically, black and Indian Christians who became celebrities were constantly reminded of—and prompted to promote—their racial roots and their cultural origins. Celebrated converts such as Phillis Wheatley and Samson Occom discovered that the more completely they mastered English culture, the more successfully they displayed their refined sensibilities, and the more public recognition they won, the more they found themselves defined racially, as prodigies, examples, or exceptions. Wheatley would always be noted as the African poet, Occom as the Indian minister. This racial narrative of conversion was not so much false or forced as it was the key to their celebrity.

It was no accident that one of the first letters the young Phillis Wheatley wrote was to the Reverend Samson Occom in the 1760s, while he was touring Britain: his celebrity also hinged on his origins as a benighted heathen. Since his ordination as a Congregational minister in 1758, Occom had become a public symbol of the potential and danger of colonial conversion. As an Indian minister, Occom knew that he had a reputation to protect and project: he embodied the power of conversion to redeem, transform, and civilize. At the height of his fame, Occom was repeatedly attacked—forced to defend not only the completeness of his conversion and his mastery of polite culture but also his authenticity as a heathen-born Indian. During his British fund-raising tour in the mid-1760s, he was attacked by a pamphlet writer who asserted that Occom's origins were not as benighted as he led the public to believe. In fact, the writer claimed, Occom had been born into a Christian community. Occom took the charge seriously enough to respond with the publication of an autobiographical narrative: "I was born a heathen, illiterate, in a swampy patch of land not stolen from my conquered ancestors." He emphasized his indifference to the overtures of an Old Light minister who tried to teach the local Indian children to read and his dramatic spiritual rebirth at the time of the Great Awakening. Meanwhile, Occom was disparaged by others—including Wheelock, who came to fear his power—who claimed that he was prone to characteristically Indian bouts of drunkenness. For Occom, his origins, a conflation of race and culture, were central to his public image (fig. 9). Of course, this view was also beneficial, because he knew that many would favor him as a manifestation of racial transformation. That, after all, is what gave him the ability to raise money so successfully in England.[46]

Wheatley's own poetry frequently played on her self-image as a formerly benighted African. She began a poem to Harvard students with an autobiographical contrast: "'Twas not long since I left my native shore / The land of errors, and *Egyptian* gloom." Wheatley consistently bore witness to the basic tenet of colonial missionary propaganda: Africans were so culturally deprived that even the ordeal of enslavement became worthwhile when attached to the benefits of cultural enlightenment and spiritual salvation. Wheatley's story of herself as a converted pagan is sometimes taken to suggest that she loathed her African self. Indeed, the question is valid: Why would she accept this image and perpetuate this narrative of her life? She was hardly obtuse; her poems are infused with critiques of Eng-

FIGURE 9. "The Reverend Mr. SAMSON OCCOM, The first Indian Minister that ever was in Europe"—so begins the caption
on this 1768 copy of a portrait painted during Occom's tour of
England to raise money for Wheelock's Indian school. The
clerical garb and the Bible represent his piety and civility; the
bow and arrow in the background emphasize his Indian roots.
Engraving by J. Spilsbury after a now lost oil painting by
Mason Chamberlain. Courtesy of Dartmouth College Library.

lish racism and wry assessments of colonial protests against imperial slavery: "How
well the Cry for Liberty, and the reverse Disposition for the Exercise of oppressive
Power over others agree,—I humbly think it does not require the Penetration of a
Philosopher to determine." Apparently, Wheatley's vision of Africa was neither an
ironic exaggeration nor just a public pose. In a private letter, she encouraged her
friend Obour Tanner: "Let us rejoice in and adore the wonders of God's infinite

Love" in bringing them from Africa to America. "Here the knowledge of the true God and eternal life are made manifest; But there, profound ignorance overshadows the Land."[47]

In fact, Wheatley's narrative of African origins, far from a handicap, was her star quality. When they were published, her poems were prefaced by testimonials of authenticity, one by her master and one by a set of gentlemen that included the governor of the colony. This was not so much to dispel doubt that she had written them. If her supporters had wanted to avoid such doubts, they could more easily have omitted the engraved portrait they had commissioned for the book's frontispiece or the repeated references to her African origins. But then who would have paid attention to the book? Rather, they were promoting Wheatley as a spectacle of cultural virtuosity: these poems, they declared, were written by "a young Negro Girl, who was but a few Years since, brought an uncultivated Barbarian from *Africa*, and has ever since been, and now is, under the Disadvantage of serving as a Slave."[48] Without such a story she would have been another obscure and probably unpublished poet. Without her poetry she would have been another pious slave sitting up in an obscure Negro box. But the combination of her story and her skill made her, for a time, an international sensation. Her proponents were selling not just her poetry but also a story of cultural metamorphosis.

Refined and modest as Wheatley may have been, she was also determined to hold colonists to the cultural bargain of conversion. "'Twas Mercy brought me from my pagan land," she wrote in one poem, echoing the dominant imperialist narrative of enslavement in America as a spiritual benefit to African pagans. But in the next line, she turned the tables: "Remember, Christians, Negroes black as Cain may be refined and join the angelic train."[49]

||| Preaching to the Converted |||

One day in the summer of 1768, the Reverend Joseph Fish pushed his horse deep into the Narragansett enclave, up and down steep slopes, crashing through the thick hedges that surrounded fields, making token efforts to repair the damage. For several years, Fish had been visiting the Narragansett enclave regularly to deliver Sabbath lectures to supplement worship at the Indian church and to supervise a mission-sponsored school. At first, he had carefully avoided describing himself as a missionary—the Indians had converted to Christianity decades earlier and were jealous of the independence—but that was how he saw his role. Over the years,

Fish's belief that the Narragansett church was full of dangerous errors had become more apparent, and members of the Indian church began drifting away from his lectures. On this occasion, he presented himself at the wigwam of Tobias Coheis. At age eighty-six Coheis was the oldest man in the tribe and, although not a regular churchgoer anymore, was reputed to be a pious Christian. He had lost his sight in old age, but he retained a visionary faith. In response to Fish's curiosity about his beliefs, Coheis talked freely of death and heaven. He told how he "longed to go Home to his Father's house." On another visit, several years later, the blind old man related a vision that stunned the white-wigged parson: "Sometime ago, been home, (meaning, to Heaven). Had seen the *Great God*, and that he was a Great Gentleman. Had seen Jesus Christ, A handsome Man. Seen also a Multitude of Folks in Heaven. Resembling Butterflies of Many Colours, etc." Fish was appalled. Ever since the Awakening had threatened to split his own parish in Stonington, Connecticut, Fish had been a prominent antagonist of New Light religion. Although Coheis's vision would seem to have had strong spiritual ties to the ancient cosmology envisioning an afterlife in "Cautantowwit's House," Fish was preoccupied by its resonance with evangelical practices. The New Light inclination to venerate such visions and inward impressions, he thought, too easily deluded ignorant people from the plain Bible truths revealed on the printed page. "Strange, Gross, Horrible Ideas!"[50]

Recently, the Old Light parson had taken it upon himself to "correct" various other aspects of the Narragansetts' New Light style and had provoked increasingly grave conflicts with the illiterate pastor of the Indian church and his followers. Soon, the Indian pastor and the white-wigged parson were openly accusing each other of doing the Devil's work.

For most Indians in eighteenth-century New England, conversion to Christianity had been a self-conscious choice: an acknowledgment that their old system of beliefs had lost its power in the face of a superior God. For generations, the Narragansetts and other Indians across New England had tolerated Christian settlers seeking them out, investigating their rituals and beliefs, and pointing out their religious errors. The Narragansetts had responded to ambassadors of English religion aware that they lived on the grounds of an ancient ancestral past. Despite the disruptions of conquest and forced servitude, the natives of New England struggled to retain their autonomy; they remained jealous of their cultural coherence—and aware of its importance as a symbol of resistance to English domination. Yet their old religious system was falling on hard times.[51]

As he traveled through the landscape, Ezra Stiles kept an eye out for "stone gods" or carved idols, which he found abandoned at springs or incorporated into settlers' stone walls. He made detailed observations, sometimes took sketches, and sometimes hauled entire objects off to the Yale College museum. He was also curious about other customs that Indians continued to honor. The roadways of southeastern New England were punctuated with spots, typically marked by large stones, that native peoples, although Christian, continued to venerate by placing more stones or twigs on them whenever they passed. When settlers did not hesitate to express their contempt for such superstitious behavior, the Indians learned to avoid conflict. Stiles observed, "The Inds. continue the Custom to this day, tho' they are a little ashamed the English should see them, & accordingly when walking with an Eng. they have made a path round at a quarter Mile's Distance to avoid it." In general, he concluded, "The New England Indians, upon the accession of the English were so soon ashamed of their old religion, or rather findg it ridiculed by us & considered it idolatrous, that they concealed much from us."[52]

Even when Indians expressed openness to Christianity and invited English preachers and schoolteachers, the resulting encounters left both parties feeling angry, humiliated, and betrayed. Sachem Ninigret rebuffed the overtures of missionaries early in the century, but around 1728 his son Charles granted a substantial tract of land to the Church of England and asked King George III to send to his people a minister who would learn their language. He explained that his conquered and impoverished people were convinced that their native gods were no longer serving them and were curious to understand Christianity. In response, the Anglicans erected a church, which was hardly under construction before the competing Congregational missionary society built a meetinghouse of its own across the road. But the local Anglican cleric, James MacSparran, made only sporadic visits from his home in South Kingstown, and the Congregational minister, Joseph Park, was ineffective. Within a few years, a demoralized Park was describing himself as spiritually "dry." Soon thereafter, the sachem's English attorney took possession of the neglected Anglican church, tore it town, and built himself a tavern.[53] English religious authorities competed with one another, lacked spiritual power, and shamelessly seized every chance they had—not to help the Indians but to fleece them. What the Narragansetts learned from this series of encounters was that English Christians seemed to have little to offer other than bad faith.

This dynamic of rapprochement, betrayal, and alienation changed very little even after most Narragansetts had become Christian. The Narragansetts converted suddenly at the height of the Awakening in the early 1740s. The conversion of the Narragansetts—and the demoralized missionary Joseph Park, as well—was spurred by the visit of the extravagant evangelist James Davenport to nearby Stonington, Connecticut, in February 1743. "I had heard many strange Things of him, and strange Effects of his preaching," Park later reported. And so had the Stonington Pequots, who invited their Narragansett friends to see what all the excitement was about. They were not disappointed. Davenport's preaching converted some hundred people in Stonington, including many local Negroes, and it deeply affected a large number of the local Pequot Indians and visiting Narragansetts. Park himself was reborn—he described himself as previously no more qualified to preach than the Devil, but now the spirit flowed freely through him. Back in Narragansett country, he held an emotional prayer meeting with the affected Indians: "The LORD gave me to plead with him that his Kingdom might be seen coming with Power among the *Indians.* . . . A SPIRIT of *Prayer* and Supplication was poured out upon *them;* and a SPIRIT of *Conviction* upon the *Enemies* of God." Playing on a common theme, he reported that his attempt to preach on the text "Behold, now is the accepted time; behold, now is the day of salvation" was interrupted by an "*Outcry.*" Virtually overnight, about half of the tribe became Christian. About a hundred Indians began to attend public worship at his meeting, he began to employ an Indian woman to "keep *School* in a *Wigwam*," and within a year some sixty-five were members of his church.[54]

The same dramatic pattern was repeated up and down the coast in enclaves that had hitherto resisted Christianity. As one settler near the Mohegan enclave recalled, during the "great reformation of 1741, Indians brot in & gave up to the English a number of stone & wooden Idols & . . . worshipped none since."[55] These conversions were, in fact, renunciations of old systems of worship and adoptions of entirely new ones. Indeed, the notion of dramatic "spiritual rebirth" was as central to the appeal of awakened Christianity for the Narragansetts as it was for other people on both sides of the Atlantic. They hoped it would be a radical and influential replacement for impotent religious traditions.

For Park, the Narragansetts' conversion promised to end the colonial cultural battle. He saw the Narragansetts adopting along with Christianity the whole system of English civility: "There is among them a change for the good respecting the *outward* as well as the *inward* man. They grow more decent and cleanly in their outward dress, provide better for their households, and get clearer of debt." Resonance with their familiar customs and current social position clearly smoothed acceptance of this change in religious affiliation for the Narragansetts. The New Light emphasis on oral communication and powerful emotional experience appealed to the Narragansetts, many of whom did not speak, much less read, English. New Light religion also had parallels with the Narragansetts' religious traditions. Awakened Christians grounded religious authority in direct revelation to individuals through visions, trances, dreams, and other intense personal experiences, an authority that echoed the Narragansetts' shamanistic tradition. Just as local pagan rites across Europe had gradually become incorporated into Christian holidays, so the Narragansetts adapted their familiar customs to their new religion. Their most important annual ritual, the ancient Green Corn festivals, for instance, had striking similarities to the large intertribal prayer meetings that soon developed at the same time of year, the end of August, and featured the similar activities of feasting, dancing, praying and singing.[56]

Yet Park's initial optimism was premature: soon Christian Narragansetts would find themselves at the center of new struggles over religious style, power, and respect. Much of the appeal of New Light Christianity for the Narragansetts stemmed from its place at the center of conflict among English settlers over religious style and civil authority. Bridging commonly accepted racial divisions, Park's church united in fellowship ordinary English, Narragansetts, and Africans—all of whom faced common struggles against poverty, landlessness, and political disfranchisement in a gentry-dominated political order. The antiauthoritarianism of the New Light sensibility had special appeal to Narragansetts, who had experienced so much exploitation by powerful settlers and government officials. Within years, Park's church would face repeated conflicts over leadership and two schisms, leading to the establishment of a separate Indian church. New Light sects were often plagued by divisions over style, theology, and leadership. These difficulties took on racial meanings for the Narragansetts because of their often bitter interactions with English Christians and their experience of settlers' bad faith. Ironically, even when native New Englanders converted to Christianity and became more integrated into provincial culture, they became increasingly alienated from local settlers and conscious of their identity as Indians.

The promise of New Light religion for the Narragansetts came closest to fulfillment in the career of Samuel Niles, who in 1743 was a middle-aged ritual leader, or powwow—a member of one of the groups most threatened by Christianity. In 1728, he conducted the marriage of Charles Ninigret to Tobias Coheis's daughter Betty; he was in charge of funerals for the sachem's family; and in 1741, at the beginning of the dynastic disputes over the sachemdom, his influence was strong enough that old Queen Toccommah rewarded his loyalty to George Ninigret with a special grant of land. In other cases, confrontations often occurred between ministers or settlers and powwows because the acceptance of English religious authority threatened to displace the powwows' authority and their roles. But Niles evidently decided to play his card differently. He was one of the early members of the tribe to "improve" his farms in the style of English husbandry and built a neat English-style wood-frame house for his family.[57] And in 1743, he was one of the first Narragansett converts to New Light Christianity and was admitted to Park's church.

But Niles's conversion led to trouble as he tried to translate his role as a spiritual leader within the tribe into a leading role within Park's church. Like many New Light churches, it was riven with division and acrimony, but in this case the main division fell along racial lines. In these early years, members of Park's church often fought over leadership and practices. For example, they reprimanded a settler, Deacon Stephen Babcock, for his "overbearing and censorious" manner. Around the same time, they also formally reprimanded Niles for "exhorting in the Congregation." Although not stated explicitly, Narragansett church members clearly interpreted the reprimand in racial terms. In response, Niles withdrew from the church, and about a hundred other Narragansetts did, too: they agreed to "walk together" as a church. Park, who continued to collect a stipend for work as an Indian missionary years after his flock had deserted him, did little to make them regret the decision.[58]

Samuel Niles and the other Indians were jealous of their independence. They built their own meetinghouse in the enclave—a twenty-five-foot square wood-frame structure for which they likely milled the wood themselves. When the censured Babcock tried to assert control over their church—after a vision in which he was called to "preach the Gospel . . . to strange Nations"—they rejected his claim to authority. They wanted not only an Indian pastor but also the ability to make their own choice. In the 1750s, when Babcock and other settlers such as Isaac Backus favored the naming of the Pequot Indian James Simon as their elder, most of the tribe sided with Samuel Niles. The bitterness of the ensuing struggle over the true forms of worship, church discipline, and the choices of a pastor was plain in a letter they wrote to a nearby Separate Baptist church. "Dear Brethren, We are Wading through many Tribulations Toward the Blissfull Shores of Eternal Day where we Shant Stand in Need of Council to Inlighten and Direct us." But in the meantime they viewed their struggle in millennial terms: "Help, help, help, we Cry

Gird on your Sword, Mount the White hourse, and Come forth to the help of the Lord against the Mighty." Despite these appeals for guidance from English-dominated churches, the Christian Indians resolved the conflict in their own way. Niles retained control of the meetinghouse, and his rival Simon, after holding worship for a handful of followers in a private home, eventually moved away.[59]

Even then, the struggle was not over, for English New Lights refused to recognize Niles's legitimacy. Several years later, Niles himself told the story to the erudite Newport minister Ezra Stiles. After winning the battle with James Simon, the Indian church members were ready to ordain Niles as their minister, but local English New Lights refused to participate in the ceremony. Eventually, the Indians decided simply to hold the ceremony themselves. The event, presided over by William Coheis, was powerfully emotional: "Such a Spirit was outpoured and fell upon them," Niles related, "that many others of the Congregation prayed aloud and lift up their hearts with prayers and Tears to God." For Niles it was a good sign that this emotional outpouring went on for the better part of an hour. But he was aware that "the white people present taking this for *Confusion* were disgusted and went away." English settlers had little tolerance for Indian Christianity, and Niles saw this hostility as an argument for separatism: it allowed the Narragansetts to seize their independence.

During their meeting, Niles struck Stiles as pious man doing good work among the Indians, which belied the worst fears of his critics. He no doubt encouraged a kind of emotional abandon that even many evangelicals found excessive and likely embarrassing. And he was illiterate. But, Stiles observed, he also seemed to know the entire Bible by heart—and accurately. Another of Niles's problems may have been his sense of honor. Ezra Stiles noted the Narragansett pastor's low tolerance for condescension when he took the illiterate Indian into his book-lined study and called his attention to a globe, explaining that the world was not, in fact, flat. Taken aback, Niles retorted that he had always known that the earth was round like a ball.[60]

Separate Indian churches also sprang up in enclaves across southern New England and Long Island, in response to the same factors that shaped the founding of the Narragansett Indian church. Repeatedly Indians were attracted to the style of Awakened religion, but they refused to submit to the arrogant leadership of English settlers. Around 1760, Fish reported that the Narragansetts were "mortally afraid of the *Standing* Minister," presumably Park: "I don't learn They Are Visited and Instructed by Any english Ministers; Unless it be now and then *One* of the Separate Stamp. I have not heard of any One of our regular Standing Ministers, being among them for Many Years." Fish knew from experience just how wary the Pequots had become of English figures of authority: they sought funding for a school from a Boston missionary organization, but they insisted that their teacher be an Indian and a woman, since their prospective students were mainly girls. Fish was dismayed, but he consoled himself that an Indian woman would at least cost much less than an Englishman. Although wary of English settlers encroaching on their autonomy, these congregations did include some whites and blacks. And they developed active and wide-ranging relationships with one another. The Narragansetts on occasion traveled twenty miles to worship with the Stonington Pequots, and their elder, Samuel Niles, also went to administer communion to Separate Indian congregations in Groton and Mohegan, Connecticut. As early as 1760, the Narragansett church was visited by Pequots from Stonington and Groton, Mohegans, Western Niantics, and Montauks from Long Island. In the years to come, these networks expanded further, fostered by the travels of preachers and exhorters. The Reverend Samson Occom, for instance, traveled up and down the New England seaboard, preaching sometimes to English congregations but especially to Indian congregations from Cape Cod to Long Island.[61]

Even as they separated into independent churches and developed wide-ranging networks of Christian Indians, members of these tribes deliberately solicited relationships with certain English clerics whose patronage they wanted. These relationships were inevitably tense, but both New Light Indians and Old Light ministers had incentives to foster a middle ground of mutual compromise. Like the Pequots, the Narragansetts wanted a school for their children—largely because they recognized the power represented by literacy in making contracts, defending their interests in the colonial legal system, and seeking patronage from settlers and imperial officials. The Narragansetts knew from the Pequot experience that several organizations would pay for such a school if they could find an English Old Light minister to superintend it. At the same time, the tribe was in a state of political and economic crisis, and its members hoped this clerical patron would help them secure the assistance of British officials. But they were extremely wary of losing power and independence. In the late 1750s, they began with overtures to Park. "Some have come to meeting with us," he reported with evident pride in 1757, "others have told me they designed to come, and others have said they believed it would have been better for them if they had not gone away." In turn, he solicited missionary money to seize this opportunity to establish a school and "to reduce the Indians to Gospel faith and order."[62] The Narragansett negotiators, however, rejected Park's response as too condescending. They looked farther afield and settled on two candidates—who were also both staunch opponents of New Light religion. The Anglican Matthew Graves of New London had a very dim view of his fellow colonists and was inclined to believe the worst of the Indians' allegations about Rhode Island officials—he himself believed that what local settlers really needed was an Anglican bishop to fix them up. Similarly, the Congregationalist Joseph Fish had been active in pointing out the "errors" of the New Lights since fighting to quell a revival and prevent a separation in his own parish during the Great Awakening of the 1740s.[63] The Narragansetts warily played the two clerics off each other, negotiating for the better deal, seeing what each could deliver. They eventually settled on Fish. Through his work with the Pequots, he had learned the importance of treating Indians with tact and respect.

The style that Fish encountered in the Narragansett church was, in many ways, classically New Light, with an emphasis on oral relations of personal experiences, emotional intensity, and a disinclination to depend simply on biblical authority. Perhaps the best description of the Narragansetts' practices comes from the journal of a prospective missionary who paid them a visit in the summer of 1768. David McClure, a Yale student and protégé of Eleazar Wheelock, joined about fifty men and women when they gathered at the Indian church. He observed as they sang, prayed, and exhorted and was struck by their emotional intensity. "They were all very earnest in voice and gesture, so much so that some of them foamed at the mouth and seemed transported with a kind of enthusiasm." McClure did not approve when the Narragansetts practiced this cacophonous New Light style of simultaneous praying and singing. He complained, "When they prayed, all spake audibly, some in english and some in Indian. It was indeed a confused noise." There were also a series of individual speakers. McClure stood next to a man who led the prayer in celebration of the forgiveness of sins: "'Lord, thou knowest what a poor vile sinner I have been; how I have been a vile drunkard, and like a beast have lain drunk in my own spue, all night at taverns and on the road; but O Lord, thou has forgiven me my sins, for the sake of our blessed Saviour Jesus Christ, who can save the vilest sinner' &c." Several other men and women also delivered exhortations that combined the mystical and the mundane into stories of salvation. One spoke of standing on the dock at Newport and watching loved ones sail away. These exhorters exemplified the New Light ability to solace those who were "weary and heavy laden." Another said, "I have been up the Northward in the french war, and when cold weather come on orders come—Go into winter quarters. This was dreadful news, to stay there all winter in cold and hunger; but soon word come again, strike your tents and home boys home. Then all was glad, and so it is with a christian going to Heaven." Such stories captured the essential vacillation of New Light Christians between the suffering of those doubting their salvation and the joy of those assured of their salvation.[64] The emotional value of New Light Christianity for Indians whose lives were transformed and dislocated by English colonization might well reside in these parables of saving grace that allowed them to transform ordinary suffering into the joy of eternal salvation.

By then, long-festering tensions with Joseph Fish over religious style had erupted into an open conflict. Although this debate was explicitly framed in the terms of the controversy over Old Light and New Light assumptions about spiritual authority, the nature of conversion, and the importance of Bible-reading versus personal experience, it took on powerful racial meanings. From the start, the Narragansetts' evangelical style had struck Fish as, at best, dangerous and, at worst, deluded. For the first few years of his relationship with them, he kept up a tactful facade—not pointing out what he thought was wrong with their practices but merely pointing the way to what he saw as right. But any semblance of mutual tolerance ended in the summer of 1768 when news reached the Narragansett enclave that Fish had published a tract attacking evangelical errors and warning that New Lights were risking damnation. Narragansett Christians eagerly consumed the riposte by New Light leader Isaac Backus, *A Fish Caught in His Own Net.* The stock terms of the debate between Fish and Backus, which resonated with a generation of Old Light/New Light controversy, had special appeal for the Narragansetts. They attacked Fish as a "white wig," which was an epithet for the standing clergy; and, indeed, Fish's own wig was described by contemporaries as the "crowning glory" of his person. For Indians, ordinary New Light fear of the standing clergy was combined with their general wariness of the English. The Narragansetts also attacked Fish as a "hireling"; and again, the pervasive New Light disapproval of men who took money for doing the Lord's work was combined with Indians' suspicion that the English never appeared to help them without trying to fleece them.[65]

At the core of this polemic were competing notions of the nature of preaching—and here, too, the stock polemic had a special resonance for the Narragansetts and other southern New England Indians. Old Lights such as Fish believed that the purpose of Christian worship was to understand and explain the plain Bible truths revealed in the written text of Scripture. The role of the preacher was to explain biblical texts and apply their lessons to the ethics of ordinary life. In contrast, the Narragansetts believed that the authentic purpose of worship was to create emotional impressions, which they did by relating personal religious experiences from daily life, visions, and dreams. Samuel Niles himself finally abandoned his statesmanlike neutrality and openly attacked Fish and other Old Lights: "These learned Ministers Are Thieves Robbers Pirates." Like other New Lights, Niles argued that Old Light preachers were wrong to depend on the Bible as their only source of divine revelation. Mere exegesis of biblical texts missed the true essence of divine revelation, which was not the literal text of Scripture but the direct communication with the Holy Spirit that it embodied. "God told the Prophets the words they Spoke: and These Ministers Steal that Word." For Niles, the Old Lights were mimetic—bad copies of true Christianity. The Narragansetts, in contrast, had "their Teaching directly from the Fountain."[66] However closely the Narragansetts and their English critics echoed the idioms of a transatlantic debate, the fact that the Indians were evangelical and the English took the part of the standing churches gave this Old Light/New Light debate a powerful racial edge.

This sense of Indian identity was further expanded by missionary networks and the bureaucracy of the British Empire. When the Narragansetts sent children to study at Eleazar Wheelock's school, they joined Indians from Stonington, Mohegan, Stockbridge, Montauk, other New England enclaves, and as far away as Delaware and Iroquoia. The correspondence of these students from far-flung backgrounds shows how the experience of living at Wheelock's school fostered a strong sense of common identity. These students shared a common Christian culture, resented the disrespect and betrayal they so often experienced in relations with English settlers, and worried about the future of their peoples. Young men and women at the school courted, and students visited one another's homes—as when Hezekiah Calvin, a Delaware, visited the Narragansett enclave in 1768, bearing news of the young Narragansetts at Wheelock's school and bitterly describing their experiences with Wheelock.[67] Wheelock's basic assumption that the goal of educating Indians was to prepare the boys to serve as missionaries and the girls to serve as their wives further extended the ties of Indian identity. When Samson Occom was ordained in 1759, it was assumed that he would labor among benighted Indians. He accepted a position among the Montauks on Long Island, though it rankled him that his sponsoring missionary organization paid him about half what it paid his English colleagues, and he later made several missionary visits to Oneida country before settling down in his hometown of Mohegan, Connecticut. Wheelock sent several of his other students to serve not in their own communities but rather as missionaries among the largely pagan Iroqouis nations. Jacob Fowler, a Montauk Indian who grew up on Long Island, was sent to serve as a schoolteacher at the Oneida village of Kanawoharem, where he struggled to learn the language and carve out for himself and his new wife some semblance of a civil life. Ties among the various New England Indians and the Iroquois were reinforced and extended though the mediation of Sir William Johnson, the imperial superintendent of Indian affairs for the northern region of British territory. Thus, Christian networks prompted native peoples in New England to recognize a shared identity as "Indian" even with pagan peoples who lived hundreds of miles away, led dramatically different styles of life, and did not even share a common language.[68]

The Narragansetts came to view their religious style not just as evangelical but as distinctively Indian. This point was firmly driven home to visiting observer David McClure as he left the Indian meetinghouse that Sabbath. He was accosted by several participants, conscious of his role as an outsider, observer, and critic. One man asked, "How do you like our way of worship?" McClure gave tactful faint praise before asking if it would not be more "edifying in prayer for one to pray and the congregation to join?" The Narragansett man made it clear that he, like other evangelicals, was less interested in harmony and refinement than in uninhibited personal impulse, collective participation, and enthusiasm. He replied wryly, "*That will never do. Must make 'em all pray.*" Otherwise, they were "*apt to cheat.*" Once again, the Narragansetts, like other New Lights, thought Old Light concern for decorum and harmony to be vainglorious and worldly. They did not want, for instance, a congregation listening to a choir perform: they wanted everyone in the congregation singing. For them, true worship relied on the active, direct, emotional involvement of each worshiper—and if the result was messy, that rough edge helped make it seem authentic.

As McClure was leaving town that Sunday, observing who had the "best farms," a man in his doorway stopped McClure. By this time the battle with Fish had escalated to the point that it was clear that the white-wigged interloper's days in Narragansett country were numbered. The Indian man did not bother asking for the Yale student's impressions but bluntly declared: "This is the way that we Indians have to get to Heaven. You white people have another way. I don't know but your way will bring *you* there, but I know that our way will bring *us* there."[69]

||| "From Black to White" |||

Even when blacks and Indians became Christian and actively defended the authenticity of their spiritual style, settlers were still able to make it seem that there was something strange about Christians of color. Although the implication of apishness, of bad imitation, is particularly salient in colonial contexts, it seems endemic to self-conscious social structures in which legitimacy is grounded in appeals to authenticity. This was a particularly powerful way in which the experiences of Christian fellowship made racial identities more compelling, more expansive, and seemingly more natural. "Old Light," "New Light," "a land of Light"—settlers had long associated true religion with enlightenment, with whiteness.[70]

Such associations of racial and religious identities were most vivid in images of the resurrection of the body. One evangelical was caught up in a mystical vision in which he flew over the landscape to a place where, he was told, he would be given a crown in the "Peesalbe Kingdom" Christ was to establish. Then he noticed that there were also "Black People" up there. He was so startled that he woke up.[71]

Even for sympathetic settlers, the notion of a converted Indian could seem anomalous. A Boston merchant visiting Wheelock's school was disappointed that he missed seeing the Mohegan Samuel Ashpo and thus "lost the opportunity of seeing Mr Wheelock in him & more especially of seeing Christ's Image in this Tawny Man." Fortunately, he did get to see one of Wheelock's model young women, and "the pleasure was exquisite to see the savageness of an Indian molded into the sweetness of a follower of the Lamb."[72]

The celebrated Reverend Samson Occom, a Mohegan who was Wheelock's star pupil, knew well that much of his success followed from such curiosity. His tour of Britain was calculated to play on such exoticism and was spectacularly successful in raising money for Wheelock's school. "I was quite willing to become a Gazing Stock, Yea Even a Laughing Stock, in Strange Countries." But Occom also knew how to put the lie to such logic—the insinuation that Europeans had a racial monopoly on authentic Christianity—by pointing out that the English themselves had no original claim to Christianity. Were the ancient Britons, he was fond of asking, not themselves heathen?[73]

However strained their logic, many New Englanders so strongly associated Christianity with whiteness that they imagined Indian and African converts physically changing color. Many Christians of color, such as Phillis Wheatley, found special solace in John 1:7—"The blood of Jesus His Son cleanses us from all sin." This image of salvation as cleansing was employed by Phillis Wheatley in her poetry and held profound racial meanings for many other contemporaries. One of them was Joseph Johnson, who studied with Eleazar Wheelock, lived briefly in Providence, and then became a schoolteacher in Mohegan; during a wrenching rebirth as a Christian in the early 1770s, he repeatedly returned to John 1:7 in his spiritual exercises and prayers. In the world of print, as well, the image was echoed: in his autobiographical narrative, the notorious black criminal John Marrant also invoked the theme of spiritually turning from black to white. One sentimental story, excerpted in the *Newport Mercury*, described a pious slave as like a potato—brown on the outside and white on the inside.[74]

Some of the most explicit images of such racial transformation were carved into the gravestones of African New Englanders. For example, "Caesar the Ethiopian" was buried by his master's family in Attleboro, Massachusetts, in 1780. His epitaph praised him as the "best of servants" and deserving of a place among the just:

> His faithful soul has fled
> To realms of heavenly light,
> And by the blood that Jesus shed
> is changed from Black to White.[75]

The implication was that Christianity could in fact transcend race by transforming blacks into whites. The prospect that conversion to Christianity would erase racial differences had long extended to people of color the promise of a new identity and had long threatened settlers with the problem of equality. In eighteenth-century New England, racial divisions were not in fact reconciled by religious conversions but rather reinforced and made to seem more natural. Yet here the promise came on a gravestone.

Half a century later, a similar epitaph linking color and Christianity was carved into a stone commemorating Mrs. Lucy Haskell in the common burying ground in Providence. Although she died in 1812, in her early thirties, it was not until her husband died in 1833 that a white employer or patron erected the couple's matching markers. The epitaph described her as

> a professed disciple of Jesus Christ
> who lived in the practice of his precepts
> and died in hope of reaping
> the rewards of grace in his kingdom,

> where every *complexion* will unite
> in praising Him who has washed their robes
> and made them *white* in his own
> blood.[76]

Salvation would eradicate racial differences. But not in this world.

PART II

Living Together

It is not enough to conquer,
one must also learn to seduce.

VOLTAIRE

CHAPTER FOUR

Strange Flesh

||| Charlestown, Massachusetts, 1755 |||

When Paul Revere set out on his midnight ride in April 1775, one of the first land-marks he passed was the body of a long-dead slave—a figure that represented, no less than the Sons of Liberty themselves, a colonial family drama of abused pater-nal authority, emasculating enslavement, and rebellion. Revere knew the body by name. Mark's remains, suspended in a metal gibbet overlooking the road, had been greeting travelers for some twenty years—since 1755, when he was hanged. His ac-complice, Phillis, was burned at the stake. Their crime had been killing their mas-ter, Captain John Codman of Charlestown. In the eyes of the patriarchal Puritan statute that prescribed their fate, this act was worse than murder: it was a form of treason. Like children who cursed their parents, servants who rebelled against their masters threatened a series of social hierarchies extending even to the king him-self—the "father of all his people." Slavery in the Codman household, as trial records reveal, had all the intimacy and intrigue of family life. After Phillis gave her master a fatal dose of poison in a porringer of gruel, it was she—not one of his daughters—who sat by his bedside all night, assuring him that she "wish'd he was as well as she was." At times, Mark testified, she stole outside and danced about in the dark, mimicking her master's gestures as he writhed "in the bitter pangs of

Death." Such emotional dynamics were of less interest to colonial magistrates than the practical moral that dependent members of household should defer to their domestic governors. Responding to pressure, Mark publicly confessed his crimes and exhorted his fellow servants, "especially the women," to respect their stations. When huge crowds gathered to witness the spectacle of the execution—the likes of which had not been since in almost a century—a printer hawked a broadside expressing the pious hope that servants, "black and white," might each "in their own Place, the Masters serve with Fear."[1]

The prosecution and ensuing publicity emphasized the family relations of master and servants, but obscure transcripts of Mark's and Phillis's first interrogation by Boston magistrates reveal another set of family dynamics. What drove Mark and Phillis to murder was their master's refusal to honor their own, independent family lives. Over the years both Mark and Phillis had developed social networks that ranged far beyond their master's home in Charlestown and into a large community of slaves across the river in Boston. It was from the slave of a Boston apothecary, for instance, that Mark had procured the poison. Initially, Codman had allowed them some autonomy. As Mark declared: "My Master let me live in Boston with my Wife and go out to work." But early in 1755, Mark had run into trouble making ends meet, and that spring the overseers of the poor formally warned him out of town. Meanwhile, Phillis had developed a relationship of her own with a Boston man named Quacko. As Mark explained, Quacko had been "contriving all he could to get her over to Boston to live with him" and even declared himself willing to spend forty pounds to convince Codman. Only when these negotiations failed did Mark and Phillis decide to kill their master.[2] Even then, their goal was not freedom. Mark and Phillis wanted what they ominously reported other slaves they knew had accomplished: to replace an intransigent master with someone who would be more willing to accommodate their desire to establish families of their own.[3]

The overlapping family lives of masters and servants suggest some of the powerful and subtle ways in which sexual lines of color served to represent, even to embody, the boundaries of the body politic. Many of these issues were raised as early as 1705 when the Massachusetts General Assembly considered a harsh bill "against fornication, or marriage of White men with Negros or Indians." As originally proposed the bill delineated a clear sexual boundary between whites on the one hand and blacks and Indians on the other, representing in a particularly profound and intimate way the social divisions within colonial society. Settlers had long since abandoned any openness to intermarriage with Indians or Africans they may have entertained in the early seventeenth century. By the turn of the century, when he published *The Selling of Joseph*, Samuel Sewall was only expressing common wisdom when he claimed that the physical and social differences between the English and Negroes were too great for the two peoples ever to "embody" together. Nonetheless, even he found the terms of the 1705 bill excessively harsh. In private negotiations, he "got the Indians out of the Bill" and mitigated penalties against Negroes. He also managed to add to the bill a clear mandate: "No master shall unreasonably deny marriage to his negro with one of the same nation." This protection was necessary, he argued, because masters had practical reasons for preventing servants from marrying anyone, even each other: "It is too well known what Temptations Masters are under, to connive at the Fornication of their Slaves, lest they should be obliged to find them Wives." In addition, legislators quietly dropped any mention of fornication by the time they passed "An Act for the Better Preventing of a Spurious and Mixt Issue."[4]

The notion that legislators might regulate *sex* by passing a law that mentioned only *marriage* was not necessarily as naïve as it might seem. It is not difficult to imagine that their goal was less to keep the races apart than to keep relations of power clear. Marriage offered legislators little room for ambiguity. It was, by definition, a public relationship that served not only to unite individuals but also to merge families and fortunes and seal alliances. In this sense, marriage affirmed identity and equality in a way that required public consent and legal authorization. Thus, repudiating interracial marriage was a powerful way to repudiate racial equality. In contrast, sex outside marriage required much more flexible regulation, at least if relations of power were to remain unequal. An illicit relationship could remain private, be tolerated, be quietly celebrated, or even be prosecuted as a crime. Much of the public meaning of illicit sexual relationships—whether an amorous liaison or a violent rape—was dependent on the ability of the parties involved to control knowledge about it. Settlers themselves were aware of this sexual double standard and were not above using it against one another. In a play performed by British troops occupying Boston during the Revolution, a black prostitute named Fanfan rebukes ostensibly chaste Sons of Liberty for their hypocrisy: "Tho' in Publick you scoff, I see many a Spark, / Would tink me a sweet pretty Girl in the Dark." By speaking the scandalous truth Fanfan was able, for a moment, to turn the tables of power. Whether considered in the abstract or made public, illicit relations could have different implications depending on the race and social rank of the men and women involved. Pennsylvania legislators recognized this in 1700 when they defined rape in different ways for blacks and whites: black men guilty of attempting to rape white women were to be castrated, but there was no penalty for men of any race who raped black women. Neither sex nor violence lay at the root of such laws. Ultimately, the issue was honor—that is, the power to control reputation and public meaning.[5]

Legislators enhanced their own personal, sexual, and racial honor by establishing legal double standards that expressed the privileges of men over women and of whites over people of color. An early Rhode Island statute defined adultery as the crime whereby married men "burn in their lusts toward strange flesh," but in many colonies it was a crime that could be committed only by married women. The Massachusetts law of 1705 prohibiting interracial marriage was apparently prompted by two lawsuits that came before the General Court involving fornication between black men and white women. Legislators had shown no such interest in a series of previous cases that had involved black women suing white men. Over the course of the eighteenth century, overlapping double standards of gender, status, and race shaped the implications of sexual honor and citizenship. By proscribing marriage between blacks and whites, colonists repudiated the prospect of racial equality and symbolically dishonored black men and women. By declining to enact firm sanctions against illicit interracial sexual behavior, however, white male legislators gave themselves and their peers license to behave in ways that expressed and further enhanced their dominance.[6]

In this context, the symbolic as well as practical problems represented by slave marriage become clearer. Like Captpain Codman, many masters discouraged not only illicit sexual relations and childbirth among their servants but also lawful marriages. To be excluded from marriage was to be excluded both from the realm of sexual legitimacy and from an important symbol of citizenship. In colonial society, marriage typically marked the point at which men moved out of their parents' households, established their social independence, and accumulated enough property to vote. But slaves did not become independent, were always susceptible to being separated by masters, and did not legally own property. These tensions can be explored in records of negotiations between individual slaves and masters and in public debates about the legitimacy of slave marriages. The same issues of honor and respectability were also at stake for men and women involved in or affected by illicit sexual relations. Even as sexual cultures in New England were changing, there was never any simply black-white line of color. Records of rape in personal documents, legal records, and published texts provide opportunities to explore the dynamics of selective sexual regulation and reflect on how double standards of gender and status were extended, exaggerated, or challenged by the dynamics of race.

Meanwhile, free blacks and Indians across New England were making their own choices about sex and marriage, choices that reflected their own values, identities, and political options. Particularly in Indian enclaves in the latter part of the eighteenth century, as gender roles changed, political conflicts came to a head, and land became short, the question of intermarriage with whites and Negroes became increasingly charged and controversial. These conflicts suggest, in part, how Indians were prompted to think of themselves in more rigid racial terms and to redefine the boundaries of tribal bodies. In the eyes of Indians and Anglo-American observers, the dynamics of interracial marriage embodied, blurred, and occasionally transcended colonial assumptions about citizenship.

||| "As Man and Wife" |||

When Pompey was born in Newport in 1763 as the child of an unmarried woman, he had "no blood" in him, at least legally speaking. As a bastard, he was the son of nobody. Yet when he died two years later, he was mourned by two fathers. Pompey's parents were Sarah, the slave of the Reverend James Searing, and Cesar, the slave of the prosperous merchant Josias Lyndon. Like many slaves, they were not legally married, but they were often regarded as man and wife. Cesar mourned his son's passing in the privacy of a journal he kept during these years: "Our little Darling Pompey was born th^e 2nd Day of May 1763 taken ill in the night Thursday with the Bloody Flux Sept.5.1765 and died Wednesday Morning ab^t ¼ after 9 o'clock." Also affected by the boy's death was Cesar's master, Josias Lyndon. Legally speaking, Lyndon had no relationship to the child: the father, his slave, was not lawfully married to the mother, and the mother and her child belonged to Searing. Nonetheless, Lyndon chose to honor the child as a member of his own extended family and commissioned gravestones—a small footer and a larger headstone—to mark his burial. Strikingly, at this most public moment of death, Lyndon chose to emphasize not the child's tangle of family relationships but rather the primacy of his own role. The epitaph was cut by one of the stone carver's slaves into a small, smooth, slate headstone: "Pompey (a beloved servant of Josias Lyndon)."[7] To this day, only an obscure journal in the archives of the state historical society in Providence links the boy to his parents. But the headstone still stands, a perennial reminder of Lyndon's desire to be remembered as a loving master (fig. 10).

FIGURE 10. Pompey Brenton headstone (1772), carved by John Stevens III. Like many men's stones, this one gives no indication of whether he was married or had children. The overlapping families of masters and slaves were, however, represented on many of the other stones in the segregated section of the burial ground in Newport reserved for black and Indian servants. Newport Common Burial Ground. Photo by the author.

Pompey's grave lies in a remote corner of Newport's Common Burial Ground reserved for the public remembrance of slaves. Most of the markers in this city of the dead were paid for by masters, and as such they present an idealized view of the family lives of masters and slaves. Such public recognition of slaves was not unprecedented—European masters from time to time honored particularly "faithful" domestic servants with public grave markers—but it was unusual. In many places, such as in the Anglican churchyard in South Kingstown or in New York's Potter's Field, slaves were buried anonymously, in unmarked graves. To be sure, the Newport stones are not only segregated geographically but conspicuously smaller than the stones of English settlers. Stones for adult male slaves were about the same size and cost about as much as stones for their masters' children.[8] Many of these stones, like Pompey's, simply identify slaves as members of their masters' households. One even gives a chronology of masters: "Here lyes the Body of CATO formerly Servant of Mʳ Jᴏʙ Aʟᴍʏ & lately a serv to M Sɪʟᴀs Cᴏᴏᴋ of this *Town*." But other stones emphasize the slave's own family bonds, remembering Violet as the "daughter of Chloe" or Phillis as the "Wife of Diego." Indeed, the stones themselves echo the patriarchal order of the English section of the graveyard, albeit on a smaller scale: they are generally grouped in family clusters, the stones of children the smallest, the stones of women larger, and the stones of men the largest. In fact, some stones make explicit the overlapping family lives of masters and slaves. Consider the epitaph for Caesar Lyndon's fellow servant Phillis, who died in 1773: "ɪɴ ᴍᴇᴍ-ᴏʀʏ of ᴘʜɪʟʟɪs a late faithful Servant of ᴊᴏsɪᴀs ʟʏɴᴅᴏɴ Esqʳ and Wife of ᴢɪɴɢᴏ sᴛᴇᴠᴇɴs."⁹ Zingo, for his part, was one of several slaves owned by the local stone carvers.

As these stones suggest, at the heart of the overlapping family lives of masters and servants was the problem of marriage. Masters liked to think of slavery as a kind of familial relationship. Slaves were like perpetual children: dependent, governed by the head of their household, and excluded from political recognition. Marriage represented a problem because it not only regulated the transmission of property and established the legitimacy of children but also was strongly associated with the privileges of citizenship. Settlers typically saw marriage as creating a separate household, the basic unit of economic, civil, and religious life—a domestic "Little Commonwealth" that composed the basic unit of the body politic. The role of men as the public representatives of their families is suggested by their gravestones: in addition to being the largest, they varied most widely. In 1750, Josias Lyndon paid £188—almost ten times the usual amount—for a massive tombstone for a particularly distinguished politician. If families were ranked around men, men were ranked in relation to one another. In this context, the extension of patriarchal authority over subordinate men worked best when relationships of dependency were either temporary, such as childhood or a term of indenture, or when they were distant, such as those between manorial lords and their serfs or between early colonists and the British monarch.¹⁰ But for slaves, dependence was not ever supposed to end. And few settlers owned large enough estates to distance slaves in outbuildings. Consequently, the marriage of slaves was the site of perpetual conflict and negotiation.

Samuel Sewall himself knew how difficult it was to reconcile marriage with household slavery: his diary records several instances in which he helped enslaved men and women broker marriage deals with their respective masters and mistresses. One such case involved a Massachusetts slave whose master agreed in principle "to buy a yoak-fellow for him." When the man subsequently developed an active "Desire to Marry," the master balked. Ultimately, they agreed on another solution: if the man worked faithfully for fifteen more years, he would be allowed to purchase his own freedom. In 1710 Jack, a "Negroman Servant," seeking to marry Esther, a "Negro Woman Servant" to another master, used the 1705 Massachusetts law to petition a Court of General Sessions, which ordered that he "be not denied marriage provided he attend[ed] the Directions of the law for the Regulation of Marriages." But this law soon fell into obscurity and disuse, and most slaves ended up negotiating on their own. Church records from across New England suggest that some masters did allow formal marriages among slaves, particularly when a single master owned both the man and the woman.[11]

Unlike southern slave owners, however, few New England settlers owned more than one slave. In cramped New England houses, the birth of a child to a slave was disruptive and rarely profitable. Massachusetts Historical Society president Jeremy Belknap exaggerated only slightly when he recalled in 1795 that "negro children were considered an incumbrance in a family; and when weaned, were given away like puppies." The market for the sale of young slave children was very limited: it was generally less expensive to buy an adult slave than to rear one from childhood. Advertisements for free children appeared in the colonial newspapers: "A Young Indian Child to be given away; enquire of the Printer." More often, masters sold women who had too many children. In 1759, the *Newport Mercury* advertised the sale of a young woman *"For no other Fault than being a notable Breeder."* In 1764, South Kingstown attorney Hezekiah Babcock offered to sell his Negro woman and her two-year-old boy *"Cheap"*—because he was "desirous of reducing his Family to a smaller Number." The language of "breeding" was common and associated enslaved women with livestock, emotionally distancing the figure of the slave mother from the regard and respect ordinarily accorded maternity.[12]

The journal of Anglican cleric James MacSparran chronicles an unending series of attempts to suppress the sexual activities of his slaves. On various occasions he whipped both Maroca and Hannibal for their affairs with other local slaves. Although MacSparran was unusual in that he punished male as well as female slaves for fornication—perhaps because of his religious outlook—he was like many masters in focusing his attention on the young woman. MacSparran was particularly peeved that Maroca, who professed herself a Christian, could behave in such an immoral manner. But on several occasions when Maroca became pregnant, MacSparran did not attempt, as it were, "to make an honest woman of her." At a time when as many as a third of all brides in New England were pregnant on their wedding day, many young people were able to use the threat of publicly disgracing their families to pressure their parents to agree to otherwise unacceptable unions. In other ways as well, a woman's reputation was easy enough to protect if she had sufficient resources. But MacSparran and other slave owners showed little interest in their slaves' sexual respectability. Instead of encouraging Maroca to marry her longtime suitor Caesar—who lived on a nearby farm—and make her sexual activity legitimate, he did his best to force her to break off the relationship, punishing her severely on one occasion when he discovered that Caesar had given her presents. Nor did he see any need to respect her maternal feelings. When her children were born, he waited until they were weaned, then baptized them, and quickly gave them away.[13] By such practices, enslaved men and women were conspicuously excluded from the bounds of colonial sexual respectability.

Suppressing premarital sex was relatively common in colonial households and families, but the position of slave masters was almost unique. They were among the only father figures in colonial New England who could not shunt the costs of rearing a bastard child onto someone else. Town "fathers" typically bore the cost of poor women having children and generally did their best to reduce costs by keeping them out of their jurisdictions whenever possible, attempting to identify fathers and get them to pay and binding poor mothers and their children out to service to subsidize their costs. Early in the century, even servants such as a "mulatto" woman who worked for Benjamin Brooks in rural Massachusetts were able to prosecute settlers successfully for paternal support. But over the course of the century, many unmarried women found it more difficult to collect child support from fathers. Increasingly the burden fell on poor women alone. The celebrated minister Lemuel Haynes, born about midcentury in West Hartford, Connecticut, was the son of a black man and an unmarried English servant woman; his mother was fired as soon as he was born, and he was bound at the age of five to a local minister.[14] Slave owners, however, could neither get town officials to assume financial responsibility nor force enslaved women and their children to serve longer terms. Instead, they often focused on discouraging slaves from having children under any conditions.

Consequently many enslaved women regarded pregnancy with fear and desperation, emotions most sorrowfully apparent in prosecutions of mothers accused of killing their babies. Indictments for infanticide constituted a large portion of all murder indictments in colonial New England, and the accused were overwhelmingly domestic servants. The enslaved Newporter Jenny admitted that when she found herself pregnant in 1767, she was stricken with terror. She feared that her abusive master would punish her even more cruelly if he found out. Therefore she carefully concealed her pregnancy, and when it came time to give birth, she crept up into the attic alone. After secretly giving birth, she took a brick and smashed her infant daughter's head. When she still saw signs of life, she smashed it again. Jenny then hid the body in a barrel of ashes. Soon it was discovered, and she was charged and confessed. She was convicted and sentenced to hang. But a group of prominent local settlers intervened and petitioned the king to pardon her. These sympathetic observers were moved by her apparent "idiotism" and by the knowledge that her master had brutally abused her: she was crippled so badly that she could not walk, only drag herself around.[15] The thirteen other women accused of infanticide in eighteenth-century Rhode Island all had their wits about them enough to plead not guilty after dead infants were found in shallow graves—or, gruesomely, rotting under beds. Each of them shared Jenny's predicament: they were all poor, single women, and most of them worked as domestic servants and lived in their masters' households.[16] For them pregnancy and motherhood meant not the start of a new family but punishment. And juries apparently sympathized with their plight: All but Jenny were found not guilty.

Another reason masters sought to suppress slave family ties was to avoid pressure to keep slave families intact. Many New Englanders would have agreed that, ideally, masters ought not rend slave families asunder through sale. "Masters of Negroes ought to be men of great humanity," one Congregational minister noted in the 1760s; "they have an arbitrary power, may correct them at pleasure, may separate them from their children, may send them out of the Country." Sometimes masters went to some effort to sell slave families as a unit. The *Providence Gazette* in 1777 advertised the sale of a "Likely Negro man, with his wife, and one child, about 14 months old; the man about 25 years of age, and the woman about 21." But few masters owned both members of a couple. A typical series of conflicts developed after an enslaved woman, Juno Larcom, formed an attachment with another slave in Beverly, Massachusetts. During the 1750s they had several children and eventually were formally married in a local church. But this legal sanction did not prevent the male slave's master from selling him to a family far away from her. In order to keep the couple together, the man's master would have had either to forgo the sale or to convince the other master to sell Juno and their children as well. Neither showed interest in any such compromise. Later, when Juno's master threatened to sell one of her children to someone far away, she openly rebelled, ran away, and filed suit against him, claiming that as a part Indian woman she was legally free.[17]

When selling slaves, masters could rarely respect the integrity of slave families without compromising their own sense of patriarchal authority and economic independence. On the other hand, many masters found it more convenient to keep women and children together. Typically, a Newporter in 1762 offered for sale "a likely, notable Negro Woman . . . with her two Children." This matrifocal redefinition of the slave family was a hallmark of slavery in North America. In colonial New England, lawmakers did nothing to discourage masters from splitting up families. Only as slavery was waning in the early nineteenth century did New York legislators prohibit the separation of husbands and wives in slave sales.[18] Just as the societal convention that the slave or free status of children would follow that of the mother and not the father, the casual disregard of the rights of couples to remain together and of fathers to retain control of their children denied enslaved people the patriarchal privileges most free settlers took for granted.

The stones in the Newport graveyard, however, are one sign that some masters felt increased pressure to honor slave families in the 1760s. By this time, the charge that masters valued market prices over the family ties of slaves became a prominent trope of abolitionist discourse. Early in the century, slaves were most often described as "faithful" to their masters. No doubt masters intended these gravestones, at least in part, to emphasize the message that good service would be rewarded with enduring recognition, whereas bad behavior would be punished with eternal ignominy. Masters likely saw these stones not just as reminders to their peers and other townspeople that they had wealth and good taste but also as outward signs of their inner benevolence. Particularly in stones dating from after the 1750s, masters emphasized that they rewarded faithful servitude with love. One man was remembered as "Faithful and well Beloved of his Master." Young Pompey was simply "beloved." Such public and lasting declarations of ownership, servitude, and fidelity show that some masters were deeply invested in publicly commemorating themselves as masters benevolent enough to regard with honor and love even the most humble members of their families.[19] By the 1760s, it became a point of honor for masters to display their benevolence specifically by demonstrating that they respected their slaves' family lives. In these memorials, masters advertised not only their love but also their respect for their slaves' familial autonomy.

This comforting paternal vision did not always satisfy slaves who were still alive. When a group of black Bostonians seeking freedom in 1774 petitioned the Massachusetts government, they emphasized, along with political notions echoing the escalating imperial crisis, the crisis of slave family life. In doing so, they claimed as personal the images that had become staples of antislavery writing in the previous decade. Under slavery in America, they were deprived of "everything that makes life even tolerable." They claimed further, "The endearing ties of husband and wife we are strangers to for we are no longer man and wife then our masters or mestresses things proper marred or onmarred. Our children are also taken from us by force and sent maney miles from us wear we seldom or ever see them again." Some infants died when snatched too early from their mother's breast. "Thus our Lives are imbittered to us." They ended the petition with a plea for respect for the divinely ordained hierarchy of authority within families—in language reminiscent of the kinds of patriarchal logic previously used to justify slavery. Under slavery, they asked, "How can a husband leave master and work and cleave to his wife How can the wife submit themselves to their husband in all things. How can the child obey thear parents in all things."[20]

Indeed, one powerful sign of masters' desire to deny or disregard slaves' need for lawful marriage and its privileges is the development of a separate, informal tradition of "Negro marriages." It became common for black and Indian men and women to describe themselves as married, but not "in the manner of the white people."[21] One Newporter in 1815 recalled a black couple who, since the mid-eighteenth century, "lived constantly & faithfully together as husband and wife from their first connection till they were separated by death—even though without the legal forms of marriage—as was pretty generally the custom, even with reputable people of their colour, sixty years ago." Alliances that would not have been recognized among white people were often considered good enough for people of color. Informal "Negro marriages" did not accrue the same legal privileges as old-style common-law marriages; they did not unite family, property, and governance. It was during these years that British officials were systematically trying to stamp out most other forms of "common-law" marriage. Particularly striking was the case of Flora, which came before the Massachusetts Supreme Court in 1758: it held that the child of an enslaved woman and man "never married according to any of the Forms prescribed by the Laws of this Land" was, nonetheless, not a bastard. The implication of this decision was that, for slaves, the general laws concerning the lawful forms of marriage did not apply and that any "actual marriages" were deemed valid even without formal solemnization before a clergyman or magistrate.[22] Once again, people of color were placed outside the domain of civil respectability reserved for settlers. This separate standard for "Negro marriages" denied slave women sexual honor, their children true legitimacy, and men the distinction of heading a family.

Of course, "lawful marriage," "Negro marriage," and unceremonious sexual alliances did not necessarily mean the same things to slaves that they meant to settlers. These less formal arrangements may have appealed to African immigrants who may not have found English rituals or sexual ideologies particularly compelling. Like enslaved Africans, many Indians, even those living outside enclaves, declined to adopt English forms of lawful marriage. An Indian woman named Mary Fowler, who had grown up in South Kingstown as an indentured servant, testified before poor-relief officials: "[She had] lived with a person of the name of James Fowler, a mustee, for about thirty years, and had ten children by him, all born in South Kingstown, but never was married to him in the manner in which white people are married in these parts." One of her daughters, examined at the same time, testified along the same lines: "She hath lived with a person of the name of John Champlin, a mustee man, as his wife eleven years . . . and has had six children by him, but never was married to him according to the form used by the white people in these parts."[23]

For some individuals, such as Cesar Lyndon, attitudes toward lawful marriage changed over time. For many years after the birth of his son Pompey, Cesar remained closely involved with Sarah Searing, but they were not formally married. In the summer of 1766, for instance, he whitewashed Sarah Searing's bedchamber and painted the woodwork blue. And his social circle included a number of apparently unmarried black couples. Only a couple of years later does his journal suggest that he began to contemplate formal marriage. In 1768 he recorded ceremonies marking the marriage of his master's son and, some time later, the marriage of the Reverend James Searing's daughter. Soon thereafter, his fellow servant Phillis and Zingo Stevens, both of whom had been born in Africa, were married. Both had recently experienced spiritual conversions and joined the Second Congregational Church; their formal marriage by the Reverend Samuel Hopkins no doubt was related to their newfound Christian faith. Lyndon shared little of their fervent piety, but he did strive for respectability. Several months later, on a Tuesday evening in October, he and Sarah Searing were married by the Reverend Dr. Ezra Stiles.[24]

Some of what marriage meant to Cesar Lyndon is suggested in his response to a romantic imbroglio involving his son during the waning days of the Revolutionary War. In the spring of 1781, Cesar Lyndon was confronted with a letter written by a free black man in Providence named Prime Brown. Lyndon's son had appar-

ently become friends with Brown, moved in with him and his wife, and then seduced her. When they eloped together, Brown was enraged. "He had better not
marry her—his Life will be in danger," he fumed, letting it be known that he was
having trouble "governing" himself. Cesar Lyndon assumed the fatherly duty of
vindicating his son by composing a response, which he sent not to the enraged
cuckold but rather to his former master, Moses Brown. "My Countryman M^r
Prime," he explained, had heretofore been under "your good Government." Apparently, Cesar Lyndon, himself still a slave, was quite comfortable with the paternalistic hierarchies of slavery—and apparently unbothered that this relationship
had been severed almost eight years earlier. His wry epistle made a clear distinction between informal unions and lawful marriages in matters of sexual honor.
Prime's claim hinged on the implication that, since he was married, he had a right
to exclusive sexual possession of his wife. Lyndon twisted the proverbial knife: "I
should think the Female Sex about which he is so anxious has none, or but little,
regard for him, or she would not keep another's Company, while he was alive." In
any case they were not really married: "As far as I can learn, the Woman, is no Wife
to Mr Prime.—they only have kept each other Company, for so long a time, as they
could agree; which time seems now to be at an End." In closing the letter, Lyndon identified himself as a servant living "under the Government" of the late governor Josias Lyndon's esteemed widow.[25] Just as striking as Brown's attempt to assert his patriarchal independence through his sexual claim to a woman is Lyndon's
attempt to pull rank by emphasizing his dependence on a woman who represented
an intricate chain of hierarchies. If this letter makes anything clear, it is that the
struggles of men and women of color to establish their own families would always
be implicated in claims to respectability and models of citizenship.

To some observers it seemed open to question whether the civil or sacramental
status of marriage really applied to men and women of color in the first place. Some
theologians publicly questioned whether English forms of marriage were proper
for slaves in the Americas. As part of a broader debate over whether Church of
England forms should be adapted to American conditions in the wake of the rock-
ing revivals of the 1740s, one question raised was the topic of slave marriage. In 1748,
Anglican minister Noah Hobart complained that the liturgical forms of the
Church of England were too inflexible to adapt to the special circumstances of
colonial life; he particularly objected that the Office of Matrimony used phrases
such as "with all my worldly goods I thee endow, in the name of the Father, and
of the Son, and of the Holy Ghost." This oath flew in the face of reality because

slaves controlled no property. Hobart insisted that such an inappropriate oath in slave marriages made the forms of the church either sacrilegious or farcical. Other clerics took up the debate.[26]

In one striking attempt to resolve the problem of slave marriage, a conservative Congregational minister literally rewrote the text of the marriage vows. His new vows were modeled after the standard form but clearly emphasized the authority of masters and the subordination of slaves' marriage to their masters' convenience. This union would be neither independent nor permanent. The ceremony began with the minister reading the oath to the groom and asking his assent:

> You S: do now in the Presence of God, and these Witnesses, Take R: to be your *Wife;* Promising that so far as shall be consistent with ye relation wch you now sustain, as a Servant, you will Perform ye Part of an *Husband* towards her; And in Particular, you Promise that you will *Love* her: And that, as you shall have ye Opportty & Ability, you will take a proper *Care* of her in Sickness and Health, in Prosperity & Adversity: And that you will be True & *Faithful* to her, and will Cleave to her *only, so long* as God in his Provdce, shall continue your and her abode in Such Place (or Places) as that you can conveniently come together.

Then he administered a similar vow to the bride. The minister then concluded:

> I then, agreeable to your Request, and with the Consent of your Masters & Mistresses, do Declare, that you have Licence given to you to be conversant and familiar together, as *Husband and Wife,* as long as God shall continue your Places of Abode as afore-said; And so long as you Shall behave your-Selves as it becometh Servants to doe:
>
> For, you must, both of you, bear in mind, that you Remain Still, as really and truly as ever, your Master's Property, and therefore it will be justly expected, both by God and Man, that you behave and conduct your-selves as Obedient and faithfull Servants towards your respective Masters & Mistresses for the Time being:
>
> And finally, I exhort & Charge you to beware lest you give place to the Devil, so as to take Occasion from the Licence now given to you, to be lifted up with *Pride.*[27]

Although married—after a fashion—they were still first and foremost slaves.

||| "Irreconcilable Aversion" |||

When sex was clandestine, the tables of power could be dramatically turned if someone managed to pull back the veil of secrecy and make a formerly private affair into a public scandal. Few eighteenth-century New Englanders knew this better than Elizabeth Maloney, the wife of a Providence barber, who had too long endured in silence the humiliation of her husband's philandering. One day she was talking with several men on the first floor of their house, which was probably used as her husband's shop, when he arrived in company with a "Negro or Mulatto Girl." The two quickly disappeared into an upstairs bedchamber and soon could been seen enjoying a deep postcoital slumber. We know this because Mrs. Maloney not only went upstairs to check on them but paraded her guests upstairs as well. As witnesses recalled, she made a show of stripping back the bedclothes to reveal her husband and the girl lying naked together "like man and wife." Soon thereafter, the witnesses' testimony became part of the official state record when she filed for divorce. In numerous other cases, illicit affairs came to light in divorce cases in which one humiliated spouse or the other sought to restore their honor publicly. In 1742, Jethro Boston, a black slave in Massachusetts, divorced his wife when she admitted that the father of her suspiciously pale child was a white soldier named William Kelley.[28] In each of these instances, control of knowledge about illicit sex was about honor and about power.

In 1768, when a gentleman in a Connecticut tavern forced a prospective missionary to admit that he would not allow his daughter to marry an Indian, it was easy enough to announce a sweeping conclusion: "I am also well acquainted with human nature, as to know the irreconcilable aversion, that white people must ever have to black."[29] Aversion to what, one wonders. To black bodies? Or to black equality? Sex outside marriage was by definition illicit and therefore generally clandestine. The definition of rape and the prosecution of coerced sex provide one window into these power dynamics. The way in which rape was defined in law and popular culture, as well as patterns of prosecution, changed during the eighteenth century. Over the course of the century, whether an incident would be legally classified as rape, whether it would be prosecuted, how the defendant would be charged, and what decisions judges and juries would come to all relied heavily on not just what had been done but also on who had done it to whom. As a broad fraternity of local white men found themselves able to defend themselves against charges of sexual misbehavior and even violent assaults, women were not the only ones to suffer. Increasingly, black and Indian men, along with other outsiders such as transients and non-English immigrants, were conspicuously excluded from this form of sexual citizenship. And, always, the line between public and private knowledge was crucial (fig. 11).

FIGURE 11. This early political cartoon shows how public exposure could dramatically change the meaning of sexual interactions. It attacks "Indian-lovers" Benjamin Franklin (*center*) and Quaker leader Israel Pemberton (*right*) for their opposition to the anti-Indian violence of the Paxton Boys in Pennsylvania in 1764. Pemberton is shown embracing an Indian woman and failing to notice as she steals his watch. Pemberton is thus dishonored by his (alleged) inability to control his "lustful passions." Detail of James Claypole, *Franklin and the Quakers*, Philadelphia, 1764. Etching. Courtesy of the Library Company of Philadelphia.

Men often flirted with the line between private knowledge and public scandal. In diaries, letters, and tavern talk, men often told about their sexual desires and illicit affairs in order to affirm their sense of masculinity and to impress one another. One example appears in a diary once owned by James Wilson, a preeminent Philadelphia politician and legal thinker whose public lectures extolled the "beautiful and striking" principle that husband and wife were legally united in marriage and that the law granted broad discretion to the husband as the legal representative of his wife. The diary, apparently later used by an employee, carried a running chronicle of sexual adventures: under the date of 15 February, the diarist wrote: "Lay too all night with a black wench—in the Inn—Foul in Odor but in the *breech* much the same as the white. Her parts were small. She saying that she never before enjoyed a man. She shrieked. . . . She caused me much fright, asking me where I dwelleth so that in case of increase [pregnancy] from contact she could make known to the fact. I said I lived in the Carolinas—and fled." Correspondence between men, as well, often included sexual banter. Traveling gentlemen often began their letters to male friends with descriptions of local women, their attractions, and impressions of their sexual pliability. Men liked to brag to their peers about their sexual conquests—including the special pleasure of cuckolding other men—but this kind of banter could get out of hand. Settler Thomas Cross bragged to fellow drinkers in a Newport tavern that he had had sex with Thomas Ninigret's mulatto wife at least a hundred times. Soon thereafter a report of this claim formed part of the Narragansett sachem's divorce case.[30]

Even within the same household, men and women could have very different attitudes toward rumors of illicit sexual activity. The household of James Bowdoin, sometime governor of Massachusetts, was shaken in 1763 by a startling revelation: "My Man Cesar has been engaged in an amour with some of the white ladies of the Town." The amused tone of this letter suggests that he viewed the matter with cosmopolitan indulgence, suggesting perhaps a fraternal identification across lines of color and station. But his wife's reaction was very different. She was upset and possibly afraid. Indeed, Bowdoin explained to his correspondent, his wife refused to let Cesar back into their house. To resolve the crisis, Bowdoin arranged to sell Cesar in the West Indies. Although the gentleman may have identified with his servant's sexual adventuring, the lines of power were clear. Cesar paid dearly for his indiscretions—banished from his home and condemned to slavery in a place where he could not be expected to live more than a few years.[31]

By the mid-eighteenth century, about the worst consequences most New England white men were likely to face as a result of any illicit sexual activity were the threat of divorce or a claim for child support. This is because government officials, legal authorities, and juries had dramatically reshaped the much more invasive and egalitarian policies of the seventeenth-century Puritans. In the seventeenth century, Puritan New England had been unique in the English-speaking world by making much sexual behavior "public" and punishing perpetrators responsible with remarkable even-handedness. Whatever the context, illicit sex disrupted the public order and violated God's will. Adultery, although selectively defined as sex between a man and a married woman, was a capital offense because it violated the sexual possession of husbands and threatened the marital union. Bastardy and fornication had been crimes for men as well as women. And rape was relatively easy to prosecute. But by the early eighteenth century, public officials were treating most sexual crimes, including adultery, as private concerns. Around 1720, New England authorities stopped prosecuting white men for fornication and rarely held them liable for the support of bastards. At the same time, these white men could—if they wanted to—usually avoid marrying women they had seduced.[32] Rape prosecutions increasingly focused on the public reputations of the individual men and women involved.

It was no accident that the only recorded rape charge by a black woman against a white man to reach the New England courts happened toward the end of the Puritan legal regime. In Plymouth, Massachusetts, in April 1717, Justice Samuel Sewall was sitting when an "Ethiopian woman," supported by her English mistress, came forward to press rape charges against an English settler. When first accused, the settler had proclaimed his innocence on his honor—saying that "if he were guilty he wished he might never get alive to Plymouth." Honor, in such cases, represented not merely a claim about an individual's more or less righteous behavior but also, and more important, a claim to the authority to control the publicly accepted version of events. Despite his notorious debauchery and public drunkenness, this defendant clearly outranked his accuser, but nearly everyone was surprised by the end of this story. Inside the courtroom in Plymouth, those gathered for the trial were amazed to receive the news that, on his way to court, the man had fallen from his horse and died.[33] Few other women had their sexual honor vindicated by acts of God.

By the 1720s, white men with ties to New England communities became virtually immune to charges of rape. This is not to say that evidence of guilt could always be ignored. In 1756 Amos Lewis violently assaulted a white woman, stripping off the lower parts of her clothing, "picking the Hair out from off her Private parts," and attempting to "have the Carnal knowledge of the body . . . against her inclinations." He might have gotten away with it if he had not committed the crime in the middle of a crowded tavern. Nonetheless, high rank and local connections protected white defendants on their journey through the legal system. In contrast to laborers and servant, artisans and farmers were less likely to be accused, indicted, convicted, and punished harshly. In Amos Lewis's case, his standing as a gentleman and a merchant probably gained him the judicial leniency he enjoyed: prosecutors brought charges into the lowest possible court—the local court of General Sessions of the Peace—and the presiding justices let him off with a fine.[34]

As the prosecution of all sexual crimes became more selective, the very definition of rape changed significantly. Seventeenth-century officials prosecuted all sorts of sexual coercion and even occasionally punished assaults between men. By the mid-eighteenth century, New England prosecutors, judges, and juries substantially narrowed the kinds of assaults that could be effectively prosecuted as rape. Partly this was a response to English legal writings, which made sexual assaults more difficult to prove. Legal experts, for instance, increasingly agreed that "penetration" was necessary for an assault to be classified as rape, which made the crime even more difficult to establish. And all women found that their testimony was increasingly suspect as colonists adopted the advice of English legal experts. Typical was Sir Matthew Hale's warning that rape was "an accusation easily to be made and hard to be proved, and harder to be defended by the party accused, tho never so innocent." He and other popular jurists suggested assessing a woman's veracity by indirect tests of her character and reputation, by signs of whether of violence took place, or by determining whether the crime was in a remote location where a woman's cries for help would not have been heard. William Blackstone, in his *Commentaries on the Laws of England* (1769), dwelled on the presumed problem of "malicious accusation" and went on to observe, "The civil law seems to suppose a prostitute or common harlot incapable of any injury of this kind: not allowing any punishment for violating the chastity of her, who hath indeed no chastity at all, or at least no regard for it."[35]

Implicitly, rape was being redefined as a violent violation of a woman's emotional innocence rather than of her physical body. This narrowed sense of what rape meant placed much heavier weight on the social identities of the perpetrators and their victims. On the one hand, men with prestige and authority, for instance, could often avoid overt violence by using other forms of coercion against women such as servants, daughters, and even women they were courting. On the other hand, men of low rank assaulting women of higher status were most likely to resort to brute force. For victims of sexual assault, the ability to press charges—to obtain public redress and assert their honor—also depended largely on their status. Although it was not a firm rule, married women generally found it easier to secure convictions than single, young women did. At the same time, the violent rapes that were easiest to prosecute under the new legal standard tended to involve men of lower standing than their victims. Black men and women were, naturally, the lowest in social standing and consequently the most likely to be prosecuted for rape, on the one hand, and to suffer sexual assaults, on the other. The few white men successfully prosecuted for rape and attempted rape tended to be not only men of humble status but also "strangers" in the land—transients and foreigners from

France, Britain, and Ireland. The only other white man to be convicted of rape in eighteenth-century Rhode Island was a transient: he was hanged. Across southern New England, the crucial variable for white men by the mid-eighteenth century was not social status but simply membership in a local community.[36]

Consider a scenario in which a master sexually assaulted a servant. Generally by the mid-eighteenth century, the master would be able to keep such matters private. In one case of braggadocio getting out of hand, a married man told a friend that he had sex with a woman other than his wife every week of the year and that "he would not hier no maid except they would have do with him." His wife used this evidence of adultery in her suit for divorce, but the servant women he seduced or assaulted had no legal recourse. Nor did other women in similar circumstances. Local men of standing were sometimes able to quash unseemly rumors. In the farming community of Little Compton, Elizabeth Palmer and her daughter spread the rumor that the local innkeeper John Briggs "had offered to be naught with his Negrow woman in attempting to have Carnell Knowledge of her body." When the case went to court, it was not because charges had been filed against him. Rather, he was prosecuting them for defamation. In court, the women were forced to sign a public retraction.[37]

Most conspicuously excluded from the evolving fraternity of white men were local black men. A notice published in the *Boston News-Letter* in 1718 set an ugly precedent, categorically warning "all Negroes meddling with any White Woman." The account was of brutal vigilantism: "A Negro Man met abroad an English woman, which he accosted to lye with, stooping down, fearing none behind him, a Man observing his Design, took out his Knife, before the Negro was aware, cut off all his unruly parts Smack and Smooth, the Negro Jumpt up roaring and run for his Life; the Black is now an Eunuch and like to recover of his wounds & doubtless cured from any more such Wicked Attempts." In legal prosecutions across British North America, black men were indeed particularly vulnerable to accusations of rape. By the end of the century, black, Indian, and mulatto men accounted for almost all the rape defendants, and they were convicted and executed with wide publicity. In some ways, this pattern reflected the association of low status with susceptibility to rape prosecutions, since blacks were largely slaves and laborers.[38] In other ways, black men's experience diverged from the dominant trend for white men.

All these issues were apparent in a particularly well documented rape in Rhode Island. One day in the fall of 1742, the widow Comfort Taylor boarded the ferry at

Bristol; the enslaved ferryman Cuff shoved off from shore, and they were alone. Not much water had passed under them before he grasped her neck and pressed his lips against her skin. He threatened to strangle her if she cried out, and he swore he would "fucke" her. Falling astride her, he thrust a menacing hand at her throat and ran the other one up under her clothes. The boat drifted aground on a sandy island. She screamed: "Murder murder for God Sake help If you Love a woman." Two men working on the shore, an Indian and an Englishman, heard her, raced across the water, and rescued her.[39]

Recovering from the assault, badly bruised, and walking with a limp, Comfort Taylor found that her struggles with male power were not over. Cuff's owner tried to head off the expense of legal action by offering Taylor both vengeance and restitution: he offered to punish Cuff in any way she wanted and even to pay her damages. At first she agreed, but the next day she changed her mind. She filed a criminal complaint against the "black beast," explaining that she needed the law to vindicate her reputation.[40] In insisting on a formal legal proceeding, the widow Taylor asserted her right to be heard in the public forum of the law, proclaiming her membership in the polity. She defied the authority of Cuff's master by refusing to allow him to resolve the dispute privately. A widow who managed her own affairs, she perhaps felt it was important to take advantage of the civil recourse available to her to demonstrate that she could neither be assaulted by a slave with impunity nor be subordinated to the patriarchal authority of his master.

For Rhode Island officials, the matter had little ambiguity. The officers of the king's law quickly indicted and convicted Cuff of attempted rape; Taylor filed a civil suit and won damages of two hundred pounds. In order to recover the money she petitioned the General Assembly not to execute or imprison Cuff but rather to sell him as property. Accordingly, Cuff was solemnly banished from the colony and sold.[41] Then, Rhode Island officials sought to make explicit that whatever complex personal, human, or other dynamics the case of Comfort and Cuff embodied, it pertained most significantly to the subordination of blacks to whites. In the aftermath of this case, the General Assembly passed a harsh act "for the more effectual punishment of negroes" who attempted "to commit rape on any white woman."[42] This law, which enshrined the enduring icon of the brutal black rapist and his innocent white victim, was as categorical as the regulation of illicit sex in eighteenth-century New England ever became.

Black men in eighteenth-century New England were doubly dishonored: they had neither the ability to protect their wives and daughters from sexual predators nor the right to form sexual alliances of any kind with white women. Yet the law was mostly an extreme codification of more subtle and broad-ranging changes in the social meanings of extramarital sex during this period. The crime of rape itself had been largely redefined to refer only to acts of sexual coercion marked by violence or committed by marginal men. This more selective prosecution of rape coincided with the general indifference of officials to most acts of consensual sex not sanctioned by marriage.

This type of double standard became only more entrenched toward the end of the century. After the Revolution, prosecution for rape, a capital crime at a time of increasing unease about the death penalty, diminished dramatically through the end of the century across southern New England. Even victims became more reluctant to accuse their assailants; as one hesitant Connecticut woman who had been raped explained her reluctance to testify against her assailant, "I was afrayd Least it would take away his Life." But these concerns did little to help black men accused of rape. In Connecticut, five men were convicted of rape between 1743 and 1791: the legislature commuted the sentences of the two whites; the three black men were hanged. As attorneys pleading to commute the death sentence imposed on one black man in Connecticut put it, "We cannot see however some may think and talk tht the Life of a Slave etc. may be treated other than the Life of another." But this plea for equal treatment fell on deaf ears.[43]

When a "negro man slave" was hanged in 1763 in New York for the attempted rape of a young white girl, the bloodthirsty crowd reportedly could not get enough gore. The *Newport Mercury* professed disgust while recounting lurid details: a mob overpowered officials and cut the hanged body down and dragged it through the streets until they were stopped by a gentleman. After that, the body was sent to be mutilated as a cadaver used by medical students studying anatomy—"The body has since been taken up, and likely to become Raw-Head and Bloody-Bones, by our Tribe of Dissectors." As the dissection presented as the ultimate punishment in William Hogarth's "Cruelty" engravings suggests, dismemberment was the ultimate horror to people in the Anglophone world. In New England's public culture as well, the image of the black rapist was disproportionately emphasized. Even though black men constituted only a very small percentage of the population and were not even a majority of those convicted of rape, the readers of New England were offered three times more narratives of rapes committed by blacks than by whites.[44]

This prurient, even pornographic, interest in the sexual, suffering bodies of black men was the flip side of the culture of sensibility that was redefining the crime of rape and its social meanings. Newspaper editors echoed the courts' new lenient attitude toward white men's indiscretions and the primacy of white women's reputations. In the 1760s, the *Newport Mercury* dismissed one rapist as "a foolish young Fellow" and approvingly noted the extralegal action of a mob in punishing another "young country man" by ducking, tarring and feathering, and riding him out of town on a rail. Humiliating and painful as this ritual may have been, it was a far cry from a legal prosecution for a capital crime. Although this may have served as a warning to others "from practicing vile artifices for the delusion and ruin of the virtuous and innocent," it was hardly as severe as the penalty prescribed by law. In 1791, the *Mercury* approvingly noted another "NEW SPECIES OF PUNISHMENT" in which a married woman agreed not to prosecute a man who had "very grossly insulted and abused" her on condition of his "publickly asking her pardon."[45] In these efforts, rape had become not an act of violence but an affair of honor: the symbolic resolution of the crime was the woman's public vindication and the man's shame. Conversely, the best protection against prosecution became a man's "honor"—his power to preserve his public reputation for chastity.

The legal and informal regulation of illicit sex in eighteenth-century New England reflected a changing social order that increasingly emphasized the private status of women and the fraternal bonds of male citizens.[46] As the public prosecution of sexual crimes became more selective, the law moved away from prosecuting acts to regulating identities. In general, the public and private regulation of illicit sex served most consistently to reinforce hierarchies of gender and race. The sexual comportment of women, whether white, Indian, or black, was usually of little public consequence and was generally left to the government of fathers and husbands. For women who suffered sexual coercion, obtaining public recourse became difficult unless the assault was so violent and disturbing that it could not be kept private. Popular culture polarized female roles, exalting "good" women as exemplars of the virtues of the home and, in an expanding genre of misogynist humor, denigrating "bad" women as slatternly and debauched.

White men were allowed great sexual license; and except in egregious circumstances, their acts were rarely exposed to either public scrutiny or legal prosecution. Among white men, distinctions of status were increasingly less important than the simple fact of their whiteness. These distinctions shared a focus on white purity and black promiscuity, once again subtly transmuting dynamics of class into racial terms that allowed white Americans to imagine themselves as equal (to one another) yet superior (to people of color). Among men, social status assumed a lesser role, particularly among white men, as distinctions among them were elided into a kind of sexual fraternity. These changes in sexual honor allowed white men to enjoy wide sexual latitude with impunity. The "sexual system" of eighteenth-century New England functioned not so much to prevent illicit sex as to regulate its social consequences.

These overlapping double standards of sex and race powerfully embodied membership in the colonial body politic. Nowhere was this more clear than in 1762, when a minister from rural New York attempted to rally support for a local white man who had been indicted for having allegedly "abused a Mulatto Wench." As in so many cases, the minister cast the accusation in terms of the reputations of the man and woman involved. The minister dismissed the charge as a "malicious Indictment" and disparaged the accuser as a "most infamous ~~whore~~ Creature." However unappealing the woman's character and behavior may have seemed, the minister showed little interest in the facts of the case. Instead, he was more concerned with the dynamics of power at stake. He emphasized that the accusation threatened not just the solidarity of men of standing but the entire edifice of racial hierarchy that for many settlers defined the American way. Nowhere was the power of illicit sex to threaten, or to confirm, social hierarchies in the northern colonies expressed more explicitly. "If Negro's are protected in their insolence . . . but an old Country Man indicted for every little Crime, twill be time for us to leave this Country."[47]

||| Elective Affinities |||

Passing along the post road near the Narragansett enclave in 1761, the Reverend Ezra Stiles had sex on his mind. Spotting John Paul, a middle-aged Narragansett man he had spoken with before, Stiles asked him about lurid stories he had heard about premarital promiscuity among local Indians. He was puzzled, he said, because he had also heard that Indians abhorred bastards. Didn't the two, as it were, go hand in hand? Paul assured him that it was true that young Indians in times past felt no shame about premarital sexual dalliance; young women would even "talk over before Fathers & mothers their Amours, & tell who had to do with them at such a Time & who at another." Yet it was also true that the Indians "abhorred Bastards & their mothers, & he believed would put to death both [if] they were catched, before the English came." Paul pointed out a place called "Bastard Rocks" where so many infants had been killed that their bones littered the ground. However, Paul emphasized, the English presence had changed this practice: "Now for a long Time the Squaws being able to fly to the English & sheltered have very much dropt both these Customs & especially the last, so that they never kill any Bastards, or if they do, it is done with greatest Secrecy." Traditional Indian marriages had also fallen out of favor. Nowadays, he observed, we "mostly disuse this Ceremony, and are either married according to Eng. Custom or take one another without any Ceremony." Other evidence complicates this simple narrative. Early in the century, for instance, colonial officials prosecuted a young Narragansett woman in South Kingstown for infanticide—and in these proceedings an elderly Indian herb doctor testified that a local settler had threatened to prosecute her if she continued to purvey abortifacients.[48] Nonetheless, Paul's emphasis on the ability of Indian women to take selective advantage of differences between English and native customs is suggestive. Changes in sexual customs represented not just distinctions between settlers and Indians but also struggles over power within native communities.

By the 1760s, open conflicts emerged in many enclaves in southern New England over the legitimacy of Indian women's marriages to men some considered outsiders, particularly black men. In part, these conflicts were responses to fears of English encroachment, land shortages in enclaves, and anxieties about cultural changes. Tribes such as the Narragansetts had long held fluid notions of membership. After King Philip's War in the late seventeenth century, residents of many local villages came together to form the Narragansett tribe—including, for instance, members of the extended Harry family who abandoned Block Island around 1720, some coming directly to the enclave and others, such as Handsome Hannah, working in Newport first. Despite conflicts over Catherine Harry's marriage to Sachem Charles Ninigret, there was no question that members of the family belonged in the enclave. Nonetheless, by 1760, records of a distinction between tribe members and "strangers" began to emerge in enclaves across New England. Some of the earliest conflicts developed in Massachusetts enclaves organized on the model of seventeenth-century praying towns, in which land was divided among a specific roster of "proprietors" who passed their rights on to their children. By the 1750s, many Indians in the Natick enclave were not proprietors and thus had little claim to the enclave's increasingly private resources. In 1761, many Mashpee residents sought more control over tribal membership. They successfully petitioned the provincial government that "we may be allowed to vote on and receive any other Indians or mullattoes to share with us in our privileges or properties."[49]

In the Narragansett enclave, concerns about "strange" Indians were first voiced in the years when Sachem Thomas Ninigret's massive sales of land were worrying many tribe members. In this context, the allocation of land rights among tribe members—whether communal or individual—aroused bitter fears. Around 1762, the Narragansetts took a census of tribe members to document their need for a schoolmaster; they included some six hundred people "belonging to Ninegret's Tribe" but pointedly excluded an undefined number of "other Indians." In addition, the partisan divisions that wracked many enclaves in the 1760s further heightened consciousness about tribe membership. The strategies of staging popular votes and supporting petitions to colonial authorities with long lists of signatures put a premium on mobilizing large numbers of supporters. Partisans on both sides accused each other of packing their ranks with strangers who didn't really belong to the tribe. In 1765, an English schoolmaster reported that among those living in the Narragansett enclave were "sundry families of Indians which properly Belongs to other tribes" as well as "a considerable Number of mixtures as melattoes and mustess . . . which the [tribal council] Disowns."[50]

In many of these disputes, concern focused pointedly on the specific pattern of Indian women marrying black men. Although the cosmopolitan minister Samson Occom labored in the early 1770s to encourage Indians across New England to recognize their common interests, he also did his best to exclude outsiders. His views were influenced by his experience in Mohegan during the 1760s trying to wrest control of tribal resources for the tribe's last sachem, who died in 1769. Occom was broadly concerned about non-Indians, including whites, gaining control of tribal resources, but he focused special attention on black men. In 1773, Occom spearheaded a Mohegan drive to expel any Indian women who married outsiders and to exclude the children of Negroes from inheritance rights in tribal property. Strikingly, the Mohegans divided over the issue. Supporters of the late sachem resisted Occom's exclusive vision of Indian identity. Instead, they pushed through rules that less drastically restricted the ability of any "foreign" people—Indian as well as Negro—to join the tribal community.[51] As in other similar conflicts, one enduring result was the development of new legalistic definitions of tribal citizenship.

Black men were targets of concern not only because Indians were adopting English prejudices but also because they were the group most likely to seek—and gain—entrance into tribal communities. By the 1760s, an increasing number of blacks were becoming free and were seeking to begin new, free lives. Often they faced poor opportunities among the English and so looked to Indian enclaves as alternative communities. And because of the economic dynamics of the international slave trade, there were still substantially more black men than women in New England. Over time, this imbalance was beginning to diminish, but censuses for Massachusetts, Rhode Island, and Connecticut around 1770 each identify about half again more black men than women. At the same time, so many Indian men had died fighting colonial wars, especially the Seven Years' War, which ended in 1763, that in most enclaves Indian women far outnumbered surviving men. Ezra Stiles, for instance, tallied large numbers of widows and entire Indian villages without men in the early 1760s. The Rhode Island census of 1774 listed half again more Indian women over sixteen than men.[52]

The marriage of Indian women to black men and other outsiders had cultural implications that were provocatively suggested by the family traditions of the nineteenth-century autobiographer William Brown. According to his 1881 memoir, Brown's grandmother and her sister both married men from outside the Narragansett community around 1760. One of the sisters married a white man. The other sister, Brown's grandmother, married a Negro man—and as a consequence faced disinheritance from her father. Brown reported that Cloe Prophet purchased her Negro husband "from the white people." She did this, he explained, "in order to change her mode of living." Brown sympathized with her preference for "civilized to savage life." "It was customary for the woman to do all the drudgery and hard work in-doors and out. The Indian men thought it a disgrace for them to work; they thought they did their part by hunting and procuring game. The Indian women observing the colored men working for their wives, and living after the manner of white people, in comfortable houses, felt anxious to change their position in life; not being able to carry out their designs in any other way, resorted to making purchases." Although this account was clearly shaped by Brown's lifelong residence in the city of Providence, his faith in the capitalist virtue of industry, and his sense of himself as a "man of color," the dynamics he identifies were undoubtedly important to the inhabitants of eighteenth-century Indian communities. Certainly he was right that decisions by Indian women to marry black men sometimes "created a very bitter feeling among the Indian men against the blacks."[53]

In the 1760s, Indian men and women across New England were grappling with new, English ways—building houses, fencing in farmland, practicing husbandry and housewifery. Many Indian women learned English ways while working in colonial households as domestic servants, often alongside enslaved black men. And black men, including former slaves, were well established in these roles and values.

Ironically, in fact, black men were more likely to be comfortable with English-style economic and domestic roles than they were to have access to the resources they needed to fulfill them. For many free black men, emulating English ways became possible only when Indian woman offered them access to land.

Sarah Muckamugg was a young Indian woman living in Providence early in the century, probably working as a domestic servant. Over time she developed an intimate relationship with Aaron, a black slave owned by her master's son. In 1728, their union was sealed by some kind of ceremony at the home of a local settler, which members of her master's family witnessed. But her master's children later testified that they were not actually married, and the town clerk found no record of any certificate. Indeed, although they had several children, Aaron did not always act the part of a colonial father. Sarah took it upon herself, for instance, to bind out her first three sons, and her master's amazed children recalled that "Aaron had no concern about this." In 1740, the birth of their fourth child, Joseph, apparently prompted Sarah to clarify her relationship with Aaron. But when she pressed him to marry her formally, he broke off his relationship with her. She left town, distraught, heading for the enclave at Grafton, where her parents were living. Along the way she told a farmer's wife that her former husband "had got another Squaw that he Loved better" and had told her that "he never would Live with [her] any more neither would he help maintain the Children." When Sarah reached the Hassinimisco enclave, she claimed the proprietorship due to her through her mother. By the time she died in 1751, she had married another African, this time a free man, and they had had a daughter. We know this story because twenty years later her son Joseph left Providence and came to the enclave to claim land so he could establish himself as farmer, and a conflict emerged over his right to claim a portion of his mother's proprietorship.[54]

If some Indian men felt that black men threatened their accustomed ways, they may well have exaggerated the extent of the danger. Some of the most precise records of intermarriages in any New England enclave were kept by the missionary Gideon Hawley, who lived on the Mashpee reservation on Cape Cod. He was struck by the fluidity of the community and, over time, noted immigrants from other native enclaves at Narragansett, Natick, Middlebury, and New Bedford. When he took a census of the enclave's inhabitants in 1776, however, he carefully distinguished between the enclave's 313 Indians and its 14 Negroes. He explained that the high proportion of widowed natives—there were 33 widows and only 64 married couples—led some of them to marry men of African descent. Among the married couples, as many as 12 consisted of Negro men and Indian women. Hawley also noted several white men living in the enclave. As he later explained, during and after the Revolution several Hessian men who had served as mercenaries fighting for the British ended their strange journey from the Palatine by settling down in Mashpee. Apparently, the Mashpee perceived these Hessians not as white but as non-English.[55] Excluded from citizenship in the new Republic, the peoples of Mashpee—as did blacks and Indians in enclaves throughout New England and New York—came together in recognition of their common dispossession.

Hawley's census also provides some surprising clues about the cultural affiliations of the black men who were marrying Indian women. Since he was concerned about changing cultural and economic ways, Hawley carefully noted whether each household lived in a house or a wigwam. The total number of houses, thirty-nine, was almost the same as the number of wigwams, thirty-seven, and married couples were much more likely to live in houses. Yet Indian husbands were even more likely to live in houses than Negro husbands. Indeed, most Negro husbands lived in wigwams. This is the reverse of what we might expect if black men were being used by Indian women to push the enclave toward more English ways. Similarly, in 1807 an English sailor who had married a Mashpee woman lived in a wigwam.[56] It may be that male "outsiders" felt—and responded to—pressure to demonstrate fidelity to native ways, even as Indian men were often embracing English ways.

To many English observers in the late eighteenth century, evidence of Indian intermarriage seemed to reinforce their sense that Indians were doomed to disappearance. Increasingly, English settlers used the concept of "pure blood" to distinguish between authentic Indians and debased "mongrels." As early as 1788, Hawley reported that few children at Mashpee—or in other local enclaves for that matter—were "now born without a tincture of foreign blood." By the turn of the century, he was describing Mashpee as "an asylum for Indians and their mixt posterity." Other observers used evidence of the supposed disappearance of "pure Indians" to suggest that Indians as a whole were disappearing from the New England landscape. One Nantucket man, Abraham Quarry, profited from his reputation as the island's "last Indian" and in the early nineteenth century emerged as something of a local celebrity. But for Indians as a group, the implications of the notion that they were "disappearing" would occupy local and national politics for much of the next half century.[57]

In part, Indians seemed to be "disappearing" because they were being written out of official existence. In the 1770s and 1780s, local officials in many jurisdictions continued to label individuals by race, but they often had trouble identifying a person consistently. Sometimes a person was labeled "black" in one document, "Negro" in another, and "Indian" in a third. In certain contexts—such as lawsuits in which people claimed they had been wrongfully enslaved—certain patterns are clear: people trying to claim freedom represented themselves as Indian, whereas those trying to enslave them represented these same individuals as black. But in most cases, the only clear pattern is confusion and apparent lack of concern. Across Rhode Island, local officials seemed increasingly inclined simply to lump all Indians, "mulattos," mustees, and Negroes together under the broad category "people of color."[58] This is particularly clear in the shift from colony and state censuses in the Revolutionary period to the early federal censuses in 1790 and afterwards. The colonial censuses carefully distinguished white, blacks, and Indians, and Rhode Island's 1782 census even added a fourth category for "mulattoes." In contrast, the first federal census of 1790 divided the white population into a variety of age and sex categories but showed no such concern for people of color. Indians who did not pay town taxes—such as those living in most enclaves, including the Narragansetts—were not listed at all. Slaves of all ages and sexes were listed in a single column. And everyone else was relegated to a single column labeled "all other free people." If Indians were not disappearing, there was no way to tell from this kind of enumeration.[59]

Some Indians immediately recognized the political danger implied by attacks on their racial purity, and some even challenged the methods of Anglo-American census takers. For instance, there was a public argument about Indian-Negro intermixture on Martha's Vineyard. In 1790, the Massachusetts Historical Society published a report claiming that Indian women on the island had begun marrying black men around 1765 and that the proportion of "pure bloods" among the five local Indian villages was, a generation earlier, "hardly more than a fifth." In response to this or a similar report, the Indian minister at Gay Head, the island's largest Indian village, compiled a census of his own. In contrast to other census takers, he used classifications that discriminated among Indians of mixed ancestry, distinguishing those who were part Negro, part white, and, in part, both white and black. His tallies minimized Negro intermixture and emphasized that most intermixture among tribe members was with whites. Some 27 inhabitants of Gay Head were part white, 19 part black (mostly children in two large families), 9 part white and black, and 122 "pure."[60]

Indians and Negroes of mixed descent were moving across the New England landscape, and their children did not simply adopt Anglo-American fantasies about who they were. Many individuals moved into and out of enclaves and manifested little anxiety about their hybrid identities. In 1782, when Mary Fowler, "alias Mary Cummock, an Indian woman," was examined by town officials in South Kingstown, she declared that she had been born in South Kingstown and had served out an indenture to Caleb Gardener, Esq. She said that "her mother's name was Sarah Cummock and thusly she belonged to Charlestown"; in addition, she had "heard people say that her mother was one of the tribe of the Indians in Charlestown." Both Mary and her mother married African men but remained conscious of their mixed heritage and Indian identity.[61] A century later, William Brown, who identified himself as a "man of color" on the title page of his autobiography, cultivated memories of both his enslaved African grandparents and his free Narragansett ancestors.

Nonetheless, after the Revolution the issue of Indian intermarriage with blacks remained heated in many enclaves. A group of Mashpee men in 1788 complained to the state legislature of being overrun by "Negroes & English, who, unhappily planted themselves here." They continued, "It is to be feared, that they and their Children, unless they are removed, will get away our Lands & all our Privileges in a short time." Subsequently, marriage became the only route by which non–tribe members could gain access to Indian land, and even full proprietary rights passed only to their children. Even former residents of the enclave returning after a long absence had to prove that they were "descendants of proprietors" to claim land. In 1789, Samson Occom made a similar attempt to exclude blacks from the Mohegan tribal registers. He argued that if a mulatto child were accepted into the tribe, not only "guinny Children, but European children and some other Children" would take root in the tribe. Around the turn of the century, many Indian men in Chappaquiddick and Christiantown on Martha's Vineyard were upset "oweing to their Females Marying Negroes whom they did not wish to have any right to their lands." Two went so far as to file lawsuits between 1805 and 1811 to prevent African American men from marrying Indian women.[62]

Like many tribes that addressed the issue of membership and intermarriage in the late eighteenth century, in 1790 the Narragansetts created a more rigid set of rules governing tribal citizenship, rules that announced a significant shift in the roles of men and women. Land and tribal membership were crucial issues at that time, for after decades of bitter factional strife that had sadly depleted the enclave's meager landholdings, a new political coalition was trying to establish regular procedures for allocating land to individuals. The new rules limited the right to vote for members of the governing tribal council to "every Male Person of Twenty-one Years, born of an *Indian* Woman, belonging to said Tribe, or begotten by an *Indian* man, belonging thereto, of any other than a Negro woman." This provision clearly singled out Negro women as inferior and limited the political power of their children, but it did not entirely bar the children of these women from being considered members of the "community." Indeed, it may have broadened entrance to the tribal community. Later the council noted, "It has been a former Custom by this tribe that when any of the tribe Married any other [woman] that Did not belong to sd Tribe to take their wife away unless the Council pleased to let them stay in the town." Now such wives could stay without question. And the children of white, Indian, and possibly mulatto women were full members of the tribe. In a way this suggests a continuing emphasis on "ethnic"—that is, cultural and social—identities rather than abstract "racial" identities. The new rules recognized the continuing importance of maternal lines of kinship: anyone born to an Indian woman could vote, but only some children of Indian men could do so. And yet the new rules also increased the importance of male lineages and explicitly excluded women from voting rights. Previously women and children had shared equal voices in collective decision making. Now women did not vote because they were not independent and because their husbands spoke for them. Models of Indian citizenship were becoming more English—and more patriarchal. In the decades to come, the question of marriage outside the tribe would continue to spark conflict—in large part because of the increasingly strenuous insistence of Anglo-American writers and politicians that one could be a real Indian only if one was of "pure blood."[63]

||| Love and Unity |||

During the heady days of the Revolutionary War, a few New Englanders challenged convention and publicly broached the sexual color line. In Warren, Massachusetts, a black man and a white woman approached a justice of the peace and asked to be married. When he refused, they "took Each other as husband and wife and . . . dwelt together Ever since." This small transgression would have passed unnoticed if the woman had not then attempted to join the local Baptist church. Many radical evangelical churches during these years had a reputation for blurring color lines, and this church gave the matter careful consideration. Although her cohabitation was clearly illegal and would normally have seemed immoral, members of the church were surprisingly sympathetic. They declared themselves convinced that the two would have married except that it was "not lawful for such to be married" and that she was otherwise a "meet subject" for membership. Nonetheless, they did not simply admit her into Christian fellowship. Instead, they referred the matter to other authorities, whose response is not recorded.[64]

Meanwhile, a similar choice confronted the Second Congregational Church in Newport in 1782. The Reverend Samuel Hopkins had become a prominent antislavery activist and braved considerable local opposition for his firm opposition to slavery and the slave trade. He also felt that his white parishioners were not happy about the black prayer groups he had been sponsoring. But Hopkins drew the line at intermarriage—a dramatic symbol of human equality. One of the church's few black communicants was Kingstown Pease, who had been living with a white woman. Pease had likely become free only a few years earlier at the death of his master, Simon Pease, one of the town's richest merchant and slave traders. By the time a census was taken in 1782, Pease was living in an independent household that included two white women and a black girl. Pease and the woman he was living with even attempted to get married, which in Rhode Island, unlike Massachusetts, was legally possible at the time—but not in practice. The church officially confronted Pease and soon thereafter voted to excommunicate him. His relationship, they declared, was "Contrary to the Distinctions that God Made."[65]

During and after the Revolution, when many blacks in the northern states were becoming free, the sexual color line remained a matter of public concern. If anything, legal and customary prohibitions against interracial sex became more consistent and urgent in the face of black freedom—anticipating, albeit in a much less drastic and violent way, the pattern in the post–Civil War South. A number of states considered the prospect of interracial sex and marriage as part of legislation intended to end slavery. In Pennsylvania, legislators had long considered free blacks a special sexual danger: in 1725–26 they decreed that free blacks convicted of marrying whites could be sold into slavery and their children into servitude to the age of thirty-one. The 1780 Gradual Emancipation Act likewise originally included a provision barring interracial marriage, though it was quietly dropped before the law was enacted. In New York in 1785, legislators considered a gradual manumission bill that would have disfranchised blacks and barred them from marrying whites. The senate rejected the intermarriage clause because it considered this a private matter. As one senator wrote to his wife, "In so important a connection they thought the free subjects of this State ought to be left to their free choice." Apparently marriage seemed to him a more urgent right of humankind than the franchise. In any case, the bill was eventually defeated.[66]

Meanwhile, in Massachusetts, almost all blacks in the state had already become free by 1786, when legislators passed an act on the "Solemnization of Marriage" that reaffirmed the colonial ban on whites marrying people of color. This time they extended the prohibition to include Indians as well as Negroes. In 1798, again long after most black people across the region had become free, Rhode Island passed a similar law prohibiting the marriage of "any white person with any Negro, Indian or mulatto." Around that time, a prominent judge and president of the Providence Abolition Society was named by a black woman in a claim for paternity support. The Rhode Island legislature was apparently less concerned about the cost of supporting such children out of public coffers than the threat this suit posed: it allowed poor black women to invade respectable white men's privacy and impugn their sexual honor. In 1800, the legislature voted to categorically deny black women the right to sue white men for paternity.[67] In yet another way, the sexual fraternity of white citizens was reaffirmed and the rights of blacks denigrated.

Despite these humiliations, many free black New Englanders recognized the link between sexual respectability and claims to citizenship. Many former slaves, as soon as they became free, sought out lawful sanction for their marriages. One ironic indication of this trend is the appearance of the first black divorce petitions in the 1790s. Around this time, Joseph Nightingale published a newspaper advertisement complaining that his wife had left him and that he would not be responsible for her bills—and he pointedly signed the notice by identifying himself as "a black man." By the 1790s, free black voluntary associations in many northern cities urged their members to marry according to lawful forms and publicly register their marriages and the births of their children. One enduring testament to the importance of family ties to newly free black men and women in towns such as Providence and Newport is the new gravestones that appeared in the segregated, black sections of common burial grounds. A surprising number of poor men scraped together the means to honor their family members with public markers. Kingstown Pease, for one, paid £1 4s cash in 1786 for a pair of gravestones for a relative named Stellar Pease. A couple of years later, Cato Thurston commissioned a handsome pair of stones for his wife, Violet. He paid the cost of £1 16s with credit he had accumulated over the previous year, furnishing five bushels of potatoes and sawing three-quarters of a cord of firewood.[68]

The response of the white public to these efforts could hardly have been encouraging. Often blacks appeared in the popular press as agents of sexual disorder. Lurid newspaper accounts, broadside confessions, and trial reports continued to exaggerate the image of violent black male sexual aggressors suggested by uneven judicial proceedings. And an image of black women as slatternly sexual threats to the virtue of white men was reinforced by a series of brother riots in towns such as Boston and Providence. At the same time, this popular fascination with black sexuality suggests not just disapproval but also a sometimes discomforting sense of attraction. The increasingly popular abolitionist narratives and images, for instance, focused attention on suffering black bodies that bordered on the pornographic. The sexual valence of William Blake's engravings of scantily clad young women tied at the wrists and hanged in a gallows seems readily apparent. More curious are representations of black men's bodies in the popular press that border on the erotic.[69]

Suggestively, a number of jokes in the popular press focused on black efforts, in the aftermath of slavery, to emulate white models of marriage. One "amusing anecdote" in the *Columbian Almanac* featured a black man courting a "wench" who was the servant of a local minister. Her master, embracing the role of surrogate father, objected to the match. As in so many stories about black people in the popular press, it is unclear whether these two were enslaved. What the joke does make clear is a measure of sympathy for this man's plight. He challenges the paternalistic minister by asserting his fraternal independence, although with slavish deference and in an uncouth dialect: "*Maser no wat the elebenth commandment be?*" The poor parson could not tell. "*Well*," the suitor explained, "De elebenth commandment is, BES WAY EVERYONE MINE HE OWN BUSINESS." Other anecdotes burlesqued free, urban, black couples—portraying both black men and women as lacking the emotional sensibility necessary to do anything more than mimic the romantic ideals celebrated in the popular press. In one joke, a termagant wife begs her long-suffering husband not to carry through with a threat to beat her into submission. Can we not live, as we used to do, she pleads, "in lub and unicorn"?[70] Her request could just as well be addressed to the white public, a plea for racial reconciliation in the aftermath of slavery. Perhaps that's why it seemed so absurd.

CHAPTER FIVE

Men of Arms

||| Hartford, 1776 |||

On the evening after the general election in May 1776, Hartford hosted a second gubernatorial contest. Fascinated, a British officer who had been living there as a prisoner of war reported that "the Negroes, according to annual custom, elected a governor for themselves." Afterwards, the victor "gave a supper and a ball to a number of his electors, who were very merry and danced till about three o'clock in the morning." For decades, such rituals had been celebrated in black communities from the Massachusetts seacoast to the Hudson River valley. Resonant with West African culture, these elections were also closely modeled after colonial elections with their alcohol-rich and sporting revelries. On this occasion, British war prisoners watched with special relish: the man chosen as the new Negro governor was John Anderson, the servant of their top-ranking officer, Philip Skene, lieutenant governor of Ticonderoga and Crown Point. The British officers were so pleased that on the following Friday evening they hosted an "entertainment" for the new Negro governor and his supporters. Patriot officials were less amused. The local Committee of Safety, smelling a Tory plot, launched an investigation that reveals how the outbreak of war in New England challenged basic assumptions about the meaning of citizenship.

When interviewed by the Committee of Safety, the imprisoned master of the new black governor insisted that he had no hand in swaying the election. Philip Skene had overheard "a few words that passed between a Mr. williams and his negro, which he supposed was mere sport." And he had given his man "a half-joe to keep the election"—but not any "money to make a feast for the negroes." For his part, the newly elected Governor Anderson stated that he had heard that the local blacks chose a governor annually and "had the curiosity of seeing an election." The possibility of his standing for the governorship was first mentioned by a local named Sharper, and, he insisted, no regulars had been involved. Anderson had earned money living in the vicinity of Ticonderoga by "going in a vessel on the lakes, where he had certain perquisites of his own," and had evidently retained some savings. Learning that cash would be the key to electoral success, he "informed the negroes that if they would elect him, he would treat them to the amount of $20." It ended up costing him $25. Anderson insisted on his political neutrality: he had "done it as a matter of sport, and intended no injury to the country."

The ousted incumbent, Cuff, told a more sinister story. He had given up his office to Anderson only under pressure from some of his "black friends" and "some of the regulars." When some of the local blacks "declared they would not have a tory for a governor," Cuff was forced to avoid an electoral contest and simply appoint Anderson. His resignation letter is certainly plaintive: "I, Governor Cuff of the Niegro's in the province of Connecticut, do Resign my Governmentship to John Anderson, Neigor Man to Governor Skene. And I hope that you will obeye him as you have Done me for this ten years past, when Colonel Willis's niegor Dayed I was the next. But being weak and unfit for that office do Resine."[1]

In the context of war—at a time when Committees of Safety across New England were hounding out suspected Tories—the meaning of black political life suddenly appeared in a different light, representing new dangers and new opportunities. Normally, "Negro elections" were considered harmless, if occasionally inconvenient. Employers docked the pay of black workers who lost time at elections, and slave owners grumbled about the cost of the festivities. In one oft-told story, Rhode Island politician William Potter, distressed by the cost of electioneering, told his slave, the local Negro governor, that one of them was going to have to get out of politics. As settlers such as Potter may have seen it, slaves were so far outside the political system that their elections seemed a kind of burlesque, a mimetic imitation of the "real" political process: they represented a dramatic reversal of roles, or a temporary adoption of forbidden ones, but not a challenge to the dominant civil structure. For slaves such as John Anderson—not particularly invested in local communities—these rituals may well have been simply carnivalesque festivities. But for many local slaves and free blacks, these elections may also have served to expand their sense of solidarity and to suggest new political possibilities.[2] In this election, there is evidence both of the social death of slaves and of their political life. On the one hand, Anderson was clearly assumed to represent the politics and status of his master, as though he had no autonomous political identity of his own. On the other hand, his action in assuming the governorship was seen as possibly subversive, which, by implication, made him a potential political actor in his own right.

Across New England, the Revolution challenged basic assumptions about the meaning of citizenship. The escalation of the imperial crisis into a movement for colonial independence required developing a persuasive new sense of national identity. The outbreak of fighting provoked internal divisions between Tories, Patriots, and the indifferent. And the waging of a lengthy war exposed long-suppressed conflicts about the status of blacks and Indians in the colonial body politic. Slaves, conquered Indians, and free people of color, who had long appeared safely outside the political order, were now recognized as potential enemies—or allies.

If the experience of war made anything clear, it was that English settlers, African slaves, and free blacks and Indians often held quite different understandings of the meanings of liberty, independence, and freedom. The military struggle offers opportunities to explore these ongoing negotiations of citizenship in a range of contexts—in the literary fantasies of wartime propagandists, in policy debates about military recruitment, and in the experiences of slaves and free people of color choosing sides and pursuing their own dreams of liberation.

||| Sons of Liberty |||

Around the time the Continental Congress finally agreed to declare national independence in July 1776, advertisements began to appear for a call to arms, a play by John Leacock optimistically entitled *The Fall of British Tyranny*. It encouraged Americans to "wish, talk, write, fight, and die—for Liberty."[3] One handbill emphasized the play's comic centerpiece, a "very black scene" between Lord Kidnapper and Major Cudjo. Kidnapper was a thinly disguised lampoon of Virginia's beleaguered royal governor, John Murray, Lord Dunmore, whose antics during the previous year needed little embellishment: he antagonized the colony's assembly so badly that he had to abandon the governor's palace and attempted to rule from a ship harbored in the Norfolk River. After that he attempted to instigate the Delaware Indians to attack the colony's western settlements; schemed to kidnap General George Washington's wife; and, in December 1775, issued a proclamation inviting his subjects' slaves to abandon their masters and join his army. The arrival of these black recruits on the governor's ship forms the comic centerpiece of the play. After interviewing Cudjo (whom he designates "Major" in order to symbolically outrank his former master, a colonel in the Virginia militia), Kidnapper publicly orders the black recruits to be incorporated "among the regulars and the other Whites on board." Then, in an aside, he directs that they be disarmed and guarded at night: "For who knows that they may cut our throats."[4] Such duplicity is obviously sinister. By why, in dramatizing British tyranny, did this Son of Liberty choose to focus on the image of a governor encouraging slaves to claim their freedom and proposing to treat black and white men as equals? And why, in another scene, did Leacock use an outlandish, supposedly historical Indian figure to epitomize the intrinsic American love of liberty?

During the imperial crisis of the 1760s, colonists often claimed that the British were attempting to reduce them to a state of "slavery." Colonial protestors also often compared themselves to Indians, represented themselves symbolically as Indians, and sometimes even dressed up as Indians. Today, historians debate the meanings of these associations. When colonial writers said "slavery," were they talking about it simply as a philosophical concept, or were they also thinking about black people, who were so widely enslaved in the colonies? As *The Fall of British Tyranny* makes clear, references to "slavery" and "liberty" were not only philosophical abstractions and rhetorical exaggerations; they were also densely packed with associations about idealized national characters, colonial fantasies of conquest, and enslaved Africans. Indeed, the significance of race and its complex relationship to notions of nationalism in the years before and during the Revolution has not been fully appreciated.[5] John Leacock's play, a chronicle of the military and political events of 1774 and 1775, was certainly partisan: he urged colonists to rise up in arms against the British. Yet the themes he drew on were quite common. The play—intended primarily to be read or, perhaps, to be acted out in private groups—was popular enough to warrant rapid republication in Boston and Providence. Considered alongside a range of Whig and Tory propaganda in contemporary newspapers, pamphlets, and other dramatizations, the play offers an opportunity to explore the themes of race and nationalism at the outbreak of the war. Indeed, the main theme of the play is that devotion to liberty and virtue is intrinsic to the Anglo-American character. In the play—as in other dramas, tracts, and newspaper accounts—this American love of liberty was contrasted with three counterparts: the degeneracy of contemporary England, the savage independence and doomed nobility of Indians, and the slavish subservience and brutish ignorance of colonial blacks.

At the start of the play, the Goddess of Liberty exhorts Americans to "Fight and be free! / Or be ye slaves—and give up liberty!" To explain this danger, the action opens in Britain, where the evil Lord Paramount (a caricature of the Scottish Lord Bute, Britain's erstwhile prime minister) explains his plans to enslave not only the colonies but also the mother country. Paramount claims that he will extend his domination even if it means annihilating "charters, magna chartas, bill of rights, acts of assembly, resolves of congresses, trials by juries (and acts of parliament, too)." If "spirited measures," "deception," and the "accumulation of power" are not sufficient to hoodwink the "ignorant multitude," he will use military force to achieve their "absolute submission." Indeed, during the imperial crisis newspapers in both London and North America revived fears of a Scottish conspiracy to usurp power that dated from the 1745 rising of Bonnie Prince Charlie and the 1688 revolution that displaced the Stuart dynasty. In the play, the Bute's sinister plans for the American colonies are part of this tyrannical vision. Invoking for himself the image of the Egyptians enslaving the Israelites, he declares of the colonies: "I'll . . . convince them the second Pharoah is at least equal to the first."[6]

This narrative helped explain how Americans had become the unique inheritors of the ancient English birthright of freedom. In patriotic British propaganda, symbolic resistance to "slavery" was at least as old as the familiar anthem "Rule Britannia" (1741). The refrain, "Britons rule the waves / Britons never shall be slaves," composed while Britain was reeling from a series of military defeats on land, emphasizes the glory of domination over other nations. During the imperial crisis, Whig propagandists turned this image against the mother country, comparing the status of colonists in the imperial system to that of slaves. Leacock's play contrasts America to Europe: "Blest Continent, while groaning nations round / Bend to the servile yoke, ignobly bound / May yet be free." Lord Wisdom (the earl of Chatham) acknowledges the colonies' unique devotion to liberty—"Who can blame a galley-slave for making his escape?"—warning that the war will be the downfall of the British, because subduing America will prove impossible. "Liberty flourishes in the wilds of America." Such rhetoric implied that America's pristine character followed from its early colonial history: the proud ancestors of American Whigs escaped just in time and were thus untainted by the subsequent degeneration of Britain.[7]

The notion that military struggle was a matter of character, rather than munitions and manpower, resonated with much other propaganda. In the play, a British colonel warns ministerial warmongers that "when a brave people, like the Americans," who have inherited liberty "as a birth-right" face attempts to reduce them to slavery, they will defend themselves to the bitter end. British soldiers may be motivated by national glory, he admits, but "what is national glory . . . when put in competition with liberty and property"? Of course, even the most honorable motives were not always enough to secure military victory. Toward the end of the play, an indomitable Whig prisoner in a British dungeon after the battle of Ticonderoga exhorts:

> Oh! my lost friends! 'tis liberty, not breath,
> Gives the brave life. Shun slav'ry more than death.
> He who spurns fear, and dares disdain to be,
> Mocks chains and wrongs—and is forever free;
> While the base coward, never safe, tho' low,
> Creeps but to suff'rings, and lives on for woe![8]

If the love of liberty cannot always vanquish tyranny on the battlefield, it can always succeed on the field of honor: independence, here, was redefined not as autonomy but simply as resistance.

Slavery in such political propaganda was closely associated with enslaved blacks. In the play, a Bostonian Whig insists that Britain will not "make slaves of American freemen"—"We are not Africans yet." In fact, Whig anxiety about enslavement in the 1760s had been closely linked to the special danger of black-white equality. When the British occupation of Boston began in 1768, the local Sons of Liberty dramatized military misrule with images of racial inversion. One early report in Samuel Adams' "Chronicle of the Times," reprinted in colonial newspapers up and down the Atlantic seaboard, complained that when British soldiers punished liberty boys for various misdemeanors, they had them publicly whipped not by white soldiers but by the drummers, who were often black. Imperial military officials could not have found a better way of humiliating settlers: "To behold Britons scourg'd by Negro drummers, was a new and very disagreeable spectacle." Shortly thereafter, Samuel Adams and his fellow propagandists reported on official proceedings by the Boston selectmen against a British officer accused of inciting a bloody slave revolt. The officer reportedly promised one slave, "Now the soldiers are come, the Negroews shall be free, and the Liberty Boys slaves."[9]

The war of words and images that developed around the so-called Boston Massacre also played on these national and racial images. On 12 March 1770, several members of a Whig mob in Boston taunted British soldiers until their targets panicked and opened fire, killing several. The Sons of Liberty, in their accounts of the event, lionized the virtue and innocence of the victims. In doing so, they downplayed the fact that one of the five men killed, Crispus Attucks, was a man of mixed Indian and African ancestry—and, quite likely, a runaway slave. Paul Revere's engraving of the "Bloody Massacre," like the painting it copied, does not distinguish Crispus Attucks by skin shading or other distinctive attributes: as a hero of Whig resistance to British slavery he was imagined as both free and white. In contrast, attorney John Adams, who was assigned the duty of defending the British soldiers at their trial, attempted to mitigate their crime by dismissing the alleged victims as unmanly, nonwhite, non-English, and otherwise "obscure and inconsiderable." The principal provocateur was Attucks, "whose very looks was enough to terrify any person." The other rioters, he told the jury, were "a motley rabble of saucy boys, negroes and molottoes, Irish teagues and outlandish jack tarrs."[10]

In this climate of shared racism, propaganda such as *The Fall of British Tyranny* could do little to convince British Tories, who prided themselves on inhabiting the most free nation in the history of the world. They were quick to turn the language of slavery against the colonists. The London wit Samuel Johnson, always an opponent of "universal" claims to freedom, dismissed Whig complaints about tyranny in the colonies: "Why do we hear the loudest yelps for liberty from the drivers of negroes?" Indeed, a highly publicized legal decision in London had freed a Massachusetts man named Somerset in 1771, arguing that he was free while on English soil and could not be forced to return to slavery. Lord Mansfield's decision in this case helped British and American Tories claim the moral high ground on the issue of slavery. One of many versions of "Yankee Doodle" that mocked the colonists for their crude provincialism and inflated pride was subtitled "The Negroes Farewell to America." The song depicts a black man abandoning his miserable life as an American slave and fantasizing about living in Britain, "where Liberty reigns / Where Negro no beaten or loaded with chains" (fig. 12). Colonial Tories were not slow to take up this line of attack. In Concord, Massachusetts, a Tory gadfly, Daniel Bliss, was run out of town by the local Committee of Safety after he erected a grave marker for an African-born man named John Jack in 1773. Bliss composed an epi-

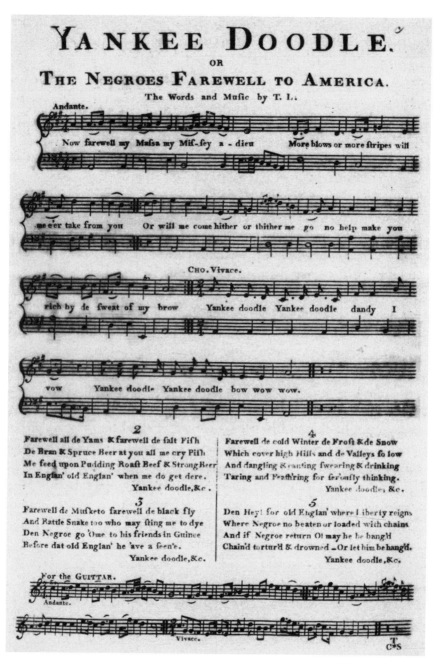

FIGURE 12. "Yankee Doodle, or, The Negroes Farewell to America" (London, ca. 1778) mocks both the rebels and black Loyalists. Courtesy of the Boston Public Library.

taph (quickly reported in London newspapers) that observed that although Jack died in a self-proclaimed "land of liberty," he had "lived as a slave."[11]

Of course, Bliss had not been much help to Jack before his rhetorically convenient death—any more than Leacock's play showed much sympathy for the character of Major Cuffe. For partisans on both sides, chattel slavery and blackness were crucial negative images in their definitions of liberty and English identity. At one level, the Whig image of imperial tyranny as slave mastery implied recognition of the greed, treachery, and violence practiced by colonial slave owners themselves. Yet these texts betray little sympathy for enslaved African Americans and even suggest that the colonists' worst nightmare was the prospect of being degraded to equality with blacks. Indeed, it may well be that the notion of absolute subjection, exemplified in chattel slavery, provided settlers with a way of imagining absolute freedom—a notion previously imagined only in certain strains of theology as a spiritual condition. In politics freedom was always imagined as limited, circumscribed, situational, and conditional.

The Americanness of such "give me liberty or give me death" bravado was often epitomized in colonial texts by the figure of the noble savage. In *The Fall of British Tyranny*, the figure of the noble Indian is played by the mythic King Tammany. Conforming to the standard trope, this heroic Indian is represented as indomitable and, as a consequence of this virtue, vanishing. This image had several relevant antecedents. A longstanding tradition, still alive in political cartoons of the Revolutionary period, represented America as a generic Indian woman, in contrast to the more recently developed character Britannia, who was rendered as a matronly white woman. In late colonial newspapers, tracts, and dramas, actual Indians were most often represented as savage, cruel, violent, and, during the war, allied with the British. In Whig propaganda, however, noble, idealized Indians—generally dead, largely mythic, and always masculine—invoked the essence of true liberty and allowed colonists to imagine an expansive, if fantastical, vision of a free nation. The figure of Tammany had a complex history in the region around Philadelphia during the previous century. After a minor role in the original founding of the colony of Pennsylvania, Tammany was revived in 1732 as the festive patron saint of the Schuylkill Fishing Company. An annual feast day on 1 May marked the legal opening of the fishing season, featuring maypoles, flowers, and dances. In May 1772, a radical, pro-independence faction of the local Sons of Liberty split off and called themselves the Sons of Saint Tammany—and one early member was John Leacock. The next year, King Tammany was chosen as the patron saint of the Pennsylvania troops and, over the course of the war, was adopted by the Continental Army.[12]

In the play, following a pastoral scene that narrated the ill-fated British raid on Concord in April 1775, two shepherds observe the springtime festival of "glorious St. Tammany's day." A bard narrates King Tammany's legendary story, which was evidently familiar enough to leave a bit elliptical. The song begins by identifying Saint Tammany as the American counterpart of Hibernia's Saint Patrick and the Scot's Saint Andrew. In fact, by the early 1770s, competing societies dedicated to these saints had been organized in Philadelphia by groups of Irishmen and Scots. The American saint Tammany is presented as an exotic, if crude, idealized monarch: "Whilst under an oak his great parliament sat, / His throne was the crotch of a tree." This rustic monarch had no need of statutes or books to give his decrees, and his subjects received his will silently:

> No duties, nor stamps, their blest liberty cramps,
> A king, tho' no *tyrant*, was he;
> He did oft'times declare, nay, sometimes would swear
> The least of his subjects were free, my brave boys.

Such associations emphasized his ties to natural reason and his unswerving devotion to liberty.

Throughout the song, the freedom of Tammany's subjects is linked to his simple wants and manly pleasures. His nobility and masculine skill are shown in his generous hunting style and precise marksmanship. Although crude—"His table he spread where the venison bled"—he ate the king of meats and never went hungry. And, despite his advanced age, he was sexually potent: "With a pipe in his jaw, he'll buss his old squaw, / And get a young saint, ev'ry night, my brave boys." Tammany's satiation, both alimentary and sexual, flows from his recognition of his people's right to liberty, lawful government, and fatherly protection. Crucial to this image was the fact that King Tammany chose death rather than any form of dependence. According to the common lore, when Tammany finally sensed he was losing his independence, he killed himself by lying down in his wigwam and setting it on fire. In fact, some Tammany Day celebrations involved constructing and then burning wigwams. At the end of the play's song, the Indian king grows "blind, deaf and dumb." Refusing to accept such indignity, he "bid adieu to his wife, / And blazed like the tail of a comet."[13] He echoes here the standard trope of the noble savage—

always already disappearing because he refuses to submit to the domination of English settlers, who embody historical progress.

By this time, New Englanders had also developed their own distinctive style of acting out Indian identities: in extralegal actions enforcing customary standards, male settlers dressed up not only as women, which was the tradition in Europe, but also, sometimes, as Indians. The Boston Tea Party crowd, for instance, dressed as "Indians" by putting on buckskin hunting shirts, painting their faces, putting feathers in their hair, and carrying tomahawks. Reports frequently emphasized this Indian cross-dressing by identifying the rioters as members of a particular tribe—often Narragansetts, evoking memories of King Philip's War a century earlier. As the *Boston Gazette* reported: "His Majesty OKNOOKORUNKOGOG King of the Narragansett Tribe of Indians, on receiving Information of the arrival of another Cargo of that Cursed Weed TEA, immediately Summoned his Council at the Great Swamp . . . who did Advise and Consent to the immediate Destruction thereof." This kind of racial cross-dressing used identification with Indians both to evoke the menace of the "savage" and to assert a sense of local "custom" that they would defend against imperial incursions. Since the 1760s a tradition of protest in both regions had involved dressing up in Indian buckskin—and colonial militiamen were commonly called bucktails. In a merging of these traditions, the Paxton Boys—a group of two hundred volunteers naming themselves after the group famous for its bloody 1763 rampage against Christian Indians on the Pennsylvania frontier—were observed passing through Hartford in the fall of 1775 on their way to join Washington's army in Cambridge, Massachusetts, "dressed and painted in the Indian fashion."[14]

Like colonists putting themselves in the symbolic position of slaves, identifying themselves with fiercely independent Indians had both great symbolic power and discomforting implications. The imaginary self-identification of Patriot propagandists with Indians emphasized their claim to be descendants of the pure founding settlers (i.e., they were almost indigenous) and suggested that they drew strength from the landscape. In this complex set of associations, the pastoral landscape of America nourished simple virtues and independence, in contrast to the decadent influences of cosmopolitan civilization. Unlike the inspirational but dead Tammany, actual Indians in the play appear as threatening outsiders to the colonial order—as vicious savages allied with the British. The play's paean to King Tammany has the exaggerated tone of a tall tale, a charming but dismissible invention of patriotic imaginations. Leacock seems to have felt no need for authenticity, to have Tammany appear to be a real personage. In some ways, this disregard for verisimilitude emphasizes the mastery of settlers over Indians: colonial writers could appropriate Indians facilely and manipulate their images at will. The utterly fantastic nature of this Indian identity underscores the Indian's separation from normal society—a temporary deviation before things return to normal. At certain moments, people have to call on their primitive powers to resist the corruption of civilization. In the play, after this wild, fantastic episode, the serious drama of the war resumes.

By 1776, when *The Fall of British Tyranny* was written, the real nightmare for rebellious colonists was the prospect that the British, instead of simply attempting to enslave the free, were attempting to free the enslaved. Prodded by Virginia slaves, Lord Dunmore had proclaimed in November 1775 that all enslaved Negroes and indentured servants of rebels who were willing to join His Majesty's troops would be welcome and would receive their freedom. Within weeks, the *Maryland Gazette* reported with distress, hundreds of escapees from Virginia masters were organized into a separate "Ethiopian" regiment and outfitted with sashes that proclaimed "Liberty to Slaves." As Dunmore was well aware, this move was both strategically desperate and symbolically outrageous. Undermining slavery threatened to destroy the property of the colonial gentry and the entire economic system imperial officials were attempting to control and regulate. Colonial Whigs and even many British officials such as Edmund Burke were appalled. In the play, it was a tyrannical attempt to cut off the colonial nose to spite its face—to destroy colonial society rather than simply try to bring it under the protection of the Crown. Perhaps because the practical danger of slave insurrection was clear enough to colonists, *The Fall of British Tyranny* focuses on the symbolic outrage of colonial slaves being transformed into British soldiers. Lord Kidnapper relishes the irony: "I look upon this to be a grand maneuver in politics; this is making dog eat dog—thief catch thief—the servant against the master—rebel against rebel."[15]

Leacock's depictions of Kidnapper and Loyalist blacks were part of a sustained attack on a British military manned by unprincipled Tories, vagabonds, criminals, and impressed sailors and soldiers. The slaves-turned-soldiers are just an exaggeration of this basic danger of the standing army—its whorish subservience to tyrannical powers. It was well known that the British navy itself consisted largely of men forced into service by impressment. As republican theorists argued, soldiers in imperial troops could easily become agents of tyranny because their actions were not guided by either inner virtue or a real stake in conserving the social order. In large part, these images of black soldiers were so powerful because of the way in which freely chosen military service in the colonial period had come to represent citizenship in the still unformed nation.

In the play, the full depravity of Kidnapper's strategy unfolds gradually. When the black recruits first arrive on board Kidnapper's ship, the crew looks on with disgust. Asked where the blacks had come from, a sailor replies, "From Hell, I suppose—for they're as black as so many devils." Through a welter of hostile comments and racial puns, it becomes clear not only that Kidnapper lacks confidence in the loyalty of the black recruits but also that he does not plan to pay them wages and that he might ultimately betray them. When the black recruits have done their fighting, the boatswain suggests to Kidnapper, "Your honor can sell them in the West-Indies, and that will be something in your honour's pocket."[16]

This scenario of betrayal was lifted directly from attacks by Whig newspapers on Dunmore in the months before the play was written. In November 1775, the *Virginia Gazette* printed a letter explaining why slaves ought not to enlist with the British. The first argument was that the British ministry had thwarted an attempt by the Virginia government to restrict the slave trade and therefore was the Negroes' real enemy. (Thomas Jefferson later included a version of this argument in his first draft of the Declaration of Independence, though it was stricken for its patent absurdity.) Second, Dunmore himself despised Negroes, had been cruel to his own slaves, and was likely to betray those who joined him by selling them in the West Indies—where their condition would be "ten times worse" than it was at home. Finally, slaves should understand "the necessity of the different orders of men in this world" and seek a better condition in the next world. The following week the paper assailed Dunmore for, among other things, his cruelty in offering freedom only to such able-bodied male slaves as could be of use to his army and showing no "tenderness" even to them. In the event, Dunmore did not fulfill these appalling predictions: most of the black recruits died of disease soon after joining his ranks, and when he evacuated Virginia in the summer of 1776, he took the survivors with him to British-held New York. This fact did not prevent Jefferson from (wrongly) reporting in August that Dunmore had "shipped off" his black recruits to the West Indies.[17]

Alarm was felt far into the northern countryside. In response to reports that the "king's party" was trying to incite slaves to "Insurrection" in the southern colonies, Eleazar Wheelock proposed to send a "molatto" man he had educated to help rally southern slaves to the Patriot cause. At the same time, the loyalty of northern blacks came under public suspicion. As early as December 1775, a New York newspaper carried the story of a Negro man in Philadelphia who, after jostling whites on the street and being forced out into the muddy portion of the road away from the buildings, had defiantly warned them to wait until Lord Dunmore and his black regiment arrived: "Then we will see who is to take the wall." The Whig press was full of stories about slaves getting caught in desperate attempts to flee across the water for British protection. One such unlucky individual named Robert ran away from his master, stole a rowboat, and hailed what he thought was a British vessel but was actually a French privateer; he was taken captive and was soon put up for sale at a public auction in Newport. Newspaper reports emphasizing a racial double standard in the treatment of traitors to the rebel cause were reprinted even in New England, where they could not have been much practical use in intimidating Chesapeake slaves.[18]

Through all of this, the black rebels in the play are depicted as less fearsome than foolish. Whereas the crew speaks with a mild accent, the one black recruit given a speaking role talks in a thick dialect, referring to his white superiors as "massa." This scene represents Cudjo not as a fearsome rebel but as a foolish, inarticulate, and gullible follower of a manipulative tyrant. Like the Tory song "The Negroes Farewell to America," the play uses blacks to condemn the British but also to disparage all Africans. Back among his mates, the boatswain goes so far as to suggest that he'll try to convince Lord Kidnapper to sail to the coast of Guinea and "beat up for volunteers, there he'll get recruits enough for a hogshead or two of New-England rum, and a few owld pipe-shanks."[19] The commercial naiveté attributed to Africans illustrates contempt for them and fantasies of domination over them similar to stories about the ability of early settlers to purchase valuable tracts of land from native peoples for trinkets and baubles. All of this makes Kidnapper's name significant, for the nickname dismisses the slaves' own agency and even makes their liberation into an act of imposed aggression.

As the war continued, settlers harped on this theme of the British enslaving them by freeing their slaves. In 1779 colonists howled in protest when the British general Henry Clinton announced an extension of Dunmore's offer to slaves of rebels not just in Virginia but in all the revolting colonies. The *New Jersey Journal* mocked Clinton for this racial inversion:

> A proclamation oft of late he sends
> To thieves and rogues, who only are his friends;

> Those he invites; all colours he attacks,
> But deference pays to *Ethiopian blacks.*[20]

Colonial Whigs objected not only to their property being enticed away but also to the notion that blacks might receive "deference" in the British army. Although there was little evidence to support that notion—if anything, British officers treated black recruits with more contempt than they showed for their regular soldiers—for colonial propagandists preserving the sanctity of white preeminence was essential.

The colonists' interest in white preeminence gave the British a ready target when they wanted to mock them. As early as 1775, a British song about the Patriot militias converging on Cambridge in 1775 ridiculed them for including black men among their ranks. This image only exaggerated the contempt the British expressed first during the Seven Years' War and then in endless variations of the song "Yankee Doodle," which lampooned the provincial militias for their rusticity, pride, and lack of discipline:

> The rebel clowns, oh! what a sight!
> Too awkward was their figure.
> 'Twas yonder stood a pious wight,
> And here and there a nigger.[21]

Unfortunately for rebellious colonists, they not only shared these values but also were conspicuously vulnerable to such attacks. As the war unfolded, American liberty would depend to an uncomfortable degree on the military service of men excluded from citizenship.

||| Citizens and Soldiers |||

As the first alarm of the British foray out to Concord in April 1775 rippled across the countryside, the militia companies that rushed to the scene were manned by blacks and Indians, servants and slaves as well as free men. One of the minutemen on the Lexington common who confronted the redcoats that morning was Prince Esterbrook, probably the slave of a local farmer. Although black and Indian men were by law excluded from membership in colonial militias, when actual fighting broke out, men such as Esterbrook were sent off as substitutes for men who were considered full citizens. Standing in the place of a local settler—probably his master or his master's son—Esterbrook saw battle that day and was wounded. The Patriot casualties that day were immediately hailed as martyrs. A black-bordered broadside, headed by a funereal skull and crossbones, listed the names of sixty-one men from twenty-three towns. Esterbrook was included, but his name stands out. Unlike every other man, he was not dignified with even the courtesy title "Mr.," and a parenthetical gloss identified him as "a Negro Man."[22] Although black and Indian men served in Patriot military forces throughout the war, their service and its meaning was contested.

At the heart of conflicts about who should be allowed the honor of defending American liberties lay unresolved questions about the nature of the fighting force the Patriots should muster and their assumptions about who truly belonged to the American body politic. In the Continental Congress, struggles to define the meaning of *inhabitants* for the purposes of taxation and representation revolved around the status of slaves. Since states were taxed according to their population, northern representatives wanted slaves counted as inhabitants for that purpose, but southern representatives did not. In the name of regional harmony they generally compromised by counting each slave as three-fifths of an inhabitant. Meanwhile, Massachusetts delegate John Adams urged legislators in his home state to lie low on the issue of antislavery: "We have Causes enough of Jealousy, Discord & Division, and this Bill will certainly add to the Number." Early in 1776, Adams did his best to quash a New Jersey delegate's suggestion to supplement the state militia there with an all-black unit: "S. Carolina would run out of their Wits at the least Hint of such a Measure." Indeed, to many members of the Continental Congress, worse than physical deprivations of war were the symbolic outrages of social and racial leveling. In 1777, the Executive Committee complained about British admiral Richard Howe's practice of placing prisoners on prison ships with "no distinction between Master, Mates, Foremast Men & Negroes," which the committee saw as "an unnecessary cruelty."[23]

As the invective against Britain's professional army in *The Fall of British Tyranny* suggests, the Sons of Liberty valorized their militia tradition—and nowhere was this tradition more alive than in New England. Writing at the time of the Revolution, John Adams argued that militia drills were one of four institutions that formed the special "virtues and talents of the people" of New England. Generally held in early June after the rush of spring farmwork was over, these performances of citizenship affirmed the mission of God's chosen people in America, the military spirit of ordinary men, the need for New Englanders to honor a proper gentry class, and above all a sense of communal solidarity. Training days had the aspect of large local festivals, combining elements of a parade, communal holiday, political rally, worship service, and sports event along with military training. Although many blacks and Indians joined white women, children, and the aged who gathered to enjoy the festivities, they were pointedly excluded from militia service. Perhaps the only blacks allowed in colonial New England militia drills were drummers, a traditionally boyish occupation. In some places there were separate "Negro Training Days" with no arms and only festivity. In lieu of militia service, Rhode Island men of color were ordered instead to be liable for watch service. In Massachusetts they were assigned to labor such as repairing roads.[24]

When fighting broke out, as during the Seven Years' War between France, Britain, and their Indian allies, it was often the men excluded from the militias who were most likely to be sent off to the front lines. For long-term service far from home, recruiters turned to men without property, transients, indentured servants, Indians, and blacks—the men with the fewest options being the most willing to suspend temporarily their "civil liberties" and home comforts in exchange for military wages. So many slaves "with a view to procure their freedom" had enlisted in the army and navy during the two previous wars, reported Jeremy Belknap in 1763, that the total number of slaves in Massachusetts had substantially declined. Many Indians struggling against poverty and motivated by ideals of masculine military honor also enlisted—included the Pequot schoolteacher Sampson Wayboy, forced into the army to escape creditors. As Ezra Stiles knew all too well, the large number of Indian men who went off to fight was represented after the war in the large number of widows and orphans in New England enclaves. For many of these long-term soldiers, their memories were not of honor and glory but of subordination and hardship. Several years afterwards, one exhorter in the Narragansett Indian church recalled his military service: "I have been to the war up north, and heard orders to camp for the winter, and then, instead, to go home, boys, home—and that is what it is like for a Christian to go to heaven."[25]

Ironically, the experience of fighting and the British victory helped reinforce many New Englanders' faith in the militia ideal. Many New England militiamen who went off to fight rankled against British military discipline and were stung by the open contempt British officers heaped on them. This personal experience confirmed a longstanding transatlantic tradition that anathematized standing armies as mercenary, brutish, and servile instruments of tyranny.[26] And although British military officials considered the provincial militia of little military value,

New Englanders themselves were inclined to believe that victory had ultimately been secured by their own bravery and character. In the years to come this only increased tensions with the imperial government, which was seeking to raise huge sums of money to man a large standing army along the colonial frontier. These opinions were further polarized after 1768, when the military occupation of Boston inspired Whig propaganda characterizing British soldiers as agents of tyranny and calling for renewed militia vigor.

It was with this conflicted legacy that New England faced the prospect of battle in 1775 and the question of what to do about black and Indian men who discreetly slipped into service. Early in the war, while the populace looked forward to a limited, brief military struggle and was inflamed by an optimistic sense of *rage militaire,* the militia ideal was strong. Benjamin Franklin marveled at efforts to fortify Philadelphia when it first faced British attack: "You can have no Conception of Merchants & Gentlemen working with Spades & Wheelbarrows among Porters & Negroes." The spirit of voluntarism provided ample recruits in 1775, and through 1776 the military burden was widely shared, with a large portion of able-bodied men going for active duty. Nonetheless, there was concern that not only the right kind of men were passing muster. In October 1775, complaints reached John Adams in Philadelphia, where he was serving as a delegate to the Continental Congress, that "the Massachusetts Forces contain[ed] a great Number of Old Men, Boys and Negroes, more in Proportion than the Troops of the other Colonies"—all of whom he considered "unfit for service." The New England companies did have more Negroes, one soldier later recalled, "which to persons unaccustomed to such associations, had a disagreeable, degrading effect." In response, some attempts were made to defend the potential of black recruits: fourteen Massachusetts officers were so moved by the courage of Salem Poor that they petitioned the General Court to award him some token of distinction: "In the person of this said negro centers a brave and gallant soldier."[27]

Early in the war, embarrassment about Negro soldiers prevailed, and government officials passed a series of measures to exclude men of color from service in both state militias and the more professional Continental Army. As the first season of fighting ended, in late 1775, the Continental Congress forbade recruiting officers from signing up "Negroes, Boys unable to bear Arms nor Old men unfit to endure the Fatigues of the Campaign" and decreed that "Negroes" alone would not be allowed to reenlist. During the summer of 1776, when the Declaration of Independence was adopted and published, the populace of New England remained mobilized at a huge level, largely by volunteers. By this time, most state and local authorities had adopted policies restricting the recruitment or reenlistment of Negroes—both slaves and free men—as well as Indians. These bans often distinguished between the state militias, from which blacks and Indians were more completely excluded, and the Continental Army, in which more loopholes were left open. As early as May 1775, the Massachusetts Committee of Safety decreed that allowing anyone but "freemen" to serve as soldiers would be "inconsistent with the principles" that were to be supported and would reflect "dishonor" on the colony. Less than a year later, in January 1776, Massachusetts barred even free Negroes, Indians, and mulattos from its militia. Finally, in early 1777, Massachusetts prohibited men of color from entering the Continental Army even as substitutes.[28]

Yet by this point the spirit of voluntarism was waning, and many politicians were coming to agree with military leaders that in order to beat the redcoats they would need a more professional army. Even before the peak of Continental strength was reached in 1777, concern began to emerge that the early spirit of voluntarism would wither. "These are the times that try men's souls," wrote Thomas Paine in late 1776, in an effort to rally support for the war effort: "The summer soldier and the sunshine patriot will, in this crisis, shrink from the service of their country; but he that stands by it NOW, deserves the love and thanks of man and woman." Indeed, throughout the war, many New Englanders served brief stints, but most served less than a total of six months—their experiences convincing many to desert, decline to reenlist, or even discourage others from signing up. "Novelty and the first impulse of passion had led them to camp; but the approaching cold season, together with the fatigues and dangers incident to war, induced a general wish to relinquish the service," David Ramsay explained in a history of the Revolution published in 1789. Many soldiers were discouraged by "military ideas of union, subordination, and discipline."[29]

These were precisely the qualities that General Washington thought the Continental Army needed. "Discipline," said the plantation master, "is the soul of the army." He particularly deplored the relative lack of respect for social hierarchy among the New England units. The key to achieving discipline was longer terms of service, and in 1777 Congress followed the request of General Washington to allow for enlistment as long as three years or the duration of the war. Just how far the struggling nation had come from the militia ideal is suggested by the attitude of General Alexander Hamilton. With "sensible officers," he opined, "soldiers can hardly be too stupid." This may help explain why, in 1779, Hamilton argued in favor of recruiting black regiments in the southern states. Hamilton believed that in a standing army the ideal solider—like the ideal slave—should work with unquestioning obedience: "Let the officers be men of sense and sentiment, and the nearer the soldiers approach to machines perhaps the better."[30]

The states struggled to meet large recruitment quotas that included more onerous long-term enlistments—and responded by instituting new draft systems and by reopening military service to men of color. As the war dragged on, the revolutionaries increasingly found themselves dependent on black and Indian fighting men. At least five hundred black and Indian men have been identified in the Massachusetts rolls, some three hundred for Connecticut, and some six hundred for tiny Rhode Island. In some cases, these men were official substitutes, encouraged by recruitment policies that allowed individuals and draft classes to send substitutes in their own places. In other cases, the solders were surrogates only in the sense that people saw them standing in the place of citizens. In many cases, the states decided to exclude blacks and Indians from the draft but to allow them to serve as substitutes for citizens who were drafted. In Connecticut, a bill promising to pay owners for enlisted slaves was proposed, and the state government did ease restrictions on manumission—in addition to removing color restrictions on draft substitutes. Massachusetts went further: in 1777, the state officially exempted only Quakers from the draft; in 1778, the state explicitly sanctioned the enlistment of Negroes and removed color restrictions on draft substitutes. But Massachusetts also passed laws in 1778, 1779, and 1780 explicitly prohibiting the enrollment of Negroes and Indians in units intended to serve specific assignments in defense of the state.[31]

Increasingly, the men sent to the Continental Army—and, it seems, the state militias as well—were those with the least stake in civilian life: single men, those without property or a trade, servants, Indians, slaves, and free blacks. In many places, two militiamen could hire one man for three-year terms in the Continental service and be exempt from draft as long as their substitute remained in the army; in addition, the substitute's service would count toward the hometown of his hirers. Local draft policies were sometimes adapted by town fathers: in Concord, after April 1778, instead of pursuing the more egalitarian draft ordered by the Massachusetts General Court, the town instead filled its quota of long-term enlistment by hiring men to sign up. A number of states even sanctioned the enlistment of slaves at different points in the war. Soon, the citizens of America were hiring a professional army to fight for their freedom.[32]

The public, however, clung to the militia ideal and resisted acknowledging blacks and Indians as potential soldiers. In 1777, Rhode Island ordered a census of potential fighting men and pointedly instructed the enumerators in each town to count adult white men in various age categories; to note whether they were able to serve, were conscientious objectors, or were already in service; and also to count black and Indian men. The local officials who actually journeyed from house to house tallying the census in each town interpreted these guidelines in various ways. The Tiverton clerk declined to distinguish men of color in any way, naming them as he did other men and leaving the column for race blank. For instance, "Cato Slocum," a man with a typically black name, was identified only as an able man between fifty and sixty years old. In Charlestown, the clerk collected all the relevant information but set men of color apart in separate columns below the white men. In South Kingstown, Negroes were named but not listed by age or ability—as though the census taker began with the assumption that their potential for military service was not relevant; strikingly, he apparently recognized that this was not his decision to make and added: "N.B. all the Negars and Indians are able to Bear Arms." In all other towns, officials counted the number of black and Indian men but recorded only incomplete information about them, omitting their names, ages, ability to serve, or all these details. The Providence census taker Martin Seamans refused to name men of color, writing instead labels such as "One Negro Man" or "one Indian man." At one point he seemed to make a mistake: he wrote "Jack Car Negar Man" before striking the line out and writing "A Negar Man" then serving in the state militia. Despite the general doubt or hostility the census takers showed toward the possibility of black soldiers, their tallies make it clear that many Negro and Indian men were already serving in the state militia and in the Continental service. The South Kingstown clerk also noted two "mustees" currently in service: one in the state militia, the other in the Continental service.[33]

The draft system allowed hundreds of New England men of color to enter the militias and the Continental Army as substitutes. This was apparent even to Hessian mercenaries fighting for the British: "The Negro can take the field instead of his master; therefore no regiment is seen in which there are not negroes in abundance, and among them are able-bodies, strong and brave fellows." London Hazard of Rhode Island was one slave who entered the war as a substitute in the militia and served a series of brief stints: in the fall of 1777 he served one month in a militia company as a substitute for a relative of his master, then served similarly short terms for another eleven months, substituting in the same company and other companies for other relatives and neighbors of his master. Many of these men remained slaves while in service. Naturally, this system was prone to various kinds of abuse. In some cases, agents bargained with different draft companies to fetch the highest price for individual substitutes, as in the case of a jailed New York runaway who was purchased from the jailer to serve as a substitute for one company and then sold behind its back to another company willing to pay substantially more.[34] Slaves naturally often sought to enlist in their own names behind their masters' back. Israel Ashley of Westfield attempted to enlist his slave Gilliam as a substitute, only to discover that the man had already enlisted himself. The master complained to General Horatio Gates, who declined to return the man, explaining that state policies were unclear. The general clearly sympathized with "slaves who have or will assist us in securing our freedom at the risk of their own lives." Increasingly as the war went on, some slaves who started out serving as substitutes reenlisted in their own name. Although extremely hostile to black soldiers, even Maryland and Virginia eventually allowed slaves to substitute for masters.[35] Apparently many white Patriots found the notion of a slave serving as a substitute less threatening than the notion of a black man enlisting in his own name—perhaps because in the former role his identity was covered by the social death of slavery and in the latter role he would have to be acknowledged in the role of a citizen.

Even as standard policies about men of color in the armed forces were pretty much resolved, controversy continued. In the fall of 1777, the front page of the *Boston Gazette* was taken up with a long essay attacking the hypocrisy, danger, and wastefulness of the substitution system—and particularly its reliance on slaves. Originally published in Philadelphia earlier that summer, *Observations on the Slaves and the Indented Servants, inlisted in the Army* begins with the notion that a "land of liberty" should not be defended by slaves: "They share in the dangers and glory of the efforts made by US, the freeborn members of the United States, to enjoy undisturbed, the common rights of human nature; and THEY remain SLAVES!" This was not only unjust—and therefore "too painful, too humiliating" for true Patriots to bear—but also too expensive. "An amazing number of these men eagerly seized the unexpected opportunity offered them," but these conditions impressed "no idea of gratitude on their minds." As it was, the prevailing situation was dangerous: "Our non-emancipated soldiers are almost irresistibly tempted to desert to our foes, who never fail to use them against us." The essay argued that this problem was expensive, since individuals without any sense of loyalty—bound servants of all types—were inclined to enlist, collect their bounties, and then desert and reenlist again somewhere else to collect another bounty. This also had the effect of defrauding individuals who hired substitutes with private payments. The author argued that to gain the loyalty of these men, freedom should be granted immediately and absolutely—not as a loan to be repaid or as a condition of further service. The essay ends by invoking the language of the Declaration of Independence to exhort Americans to live up to their ideals and be the "'VIRTUOUS PEOPLE'" that we have often declared ourselves to be."[36]

This author's worst nightmare may well have been embodied in the character of a man named Moses Hazard, who demonstrated, at least, that one did not have to be a slave to be manipulative and disloyal. Hazard came to official attention when he signed up first on board the Continental ship *Warren* and then enlisted into one of the Continental battalions. The Rhode Island War Council applied a pragmatic racial logic to the dilemma of where he should be sent to serve: because few Indians survived very long on board ships of war, Hazard should remain in the land service. Under orders to repay the ship captain for any bounties, wages, and other debts he had accumulated, Hazard enlisted into Colonel Joseph Stanton's regiment in the Rhode Island militia, along with a number of other Indians and black men. Then, in the fall, he deserted—a newspaper advertisement described him as "a Mulatto, about 5 feet 6 or 7 inches high, a sturdy, well built fellow, with long black hair." Such unreliable recruits were a publicly acknowledged problem, as the Tory *Newport Gazette* gloated: "None can be persuaded to inlist during the War, except a few Vagabonds whose abandoned thoughtlessness is such that they can dispose with the enormous Bounty which is given to them in two or three Days; and frequently when they have done it, go and inlist themselves again with some other for the sake of again obtaining the Bounty."[37]

Such spectacles and the lack of soldierly virtue they represented were not welcomed by the New England public, which failed to come to terms fully with the practical failures of the militia system and clung to the citizen-soldier ideal. Recruitment propaganda of the Continental Congress continued to emphasize a family ideal, warning in 1777, "Your foreign alliances, though they secure your independence, cannot secure your country from desolation, your habitations from plunder, your wives from insult or violation, nor your children from butchery." At the same time, increasing resistance to the prospect of volunteering for the Continental service, particularly after 1778, was accompanied by a public tone of civil antimilitarism that blamed the army for endangering the virtue of society. Whereas clergymen blamed sinfulness and war profiteering for God's punishment of the populace with a prolonged war, the people of Connecticut found the army a more

attractive object of blame, focusing on the profanity of camp language and inde-
cent behavior by officers. Respectable New Englanders increasingly viewed the
army as immoral, degrading, and brutal. Officers themselves recognized this growing gap in opinion and presented a memorial to the General Assembly in October 1778, expressing their fear that citizens were coming to view soldiers as "a people
with separate and clashing interests."[38]

The kinds of military units that blacks were accepted into helped to mitigate
their symbolic challenge to the citizen-soldier ideal. Although some substitutes
served in militia companies, most blacks—like most other undesirable recruits—
were signed up for distant, long-term service.[39] Many black and Indian soldiers
served alongside their white peers, though probably disproportionately in the auxiliary roles of drummer or fifer or in the support positions of teamsters, wagoners,
and servants to officers. It was also repeatedly proposed that black soldiers be segregated into separate, all-black units, which were actually formed in many states.
Connecticut founded a black company in 1781 with all white officers. One black
Massachusetts veteran remembered being switched into a "black company"—and
it may be that officers sometimes reorganized black troops from dispersed units
into more segregated companies. John Hancock himself presented a battle flag to
one black military unit, known as the "Bucks of America," which may have served
a watch in Boston.[40]

Separate black units were controversial. One argument for raising a specifically
black organization headed by white officers was articulated in 1778 by artillery
officer Thomas Kench, speaking to the Massachusetts General Court at Castle Island. He argued that a force of some two or three hundred Negroes could be
quickly raised, and he proposed a psychological rationale for keeping them separate: "We have divers of them in our service, mixed with white men. But I think it
would be more proper to raise a body by themselves, than to have them intermixed
with the white men; and their ambition would entirely be to outdo the white men
in every measure that the fortune of war calls a soldier to endure." He evidently assumed they would be slaves and proposed freeing them at the end of the war. The
Massachusetts legislature voted instead to continue its previous practice and quietly enlist black men as individuals.[41]

In early 1778 the Rhode Island legislature began to organize a battalion of
slaves—a move proposed by officers in the state's two current battalions of the Continental Army, greatly undermanned at Valley Forge. Although it ultimately prevailed, the plan roused stiff opposition. Six legislators attacked the proposal as im-

practical—there were not enough slaves in the state, the expense of purchasing them was exorbitant, masters would be aggrieved. They also argued that it would be a public embarrassment: "Opinion would go abroad that the State had purchased a band of slaves to defend the rights and liberties of the Colony." Arming slaves would expose Patriots to the kind of ridicule that they had so liberally bestowed upon the British when Lord Dunmore had to begun to recruit black soldiers. (Indeed, the Tory *Newport Gazette* did mock Patriots in just this way.) Furthermore, the legislators objected, black soldiers would be regarded as "contemptible" and "not equal" by other soldiers.[42] This prediction at least had the potential to be self-fulfilling; the legislature was too desperate for recruits to avoid relying on the manpower of the state's slaves but was reluctant simply to integrate them with the state's white soldiery.

Not content to register their grievances in the General Assembly, opponents of the black regiment went so far as to interrupt recruitment meetings. On 19 March 1778, Captain Elijah Lewis—who, like the other captains chosen for this unit, had had many black soldiers in his company since early 1777—held a recruitment assembly in South Kingstown, the heart of slave country, and was pleased that a "large number of Negroes collected together apparently desirous of Enlisting." One prominent local slave owner disrupted the proceedings. Hazard Potter, the captain complained, "endeavoured to deter them from entering into the service" by predicting that, as Negroes, they would be treated badly and ultimately betrayed. Potter told them that "the Negroes were to make Breast Works"—that is, the most inglorious labor of constructing earthen fortifications. At a time when the American militias did not have the courage or discipline to withstand deadly British bayonet charges, Potter predicted that the Negroes "were always to be employed upon the most dangerous service, to be put in the Front of the Battle as the Hessians were in the British Army." Moreover, he told them that when Negroes were "taken prisoners they would not be exchanged, but were to be sent to the West Indies & sold as slaves."[43] Indeed, these were precisely the same warnings made by Virginia planters when Lord Dunmore offered to enlist slaves into his army.

Nonetheless, many slaves were not discouraged, and many masters were happy to cash in. In fact, about a third of the men who were subsequently sold to the state in exchange for their enlistment in the black regiment in early 1778 had already enlisted for a year or more. At least one—Jacob Hazard, the slave of Carder Hazard of South Kingstown—had enlisted as early as September 1776. At least twenty others enlisted in 1777, most of them for the duration of the war, most of them in one of three companies under Captains Ebenezer Flagg, Thomas Cole, and Elijah Lewis (and one in John S. Dexter's and one in John Holden's). All of these companies had been largely black since 1777. Thus, it would appear that many slaves who had already negotiated manumission agreements with their masters—or at least whose masters had resigned themselves to their loss into the army—were sold again to the state the following year with no benefit to themselves and with additional profit for their masters. Others, including some free men and runaways, joined the regiment later. Some 250 probably served in this unit during the war.[44]

After two months of recruitment, the Rhode Island governor proudly reported that the 140-odd members of the state's black regiment were outfitted far better than most of the state's ill-outfitted troops, in a "very handsome Uniform," and that most been inoculated for small pox. These unusually lavish uniforms—blue suits with hats adorned with golden anchors and ostrich plumes—were similar to the outfits worn by some of the most elite of the private militia companies such as the Newport Artillery Company and may have been meant to encourage the recruits to believe they were being received into service with dignity. At the same time, the uniforms may have been intended to protect the state from accusations that they were sending lowly recruits. Governor William Greene, who had sold at least one of his own slaves into the battalion, considered the black recruits attractive because of their low cost: "[They] are good soldiers and Serve during the War without any other allowance then what is paid them by the Continent when the others doing the same duty with them are allowd what is calld subsistance Money." This subsistence money, he calculated, often cost more in a year than any of these slaves' total sale price. Meanwhile, the former slaves in Colonel Christopher Greene's regiment were excluded from a $300 bounty paid to all other Rhode Island troops to encourage recruitment and to those already enlisted to continue in the service through the end of the war. As the governor saw it, the ones who had been shortchanged were the former masters. The Rhode Island law had capped the value of slaves at $400, but when Congress recommended that southern states raise black troops in a similar way the following year, it suggested that owners be paid $1,000.[45]

Just as black soldiers were most openly accepted when the demand for manpower was highest, so the New England states began to reverse their policies and restrict black service again as the fighting moved into the Deep South and long-term recruits manned the army. In May 1778 the Rhode Island legislature proclaimed the act authorizing slave enlistment into the black battalion a temporary measure, and it announced the end of slave enlistment on 10 June 1778. Although those already enlisted continued to serve and others made their way into the militia and Continental Army, the state consistently excluded men of color, along with deserters, from draft classes. A roll of recruits from the calls of June and July 1780 lists 500 men, of whom 35 were Negroes or mulattos, 28 were Indians—and 160 were boys under age eighteen. Even though recruiters were clearly desperate, men of color were not recognized as full citizens and hence were not liable to be drafted, though they could still volunteer and serve in the place of their white peers. In Connecticut, by the early 1780s blacks and Indians were formally excluded from the state militias and Continental Army drafts.[46]

Among those who turned vocally against black military service was Colonel Jeremiah Olney, the man who commanded Rhode Island's black regiment after Colonel Greene's death. In January 1781, Olney announced that his regiment would hold musterings at Providence and East Greenwich, but, as the newspaper announcements read, *"Negroes will not be received."* Whether this was an attempt to boost enlistment by appealing to white pride or whether he really did not want black soldiers is unclear. In fact, despite the announcement, in May 1781 the *Providence Gazette* advertised the desertion of eight recruits on furlough from Greene's company—including several Indians, a Negro named Levi Thurston, an Englishman, and an Irishman. A year later, Olney more explicitly declared that men of color did not make good soldiers: "It has been found from long and fatal experience that Indians, negroes and mulattoes do not (and from a total want of Perseverance and Fortitude to bear the various Fatigues incident to an army cannot) answer the public service, they will not therefore on any account be received." Emphasizing that blacks and Indians stood outside the body politic in this essential sense, Olney's mustering orders asserted, "Experience also confirms how little reliance we can place on Foreigners." With such declarations, leaders of New England military forces began to shape the place of people of color in the new Republic.[47]

||| Divided Loyalties |||

One of the many slaves who ran away to fight in the war was Jehu Grant, a rural Rhode Islander who told his story some fifty years later in an application for a veteran's pension. Grant claimed that he had not really been a fugitive: his master had been a traitorous Tory, so he, a staunch Patriot, had merely been escaping from behind enemy lines. When fighting broke out, he was about thirty years old, "grown to manhood, in the full vigor and strength of life." He "heard much about the cruel and arbitrary things done by the British," and he knew that his master was illegally trading with enemy ships hovering offshore in Narragansett Bay. Not only that, Grant "suffered much from fear" that he would be sent aboard one of these British vessels. When the British burned the nearby town of Danbury, Connecticut, Grant made his choice. Inspired by "liberty poles and the people all engaged for support of freedom," he left his master and enlisted as a private soldier in the Continental Army. Grant was put to work as a wagoner during the summer, as a servant to the wagon master general that winter, and as the wagoner in charge of the general's personal baggage in the spring. In June, while stationed close to the lines of battle on the Hudson River valley, the long arm of his Rhode Island master reached out and brought him back to the farm, where he spent the rest of the war as a slave.[48] Half a century later, Grant's patriotic war stories failed to convince the bureaucrats in John C. Calhoun's pension office, who considered him to have been a fugitive slave and therefore not a legitimate soldier. Nonetheless, his account of the war highlights crucial aspects of the war as it was experienced in the northern states: tensions between the language of liberty and the status of slaves; divisions between Tories and Patriots; and conflicts between citizens and those claiming citizenship. Throughout the war, slaves and free people of color did their best to turn all these tensions to their advantage.

The imperial crisis and the ensuing war gave some black New Englanders the confidence to attack slavery publicly and claim recognition as equal citizens, but they did so under scrutiny and with considerable constraint. Phillis Wheatley's published poems, for example, were far more oblique than her private correspondence. Lemuel Haynes, who himself served in the war, left his 1776 essay "Liberty Further Extended" unpublished. Other New England slaves and free blacks publicly asserted themselves in petitions. In 1774, one group of Massachusetts slaves emphasized their "naturel right" to freedom and their status as "sincear" members of the Church of Christ. After the outbreak of war, black petitioners from across New England explicitly associated their claim to freedom with the "present Glorious struggle for Liberty" and invoked the language of the Declaration of Independence. Paul Cuffe and a number of other free men of color argued that they should not be taxed if they were not represented by the right to vote.[49] In such public interventions, black New Englanders sought to shape and help define the meaning of liberty in an age of revolution.

The outbreak of war offered more mundane opportunities for many New England blacks and Indians to better their lives—and more practical grounds on which to stake their claims to citizenship. Like apprentices and indentured servants, some slaves took advantage of wartime disruptions to run away. Free men and women, too, found opportunities in military service as soldiers or in auxiliary roles such as servants to officers, cooks, or laundresses. Many slaves secured their freedom not by running away but by negotiating with their masters: military service provided such men with access to substantial bonuses and stable income with which they could purchase themselves.[50] Many who became soldiers were ambivalent about the experience of fighting in the Continental Army. To some extent men of color shared the same hardships and duties of other soldiers, but they were often also set apart and demeaned in practical and symbolic ways. After the war the meaning of their service continued to be contested.

Divisions between Whigs and Tories provided some enslaved New Englanders, as well as many free people of color, with opportunities to cast their lot with one side or the other in order to improve their own situation. Such opportunities were limited, however, because throughout the war the British were confined largely to a single town in New England—Boston from the outbreak of war until 1776 and then Newport until 1779. After that, the principal British stronghold in the northern states was New York City. Opportunities for slaves and free people of color appeared mainly along the heavily guarded but not impermeable boundaries between British territory and the surrounding countryside and by the disruption created when the British raided Patriot towns or evacuated their seaport strongholds.

Attempts by the British to recruit the loyalty and service of local blacks stemmed in part from their desire to tweak rebel sensibilities and in part from their need for workers, servants, and soldiers. In March 1775, with the threat of war looming, British troops in Boston offered membership in a regimental lodge of Free and Accepted Masons to fifteen black men. The leader of this group of black Masons was Prince Hall, a former slave who had been freed shortly after the Boston Massacre; after the war, he used his position as master of the African Lodge to organize Boston's black community and to speak out against racism. Before and during the war, British officers also sought out black men and women as personal employees, as when one officer in Newport advertised for "a Negro Servant, who can be well recommended, and take care of horses." The British occupying the city did their best to encourage people of color, particularly slaves, to come to them. The British *Newport Gazette* proudly reported the arrival of refugees and bad news about the rebels. In 1778, General Clinton went further and announced that he would allow escaped slaves of rebel owners to fight for the British and receive their freedom but that he would also punish enemy Negroes. "Whereas the enemy have adopted a practice of enrolling NEGROES among their Troops, I do hereby give Notice, That all NEGROES taken In Arms or upon any Military Duty, Shall be purchased for a state Price, the Money to be paid to the Captor." Some time later, British lieutenant Frederick Mackenzie complained that relatively few locals accepted this offer: "The Negroes on this Island have been invited to join the King's Troops, and have been promised pay and provisions; but very few of them having come in." Desperate for wagon drivers and other laborers, Mackenzie resorted to drafting all black men in town who were "capable of any service."[51]

Some sense of the difficulties faced by black men and women living in these besieged British strongholds is suggested by the testimony of Anthony Johnson, a free black Newporter. Having no means of support other than his daily labor and "no Connection but those he had found on the Island," Johnson remained with his family. In desperation, he was forced into "such abject servitude" to a Tory master that when the British evacuated he was compelled to go along. At the end of the war, he made his way back to Rhode Island, where he was imprisoned as a traitor and charged with "taking up arms against the united states." He protested, claiming in fact to be a loyal American.[52]

Indeed, a large number of black men and women who lived in these British towns left with the British when they evacuated. Some slaves were clearly taken away forcibly by Tory masters, but many others escaped with the British to claim their freedom. Almost half of the thirty-nine black Rhode Islanders who became Loyalist refugees in New York reported leaving their masters at the time the British evacuated the city in October 1779. Similarly, many of the white Tories who eventually left the United States also started off in the British-occupied towns of Boston and Newport. For both white and black Loyalists, control of an area by the British made it easier to openly side with them and seek military protection. Indeed, it appears that many of these black Loyalists already had jobs working for the British before evacuations were organized. Those slaves who ran away with the British were from a much broader cross section of the population than the narrow band of young men who typically ran away in the colonial period. More than a third were women (eight out of eighteen Massachusetts slaves; nine out of twenty-seven Rhode Island slaves). In addition, many black men and women who left with the British seem to have already been free (fourteen out of thirty-nine in Rhode Island). Of course, not all slaves in areas controlled by the British made the same decisions. One Tory slaveholder, John Warren, stayed behind after the British forces abandoned Newport in October 1779. He had hoped to protect his property but instead was imprisoned as a traitor. While he was in jail, one of his slaves ran away into the British service, another into the American service.[53]

One of the black Bostonians who declined to evacuate the city with the British army was Scipio Fayerweather, a former slave who had worked hard to accumulate some property on Belknap Street, where he had built and furnished a thirty-by-seventeen-foot house. This may have been one of the reasons that he resisted pressure to join the British when they prepared to abandon the city. But, as he emphasized in a petition to the Massachusetts government, his loyalty to the Patriot cause had cost him dearly. His petition, written in formal language in the third person, emphasizes that although the British troops used every method they could to persuade him to join them, he refused: "Gratitude to this beloved Country in which he has lived from a Child made him shudder at the thought of taking up Arms against a People to whom he is under many Obligations both of a spiritual and Temporal Nature." This loyalty enraged the "Tirannical Troops," and they "not only pull'd his House down to the Ground but Entirely ruined & destroyed all his sd. Furniture." Fayerweather, who had long lived in the household of a prominent politician, was savvy enough to turn to the state legislature for reimbursement for the cost of his damaged property (eighty pounds)—and he was also aware that it might question or dismiss his professed political loyalties because he was not white. Fayerweather emphasized that his race should not impugn his standing as a Patriot, concluding that "he most humbly Prays (and doubts not altho he is a Black man) so that he would be granted some appropriate relief."[54]

When Tory masters fled the countryside or evacuated with British troops, their slaves often did their best to stay behind, but they were not always home free. One problem they faced was that the Patriot governments generally confiscated the property of fleeing Tories—and slaves were, after all, legally property. Several did their best to convince cash-strapped Patriot governments that they should be considered not confiscated property but loyal citizens. Pomp was one of several slaves who won the sympathy of the Connecticut government and were granted their freedom. The Rhode Island government equivocated about several cases: the Council of War postponed a decision in the case of Tony Rome by renting him out to a series of masters over the course of the war. Perhaps the most poignant petition came in the name of Great Prince, Little Prince, Luke, Cesar, and Prue and her three children. Their petition emphasized their equality and patriotism: "That your memorialists, though they have flat noses, crooked shins, and other queerness of make, peculiar to Africans, are yet of the human race, free-born in our own country, taken from thence by man-stealers, and sold in this country as cattle in the market . . . but we hope our good mistress, *the free State of Connecticut,* engaged in a war with tyranny, will not sell good honest Whigs and friends of the freedom and independence of America, as we are. . . . The Whigs out to be *free,* and the *Tories* should be sold." Like Jehu Grant's similar argument fifty years later, this claim was also denied.[55]

More convincing were slaves who managed to escape from behind British lines into Patriot-controlled territory. Jane Coggeshall, William Carpenter, and Violet Pease escaped from British-controlled Newport in March 1777—they presumably took a boat and made it across the bay to Point Judith, where they stopped and were secured by soldiers. An armed guard carried them to South Kingstown, where the General Assembly was meeting. They gave such useful information about the British garrison at Newport that they were declared free and given a pass to go to any part of the country to pursue their livelihood. Quacko Honeyman was another Newporter who escaped across the bay and received official protection from the Rhode Island government: after spending most of the war in the occupied port, he ran away only after his master sold him to a British officer who was preparing to evacuate the city.[56]

Conversely, many Patriot masters in the countryside feared that their slaves would run away and slip behind British lines, but although the disruptions of wartime did encourage runaways, the British presence was little encouragement except along the thin margin of coastline bordering on British strongholds. In October 1777, one master announced that his slave Diamond had run away from Patriot-controlled Boston (taking with him not only clothes but also his violin, of which he was "very fond, tho' a miserable Performer") and had been heard to say that he "would go to Newport," the closest British stronghold. Starting in the late 1760s the number of servants of all kinds running away from their masters increased substantially across the northern colonies. The Revolutionary War inspired more. But relatively few ran to the British. Patriot control of the New England countryside was tight. Committees of Safety policed local Tories and slaves as well as shorelines and sensitive travel junctures. The few runaways who made it behind British lines started out on the borders of occupied territory. A substantial cluster of Massachusetts runaways started out on the southern coast of the state and fled, apparently, to British-controlled Newport. Almost all Connecticut slaves who joined the Loyalists during the war ran away from towns on the outskirts of New York, which the British controlled for most of the war. Black people running away to the British from the New England countryside generally followed the demographic profile of colonial runaways: they were almost all escaping servitude and were overwhelmingly young men, like Boston King, who later told a dramatic story of his escape from rural New Jersey to the British-controlled city of New York.[57]

Even during the sporadic British raids along the Connecticut shoreline in 1779, led by the notorious traitor Benedict Arnold, most slaves who ran away headed not toward the British but rather into the Patriot-controlled countryside. One of these was a rebellious young woman named Abigail. When the British invaded New London and started to burn the town, her master's family rushed to remove what they could from their house and load it up on wagons. Abigail gathered her own family and loaded up another wagon with whatever she could salvage. Taking advantage of the panic, she decided not to follow her master's family but rather headed off in the other direction toward her hometown of South Kingstown. In subsequent years, she warded off repeated attempts by her master to reclaim her as a slave.[58]

For many enslaved New Englanders, the best opportunities for securing their freedom lay not in joining the British or running away but rather in signing up for military service in local militias or the Continental Army. Just as many other New England recruits joined the army to escape debt or poverty or demeaning relations of servitude, so many slaves found opportunities in military service to become free.

Many New Englanders assumed that military service implied freedom: the *Boston Gazette* contained a story on 13 October 1777 about a slave claiming his freedom on enlisting in the army. But, as Jehu Grant's story suggests, this expectation was not always honored. In June 1780, the selectmen of the town of Sandwich, Massachusetts, agreed to pay a local attorney twenty dollars a month as wages for "his Negro Boy Named Jack," who was then "a Soldier ingaged in the Continental Service for the Term of Six months," for as long as he served. But this detailed agreement made no mention of Jack's freedom. Only in 1781, near the end of active recruitment in New England, did the town of Derby, Connecticut, vote to emancipate all Negroes who enlisted, which implies that this had not been its practice previously. Nonetheless, for many slaves in Rhode Island, as elsewhere across the rebelling states, the need for manpower and the social disruptions caused by the war provided opportunities to become free. Thus, Cato appears on the Durham County, Connecticut, bounty list for 9 December 1777, having been hired by two men: his bounty was listed as "freedom."[59] For many of these men, freedom was not a simple consequence of enlistment; rather, it was the end of complicated and often tense negotiations. In these negotiations, the compensation and exemptions offered by the state—as well as perceived opportunities for escape raised by the war—provided slaves with crucial bargaining chips.

Many slaves attempted to reap the benefits of enlistment without seeking their masters' consent. Some simply ran off and joined the service under recruitment officers who were not overly concerned about their background or veracity. Early in 1778, fourteen-year-old Sipio followed the lead of his fellow slave Tom and enlisted in the army, serving five years as a drummer or musician. Their master, Sheriff Beriah Brown of North Kingstown, drafted two letters to military officials, explaining that he was an old man and complaining, "I now have no Boy to Do any thing for me." Concerned that he might be considered unpatriotic, he insisted, "I am willen to Defent my Countrey as any man." But he never actually sent the letter and never publicly advertised for Scipio's return. In other cases, less ambivalent masters did catch up with their slaves. One Cranston man filed suit against a recruiting sergeant for enlisting his slave into the Continental service and managed to have both of them jailed until the state Council of War intervened.[60]

The recruitment process often gave slaves new allies in negotiations with their masters: recruitment officers in need of men, draftees seeking to hire substitutes, and town officials struggling to meet quotas. Freelance recruiters could be aggressive in encouraging slaves to run away and join the army. As Isaac told his story, he was about twenty-five years old and living in New London when he was approached by a man who asked him to enlist and to whom he belonged. Isaac gave the name of his master, and the procurer told him to come across the state border to Coventry, Rhode Island, where he would give him one hundred dollars in hard currency bounty and six dollars a month for his service. A few days later Isaac returned to the man and told him he was now "ready to Inlist" if the man "would be up to his promise." The procurer told Isaac to identify himself to the muster master as Isaac Scranton, born and bred on Long Island. Isaac did so and was assigned to Colonel Greene's regiment. The procurer, who had provided other men to substitute for a number of draft classes, managed to bargain the Coventry draft class up from $150 to $200 for Isaac, and as soon as it received the certificate of Isaac's enlistment from the muster master, it paid up, allowing him to pocket half the money as his profit. In this case, Isaac's master did eventually reclaim him.[61]

On the other hand, enlistment also provided masters with incentives to allow their slaves to earn their freedom. The relatively secure income provided by such military service provided a number of slaves with the opportunity to buy their way out of slavery. Edom London was one slave who used his ability to escape and sign up in the military to make life miserable for a series of masters until one finally gave in and allowed him to purchase his own freedom by enlisting. Priamus, a Rhode Islander in his middle twenties, agreed with his master during the war that he would go on three voyages on a privateer: his master would receive his wages, and at the end of the last voyage he would become free. At the same time, slaveholders also found themselves in a position to ask state governments, desperate for recruits, to release them from liability for financial responsibility for their former slaves or to actually pay them for their slaves. In addition, some of those negotiating manumission through military service already had been part of complex labor negotiations. One slave named Frank Duncan was bought by the owner of a Massachusetts iron forge to work as a bloomer in 1770; they agreed that Duncan would work for ten years and then become free, receive a yoke of oxen, and be granted ten acres of land to farm. The forge owner did not believe in holding slaves any longer than the point at which they had earned back what he had paid for them. The war offered an opportunity for these men to renegotiate, and in 1777 Frank convinced his master to allow him to buy out his last three years of service by paying him thirty pounds, which he would obtain as bounties and wages when he enlisted in the Continental Army.[62]

The experiences of black and Indian men who served in the state militias and the Continental Army were similar to those of the "hard core" white soldiers who served long terms in the Continental Army, particularly after the harrowing winter of 1778 at Valley Forge. For years on end, these men endured the demeaning anonymity instilled by unit cohesion training, the physical punishment inflicted on all private soldiers, and the conditions of privation, poor pay, and low morale that often prevailed. Cato Baker was one slave who bargained for his freedom, and his letters home sound familiar themes of hardship and betrayal. Written to his former master and to the local minister who had helped secure his freedom, they not only emphasized his constant Christian piety but also displayed a gradual shift in tone from plaintive to bitter. In the summer of 1778, he reported that he although he had contracted smallpox at Valley Forge in March, he was now in good health. But he was desperately short of money, for the soldiers often had to use their wages to supplement the inadequate clothing and food with which they had been supplied. A year later, he expressed his dissatisfaction with his wages of forty shillings a month: "[For this paltry sum] We Men Riske Our Lives & Every thing that is Deere." He hoped that the people of New Hampshire would "take it into thar Wise Consedration & Make the Soldiors Som small Satsfytion."[63]

The treatment of black and Indian men serving in segregated units was probably not much harsher than that of white soldiers—at least that is the impression conveyed by the orderly books of Christopher Greene, commander of the Rhode Island black regiment. Like many other commanders, Greene had a dim view of his soldiers and repeatedly lamented the lack of discipline that led them to get sick by sleeping on damp ground, eating half-cooked food, not having their hair cut "decently" short, and drinking cold water in the heat of the day. The punishment he administered for infractions of the military code was harsh and physical. In June 1779, Sharpo Gardner received a hundred lashes for stealing. Relations with civilians remained a recurrent problem. Soldiers, for their part, were ordered not to range more than three-quarters of a mile out of camp without a written permit—another echo of slave-patrol discipline, but one that was commonly extended to white soldiers as well. During the summer of 1779 a series of private soldiers, including Prince Gardner, were tried at courts-martial for "sleaping out of camp without leave" or simply being absent from roll call. Colonel Greene also tried to regulate the female camp followers. He sternly prohibited "all women following the soldiers in camp" from ever returning—excepting only the women who were "recommended by the commanding officers of Companies for wash women." As in predominantly white units, a considerable number of these soldiers deserted, mostly when the unit left Rhode Island for service in New York—their first service away from home. This was not an uncommon pattern: early in the war, an advertisement in the *Providence Gazette* listed twenty men who deserted from one regiment "on its March to New York." The disciplinary records also contain hints of low morale and financial concerns like those voiced by Cato Baker. As in many predominantly white units, private soldiers often resented their superior officers and even occasionally suspected them of malfeasance. On 22 July 1779, Private Caesor Sabins was convicted of spreading the "false rumor" that his sergeant "had cheated the Soldiers out of their allowance."[64]

For members of this all-black unit, there were not only fears that they would be assigned the most onerous or dangerous duties but also challenges to their competence as soldiers. After a fierce battle in August 1778, aspersions were cast on their performance despite the affirmations of top officers that they had served well. Major General John Sullivan initially observed: "The conduct of Colonel Commandant Greene's Regiment was not, in the action yesterday, equal to what might have been expected." He had heard that Major Samuel Ward was "much dissatisfied with their conduct." After investigation, the general concluded that the soldiers had acquitted themselves honorably in battle. "Doubtless in the heat of action Major Ward might have said something to hurry the troops on to action which, being misinterpreted, gave rise to the report."[65] Whether or not his words were insulting in a specifically racial way, it was clear that the performance of black soldiers was being judged along racial lines.

Extant military records make it difficult to determine the extent to which black and Indian men in predominantly white units were treated the same as or differently than other soldiers. It seems that blacks were very often assigned to work as drummers or personal servants and that they were also probably more likely to be assigned to the heaviest wagon train duties. But however men of color were received within the military, the public had continuing difficulty honoring their service.

One suggestion of the problem posed by black soldiers is a comic song written during the war to celebrate what was known as the Prescott raid, in which a party of Patriots captured the British commander General Richard Prescott in July 1777—one of the few Patriot successes in the region to that point in the war. In this daring expedition, a Patriot squad made it across Narragansett Bay, burst into the farmhouse where the general was sleeping, and whisked him away before the alarm could be raised. Jack Sisson, a black soldier, navigated the Patriots' boat. In the song, the scene was redrawn with Sisson as a central figure. But his character is given the generic Negro name "Cuffee," and a series of burlesque inventions characterize him as a slavish buffoon. The Patriots arrive at the front door of the farmhouse where the general was staying:

> But to get in they had no means
> Except poor Cuffee's head,
> Who beat the door down then rush'd in
> And seized him in his bed.

The song then goes on to narrate the widely repeated story that the awakened general was not even given time to dress:

> "Stop! let me put my breeches on"
> The general then did pray:

"Your breeches, massa, I will take
For dress we cannot stay."[66]

Although the Patriots were often inclined to self-parody, this hardheaded, slavish character was no Yankee Doodle.

Many black and Indian soldiers were among the hard core of servicemen who remained in the army until the bitter end. Most New Englanders had allowed the war to be fought largely by proxy since around 1778, and subsequent fighting had taken place far away, mostly in the southern states. Even after the American victory at Yorktown in 1781, when the military struggle really ended and most state militias all but disbanded, many black soldiers remained among the long-term members of the Continental Army stationed near West Point for the duration of the war. Many waited in long lines for General Washington himself to sign their discharges on 15 July 1783. Returning home, all veterans faced the economic depression that ravaged the region. Like many white veterans, black and Indian veterans were often cheated out of their back wages and bounty land certificates.[67] Unlike their white compatriots, however, a surprising number of previously enslaved former soldiers even had difficulty preserving their hard-won freedom, as white Patriots adjudicated their cases while they were building their new "free" nation.

Some of those threatened with reenslavement were Loyalists who, at the end of the war, were behind British lines in New York City. Many Patriots, including General George Washington himself, sought to identify and apprehend former slaves who had run away behind British lines during the war: "My own slaves . . . may probably be in New York," Washington wrote, though without much hope of recovering them. Other former masters hired professional agents to represent them and henchmen to do their dirty work. As runaway Boston King later recalled, just the threat of such attempts haunted black refugees in New York: "The dreadful rumor filled us all with inexpressible anguish and horror [and] for some days we lost our appetite for food and sleep departed from our eyes." The reality was no more reassuring. In one of many incidents, a local policeman, Thomas Willis, kidnapped a refugee named Cesar and delivered him to a ship sailing out of state "in return for a gold coin." Fortunately for the refugees, such actions were punished sternly when detected. Whereas Lord Dunmore sent some of those who sought shelter in his army to the West Indies and General Charles Cornwallis surrendered his black followers at Yorktown, British commander in chief Guy Carleton was intent on keeping his word and evacuating as many blacks as he could. Virtually all claims to freedom older than 1782 were recognized as valid, and the testimony of blacks about their status as slaves or free people was largely taken at face value. By the end of 1782, black Loyalists had been issued almost a thousand passes to Nova Scotia.[68]

Meanwhile, formerly enslaved Patriots faced similar threats of reenslavement. Jane Coggeshall—who had been declared free by the General Assembly for intelligence she had provided about British forces in Newport—was threatened with reenslavement in 1785 by members of her former master's family. She went to a sympathetic local gentleman who petitioned the General Assembly on her behalf: "Having considered herself ever since her Escape as a free person and enjoyed the inestimable Blessing of Liberty for over Eight Years, she feels the most dreadful Apprehension at the Idea of again falling into a State of Slavery." Her petition was quickly granted. Even a number of veterans faced challenges to their freedom as soon as the fighting was over. As late as 1789, Colonel Jeremiah Olney, who had commanded the state's black battalion in the Continental Army at the end of the war, brought to the Rhode Island Abolition Society's attention the cases of two veterans who had been freed for their military service but were now threatened with reenslavement by their former masters. Not all of these cases were won easily—and some were not won at all. One Connecticut slave, Frank, purchased his freedom during the war by paying his master out of his wages as a soldier. But on his former master's death in 1815, Frank was claimed as property by the man's son. Despite his defense, the court ruled he was still a slave—after risking his life as a soldier for the country and living more than thirty-five years as a free man.[69]

||| Sticks and Stones |||

About one o'clock on the night of Tuesday, 10 April 1781, a barracks house in the northeastern outskirts of Providence came under attack. Two young civilians, Edward Allen and John Pitcher Jr., hurled stones and wooden sticks at the building and abused the soldiers inside with a barrage of "illiberal Language." Guarding the State House and the local gunpowder reserve, the barracks was on the margins of the growing town: a few blocks to the west lay the densely built-up riverside, to the east lay swamps and farmland. Like others living nearby, Allen and his widowed mother had moved there recently and were struggling to get by. Their home was flanked by a cluster of poor, free black households—William Cesar, Jeffery Turpin, Bonner Brown, and Prince Hopkins—and other neighbors included poor widows, an Indian woman, and several middling men.[70] In contrast, on the eastern side of Benefit Street extended the pastoral estates of merchant Moses Brown and Judge David Howell. The two assailants were men of prime fighting age—Edward Allen was twenty-three—but neither seems to have served in the local militia or in the Continental Army. In this sense, the soldiers they attacked were their substitutes. Whatever touched off their anger that night was apparently tied to the fact that the soldiers in the barracks included members of at least two all-black companies. Perhaps the assault on the black soldiers was, at one level, a performance for their black and white neighbors. Indeed, perhaps it was because these young men were so accustomed to insulting local blacks with impunity that they made a fateful mistake and raised the stakes too high. Allen and his comrade broke down the barracks house door.

The soldiers had been slow to defend themselves and their honor, but this insult was too much. One "negro soldier in the battalion," Prince Greene—a dark-complexioned man, standing five foot five and about thirty-seven years old—loaded his musket and sallied forth. Clues to his courage come from several sources. It may be that he had already been a free man when he enlisted at Warwick, on 27 March 1777, and agreed to serve for the duration of the war. Very likely he was somehow connected to the town's large and well-connected Greene clan, which included the state's current governor. In any case, he had been living as a soldier for four years and had seen a good deal of combat. Like many other soldiers who sealed their newfound independence with formal weddings, Greene had married Rhoda Eldred in North Kingstown a year after his initial enlistment.[71] That night, when he burst through the broken-down door of the barracks house, the two assailants turned tail and ran away. Greene fired anyway. The musket ball hit its mark with remarkable precision: it struck the back of Allen's head, bored a hole about an inch in diameter, and shot through his forehead. He died instantly.

To a grand jury, Greene's response was not the lawful protection of a besieged barracks but murder. He did manage to survive this capital indictment, but only by depending on the sympathies of white authorities. At Greene's trial, the presiding judge was David Howell, who in the years to come became one of the city's leading abolitionists. In addition to the neighbors and officers who testified was the soldier Pero Mowry, a former slave from East Greenwich, who had only months before become one of the few black men to receive a badge of honor and to be promoted to the rank of corporal.[72] The all-white jury found Greene guilty not of murder but only of manslaughter. He had good enough legal representation to know to request the benefit of the clergy, which was granted, thus sparing his life. Judge Howell ordered him to forfeit his property, pay court costs, and suffer his right hand to be branded "M" in open court with a hot iron.[73] The burn had hardly begun to heal when Greene went off to rejoin his regiment, then stationed in upstate New York, where he remained in service for several more years. The only permanent record of his life was in obscure official papers that document the end of his military career.

In contrast, the body of young Edward Allen received a monument. His mother presumably helped choose the epitaph for his blue slate headstone: "In Memory of Mr. EDWARD Son of Mr. EDWARD and Mrs. ELIZABETH ALLEN who by Misfortune was shot by a Negroe Soldier April the 10th 1781 in the 23rd Year of his age."[74] This choice of words—adding racial insult to mortal injury—is striking in several respects. "Misfortune," seems a oddly neutral way to describe the events of that night: its accidental quality erasing the responsibility not only of Allen, who did provoke the fight, but also of Greene, who, after all, was tried for murder with malice aforethought. After thus evading the question of blame, the epitaph goes on to attack Prince Greene not as an individual but for what he represented about military manhood and white identity. Surely his name was well known, but it was not used. Instead, Allen was not shot by "a soldier" or by "a Negro" but by "a Negroe Soldier." An incident that apparently began with a young man assaulting the dignity and legitimacy of black soldiers ended with his mother carving that message in stone.

For many years, Edward Allen's epitaph stood as one of the only public commemorations of black military service in the Revolutionary War. The country paid its devotion to distinguished officers and virtually deified General Washington, whose visit to Providence a few weeks before the Allen shooting had been an affair of the greatest pomp and honor. But even before the war ended, the state governments began to refuse to give black and Indian soldiers their due. Toward the end of the war, black and Indian soldiers witnessed the shift in recruitment policies whereby all men of color were officially excluded from the honor of military service. Restrictions on their service were reinstated in Massachusetts, Connecticut, and many other states as early as 1780. By 1785, the New England states categorically excluded blacks and Indians from their militias, and the federal government had made the Continental Army all white.[75]

The war did not end well for Prince Greene. He was among those unlucky soldiers sent on the disastrous Oswego expedition in February 1783. He lost all the toes on both feet trudging through the night on snowshoes and, along with many others similarly frostbitten, was discharged as disabled.[76] Like many other veterans, he returned to a weary, economically depressed, and seemingly ungrateful homeland. In 1785, Greene gave his discharge papers to his commanding officer, Colonel Olney, to help him procure a state disability pension. By 1790 he was living outside Providence, in East Greenwich, with two other people, presumably his wife and a child. And in 1793—coincidentally on the anniversary of the Allen shooting—he received $301.11 in back wages for his military service.[77] Although he finally obtained his financial due, he and other black and Indian veterans found it difficult to claim honor and respect as citizens.

One of the first sympathetic mentions of black veterans in print after the war was an anecdote published in the *American Magazine of Wit* in 1808 that both rendered the black soldier as foolishly subservient and lamented the racism that denied black veterans respect. It is the story of a wounded Revolutionary soldier facing the amputation of two limbs with astonishing pluck: "Neber mind, massa, take um off—tank God, I got noder leg and noder arm left for um yet." This patriotic parable ends with a barb: "Had he been a freeman instead of an African, how would he have been celebrated."[78] Indeed, freedom was, for most New Englanders of color, the most obvious and important legacy of the war. But, as this anecdote's casual opposition of the categories "freeman" and "African" suggests, the process of abolishing slavery was full of its own tensions and conflicts. The experience of black veterans and others freed during the war demonstrated that freedom would always be a struggle to achieve and often a challenge to maintain. And even when secured, freedom was no guarantee of respect or full citizenship.

Negotiating Freedom

||| Providence, 1790 |||

In February 1790, a black sailor named James Tom approached a member of the Providence Abolition Society with a common enough story: he was being held in slavery but by rights should have been free. His case was notable mainly because the man attempting to enslave him, John Brown, was the city's richest merchant, the state's most vocal defender of slavery, and the elder brother of the region's leading abolitionist, Moses Brown. Almost a year earlier the two brothers had publicly locked horns in a fierce newspaper battle over the Abolition Society's goals and tactics. Angered by attempts to "blacken his character" and browbeat him into servile acquiescence, John Brown declared, "In my opinion there was no more crime in bringing off a cargo of slaves than in bringing off a cargo of jack asses."[1]

The local abolitionists took on Tom's case and dispatched a committee to visit the defiant merchant at the imposing brick mansion he had just built between Power and Benevolent Streets. Not expecting easy compliance, the committee came prepared to threaten him with a superior court lawsuit. But what happened next astonished even worldly abolitionists. Brown quietly dispatched men to seize Tom, take him aboard one of his ships, and secure him in irons. When a court officer went down to the river to serve a writ of habeas corpus, Brown's employees phys-

ically barred him from boarding the vessel. Eventually, after considerable legal pos-
turing, they negotiated a compromise. The society dropped its threatened lawsuit,
and Brown let Tom go free. Not one to leave the last word unsaid, the unrepentant
merchant complained to his brother that the Abolition Society "had as good a right
to Claim his Coat on his Back as his Negro."[2]

Whereas John Brown was outraged that moral and political standards about
slavery were changing around him, his brother Moses Brown had embraced and
actively shaped the change in public sensibilities. Like his brother, Moses had
grown up with slaves and used enslaved workers in his business and household.
And, like most New Englanders, he did not at first give any thought to slavery as
a *moral* problem. As one New Englander recalled, "It was a very rare thing to hear
the [slave] trade reprobated. Some disliked the custom of keeping negroes from
prudential considerations; but the number was small indeed who had religious scruples."[3] When a slave ran away, a master could publish his view of the facts in a
newspaper, and the public could be expected to watch out for potential runaways—
which often meant simply any unfamiliar black men—and turn them in. Public
officials and town jails commonly helped secure suspected runaways for their
claimants. Only in the 1770s was the morality of slavery publicly challenged outside the Religious Society of Friends. Moses Brown quickly converted. He soon
freed his own slaves, dedicated himself to helping others gain their freedom, and
organized the political campaigns that first restricted, then outlawed, the slave trade
and finally mandated the gradual abolition of slavery throughout the state. Although Brown's activism was exceptional, his change in views was not. By 1790,
most New Englanders agreed that the slave trade was pernicious and that slave
keeping was inhumane and unjust. It was presumed that black people claiming
freedom were free, and a wide network of antislavery activists and sympathizers
skirted laws to shelter even those known to be illegally escaping enslavement. A
crucial link in this network was Moses Brown, even as he continued to fight with
his own brother.

The Brown brothers' struggle neatly symbolizes the familiar story of abolition
in New England, which imagines settlers confronting a choice between self-interest
and ideological consistency, between the profits of slavery and the ideals ratified by
the Revolution. On a larger scale, the brothers represent an enduring struggle
between commerce and compassion, greed and benevolence, the tyranny of
paternalism and the liberating power of the market. Today, debate about the
eighteenth-century antislavery movement in New England—and in the wider At-

lantic world—often concentrates on explaining the complex relationships between capitalism and conscience. Did slavery lose out to wage labor because it was less competitive, or because it came to seem ideologically inconsistent? If conscience was the prime motive, did the impulse to recognize human equality derive from religious beliefs or natural-rights ideals? Often, answers to these questions are rosily patriotic: the invisible hand of the market made the outmoded system of slavery wither away of its own accord, or at great personal sacrifice "Americans" freed their slaves in order to honor the ideals of liberty and equality enshrined by the Revolution. Such questions are misleading—and the answers they inspire inadequate—because they focus too narrowly on the problem of slavery as a moral struggle for white people. If the problem of slavery was anything, it was a struggle over power and the most basic meanings of citizenship.

James Tom's struggle to claim his freedom reminds us, first of all, that the abolition of slavery in New England was not the result of some amorphous collective consciousness suddenly, or even gradually, changing its mind. The struggle over slavery involved not only activists, slaveholders, and enslaved people themselves but also other members of a broad civil society. To understand the contours of this struggle we need, first, to recast manumission not as the antithesis of slavery but as part of its nature. Few enslaved people got free by convincing their masters that slavery was wrong; many, however, did earn manumission as part of a more or less articulate quid pro quo. The Brown brothers' Uncle Obadiah, for instance, freed his slaves at his death in the 1750s—not to express any moral or political sentiment, but as a reward for long and faithful service. Other slaves used promises of faithful service or financial compensation—or threats of disruption, desertion, and even violence—to force their masters into more explicit negotiations. Still, any agreement forged by masters and slaves was effective only to the extent to which it could be enforced. Both masters and slaves, therefore, depended on the agency of a broader civil society. Legal disputes over manumission agreements help illuminate the triangular nature of these power negotiations between masters, slaves, and the public.

The nature of the "public opinion" that gradually turned against slavery needs to be understood in light of its dependence on specific strains of humanitarian sensibility—attuned more to questions of innocence, the "natural affections" among families, and cruelty than to questions of equality or even liberty. Attention to the centrality of emotional sensibility in antislavery propaganda helps explain both the sequence of events and their limits. Activists first targeted abuses within master-slave relationships, then slave trading, and lastly gradual—not immediate—emancipation. This sequence of priorities and tactics did not simply follow from a rationalistic application of a set of principles about human liberty and property or from a religious emphasis on equality or the golden rule. Sometimes, those experiencing this kind of sympathy even seemed to take pleasure in the suffering and subjugation of others.[4] Indeed, the language of sensibility provided such a compelling correlative to the languages of natural rights and Christian benevolence precisely because it evaded and obscured the question of equality.

Both the power and limits of humanitarian sensibility reveal new aspects of the process by which individuals held in slavery actually became free. A quick glance at census figures shows that the emancipation statutes that proliferated after the Revolution in the northern states did not end slavery in any literal sense. Rather, as legal records and the papers of abolitionists reveal, slavery crumbled largely through the actions of slaves themselves. Enslaved New Englanders seized on opportunities presented by newly organized activists and decisive shifts in public opinion. This conflicted, ambivalent process had important implications for the fate of regional identities, the role of free black people, and the meaning of citizenship in the new nation. If the story of abolition in the North is one of the great triumphs of well-intentioned activism in modern history, the process was made possible by compromises, contradictions, and limitations with which all Americans are still struggling.

||| Slavery and Social Life |||

A fat packet of legal files always holds the promise of a good story, and the sporadic challenges to illegal enslavement brought before the courts of colonial New England present dramatic and often surprising accounts of slavery and freedom. Enfolded within one file from the Rhode Island Superior Court sitting at South Kingstown in May 1772 is a deposition in which James Gardiner told the story of his son's death ten years earlier. One day back in 1763, James's wife and his brother heard a noise in the kitchen. They rushed to investigate. They found the kitchen floor flooded. Water overflowed from a large kettle over the fire. In the kettle was the Gardiners' two-year-old son. Mrs. Gardiner pulled her mortally scalded child from the hot water. Before dying, he cried that he had been pushed into the kettle by one of the family's several servants, a woman around thirty years old named Mary Wamsley. She, at that moment, was running out the back door.[5]

Oddly enough, this testimony did not form part of a murder prosecution: Mary Wamsley was never punished for that act. Rather, these files document a civil suit brought ten years later by Mary Wamsley against the dead boy's father. She accused James Gardiner of illegally imprisoning her young daughter Susanna and attempting to sell the girl into slavery. Although the members of her family had formerly been slaves, Wamsley claimed that they were now free. This claim derived from a manumission agreement in which slave and master had negotiated a contract for the slave's freedom. This practice was not uncommon in colonial New England, but the manumissions documented in court records tended to be those that one party or the other was not honoring. Recurrent legal attempts to enforce manumission agreements reveal the tense social relations of slavery and freedom in colonial communities. Such contracts were not just between masters and slaves but rested for their meaning and practical force on an unnamed party, the public: the actions of family members, neighbors, townspeople, and strangers—and access to legal arbitration—frequently determined who had to honor what contracts and who could ignore promises with impunity.

In the Wamsleys' case, the dispute over what had actually transpired and what it meant—how the Wamsleys acquired a claim to freedom, how the Gardiners kept Mary's mother, Mary, and her daughters in servitude, and how she ultimately sought legal vindication—all help explain the dynamics of manumission and the meaning of freedom in colonial New England. It was a family saga that went back more than half a century and spanned three generations of two closely interconnected families.

The story begins in November 1706, with a fateful self-sacrifice made by Mary's grandfather in the name of paternal devotion. At that time, Thomas Wamsley was a free "mulato" man living in Kingstown and married to a local "molata" woman, Patience. Around January she had given birth to their first child, whom they named Thomas. Unlike her husband, Patience was not free. She was the slave of a local farmer, Henry Gardiner, and young Thomas Jr. and any other children she bore would also be his slaves. Wamsley did not have the wherewithal to purchase his wife and newborn son; indeed, he was in debt to a local shoemaker. So he used his best asset—the value of his labor—to strike the best deal he could.

Wamsley agreed to bind himself "as an apprentice" to Gardiner for a term of five years. When the five years were up, his wife and any children under the age of one that they might have would be immediately free; in addition, they would receive one cow and a calf. The "master and servant" further agreed that any other

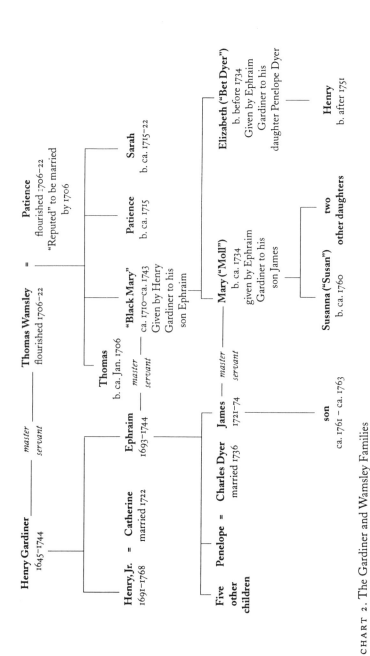

CHART 2. The Gardiner and Wamsley Families

children Wamsley and his wife might have during the five years of the indenture would be freed when they turned twenty-four years old. According to English custom, the children of servants were often liable to long indentures: pregnancy, birth, and the rearing of a young child cost the master in both expenses and lost profits, and therefore he was entitled to repayment from the labor of the child for a certain amount of time after he or she began to be productive, that is, in the child's late teens. Two neighbors witnessed the drafting of a formal contract, written in two copies on a single, large piece of paper; the signatures were sealed with hot red wax; and the page was cut with a wavy line so that the two copies could be matched against each other if their authenticity ever came into question.[6]

This contract did not, however, accurately predict what came to pass between the Wamsleys and the Gardiners. Even before Thomas Wamsley had signed his agreement with Henry Gardiner in November 1706, he and his wife, Patience, had already had one child—a son named Thomas, who had been born some months earlier (chart 2). And during the five-and-a-half-year term of the contract, while they lived and worked on Gardiner's farm, they had at least one more child, a daughter called "Black Mary," who was born around 1710. In subsequent years, they had two more daughters—Patience, born around 1715, and Sarah, born a few years later. According to the terms of the original agreement, when the parents, Thomas and Patience, became free in May 1712, they would have to leave at least two of their children behind. Thomas Jr. was not mentioned in the agreement and so would have remained Gardiner's slave. Black Mary, who was born during the term of the agreement, would have been required to continue to serve the Gardiners until she reached the age of twenty-four. As it happened, Thomas Wamsley (and perhaps his wife, as well) remained in the Gardiners' service ten years longer than originally agreed. Very likely, he agreed to the extra time in order to secure the freedom of his son—or to shorten the terms his daughters would have to serve. Certainly, in subsequent years, Thomas Wamsley Jr. was a free man: he was christened at the South Kingstown Anglican church in 1736; worked as a laborer for various locals, including minister James MacSparran, in the 1750s; married; and raised a large family in the area.[7] In any case, the elder Thomas Wamsley and at least two of his daughters were still bound to Gardiner as late as 1722.

As it happened, when Thomas Wamsley finally became free in 1722, Henry Gardiner offered a last-minute renegotiation: Wamsley could take either the cow or *one* of his daughters right away. Wamsley consulted with his wife and chose the younger of their two daughters remaining in service. (Whether this was Sarah or

Patience is unclear; it may be that one of the two had died or become free by this time.) Why the younger girl? Gardiner may have preferred to get rid of the younger girl because she was too young to be of much use around his household. By the same token, the Wamsleys may also have preferred to redeem their younger daughter because "Black Mary" was several years older and therefore would have much less time to serve before reaching the age of twenty-four. In any case, the girl they left behind was the fourteen-year-old "Black Mary."[8]

Most colonial manumissions were bargains in which enslaved men and women bound themselves to continued servitude in exchange for a promise of future freedom. There was sometimes a written contract, but more often there was an oral promise by the master: if you serve me well for a certain number of years, or until I die, then I will free you. The contractual arrangement illustrates an important feature of manumission. Most often freedom was not a benevolent "gift" from master to slave but part of a more or less explicit exchange designed to extract the most work possible for the master in exchange for freedom for the enslaved. Such contracts were typical of the constant negotiations of power between master and slave, especially in the close quarters and intimate working conditions of colonial New England.[9]

Whether a master would agree to a manumission depended on a number of variables largely tied to the value of a slave's potential labor. Often a slave was easiest to let go either when the master died or when the slave grew too old to work much. A postmortem bequest appealed to masters who wanted to benefit from a slave's labor for as long as possible. This practice was generally accepted, though heirs sometimes protested the loss of the value of the enslaved people. Freeing elderly slaves saved masters the expense of keeping them when they were no longer as productive. This tactic raised broader concerns in the community and led to legal restrictions on manumission in many states. Early in the century, the Rhode Island government restricted manumission as a precaution against mercenary slave owners shirking responsibility for their infirm, helpless, and therefore useless slaves. Similar restrictions in other states discouraged manumission, partly because of fear about free blacks becoming public charges and partly, it would seem, because the presence of free blacks was thought to undermine slavery.[10]

So, at the age of fourteen, "Black Mary" was the only member of the Wamsley family left in Gardiner's household—bound for another ten years of service. Apparently, as Henry Gardiner aged and his household shrank, he decided he did not need her any more. As the patriarch reached his late seventies, his two sons were around thirty years old and establishing their independence. The elder brother, Henry Jr., married in 1722 and settled across the bay in Newport—where his father had been born in 1645—perhaps to maintain commercial ties between the port and the large farms the Gardiners and other early settlers had begun developing in the fertile Narragansett region. The younger brother, Ephraim, remained in the Kingstown area and settled on a large commercial farm, worked mainly by enslaved laborers. It was to Ephraim that the patriarch gave the young "Black Mary."

Although this arrangement suited the Gardiners, it exposed "Black Mary" to two dangers. First, the custom of binding the children of servants for long periods of service established a vicious cycle. In the Wamsley family, the same pattern recurred generation after generation. The grandparents became free in the 1720s, but they had already had children and had to leave one of them behind. By the time "Black Mary" reached the age of twenty-four, around 1734, she had already had two daughters—the first named Mary, after her mother, the second named Elizabeth. Whatever their legal status, the fact that they were born to a woman in service gave Ephraim Gardiner the right to appropriate their labor until at least the age of twenty-four.

This vicious cycle of servitude also created confusion about the family's legal status, blurring the distinction between indenture and permanent servitude. The family was legally free but actually bound to servitude for generation after generation. Or were the Wamsleys actually still slaves for life? Ephraim Gardiner took advantage of the confusion by claiming the Wamsleys not as temporary servants but as perpetual slaves.

Attempts to resolve this claim in 1772 revolved around memories of the nature of the agreements old Henry Gardiner had made with Thomas Wamsley on the one hand and with his son Ephraim on the other. The extant copy of the 1706 indenture was apparently not available to this branch of the Wamsley family. According to Catherine Gardiner's testimony, the original agreement had made "Black Mary" a free person at birth; she were merely bound by the contract to serve a term of years. Thus, when the patriarch gave "Black Mary" to Ephraim, it was merely "to serve out her time or rather the time he had in her." According to Ephraim, however, the girl had been born a slave—and she was given to him without any binding provision for her eventual freedom. Only years after that gift did the question of freeing her come up, and even then it was only a suggestion, Ephraim insisted: "When said Negro grew to the age of a Woman my said father advised me to free her if She Lived to the age of Twenty fore years old." Whether he followed this advice was a matter of his discretion.

Around 1734, when "Black Mary" turned twenty-four, she took matters into her own hands. She left her master's farm and moved to the city of Newport. There she lived with and worked for her former master's sister-in-law, Catherine Gardiner, who, with her husband Henry Jr., operated an inn in the bustling seaport. Such a transition—mediated through an extended family—was not unusual for enslaved people beginning new, free lives. They often wanted to establish distance from their former masters to mark their independence but did not want to entirely break off relationships that could potentially be useful.[11] In this case, "Black Mary" had found an ally of enduring importance. Years later, Catherine Gardiner provided crucial testimony about "Black Mary's" status. According to Catharine Gardiner, "after her Time was expired the said Mary Wamsley . . . went at Liberty as a free Person and as such acted." Wamsley moved out of Ephraim Gardiner's household and moved in with Catherine Gardiner in Newport "as a free person."

During the time she lived in Newport, "Black Mary" was sick, and after consultations with several doctors, it was determined that she was terminally consumptive. She moved back to Ephraim Gardiner's farm and died there after a lingering illness. Catherine Gardiner later argued that she moved back across the bay only so that her daughters could nurse her.

Gardiner, for his part, claimed that she had actually become sick before reaching the age of twenty-four, implied that the move to Newport was in search of better medical treatment, and insisted that she had never actually been manumitted. He claimed that he attempted to free her but that the North Kingstown Town Council had refused to validate the manumission on the grounds that she was too infirm to support herself and too likely to require public support. Under the colony's statute, the Town Council had no such authority; it was merely authorized to require him to post a bond for her future maintenance.[12] Why he could not simply do so and accept responsibility for her support if she became incapacitated is unclear—particularly since he ended up supporting her in her final illness anyway. He claimed he had never so much as talked about freeing her two daughters. Thus, the orphaned Mary Wamsley—likely about four years old—and her even younger sister, Elizabeth, were left behind in a household in which, although they had a good claim to being servants bound only to the age of twenty-four as compensation for their upbringing, they were treated as slaves.

In this climate, the two young girls left in the custody of Ephraim Gardiner had no one to champion their cause. In the coming years, both girls went to serve

Ephraim's children. In 1736, he gave Elizabeth to his daughter Penelope, apparently on the occasion of her marriage. When James married in 1749, his father gave him Mary, who was then about fourteen. She went to live on James Gardiner's farm in North Kingstown. She remained there for fourteen years, through her twenties. During that time, she had three daughters, including one born around 1760 and named Susanna.

A crisis came in 1763. Although Mary Wamsley endured unpaid servitude into her late twenties, she did not accept permanent enslavement. And yet there was no one she could turn to for help—she had no access to the courts, no influential friends, and so she took matters into her own hands. She won her freedom from James Gardiner with the gruesome act of murdering his son. There seems to be no way of knowing why she would kill a two-year-old child or why Gardiner would decline to seek public retribution. Even in capital trials at the time, there was little attempt to capture the motives of actors or the power of their emotions. Perhaps it really was an accident that prompted her first to flee and then to make a claim for permanent freedom. Perhaps at some level she decided to make sure that, whatever the temptations and pressures, she would never be able to return to that household.

At first, some members of the Gardiner family thought that Mary had gone off to find another master to buy her. But it soon became clear that she intended to live as a free woman. She went off to find work about as far as one could get within Rhode Island: across Narragansett Bay to the city of Newport. James Gardiner did not want Mary around and did not try to stop her. His father and his brother urged him to retrieve and either prosecute or sell her. James insisted that he could not stand the sight of her and that when an opportunity appeared he would sell her. But he never did. One explanation for this puzzling behavior is that there may have been some scandalous history between this respectable farmer and his servant that he wanted to prevent from coming to light. Had the relationship between Wamsley and Gardiner been sexual? It was certainly possible. During the decade she lived in his house, Mary Wamsley bore three children, whose paternity was never mentioned in the subsequent legal testimony. Was he now afraid of public dishonor?

Viewing this story in a broader context suggests the *limits* on both masters and slaves as they negotiated power—the role of the "public." Two public institutions, the market and newspapers, would have enhanced James Gardiner's options—if he had exercised them. He was urged to sell Mary after it became clear that she was too dangerous to have around the house—as in other cases, when masters lost control, sale was their last resort. But he made no attempt to do so. He could also have recovered his runaway servant by placing an advertisement in the newspaper. Like the market, runaway advertisements were an instrument of civil society by which an amorphous "public" regulated slavery. Colonial New Englanders could be relied on to watch out for, capture, and return runaway slaves. By law, it was their obligation: a 1714 statute called on "all His Majesty's Ministers of Justice, and all other His Subjects in this Colony" to "take up" any slaves they knew to be passing through their towns without proper certificates from their masters.[13] Does Gardiner's failure to advertise for Wamsley mean that he himself knew he did not have a claim that others would accept?

One clue may lie in the even more surprising fact that when Mary Wamsley fled from North Kingstown she, like her mother, went to Newport and was taken in by James Gardiner's uncle Henry Jr. and his wife, Catherine. Several decades earlier, they had taken in Mary's mother. A decade before that, the year of their marriage, they had witnessed Mary's grandfather completing his agreement with the senior Henry Gardiner. But why would they now harbor and employ the murderer of their nephew's son? Perhaps James's aunt and uncle had some personal animosity toward him. Maybe they knew that Wamsley had been abused in some way. Maybe the younger Henry, having grown up with Mary's mother and having no children of his own, took a paternal interest in her welfare. It was only after he died in 1767 that the claim that the Wamsleys were slaves resurfaced. And when it did, his widow, Catherine, appeared in court to defend the Wamsleys' freedom against the claims of her nephew James.

When Mary Wamsley escaped to Newport, she left her three daughters behind. We know what happened only to one—Susanna. James Gardiner sent the three-and-a-half-year-old Susanna to be raised by another farmer in South Kingstown. For the next seven years this uneasy arrangement continued.

During that time, James Gardiner's finances collapsed, and he filed for bankruptcy. By 1771, almost a third of his assets, some three thousand dollars, were invested in a "negro" woman and three children: that is, Mary Wamsley and her three daughters. Despite the fact that none of them was ever legally Gardiner's slave, that Mary Wamsley was currently living as a free woman in Newport, and that he had wallowed in inaction for almost ten years, he had never quite given up his claim to them as slaves. The bankruptcy administrator, Jeffry Watson, was an old and intimate friend of the Gardiners, and he had none of James's qualms or diffidence.[14] He immediately began scheming to sell the Wamsleys. Not content to stop there,

Watson also formed plans to try to reenslave other descendants of "Black Mary," including a man named Henry Wamsley (Mary's nephew) who was then living as a free man just across the Connecticut border.

By summertime, Mary Wamsley was aware of the threat to her freedom. Over the course of the year 1771, Watson apparently made several unsuccessful attempts to kidnap her. No longer feeling safe at her home in Newport, she went to the town where her daughter Susanna was living. A farmer named Samuel Rodman allowed her to stay with him for several months.

Next, Watson trained his sights on Mary's young, and relatively defenseless, daughter Susanna, who was still legally held in indentured servitude. The administrator made plans to sell Susanna to another local man, who was to sell her to a third man in Connecticut, who was then to sell her again—probably in the Carolinas or West Indies. This complicated paper trail would disguise their shady dealings, and once they had her in the southern colonies, they knew she would never come back.

A hired man was sent to physically retrieve Susanna from the farmer who had raised her. By chance, as Susanna and the hired man were riding away, they passed the local sheriff and Samuel Rodman, the friend and ally of her mother, Mary. They accosted the hired man and asked him to identify himself. He hesitated, but Susanna told them who she was and began to cry. Both men admonished the hired man, but he continued on and delivered the girl to the first of the three prearranged buyers.

Mary Wamsley was immediately alerted of this new development by her ally Rodman. She quickly took action to void the sale of Susanna and to prosecute her kidnappers. Her first legal strategy was successfully evaded by the first buyer. But Mary's patronage network was able to secure the personal intervention of Rhode Island's governor, who issued a precept. Susanna was released, though the first buyer continued to claim ownership of her as a slave. Meanwhile, Susanna's cousin Henry Wamsley also won legal vindication against Watson's attempts to enslave him.[15]

That the intervention of neighbors prevented Mary's daughter—and nephew—from being sold into slavery and spirited far away illustrates again how communal values affected the balance of power between slaves and masters. This social consensus determined who could be enslaved, how much violence masters could use, and what room slaves had to maneuver. Over time, New Englanders were growing less tolerant of some of the basic features of slavery. Instead of taking a master's claim for granted, many New Englanders began taking more responsibility for evaluating the legal and moral bases of their own collaboration with slavery.

It is no accident that 1772 was the year the Wamsley family finally became officially free. By then, Mary Wamsley had a powerful patron. Public concern was also
responsible for an increasing number of legal actions about illegal enslavement—
and an increasing number of sympathetic verdicts. In the 1770s, many other people
of color were able to bring forward claims for freedom, and English colonists
stepped in to protect them and help them win legal vindication. Enslaved people
in Rhode Island had always fought for freedom, but increasingly they began to win.

We know about the story of the Wamsleys because, in order to vindicate her
own and her family's freedom, Mary Wamsley filed a civil lawsuit. She gained the
legal assistance of prominent Newport attorney Thomas Robinson, who would become an important Quaker abolitionist in the years to come. It was crucial for a person claimed as a slave to have a patron to get to court. There had to be someone, for
instance, to pay filing fees, to know how the procedures worked, to file a formal declaration of complaints ahead of time to get the case heard. Before 1772, only one man
in the colony of Rhode Island, Thomas Robinson's cousin Matthew Robinson of
South Kingstown, had allowed himself to be convinced to take on the case of black
people who had completed manumission agreements. He prosecuted two such cases,
winning one in the 1740s and finally losing the other after a series of appeals in 1771.

The legal strategies of the two parties suggest some of the contested symbolic
terrain of community sympathies. Gardiner defended himself by asserting that
Mary, as well as Susanna and her sisters, could hardly have been kidnapped or
wrongfully sold because they had always been slaves. The girls had been his property ever since they were born in his household, Mary since his father had given
her to him some thirty years earlier. James Gardiner had good reason to expect that
the story of his son's murder would sway the sympathies of the court and the jurors. His account was confirmed by his brother and father and denied by no one.
And yet the story failed to obscure deep conflicts within the extended Gardiner
clan. James's aunt Catherine appeared in court as an ally, not of her nephew but
of Mary Wamsley.

Winning by default in the lower court and on appeal at the superior court, Susanna and Mary Wamsley were declared free. They were awarded damages, too,
though the superior court reduced the amount from the lower court's two hundred
pounds to the more nominal fifteen pounds.[16] The official legal documents were
carefully folded, labeled, and filed away, joining a growing series of legal challenges
to slavery that were falling on increasingly sympathetic ears.

In many parts of North America in the late 1760s, those illegally enslaved were increasingly able to get into court—and sometimes they won. The pattern was observable across New England, New Jersey, and Pennsylvania and even in Virginia, where cases of people who claimed to have a good right to freedom were heard by the courts. Yet even in the colony with the strongest antislavery sentiment, Massachusetts, jury verdicts were uneven.[17] During the time the Wamsley case was in court, Matthew Robinson was still dogging the case of a South Kingstown woman named Esther and her daughters, who should have been freed when her mistress died in 1767, leaving a will that manumitted them. Instead, the mistress's heirs fought to keep the family enslaved: the parties pursued the case through a torturous series of appeals. At length, the case was decided against Esther and her children; they were declared slaves because the bond sealing their manumission had not been posted with the local town clerk.[18] Despite their uneven results, these two simultaneous cases were significant: previously, only one other enslaved Rhode Islander had managed to bring a manumission case to court.

In 1773, Deputy Governor Matthew Griswold of Connecticut summed up the new state of affairs: in cases of "outrage, undue Violence or Inhumane severity," he wrote, slaves, like other inhabitants, received the protection of the law. In cases in which the question of freedom was raised, the courts based their decisions on the merits; those illegally held in slavery were freed. And such struggles for liberation did not go unopposed. Although the trials were generally fair, Governor Griswold noted that "people of consideration" did not greatly favor them, for they feared that the freed "negroes" would prove "very Troublesome and Dangerous Inhabitants."[19]

A major reason for the increase in "freedom suits" was the development of a network of abolitionists who began to play an important role as advocates. Mary Wamsley had no advocate available in 1763, but her daughter did ten years later. By about the 1770s, a network of men and women began organizing to help people claim their freedom. This made it much easier for people of color to secure basic legal protections. And it signaled a broader shift in values that helped undermine slavery, or rather mastery, throughout the region. By the 1770s, a growing number of patrons, such as Moses Brown, began to demonstrate a more programmatic urge to curb the abuses of slavery, to ban the slave trade, and ultimately to abolish slave holding. These activists did not alone secure the end of slavery. Rather, advocates intervened as auxiliaries in ongoing struggles between masters and enslaved people. Nonetheless, their role was crucial. Their values and strategies had deep implications for how and when slavery was abolished in the northern colonies—and with what consequences.

||| Affecting Sensibilities |||

The ability of habit to inure the heart to everyday cruelties was a problem that particularly concerned Quaker writers on slavery, and Moses Brown was a case in point. Born into a family of affluent merchants, Moses Brown grew up with slaves and found it easy to take their status for granted. He felt his first moral qualms in 1763 when his brothers proposed fitting out a ship for the African slave trade. They argued him down: he kept slaves himself, didn't he? How was slave trading different? But the voyage was a disaster. The captain's letters and log book were horrifying to read. Even before leaving the Guinea coast, captives began dying; en route to the West Indies they revolted; as they approached the market, many jumped overboard in despair; dozens sickened or starved; and the rest were "so dispirited" that they brought very low prices. Nonetheless, Brown kept the slaves he owned and even bought others, priding himself on his benevolence in hiring tutors to educate them and bringing them to church for spiritual enlightenment. Brown finally came to view slave owning as wrong after a profound emotional crisis in 1773—during which his wife died, he retired from the family business, and he embraced the Quaker ethic of modest living and public service. Brown explained his motives in the formal deed of manumission that freed six men and women outright: "Whereas I am clearly convinced that the buying and selling of men of what colour soever as slaves is contrary to the Divine Mind manifest in the consciences of all men however some may smother and neglect its reprovings, and being also made sensible that holding negroes in slavery however kindly treated by their masters has a tendency to encourage the iniquitous practice of importing them from their native country and is contrary to that justice, mercy, and humanity enjoined as the duty of every christian."[20]

Even here, Brown was first moved by the evils of the slave trade and only secondarily convinced that slaveholding itself had insalubrious effects. And yet Moses Brown soon became a committed advocate of the rights of enslaved people and a crucial leader of the movement to abolish the African slave trade and to eradicate slaveholding throughout New England. Within a few years slavery was crumbling in much of the new nation, the Continental Congress had specifically suspended the slave trade, and plans for gradually abolishing slavery were under consideration in legislatures as far south as Virginia.

In the era of the American Revolution, public support for slavery was challenged less by concepts of liberty or equality than by humanitarian sensibility. As a Rhode

Islander put the problem in 1784, "[To argue that Negroes] are by Nature Free, and that they have at this Time, an undoubted Right to have their Liberty, appears to me like repeating the Letters of the Alphabet.—It is a First Principle, and is felt by all Freemen who reflect upon the Feelings of their own Minds." He was aware, however, that not all freemen actually did this kind of reflection. So he advised, "What remains therefore usefully to be said upon the Subject, should not be addressed to the Head, but to the Heart. What is necessary, is to stir up the Sparks of Compassion in the human Breast."[21] The many individuals who began to take on antislavery roles in the 1770s came from many religious traditions and varied substantially in their convictions. Many others, however, did not have to feel that slavery was wrong. Activists and restless slaves forced them to act, even if they did not want to. Neither consensus nor consistency was necessary for their efforts to undermine support for slavery at law, among legislatures, and in the more amorphous but critical domain of public opinion. And yet the agenda of activists, the sequence of legislation passed by colonial assemblies, and the tenor of the propaganda disseminated by antislavery activists all suggest the typicality of Moses Brown's emotional arguments. Colonial advocates such as Matthew Robinson in Rhode Island had attempted to redress abuses of slavery, particularly helping to free people unlawfully held in bondage. The new agenda moved on to attack first the international slave trade and then the sale of slaves within the United States and finally to promote the gradual abolition of slavery itself. In all these respects, the Quakers established during the 1750s and 1760s the basic arguments and methods that antislavery activism adopted and extended in the 1770s and 1780s. The experience of the Quakers helps illuminate how activists came to serve as a fulcrum that gradually shifted the lines of power in the ongoing struggles between masters and servants—and the limits of their goals and achievements.

By the early 1770s, Quakers on both sides of the Atlantic had developed a strong emphasis on the emotional costs of slavery in terms that resonated with a broader literary culture of sensibility. Among Quakers uneasy about slavery, the basic principle of the golden rule—the injunction to treat others as one would have them treat oneself—had long proved insufficient to persuade their brethren. Like many other local meetings in New England and the Mid-Atlantic, the South Kingstown monthly meeting had adopted resolutions condemning slavery early in the century, but many members continued to hold slaves; and when a local farmer in 1757 confronted the meeting with a forthright denunciation of slavery as selfish and unfair, his words fell on deaf ears.[22] In contrast, the 1754 epistle of the Philadelphia Yearly Meeting established a powerful strain of argument based on emotional sensibility. At the heart of the document was the fear that slave keeping had an "unnatural Tendency to lessen our Humanity." As these Quakers explained, slave keeping tends to inure our "tender and feeling sense of [the] miseries of our Fellow Creatures" and makes us "less susceptible to the Holy Spirit of Love, Meekness and Charity." In trying to help other Friends see the light on slavery, the writer of the epistle emphasized two themes that became crucial to subsequent antislavery propaganda: first, that Africans were in "good circumstances" and "happy" in their native country; and second, that forcing these "poor Creatures" into slavery was a traumatic ordeal characterized by violence and family separation—"Parents from Children, and Children from Parents." The epistle left open a loophole for slave-owning Quakers, arguing that slavery was acceptable in cases in which enslaved individuals required care, support, or supervision for "their Good." Moved by the cruelty of slavery in the 1750s, Quakers in Philadelphia and London acted first against the obvious brutality of the slave trade.

In the 1760s New England Quakers, like their Pennsylvania peers, began purging their ranks first of slave traders and only later of slaveholders. When Moses Brown joined the Society of Friends in 1774, Quaker meetings across the region were still struggling with recalcitrant slaveholders. Soon, Brown himself began participating in the process of antislavery persuasion within the Smithfield monthly meeting. One of those disowned was his friend Stephen Hopkins. Erstwhile governor of the colony, Hopkins bridled under the impertinence of the discipline committee, even though he soon became an active supporter of antislavery legislation. Only in late 1776 could the New England Yearly Meeting report to London that some recalcitrant local meetings had finally come into line with the policy that defiant slave keepers should be disowned. In many meetings, it seems that a large portion of Friends, given the choice, kept their slaves rather than their membership in the society.[23]

As Quakers and other advocates of ending slavery tried to purge others of the sin of slavery, they first intensified the old paternalistic tradition of fighting to curb current abuses, particularly by championing the rights of individuals who were illegally enslaved. Men such as Moses Brown in Providence, Thomas Robinson in Newport, Jeremy Belknap in New Hampshire, Robert Treat Paine in Boston, Elias Boudinot in New Jersey, James Pemberton in Philadelphia, and Granville Sharpe in London worked in similar ways. In dealing with the audacious kidnappers and ruthless masters, prominent abolitionists could often obviate legal action by deploying their powers of intimidation and shame.[24] Unlike earlier activists, however, this growing network encouraged the manumission even of people legally held in slavery.

As these gentlemen acquired reputations as advocates, enslaved people "anxious for . . . Liberty" sought their assistance. In early 1770, Benjamin Shearborne's slave Jinney and her husband grew "very desirous" that their two-year-old son should be manumitted, and they managed to collect the necessary two hundred pounds "from the Generosity of diverse and well disposed Persons." Gentlemen such as Moses Brown went further in pressuring masters to write manumission agreements. In one case, Moses Brown intervened when an enslaved black sailor was brutally whipped and maltreated and helped him negotiate a manumission with his master. As early as 1776, Newport resident John Quamine wrote to thank Brown for his work "in regard to the unforfeited rights of the poor unhappy Africans in this province. As "one of that nation," Quamine thanked Brown for all his "ardent endeavours for the speedy salvation of my poor enslaved countrymen."[25] The emergence of public figures willing to help enslaved people changed the state of slavery for all New Englanders.

Increasingly coordinating their efforts, activists also worked to help slaves mount legal and political challenges to slavery, even in cases in which an individual's claim to freedom was not technically clear. In Rhode Island, Moses Brown seized on a sympathetic case to rally opinion at the Providence town meeting and secure a broader mandate against the slave trade and slavery itself. For some time before his death in 1774, Jacob Shoemaker of Providence had conducted no business, living off the labor of his slaves Tom (a man in his mid-forties) and Tom's wife, who did the domestic work of the household. He promised his slaves their freedom but never got around to making a will. When Shoemaker died without heirs, his property devolved to the town. At the public meeting, the voters of Providence faced a relatively easy decision, since Tom and his family had a clear "moral" claim and no one in particular had a financial stake in keeping them enslaved. Rectifying this abuse, voters invoked the libertarian rhetoric of the escalating imperial crisis, declaring that enslaving the family would be unbecoming to "the character of freemen." Capitalizing on the sentiment aroused by the Shoemaker case, Moses Brown and other activists pushed through the town meeting a resolution calling for an end to the importation of slaves into the colony and the gradual emancipation of children born there to slave parents.

Even so, Tom, his wife, and his children were hardly free and clear. To cover the debts of their former master's estate, the freemen of Providence had voted to indenture the children to some appropriate master or mistress and to bind out Tom and his wife, as well, if necessary. Meanwhile, behind the scenes, a new threat emerged: a man in Antigua who had somehow obtained Shoemaker's slaves on that island wrote claiming ownership of Tom and his family. But the man he contacted in Providence was Moses Brown's brother Nicholas, who fended him off with a somewhat exaggerated report of the state of antislavery sentiment: "It's the opinion of some of our principal Attorney's that takeing in all circumstances, with the present disposition of People in New England against Slavery, that the Children born here, if not the others, upon a trial at Law, would be confirmed Free. There is no getting possession of them so as by any means to get them away without an exspensive Suite if it succeeded." Moses Brown himself threatened to finance any legal defense Tom's family might need.[26]

Brown seized on the political charge of the Providence town meeting and pushed for action in the Rhode Island General Assembly. He focused, like the Quakers in the years before, on a largely symbolic attack on the slave trade. With the help of troubled Quaker Stephen Hopkins, Brown drafted a bill barring Rhode Islanders from taking part in the African slave trade. Newport merchants, who were the only North Americans who controlled any substantial share of this lucrative (if risky) trade, managed to restrict the law that was passed to cover only the importation of slaves for sale into the colony—thus allowing them to take part in the trade as long as they sold the slaves in other colonies and allowing them to import some slaves they failed to sell elsewhere. Connecticut and other states soon passed similar laws. Such victories had only minor effects because so few New Englanders took part in the slave trade directly. In any case, the African trade was effectively blocked by the escalating imperial crisis. That year, the General Congress of the United States suspended the importation of African slaves as part of a more general attempt to suspend trade with Britain.[27] If opposition to the slave trade could rally only narrow victories, swaying public opinion against slaveholding was even harder.

Drawing heavily on the themes of the Quaker antislavery literature written by the likes of Anthony Benezet and John Woolman, the propaganda produced and disseminated by activists such as Brown emphasized the innocence of Africans, the violation of the "natural affections" of family members by the slave trade, and the suffering of slaves at the hands of tropical planters. During 1774, Moses Brown promoted antislavery legislation in private and in the newspapers. He planted several pieces in the *Providence Gazette*, published by the sympathetic slaveholder John

Carter. Philadelphia Quaker Anthony Benezet, in a series of influential tracts, attempted to counter the assumptions of defenders of slavery. He emphasized the innocence and happiness of Africans in Africa (they did not "need" to be rescued from backwardness); the brutality of the slave trade, particularly the wrenching separations of family members (even if they did need to be rescued, this was not the way to do it); and the extent to which mastery was characterized by violence and greed (not paternal benevolence). When the *Providence Journal* featured an extract from John Wesley's writings on the slave trade in late 1774, it described the trade, accurately, as "*very pathetic.*" In this passage, Wesley addressed slave traders: "Are you a man? Then you should have an *human* heart. But have you indeed? . . . Do you never *feel* another's pain? . . . When you saw the flowing eyes, the heaving breasts, or the bleeding sides and tortured limbs of your fellow creatures, was you a stone or a brute? . . . When you squeezed the agonizing creatures down in the ship, or when you threw their poor mangled remains into the sea, had you no relenting? Did not one tear drop from your eye, one sigh escape from your breast?"[28]

The atrocities of the slave trade were relentlessly exploited by antislavery writers, precisely because they made the moral and emotional problems of slavery so clear. Like many other writers in the 1770s, the Newport Congregationalist minister Samuel Hopkins assumed that the public opposed the transatlantic slave trade and devoted his persuasive energy to proving that purchasing or merely keeping slaves was the same as participating directly in the slave trade. Throughout the 1770s, Hopkins could not convince Newport newspaper editors to print his forthright indictments of slavery. The *Newport Mercury* did, however, publish pieces that evoke the moral problem of slavery in less direct and more ambiguous ways.[29]

The extent to which abolitionist discourse resonated with a broader culture of sensibility is clearest in the proliferation of poetry, polemical tracts, and travelers' accounts about Africans and slaves in the New England press. Suicide, a salient trope in the literature of sensibility, was commonly used to evoke sympathy for slaves and dramatize the nobility of the proud, African character. At a time when the tender affection of family ties was becoming an increasingly vaunted ideal, the slave trade inherently involved separating families. Sentimental poems and tracts focused on the suffering of blacks separated from families. A writer to the *Providence Gazette* offered a "striking instance of this kind" involving a Negro residing near Philadelphia: "From his first arrival he appeared thoughtful and dejected, frequently dropping tears, when fondling his master's children; the cause of which was not known till he was able to be understood, when he gave the following account:

That he had a wife and children in his native country; that some of their being sick, he went in the night time to fetch water at a spring, where he was violently seized and carried away by persons who lay in wait to catch him, from whence he was transported to America; that the remembrance of his family and friends, whom he never expected to see any more, were the principal cause of his dejection and grief."[30] A characteristic engraving was produced by Philadelphian Thomas Brannagan in 1805, emphasizing the traumatic separation of family members (fig. 13).

The culture of sensibility particularly valued the ability to feel the pain of others—and captives in the slave trade and slaves on tropical plantations were described with special attention to bleeding, torture, and anguish. Sheet music published in London during the 1770s included a song called "The Suffering Negro." Generally, these works did not include forthright statements of human equality—a close parallel to it was the growing fashion for expressing antipathy for cruelty to animals. After featuring abolitionist propaganda on the first page of one issue, a Providence newspaper featured, on the second, a report from Bath about a local butcher who had adopted a new, painless method of slaughtering cows—not for the ignoble purpose of gaining business from members of the local Society for the Prevention of Cruelty to Animals but "from motives of humanity only."[31]

As scrutiny into the status of those dubiously enslaved increased, and as support for slavery flagged, many masters took advantage of regional differences by selling slaves southward. Abolitionists intervened in several of these cases, which concerned them especially because of the southern and West Indian colonies' association in abolitionists' minds with the slave trade and with cruel conditions. Consider the case of Priamus, a Revolutionary War veteran from Rhode Island who had completed the terms of a conditional manumission in 1779. By a quirk of fate, he was captured by the British, was taken to Philadelphia, and then stayed behind when the British evacuated the city. Neither their previous agreement nor physical distance prevented his former master from selling him. During the brutal winter of Valley Forge, Priamus attracted the attention of abolitionists in Philadelphia, who anxiously reported to their counterparts in Providence that he was ill clothed, badly fed, and in danger of being sold again southward, where they would not be able to obtain legal recourse. Ultimately, Priamus, who had justly earned his freedom, was vindicated before the law. In another case, Quakers in Newport and New Bedford joined forces with Moses Brown to prevent a woman named Binah from being sold to a "Carolina" man. In yet another case, a girl named Sarah, born free to a white mother, had been illegally held in slavery for more than

FIGURE 13. "The husband and wife, after being sold to different purchasers, violently separated." This image of the slave trade in Africa appeals to "natural affections" and plays on
the sympathies rather than the ethical principles of the viewer to arouse antislavery sentiment in America. It further plays on the viewer's sensibility by depicting all Africans as
innocent victims of white kidnappers and omitting the complex economic and political
networks that sustained the slave trade in West Africa. Thomas Brannagan, *A Preliminary
Essay on the Oppression of the Exiled Sons of Africa* (Philadelphia, 1804), frontispiece. Courtesy of the Library Company of Philadelphia.

a decade without public notice—but immediately after she was sold to a North
Carolina merchant, her status was challenged in court. On the verge of being
shipped off southward, she was liberated.[32]

The case of Abigail suggests how strongly people responded to the sentimental arguments associated with the threat of "sale south." In the late spring of 1779,
North Carolina resident John Rice traveled through New England buying slaves
to bring back to his home state. Aware of popular opposition in New England
against selling slaves southward, he claimed to be from Hartford, Connecticut.

Passing through South Kingstown in May, he purchased Abigail and her three young children, who seemed quite happy to live with him in Hartford. Rice continued north, leaving Abigail and her children where they were, and returned with a wagon a month later. He picked up Abigail and her children and stopped in the adjacent town of Charlestown to spend the night. His real intentions became clear, and Abigail was joined in her resistance to being sent south by a number of other locals who took it upon themselves to intervene. Rice awoke the next morning to find Abigail and her children gone, and he was threatened with personal danger if he went after them.[33] Revulsion against trading slaves southward was so powerful that in the fall of 1779, when Abigail's case came before the Rhode Island legislature, it was officially enshrined in law. The General Assembly ordered Abigail and her children to be kept within the state and passed a law to prevent the sale of slaves out of state without their consent.[34] As other northern states passed similar laws, an older paternalistic distinction between "good" masters and bad ones was redrawn on a regional scale. If slavery at home was tolerable, slavery in other places was not.

As public opinion shifted, as war disrupted everyday life, as public collaboration and activism against aspects of slavery increased, masters were encouraged to give up—or at least to compromise. In Massachusetts, superior court justice John Cushing promised to free one of his own slaves, and when he refused to follow through, he found himself faced with a lawsuit backed by the state attorney general. He let the man go. Several years later, a similar case came before him. In 1781, Quark Walker had given up waiting for his master to honor the agreement they had made. He claimed his freedom by leaving his master's farm and finding another job. His master pursued him, beat him up, and dragged him back to captivity. By the time the case made it to the superior court, the attorneys and Judge Cushing had made the issue less manumission agreements than the natural right of freedom. In his charge to the jury, Cushing argued that the time had come for the people of Massachusetts to wash their hands of slavery. "Whatever sentiments have formerly prevailed," he declared, "a different idea has taken place with the people of America, more favorable to the natural rights of mankind, and to that natural, innate desire of Liberty, with which Heaven (without regard to color, complexion, or shape of noses, features) has inspired all the human race." Walker won. The verdict was widely believed to have dealt a "mortal wound to slavery," though the patient lingered on for some years. Slaves continued to be bought and sold in Massachusetts, and even the census of 1790 may have obscured slaves still held there. According to one report, a number of slaves were still held in the state in

1790, but they were not classified as such: when the marshal conducting the enumeration "inquired for *slaves,* most people answered none,—if any one said he had one, the marshal would ask him whether he meant to be singular, and would tell him that no other person had given in any." None did.[35] In any case, public opinion had shifted decisively.

By the early 1780s, many understood that slavery was ending—at least in New England and Pennsylvania. Vermont had prohibited slavery in its constitution of 1777. In 1782 New England Quakers could report that they had finally purged their ranks of slave keepers. In states south of Massachusetts, however, slavery did not just dissolve by force of public opinion and the gumption of slaves; it required formal legislative action. Pennsylvania activists pushed through a gradual emancipation law in 1780.[36] Such laws can be seen as a last negotiation between slaves, masters, and the public—in which masters and slaves were forced to compromise and the public's actions were shaped by specific priorities and fears, particularly about the role of free blacks. Moses Brown spearheaded the campaign for gradual emancipation in Rhode Island in late 1783.

Early plans to abolish slavery were gradual, limited, and preoccupied with the future place of free blacks in civil society. The first bill in Rhode Island had been proposed in 1775 and was fairly typical. It was devised, in part, by Moses Brown after corresponding with the Connecticut attorney Levi Hart, whose elaborately argued plan it closely resembled. Like other proposals, it did not call for immediate or universal emancipation but instead proposed that everyone currently enslaved would remain so: only children born after a specified date would be freed, and even they would be required to serve their mother's master for a term of some twenty-one years. Such plans solved a major problem activists foresaw: they preserved the property rights of slaveholders. Statutes freeing those not yet born took no current property away, and freed children's work would reimburse masters for the expenses of their upbringing and education. Even some of the petitions by New England slaves in the early 1770s, which gave rigorous libertarian arguments for their freedom, offered similar concessions in practice. One proposed that children serve terms of servitude before becoming free. Another offered that freed blacks would vacate the region and sail "back" to Africa.[37]

The future of free black people was the other major problem activists foresaw. Many citizens of the United States feared that freed slaves would overrun their communities with thievery, idleness, and debauchery, destroying civil life. Moses Brown himself shared some of these concerns, though he did not allow them to serve as an excuse for inaction. On a personal level, in his 1773 deed of manumission, Brown made specific provisions for the education of the children he freed and offered financial assistance, including free use of land on his farm, to the adults. He pointedly exhorted them to practice "sober prudence and industry," encouraged them to save money for their old age, and cautioned against "stealing, lying, swearing, drinking, lusting after women, frolicking and the like." As antidotes to such temptations, he advised Bible reading and self-examination. The long terms of servitude provided in gradual emancipation proposals were, in part, an attempt to solve this problem in less egalitarian terms. A postnati statute would prevent any sudden influx of free blacks into the local population, and keeping children in servitude for a long period would keep them under control during that term. Indeed, the provision seemed intended to inculcate the habits of slavelike social relations.

The paternal assistance offered by Brown translated poorly into legislation, such as the Rhode Island Gradual Emancipation Act of 1784. Although it was couched in the enlightened language of natural rights and universal truths, its practical provisions embodied more ambivalent values. Children born after 1 March 1784 would be free but were required to serve long indentures. Masters were exhorted to provide them with decent care and appropriate education but were not required to do so. Other provisions eased current restrictions on manumission, allowing masters to avoid posting any bond when freeing able-bodied men and women in the prime of life. For children and adults over thirty-five years old, the same hefty bonds were required to make manumissions legally binding. Brown was crushed when a comprehensive ban on slave trading was cut from the bill. Were the citizens of Rhode Island abolishing slavery to eliminate a burden of guilt, to put principle into practice, or to assist exploited individuals? Or, under the pressure of shifting public opinion, did they divest themselves of an institution they no longer found to be to their advantage while extracting a final economic benefit? If people thought the act resolved any of these issues, they were wrong. Rhode Island lawmakers had managed to eliminate slavery but did not recognize immediate equality. Masters were forced to submit to the abolition of slavery, but they were able to demand that prevailing social relations be disrupted as little as possible. Thus, the act reflected not so much enlightened libertarian ideology as the sentimental values and paternalistic motives that had mobilized antislavery activists for the previous decade.

It was difficult for these same legislators to apply the natural rights of black people *in practice*. A striking example of this was a case of illegal enslavement that struck many as extraordinary. Shortly after the passage of the Gradual Emancipation Act, Moses Brown had stopped a young woman on the street: although Amy was enslaved and identified her mother as a local Negro woman, she looked "clear white." After some investigation, it turned out that twenty years earlier she had been born to a white woman. In order to shield herself from the shame of bastardy, her mother had concealed her pregnancy, and as soon as the child was born, she gave the infant to one of her slaves, who they agreed would pretend to be the real mother. To cover her tracks, the white mistress then sold both the surrogate mother and her daughter. The adoptive mother proved a good accomplice, publicly accepting Amy as her own daughter. When first confronted by Brown, the "Negro" mother insisted that the "white child" was her own, but the truth soon came to light. This young woman's story shocked the General Assembly, which quickly declared: "Her being holden in slavery is an unjust deprivation of her natural right to freedom." She was "immediately" freed and "restored to the free exercise of all the rights and privileges belonging to the natural free-born citizens of [the] state."

Unlike other cases in which legal assistance and public action turned on appeals to sentimental feelings about abuse, cruelty, and family separation, the legislators found this case as clear as black and white, slave and free. Their resolution began, "Amy is a white person, and of course was born free."[38] There was no talk of freeing her adoptive mother.

||| States of Freedom |||

For a time it seemed that the cause of antislavery might unite the entire nation. When St. George Tucker, a Virginia planter and legal scholar, looked northward in 1795, he saw a landscape from which slavery was rapidly disappearing. Emancipation was largely complete in northern New England, proceeding rapidly in southern New England and Pennsylvania, gaining support in New York and New Jersey, and publicly advocated in the Chesapeake region. Tucker himself hoped to overcome objections to abolishing slavery in Virginia—in part with legal arguments and in part with elaborate demographic tables, which he used to show just how gradual the process could be. In order to find out how the process had unfolded in Massachusetts, he wrote to Jeremy Belknap, president of the new state historical society. Belknap, a longtime antislavery activist, circulated Tucker's queries among the most influential politicians, jurists, and civil leaders of the region—including John Adams and Prince Hall, leader of Boston's black Masons. These men gave divergent answers, some of them quite angry. To the question of how slavery had been abolished, Judge James Winthrop responded tartly: "By a misconstruction of our State Constitution, which declares all men by nature free and equal, a number of citizens have been deprived of property formerly acquired under the protection of law." Others warned that the "common people" would never accept free blacks as equals. But Belknap came to this conclusion: "The general answer is, that slavery had . . . been abolished here by publick opinion; which began to be established about 30 years ago."[39] Over the course of the next thirty years, slavery would come to divide the nation into increasingly distinct northern and southern regions.

Even in those states with carefully planned abolition statutes, the end of slavery was unexpectedly rapid, largely unregulated, and the result of an amorphous shifting of power between masters and slaves in which the public played a pivotal part. The Rhode Island Gradual Emancipation Act of 1784 illustrated how little the specifics of a law had to do with the actual process of abolition. Under the terms of the law, amended a year later to raise the ages at which boys and girls would become free—from eighteen to twenty-two for boys, and from twenty-three to twenty-five for girls—the earliest anyone would be released would be 1802. Yet, according to the first federal censuses, two out of three of Rhode Island's enslaved people were free by 1790, nine out of ten by 1800. In other northern states as well, enslaved people were able to seize their freedom far more rapidly than legislators anticipated.[40]

At the same time, enslaved people continued to face serious challenges to securing manumission, and free people of color often found their freedom fragile. The Rhode Island Gradual Abolition Act, like similar laws in other states, made little provision to safeguard the interests of those it liberated. In this climate, scenarios familiar from pre-Revolutionary court cases recurred, and new modes of malfeasance emerged: masters and their heirs reneged on manumissions; indentured servants, debtors, and other free people were sold as slaves; free immigrants were claimed by so-called slave hunters; and others were kidnapped.[41] Taken together, records both of these private negotiations and of conflicts that went to court show how often masters were forced to compromise, how difficult the struggle for freedom was for enslaved people, and how crucial was the role played by antislavery activists and a much wider range of men and women.

In these ongoing struggles between slaves and masters, antislavery activists remained influential; but as the dynamics of slavery shifted, their outlook became increasingly regional. The Rhode Island Abolition Society, organized by Moses

Brown in 1789, was fairly typical of such organizations: its members were white gentlemen whose first priority was ending the international slave trade. They were also dedicated to curbing egregious abuses of the manumission process. Disputes over reneged or disputed manumission agreements, familiar from the colonial courts, proliferated in Rhode Island after 1784. In many such cases, members of the Abolition Society were pleased to report, they could often secure the aggrieved party's freedom simply by visiting, prodding, and threatening the claimant.[42] As a group, they tended to favor persuasion over legal coercion and often settled cases in ways that left men and women serving long indentures rather than insisting on their immediate freedom.[43] After 1793, when federal laws came to protect the property claims of slaveholders more firmly, these activists became more radical in their approach to the problems of thwarting kidnappers and assisting fugitive slaves. At the same time, the transition in cultural values abolitionists spearheaded did not result in dramatic changes in the status of free people of color. Antislavery activists combined their sentimental arguments against slavery with an increasingly regional slant that allowed many people to imagine that slavery as practiced in other areas, however unfortunate, was not their problem. By the time the federal government acted in 1807 to outlaw the international slave trade, many of these gentlemen felt their work was done—leaving unresolved both the place of free blacks in northern society and the rapid expansion of slavery in the South.

New England slaveholders, by and large, didn't relinquish their slaves freely. As people such as Jeremy Belknap's correspondents or members of abolition societies knew, when slaveholders gave up their hold on people they claimed as property, it was most often not because the postwar depression reduced their need for slave labor, nor because wage laborers became more available. It was most certainly not because they developed an ideological distaste for human bondage. Rather, most masters let their slaves go only when changing cultural values made keeping them in bondage less profitable than letting them go. A superior court justice observed of legal challenges to enslavement that "the defense of the master was faintly made, for such was the temper of the times, that a restless discontented slave was worth little." The more members of the public sympathized with slaves' claims to freedom, the more slaves were encouraged to resist, and the more difficult it became for masters to keep them enslaved. Although rather unsympathetic, John Adams got to the heart of the matter when he observed that slaves had became "lazy, idle, proud, vicious, and at length wholly useless to their masters, to such a degree that the abolition of slavery became a measure of œconomy."[44]

Bitter slaveholders were much more eager to pin the blame on specific abolitionist activists. The organization of the Providence Abolition Society in early 1789
provoked an angry newspaper debate. John Brown, thinly disguised by the pen
name "A Citizen, and true Federalist," railed against attempts by activists—including his brother Moses—to "browbeat" himself and others into giving up the
slave trade and slave keeping. Beneath his defiance was recognition of their power.
He labeled the practices of abolitionists "slave-stealing," demanding: "What ought
you and your adherents . . . be called for stimulating and encouraging our servants
(who are by law as much our property as the coat on your back is yours) to run away
from or absent themselves from their masters employ, by which from the encouragement given them by [the abolitionists] . . . the slaves are ruined, and become a
bill of expense to their owners rather than a profit; and when their owners endeavor
to bring them to reason, they are told by their slaves that Mr. Counsellor, &c. &c.
inform them by their writings and otherwise, that their masters have no right to
their servitude."[45]

Particularly early on, members of the Providence Abolition Society sought to
insulate themselves from such criticism by focusing their efforts on sympathetic
characters. People seeking their help had to establish their good reputation among
respectable members of the community. East Greenwich resident Cloe Tibbitt, for
instance, was one of many slaves who reached a manumission agreement with their
masters but failed to secure a formal contract sealed by the posting of the required
bond. When her master died in 1790, his heir refused to set her free. She sought
out the support of a local gentleman who, in turn, solicited the help of Moses
Brown. In his appeal to Brown, he accented that her story was true, that she was
of good character, and that she was desperate: "It seem like Death to her to go back
to her Masters again." Because these qualities appealed to Brown's sense of who
deserved protection, he agreed to help Cloe. But in other cases he declined to become involved. Likewise, Colonel Jeremiah Olney, who had commanded the state's
black battalion in the Continental Army, brought to the society's attention the cases
of two veterans who had been freed for their military service. Both were claimed
by their former masters as slaves. The society resolved to help one, Jack Burrows,
but deemed the other, Jack Champlin, "not to be properly an object of this Society"—perhaps because a few years earlier he had been indicted for petty theft (he
had found a pocketbook on the street and kept the cash he found in it). Burrows
led a long, if difficult, life as a free man and claimed a veteran's pension in his old

age. There is no record of Champlin's fate. Concerned about its public image, the Abolition Society moderated its legal attacks on slave traders to prevent accusations of self-interest. It even declined to claim punitive fines against slave traders it prosecuted, since part of this money would have come to the society. The result was that slave traders lost individual cases, but not enough money to drive them out of the business.[46]

Those cases the Abolition Society did take on illustrate its role as an auxiliary in ongoing struggles initiated by enslaved people themselves. In the spring of 1789, a man named Robert arrived in Providence, sought out Moses Brown, and regaled him with a dramatic life story that revealed the sacrifices he had endured to achieve full freedom. Robert had been born into slavery in Virginia on a plantation where his father worked as a cook. Heeding British offers to free slaves who joined the Loyalists, Robert and a number of others seized on a moment of wartime confusion, took a boat, and headed off to find a British ship. Mistakenly, they hailed a French privateer allied with the Patriots, who took them to Newport, where they were put up for sale on 13 July 1781 at a public auction, evidently in violation of the terms of the 1774 law barring slave imports.[47]

At the market, Robert negotiated with several prospective buyers, finally agreeing to be purchased by baker Godfrey Wainwood in exchange for an agreement that he would be set free after seven years of good service. Such negotiations were not unusual: in the close confines of New England slavery, good working relations were important to masters. Wainwood submitted the highest bid, and the two went off together to an attorney who drafted a nine-year indenture. Despite this sly shift in terms, Robert thanked the lawyer and gave his copy of the indenture to Wainwood for safekeeping. Gradually, however, Robert realized that Wainwood was not trustworthy and intended to keep him enslaved. As the end of his indenture approached, Robert took matters into his own hands. On the night of 9 May 1789, he broke into a closet, removed his indenture papers, and ran off thirty miles to Providence. Robert barely had time to contact members of the Abolition Society before Wainwood filed a formal complaint that he was a runaway slave, charged him with theft, and had the local sheriff apprehend him. For two months, Robert remained in jail while members of the Abolition Society and Wainwood fought in the courts.[48] Without Robert's own initiative, the Abolition Society would not have done anything. In almost every case it was the complaint of an enslaved or falsely enslaved person that brought the society into the legal fray.

Once spurred into action, the Abolition Society was increasingly influential. As the society noted in its record book, Robert's owner, Wainwood, was not one whom they could persuade by merely threatening legal action. Ultimately, Robert both lost and won. The jurors ruled that he was still the slave of his Virginia master; the judge amended the verdict, assigning ownership to Wainwood; but Moses Brown and another Abolition Society member finally convinced Wainwood to let Robert go free in exchange for dropping his claim for eight years' worth of unpaid wages.[49]

Slave owners were conscious that their ability to keep people enslaved was slipping. Many, unwilling to negotiate manumission agreements or give in to the arguments of abolitionists, turned to the market to cash out on failing relationships. In a few cases, masters sold slaves to themselves or to their parents to avoid having to post bond and be liable for their future upkeep: thus James Gardiner's brother Richard sold a baby girl to her mother, Freelove Gardiner, for the nominal sum of six pence. In December 1784, the son of aging attorney Matthew Robinson, William Robinson, was dismayed when his slave Lucy took her son, moved across the bay to Newport, and set up house with her husband, Cudjoe Heally. "She is struggling with me to have her Freedom, which I never will give her," he explained to a Newport associate and offered to sell the woman and her child if his correspondent could "prevail on them to go with you."[50]

The decline of public support for slavery is clear in the increasingly plaintive and frustrated tone of runaway slave advertisements in Rhode Island newspapers. Increasing scruples about slavery seem to have had little effect on the regulation of other forms of servitude: Moses Brown himself advertised for the return of a runaway German servant in 1786. Advertisements for deserters, thieves, and indentured servants offered substantial rewards of five, ten, twenty dollars and more. But the trend in advertisements for slaves was different. The end of the war saw a brief increase in the number of runaway slave advertisements, which suggests that the rate of running away was increasing (since the total number of people enslaved had declined). At the same time, a number of masters began including in their advertisements appeals to the sympathy of readers. As early as 1775, when Moses Brown's brother Joseph advertised for a runaway slave, he described distinctive scars on the man's back and arms—and quickly added that they were not his fault but had been "occasioned by his having been severely whipped in Surinam." One master in the 1790s played on the prevalent "broken family" theme of abolitionist propaganda to turn sympathy against his slave: "Runaway from the Subscriber on the 28th Inst. a Negro Man named GEORGE, supposed to be seduced by a black Wench he kept with, and has left an aged Mother, a Wife and Daughter, all blacks, who are in good Credit." In other advertisements masters were careful to show the public that their runaways were not actually slaves. Thus, one master pointedly noted that a Negro man fleeing his service was "only" indentured. Another master, in 1799, detailed the manumission agreement he had made with "a lusty, middle aged" black woman named Rose Phillips: "The woman was purchased by me and set free on Condition of serving Three Years; of which Term, about one Half remains unexpired."[51]

During the last few years in which runaway slave advertisements appeared, masters began to offer only token rewards—"one pence," "two cents," even half a cent. Presumably, these masters did not really expect the readers to help them apprehend, secure, or return fugitive slaves. In a unique newspaper exchange about a young white apprentice who had run away from the editor of one of the Newport papers, publicly claiming that he was abused, underfed, and otherwise treated "worse than a negro," the runaway's brother described the master's newspaper notice as merely vindictive: "It could not be with an expectation of getting him back again; but to prevent him from getting employ where he might obtain his bread." By law, anyone who harbored, sheltered, or employed a fugitive servant or slave was liable to stiff penalties, and though public notice was not required by the statute, the effect of advertising was intended to put the public on notice.[52] Token rewards reflected the anger and frustration of many masters and sent an insulting message to their runaway servants: their return was worth only one cent. By 1800, the few New Englanders who still owned slaves gave up on runaway advertisements altogether.

There were other signs during these years that the old system of surveillance that had monitored the legal status of blacks was eroding. Across New England, another kind of public notice also disappeared from newspapers—notices from local sheriffs who had "taken up" strange black, mulatto, or Indian men, whom they suspected of being runaways. Such advertisements described the individual and asked the (presumed) owner to come claim his or her property. Although ads such as these had never been frequent, they all but disappeared in the 1780s. In 1793, a Connecticut man was "taken up" on the outskirts of Norwich on suspicion of being a runaway. In an unprecedented move, he filed suit, claiming that he was being unlawfully imprisoned. The case came up before a sympathetic jury that refused to consider whether he was a runaway slave and ruled that he lived in the vicinity of the city of Norwich and therefore had not been "wandering" out of the place where he belonged. By 1788, Moses Brown reassured two free black sailors in an alarmingly common predicament—they had been captured by a privateer and then sold into slavery—that "in a free Country a bare assertion of Rights ought to be Considered as Vallid Evidence until the Contrary appears."[53] Increasingly, throughout New England, people of color could enjoy this presumption.

As changes in public opinion shifted relations between slaves and masters, regional differences in the treatment of slaves became increasingly prominent both in challenges to slavery and in people's imaginations. In the colonial period, boundaries between different legal jurisdictions had been important mainly for owners with dubious legal claims who attempted to create paper trails too convoluted to trace—as in the case of Susanna Wamsley, whose kidnappers arranged a quick succession of sales first within and then beyond Rhode Island's borders. But as northern New England states abolished slavery and then southern New England states and Pennsylvania followed suit, these areas developed reputations as places where slavery was more difficult to defend and freedom easier to preserve. Long before a clear North/South division over slavery emerged, critical differences between the "northern" states remained serious practical matters for individuals seeking to escape slavery or avoid illegal enslavement.[54]

As late as 1800, differences between the legal cultures of states within New England were still distinct, with Massachusetts enjoying a reputation as the state where people escaping slavery were most likely to obtain support. In his autobiography, Connecticut-born James Mars explained how his family thwarted their master's attempt to take them to Virginia. There, he and his brother, born free under Connecticut's gradual abolition law, would have faced permanent enslavement, and his parents would have been subjected to a severity of physical abuse unparalleled in New England. Mars recalled hearing his southern-born mother say "she had often seen her mother tied up and whipped until the blood ran across the floor." His master's wife threatened his proud father that when she got him to Virginia, "where she could have at her call a half dozen men, she would have him stripped and flogged until he was cut in strings, and see if he would do as she bid him." Around 1798, these threats seemed dangerously close to becoming real. Clearly, this family had a strong sense of the regional differences in slavery in Connecticut and Virginia, but, in the end, their fate hinged on differences between neighboring towns. Mars's father spirited the family away and sought refuge just across the Massachusetts border. There they received shelter in a succession of homes. They were secreted so successfully that, as in the case of Robert in Rhode Island, they wore down their tenacious owner and were able to negotiate a settlement under which the entire family became legally free and remained in Connecticut.[55]

Around 1800, when she was a teenager, the New Jersey–born slave Nancy Thompson convinced her master to allow her to purchase her freedom over time. Under this arrangement, she moved to New York City, where her sister was already living. Probably with her sister's help, she found a series of jobs as a paid domestic servant. Thompson saved her wages and periodically took them to her master in New Jersey until she had made up the agreed twenty-five pounds. Around this time her sister died, leaving behind a young son. In the spring of 1812, in her early twenties, Nancy decided to unite her family—her mother and orphaned nephew. They packed their belongings in a chest and a trunk and set out together to begin a new, free life in Providence.

Following quickly on their heels, two professional slave catchers arrived from New York with a warrant to arrest the Thompsons for stealing their own clothes. In Rhode Island, the kidnappers convinced a local justice to give them a new warrant, enabling them to arrest whoever was found in possession of the clothes. When the men soon caught up with the Thompson family, they confiscated the trunk and its contents and remanded the captive family to jail.

The Abolition Society was immediately alerted and obtained a writ of habeas corpus. Appearing with counsel before Rhode Island's chief justice, the men from New York claimed all three as runaway slaves as well as thieves. The judge dismissed this runaway claim and scheduled a hearing for the charge of theft. But instead of waiting for the trial, the kidnappers attempted to spirit the Thompsons away. They had the trunk of clothes trucked onto a packet then embarking for New York and hired a carriage to smuggle the Thompson family just across the state border where the ship was to pick them up. Because the wind was low that day, there was sufficient time for those waiting at court to discover the treachery and send a rowboat off in pursuit of the packet. The Thompsons were safely escorted back to Providence while the kidnappers, and the trunk of clothes, headed on to New York. The charge of theft dismissed, the Thompsons were again free, though bereft of clothing. In the lost trunk were woolen blankets given to Nancy by the owner of the boardinghouse at which she had worked to buy her freedom, clothes her late sister had made for her nephew, silk cloaks, petticoats, and frocks, calico shifts, gloves, and handkerchiefs.[56]

The problem of state boundaries soon became a national concern. Disputes over fugitive slaves and kidnappers between Virginia and Pennsylvania led to the passage of the federal Fugitive Slave Law of 1793, which attempted to establish common standards for the treatment of runaways throughout the nation, made it eas-

ier to legally seize a claimed runaway, and imposed hefty fines on those who harbored runaways. But this draconian new law failed to satisfy slaveholders and outraged abolitionists. Regional cultures grew increasingly polarized as northern abolitionists became more comfortable ignoring, evading, and defying the law.
Typically, on a January evening in 1794, Moses Brown's aunt Mary stood down a
slave catcher looking for a boy named Jack who was working in the family shop,
refusing to accept the out-of-state warrant he proffered. Although he was on strong
legal ground under the terms of the Fugitive Slave Law, he backed down and left
town the next day—taking with him the boy's brother, who had evidently not been
so effectively sheltered.[57] In this climate, abolitionists began defying the law more
concertedly and developed extensive networks to hustle fugitive slaves to safety.
These dramas were early precursors of the antebellum Underground Railroad.

Meanwhile, northern free people of color continued to be kidnapped and sold
into slavery in the southern colonies and the West Indies. Applauding the organization of the Providence Abolition Society in early 1789, a correspondent to the
Providence Gazette reported several outrageous kidnappings in nearby Bristol, Massachusetts. Members of the Abolition Society described two common ploys. Some
would-be kidnappers apprehended their victims merely on the strength of their
word, having no legal title or claim of any sort. Others resorted to what the society
considered the "more dishonorable method" used in the Nancy Thompson case:
charging "black People" with theft in another state, obtaining a warrant for their
arrest, and apprehending them to be brought back for trial in "the place of the pretended theft." Generally, these were not simply random attacks on clearly free
people. Those most at risk of sale out of state were people already in states of dependence—people legally enslaved or formerly enslaved and people bound by indentures, confined to jail, or working on ships.[58]

The sale out of state of people legally enslaved alarmed activists and politicians
as early as the 1770s, and the problem escalated in the 1780s. As the value of slaves
in the northern states fell, incentives for selling them southward rose. In September 1787, a Massachusetts congressman from a rural district reported that there were
"many instances of the negroes being kidnapped & privately conveyed away to
Canada where they were sold for slaves." Several years later, Jonathan Edwards Jr.
reported that, since the passing of the Gradual Emancipation Act in Connecticut, he had already heard of one man "employed in purchasing Negroes for expor-
tation" and predicted that "now the poor creatures will be carried out in ship-loads."
Not only hundreds of slaves, he wrote, but also hundreds of children serving in-

dentures under the terms of the Gradual Emancipation Act "will be sent as perpetual slaves to Carolina, where their masters are not answerable to the magistrate for the murder of them, & every master who teaches his Negro to read is liable to a fine." Clearly, the problem was not just enslavement but enslavement under the allegedly violent and brutal conditions of the South.[59]

Although the sale of slaves out of state was restricted by law in Rhode Island after 1779, the sale of indentured servants was not—even if it was obvious to abolitionists that once they were in the South they would be enslaved and deprived of legal recourse. A number of masters exploited this loophole. Benjamin Peckham got away with selling a black boy into servitude in North Carolina because the Abolition Society could not prove that he had conspired with the purchaser to enslave the boy. Typical of the sale of indentured servants was the case of Joseph Johnson. Bound for a number of years to a farmer in Stonington, Connecticut, he was sold first in South Carolina, then taken to Hispaniola and resold as a slave. Such complex paper trails often prevented abolitionists from prosecuting anyone in such cases—or redeeming the victims. A person sold into slavery in the West Indies was unlikely ever to be redeemed.[60]

Many kidnappings happened on board ships—partly because of the self-contained and hierarchical world of sailing and partly because they often sailed to tropical ports.[61] One free black man, jailed in 1784 for a fifteen-dollar debt, struck a bargain with merchants John Clark and Joseph Nightingale. They would pay his debt, and he would repay them by working on one of their ships as a seaman for one voyage. However, when the ship arrived in the West Indies, other sailors on the ship later reported, the captain sold him as a slave. As Moses Brown observed, these Providence merchants were generally respectable and reliable but had a particularly heinous tendency to enslave free black men. Increasingly, in the early nineteenth century, Rhode Island sailors of African or native descent faced the danger of enslavement in southern ports. Traveling friends tried to keep tabs on them and communicated with their relatives in Providence, who in turn secured the assistance of abolitionists. However, these alliances of free people, their families, and activists could rarely prevent this danger from becoming reality.[62]

Over time, repeated regional dramas over state borders helped to popularize conceptions of the North as a land of liberty and the South as a bastion of slavery. To some extent, differences in legal cultures were painfully real. Into the nineteenth century, the menace of hired kidnappers was a constant threat not only to runaways but also to the legally free. But these polarized images were also promoted and exaggerated by the popular press. Increasingly in the 1780s and 1790s, poems, literary fragments, anecdotes, extracts from histories, and travel narratives concerning suffering slaves proliferated in magazines and newspapers (fig. 14). Similarly, the contentious politics of the slave trade continued to divide regions and focus the attention of northern readers on images of innocent Africans, separated families, and cruel tropical planters. In her *Vindication of the Rights of Men* (1790), Mary Wollstonecraft rebuked those who allowed such imaginary identification with slaves and victims to lull them into self-gratulatory passivity: "Such misery deserves more than tears."[63]

By 1795, when St. George Tucker prompted his New England correspondents to reflect on the process of manumission, the regional politics of slavery and freedom were becoming increasingly dichotomous. While New England and the Mid-Atlantic states were abolishing slavery, the momentum for change in the Chesapeake region and farther south was running in the other direction. By the turn of the century the victory of emancipation seemed secure in New England and the Mid-Atlantic states. As the slave trade became acknowledged as immoral and illegal in the region, ordinary people and even abolitionists worried less about the fate of those enslaved in the rapidly expanding slave states to the south. Despite the emphasis of antislavery propaganda on far-off cruelties, in fact few activists in the northern states were ready to take on the challenge of abolition in the slave states. Most were content with success at home.

The passage of the federal ban on the slave trade in 1807 was the crowning success for abolition societies from Rhode Island to Pennsylvania. After that the Providence Abolition Society became less active in helping slaves attain freedom and protecting blacks kidnapped or lured into slavery in the South. In 1818, it disbanded.

If the fate of slavery seemed clear, the role of free people of color in the northern states was fiercely contested. The emotional dimensions of freedom, though rarely recorded, were profoundly felt and fiercely fought. Many northerners in the early Republic, like white southerners after the Civil War, resisted any social or symbolic empowerment of free blacks. In 1796, a mock advertisement in the *Providence Gazette* offered a five-hundred-dollar reward for the restoration of the self-effacing industriousness that had supposedly prevailed under slavery: "Was mislaid, or taken away by mistake, (soon after the formation of the abolition society), from the servant girls in this town, all inclination to do any kind of work, and left in liew thereof, an impudent appearance, a strong and continued thirst for high wages, a gossiping disposition for every sort of amusement, a leering and hanker-

FIGURE 14. "Kidnapping." Across the Northeast in the early nineteenth century, free black people and fugitive slaves faced the threat of being kidnapped by people who claimed to own them. Like much antislavery propaganda, this image casts black people as passive victims rather than as dynamic actors. Joseph Torrey, *A Portraiture of Domestic Slavery in the United States* (Philadelphia, 1817), frontispiece. Courtesy of the Library Company of Philadelphia.

ing after persons of the other sex, desire of finery and fashion, a never-ceasing trot after new places more advantageous for stealing, with a number of contingent accomplishments, that did not suit the wearer."[64] These themes of sexual licentiousness, inappropriate consumption of petty finery, and thievery were quickly becoming standard tropes in the popular press. In magazines, newspapers, and almanacs printed across the northern states, images of blacks were increasingly polarized. Alongside the innocent Africans abused by slave traders and the pitiful slaves abused by tropical planters were comic images of blacks as incompetent citizens. The new power and autonomy exercised by free blacks were, for many northern whites, disconcerting and threatening.

Most New Englanders rallied in support of abolition less because they believed in the extension of "natural rights" to "all men" than because they were swayed by the emotional strains of sensibility. The ambiguities and contradictions inherent to this process would be the enduring legacy of emancipation.

‖‖　Absolution　‖‖

In the immediate aftermath of its publication in 1851 and ever since, Harriet Beecher Stowe's *Uncle Tom's Cabin* helped millions of American readers recognize the horror of southern slavery. More successfully than any other work of antislavery propaganda, Stowe's novel harnessed the culture of sensibility to galvanize public opinion in sympathy with the suffering of far-off strangers. As *Uncle Tom's Cabin* urged the nation closer to a sectional showdown, Stowe was mindful that there was also a long history of slavery in the North. She explored the themes of slavery and abolition in old-time New England in *The Minister's Wooing* (1859), set in Newport during the 1780s.

Curiously, the novel does not develop obvious parallels between the contemporary South and the historical North. In contrast to the earnest, emotionally searing indictment of slavery in *Uncle Tom's Cabin,* the tone of *The Minister's Wooing* is wry, even self-gratulatory. In fact, the novel even seems to accept, for New England, both the paternalistic logic of pro-slavery southerners and the white supremacy of antebellum popular culture. The characters that tug at the heartstrings of *Uncle Tom's Cabin's* readers are nowhere to be found in Stowe's evocation of eighteenth-century New England: the innocent, noble, enslaved protagonist, the selfish traders and cruel masters, and the separated families are replaced in *The Minister's Wooing* by an otherworldly, old antislavery sympathizer, a number of pious women and benign slaveholders, and a few marginal slaves who seem to have leaped directly onto the pages of the novel from the contemporary minstrel stage. Indeed, the novel is less an attack on slavery than a critique of eighteenth-century abolitionists for being everything that Stowe herself was not.

In contrast to her own enormously effective use of sensibility, Stowe depicts eighteenth-century activists, embodied in her title character, the Reverend Samuel Hopkins, as lost in abstract, principled rationalism. One of the elderly parson's only persuasive successes occurs when the pattern of rationalized debate is interrupted by the earthy candor of a slave woman complete with a turbaned head and a termagant manner. In this scene, Hopkins engages a local farmer in a debate. They begin by discussing a tract by Thomas Clarkson, consider the equivalency between slaveholding and slave trading, and debate scriptural justifications of slavery. Finally Hopkins proposes that they consult one of the man's slaves for her views on slavery. "No," Candace replies, "I neber did tink 'twas right. When Gineral Washington was here, I hearn 'em read de Declaration ob Independence and Bill o'

Rights; an' I tole Cato den, says I, 'Ef dat ar' true, you an' I are as free as anybody.'"
Hearing that, her master promptly declares, "Well, Candace, from this day you are
free." Overwhelmed with gratitude, the former slave declares that she will continue
working for her former master—only now she will work with even greater industry and devotion.[65]

Stowe's account of abolition in New England—an immediate response to the
realization that slavery violated mankind's natural rights—was familiar by the early
nineteenth century. So was her condescending depiction of the region's black inhabitants as childish and best suited for dependence. Even before slavery had been
entirely eradicated in New England and the Mid-Atlantic states, northerners began
to ponder the story of how it happened and what it meant.[66] In fact, when Stowe
told the story of her fictional master's epiphany, she was rehabilitating an old chest-
nut.[67] The preferred narrative, draped in the mantle of the Revolution, asserted that
liberty loving and slaveholding constituted a contradiction so powerful that, once
pointed out, it required immediate resolution. Such stories obscure the actual
process by which slavery in the North was abolished. In fact, Hopkins' ideas and
tactics were not that far removed from the emotional sensibility of nineteenth-
century activists such as Stowe. This distorted, abstracted narrative begs the
opportunity both to reflect on the appeal of the natural-rights narrative and to consider the limits and dangers of motives rooted in sensibility.

The notion that abolition in the North was a matter of resolving ideological
contradictions was widely encouraged at the time and in the early years of the Republic. And these associations were already present in the formal documents of the
Revolutionary period: after political battles had been fought and won on the
grounds of sentiment, the legislation was drawn up in the language of natural
rights. In 1789, when a prominent Revolutionary War hero agreed to free his slaves,
abolitionists planted a newspaper notice that closed with the prediction that "this
sacrifice of his interest, in behalf of the helpless victims of arbitrary power, would
add the *capsheaf* to his fame—*as a son of liberty.*" A decade later, when the New York
legislature finally came around to enacting a manumission statute, it fixed the end
of slavery on the symbolic Fourth of July—as though the Declaration of Independence had somehow been the agent of this liberation. At a time of bitter conflicts over white supremacy, this facile association was offensive enough to many
black New Yorkers in the 1820s that they celebrated emancipation on the fifth. By
associating the abolition of slavery with the legacy of the Revolution, northerners
implicitly countered the charges of hypocrisy leveled at Patriots during the war.
Retroactively, abolition proved the ideological purity of Americans—or, at least, of

northerners. Long before freedom was either universal or entirely secure in the North, slavery was presented as the special problem of the South—and with the implication that northerners were morally superior. Ironically, their antagonists in the war, the people of Britain, soon developed a strikingly similar brand of libertarian patriotism.[68]

Such selective memories would hardly have been necessary if that was how slavery had been abolished; and such self-congratulation would hardly have flourished if it was not, somehow, necessary. In fact, everywhere across the northern states, the abolition of slavery had involved bitter conflicts and the negotiations and accommodations of numberless individuals. By presenting abolition as a unanimous, principled agreement, retrospective histories tended to deny the agency of activists, community members, and people of color themselves. Many northerners did not oppose slavery in principle but were swayed by images of violence and cruelty, particularly those from the South and the West Indies. Many others never had to agree with antislavery principles or sentiments because their motives were simply prudential: they agreed to release slaves when it was no longer worth denying them freedom.

Powerful as it was, the language of sensibility held its own limits, pleasures, and dangers. The proliferation of sentimental images in the popular press emphasizing the distress of blacks in far-off places pointed to one danger: the sadistic pleasure of imagining another's pain. Critics at the time were wary of how empathy could verge from prompting political action to encouraging passive self-satisfaction. At the same time, an antislavery sensibility set itself up for the development of a complementary pro-slavery ideology. Sentimentality presented the problem of slavery not in terms of justice or equality but in terms of comfort and happiness. To many slaveholders, the alleged innocence of Africans, the "natural affections" of separated family members, and the cruelty of individual masters seemed to call out for rebuttal. The ever pugnacious John Brown himself could draw on a growing pro-slavery literature in 1789 to support his claims that Africans were barbaric, cruel, and distinguished by nature for their station in society; that slave traders were not responsible for family separations accomplished by Africans in the process of enslaving one another; and that if masters acted cruelly, the solution was not to free their slaves but to help the masters behave more reasonably. His brother Moses was left trying to counter these claims using different authorities, in much the same way that Harriet Beecher Stowe found herself trying to validate the claims of *Uncle Tom's Cabin* with the documentary key she published the following year. By the mid-nineteenth century, the logic of antislavery sensibility was vigorously appropriated by southern politicians and clergymen who defended the peculiar institution as a bulwark of paternalism, affective family values, and their entire social order. Pushing this argument further, they attacked the callous cruelties of northern wage slavery that so woefully degraded the lives of northern workers.[69]

This regional polarization of slavery and freedom tended to obscure the ways in which the colonial legacy of white supremacy continued to undergird social relations and senses of self throughout the new Republic. The legacy of abolition in the North was profoundly ambiguous: if it established the principle of universal freedom, it evaded the question of equality. For New Englanders of native and African descent, freedom often proved a struggle to achieve and required constant vigilance to maintain; for many it came only compromised or postponed, and for others it proved precarious. Nowhere during the era of independence did people of color have the same freedom enjoyed by their "clear white" compatriots. The North emerged in the early years of the Republic as a place where people of color would be free but not equal—and as the site of continuing struggles over the meanings of American citizenship.

PART III

Moving Apart

Now I am ready to tell of bodies
changed into other bodies.

OVID, *Metamorphoses*

Conceiving Race

||| Providence, 1803 |||

When Henry Moss visited Providence in 1803, he was in the midst of one of the strangest metamorphoses possible in eighteenth-century America. Spot by spot, the forty-six-year-old black man was becoming white. He called on antislavery activist Moses Brown, who was fascinated. About eight or nine years earlier, Brown reported, Moss "began about the roots of his nails to grow white as far as the first joint of his fingers, and then on the back of his neck, and since has been generally whitening in various parts of his body." Brown made an exhaustive examination of Moss's body, including his anus, and emphasized the change: "His back below his shoulders is mostly as white as white people of his age, as are parts of his breast and even his nipples. The white parts of his skin and especially his arms are so transparent as to show the vains as distinct as a white mans." This continuing transformation—which nowadays would likely be diagnosed as vitiligo, a pigment disorder of unknown origins—amazed the most enlightened gentlemen of the day. President Washington himself examined and verified Moss's condition, as did Thomas Jefferson, then secretary of state. "He needs no certificate that he has been a black man," Brown added, "tho' he appears now to be neither wholly black or white." The implications of this transformation were profound. "Me thinks it is an evidence of the sameness of human nature and corresponding with the declaration of the Apostle, that, 'God hath made of one blood all nations of men.' For we see in him one and the same blood sustains a man that appears to our sense, both black and white."[1]

In the early years of the Republic, the egalitarian strains of revolutionary thought and the abolition of slavery in the northern states prompted a new interest in human nature in general and race in particular. Did the peoples native to Europe, Africa, and the Americas have essentially different bodies and distinct characters? The ways in which racial nature was investigated, and the conclusions that were reached, were strikingly different from the confident racial biology of the nineteenth century. For one thing, the problem of race was never entirely separate from broader questions about human nature raised by experiments with republican government and by new confidence in the power of education to liberate human potential. Moreover, the eighteenth-century tradition of natural history embraced a range of interests including much of what we now think of as biology, botany, anthropology, archaeology, and even medicine, and it was both less specialized and less professional than the scientific disciplines that emerged later. Typically, in Henry Moss's case Moses Brown, a prosperous merchant with antislavery sympathies but no special medical knowledge, participated in the process of examining, documenting, and lending authority to the most pressing and mysterious problems. Indeed, natural historians used dramatic public spectacles to display the marvels they were investigating, illustrate their conclusions, and establish their authority. This tendency blurred a line that would later be drawn between circus spectacles and serious research.[2] Indeed, what is most striking about the natural history of race in the early years of the Republic is the way in which its basic assumptions and most optimistic conclusions ran against the grain of widely shared popular prejudices.

Conventional natural historians understood variation among humans in terms of changes produced by different climates. Although all derived from the same biblical ancestors, fair-skinned peoples lived in colder regions of the north, darker people lived in the temperate zones, and the darkest people of all lived in the equatorial Tropics. The classification scheme developed by Carolus Linnaeus between 1735 and 1758 literally begins by diving humankind into varieties distinguished by both physical appearance and qualities of mind. The European's body was "fair, sanguine, brawny," and his character "*gentle*, acute, inventive." The Asian was "sooty, melancholy, rigid," as well as "*severe*, haughty, covetous." The American was "copper-coloured, choleric, erect," and "*obstinate*, content, free." The African was "black, phlegmatic, relaxed," "*crafty*, indolent, negligent." Other natural historians such as Johann Friedrich Blumenbach criticized this scheme as too rigid. He argued that "*Innumerable varieties of mankind run into one another by insensible degrees*," but he, too, was interested in identifying distinct regional and national types. The French natural historian Comte Georges Louis Leclerc de Buffon raised the ire of the United States' wartime ambassador, Thomas Jefferson, by arguing that the American climate produced small, feeble, and otherwise degenerate varieties of Old World species. If the climate of North America had turned Indians red and savage, what future could be expected for European settlers living there? Jefferson fought back in kind. He extolled the strong bodies and noble character of Indians and presented the Paris salons with the skeleton of an enormous American moose.[3]

Even at the heady height of Revolutionary egalitarianism, the most radical racial theorists—those who questioned whether the races really were different, much less unequal—alarmed even themselves. In 1776, Providence newspaper editor Bennett Wheeler was powerfully moved by gratitude for a black woman who nursed him while he suffered a long illness: "Black or white, their Claims are equal when they behave alike." This line of thought led him to a tentative reflection on racial equality: "That *Mankind* are born equal is not a Truth—that Man is *Man*, black or white, I believe—but that there is not essential Difference between 100 white Men & 100 black men . . . find them where you will (either in the Wilderness, or in a civilized City) *I doubt* for the Cause of Such difference I do not seek. Perhaps I may Err."[4]

By the end of the American Revolution, the attention abolitionists had drawn to human equality and the natural unity of humankind had begun to inspire rebuttals. These writers emphasized in a new way that racial differences were permanent, major, and hierarchical. Jefferson himself was influenced by Edward Long's *History of Jamaica* (London, 1768). Responding to Anthony Benezet's sympathetic *History of Guinea* (1765), Long devoted a chapter to "the Gradation in the Scale of Being between the Human and Brute Creation." He began with the assertion that "Negroes, or their posterity, do not change colour"; even though they had lived in the American environment for more than a century and a half, they retained their original African appearance. Moreover, their anatomy manifested their "dissimilarity with the rest of mankind." Blacks had not only dark skin but also "wool, like the bestial fleece, instead of hair," flat noses and thick lips, a particular "bestial" smell, and only meager mental capacities: "All people of the globe have some good as well as ill qualities, except the Africans." He concluded with an extended discussion of orangutans, which he argued Negroes closely resembled. Several years later, the Scottish natural philosopher Lord Kames published the novel argument that the varieties of humankind were not in fact the descendants of common ancestors but rather had separate origins. Jefferson developed his own views in *Notes on the State of Virginia* (1785), first published in Paris, where his household included, among other favored slaves, his late wife's half sister Sally Hemmings. He, too, emphasized the physical and intellectual differences among whites, Indians, and blacks. In a haunting passage that echoes Long's discussion of orangutans, Jefferson argued that blacks are ugly and brutish. Blacks preferred white sexual partners, he wrote, "as uniformly, as is the preference of the Oran-ootan for the black women over those of his own species."[5]

This debate over racial natures took place in the context of a much broader set of discussions. At this time, human nature became central to theories of republican citizenship, the significance of emerging national boundaries, and more subtle ways in which physical appearances might manifest invisible qualities of mind. Although the universalism of the Enlightenment argued that all *men* were equal by nature, republican political theory required a polity composed of virtuous and reasonable citizens. The American Revolution therefore gave new urgency to the question of whether ordinary people—few of whom had the benefit of a liberal, or "free," education—could rise to the occasion. Many grounded their hopes on the transformative power of education. Yet at the same time, physiologists and anatomists were mounting an increasingly sophisticated and vigorous effort to find physical evidence of "character" in the bodies of individuals and to make broad generalizations about sexual, racial, and national types.

The problem of racial nature in the early Republic elicited widespread curiosity and debate not only among educated experts but also among members of a broad public. Henry Moss represented one focus of attention. For a short time around the turn of the century, the phenomenon of people of color who seemed to be turning white became a matter of intellectual concern and public interest. Other physical mysteries, too, challenged easy assumptions about the inheritance of supposedly racial features. A remarkable paternity suit in New York City in 1808 presented the case of a mulatto woman with a baby who seemed too white to belong to the black man she named as its father. Was she simply lying? Or could this anomaly be explained by the ancient theory of maternal impression, which held that strong influences on a mother during her pregnancy could become dramatically imprinted on the body of the unborn child? Finally, even if bodily difference could be understood, was its meaning more than skin deep? Political policies and popular humor suggest that few worried much about the practical implications of the race question. Most Americans of the early Republic seemed quite confident that whites, Indians, and blacks had not only different bodies but also distinct characters. Were these racial characters, however, produced by some form of heredity or by experiences? Some intellectuals sympathetic with the challenges faced by Indians and free blacks in the new Republic raised the possibility that white prejudices were not so much a natural response to racial differences as a major source of the problem.

||| American Metamorphoses |||

When Henry Moss appeared in Philadelphia, the nation's capital and largest city, in late July 1796, leading statesmen, merchants, and medical experts alike flocked to examine for themselves the wonderful changing man. An ambitious medical student, Charles Caldwell, secured Moss lodging in order to keep an eye on him and offered "small rewards" to entice him to submit to a series of experiments.[6] Amid a parade of gentlemen who personally examined the mysterious transformation, only Dr. Benjamin Smith Barton, one of Caldwell's professors, noted that Moss himself seemed distinctly gloomy. His thoughts, Barton reported, were chiefly of a "serious kind." For example, Barton wrote, attempting to reproduce Moss's speech, "Since Providence began to work the miracle, his reflections run much to the future." Such faith in the "*immediate* interference of a God" seemed "superstitious" to the Edinburgh-trained physician, but he was not without some compassion. "If the philosopher contemplates with astonishment such a change as this, it must appear miraculous in the sight of this poor, ignorant man." In the months to come, neither Barton nor any other enlightened Philadelphians who shared his appreciation of the "the immense agency of physical causes" could find any compelling explanation for Moss's mysterious metamorphosis.[7]

Because it was so mysterious, Moss's case played a central role in a broader debate among natural historians about the rigidity of racial distinctions. Conventional natural historical wisdom emphasized the fundamental unity of the human species and explained national and racial variations as a consequence of degeneration from common ancestors. But the abolitionist propaganda of the 1760s had politicized the question of the natural equality of humankind. It was one thing to entertain this possibility in the abstract. It was quite another to confront it as a political challenge to immensely profitable colonial plantation regimes. Consequently, pro-slavery natural historians began emphasizing and exaggerating the differences between the races and arguing that their differences were fixed. The spectacle of a person of color turning white challenged these views and encouraged individuals who wished to entertain the possibility that racial differences were superficial—even completely mutable. To individuals such as Moses Brown and Philadelphia physician Benjamin Rush—who had labored hard for abolition of slavery in the era of the Revolution and who now looked on the state of race relations in the emerging Republic with increasing apprehension—the image of a changing man metaphorically represented the hope that free blacks in the North could successfully emulate the model of white citizens. Narcissistically, but with the best intentions and faith in human potential, they hoped that blacks could become white.[8]

Long before Henry Moss was born in rural Virginia around 1754, amazing stories about dark-skinned Africans and Indians turning white had attracted the curiosity of European natural historians; unlike later American cases, however, these early cases elicited remarkably little interest in the process of change. Knowledge of the case of Maria Sabine moved back and forth across the Atlantic in particularly dramatic and influential ways. Sabine was born around 1736 to a slave on a plantation owned by the Jesuit college at Cartagena in New Spain. Although both the mother and father were of a normal black complexion, the child was marvelously spotted, with patches of dark and white skin. The director of the college included an account of her in the natural history of the Orinoco region he published in 1745. Meanwhile, at least two portraits were painted and shipped back to Europe, though both were diverted by the outbreak of the War of the Spanish Succession. A portrait on a captured Spanish ship ended up in Charlestown, South Carolina, and a portrait on a captured English ship ended up in the hands of the great French natural historian Buffon. He discussed the case in a volume of his monumental *Histoire naturelle* published in 1777 and included a copy of the painting, which shows the plump baby standing with a parakeet perched on her raised right arm. Buffon not only suggested that this remarkable birth might be due to the degenerative effects of the American climate on African bodies but even went on to propose that if there were cases of blacks becoming white, it was only logical to assume that there were whites becoming black.

The influence of this account was clear a few years later when attention turned to a spotted baby girl, named Adelaide, born on a plantation in the West Indies owned by the French king's dentist. A wax anatomical model of Adelaide, posed in the same way as Sabine's published portrait, became the first object acquired by the museum collection of the new Harvard Medical College in 1783. The following year, when Philadelphia physician John Morgan presented the case of Adelaide to the American Philosophical Society, he explicitly referred to Buffon's account of Sabine's birth.[9] Evidently, there were at least two kinds of "spotted" individuals— those who were born with unusual skin pigmentation, features that did not change over time, and individuals who, at some point, gradually began to develop patches of fair skin that sometimes grew, proliferated, or went away. Many early investigators such as Buffon and Morgan focused on the former category because they were less interested in debating the nature of race than they were in exploring the mystery of reproduction.

Failure to manifest change over time did nothing to diminish the appeal of John Bobey in his long career as an object of scientific inquiry and popular curiosity. As a small child in the 1770s he was transported from the West Indies to London, and a decade later he was attracting more attention than ever. An engraved portrait of him in 1789, sent by a London gentleman to the Library Company of Philadelphia, shows him standing against a background of palm trees, naked except for a loincloth, gazing innocently at the viewer; he is holding a miniature portrait of himself as a small child, which appears, if anything, more white instead of less. By 1789, in fact, he had been bought by a London showman who exhibited and sold exotic animals at Exeter Change. That was where he was examined by Johann Friedrich Blumenbach, who included an engraving of Bobey in his *Beyträge zur Naturgeschichte* (1790) and discussed him again in *On the Natural Varieties of Mankind* (1795). Blumenbach distinguished between cases of people, such as Bobey, who were "piebald" and cases of dark-skinned people who seemed to be changing color, but he was more interested in the former because they seemed to confirm his theory that skin color was caused by carbon excreted from blood vessels. Subsequently, Bobey married an Englishwoman who also worked for the "circus" and continued to attract audiences. A portrait published in 1803 shows him looking different culturally but not physically. Now dressed in genteel English clothing, he appeared more distinguished and less innocent (fig. 15). Unlike the earlier portrait, which depicted a naïve youth, this image, with its pulled down stockings, partly unbuttoned shirt, and carefully tied cravat, emphasizes his composure in the face of the spectator's intrusive gaze. But the world was also changing around him. Instead of being published in a serious natural historical text, the portrait of this seasoned showman

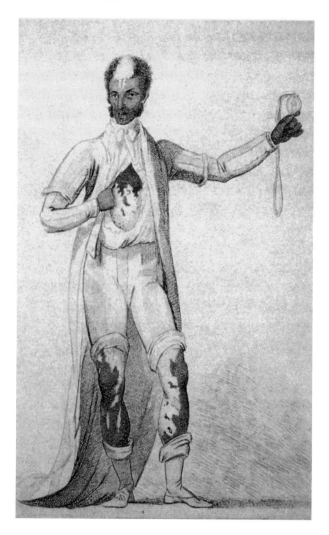

FIGURE 15. "The Wonderful Spotted Indian John Bobey."
John "Primrose" Richardson Bobey was born into slavery in
the West Indies around 1773 and several years later was sent to
London. There he was inspected by intellectuals and earned a
living exhibiting himself as part of a commercial show. In this
portrait, he is shown toward the end of a long career as a
showman: poised as he dramatically pulls back his clothing.
New Wonderful Museum, and Extraordinary Magazine (London, 1803). Courtesy of the National Library of Medicine,
Bethesda, Md.

appeared in a popular entertainment entitled the *New Wonderful Museum, and Extraordinary Magazine.*[10]

Around the same time, American natural historians focused particularly on cases of "White Negroes" who seemed to be actually changing color because these cases promised to provide evidence about the nature of race. Their motives were mixed. As gradual emancipation laws took effect in northern states and the question of slavery was at the center of national politics, long-forgotten stories from decades earlier were suddenly given new life. In 1787, for instance, the president of Yale, Ezra Stiles, recorded a story going back thirty years of a minister traveling on Long Island who came across an "Indian Man grown white in spots or pyed all over." Other cases of "white Negroes" from before the Revolution, first published in London, were reprinted in the late 1780s by journals in Philadelphia and New York.[11] Such curiosities now emerged as a compelling mystery to Americans of reason who were determined to make their own contributions to the knowledge of the world. In 1791 Charles Willson Peale, founder of the nation's first natural history museum, in Philadelphia, championed the case of an enslaved man named James, "a NEGRO, or a very dark MULATTO, turning WHITE." His account—published at least four times in newspapers and magazines—and the portrait he exhibited in his museum emphasized a crucial point of little interest to earlier natural historians: the man was changing.[12]

This emphasis on black bodies turning white was at the heart of America's most prominent contribution to the natural history of race. In 1787, Samuel Stanhope Smith published his *Essay on the causes of the variety of complexion and figure in the human species.* The pious president of the College of New Jersey, Smith took the Mosaic creation story as clear evidence of the single fatherhood of humankind. Smith wrote in response to the Scottish natural historian Henry Homes, Lord Kames, who argued that the various races of mankind were distinct species and had separate origins and sought to discredit earlier theories that the influence of climate had produced human variation. Smith sought to rehabilitate the climatic theory by refining and extending it: he argued that complexion was governed not just by climate but also by what he called "state of society" and "mode of living." Indians, for instance, would not turn white just because the landscape around them had been tamed unless they also started living in a civil manner. But if they did, they might. His argument was remarkable for its kind of cultural relativism. But there was little doubt in any of this discussion that whiteness and European civilization were the standards and everything else was deviation and degeneration.

Eventually, he argued, even enslaved blacks in North America would end up civilized and white. While Smith's analysis gave new credibility to the climatic theory of variation, he did not convince everyone: one skeptic was the young Philadelphian Benjamin Smith Barton, then a medical student in Edinburgh.[13]

In this atmosphere of debate, Henry Moss used his changing skin color and his status as a free man to exploit his own celebrity. His story began in Gluckland County, Virginia, where he was born free—and with uniformly black skin—about 1757. He was apparently indentured to Major John Brent of Charlotte County and afterwards established himself as a farmer and put down deep roots in the community. He spent six years as a private soldier in the Continental Army, serving in a number of different regiments in the Virginia line. A later report specified that he served as a pioneer—that is, part of the corps of soldiers detailed to the heavy labor of clearing roads and constructing fortifications. Military records confirm that he was honorably discharged in 1783 and was awarded a modest hundred-acre land bounty. After that he married but did not have children. His skin first began changing color in February 1792. Soon he was exhibiting himself, at least locally. In late 1794, he obtained a certificate from a white Virginian, Joseph Holt of Bedford County, who attested that he had known "Harry" Moss for some thirty years, that he had an "Honest Character," and that his skin really had been as dark as any African until, "without any known cause," it began to change. The duc de La Rochefoucauld-Liancourt reported that Moss carried such certificates to satisfy those inclined to doubt his story while traveling "about the country to show himself for money." By the time he arrived in Philadelphia in the summer of 1796, Moss had apparently already been on the road for at least several weeks.[14] Soon he was staying at the Black Horse Tavern and exhibiting himself both privately to interested gentlemen and publicly for money.[15]

Natural historians such as Barton were particularly interested in aspects of Moss's habits and past that might explain his condition. Little unusual was discovered. He had not worked exceptionally hard, eaten unusual food, or drunk to excess. Fishing about for relevant information, Barton added, "Perhaps, it is not important to observe, that *he* says, that his ability for the enjoyment of venereal pleasures is not impaired." Moss's examiners paid more sustained attention to the possibility that his ancestry had something to do with his changing skin. In fact, Barton acknowledged, Moss was "of a very mixed breed, if I may be allowed the use of an expressive phrase, which is frequently employed by naturalists when treating of other animals." A German-language almanac gave the most precise genealogy. Moss's father, although born in Virginia, was "a very black negro," whose mother was Indian and father African-born. Moss's mother, Hannah Lewis, was born in Virginia and was a "dark mulatto": her mother was an Irish woman named Mary Lewis; her father, named Primus, had been born in Africa. Despite his mixed ancestry, Moss told Barton that he was originally very black—"as black as the un-mixed negroes of this country commonly are." He assured Barton that now the darkest parts of his body were "not near so dark as they were before the change of his body first began to take place." Consequently, other observers simply de-scribed Moss as pure black. Caldwell, for instance, described him as "nearly full-blooded African." Some even suggested he was born a slave, as if to accentuate his blackness.[16]

Despite their inability to come up with compelling explanations, witnesses were fascinated with the fact that he seemed to still be in the process of changing. Moss told La Rochefoucauld-Liancourt that during his travels in the summer of 1796 alone "a sensible progress has been made in this metamorphosis of his person." Bar-ton noted that the way the skin changed followed the pattern observed by Peale in James's case: "A portion of the black becomes of a reddish brown by degrees, and remains so about six months, when it changes farther and becomes white—upon this change the white parts are very tender, and are soon burnt by the sun, even to their becoming sore for a time." Moss reported that during the colder winter months his color remained entirely stationary and that it changed most during the warmer months. Emphasizing this point, Barton also reported Moss's belief that the change had something to do with perspiration. The Philadelphia abolitionist James Pemberton also emphasized that the change was still happening. When he was visited by Moss on 13 September, not more than a square foot of the "negro skin" remained. Several weeks later, on 22 November, he was able to report, "The black parts are considerably diminished since I saw him last." Likewise, La Rochefoucauld-Liancourt concluded that there had been several other similar in-stances of Negroes, mulattos, and Indians changing their color but that Moss was unique in the completeness of the transformation. He even predicted that in a short time the change would be complete.[17]

Observers were determined to establish that Moss's skin really was turning *white*. Barton and others dismissed the possibility that Moss was an albino or suffered from morbid disease: rather, his skin had a healthy "sanguine-white colour." Emphasis on the beauty and sensibility of the white parts of his skin suggests the narcissistic European assumption that white people are the ideal from which others degenerated. James Pemberton not only examined Moss's skin with a magnifying glass but also passed his fingers through his hair to confirm that the white parts were softer and tested whether the white skin was healthy. "On pressing his skin with my finger, the part which I pressed appeared white; and on removing my finger, it was suffused with blood, as happens in Europeans." Emphasis on the health of the skin and the superior beauty of white skin was common to many of these accounts. As Peale had previously written about the mulatto James, "His skin is of a clear wholesome white, fair, and what would be called a better skin, than any of the number of white people, who were present at different times when I saw him." Moses Brown concurred in perceiving a greater softness in the white portions of Moss's skin. Barton initially believed that the white parts of his skin were "the smoothest and softest," but subsequent examination convinced him that he was mistaken, perhaps driven by a "pre-conceived theory" and a fact mentioned by another author. Barton nonetheless confirmed that the white skin did have an "increased sensibility." Moss told him that he had become less capable of supporting heat, that the sun now, in his words, "burns" his naked skin. He had even had to change his clothing. Formerly the farmer-turned-showman "wore a coarse brown linen; but of late he has been under the necessity of laying it aside, by reason of the pain or uneasiness which it excites on the skin. He, at present, wears cotton and finer linens."[18] All these associations suggested that his skin shared not only the appearance of white skin but also its qualities.

At the same time, Dr. Barton's careful physical examination of Moss on 19 August revealed ambivalence about the true seat of racial identity—whether it resided in the skin or in interior parts of the anatomy. Following published theories of racial difference, Barton described Moss as having the "negro physiognomy." That is, Moss had the short forehead, squashed nose, and curved calves "so common among blacks." By this time, the shapes of skulls were increasingly used to classify ethnic, national, and racial groups—with the high foreheads idealized in Greek sculpture held up as the most perfect form. In addition to "crisped hair, or wool, upon his head," Moss also had the "heavy eye of the blacks." Barton paid special attention to perspiration and smell, because it was widely believed that the "peculiar odour of the perspirations of the blacks . . . [was] necessarily connected with the colouring matter" of the skin. Moss reported that he sweated more now than previously. Yet Barton noted that Moss did not have "much, if any," of this special odor.[19] The implications of these observations are not entirely clear from Barton's account. On the one hand, establishing that Moss was physiognomically Negro added credibility to the notion that he actually had been black and was now turn-ing white. On the other hand, proving that he did not have other supposedly Negro traits, such as the alleged smell, suggested that Moss had always been in a sort of racial limbo.

The emphasis on smell draws attention to the ways in which the specific phys-ical differences emphasized in racial taxonomy were also powerfully associated with class distinctions—among which the most peculiar to modern sensibilities is prob-ably the Negro's supposed crooked shins. It seems obvious enough that gentle-men such as George Washington who didn't work, had access to bathing water, and wore an orange-scented cologne didn't smell the same as poor, laboring people who rarely owned more than a single change of clothes. Meanwhile, the *tibiae in-curvae* that Barton identified in Moss's body had become a standard trope of racial differences. Blumenbach cited Aristotle as an authority on the Ethiopian's "bandy" legs. He explained this, like a number of other supposed racial features, in terms of environmental causes. The Negroes acquired their curved legs, he argued, through the posture of infants when suckling, in which they were obliged to hold tight around the mother's torso with their legs. In fact, it seems unlikely that black people in eighteenth-century America actually did have particularly crooked legs. Ar-chaeological evidence at the New York African Burial Ground suggests widespread malnutrition, especially among children, but not rickets or curved leg bones. In fact, the perception that black people had crooked legs seems to have followed first from received wisdom and second from the specific meanings of shins at this time. In the eighteenth century, genteel clothing obscured almost all of a man's body ex-cept the calves, which were encased in stockings up to the knee—at least if he was wearing breeches. The form of the calf had become a major symbol of male phys-ical beauty, to the extent that many men of fashion padded their stockings with prosthetic calf enhancers.[20] The class meanings of the gentleman's exposed calf were powerful enough to become a salient political symbol during the French Revolu-tion, when "san-culottes"—men without breeches—became not only the name of workingmen but also a symbol of the new republican citizenry. In the United States, racist attacks on blacks well into the nineteenth century focused on a trin-ity that included crooked shins, big lips, and thick skulls. In this indirect way, it may be that the myth of the black man's crooked shins was a fading legacy of this class politics of white men's beauty.

In any case, Moss submitted himself to a variety of experiments in addition to Barton's physical examination. Since the coloring matter in the skin was thought by some to be washed away from the skin by perspiration, Caldwell sought to test the proposition. He "induced him frequently to excite, by exercise, a copious perspiration" so that he might test the perspiration to see whether the portion coming from dark skin was itself colored. It was not. Caldwell also tried to blister Moss's skin—a painful procedure that involved either applying a caustic chemical on the skin or creating a vacuum over part of the skin with a heated glass, which then cooled and sucked up the skin, thus separating the skin layers. Once a blister was raised, the fluid could be drained, as in bleeding, to restore humoral balance. As Moss later told Moses Brown, Dr. Rush also experimented with blisters, thinking that he could induce a change in color by raising them; but once the blisters healed, the black skin returned.[21]

His mystery still unexplained, Moss apparently left Philadelphia toward the end of 1796, leaving Dr. Rush, among others, speculating about what his story said about the nature of race. Perhaps he left to avoid the great yellow fever epidemic, which provided another tragic opportunity to test the nature of racial difference. Early on it was imagined that blacks were largely immune to the disease: the city's African American leaders organized and offered their services to the stricken whites, nursing the sick and burying the dead. Only too late did it become clear that the city's blacks did not, in fact, enjoy immunity, and they died in large numbers.[22] For his part, Dr. Rush returned to Moss's case when he developed a theory that black skin and other aspects of Negro physiognomy were not really natural features but rather a symptom of a form of leprosy. Once acquired by disease, these traits and the disease itself were passed from generation to generation. This theory had very little convincing evidence behind it, but it illustrates Rush's *desire* to believe that racial characteristics were mutable.

In a letter to Thomas Jefferson, then secretary of state, Benjamin Rush described a paper he was preparing that would attempt to prove that the "black color (as it is called) of the Negroes is the effect of a disease in the skin of the leprous kind." Although his paper would be benevolently disposed to Negroes, it would not be radically egalitarian. "The inferences from it will be in favor of treating them with humanity and justice," he assured Jefferson, "and of keeping up the existing prejudice against matrimonial connections with them."[23]

Additional attention to Moss's case appeared from time to time in print, most prominently in the controversy that greeted the second edition of William Stanhope Smith's *Essay on the Varieties of Complexion* in 1810. In it, Smith included a secondhand account of Henry Moss, whose case, after all, tended to support his theory that free blacks living civil lives would eventually turn white. But by then the tide of opinion was turning. One of the most vigorous attacks on Smith's work came from Dr. Charles Caldwell, the young medical student who had taken special interest in Moss back in 1796. In an extended series of reviews published in 1814, he used Moss's case to attack Smith's methods and conclusions. Caldwell denied the charge of critics that his intention was "to degrade the African race, and to prove them, from their physical structure, to be fitted only for a state of slavery, or some very subordinate station in society." In his vigor to refute Smith, however, he did introduce some novel assertions about Henry Moss. First, he claimed that Moss's skin manifested neither "real whiteness" nor albinism but rather had its own "unnatural" hue that he said must have proceeded from some kind of disease that removed the layer of skin in which the pigment resided. In any case, Moss was not turning white, since his features remained "Negroid." Caldwell even claimed to have seen Moss recently and that, far from completing his transformation, he had returned to black.[24] Here, at least, Caldwell seems to have been making his facts up.

The following year, Henry Moss seems to have been whiter than ever. In 1814, Dr. J. V. Weisenthal, a correspondent to the *New England Journal of Medicine*, reported seeing him on exhibit in Baltimore. The fifty-eight-year-old man's skin had "nearly lost its native colour and become perfectly white." Weisenthal's account of this "wonderful change" corresponded in almost all respects to those heard some twenty years earlier in Philadelphia—except in its chronology. Apparently, over the past twenty years, Henry Moss had been enhancing the drama of his story by moving forward in time the date at which he began changing color. He originally told observers in Philadelphia that the change began in February 1792. In 1803, he told Brown that the date was around 1795. In 1814, he told Weisenthal that the change had begun about four years earlier. Rapid change, Moss knew, is what his audience wanted. Sure enough, Weisenthal breathlessly reported, "Since he confined himself for exhibition the change has been much more rapid." Apparently, the amazing changing man needed always to be changing, always on the verge of becoming white.[25]

If Moss's representation of himself remained essentially the same, the times were changing around him. Twenty years later, Moss would have ended up as just another freak; perhaps, like John Bobey, he would have joined a circus such as P. T. Barnum's, which exhibited all sorts of strange and grotesque wonders. And by the 1830s, Dr. Charles Caldwell, his eager patron in Philadelphia forty years earlier, would be at the height of his career, established in his reputation as a phrenologist on the vanguard of American racial science, lining up skulls to show how purported gradations in cranial capacity reflected the natural hierarchy of America's social order.[26]

III   Maternal Imaginations   III

As Lucy Williams told the story to New York City officials in June 1807, her descent into unwed motherhood and poverty was an all-too-familiar tale of seduction, coercion, and betrayal. Almost two years earlier she had first met the man responsible, Alexander Whistelo. They had courted intermittently for about eight months—like many black men in the city he worked for a time as a sailor—until one Sunday in April 1806, when he proposed marriage. She declined. "I did not love him," she explained. "He then carried me to a bad house, and locked the door—I scuffled with him a long time, but at last he wore me out." Soon thereafter she realized she was pregnant. Nine months later, in January 1807, she gave birth to healthy baby girl. Lucy Williams was a relatively light, or "yellow," mulatto (her father being Scotch and her mother only part black), and her baby had remarkably fair skin, even paler than Williams' own. But, as the attending doctor remarked, it often took a week or more for black babies to darken to their true color. Williams and her daughter soon ended up in the New York City almshouse, where she was pressured to name the child's father. Yet Whistelo refused to acknowledge paternity, and the commissioners of the almshouse took their claim to court. The magistrates' court needed little more than one look at Whistelo to determine that he was not the child's father. At six months old the baby was still almost white. And Whistelo was far too dark to have been her father. When the almshouse commissioners appealed to the Mayor's Court, a publisher sensed the case's sensational potential and arranged to procure a transcript of the proceedings—which, indeed, provide a "very remarkable" opportunity to explore medical and popular notions about reproduction, heredity, and race at the opening of the nineteenth century.[27]

Although Alexander Whistelo was man of limited means—at the time of the trial he was working as a private coachman—he managed to put on a vigorous defense that did more than simply attack Lucy Williams' credibility and virtue. It was probably his employer, a prominent physician, who arranged for his two attorneys and a host of medical experts. Together, they transformed the case into a very public referendum on the state of knowledge about racial features and sexual reproduction. How could a black man have a white child? Testimony centered around the theory of "maternal imagination," the ancient belief that the thoughts or emotions of the mother (or father) at the moment of conception could become impressed physically on the child. In a widely cited biblical story, Laban induced his solid black and white sheep to produce spotted lambs by placing in front of them rods that he had made speckled by stripping off parts of the dark bark to reveal the white wood underneath. In the eighteenth century the theory was widely circulated, but with varying degrees of credulity. For instance, parental imagination was central to the plot of Laurence Sterne's popular but satirical novel *Tristram Shandy* (1761–68).[28] In the case of the almshouse against Whistelo, the possibility of maternal imagination, like the mystery of "white negroes" in previous decades, suggested that skin color might be a superficial, even malleable, characteristic instead of an indelible emblem of essentially different racial natures. But the trial also suggests a significant change in sensibilities: away from the cautious natural history of human variation of the eighteenth-century Atlantic world and toward the confident scientific racism of antebellum America.

The trial opened badly for Lucy Williams. In an extended cross-examination, the opposing attorney undermined her credibility and associated her with lurid images of urban sexual disorder. There was no question that the encounter between Williams and Whistelo on 13 April 1806 had been sexual. But in her original testimony Williams presented herself as an innocent woman who had been misled and then raped. Under cross-examination it was revealed that she had voluntarily entered the "bad house"—explaining that she thought he was taking her to visit a cousin. She learned it was a bad house only after entering, when it became clear that no respectable establishment "would take in a man with a strange woman in that manner." After asking about the timing of her pregnancy and Whistelo's reactions when she told him he was the father, the opposing attorney returned to the scene of their encounter on 13 April. He demanded, "[On that occasion] had you not a white man in bed with you"? She attempted to dismiss the question—"I had a scuffle with one once—I knocked off his hat." But eventually she admitted that this unnamed man had burst into the room brandishing a pistol, had turned the "black man out" of the bed, and attempted to take his place. The defense attorney insinuated that they had then had a "connection." Williams insisted that he could not have impregnated her because she "*fit* (fought) all the while." The court reporter's unusual use of phonetic spelling here in the transcript—"fit," followed by the translation "fought"—seems to mock Williams' pronunciation and also express doubt about her credibility. The attorney then pursued a line of inquiry commonly used by defense attorneys in rape trials to undermine the credibility of alleged victims: he asked if she had cried out. When she acknowledged that she did not "hollo," he asked if she had done *anything* to stop him. Damningly, she replied, "I bid him be quiet." Worse, it turned out that she knew the man. At the time of the trial he owed her four dollars, which he was refusing to pay. Was that, the attorney could not resist insinuating, "*your charge*"?[29]

Such insinuation carried particular power because of the mounting anxiety about prostitution in the rapidly growing city and about "disorderly" blacks at a time when many of the region's former slaves were becoming free. Other contemporary trials suggest that black women were strongly associated with a voracious and indiscriminate sexuality that was considered bad for the city. Indeed, the connection between black women and sexual disorder was pervasive throughout the northern states as free black communities grew and urban populations exploded. During this period, increasingly less attention was being paid to the role of white men as these women's partners in crime. Characteristically, Lucy Williams' own medical expert, Dr. Samuel L. Mitchell, had recently published an essay on the dangers of venereal diseases that he claimed were being spread by New York's many women of bad fame.[30]

Despite these damaging revelations and ugly insinuations, the most powerful evidence against Whistelo's paternity came from a parade of medical experts who testified that he was simply too black to have been the almost-white girl's father. Whistelo's employer, Dr. David Hosack, was typical. His testimony was summarized by the court reporter: "From the appearance of the father, the mother, and the child, and the laws of nature which he had uniformly observed in such cases, he certainly would not take it for the child of a black man. But would say it was that of a white one, or at most of a very fair mulatto." Another defense witness claimed to have acquired special expertise in Negro physiognomy during time he spent living in the West Indies. Based on his examination not only of the infant's skin but also of her hair and the angle at which her shinbones joined the foot, he was certain that she showed too few "traces of the black race" to have been Whistelo's daughter.[31]

Faced with such testimony, the attorney for the almshouse was left, in his cross-examinations, suggesting the possibility that the child represented some kind of exception to the ordinary laws of generation. It was easy enough to rule out the possibility that the child was an albino. Dr. Hosack and others insisted that, although she was almost white, she showed none of the weakness, disease, or "livid color" associated with albinos. More difficult to rule out was the possibility of maternal imagination. This theory was suggested by the dramatic revelation that the white man with the pistol had interrupted Whistelo and Williams in the middle of intercourse. Could his appearance have been impressed on the child through the imagination of the mother? "Dr. Hosack," the almshouse attorney asked during his cross-examination, "might it not be possible, judging after your reading or experience in such matters, that in the early stage of pregnancy the agitation of the mother's mind, irritation, terror, or surprise, might alter in some degree the nature and appearance of the child"? Neither Hosack nor any of Whistelo's other medical experts were inclined to lend this scenario much plausibility, but most were not willing to dismiss it out of hand. One of the defense's medical experts was forced to concede that however "far-fetched" it seemed, the possibility did exist, though he considered it more likely that the consequence would be some deformity or abortion rather than a change in color. Miracles might happen, but it seemed unlikely that Miss Williams would receive the same kind of personal providential intervention bestowed on Laban and his sheep. The eighth expert to testify, Dr. Hugh Williamson, summed up the gist of the defense position, and his words in turn were summarized by the court reporter: "If this was the child of that woman, by that man it is a prodigy, and he did not believe that prodigies happened, though daily experience unfortunately proved that perjuries did."[32]

The plausibility of maternal imagination nonetheless occupied most of the rest of the trial, which focused on the theatrical testimony of the almshouse's sole medical expert, Dr. Samuel Latham Mitchell. He was a good witness. As the founding editor of the *Medical Repository*, the nation's first such journal, he could speak with authority about the current state of knowledge. In the previous hearing he had already made it clear that he believed it perfectly possible, even probable, that Whistelo was the baby's father. And he clearly relished his role in the witness stand: his colorful sparring with the defense attorney is probably why so much of his testimony was quoted verbatim in the printed report of the case. So he was ready to agree when the almshouse attorney introduced the question of whether "accidental causes sometimes operate a change on the foetus at the time of conception." Indeed, he had long manifested this view in editing the *Medical Repository*. In court, the example he used to illustrate the possibility of "accidental causes" affecting a fetus was an obscure volume on quadrupeds written by Paraguayan natural historian Felix d'Azara, which he had recently reviewed favorably. D'Azara's evidence suggested that among the changes that might take place in the human form during the time of conception, alteration of the complexion was the most common, in fact "very frequent indeed." The progeny of Paraguayan quadrupeds supported the further proposition that such "accidents" of birth might befall every human and beast to some degree and, once effected, could even "become permanent in the race by propagation from one generation to another."[33] Long before Frederick Mendel's experiments with colored peas would establish modern understandings of genetic heredity, including the principles of mutation and dominance, Mitchell was striving to reconcile commonsense assumptions with the observable variability and unpredictability of inherited traits.

Indeed, at the time, the theory of maternal impression enjoyed wide circulation. Pressed during the trial to cite authorities who supported the belief, Dr. Mitchell named writers ranging from the English poet Haddingon and the French philosopher Malebranche to the fourth-century bishop Heliodorus. Although he didn't mention it, the most widely circulated text on maternal impression was the perennially popular midwifery manual *Aristotle's Master Piece*. This mélange of seventeenth-century texts remained popular on both sides of the Atlantic well into the nineteenth century, as the numerous editions in the early years of the Republic suggest. The text warned prospective parents that at the moment of conception "nothing is more powerful than the Imagination of the Mother." It was so powerful that even if a woman was having adulterous relations, "if fear, or any thing else, [caused] her to fix her Mind upon her Husband, the Child [would] resemble him." Mere likeness, therefore, could never affirm paternity. The book's standard frontispiece was devoted to the force of maternal imagination.[34] Varying somewhat in different editions, it usually depicted "black" and "hairy" children produced by the thoughts of their white, hairless mothers. The story of the "hairy maid" derived from an oft-told Renaissance story in which the pregnant mother spent too much time contemplating the image of Saint John the Baptist, who was always depicted wearing animal skins.[35]

Eighteenth-century natural historians, as well, sometimes turned to the theory of maternal impression to explain the mystery of "white negroes."[36] In the case of Adelaide, maternal impression was suggested as the origin of her strange complexion. John Morgan reported that Adelaide's mother had a habit of lying out in the open and staring at the stars that spot the black night sky. Hence, it was implied, her dark skin was spotted with light. Did the "strong impression" of stars on Adelaide's mother cause the child's anomalous pigmentation? Morgan left the question for each reader to judge, explaining, "There [are] many who dispute children's being ever marked by the fears, longings, or impressions made by mothers on the bodies of their children, at a certain time of pregnancy; for which they endeavor to account in different ways; whilst others, who have known a variety of children born with different marks on them (which have fallen under their particular notice) are equally confident of those marks proceeding from the causes alleged." Several years later, in 1790, a country doctor wrote to Dr. Benjamin Rush in Philadelphia, insisting that the birth of a dark child to a white woman could be explained only by the fact that she had been startled by a black man during her pregnancy.[37]

Whatever currency the notion of maternal impression enjoyed in the eighteenth century, its plausibility was certainly open to question. Cross-color impressions may never have been taken very seriously in the North American colonies, probably because of a desire to keep racial categories separate. And in England, during the 1720s, a public pamphlet debate had broken out on the general plausibility of maternal impression. The popular press echoed this skepticism. In 1763, for instance, the *Newport Mercury* published an "amusing" anecdote about a woman who looked at a clock's pendulum while pregnant and whose son now looked like it, with rolling eyes. These jokes in the popular press commonly represented maternal impression as a ploy manipulated by unfaithful women. A typical anecdote appeared in the *Columbian Almanack* in 1791: "A MARRIED Lady was seized with a singular longing for charcoal and absolutely eat several pieces. In about four months afterwards she was delivered of a fine mulatto boy, and the fond husband imputed the dusky hue to the charcoal." The punch line? "Her ladyship's footman is a stout African."[38] In both scientific and humorous exchanges, late-eighteenth-century Americans entertained lively and skeptical interest in the nature and meaning of the physical differences that marked the races.

In the Whistelo trial, the defense attorney cross-examining Dr. Mitchell lost little time attempting to reduce the theory of maternal impression to ridicule. He began by asking Mitchell to share his view of what was termed "maternal affection." The good doctor rose to the occasion with the story of a pregnant local woman and her favorite cow. Despite his wife's affection for the cow, her husband slaughtered it and butchered the meat. She didn't realize what had happened until she saw the feet "hanging up in a mangled state" and recognized them. She was so vehemently moved that her son was born without arms and with distorted feet. The attorney asked Mitchell if he had actually met the parents or examined the child. Mitchell replied that he had in fact seen the child as he passed it on the street, "playing with a cooper's shaving knife between its toes." He stopped to inquire and was told the story. The defense attorney was hardly convinced. He went on to ask whether Mitchell considered it reasonable that the Dutch farmers on Long Island commonly "plough a black mare with a bay horse, to have a bay colt." Mitchell replied that there was nothing odd about ploughing horses of different color together or in a "black mare having a bay foal." In fact, not just Dutch but many farmers on both sides of the Atlantic actually seem to have used belief in the efficacy of maternal imagination in their attempts to manipulate livestock breeding.[39]

Finally, the defense attorney resorted to invoking a series of outlandish folktales to ridicule belief in maternal imagination. At one point he asked, "Did you ever hear how the mistress of Pope Nicholas III was brought to bed of a young bear?" As the story went, the pope was a member of a family whose crest bore the device of a bear, and it was to this sight that the mistress attributed the appearance of a child that did not much resemble its father. Instead of going into this account, Dr. Mitchell replied, jokingly, that he had not heard of the case but that many women certainly did have bearish children. These women, the defense attorney concluded, "might be able to bear anything."[40]

As this courtroom banter emphasized, the notion of maternal impression raised basic questions about the nature of racial difference, questions that lay at the heart of the trial. Deflecting an inquiry about albinism, Mitchell shifted the discussion to "instances of negroes turning white where there was no symptom of disease or sickness." In court, he focused on the most famous case, that of Henry Moss. But Mitchell had also published several other accounts in recent issues of the *Medical Repository,* which were included verbatim in the trial record. These accounts explicitly addressed the fundamental issue in the trial: the extent and nature of physical difference between blacks and whites. As one of these accounts concluded, "Such an alteration of color as this, militates powerfully against the opinion adopted by some modern philosophers, that the negroes are a different *species* of the human race from the whites, and tends strongly to corroborate the probability of the derivation of all the *varieties* of mankind from a single pair."[41]

The difference between blacks and whites emerged as the central theme of the closing arguments on both sides. At first, defense attorney Washington Morton began on a different note, by emphasizing the threat cases such as this posed to the reputation and property of men. In fact, he said that the case was fundamentally like an indictment for rape. This analogy allowed him to invoke arguments commonly used by defense attorneys in rape cases to discredit the allegations of female plaintiffs. The standard of proof, he argued, ought to be "equally certain, as it went to inflict what to a poor man was a very heavy penalty." Such arguments emphasized how unnatural it seemed that, in the words of one attorney in a contemporary New York rape trial, "the life of a citizen" should rest "in the hands of a woman." Again taking a page from the book of rape defenses, Morton worked on discrediting Lucy Williams' character by challenging her reputation for "virtue and good morals." She had previously lied to the police, he claimed, and now she was lying to the court. If there was any room for doubt, he argued, it would be better for the community to suffer the inconvenience of going without the cost of one man's child maintenance in order to avoid such an error in the other possibility, which would be "an insupportable oppression." Stepping in, William Samson, the second defense attorney reprised the case in theatrical terms: "Soon after the vernal equinox, in the year of the vulgar era one thousand eight hundred and six, an Adam-coloured damsel submitted to the lewd clasps of a lascivious moor, and from that mixture sprang three miracles." One of these was that she bore a child, "not of her *primitive* and *proper* color, nor yet of that of the african—but strange to tell, of most degenerate white.... And the greatest of these wonders, she remained, as the counsel for the Alms-house charitably testifies, a lady of virtue and unblemished credit!" In conclusion, he pleaded, "All the justice we ask for our poor black swain, is not to pay for a child he never got, nor be made a worker of miracles against his will."[42]

The almshouse attorney, for his part, did his best to mitigate the damage. He emphasized the plausibility of the maternal imagination hypothesis. He attempted to explain apparent discrepancies in Williams' statements. He even introduced into the courtroom another mulatto woman with a pale child who, like Williams, claimed that the father was a black man. Finally, the almshouse attorney attempted to rebut the fraternalist insinuations of the defense counsel. He argued that the public interest should override the privileges of any individual man. However "unfortunate" Miss Williams' circumstances, her case went to "deliver the community from the support of a bastard, and justly to fix the man who begot it with the maintenance of it."

But it was Samson who had the last word, and his testimony is striking for the way he sought to discredit the paternity claim by rhetorically emphasizing the gulf between black and white races. The almshouse attorney's arguments had been grounded in the assumption that skin color was a relatively malleable quality and tended to deemphasize sharp racial distinctions. The defense attorney implied exactly the opposite. He dismissed classical authorities as "heathenish" and was contemptuous of continuing popular belief in the efficacy of maternal impressions. Throughout, he invoked highly charged plays on color that represented black and white as opposites, or inversions, of each other. At one point, ostensibly worrying that he might get lost and die rebutting the long and complex testimony of Dr. Mitchell, he announced his final wish to the court: "If I should miss my way, and never return to where I set out, my will is that all concerned shall mourn for me— the whites putting on black, and the blacks white, in token of *affection*." Later he managed to work a Shakespearian allusion into his argument, quoting Iago's concern that fair Desdemona should "be got with child of a barbary horse"—that is, Othello. By this point, the noble Moor had been so commonly conflated with enslaved Negroes that the play became the butt of numerous racial jokes.[43] The defense attorney continued with another rhetorical play on color to ridicule almshouse medical testimony, stating with mock astonishment: "The world has been in ignorance on another subject, which this trial has promulgated—First, all negroes were supposed to be black. In the process of time it was discovered that some were white; and now it appears that others are pye-balled." But, he asked, if the white man who frightened the mother was the one who determined the appearance of the child, shouldn't we consider him the true father? Indeed, was the child actually "black" or "white"?[44]

The mayor, the recorder, and the aldermen sitting on the court were convinced. They concluded that the father of the child was not Whistelo but rather an unknown "white man." They disregarded the question of maternal affection and concluded that it was only reasonable to "repose less confidence in the oath of the woman, than in the opinions of the medical gentlemen who have appeared here as witnesses."[45] In this sense, the trial reflected the trend of other trials of sex crimes in this period, a tendency to excuse men from sexual responsibility in most cases. Ironically, this sense of a fraternal unity of men against women's claims for compensation after sexual encounters may have inspired Dr. Hosack to rally to his coachman's defense. Even though fraternal identification across lines of color would seem to contradict the racial rhetoric of the defense attorney's entire case, it makes sense in this broader context. In early-nineteenth-century New York it was not black men who were considered the main sexual dangers. In the eyes of white male authorities, it was the depravity of women, and black women in particular, that was responsible for urban sexual disorder. Ultimately, of course, modern genetics does support Mitchell's views, at least in the sense that offspring do not necessarily look like their parents and that "accidental" causes can indeed permanently alter the traits of a bloodline. But in the short term, the trial's conclusion was in keeping with the opinion of respectable white men of the early nineteenth century. The trial suggests a change in racial science: away from entertaining notions about unity and similarity and toward emphasizing immutable difference and polarizing black and white, physically and mentally.

||| Human Natures |||

A few hours before Hannah Ocuish's execution for a grisly murder, the local Congregational minister, the Reverend Henry Channing, delivered a sermon that made the twelve-year-old "mulatto" girl into an unlikely symbol of the unity of humankind and the transforming power of education. The daughter of a drunken Pequot and an unnamed white man, Hannah had grown up as a servant in a rural Connecticut household and went almost unnoticed until she bludgeoned and strangled to death her master's six-year-old daughter. Passing lightly over the sensational crime, Channing focused on what he saw as its ultimate cause: the failure of parents and master to provide children with proper guidance and correction. In the words of a proverb he quoted, "Just as the twig is bent, the tree is inclin'd." In contrast to Puritan theologians who viewed children as inherently corrupt until their will had been broken, Channing evinced a new, more optimistic view of children's natural innocence. Reports in local newspapers accepted the argument that "the unhappy fate of this young girl is particularly to be lamented, as it is to be charged principally to a want of early instruction and government." Channing himself linked this changing view of human nature to changing views about race. He urged his predominantly white audience, "Think not that crimes are peculiar to the *complexion* of the prisoner, and that ours is pure from these stains." Channing even compared the guilty girl's soul to a precious jewel, which, "being left in its natural state, would be *blackness and darkness forever*" but which, "polished by divine grace, would shine in yonder world with a glorious luster."[46]

As Channing's effort to dissociate complexion from character suggests, Americans in the early Republic struggled with competing impulses: to emphasize the leveling capacity of education, and to categorize and rank the varieties of humankind. Republican political theory rested on the hope that character was dependent less on heredity than on experience. To overthrow the artificial aristocracy of birth, republicans argued for a new, natural aristocracy of talents. As Americans who were concerned about the viability of the Republic and the possibility of what they called democracy, it was crucial for them to believe that education had the power to level social differences, to raise ordinary men to a genteel standard of virtuous citizenry. But at the same time, there were also strong impulses to regard physical differences as manifesting differences in character. Physiologists were arguing with new sophistication about the physical manifestation of mental character. These enlightened investigators often assumed that the races *were* different, that this difference was essential, and that the nature of this difference justified the superiority of whites. Such assertions, widely accepted as they were, were also subject to challenge.

Despite often flamboyant rhetoric, it was never entirely clear just whom the potential of education could be expected to affect. Discussions of policy most often turned on questions of class among different groups of white men or of sexual difference between men and women. Dr. Benjamin Rush himself was an early advocate of a new model of republican education, emphasizing not the dead languages of the past but a modern curriculum that was more accessible and more practical. His emphasis on a vernacular education was part of a more democratic effort to extend access to skills, knowledge, and credentials to a wider spectrum of the population.[47] During this period, the state of Massachusetts established universal public grammar schooling that reached a large portion of the population, rich as well as poor, girls as well as boys. New England public schools of the early nineteenth century commonly offered all whites a basic education but almost uniformly closed their doors to black and Indian children. And even white children seeking college preparation had to find funding of their own. The state of Virginia, at Thomas Jefferson's behest, emphasized a university that served almost exclusively the sons of planters and merchants at the top of the social order. In the absence of any public system of basic schooling, only those who could afford private tutors could even begin to prepare for college. At the same time, new anatomical understandings of male and female bodies helped justify the exclusion of women across the country from the emerging public sphere and emphasized their domestic auxiliary role. The discourse of republican motherhood emphasized the role of women in rearing virtuous citizens. It remained open to question whether the power of education to create a virtuous citizenry extended so far as to include Indians and Negroes. Jefferson clearly thought not. And he was not alone. Popular attitudes about blacks, Indians, and whites were clear enough in jokes and stereotypes dating from before the Revolution, which perpetuated stereotypes about black and Indian incompatibility with American citizenship.

These debates in the United States were part of a much broader transatlantic effort to understand human nature in terms of increasingly precise anatomical observations and abstract generalizations. Natural historians such as Blumenbach refined new techniques of comparative anatomy to define racial varieties as well as to distinguish abstract regional types and national characters. Emerging national identities were also increasingly essentialized by "bloodlines." Around the middle of the century, when Benjamin Franklin sought to express his antipathy toward German immigrants to Pennsylvania, he presented a hierarchical gradation of human coloring: Africans, Asians, and Native Americans, he declared, were either chiefly or entirely of tawny complexions. "And in Europe, the Spaniards, Italians, French, Russians and Swedes, are generally what we call a swarthy Complexion; as are the Germans also, the Saxons only excepted, who with the English, make the principal Body of the White People on the Face of the Earth. I could wish their Numbers were increased." By the late eighteenth century, English writers were invoking long-term historical arguments to suggest that their unique dedication to liberty and power, dating from Tacitus's favorable view of the ancestral Anglo-Saxons, represented a kind of essential national character. One English political writer in 1787 used such arguments to disparage the Celts: "[They] have been savages since the world began, and will be for ever savage while a separate people; that is, while themselves, and of unmixt blood." This particular characterization was subject to dispute, but the interest in the history, mythology, and languages of the northern European nations only grew more pronounced in the late eighteenth century and culminated in the folk nationalism espoused by the German philosopher Johann Gottfried von Herder.[48]

At the same time a new, more precise kind of connoisseurship of the human form was being popularized by European anatomists striving to bring new rigor and system to the ancient art of physiognomy. One influential figure was Johann Caspar Lavater, who sought to delineate consistent rules about how physical attributes reflected mental characters. He focused much of his attention on the shapes of heads, which he frequently abstracted as profiles, seeking regular geometrical rules. He grew confident enough to do things such as use biblical accounts of Christ's character to reconstruct drawings of what Jesus of Nazareth must have looked like. Lavater's plate of nine disembodied mouths is a good example of his technique. The drawing invited viewers to identify "normal" figures between deviant extremes and also suggested that "normal" meant not just most common but also most ideal. His text predicted, for instance, that the person attached to mouth number six, with its protuberant lower lip, would "not win the prize"; that number four showed signs of degeneracy; and that number seven, with its balanced rosebud shape, suggested "the greatest affinity to genius."[49]

A similar kind of association between beauty, race, and character was promoted by the meticulous architectonic drawings of comparative anatomist Petrus Camper. Although intended as a reference for students of art, Camper's drawings invited national and racial rankings. Most influential, ultimately, was his emphasis on the importance of "facial angles" and his fondness for presenting specimens from different species, nationalities, races, and time periods in a graded series. One image, for instance, compared the skulls of an orangutan, an Icelander, a Negro, an ancient Roman, and the *Apollo Belvedere*. Not surprisingly in this neoclassical age, he determined that the ideal facial angle was represented only in ancient Greek sculptures and that of contemporary peoples the most perfect facial angles were found in Europeans. Those deviating furthest from the ideal were, predictably enough, Negroes. Some of Camper's drawings show how the Negro's jutting jaw and sloping forehead could approximate the skulls of apes. Camper himself denied any taxonomic significance to these gradations. Indeed, he went out of his way to attack as "absurd" the notion that this singular resemblance suggested that Negroes were the offspring of some mingling of whites and orangutans. Yet his architectonic style of drawing influenced later biologists in their attempts to correlate the shapes of skulls with distinct national and racial natures. Even his contemporary Blumenbach, who harshly criticized Camper's methods and conclusions, made his own efforts to delineate what he referred to as "the national face" and the "racial face."[50]

The publication of the works of Lavater and Camper in the 1790s coincided with new popular interest in the abstracted shapes and peculiarities of skulls. Late in the century, the silhouette emerged as a popular method of representing individuals visually—showing both an emphasis on anatomical accuracy and a sense that the profile represented an individual's identity and, in some way, character (fig. 16).[51] Meanwhile, a craze for phrenology developed in England. The premise of phrenology was that an individual's personality was reflected by the shape of his or her skull and by any bumps or ridges on it. Consequently, a person with sufficient expert knowledge could examine the external form of the head and gain insight into the character of the individual. This fad led to the first attempts to associate specific parts of the brain with different aspects of mental functioning and char-

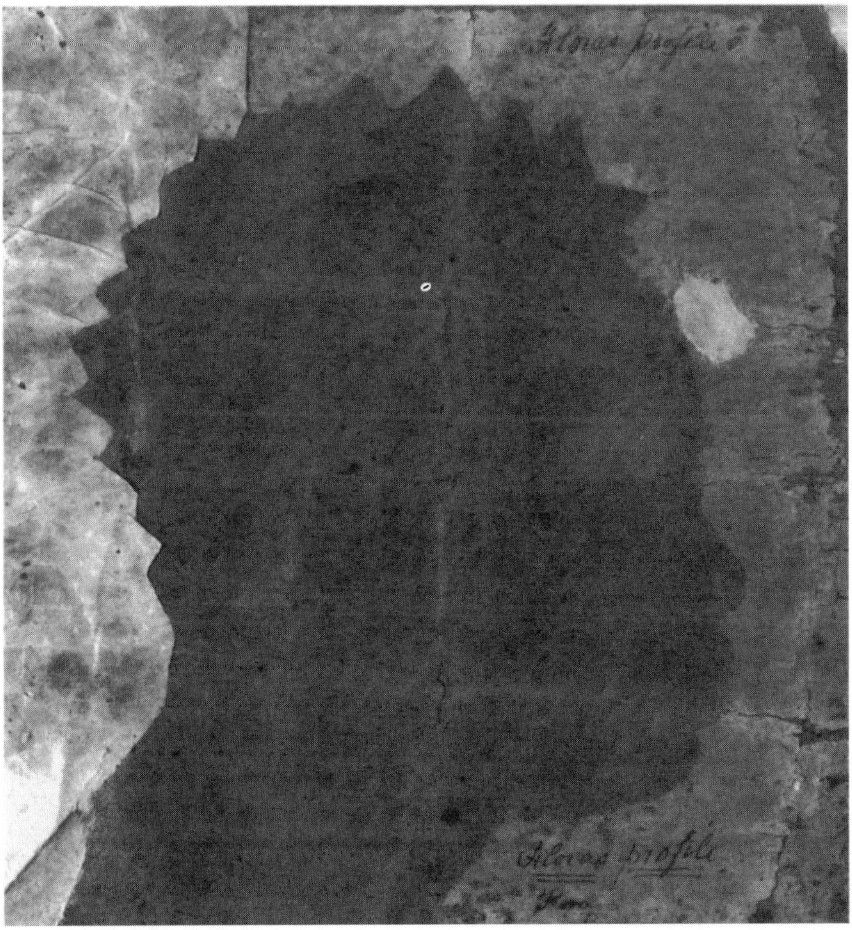

FIGURE 16. "Flora's Profile." This silhouette, cut out of paper and shaded with ink, depicts a Connecticut woman at the time she was sold in 1796. In 1815, at a time when most other New England slaves were becoming free, she died still enslaved. The image was kept, along with the bill of sale, by Margaret Dwight of Milford, the woman who sold her. Silhouette, cut paper and brown ink, 14" × 13." Courtesy of the Stratford Historical Society, Stratford, Conn.

acter and became widespread in the United States in the 1820s (fig. 17). By then, the supposition that blacks had particularly small and thick skulls was already well established—long before the racial scientists of the 1830s would attempt to confirm this conclusion with elaborate arrays of skulls and displays of precision.[52] In-

FIGURE 17. A cartoon mocking the phrenology craze. A professional "bumpologist" "pores o'er the cranial map with learned eyes / Each rising hill and bumpy knoll descries / Here secret fires, and their deep mines of sense / His touch detects beneath each prominence." George Cruikshank, *Bumpology*, London, 1826. Aquatint and etching. Courtesy of the National Library of Medicine, Bethesda, Md.

deed, the conclusion phrenologists would later "discover" through their studies of racial skulls had been widely anticipated decades earlier.

In the early Republic, for instance, representations of Indians were remarkably consistent in emphasizing their incompatibility with civilized life. Newspapers, magazines, and plays often included sentimental representations of noble savages living beyond the frontier, idealized for their natural independence and mourned because they were doomed to destruction. Anne Hunter's "North American Death Song, Written for, and adapted to, An Original Indian Air" is but one example in the sentimental vein. Jefferson particularly admired the defiant speech that Indian leader Tachnedorus, or John Logan, delivered to Virginia governor Lord Dunmore in 1774, in which he accused Virginians of having killed his innocent family despite his long alliance with them and promised that he would now fight them to the death, even though he knew that he, the last of his people, could never prevail. "Logan's Lament," as the English translation of the speech came to be known, was the most widely reproduced example of a common theme: a noble Indian betrayed by settlers and doomed to die. On the other hand, particularly in New England, newspapers and almanacs also featured jokes about Indians living with settlers— although never very successfully. Typically, one widely circulated anecdote played on the image of Indians as drunken, deceitful debtors. The Indian approaches a tavern keeper and bargains for a quart of rum in exchange for a fine fat deer he has just killed. The deer, he says, is near a tree in a nearby meadow. He gives the tavern keeper detailed directions. The tavern keeper sets out to retrieve the carcass but returns empty-handed and irate. The Indian reasons with him. "Did you not find the meadow, as I said?" asks the Indian. "Yes," replies the tavern keeper. "And the tree?" "Yes." "And the deer?" "No." "Very good, (continues he) you found *two truths to one lie, which was very well for an Indian.*"[53]

By the 1790s, intellectual observers were elaborating the conclusion that Indians were incapable of living as citizens of a civilized society. Critics of missionaries had long argued that attempts to convert and civilize Indians were useless. In the 1770s, one observer wrote, "There never was, I believe, an instance of an Indian forsaking his Habits & savage manners, any more than a Bear his ferocity." By the 1790s, a number of aging ministers living near New England enclaves were hardly more sympathetic. Typical of these men, embittered by years of failure, was Stephen Badger, the minister of the old Praying Indian Town of Natick, whose observations were published in the *Collections of the Massachusetts Historical Society* in 1797. Like many New England enclave communities, the Natick Indians were struggling for survival: impoverished, demoralized, and largely overrun by Anglo-American settlers. And, like many observers, Badger interpreted the problem not as a result of English interlopers, loss of sovereignty, or unequal treatment before the law but as a reflection of their basic character. Although he declined to say whether the difference was innate or stemmed from "accidental causes," he concluded that "there is a dissimilarity between the natural constitutions of the English and Indians." Badger retained a firm conviction that Indians were prone to "indolence and excess" and that the "general disposition and manners of Indians are so distinguishingly characteristic" that even Indian youths raised by English families—and temporarily temperate and industrious—relapsed as soon as they became independent. Badger demanded an explanation from one of those who reverted to "all the excesses of those who had not been favored with such advantages" and "became *Indians* in the reproachful sense of the word," and the good minister received the laconic reply: "*Ducks will be ducks, notwithstanding they are hatched by the hen.*" For dramatic effect, Badger also presented this aphorism in a stylized Indian dialect: "*Tucks will be tucks for all ole hen he hatch um.*"[54]

Intrigued that some writers elevated Indians as "possessed of every virtue" whereas others degraded them "below the rank of humanity," Massachusetts writer William Tudor noted, "In the mean time, the unfortunate race which is the subject of dispute, is mouldering away, and in a not remote period will have no existence but in history." Tudor focused on what at the time was a common question: "Is the red man of the American forests a species of the human genus susceptible of civilization?" No, he and other observers concluded after reviewing the history of Indians in the East. Some, like Tudor, contemplated this fate with nostalgia: "There seems something very saddening in the reflection, that the original possessors of this magnificent country . . . should be inevitably destined to destruction." In 1802 the Mashpee missionary Gideon Hawley concurred: "Mixing Indians and English in a settlement spoils and finally extirpates the former."[55] Support for the notion that Indians were disappearing from the New England landscape came partly from a perceived decline of population in Indian enclaves and partly from a sense that those who remained were increasingly losing their racial purity. The figure of the "last Indian," reinvented repeatedly across the new Republic, foreshadowed the ambivalent, anticipatory nostalgia that made Manifest Destiny such a comfort and such a sorrow to so many Americans on both sides of the western frontier.

At the same time, a number of observers in the early years of the Republic argued that the mixture of Indians with blacks might well be a good thing, at least from the point of view of heredity and character. "Since a number of Negro's have married in among Indians," Gideon Hawley wrote about the Mashpee in 1798, "they are become more temperate and more industrious than they were before." Although all these men inclined to the notion that the Indians' incompatibility with civilization was the inevitable result of their natural character, they couched their conclusions in the language of education. Regarding their "mental capacity," Gideon Hawley argued paradoxically that they were "naturally artful, cunning and insidious" because of their way of life: "Their hunting, fishing, and fowling requires the exercise of artifice, [but] their minds being always employed in small matters cannot expand." Although the childish and passionate character of Africans could only degrade white blood, and although the nobility of savage indigenes was itself undone by contact with whites, the deficiencies in black and Indian racial character complemented each other. Gideon Hawley observed about that time that the admixture of African blood made the Mashpee both more intelligent and more hardy: "As far as I can judge the Indians whose blood has been commixed were the most ingenious." He concluded: "The bodily constitution of an Indian and his original stamina is not equal to the posterity of those who came from the old continent." "Those who have mixt blood are the most capable of labor and suffering"—by which he meant civilization.[56]

The traits that seemed to exclude blacks from viable membership in civil society were roughly the opposite of those that excluded Indians: instead of being too independent and proud, blacks were too dependent and degraded. Jokes about blacks were more closely drawn from English jokes mocking servants and Irish people—all of whom were represented as foolish, lazy, and happy-go-lucky. Many jokes about black people followed the genre of self-contradictory statements, known in the eighteenth-century English world as the Irish bull. One of the most popular of all eighteenth-century jokes about blacks featured Cesar stumbling home on a very dark night, having spent the evening drinking with a friend. A friendly warning to watch his step comes too late, and Cesar trips on an old post and falls to the ground. "I wonder," says Cesar, rising and rubbing the mud from his holiday suit, "why de debil de sun no shin in dees dark nights, Cato, and not always keep shining in de day-time, when dere's no need of him." Many other jokes featured sassy servants besting their masters by playing dumb and taking instructions overly literally—another trope common in English servant jokes. One begins when a captain crossing a sandbar asks his black pilot what kind of water the ship is in. "Salt water, massa." Another frequently reprinted joke featured a black man whose very foolishness showed up a pretentious young scholar. "Boston," the youth declares, "I can take a pen and Ink, and in three minutes can cypher out and tell you how many minutes you have to live." "Canna you massa, you must be very good cypher indeed," Boston replies before proceeding to stump the young braggart with questions such as "Which can see best, a mare stone blind, or a horse without eyes?" and "'Pose fifty rail makes one load, how many he take to make a d——d great pile?"[57]

Even before many blacks became free in the North, it was common opinion that they were not well suited to the duties of citizenship. Gentlemen writing accounts of their travels through the new Republic commonly said as much. "The negro is much more susceptible of civilization," wrote William Tudor after traveling through New England. "The negro is a more gay, light-hearted, social being, than the Indian; becomes easily and permanently domesticated." Some free blacks in northern states, he added, could be observed working with some industry, accumulating some property, and sending their children to school. This progress hardly made blacks equal to whites. "Perhaps they may not be susceptible of the highest degree of civilization," Tudor concluded; "they may not have sufficient intelligence and command of their passions, to form the citizens of a free government." More confident of this conclusion was the marquise de Chastellux. In a passage from his *Travels in America* (1783) that was reprinted in the *Columbian Magazine,* the French nobleman admitted little more than that blacks and whites were "fellow creatures, at least, if not people entirely of the same species." Likely influenced by Jefferson, he claimed that blacks were suited to slavery by their diminished sensibility and even presumed to suggest that they did not actually desire freedom.[58]

The abolition of slavery and the emergence of free blacks in the northern states prompted broader reflections on their potential as citizens and relations with whites. All the gentlemen polled by the Reverend Jeremy Belknap in 1795 about the progress of abolition and the experience of free blacks in Massachusetts reported that they enjoyed at best the social status of the lowest level of the white population. Why they had not progressed further than that was the subject of some debate. All emphasized that whites insisted on their own preeminence. Some pointed to the prejudice of education. Individuals raised under slavery could hardly be expected to adapt well to the life of free citizens. A few, such as Judge James Sullivan, argued that blacks were probably simply naturally inferior. "There is no doubt a great disparity in the natural abilities of mankind, and we have great reason to believe that the organization of the Africans is such as prevents their receiving the more fine and sublime impressions equally with the white people." He felt that abolishing slavery before blacks could be exported out of country was rash. In fact, there was no historical precedent that "a man educated as a slave has been capable of enjoying freedom." Curiously, he was willing to consider the alternative possibility that the experience of social equality over several generations might "mend the race" and increase blacks' powers of perception, understanding, and analysis until they might even "exceed the white people." Yet he remained unwilling to take the risk.[59]

One of the most obvious rebuttals to claims that Indians and blacks were inherently inferior was to produce examples of individuals of distinguished attainments. Even before the Revolution, the talents, piety, and industry of individuals such as Samson Occom and Phillis Wheatley were objects of interest in North America and more widespread acclaim in England. Among the other individuals widely regarded as symbols of black potential in England and America in the late eighteenth century were Ignacio Sancho, whose letters were published in London in 1770s; Olaudah Equiano, whose incisive memoir, *The Interesting Narrative of the Life of Olaudah Equiano,* was published in 1789; and the Maryland astronomer Benjamin Banneker, who published a successful series of almanacs in the 1790s. The autobiography of Venture Smith, published in Connecticut in 1798, was also presumably intended to help combat negative stereotypes of blacks during the years when most northern blacks were becoming free. The printer, who had previously published Benjamin Franklin's autobiography, produced a volume that emphasized Smith's rustic virtues of strength, frugality, and industry. During the 1780s and 1790s, magazines published in the northern states were filled with accounts of black achievement. One almanac published in Providence in 1797 amused its readers with the story of the son of the governor of St.-Domingue, who in addition to a variety of other gentlemanly accomplishments spoke twenty-six languages and "walked round the various circles of human science like the master of each." And, the story concluded, "strange to be mentioned to white men, he was a *Mulatto,* and the son of an *African mother.*" In 1801, a Philadelphia printer republished Wheatley's poems in a book entitled *The Negro equalled by few Europeans.*[60]

Of course, such prodigies were subject to inspection and debate. "Never yet could I find that a black had uttered a thought above the level of plain narration," declared Thomas Jefferson in his *Notes on the State of Virginia.* Taking aim at the most prominent exemplar of black potential, he flatly declared that Phillis Wheatley's poems were beneath the dignity of criticism. "Religion has indeed produced a Phyllis Whatley; but it could not produce a poet." Of course, a hundred-odd pages earlier, Jefferson had gone to some lengths to defend his white compatriots from precisely the same charge. Stung by the claims of French philosophers and natural historians that the degeneracy of the American climate was evident in Americans' inability to produce works of genius in any field of endeavor, he railed against Abbé Raynall's assertion that America had not yet produced a single good poet. "When we shall have existed as a people as long as the Greeks did before they produced a Homer, the Romans a Virgil, the French a Racine and Voltaire, the English a Shakespear and Milton, should this reproach still be true," Jefferson promised, claiming for his fellow compatriots the excuse of national youth and primitive conditions, "we will enquire from what unfriendly cause it has proceeded."[61]

In this contentious climate, there were other attempts to discredit white racial arrogance. At a time when the poetic and humorous use of national and racial dialects was prominent, Jonathan Edwards Jr., the son of the great theologian, gave serious thought to the way Algonquian Indians spoke English. He had learned the Mahican language as a child and later, during a time when he was active in anti-slavery circles, published a book entitled *Observations on the Language of the Muh-hekaneew Indians* (1788). Edwards refuted common assumptions about the supposed deficiencies of Indian languages. For instance, he argued, the Mohegan language contained all eight parts of speech. "It has been said also, that savages never abstract, and have no abstract terms, which with regard to the Mohegans is another mistake." It was true, he acknowledged, that the Mohegan language had no verb *to be*, but that did not limit the Mohegans' range of expression. Instead of saying "he is a man," they used a single word, which Edwards called a verb neuter, such as "*memannauwoo*, he is a man." This feature did account for Mohegans' tendency not to use the verb *to be* when they spoke English. "They say, 'I man, I sick, &c.'" (A similar feature of West African languages accounts for the same structure in Black English.) Another difference was in the use of pronouns, which seemed redundant to those not familiar with Mohegan grammar: "They cannot say, *John loves Peter;* they always say, *John he loved him Peter; John uduhwhanuw Peteran.* Hence when the Indians begin to talk English, they universally express themselves according to this idiom."[62]

A more direct attack on white prejudices came at the hands of historian Jeremy

Belknap and geographer Jedidiah Morse in their 1796 report on the New Stockbridge and Brothertown Indians. Perhaps still thinking of the relentless emphasis
on white prejudice against blacks in his report on emancipation in Massachusetts
published the previous year, Belknap and his coauthor rejected the common argument that Indians were constitutionally incapable of surviving under civilization. One of the last queries they addressed in the report was: "Whether it be true,
as hath been strong affirmed to the Society, that the arts of civilization and industry, when adopted by the Indians, have such an unhappy effect on them, that few
of them long survive?" Clearly thinking about Badger's report on the Natick Indians, which Belknap, as president of the Massachusetts Historical Society, had
published only a few years earlier, the coauthors of the 1796 report rebutted the notion that New England Indians were disappearing: "[They] are at this day so
blended with blacks and whites, and so scattered, as not to be known or distinguished; but that these effects have resulted from their civilization and industry, is
an assertion that cannot be admitted." They went on to acknowledge that the
change from a savage to a civil mode of life is too great to be rapidly assimilated by
either body or mind. And they offered various practical explanations for why more
Indians have not become civil—including pride and force of habit—and ended
with a poignant reflection on the process of acculturation.

As Belknap and Morse saw it, the ultimate explanation for the failure of so many
Indians to become civilized lay not in their character but in white behavior. They
illustrated this point with an admittedly sentimental story about a typical Indian
youth's experiences among the English. Imagine, they asked, an Indian youth removed from his friends, family, and accustomed surroundings and taken to live
with a new people whose ways of life and thinking are entirely unfamiliar. "His new
friends profess to love him, and a desire for his improvement in human and divine knowledge, and for his eternal salvation; but at the same time endeavor to
make him sensible of his inferiority to themselves." Even at school they treat him
as a member of an inferior species. "To treat him as an equal would mortify their
own pride, and degrade themselves in the view of their neighbors." Consequently,
he acquires some knowledge but becomes progressively more demoralized. He is
reminded of his own country and desires to return to a place where he can be free
and equal. But when he returns to his friends, he discovers the real tragedy of his
fate: "He is neither a white man nor an Indian." Perhaps, if he had the strength of
mind to abandon all of his English ways, he might resume the savage life and be
received again by his compatriots, but the greater probability is that he will attempt

to drown his sorrows in liquor. "His downward progress will be rapid, and his death premature."[63] It was hard to argue with this logic.

But few observers bothered. Many recognized that Indians and blacks suffering constant discrimination could never be expected to advance to a respectable position in society—but they often heard this not as a call to reform white behavior but rather as an excuse to give up on attempting to assimilate nonwhites. The marquise de Chastellux was fairly typical in arguing that it didn't particularly matter whether the "unfortunate distinction" that set blacks apart in society was natural or social. In any case, if they were freed, they would become a plague on the landscape, forming a separate people with interests different from those of the body of citizens. "It appears, therefore, that there is no other method of abolishing slavery, than by getting rid of the negroes." William Tudor, too, claimed to be convinced that Indians could be successfully civilized if Anglo-Americans were to regard them as equals. "Savage as he is, the Indian can still see and feel the relative positions of society; and unless we surmount our prejudice against complexion, and allow the red man the same advantages as the white, what inducement can we offer them to adopt our customs?"[64] But such concessions did not lead Chastellux or Tudor to change their general sense that both blacks and Indians were doomed to degradation and exclusion from American citizenship. After 1817, this argument would be most prominently promoted by the American Colonization Society's efforts to deport free blacks and by Andrew Jackson's program to forcibly remove Indians from the path of white ambitions.

On the other hand, Chastellux and some other writers came up with another, rather surprising solution. There were, in fact, two ways of "getting rid" of black people, argued Chastellux. One solution was to deport them all to some other land, which was far from practical. The other solution involved intermarriage between white and people of color: "The best expedient would be to export a great number of males, and to encourage the marriage of white men with females." Writing specifically about Jefferson's Virginia, he noted that this would require changing the laws so that the children of enslaved women and free white men would be free. There was the problem of the property value of slaves, he emphasized; yet he continued, "It is certain, at all events, that such a law, aided by the illicit, but already well established commerce between the negresses, could not fail of giving birth to a race of mulattos, which would produce another of *Quarterons*, and so on until the colour should be totally effaced."[65] Coming from the likes of Chastellux, this seems less a serious proposal than a rhetorical reductio ad absurdum. But the fantasy that blacks and Indians would just go away was as common as the continuing desire of white Americans for their land and labor. Meanwhile, concentrating attention on black and Indian bodies served to draw attention away from the continuing, unresolved question of the meaning of equality among white citizens of the new Republic.

||| Natural Aristocracies |||

When it became clear, soon after his election to the Pennsylvania assembly in 1786, that his political career was doomed to failure, Hugh Henry Brackenridge did what any former schoolteacher with frustrated ambitions would do: he took the voters to task. During his last years in office, he completed the first two volumes of a long, satirical novel entitled *Modern Chivalry,* which he devoted to mocking the citizens of the new Republic for their democratic excesses and errors. At the time of the Revolution, he had held high hopes for the capacities of ordinary men. With proper instruction, he predicted, the honest husbandman and the humble mechanic might "rapidly improve in every kind of knowledge" and become qualified to exercise the franchise, worthy of local positions of leadership, and, perhaps, even "equal to the task of legislation." Brackenridge remained vigorously antipathetic to the notion of any artificial aristocracy: "Genius and virtue are independent of rank and fortune." Like Jefferson, he cherished the belief that virtue and talent would elicit by acclamation a new, natural aristocracy. But by the time the U.S. Constitution was being debated in the late 1780s, Brackenridge's faith in the populace had been severely tried. Too often, the voters failed to chose candidates distinguished by modesty, good sense, and education. The danger of such folly was the main theme of his novel, which chronicled the adventures of Captain John Farrago, a gentleman whose virtue was consistently overlooked, and his servant, Teague O'Regan, whose folly was just as consistently rewarded.[66] Early in the work, the natural history of race emerges as a prominent theme, but not in any way that takes seriously the question of black citizenship. For Brackenridge, the most pressing problem was the nature of equality among white men.

The novel was intended to echo the adventures of Don Quixote and Sancho Panza, unfolding as a series of picaresque narratives involving the noble gentleman and his foolish sidekick. Captain Farrago was intended as a kind of idealized republican citizen; Teague O'Regan, in contrast, was dismissed by the narrator in the first paragraph: "I shall say nothing of the character of this man, because the very name imports what he was." The fact that he was Irish apparently said it all. In the narratives that follow he emerges as the antithesis of Brackenridge's republican ideal: ignorant, foolish, grasping—and everywhere rewarded with undeserved honors and inappropriate responsibilities. Captain Farrago, who modestly demurs all attentions directed toward himself, spends most of his time trying to deter his servant from such follies as standing for election to the Pennsylvania assembly or accepting a call to become a Methodist minister. In one case, Teague is offered membership in the American Philosophical Society—which had wide-ranging interests in natural history—after he finds the body of an unusually large owl on the side of the road. A passerby recognizes the dead bird for the great rarity it is and offers to take it to the society in Philadelphia. He also offers them both memberships. The captain declines, saying that he has no qualifications for such an honor. But his servant is determined to become a philosopher. After an extended effort to reason with him, the captain finally succeeds by frightening him. Invoking the popular notion that the Irish complexion is unusually ruddy, the captain suggests that the philosophers might actually have sinister deigns on Teague. "It is their great study to find curiosities; and because this man saw you coming after me, with a red head, trotting like an Esquimaux Indian, it has struck his mind to pick you up and pass you for one."[67]

This fantasy of racial inversions on display at the Philosophical Society was too rich for Brackenridge to resist revisiting. In the second volume, the captain arrives in Philadelphia only to find Teague missing. After searching the local brothels, the captain fears that trouble might be brewing at the Philosophical Society. There he finds not Teague but a black man preparing to make an oration. Cuff, a slave in Maryland, had discovered a strangely shaped rock in a local swamp. His master forwarded it to the society, which recognized it as the petrified moccasin of an ancient Indian and invited the planter to join the society. The planter declined and nominated Cuff instead. When Cuff is invited to join the society, his master warns him that he will be expected to given an address. The master had recently read a paper arguing that "the Africans had once been white, had sharp noses, and long hair; but that by living in sun-burnt climates, the skin had changed colour, the hair become frizzled, and in the course of generation, the imagination of the mother, presenting obtuse objects, had produced offspring with flat noses." So he suggests that Cuff might want to champion the honor of his Guinea compatriots by arguing that "men were all once black" and that it was Europeans who had degenerated into whites. Accordingly, Cuff's speech, represented in a dialect so thick as to be almost incomprehensible, follows this line of argument: "Massa shentiman," he begins, "I say, dat de first man was de brack a man, and de first woman de brack a woman, and get two tree children." He goes on to explain that the rain washed them, and the snow bleached them, and their children became brown, yellow, copper, and at last quite white, and their hair grew long. Following his master's suggestion, he concludes that they got long, sharp noses by fighting with one another and "pulling on that part." The worthy philosophers greet the oration with acclaim, and the worthy captain goes off to seek his servant somewhere else.

In this novel, the natural history of race was not a serious matter. In a brief "commentary" following Cuff's performance, Brackenridge's narrator demonstrates familiarity with the standard biblical accounts of human origins, with Lord Kames's argument that the various races had separate origins, and with William Stanhope Smith's essay on the unity of humankind. "How the descendants of Adam and Eve, both good looking people, should ever come to be a vile negro, or even a mulatto man or woman, is puzzling," the narrator observers. But he cannot resist suggesting his own theory: that Adam was white, Eve black, and that their descendants, in varying degrees, inherited the traits that account for the diversity of the human species.[68] In theme and tone, Cuff's speech anticipates parodies of black learning in antebellum minstrel shows. But unlike later minstrel shows, which focused on fantastic racial inversions, Brackenridge's novel showed little further interest in black characters. In the context of *Modern Chivalry,* Cuff's performance serves largely to denigrate Teague by association—the black slave's speech is an example of the kind of speech the Irish servant might have given if he had not been rescued by the worthy captain from that vain ambition. Brackenridge writes as though the inferiority of blacks and Indians, and their exclusion from the body politic, were sufficiently obvious to require no reiteration. Indeed, Cuff's fractured English alone seems to make clear the fundamental irrelevance of the conclusions of natural historians about racial origins. For Brackenridge, the practical threat to the virtue of the Republic lay in the problem of equality among white men. If American citizens ultimately disagreed with Brackenridge's implicit elitism and expressed themselves willing to risk the dangers of a less deferential democracy, the exclusion of blacks from the political order was one thing on which they could all agree.

CHAPTER EIGHT

Manifest Destinies

||| Uxbridge, Massachusetts, 1806 |||

On Election Day in May 1806, Samuel Shoemaker went to the town common to enjoy the spectacle. Like many others who had grown up in slavery, he had probably obtained his freedom less from the liberality of the law than by his own gumption. When he had arrived in the small, out-of-the-way town of Uxbridge a few years earlier, little explanation had been either offered or demanded: it was suspected that he had run away from a master in New York, but by then opposition to slavery was strong enough that no one attempted to turn him in. A sympathetic physician offered him patronage, a job, and a little house where Shoemaker and his family could live. On the Election Day holiday, the doctor gave Shoemaker a little extra money so he could enjoy the festivities. As a black man he could not vote, but he could drink the customary libations. Somewhat inebriated, he passed the common and caught the attention of a number of white boys who were, according to an account written by the doctor's son, "at play." "Wanting more sport," the boys taunted Shoemaker. Then they began to pull at his shirt. He ignored them. Meeting no resistance, they began to poke at him. One boy threw a punch. At that, the older man finally lost his temper. He went after the boys and even blustered that he would go get his gun—although all he had at home was the broken remnants of an old pistol. At this point bystanders began to intervene. A gentleman grasped his cane and began bludgeoning Shoemaker's head; as he later explained, "he would not see white people thumped by a Negro." A crowd gathered, seized the bloodied Shoemaker, tied him up, and hauled him off to jail.

If the American North emerged in the early years of the Republic as a region of universal freedom, it remained, as it had been during the colonial period, a land of racial inequality. Shoemaker's behavior that day is striking not so much for his self-assertion as for his restraint. After risking a good deal to secure his freedom, Shoemaker did not go further and claim civil equality: for instance, he did not attempt to vote. Even when attacked by the boys, Shoemaker was slow to defend his masculine honor. Perhaps he wouldn't have fought back at all if he hadn't lost some of his inhibitions to alcohol. For their part, the boys seem to have taken it for granted that they could attack a black man with impunity. There were probably countless other incidents like this one—moments in which whites exercised the power and the pleasure of their racial privilege and in which blacks confronted their social as well as political subordination—but very few are well documented. Apparently, the only narrative of this particular conflict lies in a private letter the doctor's son wrote to recruit the assistance of Moses Brown. The citizens of Uxbridge showed their own kind of restraint. There was no talk of returning the suspected fugitive to slavery out of state, and after passions calmed, they apparently decided he had learned his lesson. Legal records show only that Shoemaker spent several days in jail, but no indictment was filed, and he was released.[1] If this story tells us anything, it is that the relative absence of open conflict over lines of color in the early years of the Republic may represent not so much a sense of racial liberality or openness as a common acceptance of the rules of racial hierarchy. Lines of color sparked violence only when they were crossed.

In the decades after the Revolution, New Englanders challenged, defended, and transformed many longstanding assumptions and practices of citizenship. It is commonplace to associate the U.S. Constitution of 1787 with a fundamentally new political order—a bold, inspired experiment in republican citizenship. Yet the politics of citizenship in the new Republic continued to reflect the colonial past—and nowhere more obviously than in continuing struggles over the civic status of blacks and Indians. Many political observers, such as Thomas Jefferson, who were comfortable enough with slaves were haunted by the prospect of living with free blacks. Many expressed doubt that blacks could ever become good citizens, and others feared that they might. Many observers simply wished that free blacks would somehow just go away. And what of Indians? Jefferson lauded their presumed nobility and independence; but, tragically, these virtues implied that Indians would never be able to submit to the restraints and discipline of civil society. The strategies pursued by both Indians and blacks suggest their fundamental ambivalence about their place within the new American Republic and also their strong desire to embody the virtues of republican citizenship. Their claims to social recognition and the rights of citizenship were not always, or even often, direct or explicit. Much of the struggle was in the more symbolic terrain in which republican citizenship was negotiated.

By the time of the Revolution, many of the most anglicized and Christian Indians in New England had given up any hope that they could have a viable future within the United States. As early as the 1760s Narragansetts talked despairingly about being forced to abandon their enclave and settle lands to the north or west. During the eighteenth century, New England Indians were increasingly forced from myriad small, separate communities across the countryside onto a few larger reservations. Constant encroachments of settlers on the lands of these reservations made it harder for their inhabitants to eke out a living, legal double standards contributed to their continued poverty, and resentment of white racism was widespread. In the 1770s, Samson Occom was able to organize seven enclave communities in New England—the Narragansett, Pequot, Niantic, Mohegan, Montauk, Farmington, and Stockbridge—to participate in a move to Oneida territory. Several hundred New England natives did move in the 1770s and 1780s, and others joined the community, named Brothertown, after the turn of the century. Their intent was to found a Christian farming community to serve as a missionary model for their Oneida brethren.[2] Other natives who remained in New England "disappeared" by moving to cities, where they often intermarried with African Americans and became part of an undifferentiated community of color. As Indians disappeared politically, though not physically, racial politics in New England became increasingly bipolar.

During the 1780s and 1790s, the emergence of free black populations in the northern cities seemed to offer a guide to how the racial future of the nation might develop.[3] Despite the enactment of gradual emancipation laws, freedom was achieved only very gradually through long struggles. Once legally free, poor blacks were not necessarily independent: some were bound by indentures, others by necessity, to live in white households as menial workers. In addition to the practical and emotional constraints with which white prejudice limited their opportunities, former slaves could not expect the kind of inheritance that was prerequisite to joining the comfortable ranks of American society. From the start of their free lives, blacks in the northern states faced steep obstacles. None were in a position to demand equality immediately. Nonetheless, the proceedings and correspondence of the Free African Union Societies in Newport and other northern cities document the development of self-conscious black communities and civic leaders in the early years of the Republic. These men were not revolutionaries. Their aspirations were remarkably modest and their strategies utterly nonconfrontational. Like native New Englanders, many free northern blacks also responded to their literal and symbolic disfranchisement in the American Republic with plans to unite racially and abandon the United States. But, instead, they staked their futures on America. Ironically, northern free blacks in the 1790s could sustain a sense of hope in the possibility of an egalitarian and racially integrated America—a hope that could be entertained precisely because it was so far from reality.[4]

Some observers at the time considered the colonial legacy of white racism to represent a fundamental contradiction to the Republic's highest ideals. In 1788, the visiting French gentleman Jean-Pierre Brissot de Warville said as much in his account of a troubling encounter in Newport. There he came across a twenty-month-old black baby who showed signs of extraordinary intelligence: "[He] repeated everything that was said to him, understood what he heard, obeyed instructions, mimicked others, danced, etc." Instead of being seen as representing black potential, the child was made an object of fun. "People amused themselves by getting him to perform spontaneously and especially by getting him to make funny faces." This seemed worse than simply cruel or thoughtless. "It was an indication of the contempt in which Negroes are still held, a contempt that Americans, above all others, must renounce if they wish to be consistent. This feeling of contempt for Negroes makes children used to too much servility, and Americans must banish, even from their children's play, the image of servility." Such comments clearly ruffled some republican feathers. When a translation of Brissot's *Travels* was published in New York in 1792, the editor silently omitted the story of the boy in Newport and other passages that called attention to white Americans' racial pride.[5] And yet, Brissot himself may have missed the depth of the problem.

The colonial legacy of white preeminence did not, in the early years of the Republic, simply survive. It took on new life. As northern blacks became increasingly independent, prosperous, and respectable in the early nineteenth century, whites responded by drawing ever more rigid lines of color. It soon became clear that humility and rectitude would not easily erase white prejudice. And, as whites increasingly emphasized symbols of equality in everyday interactions with other white people, the meaning of racial hierarchies shifted. Old rituals of deference became more egregious, more degrading, and more baldly racial. By the early nineteenth century these changes among Indian, black, and white expectations about citizenship produced increasingly open conflict.

||| Brothertown |||

Soon after the Revolution, the noted Mohegan minister Samson Occom finally gave up on the future of Indians within the American polity and undertook a long journey to an unsettling frontier outpost. There, along with refugees from seven New England enclaves, he hoped to pursue the Christian, civil life they found impossible in their homelands. Occom's diary records his departure from his Connecticut farm and his voyage, on a series of boats, along the shore to New York, up the Hudson River to Albany, westward along the Mohawk River past the fringes of colonial settlement, and finally, for the last ten or fifteen miles, on horseback through a dark forest into Oneida territory. Finally, the strains of "Melodious Singing" signaled that he had arrived. Those who had preceded him had gathered to greet him and were passing the time by singing spiritual songs. Like other settlers, the New England Indians feared the "hideous" wilderness and strove to transform it into a "Garden of God" with comforting symbols of the life they had left behind. In the fall of 1787, they formally bound themselves as a "Body Politick," to be governed by a New England–style government, which they named "Brothertown."[6]

The creation of Brothertown, planned before the Revolution and established in the 1780s, represents a turning point in ideas about the place of Indians within the American body politic—resulting in new alliances and new divisions. Occom and other leaders of the Brothertown move believed that the only hope for a viable life lay in Christianity and English-style farming, but they gave up ever pursuing this destiny anywhere near the English. The Brothertown migrants abandoned the old tribal or "town" identities that had defined the Narragansett, Mohegan, Niantic, Pequot, and Montauk Indians and forged a new kind of alliance between the Algonquian-speaking Indians of New England and the Oneidas, one of the Six Nations of the Iroquois. This transcendent sense of Indian identity—blurring historical, political, and cultural differences—reflected the influence of imperial officials, and later U.S. policymakers, who were often inclined to lump all Indians together as fundamentally the same. However, the Brothertown experiment also exacerbated existing divisions within each group. The New England enclaves were plagued by factional conflicts over religion, politics, and land use; those most determined to pursue English ways decided to leave. Similar issues divided the Iroquois: many respected the power Christianity seemed to give to white settlers, but others feared that acceptance of English ways had been the source of all their troubles. The Brothertown experiment, drawing together Indians from across New England under the authority of Christianity, was mirrored by a growing nativist revitalization movement that eventually attracted followers from Iroquoia to the Gulf of Mexico. Both groups were united by the conviction that Indians could not live together with Anglo-Americans.

The Indians of New England and Iroquoia had been brought together in the 1760s by Christian missionaries and the imperial bureaucracy. Many of the leaders of the Brothertown move, including Occom himself, had been educated by Eleazar Wheelock, whose Indian school attracted students from many New England enclaves, the Iroquois, and the Delaware. Under Wheelock's tutelage, Samson Occom, Joseph Johnson, and other later leaders of the Brothertown expedition served among the Oneidas in the 1760s as schoolteachers and missionaries—the Oneidas being the Iroquois nation most curious about Christianity. On occasion, Iroquois representatives also visited New England enclaves, as when an Oneida sachem stopped at Mohegan with Joseph Johnson in 1767 on a trip to Hartford to discuss Connecticut's claims to vast tracts of western lands. If Indians on opposite sides of the imperial frontier had little in common culturally, they did share a common problem: English settlers. Disputes with settlers brought all these Indians within the circle of the imperial Indian superintendent Sir William Johnson, whose headquarters were in Mohawk territory near Albany. During the 1760s, the Narragansetts had sent several delegations to see him in person, and Indians from across New England petitioned him for help in their conflicts with settlers. In 1768 Sir William toured New England and paid visits to the Narragansett, Niantic, Mohegan, and Montauk enclaves, "all concerning Lands." The possibility of moving New England Indians onto Iroquois territory was first suggested by Anglo-Americans thinking in terms of an imperial framework. For example, in 1767, when John Shattock and his brother stopped in New York on their way to appeal the dispute with their sachem to King George III in London, an English land speculator suggested that a better strategy would be to abandon their homes and move west. The scheme also appealed to Wheelock's missionary vision: "It may be god is designed to thrust out the christians among them, to make a new settlement; and carry ye gospel with them, among the western savages."[7] But at the time, neither the Narragansetts, Mohegans, nor any other group of New England Indians were eager to begin new lives in a remote, uncivilized wilderness.

By the early 1770s, however, it began to seem that they did not have much choice. Inhabitants of the southern New England enclaves faced debt, dispossession, and servitude: none of the enclaves had ever been given a real chance of achieving a successful and egalitarian integration into the settler economy. Matters were only made worse by the massive sales of Narragansett land ordered by the Rhode Island government and the Privy Council's disappointing resolution of the Mohegans' longstanding effort to reverse past land sales they claimed had been illegal. Occom's pessimism is suggested in a letter he wrote to Phillis Wheatley's mistress after visiting Natick, one of the remaining Massachusetts Praying Towns that had been established in the mid-seventeenth century as communities of Christian Indians. He reported that the Indians there were now "almost extinct." Such discouraging prospects provided the impetus for organizing an ambitious plan for emigration. On 13 March 1773, representatives from seven southern New England Indian enclaves met at the Mohegan enclave in Farmington, Connecticut. Joseph Johnson listed the "towns or tribes" represented as Pequots from North Stonington and North Groton, Niantics from Lyme, Mohegans and Farmington Indians, Narragansetts from Charlestown, and Montauks from Long Island. Men, women, and children of each community had appointed delegates to "seek a Place somewhere for us Seven towns to settle down together in peace." Some wanted to go as far as the Ohio River valley, but others said "it would not do to live so far from the English."[8] Although New England Indians wanted to get away from settlers, they did not want to get too far from the comforts of the life they had known.

Meeting with representatives of many New England tribes in the fall of 1773, Sir William gave his support to the idea of a removal to Indian country in the west. He sent a belt of wampum to the Oneidas to emphasize his support. Sir William had good reason to expect the Oneidas to support the plan; after the defeat of the French in the Seven Years' War, the Oneidas—along with the other Iroquois nations—found their power to manipulate the British Empire greatly diminished. The Proclamation Line of 1763 was drawn in a way that opened much Iroquois territory to colonial settlement. And years of brutal warfare had left backcountry settlers increasingly violent and hostile to all Indians. After a series of widely publi-

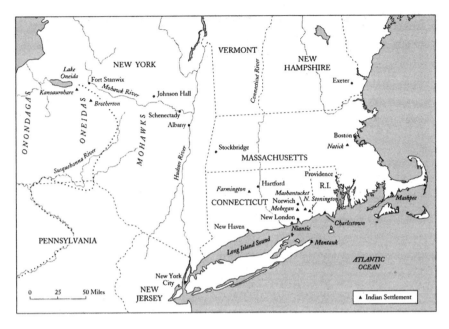

MAP 2. New England, New York, and Iroquois Country, 1774. The Fort Stanwix Treaty Line of 1768 represents the extent of colonial settlement to that point.

cized massacres, British military commander Thomas Gage reported, "All the peoples of the frontiers, from Pennsylvania to Virginia inclusive, openly avow, that they [would] never find a man guilty of murder, for killing an Indian." These pressures helped Sir William in negotiations in 1768 at Fort Stanwix, where he forced the Iroquois to accept huge losses of territory. The Six Nations were left bitter about the paltry sum they had been paid for the lands and worried that these cessations would not be the last (map 2). This context gave the Six Nations new incentives to practice their long-established custom of accepting or "adopting" different peoples to strengthen their ranks.[9]

The Oneidas took Sir William's suggestion seriously and summoned Joseph Johnson for a council meeting in early January 1774. Sir William had advised Johnson on how much land he could expect from the Oneidas, explained how he should behave at the council meeting the Oneidas would call, and gave him a silver pipe and pouch of tobacco to use as the expected diplomatic gift. Johnson needed no help explaining his people's plight in terms the Iroquois could understand. He explained their encounter with English settlers as a kind of imperial hangover:

"Whilst our forefathers were blind and Ignorant, yea drowned in Liquors the English stripped them, yea as it were cut off their right hands, and now we their Children just opening their Eyes, and knowledge growing in our hearts and just come to our Sense, like a drunken man, I say we now begin to look around and we perceive that we are Striped indeed, nothing to help ourselves. Thus our English Brethren leaves us and laugh." Indeed, the Oneidas had long been wary of English settlers. Several years earlier the Oneidas had rejected a proposal by Wheelock to establish a model white settlement on their territory: they were determined that no "white people" should ever live among them or even near them, "except ye minister and school-master." The New England Indians offered a chance to witness Christian life without the danger of a substantial white presence.[10]

On the other hand, as things stood, the New England Indians did not offer a particularly inspiring example. As one Narragansett supporter of the Brothertown move complained, "[The English] have taken away most of our Lands, and doubt-less they wou'd, many of them to have poor Indians for their Slaves." Indeed, slavery was both a metaphor and a model for the defeat, desperation, and emascula-tion the Iroquois feared. For years, nativist Iroquois had been admonishing the Oneidas to give up the white people's religion and revive instead their old customs—holding out the example of African slavery as the ominous alternative. One Seneca warned: "The spirit of the brave warrior & the good hunter will no more be discovered among us. We shall be sunk so low as to hoe corn & squashes in the field, chop wood, stoop down & milk cows like *negroes* among the dutch people."[11]

Despite any misgivings, the Oneida leaders embraced their New England brethren, declaring, "We receive you into our Body as it were, now we may say we have one head, one heart, and one Blood." They offered the New England Indi-ans a tract on the eastern edge of their territory, up against the Fort Stanwix treaty line, hoping that they would serve as a buffer against encroaching settlers. The deed by which the Oneidas granted the tract to the New England Indians was drafted by Guy Johnson, who assumed the office of superintendent of Indian affairs when Sir William died in 1774. The deed also made formal the racial anxieties both the New Englanders and the Iroquois shared. It explicitly barred "white" people from occupying the land. And it also excluded blacks—a policy Occom had previously advocated in Mohegan—stipulating that the land "shall not be possessed by any persons, deemed of said Tribe, who are descended from, or have intermixed with Negroes, or Mulattoes."[12]

The organizers of Brothertown cultivated sympathy among the Iroquois by emphasizing the depredations of English settlers, but they had to change their tune when soliciting the support of colonists. Joseph Johnson told Connecticut officials in "going out into the Wilderness, amongst More Savage Nations," the New England Indians would endeavor to "root out" the irrational prejudice that had become "very deeply rooted in the hearts of those Savages." He mourned, "Poor Creatures indeed, they vainly think themselves to be Something, when they are nothing." This deferential pose was part of a broader rhetorical strategy in which he flattered English wishes to see themselves as benevolent and guiltless, and it represented Indians as solely responsible for their own failure. In order to raise funds to finance the removal of New England Indians to Oneida territory, Joseph Johnson stopped in Schenectady, Albany, and New Haven and published plaintive letters soliciting donations in local newspapers. In these letters Johnson emphasized the "miserable circumstances" of his "poor Brethren" and frankly pleaded for sympathy. Echoing the language of the current imperial crisis, he predicted, "In short time they will unavoidably be involved in the wretched state of perfect slavery, which every rational being dreads." Yet, rather than blaming the English, he thanked them for their kind treatment of Indians in the past. Instead, he blamed the plight of New England Indians on their own imprudence, immorality, and lack of industry—which he implied comported with popular colonial stereotypes of Indian character. In a striking passage, Johnson noted that he could accept only gifts, because he could not commit to repaying loans: "To put confidence in Indians, is like a mans leaning on a broken staff."[13]

In fact, the leaders of the Brothertown move were bitterly frustrated by the lack of enthusiasm they encountered in their own enclaves. Although many of the most anglicized Indians were most likely to support the Brothertown venture, they were also often the ones with the most to lose. Just as the Narragansetts had divided in the 1760s over the management of tribal lands, the Mohegans also disagreed about whether land should be allocated privately so that individuals could "improve" it in the English manner (the position Johnson supported) or whether more of the land should be owned collectively and rented to local settlers in the hope that the Indians could live off the rent. Johnson and Occom sought to bridge these differences in various ways. In one circular letter to members of the seven New England tribes, Johnson admonished laggard members not to live up to low English expectations: "Must we let the World know that we are Indians by Nature, & by Practice?" By February 1775, Johnson could report that only fifty-eight men were prepared to make up the first party: "from Mohegan 10, from Narragansett 20, from Montauk on Long Island 13, from Nihantuck 5, from Farmington, 10 and there is two other Tribes who confess that they are So deeply involved in debt that they can not go this Season." Embarrassed, Johnson explained to the Oneidas: "True, the great drinkers & Lazy Persons are backwards in coming in these parts but we are willing to leave them there."[14]

Meanwhile, the rumblings of war realigned political alliances on both sides of the Fort Stanwix boundary line and ultimately delayed the move. In New England, the emigrants faced resistance from settlers suddenly concerned that they might join up with the feared Iroquois confederacy, particularly the Mohawks, and ally themselves with the British. In one case, a Rhode Island settler refused to pay the Narragansett man Peter Shattock twenty dollars for back wages if he went. Connecticut governor Jonathan Trumbull denied the initial party of pioneers a passport. And when the group met at Farmington, the English townspeople threatened, "It wou'd be best to knock all the Indians in the head rather than that they Shoud go to the Mohawk Country." On this occasion Joseph Johnson responded to the settlers with characteristic bitterness: "I told them I could not believe that and it seemed to Me [a] matter of great Surprize, that as the People of New England had got almost all of our Lands from Us, and thereby oblig'd us to go elsewhere, shou'd want to Stop us now, when a Year ago, they wanted to get rid of us."[15]

The pioneers had hardly arrived in Oneida country before they learned of a new danger: "the distant Indian nations" were threatening to "take up the Hatchet" against them. Some of the Iroquois feared that the new outpost was part of a scheme "formed by the People of New England to settle in that Western Country." This fear built on a longstanding antagonism to Christianity that also threatened to divide the Iroquois. One Oneida man reported to the missionary Samuel Kirkland, "We are despised by our brethren, on account of our Christian profession. Time was when we were esteemed as honorable & important in the confederacy: but now we are looked upon as small things; or rather nothing at all." The Oneidas complained that other Iroquois "twitted" them for their sympathy with Christianity. The New England settlers, fearing that the Oneidas would not be able to protect them, soon abandoned their outpost and returned back east.[16]

After the war, the Brothertown settlers returned, but they found the position of the Oneidas drastically weakened—and it was only Occom's political savvy that kept their lands from being reclaimed by the increasingly desperate Oneidas or grabbed by the ruthless government of New York. Although the Oneidas had been generally loyal to the United States, other Iroquois tribes had been staunchly Tory.

Following George Washington's orders, General John Sullivan had devastated Iroquois country. Then, at the end of the war, Britain abandoned all Indian territory south of the Great Lakes. In that context, pressure from settlers mounted, and New York's Governor Clinton pressured the Oneidas to cede land. The Oneidas attempted to bolster their numbers by inviting back not only the Brothertown and Stockbridge Indians but also hundreds of Onondagas, Cayugas, and Delawares, perhaps doubling their population to almost two thousand by 1784. But their white neighbors became increasingly aggressive and hostile, making fraudulent land purchases, defying laws regulating liquor sales, and using various ploys to get Indians into court so that they could be ordered to sell land in order to pay fines. The hostility of local settlers was keenly felt, one Indian explained: "It had become a proverb among the white people to say, '*as dirty as an Indian,*' '*as lazy as an Indian,*' '*As drunk as an Indians,*' '*lie like Indians.*' And we Indians can only say, '*Cheat like white man.*'" By early 1788, longtime missionary to the Oneidas Samuel Kirkland gave up and backed a controversial plan to lease out all their remaining territory to a white land speculation company. That summer, the governor of New York threatened to turn a blind eye to fraud, violence, and squatters unless the Oneidas gave up all their land except a 250,000–acre reservation and tracts for the Brothertown and Stockbridge immigrants. Faced with the loss of the vast majority of their territory, the Oneidas proposed to reduce the 15–square-mile tract they had given to the Brothertown Indians to the 640 acres that the early emigrants had actually occupied. But Occom, who spent much of 1788 lobbying officials in New York and Philadelphia, was able to maneuver past this threat. He had taken the precaution of having the original 1774 grant registered in the office of the secretary of state and managed to convince the New York assembly to lay out for them almost all the original tract, totaling some 24,052 acres. The assembly also stipulated that the Indians would not have any power of selling or leasing land for more than ten years.[17] Occom managed, for the moment, to protect most of their territory, but only by having the Brothertown Indians become wards of New York State.

Occom considered these restrictions necessary because factional infighting familiar from the New England enclaves had already begun to resurface in Brothertown—and he feared that the results would be catastrophic. Following the typical New England practice when settling western towns, the bulk of the property was owned at first by the town collectively and then parceled out to individual householders. Many were tempted to take advantage of this seeming abundance of land. Some leased out their original allocation and then secured another grant of land, which they rented out as well. Occom attempted to prevent the leasing of lands, because he feared it would give white settlers a way of appropriating the land. In 1791, Occom went to Albany to get the New York legislature to charter the Brothertown government, which would limit and regulate the distribution of land. By the time he returned, more than 2,000 acres had already been leased. Discouraged, Occom moved to Tuscarora country, where he died in 1792, apparently trying to find a new place for the Christian Indians of New England to settle. As late as 1795, David Fowler, a leader of the Brothertown community, originally from Montauk, still hoped that illegal leases made by "our foolish People" could be broken, as the state had already ordered: "The Indians in our Settlement will become wealthy and civilized People and also religious." Instead, the state allowed white tenants to buy any land leased to them—whether the Indian owners wanted to sell it or not. Almost instantly, more than half of the Brothertown tract was gone. By 1796, the original tract of 24,052 acres had been reduced to 9,390.[18]

Meanwhile, similar conflicts continued to divide New England enclaves—and, indeed, were exacerbated by migration to Brothertown and elsewhere. The Narragansetts finally got rid of their troubled sachems around 1777, when Thomas Ninigret's nephew George was killed in the swamp by a falling cedar tree and the Tribe's Party wrested control of tribal governance. As in Mohegan, where the political context was similar, conflict erupted over the legal status of individual tracts of tribal land. One test came when James Niles moved away from the enclave and attempted to sell his farm to a white settler. The Narragansett council objected, and ultimately the English courts agreed: they ruled that Niles did not actually own the land in fee simple and that if he or his heirs were not actually going to use the land it should revert to the tribe as a whole. This rebuff did not prevent Niles from writing a will that divided his property among several heirs; and when he died several years later, the will was not challenged by the tribe and was honored by the local town government. Other Narragansett men and women also began asserting the right to use wills to control the division of their property—at least within the tribe. Individuals also continued to lease land to "white People"—a temptation only exacerbated by migration to Brothertown and other places. In 1779, the ruling council complained, "There are many more now among us that are about Leasing out their Lands for a great Number of Years & moving away among other Tribes, & Principally those who Possess the best Farms."[19]

The deteriorating state of many New England enclaves led many Anglo-American observers to conclude that the Brothertown experiment represented the best hope for Indian civilization. In 1796 Massachusetts Historical Society president Jeremy Belknap visited Brothertown and the nearby community of New Stockbridge on behalf of a Boston-based missionary organization; he was impressed by the industry, Christianity, and relatively good husbandry of the Indian settlements. Yale president Timothy Dwight was less optimistic. He agreed that within New England there was no hope for the future of Indians. As he remarked of the Pequot enclave in Stonington, Connecticut: "The contempt which this degraded people will always experience from us, and the sense of their own degradation and our superiority, will keep them forever in their present state if they are to remain dispersed among the English inhabitants." Indeed, it was the unique opportunity to see "civilized Indian life" that inspired Dwight to visit Brothertown in 1797, where he found some forty families setting up farms. He was pleased that they spoke good English (better than the local Dutch) and that they tipped their hats and curtsied as he passed. One of three frame houses was occupied by Amos Hutton, originally from Narragansett; he had a "large barn well built," the interior of his home was distinguished by its "neatness," and "his wife was an industrious and thorough housewife." Nevertheless, Dwight concluded, the Indians' husbandry was "generally inferior to that of the white people." This, he opined, was a matter of racial nature: "Almost everywhere is visible that slack hand, that disposition to leave everything unfinished, which peculiarly characterizes such Indians as have left savage life." Dwight predicted that most of them would soon "leave their own business to labor for the white inhabitants." His conclusion was widely shared: Indians, once conquered, lost the very qualities of independence and wild nobility that made their defeat at once inevitable and tragic.[20]

In fact, the "Town Records of Brothertown," kept since the first town meeting in May 1796, trace the development of a growing and increasingly stable community. The business of the town government was largely the mundane: most entries relate to disputes over fences, highways, stray livestock, and damage done by dogs. Dancing, frolicking, traveling, or working on the Sabbath were prohibited, and stringent laws were passed against immorality, profanity, and drunkenness; idleness; concealing fugitive servants; playing cards, dice, and gambling; unfounded gossip; "abuse by foul language or assault"; and marriage with Negroes or mulattos. The Brothertown records suggest the development and maturation of the town over the next twenty years, similar in style to frontier settlement by whites. The first schoolhouse was built in 1788, and a 1796 act provided for its replacement. In 1795 lots were assigned to thirty-nine families; in 1799 there were about sixty. By

1813, two thousand acres had been cleared and were under cultivation, and the Brothertown Indians were "considerably advanced in agricultural knowledge." They also had a gristmill, two sawmills, sixteen frame houses, and eighteen frame barns. Among them were four carpenters, two blacksmiths, four shoemakers, two tailors, and five weavers. By this time, their New York superintendents concluded, "The greater part of them are men whose lives and characters would disgrace no community being temperate and industrious."[21]

Whatever the settlers at Brothertown achieved in these years, the Oneidas were not particularly impressed—and the nativist faction gained ground. Belknap reported that even though they had grown dependent on their Algonquian neighbors for corn and meat, "the Oneidas affect to despise their neighbors of Stockbridge and Brothertown for their attention to agriculture." Man, the pious visitors were told, "was made for war and hunting, and holding councils, and that squaws and hedge-hogs [were] made to scratch the ground." Certainly the presence of the Brothertown and Stockbridge Indians had not prevented the loss of most of Oneida territory in the 1780s, and the Oneidas' political betrayal by missionary Samuel Kirkland reduced support for the tribe's Christian faction. A nativist leader, called Pagan Peter, used the language of Christian Judgment to express his resentment of overweening white settlers: "The White Skin race as a body have become proud. . . . You glory in your riches, your great & commodious houses, your large fields & your abundance. You wear a white shirt & sometimes it is rufled. And you despise us Indians for our indigence, our poor huts, our scanty food, & our dirty shirts." The immorality of the whites conflicted with their undeniable power. As one Oneida explained to visiting Quakers, "[The Oneidas] looked at the flourishing state of the white people & were ready to apprehend the Great Spirit loved the white people more, because they were better, yet they saw the white People did not do right." Increasingly, the Oneidas looked not eastward toward Christian culture but westward to other Indians and nativist practices. In the 1790s, events to the west—such as Handsome Lake's revival of the White Dog Ceremony among the Senecas—encouraged confidence in traditional ways.[22] Around the turn of the century, the great Shawnee prophet Tecumseh brought together a massive antiwhite nativist movement. For a time, his spiritual and political movement united Indians from the Great Lakes to the Gulf of Mexico. But in 1813 Tecumseh's movement was defeated. And after the War of 1812, in which the Oneidas were caught between settlers to the east and the Handsome Lake revivalists to the west, talk of "removing" the Indians of the region began in earnest.

In the early nineteenth century, as New Englanders overran the region, both Brothertown's residents and the Oncidas were faced with the prospect of moving west themselves. As early as 1807, land speculators proposed moving the Iroquois, and in 1814 there was talk among speculators and the president to relocate them to the Arkansas River. The construction of the Erie Canal through Oneida territory, beginning in 1817, both raised the value of the land and increased white immigration to the area. Towns and cities developed around them, and the governor of New York continued to press them to concede more land. The Oneidas were reluctant to abandon their homeland, but the push of settlers and government officials gave them little choice. By the 1830s most Oneidas had left the region and resettled near Green Bay, Wisconsin. Soon, the residents of Brothertown and Stockbridge were forced out, too.[23]

In the early nineteenth century, as Indians along the eastern seaboard seemed to be disappearing and attention turned to the fate of the Cherokees and other great nations across the Appalachians, observers on both sides of the frontier ironically celebrated the memory of the once powerful tribes the English had first encountered in North America. References to the Narragansetts, whose devastation in King Philip's War 150 years earlier had marked the decisive victory of the New England settlers, appeared in a surprisingly wide range of sources. They served as a kind of standard referent in varying interpretations of what had gone wrong. Early in the century, the Shawnee prophet Tecumseh used the example of Christian Indians in New England to rally support for his nativist vision of Indian unity against Anglo-Americans and all they stood for. In 1813, at the height of his power, just before his decisive defeat by General Andrew Jackson, he asked, "Where today are the Pequot? Where the Narragansett? the Mohican, the Pokanoket and many other once powerful tribes of our people? They have vanished before the avarice and oppression of the white man, as snow before a summer sun." President Andrew Jackson himself used a remarkably similar argument to make his case for the removal of the Cherokees in his first annual address to Congress in 1829. Where, he asked, are the Narragansetts? Gone, he answered, the inevitable victims of civilization.[24] His implication was that removing the Cherokees beyond the pale of settlement was the only means to protect them. In fact, many of the Narragansetts were still there in their enclave in Rhode Island—where in 1832 they were confronted by the first of several attempts by the state government to dissolve the tribe legally, to abolish their political existence. One of the principal arguments raised for abolishing the Narragansett tribe was that there were no Indians of "pure blood" left.

While Narragansetts may have been surprised to hear the U.S. president and state officials announce that they no longer existed, the people of Oneida and Brothertown were also being told that they were no longer really Indians. James Fenimore Cooper's *The Pioneers* (1823) narrates the English settlement of Oneida territory in the generation following the Revolution with hardly any mention of living Indians. The main character pauses at one point to survey the vast landscape he has made his own, with the sentimental thought that "not a Redskin is left." This presumed disappearance in the novel seems to stem inevitably from the race's intrinsic character—and not, as one might imagine, from a history of warfare, power politics, threats of violence, and forced removal. Here the novel, supposedly set around the time of the Revolution, recognizes the possible exception of the Indians who were still there at that time: "unless it may be a drunken vagabond from the Oneida's or them Yankee Indians, who, they say, be moving up from the sea-shore; and who belong to none of God's creatures, to my seeming; being, as it were, neither fish nor flesh; neither white man nor savage."[25]

||| African Union |||

Around the time many Americans were celebrating their nation's independence in July 1787—and while delegates to the Constitutional Convention deliberated in Philadelphia—members of the newly formed Free African Union Society of Newport exhorted their brethren in Boston to join them in a public day of humiliation. Like days of thanksgiving, called in honor of God's mercies, days of humiliation were an old Puritan tradition, called in response to God's judgments. These occasions were marked by fasting and pious calls for reform. The members of the Boston African society agreed that the "calamitous state" of northern free blacks represented afflictions "which are like to continue on us and on our children while we and they live in this Country." Dubious about their own place within the new United States, these men expressed a profound alliance with other Africans on both sides of the Atlantic: "The many Sufferings and Afflictions we suffer hear on Earth are justly brought upon us for the Sins of us and our Four Fathers." Two years later, when the Newport society members wrote to their brethren in Providence, they emphasized the "wretched state" of hundreds of thousands of "our brethren who are in abject slavery" in the southern United States and the West Indies. And they sympathized with the "unhappy state" of "the Nations in Africa, from whom we spring, being in heathenish darkness and sunk down in barbarity." Indeed, it was because these Africans had been "so foolish and wicked as to sell one . . . another into slavery," they opined, that "many millions have either lost their lives or been transported to a Land of Slavery." Instead of pointing to European racism or colonial exploitation as the root of their troubles, they emphasized their own spiritual power. "While we are feasting and dancing, many of our complexion are starving under cruel bondage," the Newporters exhorted their Boston brethren. Any such folly, vice, and superfluity, they warned, both discourages their true supporters and "enables our enemies to declare that we are not fit for freedom."[26]

The proceedings and correspondence of the Free African Union Society document the development of a self-conscious leadership in one urban black community in the early years of the Republic. During the 1780s and 1790s these fifty-odd men sought to embody the genteel republican virtues of morality, industry, respectability—and independence. In the short run, these men did not expect equality or even relief from pressing economic afflictions, but they wanted to believe in the possibility of an egalitarian and racially integrated America. As northern blacks became increasingly independent and prosperous in the early years of the nineteenth century, many continued to entertain the possibility of moving back to Africa. This fantasy suggests their alienation from the United States, their continuing economic suffering, their resentment of white discrimination, and their sense of broad alliance with other African peoples. But by and large, they were determined to make their way in America. As the meanings of citizenship changed in the early years of the Republic, black insistence on independence and institutional autonomy grew. After the turn of the century, the emergence of separate black churches represented both the culmination of a strategy of reform and autonomy and a shift toward a more combative style of political self-assertion.

A few free blacks more directly protested their exclusion from full citizenship, often in language strikingly close to the rhetoric of the Revolution. In 1780, Paul Cuffe and other disfranchised black taxpayers in one Massachusetts town asked that Negroes be exempted from taxes because they had "no voice or influence in the election of those who tax us." These men emphasized the economic challenges they faced, having been deprived by long bondage of the "Advantage of Inheriting Estates from our Parents." And they called attention to continued discrimination. "We Poor Distressed miserable Black people . . . have not an Equal Chance with the white people Neither By Sea nor By Land." The town and state governments rebuffed this and subsequent petitions he presented, and at one point his refusal to pay taxes without representation landed him in jail.[27] Meanwhile, in Providence, one of the few men of color with enough property to be taxed was Anthony Kinnicutt, who owned a victualing business on the wharf, supplying food and liquor to ships in the busy port. In 1778, he petitioned the town, saying that "although not wholly of white blood," he had been born free, had lived in the town for some forty years, owned a house, and had gained the respect of some of the town's "Principal Men." He asked the town "to make an explicit and clear Declaration whether they will wholly forbear to tax him, or grant him the Privilege of being a Freeman of the Town like another man." The town refused even to formally receive the petition. A month later, he removed the "taxation-without-representation" language and instead simply asked for an abatement of taxes on grounds of economic hardship, and the request was honored: he and his son were dropped from the town rolls. In 1800, the town resolved the contradiction by removing all property holders of color from the tax rolls—apparently a move intended to avoid allowing them to attend the new public schools.[28] In this climate, few free blacks felt that there was anything to gain by such direct challenges to discriminatory policies.

Many free blacks were so discouraged with their prospects in northern towns that they considered moving out of the United States and "back" to Africa. In Newport one of the first acquisitions of the Free African Union Society was a copy of Henry Smeathman's book proposing a free black colony in Sierra Leone. Early in 1787 William Thornton, a West Indian proponent of the colony, visited the society. The Sierra Leone venture had been designed to provide a refuge for free blacks then living in London and Nova Scotia, where most black American Loyalists had been stationed after the war, and also to establish a model of a Christian, agricultural society that would help civilize West Africa. Within the United States and Great Britain, Thornton argued, there could be "no sincere union between the whites and the Negroes." Sierra Leone, in contrast, would be a prosperous settlement based on "freedom, self-government, schools and churches, and free trade." By the time Thornton left Newport, he could claim support from as many as seventy local blacks. Some of these Newporters wrote to their Providence compatriots that they supported the idea of a return to "their own country." Meanwhile, seventy-three black Bostonians, led by Prince Hall, petitioned their state government to support their move to Sierra Leone, despite their suspicions about the venture's white leaders. As they confided to the Newport society, "We do not approve of Mr. Thornton's going to settle a place for us; we think it would be better if we could charter a Vessel, and send some of our own Blacks." The Providence society made a similar proposal in 1794. Even as late as 1800, when reports of the calamitous state of the Sierra Leone colony were reaching American black leaders, a large number of black Philadelphians—including Absalom Jones, Wilson Gray, and Richard Allen, prominent as the organizers of that city's first independent black church—petitioned their state government for assistance in establishing an "asylum" like that of Sierra Leone "so that such of us that are favoured with Liberty may have it in our power to become more Usefull to the Community at Large who are now at a loss for a lifelyhood for ourselves & familys."[29]

Like Brothertown, the Sierra Leone colony was imaged both as an asylum for impoverished free blacks and as a missionary endeavor. At least since 1714, the idea of moving former slaves back to their "own Country" had been linked to the notion that they could also serve to Christianize and civilize West Africans. One enslaved New Englander who embraced the idea was John Quamine. A native of the Gold Coast of Africa, Quamine was sent by his father around 1760 to get a Christian education in Rhode Island, where he was instead sold into slavery. After experiencing a powerful conversion in the congregation of the Reverend Samuel Hopkins, Quamine developed an urgent wish that "his Relations and Countrymen in Africa might also come to the knowledge of and taste the same blessed Things." Then he won a lottery that allowed him to buy his freedom. He went on to pursue advanced studies at the college at Princeton to prepare him for his missionary role. For his part, Hopkins published tracts linking antislavery to an African mission and influenced the conception of the Sierra Leone scheme. In the 1780s, writing to the London antislavery activist Granville Sharpe, who headed the Sierra Leone colony, Hopkins argued that New England free blacks were doomed to remain "unhappy, while they live here among the whites."[30]

The removal of free blacks to Africa, or elsewhere, was also envisioned as a solution to the "problem" of black freedom in a white country. As Thomas Jefferson saw it, one of the main obstacles to abolishing slavery at that time was the (presumed) necessity of ridding the country of a free black population. In part this is what Prince Hollbrook had in mind in 1774 when he petitioned the Massachusetts legislature to free him and other slaves and promised that with some financial help they could all remove back to Africa. In 1793, Hopkins published a tract arguing that if colonization could "gradually draw off all the blacks in New England, and even in the Middle and Southern States," America might finally be able to rid itself of the great "calamity, and inconsistency," of slavery.[31] In this context, the interest of African Americans in the Sierra Leone colony can been seen in part as a challenge to white racists. They challenged state governments disinclined to treat them as equal citizens to put up the money necessary to be entirely rid of them. And they challenged whites who claimed that blacks could never be good American citizens to admit that they had the capacity to carve out an industrious society in the benighted African countryside and serve as models of civilization and Christian virtue.

In the end, no more than a handful of northern blacks actually moved to Sierra Leone in these years. It was one thing to embrace the idea in the abstract, quite another to contemplate actually making the move. Many simply did not want to go. When Samson Occom suggested that Phillis Wheatley return to Africa as the wife of a black missionary in 1774, she voiced support for the idea of bringing Africa from "darkness into light." But she firmly declared that she had neither the skills nor the inclination to move to that strange and threatening part of the globe. Indeed, as Noah Webster pointedly observed in 1793, the back-to-Africa scheme would have been far too expensive to put into effect. And, as Philadelphia black leaders had pointed out, the scheme had offensive implications: the goal of converting Africans could be pursued by white benefactors as well as blacks, and the notion that blacks could not remain in the United States was based on the assumption that the privilege of citizenship pertained only to whites. Although not opposing the idea of removal, they insisted that "every pious man is a good citizen of the whole world."[32] The movement is nonetheless important as a symbol of the ambivalent civic status of black northerners as they were becoming free in the decades after the Revolution. Like Brothertown, the fantasy of moving back to Africa was a complex response to the racism of the new American Republic and African Americans' cultural affinity for Christianity and republican ideals.

The strategy more actively pursued by northern African societies in the late eighteenth century was more ambitious and riskier: they sought to demonstrate that despite all disadvantages they could reform their communities and prove that Africans in America could indeed embody the rather utopian virtues associated with republican citizenship. In November 1796 the Newport society read with approval a letter "To the free Africans and other free people of colour of the United States" from the convention of Abolition Societies in the United States at Philadelphia. These gentlemen advised free blacks to act in a manner worthy of their status as free men: "It is by your good conduct alone that you can refute the objection which have been made against you as rational and moral creatures."[33] In later years, the Free African Union Society would lead to the creation of a variety of benevolent, humane, and educational institutions, but during the 1790s, it focused much of its attention on financing and organizing funerals.

In organizing what functioned largely as a burial society, the Newporters reflected both their African roots and their American aspirations. Large, collective public funerals were an important part of West African cultural and social life, and burial societies and elaborate processions developed in black communities throughout the Americas. At the same time, funerals in New England remained an important, although increasingly controversial, civic ritual. The Free African Union Society, which included professional funeral director Mintus Brenton, focused on the decorum and respectability of the public procession of mourners to the graveyard. At this time, most poor people had to rely on the minimal trappings of a pauper's burial, which nonetheless cost town governments the equivalent of a week's wages: a pine coffin, a winding sheet and shirt, grave digging, and occasionally the rental of a horse and carriage or candles for the immediate family. On such occasions, servants in genteel households often borrowed items, ranging from clothing to carriages, from their employers. In order to avoid both poor trappings and servile dependence, the members of Newport's African society agreed to buy their own set of regalia and to pay for a horse and carriage in inclement weather. They also used their dues to help bereaved families with other expenses. In 1793 the society appropriated money for Mrs. Newport Wanton "to purchase Tea, sugar and rum for the use at a funeral of her husband."[34]

During the colonial period, public funerals had offered enslaved New Englanders one of their only legitimate opportunities to gather together in large numbers. The funeral of Samuel Sewall's servant Boston in the 1729s was described in a local newspaper: "A Long Train follow'd him to the Grave, it's said about 150 Blacks, and about 50 Whites, several Magistrates, Ministers, Gentlemen, &c." Such large gatherings, which could include most of the town's black population, worried town officials. Boston selectmen ordered the number of bells that could be tolled for Negro funerals limited to one—largely to reduce attendance and prevent "Disorders." Similarly, when the Rhode Island legislature moved in 1723 to restrict Narragansett funerals, calling them "Indian dances," the grounds were nuisance—distracting servants from their work, encouraging drinking, occasioning runaways. The continuing appeal of such ceremonies forced the city's selectmen in 1735 to remind the sextons to enforce "the by-law of the town, for preventing and Reforming Disorders at the funerals of Negroes &c."[35]

These early black funerals included hints of West African cultural legacies. For instance, in 1721, Boston's selectmen ordered Negro funeral processions to "stope wending their way all over town and take the most direct route to the grave." This custom evokes accounts of West African funeral corteges that would zig and zag through a village. Such practices also took root in the West Indies. "The Negroes in general are very tenaciously addicted to the Rites, Ceremonies, and Superstitions of their own Countries," reported a disapproving Anglican parson. "There are but few Negroes who believe that they die a natural Death, but rather that they are fascinated, or bewitched. The Bearers, in carrying the Corpse of such a one to the Grave, when they come opposite to, or in Sight of the House of the Person who is supposed to have bewitched the Deceased, pretend to stagger, and say, that the Corpse is unwilling, and will not permit them to carry it to the Grave, until it is suffered to stop near, or opposite to, that House." He also described the mourners along the way to the grave: "Most young People sing and dance, and made a loud Noise with Rattles." In the excavated New York African Burial Ground, identifiably African elements are apparent in bodily modifications and in ornaments immigrants probably brought with them from their homeland: there are individuals buried with carefully filed teeth, with shells by their ears, and one with a long string of beads around her waist. At the same time, the arrangement of the bodies facing east reflected Christian influence, and wooden coffins, ornamented with hobnails, were typically English.[36]

Unfortunately for those who enjoyed them, the old Puritan style of public funeral display came under attack in the mid-eighteenth century—and in this broader cultural conflict, blacks became special targets. Early in the century observers noted resistance to the lavish consumption that often surrounded funerals. In 1721 Judge Sewall noted the first public funeral "without scarves"—one of several items traditionally distributed to mourners by the bereaved family. Twenty years later, the Massachusetts legislature officially restricted spending for funerals, ordering that "no Scarves, Gloves (except six pair to the bearers and one pair to each minister of the church where any deceased person belongs), Wine, Rum, or rings be allowed to be given at any funeral." Extravagant public displays came to seem at odds with the cult of sensibility, concern about temperance, and republican ideals of economic moderation. As settlers during the imperial crisis of the 1760s began boycotting British goods and celebrating domestic manufactures and homespun cloth, the old style of public funeral display suddenly began to seem not only old-fashioned but unpatriotic. In 1767, the *Newport Mercury* reported that a small, private funeral with modest clothing and gifts was "the most natural indication of sorrow" and that a public procession was a display of "pride and vanity." The essay ended with the acid observation: "Black at funerals is now only worn by the fashionable gentry of the Ethiopian Tribe." After the Revolution, this kind of attack on black funerals became common. The Reverend William Bentley of Salem, who preferred elaborate, formal processions, observed with a mixture of pleasure and condescension that the attendants at the funeral of a young black child were "dressed from common life up to the highest fashions . . . so that they completely aped the manners of the whites." The popular press perpetuated this stereotype. In 1794, the *Newport Mercury* published one of a series of amusing anecdotes about black funerals: four black pallbearers are halfway to the graveyard when they notice that they have not been given the customary gloves. Cuffe whispers to the bearer behind him, "Cesar, you got e grov?" "No," says he, "ask Cato." "Cato, you got e gruv?" "No, ask Toney" "Toney, you got e grov?" "No!" Feeling cheated, Cuffe suggests putting the parsimonious man's corpse down in the street: "Let he *go heself!*" The vanity and vulgarity of black funerals, it was implied, represented their unfitness for either respect or the rights of citizenship.[37]

Thus, when the African society of Newport attempted to ensure that its funeral processions were beyond reproach, it was, in a way, making a claim to citizenship. At a special meeting of the society in January 1790, the committee established a formal regulation for "funeral solemnities" in order to avoid ridicule. The committee self-consciously urged members to dress themselves decently "so they may be useful to all" and so that "Spectators may not have it in their Power to cast such Game contempt, as in times past." In the decades to come, the Newport society shifted its focus away from funerals to a variety of benevolent activities. In the early nineteenth century, it established a school for its own boys and girls, as well as a Benevolent Society and a Humane Society, both with women's auxiliaries. The society members' emphasis on self-help and moral reformation was always in part a strategy for overcoming white racism by proving themselves worthy of respect and civil rights. The efforts of the African societies in Newport and other northern towns did succeed to some extent. Observing a black funeral in 1809, the snobbish Reverend William Bentley was frankly impressed by the long, decorous procession: "80 Blacks capable of dressing themselves in good fashion & of conducting with great solemnity, without the ignorant state & the awkward manner of a new situation, is favourable to the hopes of civil society."[38]

Like the members of the Newport African society, the founders of other separate black organizations in the early years of the Republic were remarkably conservative. Consider the establishment of New England's first black church, which is documented by an extraordinary series of personal letters written by one of its founders, Peggy Harrison. Peggy had grown up in Providence as the slave of Moses Brown. She attended the Providence Baptist church along with her master and his family and remained a member of the congregation even after he became a Quaker in 1774 and freed her. At that time, he asked her to refer to him as her "Friend," not as her master. But when she moved to Boston in the 1780s and began writing to him regularly, she always began her letters "Dear Master." She emphasized her deep Christian faith in these letters and made it clear that she was attending services at the Reverend Samuel Stillman's Baptist church in Boston. Like members of Newport's African society, Peggy Harrison found solace in a remarkably humble faith, not about overcoming hardship but about learning to accept it: "i find its good to be afflicted when it comes from my lord and master and to him i look." Over the years, she took heart in the fact that she was not alone, that there were more general signs of the "work of God amongst us Colered People" in Boston. Around the turn of the century, she reported a revival of religion among the black members of Stillman's congregation: "Ther appears a great and general attention to [religion] prevailing amongst us many turning from their evil ways to serve to Lord." In this season of spiritual and communal rebirth Peggy Brown took a tentative first step toward reframing her relationship to her former master. She began one letter by writing "Dear Friend," then crossed it out and wrote instead the familiar "Dear Master."[39]

The leader of this revival was the black exhorter Thomas Paul, who had grown up in rural New Hampshire and had been admitted to a radical Baptist church in the small town of Weare in 1789. Around 1801, he began to develop a role as a lay exhorter and soon thereafter moved to Boston. There, he began to lead special prayer meetings for black members of Dr. Stillman's congregation. Indeed, the church rolls confirm that Peggy Harrison was one of a cluster of blacks admitted in 1804 into full membership in Dr. Stillman's church. One result of racial segregation within New England churches was the development of self-conscious networks among "colored" members. Such clusters are also apparent in other church rolls: in Providence, a number of Moses Brown's former servants including Peggy Harrison were among a large cluster of blacks admitted to the Baptist church in 1774. By 1811, Providence's First Baptist Church still had about twenty black members, at least some of whom felt a special tie to one another. Before Mrs. Patience

Borden died, she arranged to bequeath her savings of $230 as a fund for the relief of the "Poor of Colour of that Church." Her gravestone honors her as a "a free woman of Colour and humble disciple of Jesus."[40] But unlike Patience Borden, Thomas Paul was not inclined to endure forever the humiliation of a subordinate status within a church that pointedly discriminated against black members.

"When Thomas Paul came to Boston the Dr. told him it was *Boston,* and they did not mix colours," reported a radical tract in 1804—one of the first open critics of the prevailing system of racial ranking within New England churches. By the turn of the eighteenth century, blacks were increasingly barred from preaching to white audiences. During the Revolutionary period, Samson Occom and Lemuel Haynes had both developed careers preaching to predominantly white audiences; Haynes had served for several decades as pastor of a congregation in rural Vermont (fig. 18). Yet in 1808 he was rejected by his congregation, apparently on the grounds that its members no longer wanted a "colored" preacher. Paul himself ran into trouble when he sought permission to preach to predominantly white or mixed audiences. In Salem, one Baptist elder gambled by permitting "the Negro Minister Paul" to preach in his church and was relieved to find that "one family only disclosed displeasure." Meanwhile, "the wags of the town put a paper of doggrel rhyms in print & distributed them through the town." Preparing to leave town, Paul was barred from riding inside the stage and instead was offered a seat on top of the carriage with the driver, which he angrily refused. Other Baptist pastors were not willing to run the risk of inviting him into their pulpits. As one remarked, "There are some of my congregation who would leave the meeting if Paul should preach here . . . and as long as there are other white men to preach, I do not think it best for him to preach here." During the spring of 1805, Paul sought ordination. Rebuffed in Boston, he returned to his home church in New Hampshire, which did ordain him. Even there, the move was apparently controversial, for soon thereafter another black man was refused ordination—sparking his complaint that he had been blackballed "on account of His Color." Returning to Boston, Paul sought permission to preach in Reverend Stillman's meetinghouse—and was formally prohibited.[41]

Insulted, Paul and his black followers announced that they would withdraw from Stillman's congregation and form their own church. Indeed, there are some signs that Paul may have deliberately staged this confrontation. Some months earlier, in late 1804, Peggy Harrison, writing to Moses Brown, had asked him for a "little money": "There is now a probability of having preaching among us if there can be a little preparation made for it." A group of blacks did begin engaging

FIGURE 18. "The Reverend Lemuel Haynes in the Pulpit." Haynes grew up in the house-hold of a Connecticut minister and followed that profession. This image of him preach-ing to a white audience evokes a time in the late eighteenth century during which slavery was still being abolished and color lines across New England were not as rigid as they subsequently became. Detail of papier-mâché tray, 26 × 21″, ca. 1800. Anonymous, proba-bly English. Courtesy of the Museum of Art, Rhode Island School of Design, gift of Miss Lucy T. Aldrich.

preachers to lead meetings in a rented room. Soon they were raising money for a church for the "Black People."[42] As in so many of the black congregations founded around this time in northern states, black members of white-dominated religious societies created their own structures after running up against increasingly intran-sigent lines of color.

Dr. Stillman approved of the move. "I hope and pray," he wrote to Moses

Brown, "that Ethiopia may stretch forth her hand to the Lord." Even many benevolent Anglo-Americans who supported black preachers thought they should concentrate on the uplift of their own race. As one abolitionist wrote in support of Boston's fledgling black church: "It seems that there is a Black Man who preaches to them & who has a Good Character . . . it is of very great importance to have the Blacks instructed in Religious Duty & everything tending to improve their morals, & to make them *Industrious, honest, & prudent.*" Such thinking was consistent with less well intended concerns about racial purity. Indeed, members of Stillman's church allowed Peggy Harrison and her black brethren and sisters to withdraw to form their own church but worried that they might admit "white members" and "defeat the intention of their being an *African church.*"[43] It seems as though the real danger was racial equality.

The withdrawal into separate churches sought to achieve dignity for black people and also accepted the parameters of white supremacist thinking. Frederick Douglass later denounced separate African American churches as "negro pews, on a higher and larger scale." Indeed, it is striking how careful members of the new African church were to emphasize their deference. When the new meetinghouse was formally opened in December 1806, all those "benevolently disposed to the Africans" were invited to the dedication ceremonies. Even at the inauguration of their own church, Boston's black Baptists chose to defer to white supremacist sensibilities. Guests were assured in their invitations that the floor of the meetinghouse would be "reserved for the accommodation of the company who wish to attend." The "Africans and people of color" would sit up in the galleries.[44]

Despite its deferential style, the new African church quickly came to symbolize a new, more combative style of black self-assertion, which was met with increasingly harsh white-supremacist attacks. Soon, the African church had developed an important role in the civic life of Boston's burgeoning black community, which was taking the form of a geographically defined enclave. Within a decade, the church had more than seventy members—double or triple the number of black Baptists in Boston before the church was formed. The three-story brick structure included a schoolroom for the black children. And after 1807, the church became the focal point of an annual parade—organized by the city's African society—commemorating the abolition of the international slave trade. This procession was intended to counter the exclusion of blacks from the city's Independence Day celebrations. The bitter mockery with which white supremacists regaled the parade attested to the power of this African American assertion of civil respectability.[45]

Like the colonization movement, the establishment of black institutions admitted a kind of defeat, but such institutional independence also held the potential for changes in black public self-assertion and private senses of self. Soon after the construction of Boston's African church, Peggy Harrison finally changed the way she addressed her old master. After forty years as a free woman, she finally began to address her letters "Dear Friend."[46]

||| Distinctions |||

First performed in early 1787, Royall Tyler's *The Contrast* became the first successful American play and was acclaimed for its patriotic themes, which revolve around the republican ideal of virtuous citizenship.[47] All the characters are white, but Indians and blacks are not entirely absent: excluded from this imaginary community in the flesh, they are invoked as images to define the virtues and follies of white citizens. Early in the play the genteel heroine sits in her boudoir singing the melancholy "Death Song of Alknomook," but the role of the scene within the play has little to do with Indians, dying or otherwise: it serves to illustrate the heroine's refined sensibilities. Several scenes later, a reference to blacks serves to highlight one of the play's central contrasts. One of the play's main characters is Jonathan, depicted as a rather foolish country bumpkin who works for the play's hero, Colonel Manly. Traveling to New York City, Jonathan is greeted by a local valet: "I understand that Colonel Manly has the honour of having you for a servant." To Jonathan, this is a serious insult. "Servant!" he stammers. "Sir, do you take me for a neger,—I am Colonel Manly's waiter." Amused, the valet then sets out to demonstrate that this is "a true Yankee distinction, egad, without a difference." Jonathan is forced to admit that he performs all the offices of a servant—including "blacking" his boots—and that Colonel Manly is richer. "I am a true blue son of liberty, for all that," he insists, "no man shall master me." Back home in New England, he explains, "We don't make any great matter of distinction . . . between quality and other folks."[48]

In this scene, Jonathan acts out one of the classic stories in the history of white supremacy in America. His problem in *The Contrast* is that he held the job of servant but wanted to think of himself as equal to his employer. Contrasts between blacks and whites, servants and waiters, helped him to express his dignity and independence, even to imagine that society was more egalitarian that it really was. Elements of this story are most familiar from the open class struggles that emerged in the mid-nineteenth century, but the context of *The Contrast* is significantly different. In the early decades of the Republic, modern notions of democratic citizenship—even the idea of social equality among white men—had not yet taken hold.[49]

The play's author, for one, does not seem to have intended Jonathan's extravagant claims about equality to be taken very seriously. Tyler and many other Federalist gentlemen were inclined to think of themselves as superior in education and virtue to most poor and ignorant members of the public—white as well as black—and therefore deserving of superior wealth, moral authority, and political leadership. *The Contrast,* like Hugh Henry Brackenridge's novel *Modern Chivalry* (1792–1815), was apparently intended to help protect the new Republic from twin evils: on the one hand, false, European pretensions; on the other, abuses of the principle of natural equality. The play promulgates an idealized republican vision of virtuous leadership by meritorious gentlemen. The plain nobility of Colonel Manly and the honest foolishness of Jonathan mirror their social ranks. In this context, Jonathan's racial snobbery serves as an example of his naiveté, lack of awareness, and irrationality: black or white, he is still a servant. For Federalists, the distinction between blacks and whites was less important than the grades of social hierarchy that ordered the body politic. However, not everyone was convinced. As far as the play's readers, performers, and audiences were concerned, the play's hero did not emerge as Colonel Manly, who was perhaps too staid, humble, and self-righteous to be very engaging. Instead, Jonathan stole the show. This reversal of sympathies suggests resistance to the author's Federalist idealization of deference and republican virtue. In this sense, the audience's embrace of Jonathan can been seen as part of a wide-ranging struggle that eventually led to the triumph of a more democratic, less idealistic political culture.

What role, then, did racial identities play in this struggle over the meanings of American citizenship in the early years of the Republic? In the decades after the Revolution, many Americans looked to the status of free blacks in the northern states for signs of the nation's destiny. Many observers focused on two basic questions. Would free blacks prove themselves capable of virtuous republican citizenship? Would whites ever overcome their prejudices and allow the development of a nonracial society? Underlying these questions were political tensions between the nation's emerging free and slave sections and among segments of the northern populace. If free blacks could not succeed as citizens in the northern states, where their numbers were relatively small, then it would hardly be prudent to abolish slavery in the Chesapeake region or farther south, where the proportion of slaves was much higher. But, as *The Contrast* suggests, white racial prejudice was also connected to a broad struggle over the nature of social hierarchy and tensions between republican ideals and more democratic notions of citizenship. Even as the colonial legacy of white racial superiority continued into the early Republic, longstanding assumptions about a deferential social order were challenged and even overturned around the turn of the century. In many ways, traditional hierarchies were abandoned in the name of fraternal equality. Consequently, remaining lines of color became more conspicuous, anomalous, and contentious.

Concern about relations between newly emancipated blacks and whites particularly troubled St. George Tucker, a Virginia planter and law professor at the College of William and Mary, who labored in the 1790s to develop a plan that would allow for the abolition of slavery in his state. In 1795, he sent a list of questions about the process of emancipation in New England to Jeremy Belknap, president of the Massachusetts Historical Society. Belknap had the questions printed and solicited responses from John Adams, Prince Hall, and some twenty other local authorities. The extant replies provide extraordinary insight into how these prominent New Englanders thought about free blacks, racial equality, and white prejudice at a time when Virginia politicians, including Thomas Jefferson, generally assumed that slavery could be abolished only if a way could be found to get rid of the freed blacks. Consequently, five out of Tucker's eleven questions were about the status of free blacks—their political rights, their moral conduct, and their sexual and marital intermixture with whites. The men who answered his survey shared his anxiety about the place of Africans in the American body politic. "I heartily pitty the Southern States which still suffer the evil of slavery," offered one gentleman. "It will not be possible for them to get rid of it so easily as the Massachusetts did."[50]

The gentlemen answering Tucker's queries offered little encouragement about the state of emancipated blacks, whom they described as overrunning major seaports and demonstrating little of the decorum or industry that might make them worthy of citizenship. The condition of free blacks in Salem was "pretty miserable," reported Dr. E. A. Holyoke. "They have generally, as I am informed, left the country towns and resorted to the seaports, where, though they might all of them be constantly employed, and most of them are, yet many are not industrious, and frugality many of them seem to be utterly unacquainted with; and, having been educated in families where they had contracted habits of a more luxurious mode of living than they can now support in their present situation, they are much more uncomfortable (as they confess) than in their former state of slavery."[51]

Indeed, by the 1790s, town officials and local citizens were increasingly alarmed by the threat of black immigrants. In the years after the Revolution many towns sought to purge themselves categorically of all nonresident free people of color. In 1800, Boston overseers of the poor, prompted, perhaps, by Gabriel Prosser's bloody slave revolt in Virginia and the ongoing revolution in Haiti, printed a list of some 240 blacks, mulattos, and Indians whom they ordered expelled from town. Many of these individuals seem to have been doing their best to become respectable citizens: about quarter of those named belonged to the recently formed African Benevolent Society, a group dedicated to civic virtue and respectability; and one of them was Peggy Harrison, whose letters to her master chronicle the formation of Boston's African church. Meanwhile, in her hometown of Providence, the overseers of the poor began in the 1790s to keep separate lists of white and black transients. Local citizens complained repeatedly about immoral blacks overrunning the town. In 1806 a massive petition drive, joined by more than two hundred men, complained, "This town is now infested with swarms of idle, thievish and vagabond blacks."[52]

Whether or not blacks were entirely to blame for their plight, the respondents to Tucker's petition could easily agree that local whites were profoundly prejudiced against them. "The coloured people here demean themselves as orderly as might be expected, and are civilly treated by the whites, who employ them and pay them wages for their services; but there is a discrimination between the whites and blacks," reported Thomas Pemberton of Boston, who was more sympathetic than most. "The former are tenacious of their superiority, and it is rare for them to associate and mix together in company: whenever this happens, the whites are of the lower class of citizens." The racial pride of whites was evident everywhere—from the city's Masonic Lodges to its brothels. Dr. John Eliot emphasized the hypocrisy of Boston's all-white Masonic Lodge: "The truth is, they are ashamed of being *on an equality with blacks*." As for interracial sex and marriage, some of Belknap's informants did note that there were some sexual liaisons but emphasized that they were rare, illegal, and controversial. There was "much harmony between blacks and whites," Eliot reported, because they generally "do not associate"—except in houses of ill fame, where "some very *depraved white* females get among the blacks." Such intermingling, he hastened to observe, resulted in "contentions" including "the pulling down such houses at times, and caused several actions at Justices' Courts these two years past." Dr. Holyoke of Salem added that interracial liaisons were confined to the "the lowest of the people"—meaning white people—and even "they generally consider it an act of condescension."[53]

Like many abolitionists at the time, the respondents to Tucker's survey all agreed that that white prejudice was pervasive and vehement, but they were inclined to dismiss it as inevitable and ignore its broader implications. It is probably no accident that one of the earliest observers to call attention to the damaging effects of white prejudice on northern free blacks was an outsider, the visiting Frenchman Jean-Pierre Brissot de Warville. As he traveled across the Northeast in 1788, Brissot was struck by the practical and emotional effects of white prejudice on free blacks. The Negroes of the northern states, he reported, "are certainly happy," but he continued, "Let us have the courage to admit that their happiness and their abilities have not reached the levels they are capable of attaining." The barrier was not black ability or enterprise but white prejudice. Black shopkeepers and farmers often managed their affairs well but could never hope to expand their enterprises. This was because "the whites, who have the money, are not willing to lend a Negro the capital necessary." Brissot explained further, "To succeed in a larger enterprise, a certain amount of preliminary experience is necessary and one must have had training in a countinghouse; but the forces of reason have not yet opened to Negroes the doors of countinghouses, in which they are not allowed to sit down alongside a white man." Blame, he argued, should be placed where it was due. "If then, Negroes are limited to the small retail trade, let us not attribute it to their lack of ability but rather to the prejudices of the whites, who put obstacles in their way." This message hardly seemed likely to find a sympathetic audience in the early years of the Republic, and when the first American edition of the *Travels* appeared in New York in 1792, its editor excised Brissot's most forceful indictments of white prejudice.[54]

Even Brissot did not explore the effects of racism on white people and their political culture. Tucker's respondents and many other genteel observers were often inclined to associate racial prejudice with the lower sort of white people, even though their own attitudes were rarely egalitarian. And the nature of white racism was clearly changing in the aftermath of slavery. By the turn of the century, racial segregation in the northern states was becoming, if anything, more rigid and systematic. In part, this rigidity resulted from the loss of the "coverture" provided by slavery. As in the post–Civil War South, white supremacy became more urgent after blacks became free. For instance, skilled occupations that had seemed unthreatening to whites when performed by slaves were closed to free blacks. At the same time, this new emphasis on white superiority was related to new egalitarian ideologies among whites. Even in New England bastions of Federalism, old assumptions about social hierarchy and deferential habits were fiercely contested around the turn of the eighteenth century.

One sign of change in the social order was a broad shift in the use of public space during major civic rituals. In the colonial period, public events—such as militia training days and general elections—were attended by men, women, and children of all ranks. Despite frequent complaints about rowdy "boys and Negroes," formal ceremonies were often accompanied by raucous popular festivities, which often involved sporting, feasting, and drinking. An anonymous poem describing Election Day in Boston in 1762 suggests something of the character of these events. The governor's guard, its members resplendent in their scarlet uniforms, escorted the governor and other leading dignitaries to the Old Brick Meetinghouse for the election prayer and then hurried them to Fanueil Hall to dine and drink. Meanwhile, a varied throng of townspeople filled the streets for a day of "frolicking and mirth."

> The city swarms with every sort,
> Of black and white, and every sort
> Of high, low, rich and poor;
> Squaws, negroes, deputies in scores. . . .
> Before the sun rises,
> The blacks their forces summon.
> Tables & benches, chairs, & stools
> Rum-bottles, Gingerbread & bowls
> Are lug'd into the common.
> Thither resorts a motley crew,
> Of Whites & Blacks & Indians too
> And Truss of every sort.
> There all day long they sit & drink,
> Swear, sing, pay paupaw, dance and stink.

Across town, King George's health was "toasted round" by high and low alike. In many ways, this raucous social mixing was not threatening to elites because it occurred in a context in which the social hierarchies were explicitly marked and widely respected. At this time, everyday etiquette emphasized, at least ideally, a hierarchical code of deference.[55]

By the turn of the century the white public increasingly excluded black men and women from civic spaces during holidays. In Philadelphia, Independence Day celebrations had long been held in the square facing the old State House, where men and women of all social classes gathered for the festivities. But in 1803, the white citizens turned on the blacks present and drove them out of the square with a barrage of abuse. "It is a well known fact," James Forten complained in 1813, "that black people, upon certain days of public jubilee, dare not been seen after twelve o'clock in the day, upon the field to enjoy the times; for no sooner do the fumes of that potent devil, Liquor, mount into the brain, than the poor black is assailed like the destroying Hyena or the avaricious Wolf!" Gentlefolk also stopped attending these civic rituals, in part because of their distaste for such raucous revelries and in part because of a series of broad challenges to the political authority of the established elites. The Fourth of July became a mostly working-class white festival, a sign of a newly democratic political culture. This pattern was repeated in other northern cities: black Bostonians were forcibly expelled from the public common on the Fourth of July in 1805. As working-class whites asserted their claim to control of public ceremonies, both their social superiors and inferiors were removed from the scene; elites tacitly conceded their traditional precedence, and blacks were conspicuously excluded.[56]

In many northern towns, African Americans responded by celebrating their own holidays—and local whites countered with mockery and even violent assaults. For much of the eighteenth century, enslaved blacks in many northern communities had held separate Negro Election Days, which had always been treated with amusement and patronization by whites. During the early nineteenth century, the only time blacks were allowed in Boston Common was for the annual "Negro Elections," which continued until at least 1840. And these occasions regularly drew both complaints and scorn from white observers. Likewise, in the 1780s, when the black Masons in Boston began annual processions in honor of the feast of their patron, Saint John the Evangelist, locals responded with mockery. A newspaper soon published a facetious account referring to the "St. Black's" Lodge of Free and Accepted Masons. The next day, Prince Hall sent off a pointedly charitable response, noting, "With due submission to the public, our title is not St. Black's Lodge; neither do we aspire after high titles." He concluded, "Instead of a splendid entertainment, we had an agreeable one in brotherly love." But this did not deter subsequent lampoons of "St. Cuffe's Day."[57] News of the Haitian revolution and Prosser's Rebellion at the turn of the century may have helped inspire young black men in Philadelphia to organize their own Independence Day celebration in 1804. They formed military companies, elected officers, and, armed with clubs and swords, paraded through the streets, roughing up whites who crossed their path and attacking the house of a hostile white man—repeating the performance the next night, allegedly "daming the whites and saying they would shew them St. Domingo." Other African societies pointedly avoided the Fourth of July and organized their own, more sedate processions either on 5 July or on 14 August, the day chosen to honor the abolition of the international slave trade in 1808.[58]

In this new context, longstanding lines of color took on new meanings. The relationships between white assertions of racial preeminence and republican attacks on "feudal" hierarchies are perhaps most clear in the reorganization of seating within houses of worship. As the churchgoers of New England assembled for Sabbath worship each week, their arrangement in space represented their places in the body politic. The colonial Congregational meetinghouses—the town churches in most of rural New England—embodied an idealized model of communal hierarchy. Special committees determined the "seating" of individuals: men and women sat on opposite sides of the aisle; those distinguished by age, status, and wealth up front; those of middling and humble status toward the back; and those of lowest status in the most obscure places—children, blacks, and Indians on the stairs and in galleries. This system worked best in established town churches financed out of public coffers—such as the farming villages of Massachusetts and Connecticut.

Challenges to this orthodox vision of community were introduced by the revivals of the Great Awakening in the 1740s: "New Light" Congregationalists and evangelical Baptists attacked the standing order. They rebelled against the connection between social authority and spiritual power and blurred, even deliberately overturned, hierarchies pertaining to women and men, youths and elders, and Negroes, Indians and whites. Nonetheless, many evangelical religious societies became more conservative and respectable over time. Although the images of "silly women and foolish Negroes" continued to be staples of propaganda against evangelicals well into the nineteenth century, most Baptist and other evangelical churches soon fell into line with Anglican and Congregational practices as they became more established and respectable. When the Anglican church in Newport installed a new organ in 1772, it moved the "negroes" across the balcony; when a Baptist church in Providence remodeled in 1818, it dismantled the "upper or what was called the Negros Gallery."[59] In areas where Indians were few, they were treated as blacks; in areas with independent enclaves, it was taken for granted that Indians and the English would sit separately. By the time of the Revolution, virtually all New England churches seated blacks and Indians in separate, subordinate locations.

The Revolution, however, helped to discredit the entire system of seating in meetinghouses as aristocratic and unrepublican, and in the early years of the Republic it was quietly abandoned. The system that supplanted it represented a different logic of social order: in place of seats formally assigned by rank, churches began to sell pews and the right to sit in them. These pews were generally family-size areas, and those in better locations cost more. And in pews families sat together. The household was now the basic unit of social organization, with women, children, other relatives, and servants sitting in the pew owned by the head of the household—most often the father, as the legal representative of the family in ranks of citizens. This family model of citizenship also seemed democratic in a characteristically American sense: the explicit ordering principle became the "invisible hand" of the market, not the "dead hand" of a formal system of rank. When the formal ranking of seats in meetinghouses was contested in the name of equality and economy, it was generally replaced by the sale of pews to the highest bidders—which generally left the rich and prominent up front and center, where they had started out, the main difference being now that no one wanted to pay top dollar for the very first row of pews.[60] New Englanders, who during the colonial period lived in an economically egalitarian society but thought of the polity as hierarchical, found themselves in the early Republic in a society that was increasingly ranked economically but which they thought of as egalitarian.

Yet the new fraternal equality did not did not erase lines of color. Rather, it made longstanding racial hierarchies seem more stark and conspicuous. The segregation of blacks became more strict and uniform as various exceptions were eliminated by the demise of slavery. The seating of most black and Indian churchgoers hardly changed, and explicit racial segregation remained the norm. For instance, in the eighteenth century slaves might have sat in their master's pew, under a kind of coverture—not in their own right but as their master's servants. Such exceptions did not seem threatening, partly because they were just that—exceptional. Racial separatism was made more urgent in the early years of the Republic, not only by the abolition of slavery but by a broad change in the ideology of equality. Increasingly people of color were categorically barred from the first floors of many meetinghouses. It was most likely partially a response to attempts by black people to take advantage of this new economic equality. Dinah Roberts, for instance, a black woman employed by Massachusetts Historical Society president Jeremy Belknap, was allowed to pay $2.25 to rent part of a pew in Boston's Trinity Church in 1806. But in other cases, churches made their policy of racial segregation more explicit in the midst of routine church business. Amid decisions about repairing the belfry, whitewashing, gilding, and upholstering in velvet, the Episcopal church of Newport voted in 1818 "that in the future no colored people be allowed to sit down stairs." Such customs became written into legal documents; by the mid-nineteenth century pew deeds in New England commonly restricted their transfer to respectable white persons. White attitudes ranged from paternalistic to hostile—as suggested by the nasty new nickname for these segregated sacred spaces: "Nigger Heaven."[61]

During the early years of the Republic, independence and equality were becoming both increasingly urgent ideals and increasingly distant realities. In the northern colonies, society had validated a range of ranks through common rituals of deference, but economically it had been very egalitarian. By the mid-nineteenth century, northern society claimed to despise any hierarchy among white men, but the economy was steeply stratified, and classes were increasingly self-conscious and opposed. The ideal of democratic citizenship for all adult white men achieved legitimacy in the northern states only about fifty years after the Revolution.[62] The assertion of white pride through the insistence on superiority to all blacks gained urgency as ordinary whites sought to bridge the growing gap between the ideal of equality and the realities of inequality.

||| American Colonization |||

"What shall we do with the free people of color?" asked New Jersey clergyman Robert Finley at the first meeting of the Colonization Society of America in early 1817. As the society's founder, he had a clear, if not unfamiliar, answer in mind: remove them from the United States, preferably "back" to Africa. In a fanciful moment, he composed an imaginary dialogue set in heaven, in which the spirit of William Penn discusses the colonization scheme with two recently dead black leaders, Paul Cuffe and Absalom Jones, who were well known for their opposing views. Cuffe, a well-known Massachusetts merchant, had publicly supported the colonization scheme; he explains that the move would help free American slaves, save the nation from that great sin, and improve the lot of northern free blacks. Jones had led a dramatic Philadelphia protest against it; he argues that the scheme was insulting and injurious to free blacks, whose condition in America was actually getting better. Cuffe responds that the move was necessary because white prejudice could never be overcome: "If the Africans wish to elevate themselves to the rank and respectability of Americans and Europeans, let them establish upon the coast of Africa." Ultimately, of course, Cuffe wins the debate. Penn is convinced that the plan is benevolent, and Jones concedes that it is the best option for members of the "African nation."[63]

By 1818, when this dialogue was published, the racial politics of American nationalism had changed substantially. The Colonization Society itself reflected several important changes in political culture and regional interests. It attracted the support of many clergymen and Federalist politicians, two groups who seemed to be losing their traditional authority to new democratic impulses. The Federalists' clout had been disintegrating since their defeat in the national elections of 1800, and the doctrine of separation of church and state was finally forcing established town churches to give up their public funding and official status. The disorders of the common people who flouted longstanding hierarchies prompted the organization of new voluntary societies to promote moral reform, spread Christianity, and urge temperance. But free blacks seemed beyond hope. The experiment of black freedom had been tried, and it was a failure. Whether or not they had the capacity to become virtuous citizens, it was clear that the degrading effects of former enslavement and continuing white prejudice were too powerful to overcome. Removing free blacks would, as Reverend Finley put it, "rid our country of a useless and pernicious if not dangerous portion of its population." At the same time, the colonization movement gained support because the institution of slavery, which after the Revolution had been under attack in the northern states and also widely questioned in the Chesapeake region, was vigorously expanding into the emerging cotton belt. "Our country will be peopled," Patrick Henry observed. "The question is, shall it be with Europeans or with Africans?" Impractical and fantastic as their plan was, the organizers of the colonization movement hoped that if they could effect a gradual dissolution of slavery they might avoid the cataclysmic violence that they feared would otherwise be inevitable.[64]

The rapid expansion of slavery into the vast Louisiana Territory was possible because of decisive military conquests that inspired, in turn, new visions of a nation destined to span the continent. The British imperial policy of separating settlers from Indians was vigorously adopted by the new U.S. government under President Thomas Jefferson. After General Andrew Jackson's crushing defeat of Tecumseh's alliance during the War of 1812, the idea of removal also seemed to many national politicians the best solution to another major problem: what to do with Indians who occupied desirable territory. Already, many leading politicians were beginning to embrace the notion that the entire continent was destined to become part of the United States—and that America was providentially mandated to be a white man's country.

As Finley recognized, however, it was not entirely clear to northern free blacks—or to Indians, for that matter—that abandoning their American homelands was a good idea. Cuffe's own support of the move stemmed from a long history of disappointment and humiliation. Shortly after he joined the Society of Friends, Cuffe became interested in the prospect of sending free northern blacks to serve as Christian missionaries on the coast of West Africa. In 1815, he actually financed the settlement of thirty-eight Massachusetts blacks in Sierra Leone. His correspondent James Forten, a successful black entrepreneur in Philadelphia, reportedly concurred that African Americans "will never become a people until they come out from amongst the white people." He felt that "the more wealthy and the better informed they became, the more wretched they were made, for they felt their degradation more acutely." Cuffe was familiar with feelings of humiliation. His personal style was deferential to the point of diffidence: he made a point of declining to eat at the same table with whites, even guests in his own house. But the patronizing concern of white well-wishers could occasionally drive him to flashes of anger; he shocked one condescending visitor by declaring that "he would willing consent to be skinned if his black could be replaced by white."[65]

Increasingly, the deferential, even self-abnegating, political style of established black leaders began to seem out of touch with the feelings of many urban blacks. In January 1817, leading black Philadelphians James Forten, Richard Allen, and Russell Parrott called a meeting of the city's people of color to rally support for the Colonization Society—only to have their proposal resoundingly rejected. Some three thousand voices rose up to declare the plan an "outrage having no other object in view than the benefit of the slaveholding interests of the country." And they resolved never to abandon their enslaved compatriots—"our brethren by the ties of consanguinity, of suffering, and of wrong." As free black communities became more independent and as the new generations began to feel more entitled to freedom in the early nineteenth century, they also faced new restrictions on their rights, limits on their economic opportunities, and ugly assaults on their dignity. They responded by developing more confrontational political strategies. Echoing the rhetoric of the Revolution, opponents of the colonization move resolved, "Whereas our ancestors (not of choice) were the first successful cultivators of the wilds of America, we their descendants feel ourselves entitled to participate in the blessings of her luxuriant soil, which their blood and sweat manured; and that any measure . . . having a tendency to banish us from her bosom, would not only be cruel, but in direct violation of those principles which have been the boast of the republic."[66]

The conflict over the Colonization Society was produced by the convergence of longstanding struggles over race and nationhood. As democratic political cultures gained legitimacy and the battles over abolition in the North waned, white northerners became increasingly rigid about white preeminence. And the development of free communities of color with increasing institutional autonomy and long histories of activism prompted the more direct claims for equal rights and recognition as members of the American body politic. The stage was set for the battles over American nationalism that in the years to come would become increasingly open, antagonistic, and violent.

CHAPTER NINE

Hard Scrabble

||| Providence, 1824 |||

On the evening of 17 October 1824, a fight broke out in the streets of Providence. The conflict reportedly began when a number of black men walking around town refused to give up the "inside walk" to a group of whites coming the other direction.[1] The riot that ensued destroyed a neighborhood, sparked debates about urban vice and public order, and offers unique insight into the role of race in the emergence of American democracy.

In the days before pavement and closed sewers, the center of the road was often mucky, and the best place to walk was right up against the buildings. Even though older notions of etiquette were breaking down, walking the streets required knowing when to defer to others and when to demand deference. By the 1820s, many white men rebelled against the convention that they defer to men of higher rank or greater age; they emphasized instead their masculine equality and their common role as public protectors of women.[2] But even as they performed a new etiquette of democratic fraternity, white northerners continued to expect deference from blacks. So on that October evening when those unnamed black men decided to stand their ground, they threatened a widely shared sense of racial honor. The "insult" inflamed a large portion of the white townspeople of Providence: the next day handbills were posted calling for a rally at the Great Bridge near Market Square. That evening, white citizens decided to wreak their revenge on a notorious black neighborhood in the northeastern part of town.

As darkness fell, men streamed from all parts of Providence toward a section of low ground off North Main Street known as Hard Scrabble. Around seven, a pistol shot rang out as one member of the mob, Oliver Cummings, broke into the house of Henry T. Wheeler. But the rioter was barely wounded, and the local householders quickly abandoned any resistance. About forty or fifty men were soon at work demolishing Wheeler's house, tearing off the clapboards, chopping at the studs and posts with axes, and pulling down the weakened structure. As one observer noted, "It was pretty hard work to pull the houses down." Household furnishings were variously torn apart, smashed, or stolen. As many as a thousand spectators looked on. There was no moon that night, but the rioters had plenty of lamps. Finishing for the moment with Wheeler's home, they moved on to other houses. Around nine o'clock Cummings was seen brandishing a large club—out of fear, he was overhead to say, that the blacks would return to defend themselves against the rioters, who were "at work" on their houses. Rioters could be seen standing on the roof of Prince Condon's house, pushing the chimney off, and "halooing and telling them to cut away." One rioter, Nathaniel Metcalf, was seen working on house of Christopher Hall, "cutting one of the posts with an axe." He was accosted by a local white resident, Jesse Sweet, who shook his shoulder and demanded to know what he was doing. Metcalf ignored the interruption. He and the other rioters did not give up until after midnight, when they finally "took a vote" to adjourn.[3]

The next day one of the town's volunteer watchmen—who had stood passively by the night before—visited the scene of destruction: "It was a complete ruin, the houses demolished, the inhabitants without shelter and every thing in ruins." At least seven houses were completely pulled down, and several more were "badly shattered." That evening, the rioters reveled in their victory. Oliver Cummings spent the evening at a local cellar, drinking and bragging that he had been up to Hard Scrabble the previous night and "had worked like a good fellow." A drinking companion later testified: "He said he got shot there and showed me the place in his mouth, but I couldn't see nothing but a scratch like, and I thought if he had been shot in the mouth the wound would have been more injurious—that was what I thought."[4]

The Hard Scrabble riot was a brutal harbinger of a trend toward widespread antiblack violence in the antebellum North, a crucial turning point in race relations as the region's last slaves were becoming free. There were similar riots in the 1820s in cities from Boston to Cincinnati and hundreds of antiabolition and race riots in the 1830s across the North. These riots have been seen as marking the end of a period of potential racial egalitarianism during the early years of the Republic, when blacks were gradually becoming free from slavery and beginning to establish independent communities. To some this seems ironic, because the 1820s are also often understood to be the period in which America's distinctively "democratic" political culture first came into its own. The beginning of large-scale Irish immigration in the 1830s is often taken as the moment when struggles over identities and privileges in the Northeast first produced modern notions of whiteness. Yet the rising tide of violent conflict over lines of color resulted not from a simple intensification of racial dominance or hatred but from complex, long-term changes in the body politic.

To understand the role of "Jim Crow" in an emerging American democracy, we need to understand the place of race in broader shifts in political culture and social relations stretching back to the colonial period. The decades after the Revolution saw a broad transition from an economically homogeneous, orderly, and hierarchical society to a more economically stratified, fractious, yet democratic one. Even as the ideals of independence and equality became more widely embraced and compelling in the early decades of the Republic, they became increasingly difficult for most northerners to realize.[5] In many ways, free blacks in the North were used as foils by parties with conflicting interests in the emerging industrial society, with its increasing division of laboring and middle classes, growing economic stratification, and intensifying insistence on the overthrow of traditional social hierarchies. For both middle-class reformers suspicious of the laboring classes and working people asserting their own dignity, black men and women could help define the boundaries of respectability and disorder. At the same time, northern black communities became more prominent foci of hostility because they were becoming increasingly organized, impatient with enduring inequalities, and assertive in their political activism.

The Hard Scrabble riot provides an opportunity to explore the intersection of these themes. The political context of the riot is suggestive. The riot broke out less than a week after a Rhode Island constitutional referendum, the first effort to liberalize the state's practices of representation and franchise in more than 150 years, was voted down. The implications of this defeat can be better understood by examining the changing social geography of the rapidly expanding town. By 1830, fewer than half of the adult white men in Providence enjoyed the right to vote. Another sign of the further segmentation of northern society was Providence's black community, which was becoming more coherent, more clustered geographically, and more assertive politically.[6]

Trials that followed the riot illuminate the relationship between racial tensions and conflicts over the broader political culture. The legal arguments revolved around the character of the Hard Scrabble neighborhood and the right of white citizens to enforce public morality with violence if necessary. Town and state records reveal that for years local residents and the town fathers had been struggling in the face of rapid expansion to control problems stemming from immigration and the development of tenements, including intemperance, fighting, and prostitution. And all these urban dangers had become specifically associated with people of color. At the Hard Scrabble trial, the defense argued that the rioters had struck a blow for "the morals of the community." The prosecutor, in turn, argued that "recognition of a doctrine of this kind would tend to the subversion of all order in society."[7]

The trial was hardly over before the riot took on a new life in print culture. Early in 1825, a Boston printer produced a humorous broadside burlesque of the riot's victims. *Hard Scrabble, or Miss Philises Bobalition*—that is, "abolition"—was but one contribution to competing public discourses about the status of "colored" people as citizens. Elaborate broadsides written in stereotyped Negro dialects and often featuring satirical cartoons depicted pretentious black urbanites in ways that anticipated blackface minstrel productions of the decades to come. In the face of these attacks on their respectability and potential for citizenship, free blacks in the North launched into the world of print with a proliferation of publications in the 1820s. In bold new ways, northern blacks began to attack racial prejudice, claim equal rights, and question popular assumptions about the character of the American nation.

||| Democracy and Its Discontents |||

One of the basic paradoxes of early American nationalism was a tension between the desire to imagine the Republic as purely white and a constant fascination with racial divisions and hierarchies. One example of this ambivalence is the first town directories created for the rapidly expanding town of Providence. The first "complete Directory" of the town was compiled at the time of the riots in 1824: it presented a fan-

tasy of the town as composed exclusively of "white male inhabitants," "white females, heads of families," and major commercial and public establishments. The
compiler of names, occupations, and addresses, as he traveled through town, made a
few exceptions—an occasional black barber made it onto the list, though not denoted
as such—but the people of color in Hard Scrabble are absent from this conceptual
townscape. Some of them might have suspected that this was what members of the
American Colonization Society might have wanted—a republic pure in its whiteness. Eight years later, the 1832 edition of the directory changed policies and included a separate list of "colored people" at the end.[8] Like the fantasy of an all-
white citizenry, this explicit segregation offered the people of the North an elusive
vision: a racial division that was simple, complete, and clearly ranked. Yet by this
time, both fantasies of white purity and white supremacy were becoming more
difficult to take for granted. Despite the idealized logic of the directories and substantial geographic clustering, both black and white residents lived throughout the
town, often cheek by jowl. And as they moved through the town's public streets,
they were constantly faced with each other—sometimes literally bumping into each
other, as in the case of the sidewalk dispute that sparked the Hard Scrabble riot.

When those anonymous men refused to give up the "inside walk" on 17 October 1824, they stepped into a zone where the politics of manly honor ran up against
changing conceptions of the social order, the rights of citizenship, and urban space.
Within growing commercial centers such as Providence, the organization of space
changed to reflect new modes of transportation, new visions of independence, and
new labor relations. These social changes were connected to a broad shift in political sensibilities and economic realities that came to a conspicuous head in Rhode
Island's constitutional convention during the summer of 1824. The delegates—a
leader among them being the attorney general, Dutee J. Pearce, who prosecuted
the rioters the following fall—quickly agreed on a proposed constitution that focused on the question of "representation" among Rhode Island towns at a time
when the state was being transformed by dramatic economic and demographic
change. Meanwhile, at the time of the riot, the dramatic Electoral College struggle between Jackson, Adams, Clay, and Crawford dominated the political columns
of local newspapers. The proposed Rhode Island constitution of 1824 sparked a debate that, at least in Providence, focused on a battle between tradition and progress
and was frequently cast as a fight of brothers against patriarchs. Although this
broad transition in political culture did not invent white supremacy, it did change
the context and meaning of racial segregation. And closely related to all these trends

was the development of concentrated communities of color that supported new, independent institutions and inspired new challenges to longstanding lines of color.

Ever since the prominent merchant Moses Brown sponsored the first textile mill in the region a generation earlier, Providence had been at the heart of the industrial revolution. Since the turn of the century, the town had grown steadily. Much of this population growth came from internal migration within the state—away from the impoverished agricultural economy of the southern and western towns into the new manufacturing and urban economy of the northeastern area of the state. In 1800, the population of Providence remained under 10,000 and was largely concentrated on the east side of the river, the area settled first by Roger Williams and his followers in 1636. Only a few buildings and roads had been constructed across the bridge to the west side of the river. By the early 1820s, the town was growing explosively. The *Providence Directory* of 1826 published statistics from a town census taken in November 1825, showing that the population had risen by almost 5,000 since 1820—from about 11,000 to 15,941—a gain, in just five years, of more than 40 percent.[9] This massive shift of population created major political problems: although the southern and western regions in Rhode Island declined in population and economic importance, they continued to dominate state government because of outdated rules that regulated the apportionment of representatives among towns and qualifications for voting rights. For instance, Attorney General Dutee Pearce was able to win elections by capitalizing on his strong support in the economically marginal but politically dominant town of Newport, even though he enjoyed little support in the larger and more dynamic town of Providence.

The constitution proposed in 1824 was designed to mitigate the crisis of political representation among the state's towns without actually expanding the franchise. It increased the number of representatives from the dynamic northeastern towns, decreased the number of representatives from the declining southwestern towns, and made senators immune to local districting by having them elected at large across the state. As a writer to the *Rhode Island American* put it, the new constitution put "representation . . . upon a principle of more equality"—better balancing the interests of the "agricultural" areas with the "great increase and preponderance of the commercial and manufacturing towns." Providence newspapers attacked Newporters for their opposition to the new constitution, which would diminish their disproportionate power: "They are the PEOPLE who are implored not to yield this power to these upstart demagogues, the freemen of the north counties, who have dared to outstrip them in wealth and population!"[10]

Despite this unifying language of progress, the changes that industrialism brought were far from even—and nowhere were economic and social divisions more apparent, or increasing more rapidly, than within the town of Providence. Some of these changes can been seen in the shifting organization of residential and commercial space within the town. At the turn of the century, Providence—like most colonial seaports and European cities—was "vertically zoned." That is, members of varying social ranks lived close to one another, often in the same buildings. Servants and other workers frequently lived in the cellars or garrets of their masters or employers. By the same token, mansions were often next to shacks. Merchants lived a block or two up the hill overlooking their wharves. Poor people, including blacks, lived in garrets, cellars, or alleys—right in the midst of the rich. Businesses and residences were close to each other, often in the same buildings. In the town as a whole, most blacks were free from slavery, but most still lived in white households—just over 60 percent in 1800. Of course, the fact that people lived in close quarters did not mean they thought of one another as equals. Like other societies that have vertical "zoning," Providence still maintained a range of clear social hierarchies.[11]

By the 1820s, the rapidly expanding city was becoming more "horizontally" zoned. It was becoming more like other societies with both more precarious and mutable social boundaries and clearer geographic distinctions. The landscape physically manifested the segmentation of the city by categories of use, class, gender, and race. Most obvious was the development of the commercial center at the heart of the town—at the bridge between the older East Side and the expanding West Side—with banks and businesses, but not residences, surrounding a central market square. Manufacturing and retailing, previously united in the same buildings, were increasingly separated, even when conducted by the same firms. Shortly after the riot, a huge granite arcade modeled after a Greek temple was constructed nearby to provide an alternative to the bustle of shopping on the street: it was a quiet, convenient, and semipublic palace of consumption.

Meanwhile, new kinds of neighborhoods, often segregated by class and race, were emerging. "Respectable" residential neighborhoods included the elaborate homes of the very rich, accompanied by the more modest homes of the prosperous. Wage workers moved elsewhere because they no longer lived with employers; and as part of this trend, free blacks gradually moved out of white households into separate working-class neighborhoods, where they rented lodgings in new kinds of housing such as boardinghouses and tenements. In part, this movement reflected the physical expansion of the city and improvements in transportation, but it also represented changes in relations between employers and employees, shifts in conceptions of household autonomy and group affiliation, and new strategies of real estate speculation. This development reflected a growing economic disparity—wealth was distributed even less equally, and the rich and poor were increasingly isolated from each other.[12]

An example of this growing separation of members of different social groups was the clustering of black households. During the 1820s, the "colored" population, around 8 percent of the town's inhabitants, remained almost steady at around 1,200. Indeed, it seems to have fallen in the years after the Hard Scrabble riot: the town census of 1825 reported 1,414 "colored" inhabitants, and the federal census of 1830 reported only 1,201. As people of color moved out of white households, they located their independent households close to one another, forming neighborhoods that were largely, though not exclusively, black. Between 1800 and 1810, the proportion of independent black households rose from about 38 percent to 65 percent, and it remained steady through the 1820s. A rough sense of this trend is obvious from tabulations printed in the 1830 *Providence Directory:* the town's expanding white population was evenly divided between the two sides of the river, but more than 70 percent of the "colored" population remained concentrated on the East Side. A map of black households around the time of the Hard Scrabble riot would show a broad diffusion of black households throughout the East Side, with a cluster on Benevolent Street, and another in the neighborhood known as Hard Scrabble in the northern part of town around Olney Lane. The few black households on the West Side were concentrated downtown, mostly on back streets and in alleyways. By the 1820s, a newspaper could describe Hard Scrabble as "a small hamlet, situated at the northern suburb of the town, populated principally by blacks who located themselves on that quarter to avoid any intercourse or correspondence with their hostile neighbors." Throughout the North, urban black communities demonstrated these same tendencies toward household independence and geographic clustering.[13]

Although public attacks on Hard Scrabble associated it with the town's entire "colored" population, the neighborhood was neither exclusively black nor the only place in town where black people lived. Indeed, at least one of houses destroyed during the riot belonged to the white man Jesse Sweet, who served during the ensuing trial as the prosecution's chief witness. The racially mixed nature of the neighborhood was noted in a hostile newspaper account in 1826, describing it as a refuge for "outlawed Negroes and abandoned whites." This writer was aware of the segmentation of neighborhoods by use and reputation in European cities, saying of Hard Scrabble: "Here it is that the scum of the town and the outpourings of creation, nightly assemble to riot and debauch, and in the midst of their bachanalian revels, the whole neighborhood is kept in a constant state of inquietude and alarm—A viler place never existed, and compared with it, St. Giles of London, is a school of morality."[14]

William J. Brown, a local man of color, remembered Hard Scrabble in the 1820s as a dangerous and fearsome place. "A great many colored people purchased land there, because it was some distance from town and hence quite cheap. They put up small houses for themselves, and earned their living in various ways"—many were wood sawyers and could be seen soliciting work at the crossroads of the town's bridges. A number of houses on Olney Street and Hard Scrabble were built by white men who "rented to any one, white or colored"—often on short terms and at low rates. "Some of these places had bar-rooms, where liquors were dealt-out, and places where they sold cakes, pies, and doughnuts, &c. . . . In some houses dancing and fiddling was the order of the day." Naturally, sailors coming into the port and boardinghouse residents often ended up at Hard Scrabble and sustained it with their trade. Brown remembered walking through the street as a boy on his way from his father's garden, in the company of two other boys, looking at the people as they passed along: "Some were sitting at the windows, some in their doorway, some singing, some laughing, some gossiping, some had their clay furnaces in front of their houses, cooking, and seeing us looking at them, said, 'What are you gawking at, you brats?' hurling a huge stone at the same time, and we were obliged to run for our lives."[15]

Brown's parents, anxious about their respectability, had deliberately avoided living anywhere near Hard Scrabble. Instead, they rented a two-room second-floor apartment in a building owned by the Tillinghast family near the corner of Power and South Main Streets, between the mansions of the great merchants and the busy wharves. Some sense of the strictures of propriety is suggested by Brown's recollection that at this point anything more than two rooms for a family of six would have seemed "too good" for Negroes. He was also quite conscious of the varying respectability of different establishments, noting that a neighboring boardinghouse for sailors was run by an unscrupulous black landlord.

Underlying the expansion and segmentation of the town was an economic transformation that caused another major political crisis—which the constitutional convention of 1824 deliberately ignored. During a period when many states embraced a "free" or "general" suffrage, within Rhode Island fewer and fewer men could vote. Rhode Island was still, fifty years after the Revolution, governed by its colonial charter of 1663. When granted, this charter was one of the most inclusive in North America. As in most of the British world, it grounded voting rights on a specific property qualification or "freehold." In this context, the word *freemen* designated not former slaves but rather adult white men qualified to vote. The Rhode Island charter established a low property requirement for "freemen," and it allowed the eldest sons of freemen to vote even if they lacked the requisite property. In addition, the economy was relatively egalitarian and largely agricultural, so many men owned the requisite real estate. Compared with other colonies and Great Britain, Rhode Island had a very high proportion of freemen to inhabitants. In the colonial period as many as 90 percent of all adult men had been freemen, and by the time of the Revolution the number remained as high as 75 percent. But in the early years of the Republic, although many of the new state constitutions expanded voting rights to match or exceed this level, in Rhode Island the franchise grew more restricted. A gradual transition to wage labor during the first half of the nineteenth century meant that fewer and fewer men could vote. Because it was real, not personal, property that counted for the freehold, the new landless urban workers were for the most part disenfranchised. And Rhode Island was the most urban and industrial state in the union. By 1830 only 40 percent of the state's adult white men were freeholders. In Providence in 1832, the percentage was even lower: 32 percent.[16]

By this time, a broad attack on "patriarchy" in the name of "fraternity" had forced the question of the franchise to crisis across the northern states as white men demanded the institution of a "free suffrage." During the early nineteenth century, many asserted that it was essential that all white men be able to vote. Most northern states fell into line with this demand in the years after the War of 1812. Connecticut's new constitution was adopted in 1818, New York's in 1821.[17] In many places, the old property restrictions on voting rights had created class and regional divisions. Those who did have property tended to be farmers in the rural backwater towns, not factory workers and artisans at the vanguard of economic development. The battle lines were often drawn with a coalition of "Jeffersonian yeoman" remnants and Federalist urban merchant aristocrats who joined forces against the "leveling democracy" of enfranchising this "dangerous" new urban class. Propaganda for a liberalized white franchise commonly focused on attacks on both aristocrats and African Americans: casting both groups as untrustworthy citizens legitimized the claim that poor whites could be virtuous voters. In New York during the constitutional convention, there were public accusations that the slavelike free black population was voting in league with the aristocratic Federalists to subvert the interests of the state's honest (white) working people. In most of the northern states populists succeeded in getting all white men the vote, or at least eliminating the freehold requirement. At the same time they generally added provisions categorically restricting the franchise to whites only.

In Rhode Island, legislators responded to early suffrage agitation in 1822 with a law that left the freehold requirement untouched but that explicitly disfranchised property-holding blacks.[18] In this respect, Rhode Island fit into the broad northern pattern. Previously in Rhode Island, as elsewhere, whiteness was not a formal requirement for voting: property-holding men of color should have been able to vote in some places. But informal rules probably discouraged most from trying. In Providence, the first protest against the exclusion of blacks from the franchise came in 1788, when Anthony Kinnicutt, a free black owner of a victualing cellar, called attention to this violation of the republican principle of no taxation without representation. Here he followed the tradition of Paul Cuffe and other men of color in Dartmouth, just across the Massachusetts border, several years before. But the link between taxation and individual representation was not as literal as it would later become: at this point many men could not vote—and it was not considered a right of all men. Toward the end of the century, some women and men of color began to vote in New Jersey, but both groups were soon categorically disfranchised. In 1800, after the passage of a new Rhode Island school law that provided public education to the children of taxpayers, Providence dropped black names from the town tax rolls in order to keep them out of the schools.[19]

In 1824, delegates to the Rhode Island constitutional convention rebuffed calls for a "free" or "general" franchise and offered instead another largely symbolic gesture: elimination of the old privilege of primogeniture. According to the charter, the eldest sons of freeholders were allowed to vote even if they did not have a freehold in their own name. This emphasis on overthrowing the dead hand of the past and asserting the rights of the rising generation resonated in newspaper editorials and letters in Providence during the weeks leading up to the referendum on 13 October. Generally, the Providence papers emphasized that the constitution was better than its predecessor and contained provisions for subsequent amendment. Letters in the *Rhode Island American* on 5 October 1824 emphasized that the new constitution was an opportunity for "young, generous, ambitious, and intelligent minds" to cast off the inherited customs of an aristocratic age. One correspondent wrote a letter addressed to the Freemen of Rhode Island: "Are you content to remain any longer under the Royal Charter of King Charles II, when you have the opportunity of forming a Constitution of Government for yourselves? The Constitution bears not upon its face '*the royal will and pleasure*' of a King, but in the true spirit of republicanism, it speaks the will and pleasure of 'we, the People.'" At the same time, newspaper essays in the weeks before the referendum debated the merits of free suffrage—and one reason the constitution may have failed was because it did not go far enough in satisfying the demands of disfranchised men.[20] The "mass" rallies held on 8 and 9 October, the public newspaper debate, and the constitutional referendum itself all helped encourage a sense of political entitlement among the men of Providence. Indeed, an important political function of this antipatriarchal rhetoric, focused on broad generational metaphors, was no doubt to obscure the class divisions that were becoming more problematic within the growing commercial and manufacturing towns.

This antipatriarchal language, frequently deployed in the newspaper debates, could closely link inclusive notions of "fraternity" with an exclusive emphasis on whiteness. A letter in the *Providence Patriot* the following Saturday, 9 October, insisted that the contest was between aristocratic age and regenerating youth and dismissed the opposition between manufacturers and farmers with two complementary racial analogies. Those who preferred the "savage state to the blessings of civilization" were invited to "seek their paradise among the Sioux and the Osages": "They there may find simplicity in perfection, and never be annoyed with the sight of flourishing villages and increasing towns, or fields made fruitful by an industrious yeomanry, stimulated by commerce and manufacture." In closing, the letter compared life under the Royal Charter to slavery: If you reject the constitution, the author demanded, "How will you be able thereafter to break your fetters? unless it should please your masters to give them your freedom, you can only do it by force, by revolution."[21]

In response to explicit civil disfranchisement and vigorous everyday discrimination, people of color across the North became increasingly self-conscious, moving into residential clusters and organizing independent institutions. In the larger northern cities, separate fraternal organizations were the first signs of this trend—black Masonic Lodges and Free African Union Societies were founded in Newport, Boston, New York, Philadelphia, and Providence around the turn of the century. The first "African" church in New England was founded in Boston just after the turn of the century. In Providence, the African Union Church was founded on Meeting Street in 1820, with public support and a grant of land from Moses Brown. Most of the founding members were men with independent households and children.[22] One of them was Nathaniel Paul—the brother of the Reverend Thomas Paul of Boston—who traveled across the Northeast raising money among black communities. This ecumenical church represented a new model of church polity; it was organized, at a time of bitter factionalism among Protestant sects, not by denomination but simply by race.

In Boston, the African church quickly became the staging area for the black community's claims for public recognition and respect. People of color were forcefully excluded from Boston Common on the Fourth of July in 1804, and, as in many other northern cities, they established their own civic parades. They were often divided about whether to honor Independence Day. In New York, during the 1820s, blacks began their own parades—some on the Fourth of July and some, pointedly, on the 5th. After the federal abolition of the slave trade on 12 August 1808, blacks in Boston chose that date for their annual parades. Black abolition day parades in Boston faced a harsh reception from local whites, who not only harassed the marchers but also published broadsides mocking them (fig. 19). Since the 1780s, jokes and cartoons had mocked black political speech and public assertions of civic respectability.[23] Although meeting resistance on the streets and in print, black communities were able to make provocative claims to public notice in large part because they had gained a modicum of financial and institutional autonomy.

In Providence, the founding of the African church coincided with what appears to have been a new climate of self-assertion in the everyday interactions of black and white men in the street. William J. Brown remembered the streets of the 1820s as zones of carefully choreographed etiquette, with clear rules of deference enforced by his respectable parents and reinforced by the lessons in his spelling books. He recalled, for instance, that if a boy did not defer to an elderly man on the street, he was liable to be caned. These conventions were strongly coded racially. Teaching "colored" children was considered so disreputable that one of the white private school teachers who included black children in his classes refused to acknowledge those students in public. After one boy made the mistake of raising his hat and bowing to him on the street, the Quaker teacher responded, in private, by threatening the boy with a whipping.[24]

Brown remembered the northern edge of Market Square as a racial gauntlet

FIGURE 19. *Grand Bobalition of Slavery.* One of a series of broadsides published in northern cities in the early nineteenth century, this one mocks the annual procession of the Boston African society in honor of the abolition of the international slave trade. These caricatures of black men's military pretensions strongly echo contemporary burlesques of white militia units in which working-class men mocked a militia system that they saw as elitist and unfair. Broadside, probably printed in Boston in 1819. Courtesy of the John Hay Library, Brown University.

where white men and boys would sit and harass black passersby. If black people were dressed shabbily, the whites would make fun of them for that; if blacks were dressed well, the whites would make fun of them for that, as well. Certainly the town of Providence made repeated efforts in the early 1820s to redress "the inconvenience of assembling and loitering boys and negroes on the North Side of the Market Square."[25] Brown's memories, however, also suggest that he and other blacks were becoming more assertive and combative. He recalled one particularly troubling incident when he was walking a girl home and they were mocked and bullied by a group of white boys. He was in a bad position because he was a good Christian and did not believe in violence, but he was glad when a big black man came along and put the white bullies in their place. During this altercation a white crowd gathered and almost took Brown and the other black men off to jail—but they were dissuaded by a white businessman with whom Brown had a personal relationship. Brown clearly wanted to imagine a true gentleman as being above the brutal racism of the vulgar masses.

The dedication ceremony of the Providence African Union Church in 1820 was a particularly dramatic example of these street battles over respectability. In order to dignify the founding of the new church with additional pomp, Brown recalled, a group of "young colored men" formed a military company called the African Greys to lead a procession to the new house of worship. Accompanied by a marching band, the members of the military company wore black belts and carried muskets; their officers wore side arms. Their commander was the self-styled "Colonel" George Barrett, whose competence in military tactics had been gained in service to a military officer stationed in the city during the War of 1812. The officers of the local African society carried emblems decked with lemons and oranges, representing the fruits of Africa. The president of the African society was "dressed to represent an African chief, having on a red pointed cap, and carried an elephant's tusk in his hand; each end was tipped with gilt." But the group did not always meet with quite the reception they might have desired. When they arrived at the Friends' meetinghouse to lead the Quakers to the dedication, the latter declined to be part of such a militaristic display. When they arrived at the church where the dedication was performed, Moses Brown asked the men to leave their weapons at the door.

After the dedication, the African Greys took their parade to Market Square, where they performed the complex maneuver of "making a wheel." As Brown told the story, this public display seemed destined for humiliation. As they were executing the wheel, Colonel Barrett slipped on ice and fell, to the amusement of spectators. Meanwhile, onlookers concocted a scheme to embarrass the marchers further: one of the spectators approached one of the officers in the middle of their maneuvers, presented him with a bill for a pair of boots, and demanded immediate payment of the five dollars due. This confrontation brought the company to an immediate halt. But the day was saved by Corporal Cato G. Northrup, who proudly drew out his pocketbook, took out a five dollar bill, and passed it to the officer. Having outmaneuvered their challengers, the African Greys marched on.[26]

||| "Midnight Orgies" |||

Prosecuting the Hard Scrabble rioters was one headache after another for Attorney General Dutee J. Pearce. By late November, he was able to identify only a handful of the fifty-odd rioters. He won indictments from a grand jury against ten men for rioting, disturbing "the peace of the State," and, in particular, destroying the house of Henry Wheeler—the first building targeted by the rioters. When called for arraignment, three of those indicted "could not be found." The sheriff could produce only seven for arraignment. These men pled not guilty, demanded separate trials, and were ably served by well-connected local lawyers. Defense attorney Joseph L. Tillinghast revealed his strategy early on in the trial of the first defendant, Oliver Cummings, when he confronted the prosecution's key witness. The defense attorney asked witness Jesse Sweet, a white resident of the Hard Scrabble neighborhood, what business was usually carried on in Wheeler's establishment. Sweet dodged the question by asserting that he never went there. Attorney General Pearce objected on the grounds that "neither the house nor its inhabitants were now on trial." Tillinghast rejoined that it was indeed material whether the building destroyed was a "house" or a "pig sty." The jury had a right to decide "whether this house was not such a nuisance as justified the prisoner in aiding and destroying it."[27] The court upheld the objection and barred this line of inquiry, but the ruling provided the attorney general little comfort.

Defense attorney Tillinghast had little difficulty getting witnesses—even those called by the attorney general—to put on trial not only the residents of Hard Scrabble but also the town of Providence and the court system itself. The next time Sweet came to the stand, Tillinghast got him to acknowledge that although Wheeler lived in the upper part of his house, the lower part "was used as a dancing hall by the blacks." Nightwatchman Samuel V. Allen admitted having been to the hall frequently—"but only in the capacity of a watchman." He cheerfully elaborated that "the place was celebrated in the annals of Constables and Watchmen; he always kept as far from it as possible and only went when his duty *imperiously* called him." At the time of the riot, not only was he present, but so was his file leader and at least one member of the town council, who paced back and forth but did nothing to stop the destruction. None of them considered interference prudent. Tillinghast used such testimony to argue that the houses in question were "the resort of the most corrupt part of the black population, who supported their debaucheries and riots by carrying thither the plunder of their masters and pawning it for a participation in these disgusting scenes." Hard Scrabble was, in short, a "notorious nuisance." Wary not to go too far in defending the virtue of vigilantism, Tillinghast was able to emphasize that the rioters had in fact confined themselves to responsibly and soberly removing the nuisance without being carried away by excessive violence. He insisted that the riot was not merely justified but actually necessary because the authorities responsible for curbing such threats to public morality had proven impotent. Local citizens had repeatedly sought redress from the town and in the courts, but to no avail. Was there a "sober citizen," he asked, who would blame the "populace" for taking the matter into their own hands and destroying this "sink of vice"?[28]

Attorney General Pearce was left struggling to counter this logic of "public morals" and civil impotence, which he did by emphasizing the logic of "public order." His vision rested on a society in which elite white leaders still controlled the city and the conduct of its people, white and black. His first challenge—besides the undeniable liability that he was an unpopular Newporter at a trial in Providence—was that the riot's victims were even more unsympathetic. Instead of trying to defend them from Tillinghast's aspersions, he allied himself against the residents of Hard Scrabble while trying to deflect attention back on the rioters. "The insults which the whites may have suffered from the numerous black population in this town, had no connection with the offence charged," he insisted. "If the blacks are riotous and keep disorderly houses the law is open to punish them. But if they live here and are not outlawed they have a right to be protected by the law in their persons and property." The rule of law, he urged, should take precedence over racial solidarity: Would the jury, he asked at one point, "screen" the defendant "from justice" because the house belonged to a black man instead of a white man? Presumably because he feared that the answer to this question would not help his case, Pearce had, from the beginning, cast the real victim of the riot as not the owners of damaged property but as the "public peace" that had been disrupted. Instead of bringing charges that might have provided the property holders with restitution, Pearce focused on the crime of rioting. Since it proved difficult to charge twelve armed individuals, as required under the state riot statute, the attorney general had also resorted to the more generous common-law definition of a riot: three individuals unlawfully assembling to do an unlawful act or to put such a purpose into effect in a "frightful and turbulent manner." Such a confusing indictment made it easier for the prosecution, the court, and the jury to exploit legal technicalities. This left Pearce arguing that it was not *necessary* and indeed dangerous for the people to have cast the law aside and taken matters into their own hands: "Encourage this doctrine and no man in the community is safe." Although this claim may have resonated with jurymen anxious about what might happen to their own houses if they returned an unpopular verdict, it was harder to convince them that the town government and state courts were really able to defend public morality. "We live in a land of law, and there are no evils existing at Hard-Scrabble or anywhere else that a remedy may not be found for them in the law of the land." The problem with this assertion was that for years the town and the courts had been receiving complaints about Hard Scrabble as a public nuisance but had demonstrated little success in cleaning it up.[29]

In the weeks leading up to the trial, perhaps the only public response to the riots had been an editorial in the *Providence Gazette* five days after the riot that suggests how the legal battle between public morals and public order was part of a much broader set of concerns about nineteenth-century urbanism. The newspaper complained of the burden the black population was placing on the community, noting with approval a recent action of the town council to compile a census of the Negroes of Providence to detect and root out those "addicted to idle and dissolute habits" and to remove the "undesireable" elements from town.[30] Two things are striking about this notice. First, the dissolute habits of alcohol, dancing, and prostitution were prominent public concerns in cities throughout the United States and Europe at the time. Second, the notice presents a fantasy of the city as an organism in which inhabitants are expected to be useful to the community or ranked according to the benefit they give the community. Indeed, this period is marked by a "medicalization" of the town—its treatment as a body that required the proper circulation of air, water, and sewage, as well as the proper diffusion of light. This corporeal language, although inclusive metaphorically, could be divisive. Often, middle-class reformers targeted the poor as sources of contamination. Tillinghast's arguments about public morality coincided with ongoing local struggles to police more effectively the disorders associated with the town's growth. In Providence, the town government had been attempting for years to regulate public nuisances, control immigrants, and suppress vice. Tillinghast's arguments were powerful because they tapped into a longstanding concern within the town of Providence that portrayed the city not as integrated and jointly controlled but as polarized morally and racially—emphasizing a sharp distinction between the good white people of Providence and the bad black residents of Hard Scrabble. For many members of a rapidly expanding and increasingly stratified white population, it was convenient and even comforting to focus on blacks as the main source of what were actually much broader divisions and more intractable conflicts.

By the 1820s, the town fathers of Providence were accustomed to responding to the threat of urban disorder by focusing on the specter of strange people of color. As early as the 1790s, concern about disorderly blacks sparked complaints to local overseers of the poor across New England and riots in towns such as Boston. Despite popular fears in Providence, blacks were not immigrating in huge numbers in the early nineteenth century and were not actually growing as a portion of the population. Nonetheless, the Providence town fathers targeted nonresident blacks for expulsion and made greater efforts at policing legal black inhabitants. Around 1808 the town placed a curfew on people of color. Later, this surveillance and regulation of local people of color were expanded to "any disorderly or suspicious Person." The town council authorized voluntary night patrols to apprehend such persons and convey them to the watch house. In the early 1820s, when the town's growth was fastest, redoubled efforts to regulate the town's public spaces included installing numerous street lamps. In addition to hiring more constables, the town approached the problem of policing the town by authorizing various groups of local white men—such as a group of neighbors on the West Side and a cadet company— to form volunteer watch companies to patrol the streets at night.[31]

During these years, the rapid expansion of Providence had prompted the town council and local citizens to attempt to clean up the city both literally and figuratively. Local residents focused on the problems of crowded tenements, boarding-houses, and the illicit activities of their occupants. In 1822, the town's Nuisances Committee, including Stephen Tillinghast (perhaps the brother of attorney Tillinghast), emphasized "nuisances injurious to the health of the Inhabitants of the Town"—prominent among them the "wash," or sewage, from the East Side, which required a general regulation. At one "sailor boarding house" the privy and yard were "full to overflowing." In another place, four black families had crowded into a small house: "Having no other means of disposing of their filth except placing it on the street—there will always be a nuisance created in a few days." In 1826, neighbors complained that the keepers of a "confectionary store" allowed gambling. There were also complaints about shops selling liquor improperly. By this point, the town's liquor licenses included a clause forbidding the grantee from allowing "any person of colour to take charge of his store."[32]

Groups of neighboring men repeatedly decried "disorderly houses"—and often their concerns had to do with the supposedly inadequate domestic governance of poor householders. Partly these disputes arose because people were living so close to one another. Seventeen men complained in 1817 that their neighbor James Lee, "a Blackman," was keeping a disorderly house—that he, his wife, and children were "very quarrelsome amongst themselves," that their children were "very mischievous, and seem[ed] to be under no kind of government," and that Lee himself had been "entertaining persons of very bad habits." These men, mostly employed as grocers, butchers, masons, and gunsmiths, lived within a few blocks of one another on North Main, Charles, and Orms Streets. Sixteen local men complained in 1820 that Nahum Eager was "entertaining company" in his victualing cellar on Sundays, and the town council cautioned him to desist. In early 1822, Thomas Hull complained that Judith Maxwell and Rachel Smith, who lived in the house of Isaac Angell, were disorderly persons. Peter Turner, an Irishman, appeared before the council on complaint of the overseer of the poor and promised to dismiss his disorderly boarders and, in the future, keep a quiet house.[33]

Faced with complaints about disorder in the growing city, town leaders conspicuously attacked the legal rights of people of color to reside in Providence. Since the colonial period, citizenship in New England had been fundamentally constructed by town. People had a legal residence by default in the town where they were born. When someone moved, he or she had to obtain official acceptance from the authorities in the new town. This process was partly defensive; towns wanted to avoid having to take care of poor people who "belonged" to other towns, and the poorer a person was, the less likely he or she was to be accepted in a new town. Towns struggled to maintain not only a lower tax burden but also an ideal of community that emphasized homogeneity and household autonomy. Strangers to town were routinely examined before the town fathers and either accepted or officially "warned out"—that is, given notice to leave. For example, in 1820 Libbius Prince was able to produce testimonials sufficient to convince the Providence Town Council to allow him and his family to remain as long as they showed "good behavior."[34] In contrast, in 1827, Joseph Nocake—a Narragansett Indian—was warned out of Providence as a person of "bad fame and reputation" and unsuitable to be an inhabitant of the town. But when the constable went to get him, he "had got sight of him and ordered him to stop, but he ran off and eluded him."

Sometimes those warned out were unceremoniously hauled off by the sheriff and deposited on the other side of the town line. But even forcibly evicting people from town did not always work: for instance, around 1820, the Providence overseer of the poor complained that Betsy Updike, alias Prophit, had been removed to

North Kingstown but was now back: it was ordered that she be fined seven dollars or whipped ten stripes. As places such as Providence grew larger, such warnings grew less common, but the legal system still recognized the fact that newcomers to the city needed formal approval.[35]

The result in places such as Providence was a number of individuals living and working in the town without any legal right to stay there—rather like modern "illegal aliens"—which most conspicuously placed them at the mercy of their employers or landlords. Increasingly, it was their moral character and household arrangements that were scrutinized by employers, landlords, neighbors, and town fathers. Employers dissatisfied with servants could threaten them not only with dismissal but also with bodily removal from the town. Hence, Moses Stanton, who ran a boardinghouse on the southern end of the East Side, complained about his housekeeper of several years, Mary Cooper, a "woman of color." Her bad behavior, he claimed, included stealing his belongings to purchase liquor, neglecting his children, failing to mend their clothing, and threatening to set fire to his house and kill him and his children. Fourteen male neighbors—with occupations such as grocers, house carpenters, rope makers, blacksmiths—supported his petition that she be "Banished" from Providence forever: "Her conduct . . . has been so bad & wicked of late, that she is not fit to be among civilized Society."[36]

Perhaps prompted by the statistics produced by the 1820 census, the town fathers of Providence attempted to bring boardinghouses and tenements under systematic regulation—and their initial impulse was to focus specifically on the problem of strangers of color. Around this time, the state General Assembly passed "an act for breaking up disorderly houses kept by the negroes and mulattoes, and for putting such negroes and mulattoes to service"—another echo of nostalgia for domestic slavery as a means of governing the black population. In the early 1820s, the town council repeatedly made special efforts to regulate "colored" transients, white transients, and those living in boardinghouses and tenements. In late August 1821, constables Henry Alexander and Thomas Cooke were ordered to search the town and compile a list of "persons of color of disorderly behavior and bad habits, who are housekeepers" as well as families of color who did not have a legal settlement in the town and families of color who had boarders who were not legally settled. Again, in June 1822, the town council ordered that all the "Coloured" housekeepers in town be warned that if they housed any transients—white or not—who lacked a legal settlement in the town they would be prosecuted unless they gave notice to the council. The resulting list of "colored" housekeepers and heads of families named more than a hundred individuals and counted another hundred family members living mostly in tenements owned by about fifteen mostly white landlords. In early 1823, the town sergeant was ordered to visit all the boardinghouses in town and compile a list of the "several Boarders who are Strangers." Meanwhile, the keepers of tenements and boardinghouses were required to register any strangers with the town. James Thurber, a local justice of the peace living on North Main Street, reported that he had let a tenement to William Apess of Connecticut, a "Collourd man" who said he had a wife and two children and was "to follow trucking for a Living."[37]

At the trial of the rioters, Tillinghast's denigration of Hard Scrabble focused specifically on the themes of dancing and, more obliquely, prostitution. He sardonically mused on the etymology of the name "Hard Scrabble"—he wondered whether one had to scrabble hard to get there or to get out. Perhaps, he concluded, the name referred to a style of black dancing: "the *shuffling*, which is there practiced in the graceful evolutions of this dance, or the zig zag movements of Pomp and Phillis, when engaged in treading the *minuet de la court*." This mockery was not just about black pretension or styles of dancing—he makes fun of both African-style and European-style dancing—but was also closely associated with sexual debauchery. After an argument about the riot act and the possession of the house, Tillinghast returned to the themes of immorality and justified vigilantism: "It was not a dwelling house, but a *dancing hall*, where the party-coloured votaries of pleasure assembled together, and the noise and the smoke of their incense went up to Heaven!"[38]

The blasphemy of these "midnight orgies" was not just merriment or even pleasure but sex across lines of color. Prostitution—disorderly women as well as disorderly houses—had been a public concern in growing northern towns since the 1790s. And this disorder, too, was closely associated with concentrations of free blacks in certain areas. In Boston, several local observers reported to Jeremy Belknap in 1795 that the town had already witnessed several riots whose participants tore down brothels and bawdy houses—particularly those that mixed black and white men and women. In Philadelphia and New York, prostitution became a prominent symbol of disorder and the focus of reform efforts in the early decades of the nineteenth century. There seems little doubt that the number of prostitutes and their customers increased as cities grew dramatically. Increasingly reformers saw prostitution as a distinct kind of vice and the subject of special campaigns for moral reform. These moral reform movements against prostitution grew out of changes in assumptions and class styles of romance, love, and sex. In Providence, as early as 1794, when the town still numbered fewer than ten thousand inhabitants, citizens complained that the area near the old Baptist Meeting House was infested with "notorious women." A decade later, another group of citizens petitioned the town government to "stop all vices in the boundaries of the town."[39]

By 1817, when Moses Brown headed a petition against prostitution, the association of bad women and black women was well established. As the petitioners complained: "There are within the Border of our Town Divers Houses of Bad fame not only Among the Coloured People but Even Among the Whites who come here from Neighboring States and collect Women of prostituted Character . . . for the Infamous and Degrading purpose of Seducing our Youth and Others to the Ruining of their Morrals and debaseing the Manner to their & their Parent's Grief, and the Grief of all Good Citizens." The respectable citizens who subscribed to the petition proposed that the best way to solve this problem would be to "examine all open and secret houses" that entertained the town's citizens or those who visited them "for the Criminal Intercourse of the Sexes or the Seductive purposes preparatory to such Disruptive Practices." Those not belonging to the town were to be removed and the legal inhabitants dealt with effectively. In response to this petition, the town council resolved that all citizens should report to the overseers of the poor all persons of questionable character within the boundaries of the town so they could be examined, removed, or dealt with according to law. The petition, described in the town papers as coming from a "large number of respectable citizens," was to all appearances a united front of the town's elite and middling ranks. Almost two-thirds of them appear on the 1824 city directory with residences all over town: slightly more than a third lived on the newly developing West Side, and the rest were concentrated in the long-established central portion of the East Side, between Angell and Power Streets. The signers' occupations ranged from grocers, schoolteachers, yeomen, and shopkeepers to merchants, manufacturers, brokers, attorneys, and at least two ministers—the Reverend Stephen Gano of the First Baptist Church and the Reverend James Wilson. But it was likely through Moses Brown's influence that the petition managed to attract support from such a complete cross section of the town's respectable citizens, as it was likely at Brown's behest that the petition explicitly fingered not just black but also white culprits.[40]

The notion that bad women were victimizing virtuous men epitomized common attitudes toward prostitution, gender, and class. In the 1820s, a convicted rapist from a neighboring town petitioned the General Assembly. He argued for mercy on the grounds not only that was he fifty-two years old and had a wife and children to support but also that it was his rights that had been violated: "Where is the saifty of men if every prostitute whin they git Mad can Be allowed to Destroy a man after this sort[?]" By the early nineteenth century, a "fraternal" culture of sexual license developed for most men. Male sexuality was largely distinguished for the ways it bridged lines of class and social difference. Whereas respectable women were supposed to be distinguished by their virtue and restraint, men were often indulged in their pursuit of pleasure and encouraged to think of their sexual exploits in terms of conquest. For men, sexual indulgence could provide affirmation, and in this conflation of desire and identity, race played an important role. Black men were conspicuously excluded from this sexual fraternity. Among women, class distinctions were much more obviously tied to competing sexual cultures. The sentimental cult of romantic marriage was linked to a valorization of genteel female sexual purity, which must be guarded against dishonor. But whereas middle-class women may have been obsessed with the fate of "fallen women," lower-class women often had different priorities.[41] Often this subgroup of white "bawdy wenches" was associated with black women as a whole.

In the years before the riot, the neighborhood of Hard Scrabble came under vigorous—if unsuccessful—attack by a group of white men who lived nearby. As early as 1821, the captain of the town watch had complained that the colored woman Thankful Sharpe kept a disorderly house and entertained "rude company at unreasonable hours." In the spring of 1821, Samuel Thurber, who lived high up North Main Street, complained, "Ever since Calvin Hill moved into the north part of town he has kept and continues to keep a disorderly house." In 1822, a number of "residents of Olneyville" filed a more general petition to the town, complaining of disreputable neighbors.[42] These men had no qualms about emphasizing the combined racial and sexual disorder they saw in local dance halls and bawdy houses.

In a petition to the state legislature, George Olney and a group of neighbors complained that houses of "ill fame" had plagued Olney Lane for years without redress. Particularly disturbing was the sexual mingling of black and white men and women. "In these houses blacks & whites mingle in promiscuous debauching, profanity & intoxication & the whole street is frequently made the scene of their criminal excesses." The "tardy forms of the Common law" and of the town council had been tried and found to be "wholly inadequate to the redress of these grievances." Frequent disturbances of the public peace required the intervention of "civil authority"—but without any lasting effect. Removing one bad tenant only made room for another, and such tenants could not be pursued in civil actions because they did not have enough property to make prosecution cost-effective. Sometimes, the malefactors were expelled from town only to return almost as quickly as the officers who escorted them out. Further, these local homeowners complained, most of these degenerate houses were owned by "two or three Individuals" who were "enriching themselves in letting them by the day or week to vile abandoned wretches, from who [was] extorted the most exorbitant rent, exceeding four fold the common rents in the Town." Despite this suggestion, there was little effort to turn to the landlords for redress, and public outrage continued to focus on the "colored" residents of Hard Scrabble.[43]

Widespread exasperation with the impotence of the town in the face of such public outrages made defense attorney Tillinghast's job easier. In a closing statement that reportedly lasted an hour and three quarters, he argued that members of the public had little choice but to remove a nuisance themselves when the "tardy operations of the law" would either take too long or prove ineffective. In this case, the town council had done as much as it could, and several legal prosecutions against the occupants of a disorderly house had been resorted to—but all in vain. He hoped the jury would agree that "destruction of this place is a benefit to the morals of the community."

At the same time, Tillinghast's closing statement suggests how much the public morals of Providence *needed* Hard Scrabble. The language of Tillinghast's closing statements—at least as reported in the press—suggests not merely outrage and vicarious titillation but also pleasure in describing just how debauched the victims of the riot really were. In his closing arguments, Tillinghast drifted into melodramatic vagaries and sardonic monologues that suggest real rhetorical relish. At one point he exclaimed: "The renowned city of *Hard-Scrabble* lies buried in magnificent ruins! Like the ancient Babylon it has fallen with all its graven images, its tables of impure oblation, its idolatrous rights and sacrifices, and my client stands here being charged with having invaded this classic ground and torn down its altars and its beautiful temples! I might, gentlemen, be pathetic on this subject, but I spare your feelings."

Not surprisingly, the jury returned a verdict of not guilty in Cumming's case, and it was soon apparent that no convictions were going to be sustained against the other defendants. The jury found young Nathaniel Metcalf guilty of riot at common law but recommended lenience because it judged him to be mentally deficient. After the jury found the fourth defendant guilty of riot at common law but not of statutory riot, the prosecution ground to a halt. For a time the lawyers wrangled over the common law and statutory riot codes, but then the court dismissed the conviction. Attorney General Pearce accepted defeat and withdrew the remaining indictments. Most of the file papers from the trials subsequently disappeared from the records of the court clerk.[44]

||| Bobalition |||

The black residents of Hard Scrabble, barred from testifying at the trial, made no public statements about the riot afterwards. But that did not prevent a Boston printer from producing a broadside that purported to describe the riot and its aftermath from the point of view of one of its victims. Actually, *Hard Scrabble, or Miss Philises Bobalition* (Boston, [1825]), was an undisguised burlesque. Supposedly a letter from the urban Miss Phillis to a country cousin, the text was written in a thick "Negro" dialect in verses set to the tune of the popular romantic song "O Dear, What Can the Matter Be?" The account begins by mocking "Miss" Phillis and her husband, Pompey, for their absurd aspirations to genteel respectability. The happy couple's domestic bliss—represented by a supper of clam and eel custard—is interrupted by the sound of rioters shattering windows. Phillis and Pompey scramble for cover, and the rioters tear their home apart:

> O, O, so peaceable late we lib in Hard Scrabble,
> 'Till routed and driven away by the rabble,
> Who 'tack us like furies wid a high diddle diddle!
> Demolish our dwelling, smash Beaurau and Cradle,
> My Gin Jug and Spider, my Portrait and Ladle,
> My Candlestand, Chairs, and poor Pompey's Fiddle.

Returning the next day, Phillis finds the entire neighborhood destroyed. Fields for a mile around are spread with feathers from torn-up bedding.

> De mud Clay & brick dust lay so thick in Hard Scrabble
> I was 'blige hold up my skirt to prevent it from drabble.[45]

Here, through the medium of print, the riot took on a new life—returning not just as a physical attack on specific individuals and their property, nor as a trial of specific defendants and a debate about local public morals, but as an abstracted fantasy that both repeated the humiliation of such attacks and presented it as an object of enjoyment.

Miss Philises Bobalition was but one of dozens of broadsides published in Boston and other northeastern cities in the years after the War of 1812 that mocked urban free blacks for their disorderly living, pretensions to respectability, and status as victims of assaults and derision. As these broadsides suggest, the themes of black domesticity and struggles for respectability were at the heart of the politics of race in northern cities during the 1820s. These themes, manifested in such events as the Hard Scrabble riot and the ensuing trial, reflected both developing middle-class anxieties about growing urban working classes and the emergence of increasingly organized and assertive black communities.

The characters Phillis and Pompey seem to have appeared first in *Dreadful Riot on Negro Hill!* (Boston, 1816). It, too, was a poetical letter written by Miss Phillis to a country cousin about a devastating riot in a black neighborhood that is explicitly associated with prostitution and disorderly living. Phillis explains that the riot occurred when "a great number of de white Truckerman" got angry with the people in the neighborhood because "so many bad girl lib here." The name Phillis and the verse format alluded to the celebrated Bostonian Phillis Wheatley, whose *Poems on Various Subjects, Religious and Moral* had just been republished. At least two editions of the *Dreadful Riot* broadside appeared in 1816, and other variations were printed in Boston in 1827 and after a riot in 1828 and in New York in 1832. The characters Pompey and Phillis also made frequent appearances in other broadsides; in the *Grand Bobalition of Slavery* ([Boston, 1819?]), she is the object of a romantic song, "Phillis, Rose of de Hill."[46] By 1824, the characters Phillis and Pompey were already well known in Providence: at the trial of the indicted rioters, defense attorney Tillinghast used the fictive couple to mock the residents of Hard Scrabble (fig. 20).

The word *bobalition* in the Hard Scrabble broadside refers derisively to the annual ceremonies local African societies organized to honor the abolition of the international slave trade in 1807 by the United States and Great Britain. In Boston, the first Abolition Day procession was held on 14 July 1808 and centered around the African Baptist Church on Beacon Hill, the neighborhood attacked in the *Dreadful Riot*. By 1810, the Boston African society had begun advertising invitations in local newspapers, announcing the order of ceremonies and featured speakers. A number of Abolition Day orations by black leaders in Boston, New York, and Philadelphia were published as pamphlets. Early on, Abolition Day proces-

Dreadful Riot on Negro Hill!

O ! Read wid detention de Melancholly Tale and he send you yelling to your Beds !

FIGURE 20. *Dreadful Riot on Negro Hill!* Supposedly a letter written by Phillis about a riot in which a group of white Bostonians attacked a cluster of black dwellings on Beacon Hill, this text provided the basis for the broadside about the Hard Scrabble Riot in Providence in 1824. Both broadsides mock black residents of northern cities for their pretensions to gentility and sexual disorder. In a reversal of conventional male-female roles, Phillis wards off the attackers while Pompey, wounded in the shin, limps away. Detail of broadside (Boston, 1816). Courtesy of the Library Company of Philadelphia.

sions were confronted by hostile and sometimes violent crowds of local whites, but after 1816 the attacks moved more into the realm of print.

In 1816, the same year that the *Dreadful Riot* appeared, a Boston printer produced another Negro-dialect broadside, entitled *Invitation, Addressed to the Marshals of the "Africum Shocietee," at the Commemoration of the "Abolition of the Slave Trade.* Soon, broadsides with titles like *Grand Celebrashun ob de Bobalition ob African Slavery!!!* began to appear annually in Boston and spread to other cities, including New York and Philadelphia; typically, they featured outlandish orders of ceremonies, including speeches, toasts, and songs. This running joke was taken one step further in another series of broadsides that purported to represent black responses to the Abolition Day broadsides. An early example was called *Reply to*

Bobalition of Slavery. These "reply" broadsides generally were dialogues, again spoken in thick dialect. Like the riot broadsides, they burlesqued the victims to whom they ostensibly gave voice.[47] In many ways—in their burlesque tone, their blackface character, their mixture of poetry, dialogues, speeches, toasts, and songs—these cheap, ephemeral bobalition broadsides anticipated the minstrel shows that became popular in subsequent decades.

We often think of minstrel shows by exploring what they may have meant to white audiences and especially how class conflicts between whites were often modulated through fantastic projected racial others. But this earlier genre of bobalition broadsides calls attention to a much more literal dialogue between urban whites and black leaders. Whereas early black political writings were typically deferential and optimistic, after the War of 1812 they became increasingly confrontational. Early black speeches on abolition, for instance, lavished praise and gratitude on white benefactors, anticipated the rapid end of slavery across the land, and overlooked continuing inequalities. By the 1820s, however, black writers were more likely to call attention to the enduring national crime of slavery, the racist policies of national leaders, and the inequalities of rights and opportunities endured by free blacks in the free states. These writers were, naturally, aware of the bobalition broadsides. Hartford, Connecticut, activist Hosea Easton's assessment was incisive: "Cuts and placards, descriptive of the negro's deformity are every where displayed to the observation of the young, with corresponding broken lingo." They filled the windows of popular urban bookstores and were displayed in the bar rooms of rural public houses and were thus "under the daily observation of every class of society, even in New England." Their political meaning seemed as clear as it was ugly: "What could accord better with the objects of this nation in reference to blacks, than to teach their little ones that a negro is part monkey?"[48]

More surprising, perhaps, the writers of the bobalition broadsides seem to have been paying remarkably close attention to the writings of these black leaders. The broadsides echo these black writers' common themes, arguments, and attitudes, which typically focused on respectability, politics, and the nature of prejudice.[49] Of course, the bobalition broadsides differed in tone. Black writers were trying to develop reasonable and persuasive arguments against racist politics and for the advancement of the Negro race; the bobalition broadsides burlesqued not only these goals but also their advocates. In a way, these broadsides can be seen as part of a new cult of racial insensibility, which instead of spurning callousness and prejudice—as antislavery activists urged—took pleasure in them.

The disputed terrain of respectability is nowhere more clear than in the "broken lingo" of black speakers in these broadsides and in its symbolic suggestion of exclusion from American citizenship. In the broadsides and other contemporary caricatures, Negro characters speak a thick, stereotyped dialect developed in the eighteenth century, in part by London actors using West Indian speech patterns as their model. When written, some nonstandard spellings were plausibly phonetic. For example, the use of "de" for "the" seems to have derived from seventeenth-century theatrical representations of Irish speech, which in turn derived from even earlier English representations of Dutch speech. Other common features of the alleged Negro dialect in writing did not actually represent differences in pronunciation at all. This so called eye-dialect—such as substituting "wuz" for "was"—was a visual representation of normal speech that had the effect of appearing defective. Of course, northern blacks did not often speak with West Indian accents, since most of them were born in New England and grew up in households in which English would have been their first language. Letters written by black New Englanders in the early decades of the Republic generally reflect quite standard speech patterns.[50]

Taken out of context, the broadsides' fantastic Negro dialect suggested that northern blacks were imitating white speech patterns—and failing. In many broadsides, references to "Massa Shakespole" suggest a contrast between allegedly vernacular black dialect and an idealized model of standard English. *Dreadful Riot on Negro Hill!* (1816) begins with Miss Phillis's announcement that she plans to describe the events "in de language of Massa POPE and MILTON." The authors of these broadsides seem to have taken special pleasure in transmogrifying the word *respectability* itself, as in a passage in which members of the African society describe themselves as "moss spickable brack folk of stinkation" (most respectable black folk of distinction). The importance of a standard style of speech was emphasized in these years by the publication of Noah Webster's first "American" dictionary in 1828, which sought both to help regularize regional dialects across the country and to announce America's cultural independence from Britain.[51]

The broadsides playfully suggest that their use of Negro dialect reversed the normal role of printers, which was to take a text and correct its malapropisms, grammatical errors, and misspellings. One broadside begins with the notice that the speech reprinted below had been written by the president of the African society in his presumably broken dialect and then given to "*de* Printer *to be* super-danglify *into* English!"[52] In fact, it seems that at least some of the broadsides were first composed in standard English and then, as it were, translated into Negro dialect. A telling typographical error appears in the first line of *Miss Philises Bobalition*—"What can the de matter be?" Apparently, the writer or printer changed the article "the" to "de" but then forgot to eliminate the first version of the word and redundantly printed both.

The implication of this ubiquitous stereotyped dialect was that blacks could not actually master standard, much less refined, English. This assumption lay behind the fact that when Phillis Wheatley's poems were first published in the 1770s they were accompanied by a statement from local gentlemen testifying that she had actually written them herself. Since then the language of black writers had been under special scrutiny. Peter Williams Jr.'s *Oration on the Abolition of the Slave Trade* (New York, 1808) was so eloquent that it was deemed necessary to provide readers with affidavits from the printer and others that it was composed by Williams himself and that it came from the press "with only a few immaterial verbal alterations."[53] However, by the 1820s, when the bobalition broadsides became prominent, such notices were no longer common. As more and more blacks benefited from formal schooling and a substantial body of black writing appeared in print, their literary skill could be taken for granted, and to suggest otherwise began to seem—at least to them—offensive. Of course, that is precisely why the burlesque of black speech retained its symbolic punch.

Dreadful Riot on Negro Hill!, which introduced the characters Pompey and Phillis, mocks the aspiration of urban blacks for genteel respectability by emphasizing their excessive spending on consumer goods and their sexual disorder. The narrative begins with a scene of domestic tranquility—the couple is in bed ready to blow out the candle—when they are interrupted by the sound of the gathering riot. Phillis pleads with the rioters that her home is respectable:

> I tell 'um Pomp he poor man,
> Not by keep girl he gain he food,
> For while I wash, do all I can,
> Pomp earn'd a trade sawing wood.

Even if the family was industrious and not associated with prostitution, the simple fact that Phillis was acting as her family's spokesman reversed patriarchal expectations about the proper roles of men and women. Her account goes on to emphasize stereotyped images of black bodies, including crooked shins, woolly hair, thick skulls, and dark skin: stones hurled through the window break Pompey's shin and hit baby Katy on the head, which would have been fatal had she not been "fleec'd well wid wool." Pompey then hides in a chimney and emerges covered in soot. The subsequent five stanzas catalogue the couple's "genteel" furnishings, which the rioters destroyed, including a portrait of Pompey, mahogany tables, and sofas. Phillis explains, "Common Furniture will do in de country. But in Bossun or Providencee if a body wish to be reckon anyting day muss conform to de fashion ob de place." Yesterday, she sighs, Pompey was worth a hundred pounds; now, "one broken shin now all he got."[54] The couple's domestic disorder is emphasized in the broadsides' illustrative woodcut, which presents Phillis as decidedly unfeminine and Pompey as thoroughly emasculated. In the illustration, as in the text, Phillis is assertive, facing the rioters and brandishing a broom, while Pompey, shielded by his wife, limps away on crutches.

The association of sexual desire with lust for consumer goods has long historical roots, dating from at least the first publications of the song "O Dear, What Can the Matter Be," on which *Miss Philises Bobalition* was based. In the song, a young woman yearns for her lover's return and the tokens of his affection that he was supposed to buy for her at the market. By the 1820s, when publications of the song multiplied in northern cities, both excessive consumption and disorderly sexuality had come to represent, at least for middle-class reformers, similar dangers to the social order. During the 1820s, the mass production of ready-to-wear clothing allowed individuals with modest incomes to emulate, imitate, or mock those of higher social status. In Providence, a circular printed by one of the local newspapers for New Year's Day 1825 put the Hard Scrabble riot in the context of these concerns. The daily spectacle of Market Square would shock the colony's colonial founder, Roger Williams:

> Ah! how would he sigh at beholding our fair,
> With their impudent swing and their courtezan air;
> All cover'd with gaiety, fashion and show,
> With a waist like a wasp, and a head like a cow;
> Flirting and tossing and wriggl'ing in walking,
> And drowning the noise of the street with their talking.

Several years later, a group of prominent citizens organized the Society for the Encouragement of Faithful Domestic Service in Providence. Modeled after an idea first instituted in London and copied in Boston, New York, and Philadelphia in the 1820s, the society sought to compel servants to respect their employers and maintain deferential habits. Thus, although the bobalition broadsides emphasized an image of blacks imitating whites, this theme gained meaning from a much broader set of social conflicts. Similarly, other caricatures published in northern cities lampooned black characters in ways that could also be read as cautions to lower-class whites. In one cartoon from Edward Williams Clay's series *Life in Philadelphia* (1828), an elaborately dressed black woman is asked how she's faring in the current hot weather. "Pretty well I tank you Mr Ceasar," she replies, "only I aspire too much."[55]

Working-class men, as well, were criticized for dandification, which could imply everything from sexual predation, effeminate passivity, and threats to class hierarchies. In one of the "reply" dialogues, Cato criticizes Miss Phillis's new beau, Sambo: "He got to be quite a Dandy." Sambo copied the fashion of his master's son, Tommy Tightlace, which was not only above his station but also beyond his means: "To-day he speakeee for de dandy dress, tomorrow wear him, de nez day come de tailor bill, and den the cruel constable, and lug him to jail." Scipio agrees but insists that part of the blame lies in the "bad sample set by some of de white people." Emphasizing the theme of respectable humility, Scipio concludes the dialogue by proposing to expel from the African society all those who imitated "de white dandy."[56] Apparently, this was one black attitude that some observers wished working *whites* would emulate.

In fact, the issue of respectability was crucial to many black leaders across the northeastern states. Since the 1790s, black ministers and leaders of voluntary societies had emphasized the republican virtues of industry, thrift, and modest comportment; and in the 1820s, they began to attack excess consumption within their communities with new vigor. These leaders, many of whom were ministers and small businessmen, and thus relatively prosperous, sought to reform their less fortunate, and less virtuous, peers. "I see the greater part of our community following the vain bubbles of life," complained Maria Stewart, a Bostonian moral reformer who became active after her husband, a minister, died around 1828. "Faithful are the wounds of a friend," she emphasized, aware that her comments echoed the attitudes of white racists, "but the kisses of an enemy are deceitful." She urged blacks to strive for middle-class respectability and was not reluctant to admit that they had much room for improvement. Gambling, dancing, and drinking were her main complaints, but she also emphasized inappropriate clothing and immodest comportment. Similarly, the black Philadelphia leader James Forten, son of a prosperous manufacturer, responded to white criticism: "It is undoubtedly true that, among some of our young men, there is a disposition to appear conspicuous in the eyes of the world; but I am fearful it is not of the right stamp, and will excite ridicule, instead of the approbation of the reflecting and respectable." As Stewart concluded in another address, instead of spending money and time on frivolous pursuits, blacks should turn their attention to mental and moral improvement: "Let our money, instead of being thrown away as heretofore, be appropriated for schools and seminaries of learning for our children and youth." She urged that blacks "ought to follow the example of the whites in this respect."[57]

White racism was surprisingly prominent in these bobalition broadsides. In *Miss Philises Bobalition*, the narrator is exasperated by the inequality of a legal system that allowed the rioters to evade punishment: despite the arraignment of various men, they were all declared not guilty. "Mr. Nobody did it!" Phillis expostulates:

> Mr. Nobody, wretch! some invisible d———v———l
> De bigest brick block in a moment he level
> See what he did bout tre months ago;
> He demolish a bilding near four stories high,
> And level the whole in a twink of an eye,
> Pray who did it? Why Nobody know.

It may seem odd that a broadside ostentatiously mocking the victims of the riot would include a seemingly sympathetic and reasonable critique of the biased judicial system. Others complained explicitly about racially unequal justice. In this sense, the Hard Scrabble broadside is typical of a series of bobalition broadsides that sharply point up white racism. Of course, for broadsides to emphasize blacks' reactions to racism is also, in a way, an effort to emphasize, even prolong, their humiliation and their lack of recourse. In *Reply to Bobalition of Slavery* (Boston, 1819), Cato is upset by the publication of a recent bobalition broadside; Scipio explains that he used to feel that way himself but that he's changed his mind: "I guess bess way take no notice ob um, cause den he tink me care some ting bout it."[58]

The broadside's references to white racism might also be seen, like the prosecution of the Hard Scrabble rioters, as part of a broader middle-class critique of lower-class vulgarity and rowdiness. Indeed, the kinds of attacks launched against Abolition Day festivities were also an important concern among an emerging northern middle class, which found a range of traditional ceremonies increasingly worrisome. The *Bosson Artillerum Election, or the African's Reply To the Burlesque on the late Celebration of the Abolition of the Slave Trade* (Boston, 1817) features the ubiquitous Pompey and Phillis. In it, they contrast the Abolition Day ceremonies, which they argue are in fact respectable and only unfairly attacked, with the predominantly white Artillery Election Day festivities, which they depict as rife with disorder and violence. Pompey begins by complaining about the Boston wits who made fun of the Abolition Day procession in bobalition broadsides:

> Shame! Shame! dat we cant celebrate
> As broders, countrymen and frens,
> But every lousy dog must prate
> About our wool and crooked shins!

Phillis then describes the shocking spectacle of the artillery election, which featured intemperance, brawling, destruction of property, and sexual assaults. The contrast is as clear as black and white, yet counters popular prejudices: "'Mong us, 'poor, brack, stupid, ignorant thick lip, crook shin Affrican' perfect, love, peace and unitee prevail: but mong 'de polite, de learned, de refined, de thin skull and trait shin white citizen' dare was tumult and fusion, cursing and swearing, drinking and fighting, and ebery oder indecencee you can tink ob."[59] In fact, it was for these reasons that Massachusetts officials ended Artillery Day festivals around this time. By the 1820s, temperance was already becoming a major reform movement across the Northeast. And in many states, general elections, traditionally raucous, drunken events in early summer, were moved to dates in late fall or winter in the hope that cool weather and a curtailed supply of alcohol would encourage better decorum. The concerns raised humorously in the *Bosson Artillerum Election* were thus actually part of a serious discussion of traditional public culture and a new bourgeois emphasis on order and temperance. But the tone of these broadsides is not easy to pin down. Were they primarily expressions of middle-class anxieties? Or examples of working-class resistance, displacement, or fantasy?

Some suggestions lie in the sharp references these bobalition broadsides make to specific political issues, such as the colonization movement, the status of free blacks, and southern slavery. Most conspicuously and consistently attacked was the American Colonization Society, founded in 1816. *Bobolition of Slavery!!!!* (1818) included a typical toast to Henry Clay, the organization's leading national spokesman: "[To] Massa Clay—If he want brack man to go lib in Africa why he no go show him de way heself." In a later broadside, a reference to colonization was followed

by the song "You Don Fool Me." Many broadsides also called attention to southern slavery and northern inequalities. An 1817 broadside proposed a toast to "De
Tate of Virginee—de Merican *Purgatory*": "Where de poor Affrican Emegrant
muss endure Purgation and Laceration to make um fit citizen for Boston Tate."
Bobolition of Slavery!!!! features a toast "[To] De Nited Tate—de land of liberty,
sept he keep slave at de Sout." This and other toasts from this broadside were
reprinted in the following year in an almanac published in Charlestown, South
Carolina, suggesting that no matter how sharp their implications, these humorous
attacks on colonization and slavery were not necessarily taken seriously.[60]

Indeed, other comments on slavery and freedom in these broadsides were far
less sympathetic. The *Grand Celebration! Of the Abolition of the Slave Trade* (Boston,
1817) included a toast asserting, " 'Tis better to be a well fed SLAVE den a dam poor
half starve FREE negur." Clearly the writers of these broadsides were not ignorant of
the antislavery arguments; rather, they expressed disagreement and disdain. Some
broadsides mocked contemporary antislavery writing, such as *Grand Jubelum!!!*
(Boston, 1827), which parodied the genre of sentimental captivity narratives:

> When I was a Picaninny,
> I was brot away from Guinea,
> Tore away from my poor Modder,
> Farder, granny, sisser, broder.
> My cruel Massa hard did treat me,
> Starve me, kick me, cuff and beat me,
> Call me tick-skull, wool-head mink,
> And say I lousy, rotten—stink!

Such callous mockery of black hardships and accomplishments would seem to have
been a deliberate display of insensibility—a conscious rejection of refined middle-
class values.[61]

Perhaps because of this kind of tension, a surprising number of broadsides focus
on interracial sex, placing the blame for it not on black women but on white men.
One broadside included a toast to "De Fair Sex": "If he skin is brack, white man
like him for all dat." Such aspersions may reflect class-based tensions that the Hard
Scrabble trial sought to obscure. During these years, attacks on prostitution in New
York City often expressed the resentment of working-class men and women against
the more prosperous and putatively respectable men who were assumed to be the
principal patrons of brothels. A number of broadsides more specifically referred

to riots in West Boston that, like the Hard Scrabble riot, were justified as attacks on "bad" black women. *Bobolition of Slavery!!!!* (1818) referred to a recent riot and called attention to the role of white men in creating such disorders: "De rising brack generation—only some of em half white—May de white gemmen not be so fond of crossing de breed." The 1820 *Grand Bobalition of Slavery! By de Africum Shocietee* included a toast to West Boston: "Let de bad house alone, and he no trouble you." This toast was followed by a song that admonished white men to tend to their own domestic responsibilities and not to come looking for trouble in the city's black neighborhood.[62] This logic is, of course, hard to argue with. But these references to white men indulging in disorderly sexuality were always more than calls for reform. By the 1830s, for instance, the charge that antislavery activists favored interracial "amalgamation" became a powerful rallying cry for the large portion of the northern population that opposed the abolition of slavery. And, in any case, drawing attention to white men's sexual access to black women as well as to their ability to tear down black neighborhoods functioned to humiliate, indeed emasculate, black men who could protect neither their women nor their homes.

Riots and sex were two topics that were studiously avoided by the growing body of black writers in the 1820s. But black writers did vigorously discuss the other political themes emphasized in the broadsides: the racism of the Colonization Society, the national crime of slavery, and racial inequality in the free states. On 4 July 1830, the Reverend Peter Williams of New York told his audience, "The festivities of this day serve but to impress upon the minds of reflecting men of colour a deeper sense of the cruelty, the injustice, and oppression of which they have been the victims." The colonization scheme, he argued, was disingenuous: "The colonies planted by white men on the shores of America, so far from benefiting the aborigines, corrupted their morals, and caused their ruin; and yet those who say we are the most vile people in the world, would send us to Africa, to improve the character and condition of the natives." Slavery remained a national crime: "Alas, there are slaves in the midst of freemen; they are slaves to those who boast that freedom is the unalienable right of all; and the clanking of their fetters, and the voice of their wrongs make a horrid discord in the songs of freedom which resound through the land." And in the North, blacks were deprived of their basic rights: "Freedom and equality have been 'put asunder.' The rights of men are decided by the colour of their skin." The problem northern blacks faced lay not in themselves but in white racists. "What hinders our improving here, where schools and colleges abound, where the gospel is preached at every corner, and where all the arts and sciences are verging fast to perfection? Nothing, nothing but prejudice." Other black leaders sounded similar themes. William Whipper, speaking to the black American Moral Reform Society in the 1830s, emphasized the practical effects of racial discrimination: "The lucrative avocations, mechanical arts, and civil associations by which men acquire a knowledge of government and the nature of human affairs, have been almost wholly reserved as a dignified reward, suited only to the interest and use of the fairer complexion." Another writer, Maria Stewart, expostulated on the national sins of slavery and racism: "Oh, America, America, foul and indelible is thy stain! Dark and dismal is the cloud that hangs over thee, for thy cruel wrongs and injuries to the fallen sons of Africa." She goes on: "Thou art almost become drunken with the blood of her slain; thou hast enriched thyself through her toils and labours; and now thou refuseth to make even a small return."[63]

The nature of racial prejudice was addressed in at least one of the bobalition broadsides. *Miss Philises Bobalition* ends with a curious morality of reformation and an implicit promise of respectability. Accepting the notion that the riot appropriately punished the residents of Hard Scrabble for their disorderly living, Phillis promises to reform herself and Pompey:

> So while Pomp earn a little by honest day labour,
> I'll wash and make soap for some of my neighbor,
> And lib by industry as honest folks do:
> Pomp throw by your Fiddle & I'll smash de Gin Bottle
> And soon we'll be able to build up our hovel
> And more steady course we both will pursue.

Reenacting the behavior of the rioters in her own kind of bonfire of the vanities, Phillis warns other blacks to stay away or reform. "Miss Boston keep home your lazy black rabble," she warns, because Hard Scrabble will no longer offer any haven to the unrespectable. Most striking about this narrative of reform is her confidence that the white people of Providence will recognize and honor it.

> I guess it best now for us brack folks be easy,
> And no longer live lives immoral and lazy,
> But gain honest living by sweat ob our brow;
> Depend on't de white folk won't den trouble or 'tack us,
> But de good people of Providence will always respec us,
> As they are wont to respec all good people now.

So the broadside ends, with Miss Phillis fantasizing about achieving respectability. Once again, the tone of this passage is hard to judge. The broadside seems to encourage her faith that black moral reform would be met with white respect and simultaneously to mock her naïve understanding of the nature of prejudice.[64]

In these years, moral reform and white prejudice were the dominant themes of black political writing across the northern states. David Walker's *Appeal to the Coloured People of the World* (Boston, 1828), despite its angry, even violent overtones, was in many ways typical of a growing black moral reform movement that promoted unity among the black people of the world, piety, and civic virtue. Like the fictional Miss Phillis, many of these writers argued that the result of black moral reform would be the destruction of white prejudice, a belief grounded in the assumption that prejudice represented a form of ignorance that would inevitably be vanquished by the light of truth. "Prove to the world," Maria Stewart urged her readers, that "Though black your skin as shades of night, / Your hearts are pure, your souls are white."[65] Similarly, the Reverend Nathaniel Paul, at the time of the Hard Scrabble riot the pastor of Providence's new African Union Church, called for a moral regeneration of free black communities that would overcome white prejudice. "Let us then relieve ourselves from the odious stigma which some have long since cast upon us, that we were incapacitated by the God of nature, for the enjoyment of the rights of freemen, and convince them and the world that although our complexion may differ, yet we have hearts susceptible of feelings, judgment capable of discerning, and prudence sufficient to maintain our affairs with discretion, and by example prove ourselves worthy of the blessings we enjoy." The previous generation did not have the advantages of the rising generation. And this potential justified his optimism: "We look forward with pleasure to that period when men will be respected according to their characters, not according to their complexion."[66]

These well-educated, pious, and relatively affluent leaders were aware that their audiences were not always readily inclined to accept the notion that their poverty and degraded status were entirely their own fault. Leaders such as Maria Stewart had to balance awareness of the obstacles created by white prejudice while delivering an encouraging, empowering message focusing on self-reliance. "I am sensible, my brethren and friends, that many of you have been deprived of advantages," wrote Maria Stewart, "and if any of you have attempted to aspire after high and noble enterprises, you have met with so much opposition that your souls have become discouraged." On the other hand, few could argue with her observation that black northerners had no one but themselves on which to rely. "Never, no, never will the chains of slavery and ignorance burst, till we become united as one, and cultivate amongst ourselves the pure principles of piety, morality, and virtue." Although conscious of the difficulties endured by northern blacks, she insisted a positive attitude was essential: "'I can't' is a great barrier in the way. I hope it will soon be removed, and 'I will' resume its place."[67]

Yet there was good reason to believe that American prejudice would not be overcome so easily—that prejudice might involve more than simple ignorance. The bobalition broadsides, after all, mocked free urban blacks both for their disorderly living and for their pretensions to respectability. And these broadsides showed that racists were not necessarily ignorant of black accomplishments or of their own hypocrisy. A more compelling theory of racial prejudice was developed by Hosea Easton, a minister of both African and Narragansett ancestry. He argued forcefully that the true causes of prejudice are neither color nor ignorance but rather slavery and greed. This was apparent in the radically different attitudes entertained of black men when enslaved or free. "If he should chance to be found in any other sphere of action than that of a slave, he magnifies to a monster of wonderful dimensions, so large that they cannot be made to believe that he is man and a brother. Neither can they be made to believe it would be safe to admit him into stages, steam-boat cabins, and tavern dining-rooms; and not even into meeting-houses, unless he have a place prepared on purpose. Mechanical shops, stores and school rooms, are all too small for his entrance as a man; if he be a slave, his corporeality becomes so diminished as to admit him into ladies' parlors, and into small private carriages, and elsewhere without being disgustful on account of his deformity, or without producing any other discomforture." Prejudice, he argued, "seems to possess a magical power, by which it makes a being appear most odious one moment, and the next beautiful—at one moment too large to be on board a steam-boat, the next, so small as to be convenient almost any where." In general, he concluded of prejudice, "Its malignancy is heightened in proportion as its victim in any way recovers, or has a manifest prospect of recovering the injury."[68]

||| Incorporating Providence |||

The Hard Scrabble riot did not encourage those who dreamed that Americans would one day learn to accept members of all races as equal citizens. Christopher Hall, whose house was pulled down during the riot and whose household furnishings were subsequently sold at public auction by the rioters, responded with defiance. He pulled the detached roof of his house over the cellar hole and lived there with his family all winter. Some sympathetic whites offered assistance, but he turned them down. In the spring, he rejected not just help and Providence but the entire American nation and accepted the help of a colonization organization to move "back" to Africa.[69]

The riot touched some members of the Newport black community in the same way. That fall, the elderly Newport Gardner also joined the colonization movement. After almost seventy years spent living a life of humility and rectitude, working to help local blacks become better Christians and more self-reliant, respectable, and educated, he gave up on the future of Africans in America. "I go to set an example to the youth of my race. I go to encourage the young. They can never be elevated here. I have tried it sixty years—it is in vain." At the end of that winter, he, Christopher Hall, and thirty-odd other Rhode Islanders sailed from Boston for the shores of Liberia. The *Providence Gazette* reported their departure with approval. Over the years the African-born Gardner had never forgotten his native name and had carefully practiced his native language; sadly, soon after arrival he died of a tropical disease.[70] Finally returning to Africa, he found that his body had become too American.

If the riot did not resolve the question of American identity, it certainly did not solve the problem of urban vice, even in the limited area around Hard Scrabble. The notorious Thankful Sharpe survived not only efforts to warn her out of town earlier in the decade but even the riot itself. Her nemesis, George Olney, grew increasingly frustrated. A year after the riot, in October 1825, he and a group of neighbors complained to the town council that Thankful Sharpe and Peter Brown, persons of color, owned houses in Olney Lane that admitted white females of loose character who were visited in the night by sailors. They also complained that Sharpe's son James cohabited in another such house with Marra Cleman, a "White Girl" from the neighboring town of Smithfield. Brought before the town council several days later, the mother and son, identified as "Mulattoes," were examined, the complaint was verified, and both of them were ordered to leave town within a fortnight. In accordance with a recently passed state law concerning disorderly people of color, they were told that if they returned to town they would be liable to be bound out to service. A year after that, James was still in town. In the spring of 1826, the town council summoned him and another man to be examined for keeping a disorderly house. James Sharpe evidently knew better than to appear, but the other man was a legal inhabitant of the town and was ordered to break up the disorderly house; the woman he was living with was ordered out of town. Adding fuel to the fire, a Providence newspaper published a report from the Court of General Sessions of the Peace in which John L. Jones, a colored man, was prosecuted for keeping a disorderly house. Frustrated by the town's laxity in October 1825, George Olney also circulated an angry petition to the General Assembly complaining of the "evil coming from disorderly houses in Olney Lane" and the impotence of both the town and the courts. Such complaints only mounted in subsequent years. Nostalgia for "faithful service" was also echoed in rosy memories of the domestic fidelity that prevailed under slavery—as in the newspaper obituary of Cesar Lyndon's long-lived wife who died in the 1820s.[71] By the 1830s, groups attempting to reform the problems of drinking, prostitution, irreligion, incomplete families, poor sanitation, and slavery in the southern states proliferated.

The riot also helped convince the people of Providence to accept a new conception of the local polity and the role of governance. This argument was explicitly made by the anonymous editor of the published report of the trial proceedings, *The Hard-Scrabble Calendar,* which went on sale in Providence by early 1825: "Owing to the difference in the severity of our Police and that of the neighboring cities in relation to the blacks, the number had increased in this town." Although some of these were "industrious and honest individuals" who might be useful members of society in "their department," the mass could "hardly be considered a valuable acquisition to any community, and their return to their respective places from whence they came, probably would not be considered a public calamity." This did not happen because of the "tardiness and inefficiency" of the municipal government. The writer concluded, "As we increase in population, it may be necessary to exchange [the town government] for a form that will not in fact be more despotic than the undefined powers of a Town Council, but which is fitted to carry those powers into speedy and efficient operation."[72] The rhetorical role of dissolute black people was complicated. From one point of view, they served to represent a range of urban vices on which they clearly had no racial monopoly. Thus, this rhetoric can be said to have displaced broader concerns onto the figure of disorderly blacks—symbolically uniting unhappy neighbors, the rioters, sympathetic spectators, and even those who disapproved of rioting. A range of social and cultural conflicts was obscured by the satisfying simplicity of black and white antitheses. Indeed, some may even have sought to use the association of urban vices with people of color to make them seem more distasteful to potentially degenerate whites. From

another point of view, this image of disorderly blacks can be seen as a figure standing for a broader understanding of the disorderly elements of the city, which in this
case included the rioters—a way of arguing for unpopular reforms that a minority
wished to enact on a much larger populace.

If the citizens of Providence found it easy to agree that alien people of color
lay at the heart of urban problems, they did not agree that the days of town-meeting-
style direct democracy were over. Many associated attempts at municipal reform
with business leaders and commercial interests not sympathetic to the needs of
working people. This new, stronger, more centralized model of government can be
seen as a response to the dissolution of older, romanticized communities with orderly hierarchies and deferential styles, which were being replaced with crass,
bumptious, fractious associations of competition and aggression, of fragmenta-
tion and intransigence. After another similar riot in 1831 in which several people
were killed and the militia had to be called in when the mob kept going night after
night, enough consensus was achieved that the governmental structure itself was
changed. The state General Assembly approved a new charter replacing the town-
meeting government of Providence with a city corporation, and the charter was
ratified by the voters in November 1831. The new charter gave the mayor powers to
combat vice and disorder, including authorization to imprison for twenty-four
hours "any dissolute person" who had been "fighting, or being otherwise disorderly."
He could search any building reasonably thought to be occupied by "persons of ill
fame, or to which persons of dissolute, idle or disorderly behavior are suspect to resort."[73] Ultimately, the vote recognized that in the new, large, dynamic city, groups
were too divided and the state needed more power to control them. The role of the
state was now not to harmonize interests—indeed, the electoral polity continued
to thrive on competing interests—but to regulate their interactions and to uphold
order with a supervening authority of surveillance, discipline, and police.

This new city government, a symbol of vigor in the age of industry, born out
of violent efforts to maintain white superiority over blacks, chose as its symbol a
nostalgic image of the founding of the settlement two hundred years earlier. As a
kind of origin myth, it can been seen as nativistic—in a time of increased concern
about immigration not only of Africans but also of Irish Catholics, it exalted the
city's most ancient English forebears. But it is also an image of racial encounter—
one that skipped over the ugly contemporary struggles between blacks and whites
in order to evoke, instead, a pristine vision of an earlier struggle whose ultimate
resolution was well known and perfectly clear. Indeed, to the present day it remains

FIGURE 21. In this celebratory image of the landing of Roger Williams, proud Indian men consult one another about how to greet the newcomers, while women and children cower in the background. Williams and his followers, in contrast, forge boldly forward. The rock and boat echo the iconography of the Pilgrims' landing. The hand gestures echo the Sistine Chapel ceiling: God reaching out to Adam. T. F. Hoppin, "Landing of Roger Williams," Providence, published 27 Jan. 1844. Steel engraving. Courtesy of the Rhode Island Historical Society (RHi X3 2036).

America's preferred image of racial encounter: the first settlers encountering the region's natives. Africans are nowhere to be seen.

Much of the mystery of such images, and no doubt much of their power, came from a sense of retrospective nostalgia. In 1831 President Jackson was completing what was genteelly called the "removal" of the Cherokees to open the lower South for the expansion of slavery. Local politicians were struggling with local Indian leaders to declare the Narragansett tribe legally extinct. The "colored" tenement dweller William Apess had given up his career in Providence as a truckman and had moved to Cape Cod, where he was organizing a revolt for self-governance among the Mashpee Indians. But in contemporary magazines, novels, and the theater, a revival of interest in the seventeenth-century drama of King Philip's War offered the American citizenry a vision of Indians as a race that had already been disappearing for centuries. Their fate was tragic but convenient.[74] The image chosen for the Providence city seal was drawn from a proliferation of engravings of the same subject produced in the previous decade: it is full of heroism, benevolence, and patriarchal tenderness (fig. 21). The image casts an intrepid Roger Williams, his body covered with heavy clothing, standing at the bow of a boat and reaching forward to a languid Narragansett man, almost naked, supine on the rocky shore. Their poses were familiar from engravings of Michelangelo's Sistine Chapel frescoes: God reaching out to Adam.

E P I L O G U E

Democracy in America

Out of the ashes of the War of 1812 rose the white marble dome of the new national Capitol—a building whose magnificence represented the coming of age of the new nation. As the men who had fought in the Revolution were dying and as divisions between slave and free sections of the country were coming to a head in national politics, the building embodied a unifying story of the country's common origins. Carved into the limestone over the grand rotunda's doorways were scenes representing the founding of the colonies: the two largest friezes, on opposite sides of the room, represented Pocahontas saving John Smith and the Pilgrims landing at Plymouth; the other pair presented William Penn, the celebrated pacifist, signing the Elm Tree Treaty, and Daniel Boone, the founder of Kentucky, locked in mortal combat with one Indian while standing on corpse of another. Each of the nation's overlapping regions, North and South, East and West, had its own version of the same story. Peaceable encounters must eventually yield to the forcible: the conquest of Indians by settlers prepared the way for the American nation. On the walls between the doorways hung huge paintings depicting the fathers of the nation in a series of Revolutionary tableaux: the signing of the Declaration of Independence, the British surrenders at Saratoga and Yorktown, and Washington resigning his military commission to return to civilian life.[1] This remarkably unbloody version of the war told the story of the nation's founding as a triumph of heroic self-sacrifice, manly vigor, and republican virtue.

In this vision of the nation's past, the complexion of the American citizen is as white as the limestone and marble out of which the building was constructed. Indians are ultimately vanquished—a compelling fantasy at a time when the "removal" of native peoples and the expansion of U.S. territory westward were increasingly contentious issues in national politics. And although enslaved workers rented from their masters did much of the work of physically constructing the building, black Americans were nowhere represented in these celebratory stories of national origin. By this time, slavery was already emerging as an issue that threatened to divide northeastern public opinion and split the nation into northern and southern sections. Focusing on moments of colonial encounter helped extend the narrative of the nation's origin back, well before the relatively recent Revolution into a more distant, hazy, and mythic past. And in this epic American struggle that began so long ago, the white race had been fated to prevail. The Empire of Liberty, as Thomas Jefferson termed it, was destined for power, prosperity, and an unprecedented experiment with democracy.

At the same time, this story of national origins was coming under scrutiny by observers such as the French political philosopher Alexis de Tocqueville—and under assault from a number of increasingly bold and trenchant Indian and black writers. This developing debate produced contrasting views of America's colonial past and the nature of its democratic future.

I   I   I

While visiting the city of Washington in January 1832, Alexis de Tocqueville was eager to explore the origins of America's national character. In a conversation with former president John Quincy Adams, he agreed that New England represented the best of American democracy and that the region's virtues derived from its "point of origin."[2] As Tocqueville elaborated in *Democracy in America* (1835–40), "The emigrants who colonized America at the beginning of the seventeenth century in some way separated the principle of democracy from all those other principles against which they contended when living in the heart of the old European societies, and transplanted that principle only on the shores of the New World." And of all those founders, the early New England settlers stood out: "In almost all other colonies the first inhabitants have been men without wealth or education, driven from their native land by poverty or misconduct, or else greedy speculators and industrial entrepreneurs." New England settlers, as Tocqueville told the story, were dedicated not to material gain but rather to the "triumph of *an idea*." Coming from the well-to-do classes of England, they migrated as families and devoted themselves to civil order, religious liberty, and social equality. New England was quickly distinguished by an "almost complete equality of conditions"—and, over time, the region "came more and more to present the novel phenomenon of a society homogenous in all its parts." Fortunately, Tocqueville proclaimed, the example was infectious. By the 1830s, "New England principles" had penetrated everywhere throughout the nation.[3]

Tocqueville was also aware that—unlike European nations, which were populated by "shoots of the same stock"—America was inhabited by "three naturally distinct, one might also say hostile races."[4] Tocqueville deplored the brutality of American territorial conquests, particularly President Jackson's cruel policy of Indian removal, and he was concerned about the many evils of slavery. But he could envision no real alternative. As a result of past interactions with whites—and flaws in what he viewed as their natural characters—Indians and blacks were doomed to exclusion from the American body politic.

Of course, this account of early American history is both highly selective and obviously distorted. Tocqueville's account of the legacy of the colonial past reflects the logic of a nineteenth-century "folk" nationalism. Before Europeans arrived, Indians had been a happy and tranquil, if simple, people, but a long series of brutal wars and broken treaties had left them devastated and displaced. Tragically, as Tocqueville saw it, even peaceful interactions with settlers were ultimately destructive: "The Europeans introduced firearms, iron, and brandy among the indigenous population of North America; they taught it to substitute our cloth for the barbaric clothes which had previously satisfied Indian simplicity." Colonial domination disrupted the Indians' geographic roots, family life, cultural traditions, and, ultimately, coherence as a people: "Their homeland has already been lost, and soon they will have no people; families hardly remain together; the common name is lost, the language forgotten, and traces of their origin vanish. The nation has ceased to exist." At root, the problem was not Anglo-American actions but rather the Indians' racial character—which, in this case, was tragically noble. Indians were too independent to subject themselves to the strictures of civil society.

When he turned to the place of blacks in the new nation, Tocqueville was less romantic but just as sweeping in his pronouncements. As he saw it, the problem with blacks was different, but his account of slavery and the "problem" of free blacks closely parallels his account of Indian debasement. "The United States Negro has lost even the memory of his homeland; he no longer understands the language his fathers spoke; he has abjured their religion and forgotten their mores." In addition, slavery destroyed the patriarchal African family: "The Negro has no family; for him a woman is no more than a passing companion of his pleasures, and from their birth his sons are his equals." Degraded to this extent, Tocqueville believed, blacks found freedom not a blessing but a curse. Always sensitive to the perils of unrestrained commercialism, he emphasized the special danger that market relations posed for the former slave: "A thousand new wants assail him, and he lacks the knowledge and energy needed to resist them." As such, blacks were incapable of citizenship, and since nothing could be done about the evil of slavery, one could only hope that the free black population in the North would eventually disappear. In the meantime, one could only resign oneself to the necessity of maintaining slavery in the South. All Tocqueville could offer the Negro was pity: "Ceasing to belong to Africa, he has acquired no right to the blessings of Europe; he is left in suspense between two societies and isolated between two peoples, sold by one and repudiated by the other, in the whole world there is nothing but his master's hearth to provide him with some semblance of a homeland."[5]

In the end, the history of colonialism left Tocqueville with a sad paradox: "The Negro would like to mingle with the European and cannot. The Indian might to some extent succeed in that, but he scorns to attempt it." In the face of Anglo-American dominance, the Negro's servility fated him for slavery; the Indian's pride doomed him to death.[6] For Tocqueville, the matter was mournful but not of great moment. As he saw it, this aspect of America's colonial history was merely a sidelight to his central concern: how America's experiment with democracy could provide a model that might help guide his European homeland in its struggle to reconcile a monarchical past with republican ideals and an increasingly industrial future.

| | |

Around the time that Tocqueville visited the eastern seaboard, a number of articulate northern Indian and black leaders were presenting the public with a very different account of America's colonial past. They agreed that the discovery of America opened up a new era in human history—but not, in their estimation, an auspicious one. As these leaders saw it, European colonialism had been a disaster that even the American Revolution had failed to redeem. New England Indian leaders had begun to articulate an alternative vision of colonial origins well before the Revolution, emphasizing the benevolence of Indians in early encounters and the debt that settlers rightfully owed them.[7] By the 1830s, William Apess, a Pequot-born Methodist minister, emerged as New England's most eloquent Indian spokesman.

As Apess told the story, in 1620 "the Pilgrims landed at Plymouth, and without asking liberty from anyone they possessed themselves of a portion of the country, and built themselves houses, and then made a treaty, and commanded [the Indians] to accede to it. This, if now done, it would be called an insult, and every white man would be called to go out and act the part of a patriot, to defend their country's rights." Instead, the Indians forbore the Pilgrims' presence and even provided them with protection and sustenance: "Had it not been for this humane act of the Indians, every white man would have been swept from the New England colonies." For all this the Indians received no gratitude. Instead, "they were called savages and made by God on purpose for them to destroy."[8] In a passage redolent of his calling as an evangelical preacher, Apess asked his reader to imagine the peoples of the earth assembled together—only one-fifteenth of whom, he pointed out, were white. "Now suppose these skins were put together, and each skin had its national crimes written upon it—which skin do you think would have the greatest?"[9]

Anglo-Americans were surprisingly eager to hear this harsh accounting of their ancestors' colonial crimes. In 1833, an audience at the Hall of the House of Representatives in Boston received Apess warmly, as the newly founded antislavery newspaper, the *Liberator* reported: "In several instances, the speaker made some dexterous and pointed thrusts at the whites, for their treatment of the sons of the forest since the time of the pilgrims, which were received with applause by the audience." By this time, mourning the supposed disappearance of native peoples from settled American territory was already a long tradition, going back before the Revolution. After Andrew Jackson's election to the presidency in 1828, the plight of the Cherokees attracted widespread sympathy—particularly among his political opponents in New England.[10]

This sympathy for the distant Cherokee nation did not extend to Indian groups closer to home as they struggled to rally support for their efforts to defend their territory against grasping settlers and compliant politicians. During the early nineteenth century, most of the Iroquois had been forced to move to Wisconsin, and in the 1830s the Brothertown and New Stockbridge Indians were compelled to follow them. Even within New England, longstanding enclaves on legally established reservations faced new threats. In 1832, members of the Rhode Island legislature attempted to abolish the Narragansett tribe legally and disperse its reserved lands. Apess's special concern during the 1830s was the relationship between the Mashpee Indians of Cape Cod and their state-appointed guardians, who, he felt, obstructed any prospect the Indians ever had of rising out of their degraded status. In his writings, Apess expressed his exasperation with the politics of selective sympathy: "How will the white man of Massachusetts ask favor for the red men of the South, while the poor Marshpee red men, his near neighbors, sigh in bondage?"[11]

As a descendant of seventeenth-century "sons of the forest" who lived in a house, was a Christian minister, and published pamphlets, Apess was living proof that Indians had not disappeared from the New England landscape and that they were quite capable of living civil lives. The problems faced by contemporary Indians, Apess argued emphatically, were the result of white prejudice—which, he argued, was the most conspicuous legacy of America's founding fathers. Referring to the dates commemorating the Pilgrims' Landing and the Declaration of Independence, he declared, "The 22nd of December and the 4th of July are days of mourning and not of joy." The only American principle more than "skin-deep," he quipped, was the principle that "might makes right." He used the story of his own life to demonstrate the wide range of ways in which prejudice against Indians was expressed. "About two years ago, I called at an inn in Lexington; and a gentleman present, not spying me to be an Indian, began to say they ought to be exterminated. I took it up in our defense, though not boisterous but coolly; and when we came to retire, finding that I was an Indian, he was unwilling to sleep opposite my room for fear of being murdered before morning. We presume his conscience pled guilty. These things I mention to show that the doctrines of the Pilgrims has grown up with the people."[12]

Prejudice was also evident in white resistance to Indians' Christian fellowship: "Is not religion the same now under a colored skin as it ever was? If so, I would ask, why is not a man of color respected?"[13] Sex, too, was a visceral symbol of membership in the body politic. "As soon as we begin to talk about equal rights, the cry of amalgamation is set up," he remarked in a passage that points up both the hypocrisy and the arrogance underlying this association. "Should the worst come to the worst, does the proud white think that a dark skin is less honorable in the sight of God than his own beautiful hide?"[14]

The alternate narrative of American origins elaborated by Apess (who lived in Providence with his sister for a time after the Hard Scrabble riot) echoed themes already prominent in the writings of black leaders across the Northeast. These writers often began the story of colonialism long before the Mayflower embarked, placing English colonial ventures squarely in the tradition of the anti-Spanish Black Legend. "Would to God that Columbus with his exploring schemes had perished in Europe ere he touched the American Isles," exclaimed New York minister William Hamilton. "Then might Africa have been spared the terrible calamity she has suffered." After Columbus's fateful voyage, as Russell Parrott of Philadelphia saw it, "the immense treasures that inundated the mother country, the highly coloured descriptions of its soil, climate and resources, spread such an universal desire of gain, that it pervaded all ranks of society, from the peasant to the king." Like Tocqueville, these black leaders assumed that most early settlers were motivated mainly by greed and characterized by ruthlessness; but, unlike him, they argued that this greed and the resulting history of slavery and prejudice were central to the American story. Having destroyed the native peoples of America, these writers argued, the ruthless Europeans turned to the innocent and peaceful nations of Africa to supply laborers for their ever expanding plantations. The results of slavery were the devastation of the African nations, the suffering and death of those transported across the Atlantic, and the enrichment of the American colonies through the blood and sweat of slaves.[15]

These ignoble beginnings had not been redeemed by the Revolution. In the 1770s, black writers such as Phillis Wheatley had pointed out the obvious contradictions between liberty-loving rhetoric and actual slavery and racial inequality. By the 1830s, when an articulate abolitionist movement had began to organize—often provoking a violent backlash—these black leaders viewed self-gratulatory rhetoric about liberty and equality as a humiliating reminder of the ways in which patriotic narratives ignored the presence of and injustices endured by black Americans. When James Mars published an autobiographical narrative during the Civil War, he did so in large part because "many of the people now on the stage of life do not know that slavery ever lived in Connecticut."[16] If northern whites were inclined to forget their region's history of slavery, abolitionists often seemed inclined to focus on the faraway sin of slavery rather than their own participation in increasingly rigid practices of segregation at home. Black frustration with white patriotic rhetoric only mounted. "What have I, or those I represent, to do with your national independence?" demanded Frederick Douglass in a Fourth of July oration in 1852. "Are the great principles of political freedom and of natural justice, embodied in that Declaration of Independence, extended to us?"[17]

At a time when blacks' debasement was increasingly seen in mainstream culture as a reflection of their low natural capacity, black leaders emphasized the historical and contemporary effects of white prejudice. "No, my brethren," James Forten reassured black moral reformers at a national conference in Philadelphia in 1837, "if we are inferior in any respect, it is because they have made us so; it arises from their cruel and partial laws, and customs, and prejudices." One way of defending the natural capacity of blacks was to emphasize the nobility and grandeur of the African past—particularly the role of Egypt in ancient times as the birthplace of Greek and Roman culture. The grandeur of ancient Africa only made the current debasement of contemporary African peoples more appalling, as the leaders of this moral reform conference emphasized in their opening declaration: "We have observed, that in no country under Heaven, have the descendants of an *ancestry* once enrolled in the history of fame, whose glittering monuments stood forth as beacons, disseminating light and knowledge to the uttermost parts of the earth, been reduced to such degrading servitude as that under which we labour from the effect of American slavery and American prejudice."[18]

"What, then, shall we do?" Apess asked about the legacy of colonial atrocity and Revolutionary hypocrisy. "Shall we cease crying and say it is all wrong, or shall we bury the hatchet and those unjust laws and Plymouth Rock together and become friends?" Apess and his black peers hoped that America might eventually come to embody its best ideals. Although they wanted to draw attention to the continuing realities of racial prejudice, they did not want to leave the impression that this prejudice was insuperable. This argument was an attempt to rebut a dominant trend in national politics. In these years, the American Colonization Society attracted widespread support for its assertion that American prejudice—or black inferiority, it didn't make any practical difference—was too ingrained to be overcome. As a result, slaves could never be freed until they could be transported outside the American body politic. Jackson made the same kind of argument to defend his policy of Indian removal: it was necessary to "protect" the Cherokees from the depredations of hostile settlers. In contrast, Apess remained ever hopeful of redeeming American whites: "You and I have to rejoice that we have not to answer for our fathers's crimes; neither shall we do right to charge them one to another." As for the injustice of the past, he concluded, "We can only regret it, and flee from it; and from henceforth, let peace and righteousness be written upon our hearts and hands forever."[19]

Other black northern writers began to argue that as victims, not exploiters, they were morally superior to their white compatriots and were destined to "redeem" the nation for the benefit of all. As the American Moral Reform Society declared in 1837: "We rejoice that we are thrown into a revolution where the contest is not for landed territory, but for freedom; the weapons not carnal, but spiritual; where the struggle is not for blood, but for right." After all, fighting for principle, not self-gain, was the mark of true patriots.[20]

||| ||| |||

This debate about America's colonial origins and Revolutionary legacy had wide-ranging implications, but almost all observers agreed, in the end, to focus on the same, basic question: Should American citizenship remain exclusively white or be opened also to people of color? This question has been at the heart of most debates about civil rights and citizenship ever since—in part because it avoids other questions that can seem too distracting or too dangerous. It was one thing to agree that the American nation had profited from the dispossession of native peoples and the enslavement of Africans—or that both Indians and blacks suffered grievously from the effects of white prejudice. It was quite another to ask how the national character—American democracy, in particular—was shaped by the legacy of colonial conquest, enslavement, and racial domination.

As Tocqueville saw it, Indians and blacks were "like tangents" to the national story—"being American, but not democratic." To some extent, he did acknowledge that, at least for blacks, the story was more complicated than that: "The Indians die as they have lived, in isolation; but the fate of the Negroes is in a sense linked with that of the Europeans. The two races are bound to one another without mingling; it is equally difficult for them to separate completely or to unite." But for Tocqueville, the real danger posed by slavery was the threat that it might disrupt the national union. Consequently, he found a kind of comfort in the national dedication to white supremacy. In the North, where blacks had become free, the races had only grown further apart: "Inequality cuts deep into mores as it is effaced from the laws." Unlike European distinctions of class, he argued, the physical markers of race were indelible. "In the South the master has no fear of lifting the slave up to his level, so he knows that when he wants to he can always throw him down into the dust. In the North the white man no longer clearly sees the barrier that separates him from the degraded race, and he keeps the Negro at a distance all the more carefully because he fears lest one day they be confounded together."[21] Characteristically, Tocqueville assumed that the source of racial prejudice lay in the bodies or character of people of color and not in the ideas or assumptions of white people.

Tocqueville did not turn his attention to the question of how the common colonial legacy shaped the nature of American democracy—even though the emotional tenor of his language suggests some possibilities. Along with his pity, there is something pornographic in his smug account of white claims to racial supremacy: "Seeing what happens in the world, might one not say that the European is to men of other races what man is to the animals? He makes them serve his convenience, and when he cannot bend them to his will he destroys them." Tocqueville's view of blacks as utterly dependent and Indians as implacably independent mirrored broad currents in popular culture that suggest not only disgust and despair but also hints of fantastic identification and nostalgic longing. For generations, American Indians had represented the primal masculine virtue of independence. And, as market relations transformed social relations across the Northeast, accounts of Indian independence and primitivism could express fantasies of resistance to new forms of rigid discipline, self-control, and emasculating gentility. Tocqueville's account of slaves bound helplessly to their master's hearth foreshadows the nostalgic minstrel songs that were just beginning to appear during his visit to America—and promises an equally fantastic escape from the present. The plight of the slave could represent not just the antithesis of the virtuous democratic citizen but also a longing for an authentic past, for geographic rootedness, for a secure sense of belonging that the restless, mobile, new market economy was continually unsettling.[22]

Black and Indian critics did not have much interest in pursuing this line of inquiry. They preferred to emphasize an essentially uplifting vision of American nationalism. As they framed it, the challenge was to realize America's revolutionary potential by opening citizenship to all the nation's inhabitants. This was a vision based not on descent from a pantheon of founding fathers but on the embodiment of shared values and ideals. The national narrative told by black and Indian writers of the early Republic was more troubled than that told by Tocqueville, but it was also, in the end, a story of redemption. Ultimately, they declared, America could be remade as a nation not of prejudices, bloodlines, and hierarchy but of principles, virtues, and equality.

In a tract entitled *Religion and the Pure Principles of Morality, the Sure Principle on Which We Must Build*, the incisive black reformer Maria Stewart chronicled the crimes of white Americans and the benefits they continued to derive from the exploitation of Indians and blacks. "We will tell you, that it is our gold that clothes you in fine linen and purple, and causes you to fare sumptuously every day; and it is the blood of our fathers and the tears of our brethren that have enriched your soils." And, she boldly declared, "WE WILL CLAIM OUR RIGHTS." Yet she also emphasized that this claim for civic inclusion would be accomplished not by violence but by an open-eyed recognition of a long, shared history that bound all inhabitants of the nation together—a history that included a legacy of sexual intermixture. "We will not come out against you with swords and staves, as against a thief; but we will tell you that our souls are fired with the same love of liberty and independence with which your souls are fired. We will tell you that too much of your blood flows in our veins, and too much of your color in our skins, for us not to possess your spirits."[23] Here, indeed, was an alternative to the view of the American history built into the nation's Capitol.

| | |

The nation's Capitol had hardly been completed before it began to seem too small to accommodate the needs of a rapidly expanding nation. By the 1850s, when massive additions were planned, the lands conquered during the war with Mexico had finally fulfilled the vision of a nation spanning the continent. At the same time, these and other western territories threatened to split the nation apart by disrupting the increasingly polarized balance of power between the slave South and the free North. Work on the additions to the Capitol had hardly begun before the Civil War broke out. During the war, the soaring new rotunda was completed. And in 1863, President Lincoln finally acceded to the pleas of northern moral reformers and declared Thanksgiving a national holiday—enshrining New England as America's historical point of origin and moral center. The war decisively settled the question of slavery. And soon thereafter, the subjugation of the last resisting Plains Indians in the 1880s completed the U.S. conquest of its long-envisioned continental territory. By then, after more than a decade of vigorous and increasingly violent struggle, the South had fallen into line with the northern pattern of universal freedom and racial inequality.

A century after the Civil War, the movement for civil rights finally confronted the nation with the question of legal equality for all Americans. Fittingly, it was in the 1960s—when the basic colonial questions of race and equality were engaged by the nation in new, if still limited, ways—that Malcolm X recast Cole Porter's light lyrical reference to the Pilgrims' Landing into a pointed reminder of the centuries-long legacy of American colonial domination. "Our ancestors didn't land on Plymouth Rock," the defiant black leader declared; "Plymouth Rock landed on them."[24] The ramifications of the principle of civil equality under law transformed not just the South but the entire nation. After all, when Malcolm X invoked Plymouth Rock, he was less interested in castigating southern white supremacists than northern racists. But even as the nation has come to agree on the principle of common civil rights, the divisions and dynamics of America's troubled racial past have not disappeared. If anything, we have become more conscious of the limits of defining membership in the body politic as simply a matter of legal rights and more aware of social, cultural, and symbolic ways in which Americans continue to negotiate their respective places in the nation. The colonial legacy of race continues to split Americans apart—it also binds us together.

N O T E S

Abbreviations

AHR	*American Historical Review*
APS	American Philosophical Society Library, Philadelphia
BC	Bristol County, Rhode Island
BPL	Boston Public Library
CCP	Court of Common Pleas
CSA	Connecticut State Archives, Hartford
EWP	Eleazar Wheelock Papers, microfilm ed. (Dartmouth College, 1971)
GCT	General Court of Trials
GSP	Court of General Sessions of the Peace
HSP	Historical Society of Pennsylvania, Philadelphia
JAH	*Journal of American History*
JCB	John Carter Brown Library, Brown University, Providence
KC	King's County, Rhode Island (renamed Washington County after the Revolution)
LCP	Library Company of Philadelphia
MBP	Moses Brown Papers
MHS	Massachusetts Historical Society, Boston
MSA	Massachusetts State Archives
NA	National Archives, Washington, D.C. (Revolutionary War Pension Applications)
NC	Newport County, Rhode Island
NEQ	*New England Quarterly*
NHS	Newport Historical Society
PC	Providence County, Rhode Island
PTP	Providence Town Papers, Rhode Island Historical Society, Providence
RCRI/RSRI	*Records of the Colony of Rhode Island* (1636–1792), ed. John Russell Bartlet, 10 vols. (Providence, 1856–65). Title changes for volumes after 1776 to *Records of the State of Rhode Island*.
RIH	*Rhode Island History*
RIHS	Rhode Island Historical Society, Providence
RIJRC	Rhode Island Supreme Court Judicial Records Center, Pawtucket

RI Notarial	Notarial Records, Rhode Island State Archives, Providence. Cited by volume and item number.
RI Petitions	Petitions, Rhode Island State Archives, Providence. Cited by volume and item number.
RISA	Rhode Island State Archives, Providence
SC	Superior Court
SWJP	*The Papers of Sir William Johnson. Prepared for Publication by the [State of New York] Division of Archives and History,* 14 vols. (Albany, 1921–65)
WC	Washington County, Rhode Island (before the Revolution, King's County)
WMQ	*William and Mary Quarterly,* 3d ser.

Introduction ||| *After Origins*

1. Ellouise Baker Larsen, *American Historical Views on Staffordshire China,* rev. ed. (Garden City, N.Y., 1950), 8–9.

2. Carroll Smith-Rosenberg, "Dis-Covering the Subject of the 'Great Constitutional Discussion,' 1786–1789," *JAH* 79, no. 3 (1992): 841–73. Jill Lepore, *A Is for America: Letters and Other Characters in the Newly United States* (New York, 2002).

3. Alexis de Tocqueville, *Democracy in America,* trans. George Lawrence, ed. J. P. Mayer (New York, 1988), 40. Jack P. Greene, *Pursuits of Happiness: The Social Development of Early Modern British Colonies and the Formation of American Culture* (Chapel Hill, N.C., 1988).

4. C. Vann Woodward, *The Strange Career of Jim Crow,* 3d ed. (New York, 1974).

One ||| *Common Ground*

1. *Gentleman's Progress: The Itinerarium of Dr. Alexander Hamilton,* 1744, ed. Carl Bridenbaugh (Chapel Hill, N.C., 1948), 98.

2. Hopkins to Gideon Hawley, 7 June 1762, quoted in Joseph A. Conforti, *Samuel Hopkins and the New Divinity Movement: Calvinism, the Congregational Ministry, and Reform in New England between the First and Second Great Awakenings* (Grand Rapids, Mich., 1981), 54.

3. Richard White, *The Middle Ground: Indians, Empires, and Republics in the Great Lakes Region, 1650–1815* (New York, 1991). Fred Anderson, *The Crucible of War: The Seven Years' War in British North America, 1754–1766* (New York, 2000).

4. James Merrell, *Into the American Woods: Negotiators and the Pennsylvania Frontier* (New York, 1999). Eric Hobsbawm and Terence Ranger, eds., *The Invention of Tradition* (New York, 1983), intro. See also E. P. Thompson, *Customs in Common: Studies in Traditional Popular Culture* (New York, 1991). James C. Scott, *Domination and the Arts of Resistance: Hidden Transcripts* (New Haven, 1992).

5. Wigwams of sachems: Roger Williams, *A Key into the Language of America* (London, 1643), 133; *Extracts from the Itineraries and Other Miscellanies of Ezra Stiles . . ., 1755–1794,* ed. Franklin B. Dexter (New Haven, 1916), 156 (24 Oct. 1761); hereafter cited as *Itineraries of Ezra Stiles.* Ninigret's finances: Joseph Stanton, Accounts with Charles Ninigret, Sept.

1731–Feb. 1736, Champlin Papers. Ninigret's trustees: *RCRI* 5:451. Charles Ninigret quote: examination of James Robens, 1 Sept. 1746 and Aug. 1757, in loose files associated with *Thomas Ninigret v. Charles Ninigret (in stead of Benoni Sash and Jonathan Tidal)*, CCP KC, Aug. 1757. At the CCP KC, Feb. 1756, Charles Ninigret was admitted as defendant in the case *T. Ninigret v. B. Sash and J. Tindal*, D:686, and the case was continued; in Oct. 1757, the case was appealed to the SC KC, A:229, and continued to Oct. 1759, A:258; in an unusual move, the parties agreed to try the case in Massachusetts, but subsequently they settled the matter privately. All the above at the RIJRC. These examinations of Robens were not included in the 13 Feb. 1753 copy in the Christopher Champlin Papers, RIHS.

6. Charles Augustus Ninigret to George II, king of Great Britain, Misquammacuck, alias Westerly, 13 Jul. 1727, photocopy in Campbell Collection, RIHS. Williams, *Key into the Language of America*, 132. Roger Larkin, deposition, 5 Sept. 1743, *Charles Ninigret v. Samuel Clark* (appeal), SC NC, Sept. 1743, RIJRC.

7. Paul R. Campbell and Glenn W. LaFantasie, "Scattered to the Winds of Heaven— Narragansett Indians, 1676–1880," *RIH* 37, no. 1 (1978): 70.

8. William S. Simmons and George Aubin, "Narragansett Kinship," *Man in the Northeast* 9 (1975): 21–31. Eric Spencer Johnson, "'Some by Flatteries and Others by Threatenings': Political Strategies among Native Americans of Seventeenth-Century New England" (Ph.D. diss., University of Massachusetts, 1993). *Itineraries of Ezra Stiles*, 142 (31 Oct. 1761).

9. *RCRI* 3:68, 144. Appeal to king: Howard M. Chapin, *Sachems of the Narragansetts* (Providence, 1931), 91–92.

10. Joseph Garrett challenged Ninigret in Sept. 1699: Chapin, *Sachems of the Narragansetts*, 94. Afterwards, Ninigret granted land to important settlers: deed of 1,200 acres to Samuel Sewall, 23 Sept. 1699, RI Notarial 2:102; deed of 200 acres to Benedict Arnold, 25 Sept. 1699, RI Notarial 2:107; deed of land to John Holmes, 27 Sept. 1699, RI Notarial 2:106; deed of 140 acres of land to Christopher Champlin, 21 Sept. 1700, RI Notarial 2:123. Sewall describes the process by which Ninigret signed the deeds and had them duly authorized: *The Diary of Samuel Sewall, 1675–1729*, ed. H. Halsey Thomas, 2 vols. (New York, 1971), 1:414 (25 Sept. 1699). Evidence that Ninigret was his father's heir around 1705: William Champlin, deposition, 5 Sept. 1743, *Ninegret v. Clark*, SC KC, Sept. 1743, RIJRC. An Aug. 1703 account of the Ninigret family lineage among the manuscripts of the Reverend John Callender of Newport: *Itineraries of Ezra Stiles*, 27–28 (10 July 1762). Testimony of George Wightman, 1 May 1704, and deposition of Nathaniel Waterman, 6 Feb. 1706, Indian File, NHS. Ninigret, deed of 300 acres of land to William Davell, 13 Nov. 1705, RI Notarial 3:4. Connecticut records include "Alleged Petition of Nenegrat, sachem to R.I. Assembly," Oct. 1705, and "Questions to be put to Nenegrat," Trumbull Papers 22:41, 42a–b, CSA. See also Narragansett Country material in the Trumbull Papers published in the *Collections of the Massachusetts Historical Society* (hereafter cited as *MHS Collections*), 5th ser., 9 (1885). On the Atherton Company: Sydney V. James, *Colonial Rhode Island: A History* (New York, 1975), 65–68, 85–87, 104–7.

11. Ninigret, deed, 28 Mar. 1709, RI Notarial 3:273–76. Ninigret ("Ninecraft alias Wayaconshett"), deed of 150 acres to Christopher Champlin Jr., 29 June 1712; deed of land to Christopher Champlin from "the Committee Appointed to Assist Ninnegret in Disposing

Some of his Lands," 24 Dec. 1712 (confirmed 18 June 1731), both in Champlin Papers. On William III: William Blackstone, *Commentaries on the Laws of England*, 4 vols. (London, 1766–69), 1:286.

12. Overseers appointed in 1717 included Captain Joseph Stanton; *RCRI* 4:151–52, 220–21. Ninigret, will, 15 Mar. 1717 (18–10), and Samuel Clark, deposition, 12 Sept. 1746 (20–21), in copy case of *Charles Ninigret (in stead of Samuel Clark) v. Thomas Ward*, CCP KC, May 1749, in files of the appeal, SC KC, A:33, RIJRC. Challenge of 1717: *RCRI* 4:234, 236.

13. Letter to the editor, dated Newport, 26 Jan. 1723, *New-England Courant* (Boston), 4 Feb. 1723, in response to an account of Ninigret's funeral in the no longer extant *Boston Gazette*, 21–28 Jan. 1723.

14. Pennewis: Simon Ray, deposition, 2 Sept. 1743, *Ninegret v. Clark*, SC NC, Sept. 1743, RIJRC. On the marriage of Betty Coheis, see the deposition of her father: Tobias Coheis, 3 Apr. 1741, Champlin Papers, 1:11. The Coheis deposition is an example of evidence their attorney Christopher Champlin collected but did not introduce in court.

15. Living in a house: Enoch Kinyon, deposition, 5 Sept. 1743, *C. Ninigret v. S. Clark*, SC NC, Sept. 1743, RIJRC. Ninigret's trustee paid William Stevens two pounds for a pair of gravestones on 1 June 1734: Joseph Stanton, Accounts of Charles Ninigret, 1731–36, RIHS. George Ninigret headstone (1732), Charlestown, R.I.

16. Babcock: William Basset and Experience Bassett, deposition, 5 Sept. 1743; "bastard": Roger Larkin, deposition, 5 Sept. 1743; both from *C. Ninigret v. S. Clark*, SC NC, Sept. 1743, RIJRC. Ninigret: examination of James Robens, 1 Sept. 1746 and Aug. 1757, in loose files associated with *T. Ninigret v. C. Ninigret (in stead of Benoni Sash and Jonathan Tindal)*. CCP KC, Aug. 1757, RIJRC; again, this testimony was not included in the earlier Champlin Papers copy.

17. *C. Ninigret v. S. Clark*, SC NC, Sept. 1743, RIJRC. Blackstone, *Commentaries on the Laws of England*, 1:433–40. R. B. Outhwaite, *Clandestine Marriage in England, 1500–1850* (London, 1995).

18. William Champlin, deposition, 22 Nov. 1742, *C. Ninigret v. J. Stanton*, CCP KC, Aug. 1743, RIJRC. Joseph Stafford, deposition, 11 Aug. 1746, *Thomas Ninigret v. Samuel Clarke*, CCP KC, Aug. 1746, RIJRC. Samuel Perry, deposition, 16 Feb. 1756, *Charles Ninigret (in stead of Samuel Clark) v. Thomas Ninigret*, in loose files associated with *T. Ninigret v. C. Ninigret (in stead of B. Sash and J. Tindal)*, CCP KC, Aug. 1757.

19. *New York Gazette*, 19–26 May 1735. *Itineraries of Ezra Stiles*, 130 (16 Oct. 1761).

20. On this ceremony, see the copy case of *Charles Ninigret v. Joseph Stanton (in stead of Samuel Clark)*, action of account, CCP KC, Aug. 1743, particularly the depositions of John Hill (43–45), Thomas Noyes (64), and James Congdon (65). The evidence in this case and related ones is complicated: cases were repeatedly continued and appealed, and evidence from one case was sometimes reused in another; moreover, at each stage new depositions and examinations could be introduced, old evidence was attested to by witnesses, and sometimes witnesses gave new testimony under interrogation and cross-examination. In addition, attorneys like Christopher Champlin, whose papers are at the RIHS, sometimes collected evidence that they did not end up introducing in court. For example, some of the evidence in the case *C. Ninigret v. S. Clark* was collected in Nov. 1742; Charles Ninigret then

introduced two actions against Clark at the CCP KC in Feb. 1743—and action of trespass and ejectment (for possession of land) and action of account (for money due). The action of account was continued to the Aug. 1743 term, and in the meantime Joseph Stanton successfully petitioned the General Assembly (Petitions 5:16, May 1743) to be admitted as defendant instead of Clark. Ninigret objected and in Sept. 1743 appealed the case to the SC NC, where additional evidence was collected. The case returned to the CCP KC in Feb. 1744 (B:113) and was finally decided by the SC NC in Mar. 1744 (C:148) in Stanton's favor. The SC NC denied Ninigret an appeal to the Rhode Island Court of Equity, and so his attorney promised an appeal to the king in council.

21. Belt of wampum: John Hill Jr., deposition, 4 Aug. 1746, *Thomas Ninigret v. Samuel Clark,* CCP KC, Aug. 1746, RIJRC.

22. *C. Ninigret v. J. Stanton,* CCP KC, Aug. 1743, copy case; see especially James Robins, deposition, 17 June 1742, and testimony, Aug. 1743 (36–39); Sompauwit, deposition, 17 Nov. 1742, and testimony, Aug. 1743 (49–53); John Thompson, testimony, Aug. 1743 (40–41).

23. Threat: Joseph Stanford, deposition, 11 Aug. 1746, and John Potter, deposition, 11 Aug. 1746, *T. Ninigret v. S. Clarke,* CCP KC, Aug. 1746, RIJRC. Kate's explanation: Sarah Tom, deposition, 2 Aug. 1753, Champlin Papers, 1:33.

24. Petition of George Augustus Ninigret to the General Assembly, May 1740, and Petition of Toby (Tobias) Coheis, Samson Potter, Joseph Coheis, John Tiask, Samuel Niles, William Sachem, and Ephraim Coheis to the General Assembly, June 1741, RI Petitions 4:86. Memorandum, *C. Ninigret v. S. Clark,* SC NC, Sept. 1743.

25. Blackstone, *Commentaries on the Laws of England,* 2:200–240 (title by descent), 1:454–59 and 2:247–49 (bastards). Parliament could also direct the course of royal succession (1:191–95) or even make a bastard legitimate by a special act (1:459). Howard Nenner, *The Right to Be King: The Succession of the Crown in England, 1603–1714* (Chapel Hill, N.C., 1995). On the power of symbolism and legitimacy, see Scott, *Domination and the Arts of Resistance.*

26. Mary alias Oskoosooduck, deposition, 3 Sept. 1746, *Thomas Ninigret v. B. Sash and J. Tindall,* CCP KC, Aug. 1755, copy case 59–60, Champlin Papers.

27. Tobias Coheis assault: Sarah Tom, deposition, *C. Ninigret v. S. Clark,* CCP KC, Aug. 1743, copy case 32–34, RIJRC. Kate's family: Capper Harry, deposition, 2 Sept. 1743, *C. Ninigret v. S. Clark,* SC NC, Sept. 1743, RIJRC.

28. Jonathan Kinyon, deposition, 18 Oct. 1752, *T. Ninigret v. B. Sash and J. Tindall,* CCP KC, Aug. 1755, RIJRC. Examinations of 1753: RI Notarial 6:81. War of 1745: *Itineraries of Ezra Stiles,* 142 (31 Oct. 1761).

29. Depositions of Edward Deake, Ephraim Coheis, Thomas Coheis, and Anthony King, *Nathan Kinyon v. William Welch,* CCP KC, Feb. 1772, RIJRC.

30. Daniel K. Richter, *Facing East from Indian Country: A Native History of Early America* (Cambridge, Mass., 2001), 151–88.

31. *Thomas Ninigret v. Samuel Clark,* CCP KC, Aug. 1746, copy case in 1757 appeal, RIJRC: esp. depositions of Ephraim Coheis, 4 Aug. 1746, and John Hill Jr, 4 Aug. 1746.

32. Roger Wappy's land: Jonathan Kinyon, deposition, 10 Feb. 1758, RI Petitions 10:[49]. Evidence about Thomas Ninigret's investiture: *T. Ninigret v. S. Clark* (appeal), SC NC, Sept. 1746, copy case in Champlin Papers.

33. William Crandell, deposition, 29 Aug. 1746, in loose files associated with *T. Ninigret v. C. Ninigret (in stead of Benoni Sash and Jonathan Tindal)*, CCP KC, Aug. 1757, RIJRC.

34. John A. Sainsbury, "Indian Labor in Early Rhode Island," *NEQ* 48, no. 3 (1975): 378–93. Harold W. Van Lonkhuyzen, "A Reappraisal of the Praying Indians: Acculturation, Conversion, and Identity at Natick, Massachusetts, 1646-1730," *NEQ* 63, no. 3 (1990): 396–427.

35. John Callender, *An Historical Discourse, on the Civil and Religious Affairs of the Colony of Rhode-Island* (Boston, 1739), reprinted in *Collections of the Rhode Island Historical Society* (hereafter cited as *RIHS Collections*) 4 (1838): 132–33. A similar view: George Berkeley, *A Sermon before the Society for the Propagation of the Gospel* (London, 1731). The first extant colony-wide enumeration: Census of the Inhabitants of Rhode Island, 1774, RISA.

36. Account of Christopher Champlin with "Peter Coyhese & his Squaw Betty Peter in Company," 1720-27, *Christopher Champlin v. Betty Peter*, CCP KC, June 1732, copy case in *Champlin v. Peter*, SC KC, Mar. 1733, RIJRC.

37. *Christopher Champlin v. Betty Thompson*, SC NC, Sept. 1733, files, RIJRC.

38. Account of Christopher Champlin with Betty Peter, 19 Sept. 1727-31, *Champlin v. Peter*, SC KC, Mar. 1733, files, RIJRC. The negotiation: Joseph Champlin and Ann Champlin, deposition, 27 Mar. 1732, in *Champlin v. Thompson*, SC NC, Sept. 1733. Champlin family: Ann Marie Plane, *Colonial Intimacies: Indian Marriage in Early New England* (Ithaca, N.Y., 2000), 140, 229 n. 50. Legal culture: Mary Sarah Bilder, "Salamanders and Sons of God: Transatlantic Legal Culture and Colonial Rhode Island" (Ph.D. diss., Harvard University, 2000).

39. "To the halves": James Clark, deposition, 12 Feb. 1748; workmen: Christopher Kinyon, deposition, 12 Feb. 1748; Robin living with Clark: Tacy Saunders, deposition, 4 Aug. 1757; in loose files associated with *T. Ninigret v. C. Ninigret (in stead of Benoni Sash and Jonathan Tindal)*, CCP KC, Aug. 1757, RIJRC. "Champlin's Indian": Thomas Baker, deposition, 28 Dec. 1732; "lived with": Pepewas (Peter's mother), deposition, 30 Aug. 1733; both in *Champlin v. Thompson*, SC NC, Sept 1733, RIJRC.

40. *Itineraries of Ezra Stiles*, 155–56 (24 Oct. 1761), and Stiles, "Memoir of the Pequots," *MHS Collections* 10 (1810): 101–5. William C. Sturtevant, "Two 1761 Wigwams at Niantic, Connecticut," *American Antiquity* 40, no. 4 (1975): 437–44; fig. 2c drawn by Edward G. Schumacher at the author's direction.

41. Kathleen Bragdon, "The Material Culture of the Christian Indians of New England, 1650-1775," in *Documentary Archeology in the New World*, ed. Mary C. Beaudry (New York, 1989), 126–31. The accounts of a Charlestown storekeeper show many Indians in his debt in the early 1760s: petition for bankruptcy of Peter Boss Jr., Mar. 1763, CCP KC, RIJRC. *Boston News-Letter*, 19–26 Mar. 1741.

42. *Acts and Laws . . . of Rhode Island . . .* (Boston, [1719]), 85. Complaint of Nantucket Indians: Daniel R. Mandell, *Behind the Frontier: Indians in Eighteenth-Century Eastern Massachusetts* (Lincoln, Nebr., 1996), 70. Daniel Vickers, "The First Whalemen of Nantucket," *WMQ* 40 (1983): 577–78. Excluded Indian translator: Record, *C. Ninigret v. S. Clark*, CCP KC, Feb. 1744, B:113, RIJRC.

43. Kathleen M. Brown, "The Anglo-Algonquian Gender Frontier," and Theda Perdue,

"Women, Men, and American Indian Policy: The Cherokee Response to 'Civilization,'" in *Negotiators of Change: Historical Perspectives on Native American Women,* ed. Nancy Shoemaker (New York, 1995), 26–48, 90–114.

44. Men fighting in wars: *Itineraries of Ezra Stiles,* 131–32 (16 Oct. 1761), 141–42 (31 Oct. 1761). Joseph Fish to Andrew Oliver, 12 June 1760, Misc. Bound, MHS.

45. John Daniel to Wheelock, 30 Nov. 1767, Charlestown, EWP 767630.3. Marketing fish: James Congdon Sr., deposition, 9 Apr. 1783, *Samuel Niles et al. v Peleg Cross,* SC WC, Apr. 1783, RIJRC. Taxes: petition of Thos. Ninigret and forty-four others to the General Assembly, Jan. 1757, RISA. Another Narragansett man the town unsuccessfully attempted to tax: Simeon Matthews, 26 Feb. 1765, RI Petitions 11:195.

46. On houses and wigwams: *The King v. Barsheba Harry and Betty Seepit,* SC KC, Oct. 1768, RIJRC. Mandell, *Behind the Frontier,* 80–116. A dispute within the tribe over land and timber: *Anthony Sock v. Roger Wappy and Isaac Wappy,* CCP KC, Feb. 1758, E:191; Thomas Lewis, deposition, 8 Feb. 1758; Wappy and Wappy, June 1758, RI Petitions 10:48. Sawmill: David Suketer, James Wappy, Christopher Harry, et al., 9 Mar. 1789, RI Petitions 25:69. See also Mathew Robinson to Johnson, South Kingstown, 20 Mar. 1765, *SWJP* 11:640–43. Gary Kulik, "Dams, Fish, and Farmers: Defense of Public Rights in Eighteenth-Century Rhode Island," in *The Countryside in the Age of Capitalist Transformation,* ed. Steven Hahn and Jonathan Prude (Chapel Hill, N.C., 1985), 1–50. On Shattock's house and hut: Isaac Nye, deposition, 13 Feb. 1773, *Thomas Shearman v. Daniel Knowles et al.,* SC KC, Apr. 1773, RIJRC.

47. "Thomas Ninegrett to the Commissioners for Propagating the Gospel in New England," Narragansett, 26 Apr. 1765, Misc. Bound, MHS.

48. One complaint about Wheelock came from a Narragansett father: John Daniel to Wheelock, 30 Nov. 1767, Charlestown, EWP 767630.3. Gideon Hawley to James Freeman, 15 Nov. 1802, Gideon Hawley Papers, MHS.

49. On Massachusetts: Mandell, *Behind the Frontier,* 164–202. The Rhode Island Census of 1774 identified about five hundred "Indians" in Charlestown, RIHS. According to Ezra Stiles, counts procured by the Boston commissioners around 1732 and 1740 found about fifty-one families; *Itineraries of Ezra Stiles,* 21 (2 Sept. 1761). In 1761 Stiles himself counted, in addition to King Ninigret and his wife, 42 married men, about 40 wives, 12 widows, 70 boys, and 82 girls; *MHS Collections* 10 (1810): 104. In 1762, a count by the tribe intended to "shew the Need of a Schoolmaster for the Indian children" produced a much larger figure: "about Six Hundred Souls—belonging to Ninegret's Tribe & exclusive of other Indians"; *Itineraries of Ezra Stiles,* 54 (15 Apr. 1761).

50. Wheelock to Johnson, Lebanon, 19 Aug. 1767, EWP 767469.2. James Clifford, "Identity in Mashpee," in *The Predicament of Culture: Twentieth-Century Ethnography, Literature, and Art* (Cambridge, Mass., 1988), 277–348. Ruth Wallis Herndon and Ella Wilcox Sekatau, "The Right to a Name: The Narragansett People and Rhode Island Officials in the Revolutionary Era," *Ethnohistory* 44, no. 3 (1997): 433–62. Jack Campisi, "The Emergence of the Mashantucket Pequot Tribe, 1637–1975," in *The Pequots in Southern New England: The Fall and Rise of an American Indian Nation,* ed. Laurence M. Hauptman and James D. Wherry (Norman, Okla., 1990), 117–40.

51. Around 1750 Thomas was reportedly living in Stonington, and his house was in dis-

repair; "Some Cursory Remarks made by James Birket in his Voyage to North America, 1750–1751," *RIHS Collections* 13, no. 2 (1920): 60–65. National Society of the Colonial Dames of America in the State of Rhode Island, *Old Houses in the South County of Rhode Island* (Providence, 1932). Campbell and LaFantasie, "Scattered to the Winds of Heaven," 73. Settlement: Joseph Crandal, examination, 4 June 1760, Champlin Papers, 1:93. Ninigret to Johnson, 20 Mar. 1765, *SWJP* 11:637–40.

52. James Niles and 137 others to Thomas Ninigret, [Charlestown, 6 Apr. 1766], RISA. "Act Concerning the Rhode Island Indians," 20 Aug. 1759, *SWJP* 3:124–26.

53. Matthew Graves to Johnson, [3 June 1765], *SWJP* 4:756–58. The petition of John Shattock to King George III (1768) claimed that there had been about twelve thousand acres in the 1750s and only about four thousand by 1768. Hostile attorney Matthew Robinson estimated Ninigret's debt at £50,000 to £60,000 Rhode Island "old tenor"(or about £2000 sterling); The case against Thomas Ninigret, 15 Nov. 1764, *SWJP* 11:409–12. Conversion based on John J. McClusker, *Money and Exchange in Europe and America, 1600 1775: A Handbook* (Chapel Hill, N.C., 1978).

54. Ephraim Coheis and Samuel Niles, petition on behalf of the rest of the Narragansett Tribe to the Rhode Island General Assembly, [28 Feb. 1765], *SWJP* 4:660–63; see also an undamaged copy: *RCRI* 6:357 ff. Matthew Robinson to William Johnson, South Kingstown, 20 Mar. 1765, *SWJP* 11:640–43.

55. Petition of "a large part of the Narragansett Tribe of Indians" to the General Assembly, June 1763, Narragansett Indian File 15, RISA. Tobias Shattock to Johnson, [ca. 1764], James N. Arnold, *A Statement of the Case of the Narragansett Tribe of Indians, as shown in the Manuscript Collection of Sir William Johnson . . . To which Are Added a Few Other Important Papers Illustrating the Case* (Newport, 1896), 33–35. Ephraim Coheis and Samuel Niles on behalf of the rest of the tribe of the Narragansett Indians, [June 1764], RI Petitions 11:2–89.

56. "Catalogue of the names of those who agreed to accept the sachem's offer made before the General Assembly," Aug. 1763, and Resolution of the General Assembly, 5 Aug. 1763, Narragansett Indian File 13; Report of Joseph Lippett et al., June 1764, Narragansett Indian File 16, RISA.

57. Thomas Ninigret to Johnson, 20 Mar. 1765, *SWJP* 11:637–40.

58. Ninigret's statement: Ephraim Coheis and Samuel Niles, 15 June 1764, RI Petitions 11:2–89. See also Samuel Niles, Ephraim Coheis, and thirty-six others to Johnson, 15 Nov. 1765, *SWJP* 11:412–14. Deed of 1709: Samuel Niles and John Shattock to Johnson, Charlestown, 21 Feb. 1767, *SWJP* 5:497.

59. On land tenure for three generations: Ephraim Coheis, deposition and examination, 10 Feb. 1768, *Sachem v. Niles*, SC KC, Apr. 1769, B:202, files, RIJRC. Joseph Kinson, deposition, 9 Apr. 1783, *Samuel Niles et al. v. Peleg Cross*, SC KC, Apr. 1783, C:31–33, RIJRC. On the "twig and turf" ritual: Roger Hassard, deposition, 7 Aug. 1772, *Thomas Shearman v. Daniel Knowles et al.*, SC KC, Apr. 1773, RIJRC; State of Rhode Island, *Report of the Commission on the Affairs of the Narragansett Indian . . . 1881* (Providence, 1881), 151, 100–101, 109. On the livery of seisin: Lawrence M. Friedman, *A History of American Law* (New York, 1973), 54–55, 207.

60. Work for sachems: Joseph Kinyon, deposition, 9 Apr. 1783, *Niles v. Cross*. Rent: James Daniel, deposition, 8 Feb. 1768, *Sachem v. Niles*.

61. Mary Sock (alias Mary Sam), deposition, 8 Feb. 1768, *Niles v. Cross.* Gary J. Kornblith and John M. Murrin, "The Making and Unmaking of an American Ruling Class," in *Beyond the American Revolution*, ed. Alfred F. Young (DeKalb, Ill., 1993), 28–79.

62. Depositions of Thomas Paul, Thomas Lewis, and Mary Sock, 8 Feb. 1768, *Sachem v. Niles.* Lucy Simler, "Tenancy in Colonial Pennsylvania: The Case of Chester County," *WMQ* 42 (1986): 542–69.

63. Bernard Bailyn, *The Ideological Origins of the American Revolution* (Cambridge, Mass., 1967).

64. George Ninigret: Joseph Coheis, deposition, 11 Feb. 1768, and John Shattock deposition, 10 Feb. 1768, both in *Sachem v. Niles.* Petition of James Niles and 156 others to Thomas Ninigret, 6 Apr. 1766, in Arnold, *Case of the Narragansett,* 57–60.

65. Petition of Thomas Ninigret and 121 others to the General Assembly, Aug. 1763, *SWJP* 11:406–8.

66. Examination of Alexander Huling III, petition of Thomas Ninigret for divorce, Oct. 1765, SC NC, Sept. 1766, E:320; petition of Thomas Ninigret for divorce, SC Kent County, Apr. 1769, 1:341 and files, RIJRC. *Newport Mercury,* 9 Sept. 1765 (wife), 3 Mar. 1766 (Sampson Seedux).

67. Petition of James Niles and 156 others to Thomas Ninigret, 6 Apr. 1766, in Arnold, *Case of the Narragansett,* 57–60. Of these petitioners, 14 had signed the 1763 petition supporting the sachem, and 29 had signed the 1763 petition challenging him.

68. Joseph Wanton, proclamation concerning a petition of the Narragansett tribe, Newport, 20 Dec. 1769, JCB. Petition of James Daniel et al., Sept. 1769, Narragansett Indian File 18, RISA. Petition of Thomas Ninigret, Feb. 1769, Narragansett Indian File 20, RISA.

69. "White Allies": Matthew Robinson to Johnson, 15 Nov. 1764, *SWJP* 11:405–6. Tobias Shattock to the Committee of the General Assembly, Charlestown, 8 Dec. 1767, in *Correspondence of the Colonial Governors of Rhode Island, 1723–1775* (Boston, 1902–3), 2 vols., 1:398–99. Tobias Shattock to Johnson, [1767], *SWJP* 6:58–61. Ninigret continued to contract debts that, despite repeated orders, the General Assembly ultimately honored by authorizing the sale of land. In 1767, Ninigret defaulted on a £200 mortgage of a farm and two houses to the local weaver Samuel Cross, but Cross continued to furnish him with supplies on credit: *Samuel Cross v. Thomas Sachem and Esther Sachem,* CCP KC, Aug. 1770, RIJRC.

70. Joseph Fish to Andrew Oliver, 7 July 1767, photostat, MHS. Graves to Johnson, 14 Jan. 1768, *SWJP* 6:80–82. David W. Conroy, "The Defense of Indian Land Rights: William Bollan and the Mohegan Case in 1743," *Proceedings of the American Antiquarian Society* 103, no. 2 (1994): 395–424. Leslie Weinstein-Farson, "Land Politics and Power: The Mohegan Indians in the Seventeenth and Eighteenth Centuries," *Man in the Northeast* 42 (1991): 9–16. Johnson to Wheelock, 30 Oct. 1765, *SWJP* 11:961–62.

71. "The humble Petition of John Shattock, an Indian of the Narragansett Nation in North America on Behalf of himself and of the whole of the said Indians To the King's most Excellent Majesty," [May 1768], CO5 114 08082, 124–25, Public Record Office, London (photocopy, Campbell Collection, RIHS).

72. Ninigret's finances: petition of Thomas Ninigret, Feb. 1769, Narragansett Indian File 20, RISA; Isaac Nye, deposition, Aug. 1770, *Ichabod Closen v. Thomas Sachem,* CCP KC, Aug.

1770, RIJRC. In support of the sachem: petition of James Daniel et al., the Council of Thomas Ninigret, to the General Assembly, Sept. 1769, Narragansett Indian File 18, RISA. In protest: petition of Samuel Niles, Ephraim Coheis, et al. to the General Assembly, [1769], Narragansett Indian File 19, RISA.

73. Wheelock to Johnson, 19 Aug. 1767, EWP 767469.2. Ninigret threat: Tobias Shattock to Johnson, [1767], *SWJP* 6:58–61.

74. Obituary: *Newport Mercury*, 27 Nov. 1769. Chapin, *Sachems of the Narragansetts*, 102.

75. *The Literary Diary of Ezra Stiles*, ed. Franklin B. Dexter (New York, 1901), 3:23 (28 May 1782).

76. Edward Deake to Wheelock, Charlestown, 20 Dec. 1768, EWP 768670.

Two ||| *Negotiating Slavery*

1. John Saffin, manumission agreement with Adam, 26 June 1694, certified Boston, 25 June 1701, Misc. Bound, MHS. Abner C. Goodell Jr., "John Saffin and His Slave Adam," *Publications of the Colonial Society of Massachusetts* 1 (1895): 85–113.

2. *The Diary of Samuel Sewall, 1675–1729*, ed. H. Halsey Thomas, 2 vols. (New York, 1971), 1:432–33 (19 June 1700). Samuel Sewall, *The Selling of Joseph: A Memorial* (1700), ed. Sidney Kaplan (Amherst, Mass., 1969).

3. Lawrence W. Towner, "The Sewall-Saffin Dialogue on Slavery," *WMQ* 21 (1964): 40–52.

4. A. Leon Higginbotham Jr., *In the Matter of Color: Race and the American Legal Process: The Colonial Period* (New York, 1978). Early criticism of slavery in Massachusetts: Towner, "Sewall-Saffin Dialogue," 52. Sewall, *Selling of Joseph*, 45. The *Boston News-Letter* ran a "Computation that the Importation of Negroes is not so profitable as that of White Servants," possibly by Sewell: George H. Moore, *Notes on the History of Slavery in Massachusetts* (New York, 1866), 107–8. Rhode Islanders reportedly discouraged slavery because of their "general dislike" for blacks: Governor Samuel Cranston to the Board of Trade, 5 Dec. 1708, in the *Newport Historical Magazine* 3 (1882): 197–98. Duty: *RCRI* 4:193.

5. Robert V. Wells, *The Population of the British Colonies in America before 1776* (Princeton, N.J., 1975).

6. Example of a cellar chamber for slaves: Judson House, Stratford (Conn.) Historical Society. Louis P. Masur, "Slavery in Eighteenth-Century Rhode Island: Evidence from the Census of 1774," *Slavery and Abolition: A Journal of Comparative Studies* 6, no. 2 (1985): 139–50.

7. Anne-Marie Cantwell and Diana diZerega Wall, *Unearthing Gotham: The Archaeology of New York City* (New Haven, 2001), ch. 16.

8. Sewall, *Selling of Joseph*, 10.

9. Rhode Island restricted the settlement of all "Strangers coming into this Colony, from any Parts whatsoever by Sea, excepting *Great Britain, Ireland, Jersey* and *Guernsey*"; *Acts and Laws of . . . Rhode-Island* (Newport, 1730), 185. *The Letter-Book of Samuel Sewall*, MHS Collections, 6th ser., 1 (Boston, 1886): 326.

10. *The Life, and Dying Speech of Arthur, a Negro Man . . .* (Boston, 1768).

11. On Prudence Punderson and her family, including Jenny (fig. 6), see Laurel Thatcher

Ulrich, *The Age of Homespun: Objects and Stories in the Creation of an American Myth* (New York, 2001), 209–47. Ruth Wallis Herndon, "'To Live after the Manner of an Apprentice': Public Indenture as Social Control in Eighteenth Century Rhode Island," paper presented to the Philadelphia Center for Early American Studies, May 1995. Indenture of Solomon Seasor to Joseph Clark, 24 June 1768, RIHS. Examples of English servants gaining legal redress: one woman protested when her estranged husband indentured their two daughters to a third man (*Mary Remington v. Joshua Winsor,* GSP, Providence, June 1742, RIJRC); a white laborer ran away and defended himself when a man appeared with an indenture signed by his mother (*Metcalf Bowers v. John Randall,* GSP, Providence, June 1740, RIJRC). In 1768, the transient "negro" Jack Hammon was advertised for sale to satisfy a judgment of court; *Newport Mercury,* 25 July–1 Aug. 1768. Rhode Island law: John A. Sainsbury, "Indian Labor in Early Rhode Island," *NEQ* 48, no. 3 (1975): 378–93.

12. One slave named Immanuel was abducted on Christmas Day: *Thomas Havens v. Antipas Hathaway,* CCP NC, Nov. 1738, A:571, RIJRC; *Havens v. Hathaway,* SC NC, Mar. 1739, MSA 6:579–85. Other cases: Daniel Bartlett, June 1765, RI Petitions 11:212; Nicholas Spencer, June 1768, RI Petitions 13:2–22. An Indian servant to one settler was sold into slavery by a third man: John Lewis Jr., 6 Sept. 1765, RI Petitions 11:201.

13. *Sarah Chauqum v. Edward Robinson,* CCP KC, Jan. 1734, A:121; *Sarah v. Robinson,* SC NC, Sept. 1734, B:481 and files, RIJRC; Edward Robinson, Feb. 1733, RI Petitions 2:14. The case of "Negro" servant John Wamsley pitted two putative owners against each other: *John Walmsley v. James Brown Jr.,* GSP KC, Aug. 1740, RIJRC.

14. *Newport Mercury,* 10 Oct. 1763. Cognehew: Francis G. Hutchins, *Mashpee, the Story of Cape Cod's Indian Town* (West Franklin, N.H., 1979), 73. A Spanish sailor enslaved in Boston presented a learned attack on slavery: Manuel Jalla, petition to the governor and council of Massachusetts, Jan. 1708, MS-L, MHS. Three Indian sailors from Rhode Island were held at Hispaniola and threatened with enslavement; Silas Cook, Aug. 1759, RI Petitions 10:96. Sweet: Matthew Robinson, June 1748, RI Petitions 5:165.

15. Governor George Thomas to Governor Gideon Wanton, Philadelphia, 17 Apr. 1746; Edward Frelawny to Governor Wanton, Jamaica, 22 June 1746; Joseph Espinosa to [Governor Wanton], 22 Aug. 1746; Letters to the Governor, RISA. George Wanton to Don Juan Francisco de Inumes y Harrastitas, 14 June 1746, Letters from the Governor, 1:57, RISA. William Howland to Wilkinson and Ayrault, 2 Oct. 1746, RIHS. Job Bennet Jr., June 1748, RI Petitions 5:166, 7:23.

16. J. L. Dillard, *Black English: Its History and Usage in the United States* (New York, 1972), 123–35.

17. James MacSparran, *Letter Book and Abstract of Out Services . . . 1743–1751,* ed. Daniel Goodwin (Boston, 1899), 49–50 (10 Aug. 1751), 49 (9 Aug. 1751). The manuscript is now in the archives of the University of Rhode Island.

18. *Boston Weekly News-Letter,* 9–16 July 1741.

19. MacSparran, *Letter Book,* 52–55 (29 Aug.–10 Sept. 1751).

20. *Rex v. Charles Dickinson,* SC NC, Mar. 1733, B:449; indictment of Jabez Reynolds, SC KC, Oct. 1773; both in RIJRC.

21. "An Indian Branded in 1727," *Newport Historical Magazine* 4 (1883): 115–16. Irving

H. Bartlett, *From Slave to Citizen: The Story of the Negro in Rhode Island* (Providence, 1954), 15–16.

22. *Newport Gazette*, 6 Aug. 1764.

23. Michael F. Brown, "On Resisting Resistance," *American Anthropologist* 98, no. 4 (1996): 729–35.

24. Daniel E. Williams, "'Behold a Tragic Scene Strangely Changed into a Theatre of Mercy': The Structure and Significance of Criminal Conversion Narratives in Early New England," *American Quarterly* 38, no. 5 (1986): 827–47.

25. William J. Brown, *The Life of William J. Brown, of Providence, R.I., with Personal Recollections of Incidents in Rhode Island* (Providence, 1883), 11–12.

26. Philip Morgan, "British Encounters with Africa and Africans circa 1600–1780," in *Strangers within the Realm*, ed. Bernard Bailyn and Philip D. Morgan (Chapel Hill, N.C., 1991), 157–219.

27. MacSparran, *Letter Book*, 49 (9 Aug. 1751).

28. Teddeman Hull, record book as warden, Jamestown, 24 Apr. 1742–2 Feb. 1743, RIHS. Other cases involving black and white thieves and fences: indictment of Edward Hull, GSP, Newport, May 1737; indictment of Sarah Squire, GSP, Newport, Nov. 1750; both in RIJRC.

29. Venture Smith, *A Narrative of the Life and Adventures of Venture, A Native of Africa, But Resident Above Sixty Years in the United States of America, Related by Himself* (New London, Conn., 1798); all quotations from the H. M. Selden edition (Middletown, Conn., 1897), 14–15. The best reference on Smith is Robert Desrochers Jr., "'Not Fade Away': The Narrative of Venture Smith, an African American in the Early Republic," *JAH* 84, no. 1 (1997): 40–66.

30. Ibid., 17–19.

31. Indictment of Job Almy; petition of pardon (apprentice to Almy); GSP NC, Nov. 1758, 94, RIJRC. *Newport Gazette*, 13 Apr. 1789.

32. *Rex v. Fortune*, SC NC, Mar. 1762, E:183–84 and files, RIJRC. Henry Bull, "Memoir of Rhode Island. Comprising the Period from the Settlement of the Island in 1638, to the Close of the Revolutionary War in 1783," originally published in the *Rhode Island Republican* (Newport) between 1832 and 1839, transcribed by Charles E. Hammett Jr., 1888, 2 vols., 2:215, RIHS. Jeremy Belknap, Diary, 1762, MHS. *The dying confession and declaration of Fortune, a Negro man . . .* (Boston, 1762).

33. John M. Murrin, introduction to *Princetonians, 1784–1790: A Biographical Dictionary*, ed. Ruth L. Woodward and Wesley Frank Craven (Princeton, N.J., 1991), l–li. Lotteries: *Newport Gazette*, 22 Apr. 1760.

34. Ira Berlin, *Many Thousands Gone: The First Two Centuries of Slavery in North America* (Cambridge, 1998), 177–94.

35. Smith, *Narrative*, 17, 20–22. Daniel Vickers, *Farmers and Fishermen: Two Centuries of Work in Essex County, Massachusetts, 1630–1830* (Chapel Hill, N.C., 1994), 229–47.

36. Smith, *Narrative*, 17–24. Desrochers, "Not Fade Away," 45–48.

37. Cesar Lyndon, Journal, Rhode Island Manuscripts, 10:81–85, RIHS. Olaudah Equiano also was active in private commercial ventures while enslaved; *The interesting narrative of the life of Olaudah Equiano, or Gustavus Vassa, the African* (London, 1789).

38. *Newport Mercury,* 9 Feb. 1762. Later, One's master arranged for a third party to supervise him: *Newport Mercury,* 20 Feb. 1764; 27 Feb. 1764.

39. Smith, *Narrative,* 19, 21.

40. Lyndon, Journal.

41. Kenneth Greenberg, *Honor and Slavery* (Princeton, N.J., 1996), ch. 2.

42. Smith, *Narrative,* 16–17.

43. Passes: *Acts and Laws of Rhode Island* (Newport, 1730), 72. One example of a stranger "taken up" by a sheriff: Thomas Fenner, warrant for arrest of "a Negro man," 8 Nov. 1710, RIHS. See also Simon Fuller to James Wood, Albany, 5 Dec. 1767, RI Notarial 7:682. *Newport Mercury,* 25 Aug.–1 Sept. 1766. *Newport Gazette,* 19 Mar. 1770.

44. Advertisement for Pomp, 26 Feb. 1785; Brown also drafted, but did not publish, an advertisement for the white servant William Oakley [ca. 1770]; Beriah Brown Papers, RIHS.

45. Ben: *Newport Mercury,* 19 Aug. 1765 (repeated for six weeks). Deposition of Cuff, *George Hazard v. Ben,* CCP KC, Aug. 1765; *George Hazard v. Jonathan Hazard, on behalf of Ben,* SC KC, Apr. 1766, B:81; RIJRC.

46. Servants were twice as likely to run away from March through October than from November through February. Peak months were April, August, and September. My sample shows 6 Jan., 2 Feb., 10 Mar., 14 Apr., 12 May, 5 June, 10 July, 14 Aug., 14 Sept., 10 Oct., 9 Nov., 6 Dec. One example of multiple household members "running away" involves Godfrey Wainwood: he advertised a runaway servant (*Newport Mercury,* 1–8 Aug. 1768) and the elopement of his wife (*Newport Mercury,* 22 Aug. 1774); several of his servants ran away during the war (see ch. 5 below); and his servant Robert ran away in 1790 (see ch. 6 below).

47. Ceaser, examination, 1 July 1717, MHS.

48. *The Life, and Dying Speech of Arthur.*

49. In her sample of runaway advertisements in Rhode Island newspapers between 1758 and 1776, which excludes all white servants, Lynne Withey found 48 with attributed occupations, including 16 sailors, 11 artisans, and 11 others; Withey, *Urban Growth in Colonial Rhode Island: Newport and Providence in the Eighteenth Century* (Albany, 1984), 75. York: *Newport Mercury,* 15 Aug. 1774. Similarly, Pompey had been rented by his mistress during the 1720s to a Marblehead mariner; when he ran away because of "bad usage," he stowed away aboard a ship bound for England; deposition of John Cornuck et al., 7 Oct. 1724, Bristol, [England], MHS.

50. Shane White, *Somewhat More Independent: The End of Slavery in New York City, 1770–1810* (Athens, Ga., 1991), 114–49.

51. Laurel Thatcher Ulrich, *Good Wives: Image and Reality in the Lives of Women in Northern New England, 1650–1750* (New York, 1982), ch. 11.

52. In Rhode Island advertisements from later in the century, white servants were slightly less likely to run away than blacks or Indians; but most white servants were indentured children who knew they should be free at age eighteen or twenty-one anyway. Withey, *Urban Growth,* 124–25.

53. Isaac's conviction was overturned on appeal; *Rex v. Isaac,* SC NC, Mar. 1732, B:619 and files. Jupiter's owner sued Isaac for damages but lost on appeal; *Isaac v. Benjamin Stanton,* SC NC, Sept. 1732, B:424 and files, RIJRC.

54. *Newport Mercury,* 17 July 1769. Other suspected runaways "taken up": *Newport Mercury,* 27 Dec. 1762; *Providence Gazette,* 9 July 1763; *Providence Gazette,* 10 Oct. 1767.

55. Josias Lyndon, bill of sale to Nicholas Cooke, 18 Sept. 1771, Cooke Papers, RIHS.

56. For example, the *Newport Mercury,* 3 Aug. 1772, advertised: "To be SOLD, for no FAULT, A Likely NEGRO GIRL, about nine years old." Jonah Marton to Andrew Adams, Schaticook, 16 Apr. 1794, HSP.

57. Smith, *Narrative,* 18–19. Similarly, repeated whippings and rumors of a planned escape prompted MacSparran to sell Hannibal; *Letter Book,* 55–56 (Sept. 1751).

58. Indenture of Ruth Cockaway, 1 May 1713, MHS. In the summer of 1736, an Indian servant of James Brown ran away as part of a successful negotiation to avoid serving as a sailor under a particular captain; James Brown to Captain Malebone, 14 June 1736, *The Letter Book of James Browne of Providence, Merchant, 1735–1738* (Providence, 1929), 33. Pompe: Samuel Bowman to Samuel P. Savage, 14 Oct. 1752, MHS.

59. Smith, *Narrative,* 18–19.

60. Ibid., 21–24.

61. David Waldstreicher, "Reading the Runaways: Self-Fashioning, Print Culture, and Confidence in Slavery in the Eighteenth-Century Mid-Atlantic," *WMQ* 56 (1999): 243–72.

62. Sewall, *Selling of Joseph,* 10.

63. Action of trespass against Cambridge, servant of Peter Taylor, SC NC, Mar. 1747, D:23 and files; Cambridge's bond discharged, GSP NC, 6; both in RIJRC.

64. Thomas J. Davis, *A Rumor of Revolt: The "Great Negro Plot" in Colonial New York* (New York, 1985).

65. News of the New York trials prompted vice-admiralty judge Robert Auchmuty in Boston to advertise the sale of his slave Cesar, on condition that he be transported south; Auchmuty urged other slaveholders to follow his example and called on the General Court to legislatively "correct the Licentious Behaviour of this black Crew, and timely avert what a neighboring Government providentially escaped"; *Boston Weekly News-Letter,* 9–16 July 1741. Whig propagandists complained in 1768 that British troops in Boston were encouraging slaves to "beat, abuse and cut their masters throats, promising them as a reward . . . to make them free"; *Newport Gazette,* 7–14 Nov. 1768.

66. Gordon S. Wood, "Conspiracy and the Paranoid Style: Causality and Deceit in the Eighteenth Century," *WMQ* 39 (1982): 401–41.

67. *Rex v. Cambridge,* GSP NC, 24 May 1751, 38 and files, RIJRC.

68. Wilkins Updike, *Memoirs of the Rhode Island Bar* (Boston, 1842), 58.

Three ||| *Strange Christians*

1. Stiles recorded two somewhat different versions of the story: *Itineraries of Ezra Stiles,* 142–43 (31 Oct. 1761); *The Literary Diary of Ezra Stiles,* ed. Franklin B. Dexter (New York, 1901), 1:386 (13 June 1773). William S. Simmons, *Spirit of the New England Tribes: Indian History and Folklore, 1620–1984* (Hanover, N.H., 1986).

2. *New Entertaining Philadelphia Jest Book* (Philadelphia, 1790), 31. Benjamin Franklin, *Two tracts: Information to those who would remove to America. And, remarks concerning the sav-*

ages of North America (London,1784). Robert K. Dodge, *Early American Almanac Humor* (Bowling Green, Ohio, 1987), 73, 75. "An Indian's Answer to a Swedish Missionary," 1704, HSP.

3. Quoted version dates from the early nineteenth century, Thomas Weston, *History of the Town of Middleboro, Massachusetts* (Boston, 1906), 102–3. A version published in 1800: Dodge, *Early American Almanac Humor,* 65–66.

4. Jeremiah 5:19. Nicholas P. Canny, "The Ideology of English Colonialism: From Ireland to America," *WMQ* 30 (1973): 575–98. Matt B. Jones, "The Early Massachusetts-Bay Seals," *Proceedings of the American Antiquarian Society* 44 (1934): 12–44.

5. Thomas Hariot, *A Briefe and True Report of The New Found Land of Virginia* (Frankfurt on Main, 1590).

6. Virginia statute of 1705: W. W. Henig, ed., *Statutes at Large . . . of Virginia,* 18 vols. (Richmond, 1809–23), 3:447–62. On a similar New York statute (1706): Sheldon S. Cohen, "Elias Neau, Instructor to New York's Slaves," *New-York Historical Society Quarterly* 55, no. 1 (1971): 17. Adolph B. Benson, ed., *The America of 1750: Peter Kalm's Travels in North America: The English Version of 1770* (New York, 1966), 209. On colonial opposition to British missionary efforts: John C. Van Horne, *Religious Philanthropy and Colonial Slavery: The American Correspondence of the Associates of Dr. Bray* (Chicago, 1985), 25–38.

7. Alexis de Tocqueville, *Democracy in America,* trans. George Lawrence, ed. J. P. Mayer (New York, 1988): 319–20.

8. David Crosby to Wheelock, East Hartford, 4 Nov. 1767, EWP 767604.1.

9. Joseph A. Conforti, *Samuel Hopkins and the New Divinity Movement: Calvinism, the Congregational Ministry, and Reform in New England between the First and Second Great Awakenings* (Grand Rapids, Mich., 1981), 53–54.

10. Cotton Mather's "Rules for the Society of Negroes" was drafted and printed in Boston in 1693, though no copy is extant; it was reprinted in Boston around 1706–14. See also his *The Negro Christianized: An essay to excite and assist the good work, the instruction of Negro-servants in Christianity* (Boston, 1706).

11. "Diary of Rev. Jacob Eliot," *Historical Magazine,* 2d ser., 5, no. 1 (1869): 33–35 (5 June 1742). A similar story related in 1795: Jane Marcou, *Life of Jeremy Belknap* (New York, 1847), 70.

12. Charles E. Hill, "Slavery and Its Aftermath in Beverly, Massachusetts: Juno Larcom and Her Family," *Essex Institute Historical Collections* 116, no. 2 (1980): 115. Robert K. Fitts, "The Landscapes of Northern Bondage," *Historical Archaeology,* 30, no. 2 (1996): 54–73. Dell Upton, *Holy Things and Profane: Anglican Parish Churches in Colonial Virginia* (New York, 1986). Robert J. Dinkin, "Seating in the Meetinghouse in Early Massachusetts," in *Material Life in America, 1600–1860,* ed. Robert Blair St. George (Boston, 1988), 407–18. The New England commissioners ordered that "half" of the meetinghouse to be built near the Narragansett reserve in 1734 be reserved for the Indians, and they probably meant that literally; in Sandwich the Indians complained of being "crowded out" by the local settlers; declaration regarding the meetinghouse at Sandwich, 16 Oct. 1761, Misc. Bound, MHS. When a new meetinghouse was built on the Mashpee reserve in 1757, the Indians specified a site where they would be "least troubled with the English crowding their Seats"; Gideon Hawley to the Commissioners for Propagating the Gospel [draft], 24 Sept.–3 Dec. 1757, Gideon Hawley Papers, MHS.

13. James MacSparran, *Letter Book and Abstract of Out Services . . . 1743–1751*, ed. Daniel Goodwin (Boston, 1899), 45–46 (25 July 1751), 49–50 (10 Aug. 1751). "Lord's freeman": John Callender, *A Discourse on the Death of the Rev. Nathaniel Clap* (Newport, 1746), 30–33.

14. *Literary Diary of Ezra Stiles*, 1:108 (June 1768), 1:239–40 (31 May 1772). Policies that infant slaves should be baptized by right of their master's covenant, regardless of their own parents' religious status, were adopted in 1738 by the Connecticut General Association and in 1741 by the church in Medfield, Massachusetts; William D. Piersen, *Black Yankees: The Development of an Afro-American Subculture in Eighteenth-Century New England* (Amherst, Mass., 1988), 54.

15. George C. Mason, *Annals of Trinity Church, Newport, Rhode Island, 1698–1821* (Newport, 1890) 1:192 (1789). In 1772, Stiles counted only about twenty black communicants in the various religious societies of Newport—seven out of eighty in his own church—but he observed as many as several hundred attending Sabbath worship and other prayer meetings so that his own congregation was at times as much as a third black: *Literary Diary of Ezra Stiles*, 1:213–14 (24 Feb. 1772), 247–48 (10 July 1772). Marmaduke Brown to John Waring, 1 July 1766, Van Horne, *Correspondence of the Associates of Dr. Bray*, 247–48.

16. Peter Wood, *Black Majority: Negroes in Colonial South Carolina from 1660 through the Stono Rebellion* (New York, 1974), 131–66. Thomas Pollen to [John Waring], 6 July 1755, Van Horne, *Correspondence of the Associates of Dr. Bray*, 119–20.

17. "Diary of Eleazar Wheelock, D.D., during His Visit to Boston" (1741), *Historical Magazine*, 2d ser., 5 (1869): 238. Susan Juster, *Disorderly Women: Sexual Politics and Evangelicalism in Revolutionary New England* (Ithaca, N.Y., 1994), 33. Another sympathetic story of a slave who converted his master: *The Diary of Isaac Backus*, ed. William G. McLoughlin (Providence, 1979), 1256 (27 Mar. 1789).

18. Jean R. Soderlund, *Quakers and Slavery: A Divided Spirit* (Princeton, N.J., 1985).

19. Rhys Isaacs, "Evangelical Revolt: The Nature of the Baptist Challenge to the Traditional Order in Virginia, 1765 to 1775," *WMQ* 31 (1974): 345–68. Old Light quote: Charles Chauncey, *Seasonal Thoughts on the State of Religion in New England* (Boston, 1743), 226. *Boston Gazette*, 29 Apr. 1765. One runaway servant was described as "very forward to mimick some of the strangers that have of late been preaching [in Boston]," *Boston Weekly News-Letter*, 1 July 1742. Flora: Erik R. Seeman, "'Justise Must Take Plase': Three African Americans Speak of Religion in Eighteenth-Century New England," *WMQ* 56 (1999): 397.

20. McLoughlin, *Diary of Isaac Backus*, 260 (13 Dec. 1752), 287 (23 May 1753), 370–71 (30 Mar.–1 Apr. 1755).

21. David Grimsted, "Anglo-American Racism and Phillis Wheatley's 'Sable Veil,' 'Length'ned Chain,' and 'Knitted Heart,'" in *Women in the Age of the American Revolution*, ed. Ronald Hoffman and Peter J. Albert (Charlottesville, Va., 1989), 338–444. Osborne quote: Barbara E. Lacey, "The Bonds of Friendship: Sarah Osborne of Newport and the Reverend Joseph Fish of North Stonington, 1743–1779," *RIH* 45, no. 4 (1986): 133.

22. McLoughlin, *Diary of Isaac Backus*, 1105 (14 July 1782). McLoughlin's note (1105–6) summarizes affidavits Backus collected from Lee and other eyewitnesses.

23. New England: Juster, *Disorderly Women*. More broadly: Christine Heyrman, *Southern Cross: The Origins of the Bible Belt* (New York, 1997). In 1790, the Baptist church in Prov-

idence debated whether Negro members could vote on the selection of a minister; Record Book, First Baptist Church, Providence, Records, RIHS.

24. James Axtell, "The Little Red School," *The Invasion Within: The Contest of Cultures in Colonial North America* (New York, 1985), 179–217.

25. Daniel Simon to Wheelock, Sept. 1771, [Hanover, N.H.], EWP 771540. John Daniel to Wheelock, 30 Nov. 1767, Charlestown, EWP 767630.3. Wheelock to John Sergeant, 7 Dec. 1774, Dartmouth College, EWP 774657.

26. Calvin's complaints were reported by the Narragansetts' English schoolmaster: Edward Deake to Wheelock, Charlestown, 21 June 1768, in James Dow McCallum, *The Letters of Eleazar Wheelock's Indians* (Hanover, N.H., 1932), 65. Leaders of the Narragansett Tribe's Party wrote: "Many People among us conclude 'tis best for an Indian to have but little Learning; but we are sure we are great sufferers for want of it"; Samuel Niles, John Shattock, et al. to Wheelock, Charlestown, 28 Mar. 1767, Gratz MSS 4:5, HSP.

27. *Diary and Autobiography of John Adams*, ed. L. H. Butterfield, vol. 1 (Cambridge, Mass., 1961), 152–53 (19 Aug. 1760).

28. David Fowler to Wheelock, 26 Aug. 1766, Lebanon, EWP 766476.2. Wheelock to Fowler, Lebanon, 26 Aug. 1766, Lebanon, EWP 766476.1.

29. David McClure to Wheelock, 2 Feb. 1774, Portsmouth, EWP 774152.

30. Occom to Wheelock, 1 June 1773, [Mohegan?], Gratz MSS 4:5, HSP. Occom to Wheelock, 24 July 1771, Mohegan, EWP 771424.

31. In 1773, several English students—and the Oneida Peter Pohqunnoppeet—complained about "the Indians" making too much noise; Daniel Simon et al. to Wheelock, 16 Feb. 1773, Dartmouth College, EWP 773166. In 1775, an English boy objected to sleeping in common with Indians; Colonel Sam. Stephens to Wheelock, 13 June 1775, Charlestown, EWP 775363. Williams Fund: Andrew Oliver to Jno. Stoddard, 10 Nov. 1746, Gratz MSS, 2:31, HSP. Oliver to [?] Jackson, 4 Jan. 1770; Oliver to Jasper Manduit, Nov. 1770; Oliver to Manduit, 13 Dec. 1770; Manduit to Samuel Locke, 29 Apr. 1771; Andrew Oliver Letterbook, 1767–74, Hutchinson-Oliver Papers, British Museum, London (microfilm copy, MHS). Earlier, Oliver complained that another endowment, the Sir Peter Warren Fund for the education of Iroquois children, had been diverted to the Brookfield town minister; Oliver to Wheelock, 6 July 1767, Boston, EWP 767406.2.

32. John Smith, "A Dialogue between an Englishman and an Indian," 2 Mar. 1779, in *Dramas from the American Theatre, 1762–1909*, ed. Richard Moody (Boston, 1969), 7–8.

33. Henry Abelove, *The Evangelist of Desire: John Wesley and the Methodists* (Stanford, 1990).

34. "On the Death of the Rev. Mr. George Whitefield," 1770, in *The Poems of Phillis Wheatley*, ed. Julian D. Mason Jr., rev. ed. (Chapel Hill, N.C., 1989), 55–57. Grimsted, "Anglo-American Racism."

35. "The Will of a Negro Slave in 1773," *Connecticut Magazine* 10, no. 4 (1906): 693.

36. Stevens: *Literary Diary of Ezra Stiles*, 1:355 (9 Mar. 1773). The next "colored" member of the Providence church joined ten years later; Henry M. King, *Historical Catalogue of the Members of the First Baptist Church in Providence, Rhode Island* (Providence, 1908).

37. In reports to their sponsoring agency in England, the pastors of the Anglican

churches in Newport and South Kingstown both claimed that about one hundred blacks regularly attended worship: MacSparran, *Letter Book*, 85 n. 41; Mason, *Annals of Trinity Church*, 1:76. Meanwhile, a group of slaves also attended a Congregational church in Newport: Callender, *Discourse on the Death of the Rev. Nathaniel Clap*, 30–33.

38. *Literary Diary of Ezra Stiles*, 1:213 (24 Feb. 1772), 1:247–48 (10 July 1772).

39. *Memoirs of Mrs. Chloe Spear, A Native of Africa, Who was Enslaved in Childhood, and Died in Boston, January 3, 1815 . . . Aged 65 Years* (Boston, 1832), 196. *Literary Diary of Ezra Stiles*, 278 (26 Aug. 1772). Trinity Church public catechism: Marmaduke Browne to John Waring, Newport, 4 June 1767, Van Horne, *Correspondence of the Associates of Dr. Bray*, 258–59.

40. Narratives of Susanna Low and Mary Rust (1764), "Conversion Narratives from the Seacoast Revival," box 1, folder 1b, John Cleveland Papers, Peabody Essex Museum, Salem; I would like to thank Eric Seeman for sharing his transcriptions of these documents.

41. "Land of Light": Juster, *Disorderly Women*, 73 n. 80; 70 n. 69; 62–68. Seeman, "Justise Must Take Plase."

42. *Literary Diary of Ezra Stiles*, 1:174 (13 Oct. 1771).

43. Greenwich, testimony, 29 Mar. 1754 (Records of the Canterbury Separate Church, 1733–1815, Connecticut Historical Society), in Seeman, "Justise Must Take Plase," 411–13. Ruth Bogin, "'Liberty Further Extended': A 1776 Anti-Slavery Manuscript of Lemuel Haynes," *WMQ* 40 (1983): 85–105.

44. Narratives of Susanna Low, Rachel Low, and Haskell (1764), "Conversion Narratives from the Seacoast Revival," John Cleveland Papers; transcriptions by Eric Seeman. Wheatley to Obour Tanner, 30 Oct. 1773 and 19 May 1772, in Mason, *Poems of Phillis Wheatley*, 198, 190.

45. See also John Saillant, "Slavery and Divine Providence in New England Calvinism: The New Divinity and a Black Protest, 1775–1805," *NEQ* 68, no. 4 (1995): 584–608.

46. This first letter to Occom is not extant, but in extant letters to Occom her analysis of colonial race relations is particularly acerbic: Wheatley to Occom, 11 Feb. 1774, in Mason, *Poems of Phillis Wheatley*, 181, 203. Leon Burr Richardson, ed., *An Indian Preacher in England . . .* (Hanover, N.H., 1933).

47. "To the University of Cambridge, in New-England"; Wheatley to Tanner, 19 May 1772; both in Mason, *Poems of Phillis Wheatley*, 52, 190.

48. Mason, *Poems of Phillis Wheatley*, 47–48.

49. "On Being Brought from Africa to America" [1772], in Mason, *Poems of Phillis Wheatley*, 53.

50. Fish, account of lectures, in *Old Light on Separate Ways: The Narragansett Diaries of Joseph Fish, 1765–1776*, ed. William S. Simmons and Cheryl L. Simmons (Hanover, N.H., 1982), 43–44 (20 June 1768), 93 (5 July 1773). William S. Simmons, *Cautantowwit's House: An Indian Burial Ground on the Island of Conanicut in Narragansett Bay* (Providence, 1970).

51. William S. Simmons, "Red Yankees: Narragansett Conversion in the Great Awakening," *American Ethnologist* 40, no. 1 (1983): 253–71.

52. *Itineraries of Ezra Stiles*, 159–61 (3 June 1762). *Literary Diary of Ezra Stiles*, 3:76–77 (27 June 1783). See also Simmons, *Spirit of the New England Tribes*, 252.

53. Confirming his late brother's earlier grant: George Augustus Ninigret, deed of forty

acres in Charlestown for the benefit of the Church of England, 14 Jan. 1746, Christopher Champlin Papers, RIHS, Indian Lands, 1:17. Granting an additional twenty acres and swapping land with Christopher Champlin: George Augustus Ninigret, Aug. 1746, RI Petitions 6:62. Matthew Graves to Sir William Johnson, New London, 20 Mar. 1773, *The Documentary History of the State of New-York,* ed. E. B. O'Callaghan (Albany, 1851), 4:485–86.

54. Joseph Park, "An Account of the late Propagation of Religion at Westerly and Charlestown in Rhode-Island Colony . . . ," *Christian History* (Boston) 1, no. 26 (1743): 201–8, and 2, no. 56 (1743): 25–28.

55. Ezra Stiles heard this story from the aged Deacon Avery of "Groton Pokatunnek," *Literary Diary of Ezra Stiles,* 3:508 (22 Oct. 1793).

56. *Christian History* 2, no. 56 (1743): 25. Simmons, "Red Yankees," 253–271.

57. Deposition of Tobias Coheis, 11 Feb. 1768, *William Sachem et al. v. James Niles,* CCP KC, Feb. 1768, RIJRC.

58. *Literary Diary of Ezra Stiles,* 1:232–33 (8 May 1772). Isaac Backus, *A History of New England with Particular Reference to the Denomination of Christians Called Baptists,* ed. David Weston (Newton, Mass., 1871), 2:510–11. McLoughlin, *Diary of Isaac Backus,* 260 n. 1, dates the formation of the Separate church in Charlestown at 1745, after Niles was disciplined for exhorting in a "disorderly fashion." "Acco. of the Preachers to the Jndians wth their Severeal Stipends" (1748), *Publications of the Colonial Society of Massachusetts,* vol. 16 (Boston, 1925), 850.

59. Simmons, "Red Yankees," 262–63. Letter to the Canterbury Separate Church, 26 Apr. 1752, in C. C. Goen, *Revivalism and Separatism in New England, 1740–1800* (New Haven, 1962), 91.

60. *Literary Diary of Ezra Stiles,* 1:232–33 (8 May 1772).

61. Fish to Wheelock, 31 July 1766, photostat, MHS. Fish to Joseph Sewall, [after 18 Sept. 1765], in Simmons and Simmons, *Old Light on Separate Ways,* 3–7. Fish to [Andrew Oliver], 4 Nov. 1757, Misc. Bound, MHS. Simmons, "Red Yankees," 263. William DeLoss Love, *Samson Occom and the Christian Indians of New England* (Boston, 1899).

62. Joseph Park to [the Boston commissioners], Charlestown, 17 Sept. 1757, Misc. Bound, MHS. Similarly, the Mashpees invited an English minister to join their Indian pastor at the same time that they filed a new round of grievances against local English settlers and their commonwealth-appointed overseers; Philip Tankooph et al. to the Commissioners for Indian Affairs in Boston, 4 Aug. 1757, Hawley Papers, MHS.

63. On division in his own parish: Fish to Wheelock, 3 Dec. 1741, Lebanon, EWP 741653. On his missionary work among the Pequots and Narragansetts: Simmons and Simmons, *Old Light on Separate Ways,* introduction.

64. Franklin B. Dexter, ed., *Diary of David McClure, Doctor of Divinity, 1748–1820* (New York, 1899), 189–91 (1768).

65. Joseph Fish, *The Church of Christ a Firm and Durable House . . .* (New London, 1767). Isaac Backus, *A Fish Caught in His Own Net . . .* (Boston, 1768). Account of lectures, 7 Nov. 1768, Simmons and Simmons, *Old Light on Separate Ways,* 52.

66. Account of lectures, 4 Sept. 1769; Fish to Andrew Oliver, Stonington, 25 Oct. 1769; both in Simmons and Simmons, *Old Light on Separate Ways,* 60, 62–63.

67. Account of lectures, 22 Aug. 1774, Simmons and Simmons, *Old Light on Separate Ways*, 107.

68. Love, *Samson Occom*, 84–110.

69. Dexter, *Diary of David McClure*, 189–91 (1768).

70. On mimicry, see Roland Barthes, "Myth Today," in *Mythologies*, trans. Annette Lavers (New York, 1972); Homi K. Bhabha, "Of Mimicry and Men: The Ambivalence of Colonial Discourse," *October* 28 (1984): 125–33. For an ostensibly satirical example of the use of mimicry to police membership in the British upper class: Nancy Mitford, "U and Non-U," in *Noblesse Oblige: An Enquiry into the Identifiable Characteristics of the English Aristocracy* (New York, 1956). On Christianity and skin color: Winthrop D. Jordan, *White over Black: American Attitudes toward the Negro, 1550–1812* (Chapel Hill, N.C., 1968).

71. Entry at Dartmouth, [Mass.], Dec. 1779, Anonymous Journal, Apr. 1779–Mar. 1780, RIHS.

72. John Smith to [unknown], 18 May 1764, Boston, EWP 764318.2. This logic prompted some Indians to join the growing chorus of English voices proclaiming that they could never be truly converted because civility was incompatible with their racial character. In a moment of frustration, the Delaware missionary Hezekiah Calvin wrote that his Mohawk charges would never abandon their "evil practices." "Indians," he wrote, "will be Indians." Calvin to Wheelock, Fort Hunter, 11 Aug. 1766, EWP 766461.2.

73. Occom to Wheelock, 24 July 1771, Mohegan, EWP 771424. His fund-raising tour to England was calculated to play off interest in his identity as a converted Indian. In early 1760, George Whitefield had suggested the tactic to Wheelock: "Had I a converted Indian Scholar that could preach and pray in English, something might be done to the purpose," quoted in Love, *Samson Occom*, 130. When Occom's trip was proposed, the Reverend Charles Jeffery Smith predicted, "An Indian minister in England might get a Bushel of money for the School," Smith to Wheelock, 30 Mar. 1764, Egg Harbor, EWP 764230 (see also EWP 765556.1). In his journal (30 July 1786), Occom described an outlandish Oneida man: "His appearance made me think of the old Britains in their Heathenism"; Love, *Samson Occom*, 256.

74. "On Being Brought from Africa to America" [1768]; "On the Death of the Rev. Mr. George Whitefield" (1770); both in *Poems of Phillis Wheatley*, 53, 55–57. Joseph Johnson's vow, 10 Jun 1776, EWP 776360. *A Narrative of the Lord's Wonderful Dealings with John Marrant, a Black* (1802), in Dorothy Porter, ed., *Early Negro Writing, 1760–1837* (Boston, 1971), 446. Potato: "Extract from . . . Zeluco, or various views of Human Nature," *Newport Mercury*, 10 Apr. 1790.

75. Angelika Kråger-Kahloula, "Tributes in Stone and Lapidary Lapses: Commemorating Black People in Eighteenth- and Nineteenth-Century America," *Markers* 6 (1989): 32–100.

76. Lucy Haskell headstone (1835), North Burial Ground, Providence.

Four ||| *Strange Flesh*

1. *A few Lines on Occasion of the untimely End of Mark and Phillis . . .* [Boston, 1755].

2. Boston Overseers of the Poor, Misc. Papers, 1735–1835, MHS: Mark, hometown

Charlestown, is listed as warned out on 28 Feb. 1755; a note added later reads, "since hangd."
Another example: "Cophee tells me he gives Mr Pemberton £40 for his Time, that he might
be with his wife. I have him 5ˢ help him"; *The Diary of Samuel Sewall, 1675–1729*, ed. H. Halsey
Thomas, 2 vols. (New York, 1971), 762 (13 July 1714). *The Last & Dying Words of Mark, Aged
about 30 Years . . .* (Boston, 1755).

3. Abner Cheney Goodell Jr., "The Trial and Execution, for Petit Treason, of Mark and
Phillis," *Proceedings of the Massachusetts Historical Society* (hereafter cited as *MHS Proceedings*) (1882): 122–49.

4. Samuel Sewall, *The Selling of Joseph: A Memorial* (1700), ed. Sidney Kaplan (Amherst,
Mass., 1969), 47.

5. The Blockade of Boston (1776) quoted in Kenneth Silverman, *A Cultural History of
the American Revolution* (New York, 1976), 292–93. Kenneth Greenberg, *Honor and Slavery*
(Princeton, N.J., 1996).

6. *Laws and Acts of Rhode Island . . . 1636 to 1705*, in John D. Cushing, ed., *The Earliest
Acts and Laws of the Colony of Rhode Island . . . 1647–1719* (Wilmington, Del., 1977), 65. David
D. Smits, "'We Are Not to Grow Wild': Seventeenth-Century New England's Repudiation of Anglo-English Intermarriage," *American Indian Culture and Research Journal* 11, no.
4 (1987): 1–31.

7. "Sons of nobody": William Blackstone, *Commentaries on the Laws of England*, 4 vols.
(London, 1766–69), 2:247. Cesar Lyndon, Journal, Rhode Island Manuscripts, 10:82d, 10:83c,
RIHS. Ann Tashjian and Dickran Tashjian, "The Afro-American Section of Newport,
Rhode Island's Common Burying Ground," *Cemeteries and Gravemakers: Voices of American
Culture*, ed. Richard E. Meyer (Ann Arbor, Mich., 1989), 163–96.

8. "Potters' Field": Matthew 27:8. Anne-Marie Cantwell and Diana diZerega Wall, *Unearthing Gotham: The Archaeology of New York City* (New Haven, 2001), 277–93. James C.
Garman, "Viewing the Color Line through the Material Culture of Death," *Historical Archaeology* 28, no. 3 (1994): 74–93. John Stevens II, Account Book 5, 1770–92, John Stevens
Shop, Newport. I am grateful to Nick Benson for permission to consult these records.

9. Violet: Garman, "Viewing the Color Line," 81. Phillis Lyndon headstone: Tashjian
and Tashjian, "Afro-American Section," fig. 7.15.

10. John Demos, *A Little Commonwealth: Family Life in Plymouth Colony* (New York,
1971). Nancy F. Cott, *Public Vows: A History of Marriage and the Nation* (Cambridge, Mass.,
2000). John Stevens, Account Book 4, 1743–50, John Stevens Shop, Newport. Susan Dwyer
Amussen, *An Ordered Society: Gender and Class in Early Modern England* (New York, 1988).

11. *Diary of Samuel Sewall*, 435 (26 Sept. 1700). "Desire to Marry": agreement between
Richard Smith and Jo, 10 May 1689, in George B. Loring, "Slavery in Essex County," *Essex
Institute Historical Collections* 7, no. 1 (1865): 73. Jack's petition (1710): George E. Howard,
History of Matrimonial Institutions (Chicago, 1904), 2:219. Joseph Carvalho III, *Black Families in Hampden County, Massachusetts, 1650–1855* ([Boston], 1984).

12. Jeremy Belknap, "Answer to Queries Respecting the Slavery and Emancipation of
Negroes in Massachusetts," *MHS Collections* 4 (1795): 191–211. *Boston Weekly News-Letter*, 18
June–25 June 1741. *Newport Mercury*, 31 Dec. 1764; 20 Nov. 1759; 20 Feb. 1764; 1 Jan. 1760.
Providence Gazette, 13 Feb. 1768.

13. James MacSparran, *Letter Book and Abstract of Out Services . . . 1743–1751,* ed. Daniel Goodwin (Boston, 1899), 15 (24 Oct. 1743), 29 (25 June 1745). MacSparran described Maroca as "his slave and wife to Richard african his slave likewise" when their child was baptized on 24 Feb. 1732. Daughter Beleco was baptized 27 Mar. 1741. MacSparran gave away a daughter (baptized 8 Feb. 1745) and another child (baptized 8 Nov. 1749). Wilkins Updike, *History of the Episcopal Church in Narragansett, Rhode Island* (Boston, 1907), 2:509, 521, 525, 541. One master offered to sell a woman for "Half her Value . . . for no other Fault than having Children without a Husband"; *Newport Mercury,* 28 Apr.–5 May 1766. Negotiations about marriage: Robert A. Gross, *Minutemen and Their World* (New York, 1976), 98–104. Women's reputation: Cornelia Hughes Dayton, *Women before the Bar: Gender, Law, and Society in Connecticut, 1639–1798* (Chapel Hill, N.C., 1995), 161. When an Englishwoman gave birth to a "mulatto" child in New Hampshire about 1750, the child was raised by her father, who then bound him out; Eleazar Wheelock to Governor Jonathan Trumbull, 28 Dec. 1775, Dartmouth College, EWP 775478.

14. Ruth Wallis Herndon, *Unwelcome Americans: Living on the Margin in Early New England* (Philadelphia, 2001), ch. 1. Brooks: MSA 9:393 (19 Dec. 1755). Timothy Mather Cooley, *Sketches of the Life and Character of the Reverend Lemuel Haynes, A. M.* (New York, 1837).

15. *Rex v. Jenny Chapman,* SC NC, Mar. 1767, E:325 and files, RIJRC. *Newport Mercury,* 9–16 Feb. 1767, 6–13 Apr. 1767. Walter Challoner, May 1767, RI Petitions 12:67 (includes statements by William Vinall and Ezra Stiles). The assembly stayed her execution and petitioned the king for a pardon; the governor of Rhode Island to the earl of Hillsborough, 14 Nov. 1768, Letters from the Governor, 2:15, RISA.

16. Rhode Island cases: *Rex v. Mary Roolenburg,* GCT, Newport, Mar. 1717; *Rex v. Ethalinah Steere,* GCT, Newport, Mar. 1726; *Rex v. Sarah Faroah,* SC NC, Mar. 1730, B:372 and files; *Rex v. Jane Honey,* SC BC, Oct. 1748, 1:4–5; *Rex v. Mary Elisha,* SC NC, Mar. 1750, D:184; *Rex v. Dutches, alias Dutches Mason,* SC PC, Mar. 1765, 1:394 and files; *Rex v. Sarah Crandall,* SC NC, Sept. 1771, E:491–92; *Rex v. Nancy alias Nancy Durfey,* SC NC, Sept. 1772, F:54 and files; *Rex v. Mary White,* SC PC, Sept. 1790, 3:13–14; *Rex v. Mariah Slade,* SC PC, Mar. 1791, 3:43–45; indictment of Judith Malbone, SC NC, Mar. 1796, files. Peter Charles Hoffer and N. E. H. Hull, *Murdering Mothers: Infanticide in England and New England, 1558–1803* (New York, 1981).

17. "Masters of Negroes": "Journal of Rev. John Ballantine, 1737–1774," quoted in Carvalho, *Black Families in Hampden County,* 11–12. *Providence Gazette,* 22 Nov. 1777. "Recommendation of a Negro named Exeter, whom Wheelock wishes to sell, with the Negro's wife and child, for £60," 5 Nov. 1765, Lebanon, EWP 765605.2. Charles E. Hill, "Slavery and Its Aftermath in Beverly, Massachusetts: Juno Larcom and Her Family," *Essex Institute Historical Collections* 116, no. 2 (1980).

18. *Newport Mercury,* 5 Oct. 1762. Other examples: *Newport Mercury,* 2–9 Jan. 1769 (a Negro woman and child); 12–19 Jan. 1767 (a Negro woman and her son). New York law: Nell Irvin Painter, *Sojourner Truth: A Life, a Symbol* (New York, 1996).

19. John Stevens II, Edward Collins Headstone, 1739, Newport Common Burial Ground.

20. Petition of "a Grate Number of Blacks" to General Thomas Gage, 25 May 1774, in *MHS Collections*, 5th ser., 3 (1877): 432; a similar petition, 434–35.

21. Herndon, *Unwelcome Americans*, ch. 2.

22. Mary R. Morton to Moses Brown, Newport, 21 July 1815, MBP. John R. Gillis, "Married but Not Churched: Plebeian Sexual Relations and Marital Nonconformity in Eighteenth-Century Britain," *Eighteenth-Century Life* 9, no. 3 (1985): 31–42. Eve Tavor Bannet, "The Marriage Act of 1753: 'A Most Cruel Law for the Fair Sex,'" *Eighteenth-Century Studies* 30, no. 3 (1997): 233–54. Flora's Case: Howard, *History of Matrimonial Institutions*, 219.

23. Iris Berger, *Women in Sub-Saharan Africa: Restoring Women to History* (Bloomington, Ind., 1999). Claire C. Robertson and Martin A. Klein, eds., *Women and Slavery in Africa* (Madison, Wisc., 1983). Examination of Mary Fowler, alias Mary Cummock, 14 May 1796, South Kingstown Town Council Records, 6:229 (microfilm copy at RIHS); Herndon, *Unwelcome Americans*, 60–62.

24. Cesar Lyndon, Journal, 1764–70, Rhode Island Manuscripts, 10:81–85, 10:83a, 10:84c, RIHS. Examples in the M. Chamberlain Collection, MHS: the "Negros [marriage] Intention" between "John (a negro mallato man Servant to Lieut. James Hay of Stoneham) and Phillis (a Negro ~~gerl~~ woman servant to Mr. Eleazer Poole of Woborn)," 25 Nov 1760; David Green of Reading, permit for his "negro man Jack to be married to De[aco]n Joseph Greens negro woman, cloea," 6 Apr. 1768.

25. I assume that the letter writer is the elder Cesar Lyndon ("Great Cesar") and that it was his son of the same name ("Little Cesar") who seduced Brown's wife. Cesar Lyndon to Moses Brown, Newport, 3 Sept. 1781, MBP.

26. Noah Hobart, *Serious Address to the Episcopal Separation in New England . . .* (Boston, 1748), 77, 78. In rebuttal: John Beach, *Calm and Dispassionate Vindication . . .* (Boston, 1749), 39.

27. Samuel Phillips, "Form of a Negro-Marriage," n.d., in George H. Moore, "Slave Marriages in Massachusetts," *Historical Magazine*, 2d ser., 5 (1869): 135–37. Phillips was minister in Andover from 1710 to his death in 1771.

28. Petition of Elizabeth Maloney for divorce, SC PC, Mar. 1783, files, RIJRC. Jethro Boston: MSA 9:349–52 (1750); see also MSA 9:248–50 (1742). In 1785, Pricilla Wakefield of Boston was accused of adultery with a Negro man; Increase Sumner, Notes on Law Cases, 2:293, MHS.

29. David Crosby to Wheelock, East Hartford, 4 Nov. 1767, EWP 767604.1.

30. On cartoons attacking James Pemberton by depicting him involved sexually with an Indian woman (fig. 11), see Robert F. Looney, *Philadelphia Printmaking: American Prints before 1860* (West Chester, Pa., 1976), 75–80. Account book and diary, James Wilson Papers, APS. The sex diary was probably kept by a sawyer who worked for Wilson in the early 1790s: Richard Godbeer, *Sexual Revolution in Early America* (Baltimore, 2002), 408 n. 11. Wilson's 1792 law lectures: quoted in Cott, *Public Vows*, 10–12, 161–62. Petition of Thomas Ninigret for divorce, SC NC, Oct. 1766, files, RIJRC.

31. James Bowdoin to George Scott, Boston, 14 Oct. 1763, Bowdoin-Temple Papers, MHS.

32. Dayton, *Women before the Bar*, 206.

33. *Diary of Samuel Sewall*, 853 (24 Apr. 1717).

34. Barbara S. Lindemann, "'To Ravish and Carnally Know': Rape in Eighteenth Century Massachusetts," *Signs* 10, no. 1 (1984): 63–82. Amos Lewis, GSP KC, Aug. 1757, Minute Book, RIJRC.

35. For seventeenth-century Massachusetts, see Roger Thompson, *Sex in Middlesex: Popular Moves in a Massachusetts County, 1649–1699* (Amherst, Mass., 1986), 107–8. In another case, Nicholas Sension was prosecuted for sexual assault on a male servant: Jonathan Ned Katz, *Gay/Lesbian Almanac: A New Documentary History* (New York, 1983). Matthew Hale, *Pleas of the Crown* (London, 1736), quoted in Dayton, *Women before the Bar*, 247. Blackstone, *Commentaries on the Laws of England*, 4:213.

36. Sharon Block, *He Said I Must: Coerced Sex in Early America* (Chapel Hill, N.C., forthcoming). Dayton, *Women before the Bar*, 234, 246–58. Lindemann, "To Ravish and Carnally Know," 63–82. Rape prosecutions in eighteenth-century Rhode Island include indictment of Michael Carel, GCT, Newport, Sept. 1724, RIJRC. *Rex v. Humphry Sillavan*, SC NC, Mar. 1730, B:372, RIJRC. Peter was branded "R" and sold (presumably out of the colony); Cuff was sold out of the colony to pay his fines, court costs, and civil damages; and Benjamin Smith was whipped, sold, and banished. Benjamin Smith "a Mustee or Molatto Man," SC PC, Sept. 1769, 2:11–12 and files, RIJRC. Daniel Wilson, SC PC, Mar. 1774, 2:297–98, RIJRC.

37. Ephraim Pearce, deposition, 2 May 1766, petition of Rebecca Thayer for divorce, SC PC, Mar. 1766, quoted in Sheldon S. Cohen, "The Broken Bond: Divorce in Providence County, 1749–1809," *RIH* 44, no. 3 (1985): 71. Record of settlement, *John Briggs v. Elizabeth Palmer and Phebe Palmer*, 27 July 1756, in indictment of Job Almy, GSP NC, Nov. 1758, files, RIJRC.

38. *Boston News-Letter*, 24 Feb. 1718, in Robert C. Twombly, "Black Resistance to Slavery in Massachusetts," in *Insights and Parallels*, ed. William O'Neil (Minneapolis, 1973), 33. Winthrop D. Jordan, *White over Black: American Attitudes toward the Negro, 1550–1812* (Chapel Hill, N.C., 1968), 175.

39. *Rex v. Cuff*, SC NC, Mar. 1743, C:127 and files, RIJRC.

40. *Comfort Taylor v. Cuff*, Oct. 1743, Court of Equity, 6:105–7, RISA.

41. *Taylor v. Cuff*, CCP NC, May 1743, files; *Cuff v. Taylor* (appeal), SC NC, Sept. 1743, C:127 and files, RIJRC. Comfort Taylor, Oct. 1743, RI Petitions 5:33. Through the 1770s, courts routinely ordered defendants sold for a limited term if they could not otherwise satisfy financial judgments; for instance, burglar John Ellis Noble was liable for sale for not more than seven years; SC PC, Sept. 1772, 2:190–92, RIJRC.

42. *Acts and Laws of . . . Rhode-Island* (Newport, 1745), 263. *Acts and Laws of . . . Rhode-Island* (Newport, 1767), 195–96.

43. Dayton, *Women before the Bar*, 248–55, 269. Lindemann, "To Ravish and Carnally Know," 69.

44. *Newport Gazette*, 5 Dec. 1763. Richard Slotkin, "Narratives of Negro Crime in New England, 1675–1800," *American Quarterly* 25, no. 1 (1973): 3–31. On seventeenth-century prosecutions: Thompson, *Sex in Middlesex*, 74.

45. *Newport Mercury*, 31 Oct. 1763; 13 Nov. 1769; 3 Dec. 1791.

46. Martha Hodes, *Sex across the Color Line: White Women and Black Men* (New Haven, 1996).

47. T. T. Brown to John [Tabor] Kemp, Albany, 21 July 1762, Sedgewick II Papers, MHS.

48. *Itineraries of Ezra Stiles*, 141–42 (31 Oct. 1761). *Rex v. Sarah Pharoah*, SC NC, Mar. 1730, B:372 and files, RIJRC. For complaints to town officials about Indian women abandoning "mustee" children: Ruth Wallis Herndon and Ella Wilcox Sekatau, "The Right to a Name: The Narragansett People and Rhode Island Officials in the Revolutionary Era," *Ethnohistory* 44, no. 3 (1997): 128.

49. Jean M. O'Brien, *Dispossession by Degrees: Indian Land and Identity in Natick, Massachusetts, 1650–1790* (New York, 1997). Petition of 1761: Francis G. Hutchins, *Mashpee, the Story of Cape Cod's Indian Town* (West Franklin, N.H., 1979), 76.

50. Deake to Fish, Dec. 1765, in Simmons and Simmons, *Old Light on Separate Ways,* 21–22.

51. Daniel R. Mandell, "Shifting Boundaries of Race and Ethnicity: Indian-Black Intermarriage in Southern New England, 1760–1880," *JAH* 85, no. 2 (1998): 475.

52. Rhode Island Census of 1774, RISA.

53. William J. Brown, *The Life of William J. Brown . . .* (Providence, 1883), 5–18.

54. Daniel R. Mandell, "The Saga of Sarah Muckamugg: Indian and African Intermarriage in Colonial New England," in *Sex, Love, Race: Crossing Boundaries in North American History*, ed. Martha Hodes (New York, 1999), 76–77.

55. Gideon Hawley to James Freeman, Mashpee, 2 Nov. 1802, Gideon Hawley Papers, MHS.

56. Hawley, Census of Mashpee, 1776, Hawley Papers, MHS. Edward Augustus Kendall, *Travels through the Northern Parts of the United States in the Years 1807 and 1808* (New York, 1809), 2:48–51.

57. Hawley to Shearjashub Bourne, Mashpee, 15 Dec. 1788, S. P. Savage II Papers, MHS; Hawley to Freeman, 2 Nov. 1802, Hawley Papers, MHS. William S. Simmons, "The Earliest Prints and Paintings of New England Indians," *RIH* 41, no. 3 (1982): 82–85.

58. Herndon and Sekatau, "Right to a Name."

59. For example, "Heads of Families" in the first federal census, U.S. Bureau of the Census, *Heads of Families at the First Census of the United States taken in the year 1790: Rhode Island* (Washington, D.C., 1909).

60. Mandell, "Shifting Boundaries," 477.

61. Examination of Mary Fowler, alias Mary Cummock, 14 May 1796, South Kingstown Town Council Records, 6:229; Herndon, *Unwelcome Americans*, 60–62, 210.

62. Mandell, "Shifting Boundaries," 476–82.

63. "An Act for regulating the Affairs of the Narragansett Tribe of Indians, in this State," Feb. 1792, *RSRI* 10:467. James H. Merrell, "The Racial Education of the Catawba Indians," *Journal of Southern History* 50, no. 3 (1984): 363–84. State officials used the claim that there were few "pure blooded" Indians left to argue that the tribe should be legally dissolved: Dan King, "Report of Committee on [Narragansett] Indian Tribe, Jan. 1831, Narragansett File 81, RISA; Joseph H. Griffin, *Report of the Commissioner on the Narragansett Tribe of Indians, 1858* (Providence, 1858), 4. In response to the 1831 report, which described the Narragansetts as "mongrels in which the African blood predominates," and to a similar report a year later, which depicted them as "a vagrant race of negro paupers, idle, filthy and vicious," tribe pres-

ident Tobias Ross protested that there was actually little intermixture with blacks. In 1834, the Narragansetts requested a state law expelling from the tribe women who married outside the tribe. Narragansett Council, Response to King Report, June 1832, Narragansett Indian File 86; Narragansett Council to the Rhode Island General Assembly, May 1834 and Oct. 1835, Narragansett Indian File 102, 105, RISA.

64. Elder Asa Hunt to the Warren Association, 2 Sept. 1774, in William G. McLoughlin, *New England Dissent: The Baptists and the Separation of Church and State* (Cambridge, Mass., 1971), 2:764. Around the same time, Abigail Carr, a "Negro" woman, was expelled from a Providence church because, among other things, she "both bedded and boarded with a certain white man, by the name of Simeon Anderson"; First Baptist Church Records, 1:77, RIHS.

65. McLoughlin, *New England Dissent*, 2:764–65. Simon Pease: Elaine Crane, *A Dependent People: Newport, Rhode Island, in the Revolutionary Era* (New York, 1985), 25. Kingstown Pease's household: 1782 census of Rhode Island, RIHS. Later, Pease joined—and was expelled from—a Baptist church in Newport and then was accepted by a New York Baptist church: Samuel Jones, clerk of the Second Baptist Church, New York, to Parker Hall, clerk of the Second Baptist Church, Newport, 15 Aug. 1792, Newport Second Baptist Church Records (microfilm copy at RIHS).

66. Hodes, *Sex across the Color Line.*

67. Jordan, *White over Black*, 471–72. Pennsylvania's 1725–26 manumission statute established harsh penalties for whites who "shall cohabit or dwell with any negro under pretense of being married"; A. Leon Higginbotham Jr., *In the Matter of Color: Race and the American Legal Process: The Colonial Period* (New York, 1978), 284. "An Act to prevent clandestine Marriages," *Public Laws of the State of Rhode-Island: as revised . . . and . . . enacted. . . . in January, 1798* (Providence, 1798), 483. Paternity law: *Public Laws of the State of Rhode-Island . . . Passed since . . . 1798* (Providence, 1810), 31.

68. Cohen, "Broken Bond," 67–80. Joseph Nightingale ad: *United States Chronicle* (Providence), 25 July 1799. John Stevens Jr., Account Book 6: 1786–98, John Stevens Shop, Newport: Pease, 76 (29 Mar. 1788); Newport Gardner, 134 (28 Sept.–30 Oct. 1790); Cato Thurston, 161 (1792–20 Sept. 1793).

69. John Saillant, "The Black Body Erotic and the Republican Body Politic, 1790–1820," *Journal of the History of Sexuality* 5, no. 3 (1995): 403–28.

70. *The Columbian Almanac for . . . 1796* (Philadelphia, [1795]), in Robert K. Dodge, *Early American Almanac Humor* (Bowling Green, Ohio, 1987), 69. *Newport Mercury,* 9 Oct. 1798 (reprinted from the *Salem Gazette*).

Five ||| Men of Arms

1. Royal R. Hinman, *A Historical Collection from Official Records, Files, &c., of the Part Sustained by Connecticut, during the War of the Revolution* (Hartford, 1842). Lorenzo Johnston Greene, *Negro in Colonial New England* (New York, 1942), 252–53.

2. Joseph P. Reidy, "'Negro Election Day' and Black Community Life in New England, 1750–1860," *Marxist Perspectives* 1 (Fall 1978): 102–17. Shane White, "'It Was a Proud Day': African Americans, Festivals, and Parades in the North, 1741–1834," *JAH* 81, no. 1 (1994): 13–50.

3. [John Leacock], *The Fall of British Tyranny or, American Liberty Triumphant. The First Campaign. A Tragi-Comedy of Five Acts . . .* (Philadelphia, 1776). References are to act and scene numbers.

4. *Fall of British Tyranny*, IV.4.

5. F. Nwabueze Okoye, "Chattel Slavery as the Nightmare of the American Revolutionaries," *WMQ* 37 (1980): 5–28.

6. *Fall of British Tyranny*, I.3. Scottish conspiracy: *Connecticut Courant*, 19 June 1775.

7. *Fall of British Tyranny*, prologue.

8. Ibid., V.2, III.3, II.2.

9. Oliver M. Dickerson, ed., *Boston under Military Rule, 1768–1769, as Revealed in a Journal of the Times* (Boston, 1936), 3 (6 Oct. 1768), 6 (14 Oct. 1768), 16 (31 Oct. 1768) and others. George H. Moore, *Notes on the History of Slavery in Massachusetts* (New York, 1866), 180–81.

10. Alfred F. Young and Terry J. Fife, *We the People: Voices and Images of the New Nation* (Philadelphia, 1993), 30–31. Benjamin Quarles, *The Negro in the American Revolution* (Chapel Hill, N.C., 1961), 4–6.

11. T. L., *Yankee Doodle, or the Negroes Farewell to America* [London, ca. 1778], Vocal and Instrumental Music, Dr. Arne, 2:12, BPL. Robert A. Gross, *The Minutemen and Their World* (New York, 1976), 95–98.

12. Philip J. Deloria, *Playing Indian* (New Haven, 1998), 13–58.

13. Ibid., 17. *Fall of British Tyranny*, III.6.

14. *Boston Gazette*, 14 Mar. 1774. John Andrews to William Barrell, 18 Dec. 1773, *MHS Proceedings* (1866): 326. See also Carla Mulford, ed., *John Leacock's The First Book of the American Chronicles of the Times, 1774–1775* (Newark, Del., 1987), 41, 91 n. 17. *Connecticut Courant*, 16 Oct. 1775.

15. *Maryland Gazette*, 14 Dec. 1775; see also 21 Dec. 1775, 4 Jan. 1776. Woody Holton, *Forced Founders: Indians, Debtors, Slaves, and the Making of the American Revolution in Virginia* (Chapel Hill, N.C., 1999), 133–63. Sylvia R. Frey, *Water from the Rock: Black Resistance in a Revolutionary Age* (Princeton, N.J., 1991), 63–80. *Fall of British Tyranny*, IV.6.

16. *Fall of British Tyranny*, IV.2.

17. *Virginia Gazette* (Purdie), 17 Nov. 1775, 24 Nov. 1775. The fate of Dunmore's "Ethiopian Regiment": Elizabeth A. Fenn, *Pox Americana: The Great Smallpox Epidemic of 1775–82* (New York, 2001), 55–62. Thomas Jefferson to John Pane, 20 Aug. 1776, in *The Papers of Thomas Jefferson*, ed. Julian Boyd (Princeton, N.J., 1950), 1:497–98.

18. Wheelock to Jonathan Trumbull, 28 Aug. 1775, Dartmouth College, EWP 775478. *New York Journal*, 29 Dec. 1775 (supplement), quoted in Quarles, *Negro in the American Revolution*, 31. Captured runaways: *Virginia Gazette*, 10 Jan. 1776, 13 Apr. 1776; *Maryland Gazette*, 22 Feb. 1776; *Connecticut Courant*, 27 Nov. 1775. *Robert v. Godfrey Wainwood*, SC PC, [Nov. 1790], files, RIJRC.

19. *Fall of British Tyranny*, IV.3.

20. Quarles, *Negro in the American Revolution*, 114.

21. "Adam's Fall: The Trip to Cambridge" (1775), in Frank Moore, *Songs and Ballads of the American Revolution* (New York, 1855), 99–102.

22. "A List of the Names of the Provincials who were Killed and Wounded . . . at Concord," broadside, [1775], MHS.

23. Thomas Jefferson, *Notes on the Proceedings in Congress*, 1–4 July 1776, in *Letters of Delegates to Congress, 1774–1789*, ed. Paul H. Smith et al., 26 vols. (Washington, D.C., 1976–2000), 4:438–46. John Adams to James Warren, Philadelphia, 7 July 1777, in *Letters of Delegates*, 7:308. Adams to Jonathan Dickinson Sergeant, Philadelphia, 17 Aug. 1776; enclosure in Sergeant to Adams, 13 Aug. 1776; both in *Letters of Delegates*, 4:12. Executive Committee to George Washington, Philadelphia, 9 Jan. 1777, in *Letters of Delegates* 6:71.

24. H. Tefler Mook, "Training Day in New England," *NEQ* 11, no. 4 (Dec. 1938): 675, 696. Richard P. Gildrie, "Defiance, Diversion, and the Exercise of Arms: The Several Meanings of Colonial Training Days in Colonial Massachusetts," *Military Affairs* 52, no. 2 (1988): 53–55. Fred Anderson, *A People's Army: Massachusetts Soldiers and Society in the Seven Years' War* (Chapel Hill, N.C., 1984). Benjamin Quarles, "The Colonial Militia and Negro Manpower," *Mississippi Valley Historical Review* 45, no. 4 (1959): 643–52. White, "It Was a Proud Day," 18. Negro drummers: *Boston Evening Post*, 31 Mar. 1763.

25. John Shy, *A People Numerous and Armed: Reflections on the Military Struggle for American Independence*, rev. ed. (Ann Arbor, Mich., 1990), 37–39. For example, Billeting Rolls, 1757, Notarial 7:361, RISA: Captain Whiting's company included Algonquian names such as "Joseph Wappy," "Moses Chesuck," and "James Tookup" and West African names such as "Quaco Briggs." In 1760 the Rhode Island regiment reportedly had about sixty or seventy Indians; *Itineraries of Ezra Stiles*, 119 (20 Jan. 1761). Jeremy Belknap, "Answer to Queries Respecting the Slavery and Emancipation of Negroes in Massachusetts," *MHS Collections* 4 (1795): 199. Narragansett exhorter: Franklin B. Dexter, ed., *Diary of David McClure, Doctor of Divinity, 1748–1820* (New York, 1899), 189–91 (1768).

26. Voltaire, *Candide* (1759).

27. Benjamin Franklin to Anthony Todd, New York, 29 Mar. 1776, in *Papers of Benjamin Franklin*, ed. William C. Willcox, vol. 22 (New Haven, 1982), 392–94. Adams to John Thomas, Philadelphia, 5 Oct. 1775, in *Letters of Delegates*, 2:560. Adams to William Heath, Philadelphia, 5 Oct. 1775, in *Letters of Delegates*, 2:113. Alexander Graydon, *Memoirs of a Life* (Harrisburg, Pa., 1811), 131. Salem Poor: Quarles, *Negro in the American Revolution*, 11.

28. Quarles, *Negro in the American Revolution*, 13–18. Massachusetts Committee of Safety: Peter Force, ed., *American Archives*, 4th ser., 6 vols. (Washington, D.C., 1837–46), 2:762.

29. Thomas Paine, *The American Crisis. Number I. By the author of Common sense* ([Philadelphia, 1776]), 1, LCP. Gross, *Minutemen and Their World*, 153. Quarles, *Negro in the American Revolution*, 17. David Ramsay, *History of the American Revolution* (1789), 2 vols. (New York, 1968), 1:233–34.

30. Washington: James Kirby Martin and Mark Edward Lender, *A Respectable Army: The Military Origins of the Republic, 1763–1789* (Arlington Heights, Ill., 1982), 45. Hamilton: Charles Patrick Neimeyer, *America Goes to War: A Social History of the Continental Army* (New York, 1996), 2.

31. Neimeyer, *America Goes to War*, 71–89. Quarles, *Negro in the American Revolution*, 73, 53–54. Recent studies provide larger numbers: Louis Wilson, "Genealogical and Military Data of Blacks, Indians, Mustees from Rhode Island in the American Revolutionary War,"

typescript, 1 Aug. 1996, RIHS; David O. White, *Connecticut's Black Soldiers, 1775–1783* (Chester, Conn., 1973), lists 289 black men from the military rolls and says that another 100 names are identifiably black (56–64). A. Leon Higginbotham Jr., *In the Matter of Color: Race and the American Legal Process: The Colonial Period* (New York, 1978), 88.

32. The best studies of New England are Gross, *Minutemen and Their World*, 147–52; Shy, *People Numerous and Armed*, 171–72; and Richard Buel Jr., *Dear Liberty: Connecticut's Mobilization for the Revolutionary War* (Middletown, Conn., 1980), 93–134. See also Neimeyer, *America Goes to War*, 18–27, and Quarles, *Negro in the American Revolution*, 51–67.

33. The Rhode Island Military Census of 1777, RIHS.

34. Hessian: W. B. Hartgrove, "The Negro in the American Revolution," *Journal of Negro History* 1 (1916): 126. London Hazard, Pension Application S17463, 1832, NA. *Hampshire Gazette*, 7 Mar. 1787, in William Pencak, "The Humorous Side of Shay's Rebellion," *Historical Journal of Massachusetts* 17, no. 2 (1989): 163.

35. Neimeyer, *America Goes to War*, 72–73. Quarles, *Negro in the American Revolution*, 70. William Watson, Pension Application S22035, 1832, NA. Martin and Lender, *Respectable Army*, 91.

36. *Boston Gazette*, 13 Oct. 1777. Antibiastes, *Observations on the Slaves and the Indented Servants, inlisted in the Army, and in the Navy of the United States* (Philadelphia, 14 Aug. 1777), LCP.

37. Moses Hazard: Council of War Minute Book, 1777, Revolutionary War Records, RISA, 2:7. *Providence Gazette*, 15 Nov. 1777. *Newport Gazette*, 10 Mar. 1777.

38. Buel, *Dear Liberty*, 135, 211, 179. Worthington C. Ford, ed., *Journals of the Continental Congress*, vol. 11 (Washington, D.C., 1908), 477.

39. Quarles, *Negro in the American Revolution*, 69.

40. Neimeyer, *America Goes to War*, 191 n. 54. White, *Connecticut's Black Soldiers*, 29–35. "Bucks of America": Sidney Kaplan and Emma Nogrady Kaplan, *The Black Presence in the Era of the American Revolution* (New York, 1973), 55–59.

41. Neimeyer, *America Goes to War*, 76.

42. Quarles, *Negro in the American Revolution*, 52. RCRI 8:640–41. *Newport Gazette*, 5 June 1777, 5 Feb. 1778. Sidney S. Rider, *An Historical Inquiry Concerning the Attempt to Raise a Regiment of Slaves by Rhode Island during the War of the Revolution* (Providence, 1880), 9–18.

43. Captain Elijah Lewis to the Speaker of the Assembly, South Kingstown, 13 Mar. 1778, RISA.

44. Seventy-four names from the 1778 treasurer's accounts (Rider, *Historical Inquiry*) were compared against the compilation of black veterans' records by Louis Wilson, 1996, at the RIHS: at least twenty-three had served since at least 1777. Deposition of Luke Griffith, 9 Sept. 1781, RISA. Military Papers, Revolutionary War, 3:23, nos. 1, 2, 24, 25; General Treasurer's Accounts, 1761–81, vol. 6; both in RISA. Neimeyer, *America Goes to War*, 75.

45. Governor Nicholas Cooke to General Warren, 24 Mar. 1778; Governor W. Greene to William Ellery, 21 Dec. 1779; W. Greene to Henry Marchant and John Collins, 3 Sept. 1779; all in RISA.

46. Rider, *Historical Inquiry*, 20, 26–27, 40. Rhode Island General Assembly, *July (second session) 1780. At the General Assembly of the governor and Company of the state of Rhode-Island . . .* (Providence, [1785]), 28. *Public Records of the State of Connecticut* (1782), 138.

47. *Providence Gazette*, 10 Jan. 1781, 19 May 1781, 9 Mar. 1782.

48. Jehu Grant to J. L. Edwards, 1836, and petition of Jehu Grant, 1832, in John C. Dann, ed., *The Revolution Remembered: Eyewitness Accounts of the War for Independence* (Chicago, 1980), 26–28.

49. "Negro Petitions for Freedom," *MHS Collections*, 5th ser., 3 (1877): 423–37. Petition of Paul Cuffe, Oct. 1780, MSA, in Herbert Aptheker, ed., *A Documentary History: Of the Negro People in the United States* (New York, 1951), 15. Petition of John Cuffe and six others, Dartmouth, 10 Feb. 1780, MSA 186:134–36. Thanks to Dan Mandell for sharing this document with me.

50. Benjamin Quarles, "The Revolutionary War as a Black Declaration of Independence," in *Slavery and Freedom in the Age of the American Revolution*, ed. Ira Berlin and Ronald Hoffman (Urbana, Ill., 1983), 283–301.

51. Kaplan and Kaplan, *Black Presence in the Era of the American Revolution*, 203. *Newport Gazette*, 12 June 1777; 12 June 1777, 8 July 1779. Frederick Mackenzie, *Diary of Frederick Mackenzie, giving a daily narrative of his military service as an officer of the regiment of Royal Welch fusiliers during the years 1775–1781 in Massachusetts, Rhode Island and New York . . .*, 2 vols. (Cambridge, Mass., 1930), 2:326.

52. Anthony Johnson, 4 Dec. 1783, RI Petitions 20:101.

53. Data compiled from Graham Russell Hodges, *The Black Loyalist Directory: African Americans in Exile after the American Revolution* (New York, 1996), and Peter Wilson Coldham, *American Migrations, 1765–1799: The Lives, Times, and Families Who Remained Loyal to the British Crown before, during, and after the Revolutionary War, as Related in Their Own Words and through Their Correspondence* (Baltimore, 2000), 134–47.

54. Petition of Scipio Fayerweather, 27 Apr. 1776, Revolutionary War Rolls 416–17, MSA.

55. Charles Dudley, Newport's collector of customs until 1774, lost income, his house, and two black servants (138); Connecticut widow Sarah Nichols fled with her children to Nova Scotia, leaving behind a farm, house, and a Negro man (23); in Massachusetts, Chief Justice Peter Oliver lost a "family" of slaves from his estate in Middleborough (96), and Lieutenant Governor Thomas Oliver lost eleven slaves from his estate in Cambridge (97); all in Coldham, *American Migrations*. Public Records of the State of Connecticut, 1779, Connecticut Archives, Record Group 1. Resolution re: Tony Rome, Council of War Minute Book, Revolutionary War Records, RISA, 181. Gwendolyn Evans Logan, "The Slave in Connecticut during the American Revolution," *Connecticut Historical Society Bulletin* 30, no. 3 (1965): 76.

56. Jane Coggeshall, Oct. 1785, RI Petitions 22:72. Resolution of the General Assembly declaring Quaco a freeman, RI Notarial 8:91.

57. *Boston Gazette*, 27 Oct. 1777. Of Massachusetts slaves who did not evacuate Boston with the British, most of those who ended up behind British lines were the five from the Swanzey area, of whom at least four fled during the British occupation of Newport: Hodges, *Black Loyalist Directory*.

58. Lodowick Stanton, RI Petitions 18:120.

59. Seth Freeman and Micah Blackwell to Joseph Nye, Sandwich, 14 July 1780, LCP at HSP. Derby vote (Jan. 1781): Connecticut Archives, Revolutionary War, Record Group 2:21,

CSA. Silas Loomis, petition to the General Assembly, 26 May 1777, Connecticut Archives, Revolutionary War, ser. 1, vol. 37, "Slaves; 1764–1789," CSA; Logan, "Slave in Connecticut," 75.

60. Beriah Brown, draft letter re: Scipio, North Kingstown, 17 Mar. 1778, Beriah Brown Papers, RIHS. Scipio Brown, Pension Application S38584, 1818, NA. Hobby: Gross, *Minutemen and Their World*, 151. Council of War Minute Book, 28 Feb. 1778, Revolutionary War Records 3:22, RISA. *Henry Randal v. Alexander Stewart and Prince Randal,* Council of War Minute Book, Revolutionary War Records, 3:22 (28 Feb. 1778), RISA.

61. Robert Roger and Jacob Greene, 1 Feb. 1781, RI Petitions 18:54.

62. On London: *Inhabitants of Winchendon v. Inhabitants of Hatfield,* Mar. 1808, in Helen Tunnicliff Catterall, ed., *Judicial Cases Concerning American Slavery and the Negro,* 5 vols. (Washington, D.C., 1926–37), 4:484. Scipio's story is similar; *Inhabitants of Salem v. Inhabitants of Hamilton,* 4 Mass. 676, Nov. 1808, in Catterall, *Judicial Cases,* 4:488. On Priamus: James Pemberton to Moses Brown, 16 May 1780, Philadelphia, MBP. Thomas Eyers, 27 Oct. 1778, RI Petitions 25:2–29. See also William Hall (re: London), RI Petitions 25:21. Petition of Joshua Austin, 21 Jan. 1783, Connecticut Archives, Revolutionary War, ser. 1, 37, "Slaves; 1764–1789," CSA; quoted in Logan, "Slave in Connecticut," 75. Petition of Joshua Austin, 1784, Misc. Papers, Connecticut Archives, CSA. *Inhabitants of Stockbridge v. Inhabitants of West-Stockbridge,* 12 Mass. 400, Sept. 1815, and appeal (1817), in Catterall, *Judicial Cases,* 4:491, 494. Cato Bannister: Petition of Elkanah Humphrey, 1783, Revolutionary War Records, 2:42, RISA.

63. Cato Baker to Jeremiah Belknap, Danbury, 26 Sept. 1778; Baker to Colonel Baker, Fishkill, 19 June 1779; Jeremy Belknap Papers, MHS.

64. *Providence Gazette,* 5 Oct. 1776. Christopher Greene, Orderly Book, 1777–79, RIHS, 164–81.

65. Rider, *Historical Inquiry,* 23–24.

66. *Pennsylvania Evening Post,* 7 Aug. 1777. *Diary of Frederick Mackenzie,* 2:148–49. Samuel E. Barney, *Songs of the Revolution* (New Haven, 1893), 41–42.

67. Thomas Robinson to Moses Brown, Newport, 18 June 1793, RIHS. Rider, *Historical Inquiry,* 62–64, 69–71, 79–86.

68. Hodges, *Black Loyalist Directory,* xvii–xviii. Ellen Gibson Wilson, *The Loyal Blacks* (New York, 1976), 65. Boston King, "Memoirs of Mr. Boston King," *Methodist Magazine* (Mar. 1798): 155.

69. Quaco [Honeyman], Petition, 1782, RI Notarial 8:91. Jane Coggeshall, 1785, RI Petitions 22:72. Her master: Coldham, *American Migrations,* 137. *Jack Arabas v. Thomas Ivers,* 1 Root 92, 1784, in Catterall, *Judicial Cases,* 4:422; see also Connecticut Archives, Revolutionary War, ser. 1, 37, "Slaves; 1764–1789," CSA. Jack Burrows, Pension Application S44714, NA. *Inhabitants of Stockbridge v. Inhabitants of West-Stockbridge,* 14 Mass. 157, Sept. 1817, in Catterall, *Judicial Cases,* 4:494.

70. "Elizabeth Allin" is listed as a household head in South Kingstown in the 1774 Rhode Island census, RISA. 1782 R.I. Census, RIHS, 89–92. Providence Tax Valuation, 1782, PTP.

71. Physical description from enlistment record dated Warwick, 22 May 1777, Captain Elisha Lewis's Company of the First Rhode Island Regiment, summarized in Wilson, "Genealogical and Military Data," 36. In April 1787, Prince Greene enlisted into Captain Elisha

Lewis's Company in the "Black Regiment" and served in various companies until discharged in 1783; Prince Greene, Pension Application S38754, 1818, NA. He married Rhoda Eldred, 21 June 1778, North Kingstown—Family Search International Genealogical Index v4.01 (2001). "Return of the Married Non-Commissioned Officers and Privates . . . December 22, 1782," in Rider, *Historical Inquiry*, 81.

72. Rhode Island Census, 1782, RIHS. Providence Tax Roll, 1782, RIHS, assessed: Lindsey Munro, no value; Nehemiah Sweet £10; William Wheaton £75 (or William Wheaton Jr. £60); Magg Shakelfed no value; David Burr £10; Henery Rice £120; Elizabeth Allin was not assessed. According to the Rhode Island Military Census, 1777, RIHS, Pero was a slave of Daniel Mowry Jr., of Smithfield. Pero Mawney, Pension Application S38952, 1818, NA.

73. Indictment of Prince Greene, SC PC, Mar. 1781, 2:405 and files, RIJRC.

74. North Burial Ground, Providence.

75. *The Wyllys Papers: Correspondence and Documents Chiefly of Descendants of Gov. George Wyllys of Connecticut, 1590–1796* (Hartford, 1924), 137–38. Guocun Yang, "From Slavery to Emancipation: The African Americans of Connecticut, 1650s–1820s" (Ph.D. diss., University of Connecticut, 1999), 142. In Massachusetts, when the war was over, in 1785, "Negroes, Indians, and Mulattoes were again excluded from the militia"; Higginbotham, *In the Matter of Color*, 88.

76. "List of Invalids resident in the State of Rhode Island," 1785, *RSRI* 10:162–67.

77. Prince Greene gave his discharge papers to Colonel Olney in exchange for a certificate entitling him to a disability pension as per the congressional ordinance of 7 June 1785. Payment of 1793: Wilson, compilation of Rhode Island black servicemen, 1997, RIHS.

78. *American Magazine of Wit* (New York, 1808), 51–52.

Six ||| *Negotiating Freedom*

1. J. Brown quote: *United States Chronicle*, 26 Mar. 1789.

2. Providence Abolition Society's Book, 19 (29 Feb. 1790), Yearly Meeting of Friends for New England Archive, RIHS (hereafter cited as NEYMFA). Moses Brown to James Pemberton, Providence, 26 Apr. 1790, RIHS.

3. Samuel Dexter to Jeremy Belknap, Weston, 23 Feb. 1795, in "Slavery in Massachusetts," *MHS Collections*, 5th ser., 3 (1877): 384.

4. Karen Halttunen, "Humanitarianism and the Pornography of Pain in Anglo-American Culture," *American Historical Review* 100 (1995): 303–34.

5. Ephraim Gardner, deposition, 22 May 1772, *Susannah Wamsley v. Jeffrey Watson*, SC NC, Sept. 1772, files, RIJRC.

6. Indenture between Thomas Wamsley and Henry Gardiner, 20 Nov. 1706, *Henry Wamsley v. Samuel Phelps et al.*, CCP NC, Nov. 1772, files, RIJRC.

7. On the Gardiner family, see Caroline E. Robinson, *The Gardiners of Narragansett: Being a Genealogy of the Descendants of George Gardiner the Colonist, 1638*, ed. Daniel Goodwin (Providence, 1919), 5, 13–14, 42–43. On the Wamsley family, see, in addition to testimony in the *Wamsley v. Watson* suits, the databases compiled at http://www.FamilySearch.org, version 2.2.0; James N. Arnold, *Vital Records of Rhode Island, 1636–1850*, vol. 5, *Washington*

County, 1718–1875 (Providence, 1894); "Records of St. Paul's Church, Narragansett," in Wilkins Updike, *History of the Episcopal Church in Narragansett,* ed. Daniel Goodwin (Boston, 1907), vol. 2; James MacSparran, *Letter Book and Abstract of Out Services . . . 1743–1751,* ed. Daniel Goodwin (Boston, 1899).

8. Testimony of Catharine Gardiner, 19 Mar. 1772, *Wamsley v. Watson,* SC NC, Sept. 1772.

9. Roger Richmond, bill of sale of mulatto woman Sarah Jethro and her daughter Abigail to John Mingo, Negro man, [Bristol], 10 Jan. 1746, RIHS. Orlando Patterson, *Slavery and Social Death: A Comparative Study* (Cambridge, Mass., 1982). Shane White, *Somewhat More Independent: The End of Slavery in New York City, 1770–1810* (Athens, Ga., 1991), 106–11.

10. *Rhode Island Laws* (Newport, 1730), 162. A. Leon Higginbotham Jr., *In the Matter of Color: Race and the American Legal Process: The Colonial Period* (New York, 1978).

11. Charles E. Hill, "Slavery and Its Aftermath in Beverly, Massachusetts: Juno Larcom and Her Family," *Essex Institute Historical Collections* 116, no. 2 (1980): 118 ff. Dutchess remembered by William Ellery Channing: Wilkins Updike, *Memoirs of the Rhode Island Bar* (Boston, 1842), 100–101.

12. Ephraim Gardiner, deposition, 22 May 1772, *Wamsley v. Watson,* SC NC, Sept. 1772. To validate a manumission, the master was required to post a bond with the town for the freed person's future support; "An Act, regulating the manumitting and freeing of *Negro* and *Mulatto* Slaves," *Acts and Laws of . . . Rhode-Island* (Newport, 1767), 234.

13. "An act to prevent slaves from running away from their masters, etc." (1714), *Acts and Laws of . . . Rhode-Island* (1767), 234.

14. Edward M. Cook Jr., ed., "Jeffery Watson's Diary, 1740–1784: Family, Community, Religion, and Politics in Colonial Rhode Island," *RIH* 43, no. 3 (1984): 79–116.

15. *Henry Wamsley by Elizabeth Wamsley (alias Dyer) v. Samuel Phelps and Jeffrey Watson,* CCP PC, Nov. 1772, 1:262, RIJRC.

16. *Susanna Wamsley v. Samuel Rose,* CCP KC, Dec. 1771, files; *Susanna Wamsley v. Jeffrey Watson,* CCP NC, May 1772, files; *Wamsley v. Watson,* SC NC, Sept. 1772, F:33–34 and files.

17. One of the few Rhode Island challenges to enslavement before 1770: Richard Hunt, May 1753, RI Petitions 8:110. Massachusetts and Connecticut cases were clustered around the turn of the century and then reemerged in the 1760s; Lorenzo Johnston Greene, *The Negro in Colonial New England* (New York, 1942), 183–84, 293–97. Higginbotham, *In the Matter of Color,* 82–88.

18. *John Randall v. Matthew Robinson,* SC KC, Oct. 1769, B:217; Oct. 1772, B:352–53; Oct. 1773, B:383; Oct. 1774, B:414–15 and files; RIJRC. John Randall, RI Petitions 15:50 (Aug. 1773).

19. Matthew Griswold to Governor Joseph Wanton, Lyme, 19 June 1773, in Caroline Hazard, ed., *Thomas Hazard, Son of Robert, Called College Tom* (Boston, 1893).

20. James B. Hedges, *The Browns of Providence Plantations,* vol. 1, *Colonial Years* (Cambridge, 1952), 76–81. The deed was recorded 12 Nov. 1773, Probate Court Records, Probate Wills Book 6:73, City Hall, Providence.

21. *United States Chronicle,* 29 Jan. 1784.

22. Richard Smith, bill of manumission of Jane, Groton, Conn., 1757, South Kingstown Monthly Meeting Records, RIHS.

23. Yearly Meeting of the Religious Society of Friends, *An Epistle of caution and advice*

(Philadelphia, 1754), Van Pelt Library, University of Pennsylvania. Thanks to Niki Eustace for alerting me to this text. *The Journal and Major Essays of John Woolman,* ed. Phillips P. Moulton (New York, 1971), 50. See also John Woolman, *Considerations on Keeping Negroes. Part Second* (Philadelphia, 1762). On backsliding, see the case of Hezekiah Collins in Hazard, *Thomas Hazard,* 168–70.

Although the town of South Kingstown had more than five hundred enslaved people in 1774 and a large portion of major slave owners were Friends, the number of manumissions in the records of the local monthly meeting is remarkably low—only eight woman, eight men, and two children in the three decades between 1757 and 1786. Caroline Hazard, *The Narragansett Friends' Meeting in the XVIII Century* (Cambridge, 1899), 190.

24. Thomas B. Hazard, *Recollections of Olden Times* (Newport, 1879), 20. Robert Treat Paine to [unknown], Boston, 21 Aug. 1779, MHS. Ichabod Allen, Certificate, 14 Sept. 1774, MBP; John Carter, manumission of Ingow and Fanny, 18 Feb. 1789, MBP.

25. Brown to Samuel Hopkins, 1 Sept. 1786; Hopkins to Brown, Newport, 16 Sept. 1786; both in RIHS. Benjamin Shearburne, manumission of Pompey, 11 Jan. 1770, RISA. An example of master-slave negotiations: Prince Bowen to Moses Brown, RIHS. George Irish, deposition, [1786], and attorney's notes re: *Samuel Freebody v. James Brattle,* CCP BC, July 1786, in RIHS Manuscripts 16:102, RIHS. John Quamine to Moses Brown, Newport, 5 Jun. 1776 (missing from RIHS), in Mack Thompson, *Moses Brown: Reluctant Reformer* (Chapel Hill, N.C., 1962), 105.

26. Providence Town Meeting Records 6:13–16, RIHS. Nicholas Brown to Keen Osborn, 30 Nov. 1774, JCB.

27. Thompson, *Moses Brown,* 97–99. *RCRI* 7:251. Connecticut in 1774 prohibited the importation of slaves; *Acts and Laws of Connecticut* (1796), quoted in Helen Tunnicliff Catterall, ed., *Judicial Cases Concerning American Slavery and the Negro,* 5 vols. (Washington, D.C., 1926–37), 4:413. Even many large Chesapeake planters wished to stop the international slave trade, largely to increase their profits from the domestic slave trade; Woody Holton, *Forced Founders: Indians, Debtors, Slaves, and the Making of the American Revolution in Virginia* (Chapel Hill, N.C., 1999), 66–73. Jay Coughtry, *The Notorious Triangle: Rhode Island and the African Slave Trade, 1700–1807* (Philadelphia, 1981).

28. John Welsey, *Thoughts on Keeping Negroes,* extracted in *Providence Gazette,* 22 Oct. 1774.

29. Samuel Hopkins, *A Dialogue, Concerning the Slavery of the Africans . . .* (Norwich, [Conn.], 1776). Ezra Stiles and Samuel Hopkins, *To the public* ([Newport, R.I.], 1776). Hopkins complained about the editor of the Newport newspaper in his diary and in a letter to Moses Brown, 17 Nov. 1784: Amasa A. Park, "Memoir," in *The Works of Samuel Hopkins . . . ,* ed. Sewall Harding, 3 vols. (Boston, 1865), 1:119–29. James F. Reilly, "The Providence Abolition Society," *RIH* 21, no. 2 (1962): 35–36.

30. G. J. Barker-Benfield, *The Culture of Sensibility: Sex and Society in Eighteenth-Century Britain* (Chicago, 1992). *Providence Gazette,* 30 Aug. 1783.

31. Mukhtar Ali Isani, "'Far from Gambia's Golden Shore': The Black in Late Eighteenth Century Imaginative Literature," *WMQ* 36 (1979): 353–72. *Providence Gazette,* 7 Feb. 1784.

32. Priamus appears in an extract from Thomas Hazard's account book in Hazard, *Thomas Hazard,* 118–19. See especially evidence of Robert Hazard, Warwick, 28 Nov. 1780,

in Matthew Robinson to Moses Brown, 2 Dec. 1780, MBP. William Dennis to Brown, 3 Jan. 1782, RIHS. Brown to John Pemberton, 19 Jan. 1782; Brown to John Pemberton, 14 Dec. 1781; Thomas Robinson to Brown, Newport, 1 Sept. 1781; Brown to [unknown], 10 Oct. 1784; all in RIHS. Binah: Thomas Robinson to Moses Brown, Newport, 14 June 1776, MBP. A similar case: Hazard, *Recollections of Olden Times*, 20. Sarah: *John Walker v. Edward Bliven*, SC KC, Apr. 1773, B:360.

33. John Rice, 28 Oct. 1779, RI Petitions 17:118. *RCRI* 8:576.

34. One owner sought an exemption from this law on the grounds that his slave Jack had behaved "in a villienous and unfaithful manner"; petition of Nathaniel Phillips, GSP BC, July 1794, RIJRC.

35. Higginbotham, *In the Matter of Color*, 95. *Commonwealth of Massachusetts v. Jennison*, Apr. 1783, in Catterall, *Judicial Cases*, 4:480–81. Arthur Zilversmit, *The First Abolition: The Abolition of Slavery in the North* (Chicago, 1967), 114–15. One sale: John Mory, bill of sale of Dick, 30 Jun. 1785, MHS. Jane Marcou, *Life of Jeremy Belknap* (New York, 1847), 164–65.

36. NEYMFA, 314 (1782), RIHS. Jean R. Soderlund, *Quakers and Slavery: A Divided Spirit* (Princeton, N.J., 1985).

37. "Negro Petitions for Freedom," *MHS Collections*, 5th ser, 3 (1877): 432–37. A petition by Bristol Lambee to "The Sons of Liberty in Connecticut" was reprinted in the *Providence Gazette*, 22 Oct. 1774.

38. Petition of Amy Allen to the General Assembly, Oct. 1784, *RSRI* 10:70–71. Brown to [unknown], 29 May 1786, MBP.

39. Winthrop to Belknap, Cambridge, 4 Mar. 1795, "Slavery in Massachusetts," 389. Jeremy Belknap, "Queries Respecting the Slavery and Emancipation of Negroes in Massachusetts," *MHS Collections* 4 (1795): 201. Some Massachusetts blacks who informally claimed their freedom in the 1770s later became involved in settlement disputes: for example, Romulus and Rosana, who "claimed their liberty, like other blacks, in 1776"; *Shelburne v. Greenfield, Massachusetts*; see also *Littletown v. Tuttle, Massachusetts* (1790); both in Catterall, *Judicial Cases*, 4:481–82.

40. *RSRI* 10:132. Summary of census data: Edgar J. McManus, *Black Bondage in the North* (Syracuse, N.Y., 1973), 199–214.

41. In 1775, the Charlestown clerk declared his intention of recording all manumissions but in the next thirty years recorded only two: Town Council Record Book, 2:2 (4 Sept. 1775), Charlestown Town Records (microfilm at RIHS). The South Kingstown town council heard several cases of people claiming protection under the laws; Jean C. Stutz, ed., *South Kingstown, Rhode Island, Town Council Records, 1771–1795* ([Kingstown, R.I.], 1988), 230 (London and Bristol, 8 Sept. 1788); 231 (Lydia Robinson and Peter Peckham, 18 Oct. 1788); 236 (Phebe, Phillis, and Chloe, 12 Jan. 1789); 239 (Margaret and Catharine, 9 Mar. 1788); 258 (Cato, 14 June 1789); 261 (Quos, 13 Sept. 1789); 271 (Moses Watson, 10 Oct. 1791).

42. Abolition Society's Book, 12 (21 Aug. 1789), RIHS.

43. One intransigent slaveholder: William Almy to Andrew Herr, 12 Dec. 1796; Almy to Herr, 13 Dec. 1796; both in RIHS.

44. Charge of Chief Justice Parsons, *Inhabitants of Winchendon v. Inhabitants of Hatfield*, 4 Mass. 123, March 1808, in Catterall, *Judicial Cases*, 4:484. Adams to Belknap, Quincy, 21

Mar. 1795, in "Slavery in Massachusetts," 401–11. In 1766 Adams represented a "mulatto" woman claiming freedom; Greene, *Negro in Colonial New England*, 296–297. In 1768 Adams successfully represented a slave owner in a freedom suit; Zilversmit, *First Abolition*, 103.

45. *Newport Herald*, 12 Mar. 1789. "Browbeat:" *United States Chronicle*, 26 Mar. 1789.

46. John Reynolds to Moses Brown, 22 May 1790, RIHS. Abolition Society's Book, 22–23 (20 May 1791), RIHS. *Abner Thayer v. Cuff Roberts and Jack Champlin*, CCP PC, June 1784, files, RIJRC. Jack Burrows, Pension Application 428, NA. On legal strategies, see Coughtry, *Notorious Triangle*, ch. 6. Abolition Society members were accused of selfish motives by John Brown, writing as a "Citizen," in the *Providence Gazette*, 12 Feb. 1789.

47. The Abolition Society faced a number of cases concerning men and women brought into Rhode Island after 1774 and held in slavery. The same day that Robert was arrested in Providence, the society took on the case of a man claimed by Robert Stephen; Abolition Society's Book, 28 (ca. May 1789), RIHS.

48. At least eight cases handled by the Abolition Society involved men captured by privateers, including ships owned by John Brown. In May 1789 another of these men, Liverpool, approached Abolition Society lawyer David Howell, who asked Moses Brown to broach the matter with his brother; Howell to Brown, 14 May 1789, MBP.

49. Abolition Society's Book, 12 (21 Aug. 1789), 16 (20 Nov 1789), 26 (18 Nov. 1791), RIHS. *Robert v. Godfrey Wainwood*, SC PC, Nov. 1791, files, RIJRC.

50. Richard Gardiner, bill of sale of a "Negrow femail Child Slave," Oct. 1783, RIHS. Similarly, a South Kingstown farmer sold a two-year-old girl to her parents, Prince and Violet Dyre; William Dyre, bill of sale and indenture of Violet, 24 Dec. 1791, RIHS. William Robinson to Samuel Freebody, South Kingstown, 1 Dec. 1784, RIHS.

51. *Providence Gazette*, 29 Apr. 1786. *Providence Gazette*, 12 Aug. 1786 (Moses Brown ad); 8 June 1775 (Joseph Brown ad). *Newport Mercury*, 7 May 1792 (John Slocum ad); 3 Dec. 1799 (Samuel Elam ad).

52. Before 1772, advertisers generally promised a substantial reward for the return of runaway slaves, indentured servants, apprentices, deserters, and criminals. Afterwards, advertisers for apprentices began offering only token rewards. Between 1787 and 1800, slave advertisers offered rewards below one dollar in eight out of sixteen cases. For Rhode Island runaway advertisements, see Maureen Taylor, ed., *Runaways, Deserters, and Notorious Villains from Rhode Island Newspapers*, vol. 1, *The Providence Gazette, 1762–1800* (Camden, Maine, 1994), and Maureen Taylor and John Wood Sweet, eds., *Runaways, Deserters, and Notorious Villains from Rhode Island Newspapers*, vol. 2, *Additional Notices from the Providence Gazette, 1762–1800, as well as Advertisements from All Other Rhode Island Newspapers from 1732–1800* (Rockport, Maine, 2001). *Newport Mercury*, 20 Jan. 1790.

53. Moses Brown advertised for an indentured servant, "his Mother an Indian, his Father supposed to be White," *United States Chronicle*, 11 July 1799. David Howell and James Manning advertised for the return of two "German Redemptioners," *Providence Gazette*, 29 Apr. 1786. *Pettis et al. v. Jack Warren*, Mar. 1788, in Catterall, *Judicial Cases*, 4:422–23. Moses Brown to Judge Foster, 3 Sept. 1778, RIHS.

54. Joseph Carvalho III, *Black Families in Hampden County, Massachusetts, 1650–1855* ([Boston], 1984), 6.

55. James Mars, *Life of James Mars, A Slave Born and Sold in Connecticut. Written by Himself,* 8th ed. (Hartford, 1869), 4–19.

56. Moses Brown to [unknown], 2 Jun. 1812, NEYMFA.

57. Paul Finkelman, "The Kidnapping of John Davis and the Adoption of the Fugitive Slave Law of 1793," *Journal of Southern History* 56, no. 3 (1990): 397–422. Obadiah Brown to Moses Brown, 26 Jan. 1794, RIHS. For an attempt to shelter a presumed fugitive slave in 1817, see Obadiah Brown to Moses Brown, 28 Nov. 1817, NEYMFA.

58. *Providence Gazette,* 21 Mar. 1789. Abolition Society's Book, 12 (21 Aug. 1789), 16–18 (20 Nov. 1789, re: cases pending the resolution of Robert's case), RIHS. Another case: Moses Brown to James Pemberton, 20 Jul. 1784, RIHS.

59. Peter Thatcher to Moses Brown, Boston, 21 Sept. 1787, RIHS. The Longmeadow "List of the Polls" for 1784 apparently caught Benjamin Swetland in the act of speculating in an underground slave market, buying inexpensive "slaves" in the Connecticut River valley in order to sell them downriver: his modest eighty-two-acre farm held ninety-two black people—perhaps half the black population of the county; Carvalho, *Black Families in Hampden County,* 4. Jonathan Edwards to Moses Brown, New Haven, 20 Oct. 1788, RIHS. Carol Wilson, *Freedom at Risk: The Kidnapping of Free Blacks in America, 1780–1865* (Lexington, Ky., 1994), 7.

60. John Richman was another indentured man sold into slavery in the West Indies; Philip Slead to Moses Brown, Somerset, 26 Dec. 1793, RIHS. Another case involved Peter Gum, kidnapped in Leicester, Massachusetts, and sold as a slave in the West Indies; Abolition Society's Book, 28 (May 1792), RIHS. The extensive correspondence about another sailor—Rhode Island Indian John Fry Jr., who was sold into slavery in the West Indies in the early 1790s—illustrates just how unlikely it was that anyone sold into slavery in the West Indies would ever come back, no matter how clear the proof of his or her legal freedom: Abolition Society's Book, 30 (17 May 1793), RIHS. Granville Sharpe to James Pemberton, 20 Aug. 1794; Moses Brown to James Pemberton, 17 Nov. 1794; both in Pennsylvania Abolition Society Papers, Committee of Correspondence, Letter Book, 1794–1809: 7–8, 9, HSP. Pennsylvania Abolition Society to William Weaver, 23 Feb. 1795; Pennsylvania Abolition Society to Ebenezer Edie, 23 Feb. 1795; Pennsylvania Abolition Society to Thomas Bendle, 23 Feb. 1795; Samuel Coates to William Weaver and Ebenezer Eddy, 30 Nov. 1795; Thomas Harrison to Samuel Griffiths, 4 May 1796; James Pemberton to Providence Abolition Society, 7 May 1796; Moses Brown to Pennsylvania Abolition Society, 1 Jun. 1796; all in HSP.

61. In 1799, one putative mistress managed to get a man named Lindor jailed by identifying him as a runaway servant and then compelled him to agree to serve on two long voyages to India—effectively earning for herself six years of his wages—in exchange for giving up her claim to own him; Poulain Audinet, power of attorney to Nicholas Gilbert, 26 Apr. 1799; Nicholas Gilbert and Lindor, manumission agreement, 29 Apr. 1799; NEYMFA.

62. Moses Brown to [unknown], 20 Oct. 1784, NEYMFA. Moses Brown to [unknown], 26 May 1786, RIHS. It was the vigilance of Rhode Island's communities of color, and the assistance of well-connected white gentlemen, that occasionally enabled the redemption of some of the free Rhode Islanders who had been enslaved in the South. See William Buffam to Moses Brown, 19 July 1815, Smithfield, MBP. Benjamin Hawden to [Moses Brown],

Newport, 3 Jan. 1820; memorandum regarding Thomas Francis, n.d.; B. G., memorandum regarding Olive Westey, n.d.; all in NEYMFA. The kidnapping of three men in Boston Harbor in 1788 created a sensation. About the same time, however, another man was kidnapped in a similar way in Connecticut, and the Providence Abolition Society was pressing two different cases. Belknap to Rush, 7 Apr. 1788 and 22 June 1788, B. Rush Papers, LCP at HSP.

63. Mary Wollstonecraft, *A Vindication of the Rights of Men* (London, 1790), 145; Janet Todd, *Sensibility: An Introduction*, ch. 8.

64. Rhode Island Black Heritage Society, *Creative Survival: The Providence Black Community in the Nineteenth Century* (Providence, [1988]), 46.

65. Harriet Beecher Stowe, *The Minister's Wooing*, in *Three Novels* (New York, 1982), 631–33. An earlier version of this story, told about Hopkins and the Reverend Joseph Bellamy: John Ferguson, *Memoir of the Life and Character of Rev. Samuel Hopkins* (Boston, 1830), 85–86.

66. Quoted in "Ethnic Humor in Early American Jest Books," in *A Mixed Race: Ethnicity in Early America*, ed. Frank Shuffleton (New York, 1993), 175–76. Similar stories: Zilversmit, *First Abolition*, 118.

67. One example is the oft-repeated story of Jeremiah Austin, who freed all his slaves, his only inheritance, and himself worked at day labor; Hazard, *Thomas Hazard*, 165–66.

68. "Capsheaf": *United States Chronicle*, 12 Mar. 1789. Shane White, "'It Was a Proud Day': African Americans, Festivals, and Parades in the North, 1741–1834," *JAH* 81, no. 1 (1994): 13–50. Linda Colley, *Britons: Forging the Nation, 1707–1837* (New Haven, 1992).

69. Julie K. Ellison, *Cato's Tears and the Making of Anglo-American Emotion* (Chicago, 1999). John Brown ("A Citizen") quoted a long, disparaging description of Guinea from "Middleton's *Geography*" in the *Providence Gazette*, 28 Mar. 1789. See Charles Theodore Middleton, *A New and Complete System of Geography* (London, 1777–78). Moses Brown ("M.B.") replied in the same issue. See also *United States Chronicle*, 26 Feb. 1789. Larry E. Tise, *Proslavery: A History of the Defense of Slavery in America, 1701–1840* (Athens, Ga., 1987).

Seven ||| *Conceiving Race*

1. Moses Brown to all whom it may concern, 1803, MBP.

2. Thomas L. Hankins, *Science and Enlightenment* (Cambridge, 1985), 113–57.

3. Carl von Linné, *A General System of Nature . . .*, trans. William Turton, 7 vols. (London, 1802–6), 1:9, APS. Johann Friedrich Blumenbach, *On the Natural Varieties of Mankind*, 3d ed. (1795), trans. Thomas Bendyshe (1865; reprint, New York, 1969), 265 (sect. 80). On Buffon and Jefferson: Antonello Gerbi, *The Dispute of the New World: The History of a Polemic, 1750–1900* (1955), rev. ed., trans. Jeremy Moyle (Pittsburgh, 1973), 3–34, 252–67.

4. "A Journal of the most particular occurrences of the life of Bennett Wheeler . . . Chiefly written and copied AD 1806," entry of 20 Sept. 1776, RIHS.

5. Edward Long, "Observations on the Gradation in the Scale of Being between the Human and Brute Creation," in *History of Jamaica* (London, 1768), reprinted in the *Columbian Magazine or Monthly Miscellany* 2 (1788): 14–20. Henry Home, Lord Kames,

Sketches of the History of Man (Edinburgh and London, 1774). Jefferson, *Notes on the State of Virginia* (Paris, [1785]), 253, APS.

6. Charles Caldwell, "Review of *An essay on the causes of the Variety of Complexion, and figure in the human species, &c. &.* By Samuel Stanhope Smith," *Port Folio* 4 (1814): 259–71 (on Moss); the entire review begins on p. 8 and ends on p. 457. See also Caldwell's shorter review of Smith, *American Review* 2 (July 1811): 128–66.

7. Benjamin Smith Barton, "*Account of* HENRY MOSS, a White Negro . . . ," *Philadelphia Medical and Physical Journal* 2 (1806): 4.

8. The best compilation of these cases: Karl Pearson, Edward Nettleship, and Charles H. Usher, *Monograph on Albinism* (London, 1911), pt. 1, 197–264. Barbara Maria Stafford, *Body Criticism: Imagining the Unseen in Enlightenment Art and Medicine* (Cambridge, Mass., 1991), 319–23.

9. Georges Louis Leclerc, Comte de Buffon, *Histoire naturelle, générale et particuliére . . . ,* vol. 33: supplément, tome quatrième (Paris, 1777), 555–78, APS. Pearson, Nettleship, and Usher, *Monograph on Albinism,* 229–32, plates F18, SS151, SS154, SS155. Dr. John Morgan, "Some account of a motley coloured, or pye negro girl and boy, exhibited before the American philosophical society, in the month of May, 1784," *American Magazine, or Universal Magazine* 3 (1789): 37–39.

10. "Primrose, the Celebrated Piebald Boy, a Native of the West Indies, publicly shewn in London, 1789," engraving (London, [ca. 1790]), LCP. Bobey: Pearson, Nettleship, and Usher, *Monograph on Albinism,* 197–264. Johann Friedrich Blumenbach, *Beyträge zur Naturgeschichte* (Göttingen, 1790), 96–126, APS (this copy, signed by Benjamin Smith Barton, lacks pp. 125 ff). Blumenbach describes seeing Bobey in London and criticizes Buffon's assessment of individuals such as Maria Sabine: *On the Natural Varieties of Mankind,* 218–200 (sect. 48). Bobey engraving: William Granger, *The New Wonderful Museum, and Extraordinary Magazine* (London, 1803).

11. *The Literary Diary of Ezra Stiles,* ed. Franklin B. Dexter (New York, 1901), 3:259 (5 Apr. 1787). "An Account of a remarkable alteration of colour in a negro woman: in a letter to the Rev. Alexander Williamson of Maryland, from Mr. James Bate, Surgeon in that Province, 1759" first appeared in the Royal Society of London, *Philosophical Transactions* 51 (1760): 157; reprinted in *American Museum* (Philadelphia) 4 (1788): 501–2; *New York Weekly Magazine* 2 (1796). James Parsons, "Account of a white negro," *Philosophical Transactions* 55 (1765): 45; reprinted in *American Museum* 5 (1789): 234.

12. Charles W. Peale, "Concerning a Negro Who Turned White," 2 Sept. 1791, Peale-Sellers Papers, Sellers Family Papers, APS, published first as "An Account of a Person born a Negro, or a very dark Mulatto, who afterwards became white," *National Gazette* (Philadelphia), 31 Oct. 1791, 3; reprinted in *Universal Asylum, and Columbian Magazine* 2, [no. 7] (1791): 409–10; *New-York Magazine; or, Literary Repository* 2 (1791): 634–35; *Massachusetts Magazine* 3 (1791): 744. James's portrait is mentioned in Barton, "*Account of* HENRY MOSS," 7. Also on James's portrait: *Historical Catalogue of the Paintings in the Philadelphia Museum* (n.p., 1813), 56 (#225).

13. Samuel Stanhope Smith, *An essay on the causes of the variety of complexion and figure in the human species; to which are added strictures on Lord Kaim's discourse, on the original di-*

versity of mankind (Philadelphia, 1787). On this debate, see Bruce Dain, "A Hideous Monster of the Mind: American Race Theory, 1787–1859" (Ph.D. diss., Princeton University, 1996), 99–153. Arguing against a climatic theory of color: Benjamin Smith Barton to Benjamin Rush, Edinburgh, 24 Jan. 1787, B. Rush Correspondence, 27:2, LCP at HSP.

14. Samuel M. Wilson, *Catalogue of Revolutionary Soldiers and Sailors of the Commonwealth of Virginia to whom Land Bounty Warrants Were Granted* (Baltimore, 1953), 48 (warrant #777). John H. Gwathmey, *Historical Register of Virginians in the Revolution: Soldiers, Sailors, Marines, 1775–1783* (Baltimore, 1979), 569. Barton, "*Account of* HENRY MOSS," 16–17. Duc de La Rochefoucauld-Liancourt, *Travels through the United States of North America . . . in the years 1795, 1796, and 1797 . . .* (London, 1799), 2:134.

15. "Henry Moss, ein schwarzer Mann, der sich in einem Weissen verwandelt," *Americanischer Stadt und Land Calender auf das 1797ste Jahr Christi* (Philadelphia, [1796]), 33–34, LCP. I am grateful to Ron Calinger for help in translating this text. Benjamin Rush, Commonplace Book [1792–1810], 91–92 (27 July 1795), 91–92, APS. The broadside is pasted into Rush's own account of Moss.

16. Barton, "*Account of* HENRY MOSS," 3–6. Charles Caldwell, *Autobiography of Charles Caldwell, M.D.* (Philadelphia, 1855), 163–64, 268–69.

17. La Rochefoucauld-Liancourt, *Travels through the United States of North America*, 2:134. Peale, "Account of a Person born a Negro." "Account of a remarkable Change of Colour in a NEGRO. By Miers Fisher.—Extract of a Letter from Mr. James Pemberton to Thomas Wilkinson, Communicated by Dr. Holme. Read Dec. 15th, 1797," *Memoirs and Proceedings–Manchester Literary and Philosophical Society* 5, no. 1 (1798): 314–18.

18. "Account of a remarkable Change of Colour," 316–17. Peale, "Account of a Person born a Negro." Moses Brown to all whom it may concern, 1803, MBP. Brown, "*Account of* HENRY MOSS," 11, 14–15. See also "Another Instance of a Negro turning White," *Medical Repository* 4 (1801): 199 (apparently a reprint of "Another Instance of a Negro Turning White," *Monthly Magazine and American Review* 5 [1800]: 391–92).

19. Barton, "*Account of* HENRY MOSS," 4, 14–16.

20. Blumenbach, *On the Natural Varieties of Mankind*, 250–51 (sect. 69). Zillah Halls, *Men's Costume, 1750–1800* (London, 1973).

21. Caldwell, *Autobiography*, 163–64. *Oxford English Dictionary*, s.v. "blister." Moses Brown to all whom it may concern, 1803, MBP.

22. Gary B. Nash, *Forging Freedom: The Formation of Philadelphia's Black Community, 1720–1840* (Cambridge, 1988), 121–24.

23. Rush to Jefferson, 4 Feb. 1797, in *Letters of Benjamin Rush*, ed. L. H. Butterfield (Princeton, N.J., 1951), 785–86. For Rush's paper, see Benjamin Rush, "Observations intended to favour a supposition that the black Color (as it is called) of the Negroes is derived from LEPROSY. Read at a Special Meeting July 14, 1797," *Transactions of the American Philosophical Society* (1799): 289–97.

24. Caldwell, "Review of *An Essay*," 150 (his intention), 267–68 (Moss).

25. "Case of a Negro whose skin has become white. By J.V. Weisenthal, M.D. of the United States Ship Independence," *New England Journal of Medicine and Surgery, and Collateral Branches of Science* 8 (1819): 35–36.

26. Stephen Jay Gould, *The Mismeasure of Man* (New York, 1981).

27. *The Commissioners of the Alms-house vs. Alexander Whistelo, a black man; being a remarkable case of bastardy* (New York, 1808), 12–13.

28. Donna Landry and Gerald MacLean, "Of Forceps, Patents, and Paternity: Tristram Shandy," *Eighteenth-Century Studies* 23, no. 4 (1990): 522–43.

29. *Alms-house vs. Alexander Whistelo*, 10–13. Trial strategy: Sharon Block, "Coerced Sex in British North America, 1700–1820" (Ph.D. diss., Princeton University, 1995), 123–78.

30. Marybeth Hamilton Arnold, "'The Life of a Citizen in the Hands of a Woman': Sexual Assault in New York City, 1790–1820," in *Passion and Power: Sexuality in History,* ed. Kathy Peiss and Christina Simmons (Philadelphia, 1989), 35–56. Note about brothels: *Medical Repository* 7 (1804): 89.

31. *Alms-house vs. Alexander Whistelo*, 13.

32. Ibid., 13–15, 33. Williamson later developed his ideas on complexion: Hugh Williamson, *Observations on the climate in different parts of America, compared with the climate in corresponding parts of the other continent. To which are added, remarks on the different complexions of the human race; with some account of the aborigines of America. Being an introductory discourse to The history of North-Carolina . . .* (New York, 1811).

33. *Alms-house vs. Alexander Whistelo,* 17–18. Review of Felix d'Azara, *Essays on the Natural History of the Quadrupeds of the Province of Paraguay,* trans. M. Moreau-Staint-Mércy, 2 vols. (Paris, 1801), *Medical Repository* 9 (1806): 64–70.

34. *Aristotle's Master-Piece: or, the Secrets of Generation Displayed* (London, 1695), 20–21, quoted in Landry and MacLean, "Of Forceps, Patents, and Paternity," 539. Roy Porter, "Medical Folklore in High and Low Culture: *Aristotle's Masterpiece,*" in *Facts of Life: The Creation of Sexual Knowledge in Britain, 1650–1950,* ed. Roy Porter and Leslie Hall (New Haven, 1995), 33–64. John D'Emilio and Estelle B. Freedman, *Intimate Matters: A History of Sexuality in America* (New York, 1988), 19–20, 46. Stafford, *Body Criticism,* 306–18.

35. Marie-Hélène Huet, *Monstrous Imagination* (Cambridge, 1993).

36. James Parsons, "Account of a white negro," 30 Jan. 1765, *American Museum* 5 (1789): 234.

37. Morgan, "Some account of a motley coloured, or pye negro girl and boy," 37–39. Moses Jaques to Benjamin Rush, 5 June 1800, Kennet Square, B. Rush Correspondence, 8:42, HSP.

38. *Newport Mercury,* 4 Apr. 1763. William Lilly Stover, *Columbian Almanack . . . and Magazine of Knowledge and Fun, for the year of Our Lord 1791* (Newport, [1790]), 12v.

39. *Alms-house vs. Alexander Whistelo,* 22–23, 30–31. Stafford, *Body Criticism.*

40. *Alms-house vs. Alexander Whistelo,* 30.

41. Ibid., 19. "Another Instance of a Negro turning white," *Medical Repository* 4 (1801): 199; "ANOTHER ETHIOPIAN TURNING TO A WHITE MAN [letter from A. Catlin, Litchfield, Conn., 28 June 1801]," *Medical Repository* hexade 1, 5 (1801): 83–84. "Account of a Negro growing white," *Medical Repository* 5 (1802): 83. "Account of two Albinos," *Medical Museum* 2 (1806): 284–86.

42. *Alms-house vs. Alexander Whistelo,* 34, 38–39. Arnold, "Life of a Citizen in the Hands of a Woman," 35–56.

43. *Alms-house vs. Alexander Whistelo,* 38–39, 47. For example: *The New Entertaining Philadelphia Jest-Book, and Chearful Witty Companion* . . . (Philadelphia, 1790), 15.

44. *Alms-house vs. Alexander Whistelo,* 48, 45.

45. Ibid., 55.

46. *Newport Mercury,* 22 Jan. 1787. Henry Channing, *God admonishing his people of their duty, as parents and masters* (New London, 1787), 23. Timothy Breen, "Making History: The Force of Public Opinion and the Last Years of Slavery in Revolutionary Massachusetts," in *Through a Glass Darkly: Reflections on Personal Identity in Early America,* ed. Ronald Hoffman and Frederika J. Teute (Chapel Hill, N.C., 1997), 67–95.

47. John Guillory, *Cultural Capital: The Problem of Literary Cannon Formation* (Chicago, 1993).

48. Winthrop D. Jordan, *White over Black: American Attitudes toward the Negro, 1550–1812* (Chapel Hill, N.C., 1968), 220–23, 254. Reginald Horsman, "Origins of Racial Anglo-Saxonism in Great Britain before 1850," *Journal of the History of Ideas* 37, no. 3 (1976): 392.

49. Stafford, *Body Criticism.* Johann Caspar Lavater, *Essays on Physiognomy,* 3 vols. (London, 1789–98), 3:404 (pl. 155: "Nine mouths, shaded"), APS.

50. Petrus Camper, *Dissertation physique de Mr. Pierre Camper, sure les différences réelles que présentent les traits du visage chez les hommes de différents pays et de différents ages* . . . (Utrecht, 1791), 34, pl. 1, pl. 3, APS. Blumenbach on Camper, *On the Natural Varieties of Mankind* (1795), 226–46 (sects. 55–64).

51. Lavater on silhouettes: *Essays on Physiognomy,* 2:179. Stafford, *Body Criticism,* 84–118.

52. Gould, *Mismeasure of Man,* 30–72.

53. Indian death songs: Julie K. Ellison, *Cato's Tears and the Making of Anglo-American Emotion* (Chicago, 1999), 98–100. Logan: Anthony F. C. Wallace, *Jefferson and the Indians: The Tragic Fate of the First Americans* (Cambridge, Mass., 1999), intro. Other drunk-Indian jokes: *Newport Mercury,* 11 July 1797; 6 Feb. 1799. *Providence Gazette,* 8 Nov. 1788. This joke also appears in *American Jest Book* (Harrisburg, Pa., 1796), 5–6; *Franklin's Legacy: or, The New York and Vermont Almanack for . . . 1799* (Troy, N.Y., [1798]), quoted in Robert K. Dodge, *Early American Almanac Humor* (Bowling Green, Ohio, 1987), 74.

54. Remarks on Indians, ca. 1770, Misc. Bound, MHS. Jean M. O'Brien, *Dispossession by Degrees: Indian Land and Identity in Natick, Massachusetts, 1650–1790* (New York, 1997). Stephen Badger, "Historical and Characteristic Traits of the American Indians in General, and those of Natick in Particular," *MHS Collections* 5 (1797), 32–45.

55. William Tudor, *Letters of the Eastern States,* 2d ed. (Boston, 1821), 280, 294. Gideon Hawley to R.D.S., Aug. 1802, typescript, S. P. Savage II Papers, MHS.

56. Isaac Backus to John Rippon, 10 Nov. 1798, *The Diary of Isaac Backus,* ed. William G. McLoughlin (Providence, 1979), 1437. Gideon Hawley to [unknown], no. 4, ca. 1795, Savage II Papers.

57. *New Entertaining Philadelphia Jest-Book,* 10. Reprinted in *Merry Fellow's Companion* (1789), 26–27; *Merry Fellow's Companion* (1797), 25–26; *American Jest Book* (1798), 45; *The United States Almanac . . . for . . . 1798* (Wilmington, Del., [1797]); also reprinted in Dodge, *Early American Almanac Humor,* 65. See "The Irish Bull," in Dodge, *Early American Alamanc Humor,* 55–58. *Curtis's Pocket Almanack, for . . . 1801* (Exeter, N.H., 1800), in Dodge, *Early*

American Almanac Humor, 66. *Newport Mercury,* 11 May 1789; reprinted in *American Jest Book* (1796), 24; *American Jest Book* (1798), 10. See also Robert Secor, "Ethnic Humor in Early American Almanacs," in *A Mixed Race: Ethnicity in Early America,* ed. Frank Shuffleton (New York, 1993), 175.

58. Tudor, *Letters of the Eastern States,* 301. "The State of Slavery in Virginia and other parts of the Continent, from the Marquise de Chastellux's Travels in America," *Columbian Magazine* (1787): 479–80.

59. "Letters and Documents Relating to Slavery in Massachusetts," *MHS Collections,* 5th ser., 3 (1877): 373–442.

60. Essay on a Negro man's arithmetical talents: *American Museum* (Philadelphia) 5 (1789): 62. Account of a Negro doctor: *American Museum* (Philadelphia) 5 (1789): 61. Isaac Bickerstaff, *The New England Almanac, or Lady's and Gentleman's Diary, for the Year of our Lord Christ, 1798* (Providence, 1797), D1r. Joseph Lavallee, *The Negro equalled by few Europeans. Translated from the French. To which are added poems on various subjects, moral and entertaining by Phillis Wheatley* (Philadelphia, 1801). "The Negro Equalled by Few Europeans" was also the title of a series of articles in the *American Museum* (Philadelphia) 9 (1791): 53, 99, 145, 205, 257, 313; 10 (1791): 39, 77, 129, 185, 241, 285.

61. Jefferson, *Notes on the State of Virginia,* 247–50, 257, 118–19.

62. Jonathan Edwards, *Observations on the Language of the Muhhekaneew Indians . . .* (New Haven, 1788), esp. 13–16. This essay was excerpted in the *American Review* 1 (1801): 343. J. L. Dillard, *Black English: Its History and Usage in the United States* (New York, 1972).

63. Jeremy Belknap and Jedidiah Morse, "The Report of a Committee . . . who Visited the Oneida and Mohekunuh Indians in 1796," *MHS Collections* 5 (1796): 24–30.

64. Tudor, *Letters of the Eastern States,* 280, 294.

65. "The State of Slavery in Virginia," 479–80.

66. Hugh Henry Brackenridge, "Introduction," *United States Magazine* (Jan. 1779): 10. Christopher Looby, *Voicing America: Language, Literary Form, and the Origins of the United States* (Chicago, 1996), chap. 4.

67. Hugh Henry Brackenridge, *Modern Chivalry: Containing the Adventures of Captain John Farrago, and Teague O'Reagan, His Servant,* vol. 1 (Philadelphia, 1792), bk. 1, ch. 1, p. 10; bk. 2, ch. 1, pp. 46–56.

68. Ibid., vol. 2 (Philadelphia, 1792), bk. 5, chs. 1–2, pp. 70–79. "It may be asked, How at the flood? when Noah, his wife, his three sons, and their wives, eight persons, only were saved? It is but giving some of the sons negro wenches for their wives, and you have the matter all right."

Eight ||| *Manifest Destinies*

1. Abijah Willard to Moses Brown, Uxbridge, 5 June 1806, MBP. Although not named in the letter, the man described is probably Samuel Shoemaker, a laborer from Uxbridge who was jailed in Worcester for assault on complaint of Josiah Taft, Esq.: Samuel Shoemaker's Mittimus, Uxbridge, 28 May 1806; "A List of Prisoners Confined in Gaol at June term, 1806," 9 June 1806; "Nathan Heard's account against the County of Worcester, June 1806, No. 2";

GSP Files, Engineer's Office, Worcester County Court House. Elizabeth C. Bouvier, archivist, Massachusetts Supreme Judicial Court, Boston, reports that Shoemaker was soon released: CCP, Worcester County, June 1806, 23:396: "No indictment being found against Saml. Schomaker, a prisoner in the gaol at Worcester in said County He is discharged"; the same notation is found in the GSP Docket Book. Similar altercations between black men and white boys recorded by Henry David Thoreau are discussed by Robert A. Gross, *Minutemen and their World* (New York, 1976), 96–97, 187–88.

2. William DeLoss Love, *Samson Occom and the Christian Indians of New England* (Boston, 1899), 207–315.

3. Robert J. Cottrol, *The Afro-Yankees: Providence's Black Community in the Antebellum Era* (Westport, Conn., 1982).

4. Records of the Newport Society and related organizations were preserved in the Union Congregational Church records, now held by the NHS: African Union Society, Record Book, 1789–96 (a formal copy); African Union Society, Meeting Notes, 1793–1810 (draft minutes). William H. Robinson edited the Record Book (1789), but not the draft Meeting Notes (1793–1810), in *Proceedings of the Free African Union Society and the African Benevolent Society, Newport, Rhode Island, 1780–1824* (Providence, 1976), which also includes African Benevolent Society, Meeting Notes, 1808–24. See also African Human Society, 1810–23; Union Church, Meeting Notes, 1824–63, also at the NHS.

5. J. P. Brissot de Warville, *New Travels in the United States of America, 1788*, ed. Durand Echeverria (Cambridge, 1964), 134. J. P. Brissot de Warville, *New Travels in the United States: Performed in 1788 . . .* (New York, 1792), 84, 155–65.

6. Occom diary, in Love, *Samson Occom*, 224–52 (24 Oct.–7 Nov. 1785), 272 (1 Oct. 1787).

7. Stephen Valone, "Samuel Kirkland, Iroquois Missions, and the Land, 1764–1774," *American Presbyterians* 65, no. 3 (1987): 187–94. J. Johnson and Oneida sachem at Mohegan: Willard Hubbard to Wheelock, Mohegan, 8 Oct. 1767, EWP 767558.2. Johnson, account against the Crown, 14 Nov. 1768, *SWJP* 12:644 (23 Apr. 1768). Offer to Shattock: Thomas Clarke to Wheelock, New York, 10 Mar. 1768, EWP 768210. Wheelock to George Whitefield, Lebanon, 17 Dec. 1767, EWP 767667.7.

8. Mason Case: *Connecticut Courant*, 3 Nov. 1766; 22 May 1769; 9 Mar. 1773; 6 Apr. 1773; 22 Feb. 1774. Joseph Johnson's speech to the Oneidas, Kanoarohare, 20 Jan. 1774, in Laura J. Murray, ed., *To Do Good to My Indian Brethren: The Writings of Joseph Johnson, 1751–1776* (Amherst, Mass., 1998), 206–10. Occom to Susan Wheatley, 21 Sept. 1773, EWP 773521.

9. Love, *Samson Occom*, 210–11. Daniel K. Richter, *Facing East from Indian Country: A Native History of Early America* (Cambridge, Mass., 2001), 206–15 (Gage quote, 213). Karim Michael Tiro, "The People of the Standing Stone: The Oneida Indian Nation from Revolution to Removal, 1765–1840" (Ph.D. diss., University of Pennsylvania, 1999), 68–110.

10. Johnson's speech to the Oneidas, 206–21. Kirkland to Andrew Oliver, 12 Nov. 1770, quoted in Tiro, "People of the Standing Stone," 93.

11. David Fowler to Colonel Guy Johnson, 8 Apr. 1775, in *Writings of Joseph Johnson*, 259–61. Gregory Evans Dowd, *A Spirited Resistance: The North American Struggle for Unity, 1745–1815* (Baltimore, 1992), 39. Warning of Captain Onoonghwandekha (Seneca): *The Journals of Samuel Kirkland*, ed. Walter Pilkington (Clinton, N.Y., 1980), 23–25 (7 Apr. 1765).

12. Oneidas' second answer to J. Johnson, 22 Jan. 1774, in *Writings of Joseph Johnson*, 217–20.

13. J. Johnson to the Connecticut Assembly, 2 June 1774; J. Johnson to the Gentlemen of New Haven, 21 Feb. 1774; both in *Writings of Joseph Johnson*, 233–36, 223–26.

14. J. Johnson to Jonathan Trumbull, Farmington, 11 Oct. 1773, Trumbull Papers 3:155, CSA. Farmington Indians to "All our Indian Brethren, at Nihantuck, Mohegan, Groton, Stonington, Narragansett, and Long Island, or at Montauk," 13 Oct. 1773, EWP 773674.1. J. Johnson to John Rogers, Mohegan, 15 Feb. 1775, EWP 775165. J. Johnson's second speech to the Oneidas, 24 Jan. 1774, in *Writings of Joseph Johnson*, 220–21.

15. J. Johnson to Colonel Guy Johnson, Guy Park, 25 Mar. 1775 (255–59), and David Fowler to Guy Johnson, 8 Apr. 1775 (259–61), in *Writings of Joseph Johnson*.

16. Tiro, "People of the Standing Stone," 99–101. J. Johnson to the New York Congress, 21 Jun. 1775, in *Writings of Joseph Johnson*, 264–66. Dowd, *Spirited Resistance*, 41. On Iroquois nativism, see also "Objections of the Indians to the school," David Avery, 31 May 1772, EWP 772331.

17. Love, *Samson Occom*, 247–49, 277, 286–87. *Journals of Samuel Kirkland*, 170–72 (5 Sept. 1789). See also Jacob Kunkosott to John Taylor, Albany, 23 Mar. 1815, Gratz MSS 4:5, no. 2, HSP.

18. Love, *Samson Occom*, 209, 288–97. David Fowler to [unknown], New York, 3 Jan. 1795, HSP.

19. *James Niles v. John Hanon*, CCP KC, Feb. 1779, 1:358, RIJRC. Will of Joseph Cozzens, 7 Jan. 1788, in Ruth Wallis Herndon and Ella Wilcox Sekatua, "The Right to a Name: The Narragansett People and Rhode Island Officials in the Revolutionary Era," *Ethnohistory* 44, no. 3 (1997): 119. Narragansett Council and others of the tribe, Aug. 1779, RI Petitions 17:79.

20. Jeremy Belknap and Jedidiah Morse, "The Report of a Committee . . . who Visited the Oneida and Mohekunuh Indians in 1796," *MHS Collections* 5 (1796): 12–32. Timothy Dwight, *Travels in New England and New York* (1822), ed. Barbara M. Solomon, (Cambridge, 1969), 3:14–19 (Stonington), 3:124–26 (Brothertown).

21. Love, *Samson Occom*, 301–06.

22. Belknap and Morse, "Oneida and Mohekunuh Indians in 1796," 23, 20. Peter the Pagan: *Journals of Samuel Kirkland*, 390–92 (17 Sept. 1804). Tiro, "People of the Standing Stone," 161–66, 174–80, 184–85 (Quaker quote), 203–10.

23. Tiro, "People of the Standing Stone," 211–52.

24. Jeanne Ronda and James P. Ronda, "'As They Were Faithful': Chief Hendrick Aupaumut and the Struggle for Stockbridge Survival, 1757–1830," *American Indian Culture and Research Journal* 3, no. 3 (1979): 43–55. Andrew Jackson, "First Annual Message, December 8, 1829," *Messages of Gen. Andrew Jackson: With a short sketch of his life* (Boston, 1837), 61.

25. James Fenimore Cooper, *The Pioneers, or, the Sources of the Susquehanna: A Descriptive Tale*, 2 vols. (New York, 1823), 2:324, Firestone Library, Princeton, N.J.

26. Samuel Stephens to Anthony Taylor, Boston, 1 June 1787; Newport Society to Providence Society, ca. Sept. 1789; both in Robinson, *Proceedings of the Free African Union Society*, 17–18, 29.

27. Petition of John Cuffe and six others, Dartmouth, 10 Feb. 1780, MSA 186:134–36.

Thanks to Dan Mandell for sharing this document. Sidney Kaplan and Emma Nogrady Kaplan, *The Black Presence in the Era of the American Revolution*, rev. ed. (Amherst, Mass., 1989), 151–54.

28. Anthony Kinnicutt, Petition for right to vote, 1780, Providence Town Papers 1520, RIHS. Rhode Island Black Heritage Society, *Creative Survival: The Providence Black Community in the Nineteenth Century* (Providence, [1988]), 28–32.

29. Henry Smeathman, *Plan of a settlement to be made near Sierra Leone on the Grain Coast of Africa* (London, 1786). On Thornton in Newport: Hopkins to Moses Brown, 7 Mar. 1787, in *The Works of Samuel Hopkins . . .* , ed. Sewall Harding, 3 vols. (Boston, 1865), 1:139–40. On Thornton in Boston, Newport, and Philadelphia: Gary B. Nash, *Forging Freedom: The Formation of Philadelphia's Black Community, 1720–1840* (Cambridge, 1988), 100–104. Thornton quote: Brissot de Warville, *New Travels in the United States of America, 1788* (Cambridge, Mass., 1964), 149. Anthony Taylor and Salmar Numbia to "all the Afficans in Providence," Newport, 27 July 1789 (18–19); Bonner Brown and James McKenzie, by order of the African society in Providence, to the Bretheren of the Union Society in Newport, 15 Jan. 1794 (43); Samuel Stevens to Anthony Taylor, Boston, 1 June 1787 (17–18); Robinson, *Proceedings of the Free African Union Society*. "African Petition," 4 Jan. 1787, House of Representatives, Unpassed Legislation, 2358, MSA. There was also substantial interest among black Philadelphians in the Sierra Leone move: Petition of Moses Johnson and fifty-two others, [ca. 1800], Cox, Parrish, Wharton Papers, 14:7, HSP.

30. *Boston Evening Post*, 1735, quoted in William D. Johnson, *Slavery in Rhode Island, 1755–1776* (Providence, 1894), 115. *The Literary Diary of Ezra Stiles*, ed. Franklin B. Dexter (New York, 1901), 1:366 (13 Apr. 1773). Quamine referred to his "poor enslaved country men" in a letter to Moses Brown, 5 June 1775 (missing from the RIHS), quoted in Mack Thompson, *Moses Brown: Reluctant Reformer* (Chapel Hill, N.C., 1962), 105. On Quamine: John M. Murrin, introduction to *Princetonians, 1784–1790: A Biographical Dictionary*, ed. Ruth L. Woodward and Wesley Frank Craven (Princeton, N.J., 1991), xvii–lviii. Ezra Stiles and Samuel Hopkins, *To the Public*, [Newport, 1776]. Samuel Hopkins, *A dialogue, concerning the slavery of the Africans . . .* (Norwich, Conn., 1776). Hopkins to Sharpe, 7 Mar. 1787, in *Works of Samuel Hopkins*, 1:140–41.

31. Thomas J. Davis, "Emancipation Rhetoric, Natural Rights, and Revolutionary New England: A Note on Four Black Petitions in Massachusetts, 1773–1777," *NEQ* 62, 2 (1989): 248–63. Samuel Hopkins, *A Discourse upon the Slave Trade, and the Slavery of Africans* (Providence, 1793), app.

32. Occom to Susannah Wheatley, 5 Mar. 1771, Mohegan, EWP 771205.1. Phillis Wheatley to Hopkins, Boston, 6 May 1774, in *The Poems of Phillis Wheatley*, ed. Julian D. Mason Jr., rev. ed. (Chapel Hill, N.C., 1989), 207–8. Henry Sherwood, "Early Negro Deportation Projects," *Mississippi Valley Historical Review* 2, no. 4 (1916): 484–508. The Philadelphia Free African Society to the Newport African Society, [ca. Sept. 1789], in Robinson, *Proceedings of the Free African Union Society*, 30.

33. Robinson, *Proceedings of the Free African Union Society*, 145–47 (22 Dec. 1796).

34. Jamie Coughtry and Jay Coughtry, "Black Pauper Burial Records: Providence, Rhode Island, 1777–1831," *RIH* 44, no. 4 (1985): 112. Black servants borrowing finery—including a

coach and white driver—for a wedding: Elaine Forman Crane, ed., *The Diary of Elizabeth Drinker* (Boston, 1991), 1127 (3 Jan. 1799). Robinson, *Proceedings of the Free African Union Society,* 64 (4 Mar. 1790), 69 (7 Oct. 1790), 86 (8 Sept. 1791), 93 (16 Feb. 1792), 94 (6 Mar. 1792), 103 (8 Nov. 1792), 119 (14 Nov. 1793).

35. On the day of the death, Sewall received mourners: *The Diary of Samuel Sewall, 1675–1729,* ed. H. Halsey Thomas, 2 vols. (New York, 1971), 1064 (6 Feb. 1729); *New-England Weekly Journal,* 24 Feb. 1729. Boston Selectmen's Minutes, 24 Dec. 1735, quoted in William D. Piersen, *Black Yankees: The Development of an Afro-American Subculture in Eighteenth-Century New England* (Amherst, Mass., 1988), 78.

36. Piersen, *Black Yankees,* 78. Griffith Hughes, *The Natural History of Barbados* (London, 1750), 15, APS. Anne-Marie Cantwell and Diana diZerega Wall, *Unearthing Gotham: The Archaeology of New York City* (New Haven, 2001), ch. 16.

37. Alice Morse Earle, *Customs and Fashions in Old New England* (1893; Rutland, Vt., 1973), 379. *Newport Mercury,* 14–21 Dec. 1767. *The Diary of William Bentley, D.D., Pastor of the East Church, Salem, Massachusetts,* 4 vols. (Salem, 1905–14), 2:235 (24 Aug. 1797). *Newport Mercury,* 9 Sept. 1794 (glove joke); 24 Nov. 1788 (another joke about black pallbearers).

38. Robinson, *Proceedings of the Free African Union Society,* 62 (14 Jan. 1790). African Union Society, Meeting Notes, 1793–1810, NHS. *Diary of William Bentley* , 3:437 (1 June 1809).

39. Margaret ("Peggy") Harrison to Brown, Boston, 7 Nov. 1809; Harrison to Brown, Boston, 20 Oct. 1804; MBP.

40. Nathan E. Wood, *The History of the First Baptist Church of Boston* (Philadelphia, 1899), 297. Henry Melville King and Charles Field Wilcox, *Historical Catalogue of the Members of the First Baptist Church in Providence, Rhode Island* (Providence,1908). Photo of Patience Borden headstone, North Burial Ground, Providence: Coughtry and Coughtry, "Black Pauper Burial Records," 109.

41. Elias Smith, *Five Letters with Remarks* (Boston, 1804), 18. William G. McLoughlin, *New England Dissent: The Baptists and the Separation of Church and State* (Cambridge, Mass., 1971), 2:1071 n. 17, 1:765, 2:878 n. 3. Paul in Salem: *Diary of William Bentley,* 3:490. William G. McLoughlin, *Isaac Backus and the American Pietistic Tradition* (Boston, 1967), 219–20.

42. Peggy [Margaret Harrison] to Brown, Boston, 20 Oct. 1804, MBP. George A. Levesque, "Inherent Reformers—Inherited Orthodoxy: Black Baptists in Boston, 1800–1873," *Journal of Negro History* 60, no. 4 (1975): 419–519. Wood, *History of the First Baptist Church of Boston,* 297.

43. Samuel Stillman to Brown, 30 May 1805, MBP. "There is a Black Man in town from the State of New York—who has preached—last Eveng under the Baptist meeting house," Brown's nephew wrote, suggesting that it might be good for the "Abolition Society to Encourage him"; Nicholas Brown II to Moses Brown, 21 Dec. 1792 and 14 May 1805, MBP. Wood, *History of the First Baptist Church of Boston.* McLoughlin, *New England Dissent,* 1071.

44. Frederick Douglass, *North Star,* quoted in Leon F. Litwack, *North of Slavery: The Negro in the Free States, 1790–1860* (Chicago, 1961), 212. Levesque, "Inherent Reformers—Inherited Orthodoxy," 2–3.

45. Beth Anne Bower, "Social Systems and Material Culture: Afro-Americans in

Nineteenth-Century Boston," *Man in the Northeast* 27 (1984): 67–78. Levesque, "Inherent Reformers—Inherited Orthodoxy," 499. See Shane White, "'It Was a Proud Day': African Americans, Festivals, and Parades in the North, 1741–1834," *JAH* 81, no. 1 (1994).

46. Margaret Harrison to Brown, Boston, 16 Nov. 1808, MBP.

47. *Independent Journal* (New York), 5 May 1787. Other favorable reviews: *New York Daily Advertiser*, 18 Apr. 1787; *Worcester Magazine*, 3 (May 1787): 61.

48. Royall Tyler, *The Contrast, a Comedy; in five acts, written by a Citizen of the United States, Performed with Applause at the Theatres in New-York, Philadelphia, and Maryland . . .* (Philadelphia, 1790), 26–28.

49. Alexander Saxton, *The Rise and Fall of the White Republic: Class Politics and Mass Culture in Nineteenth-Century America* (New York, 1990). David R. Roediger, *The Wages of Whiteness: Race and the Making of the American Working Class* (New York, 1991), 47.

50. Nathaniel Appleton to Belknap, 26 Feb. 1795, in "Slavery in Massachusetts," 388.

51. Holyoke to Belknap, Salem, 19 Mar. 1795, in "Slavery in Massachusetts," 400.

52. Joanne P. Melish, *Disowning Slavery: Gradual Emancipation and "Race" in New England, 1780–1860* (Ithaca, N.Y., 1998), 191–92. George H. Moore, *Notes on the History of Slavery in Massachusetts* (New York, 1866), 231–37. *Commercial Advertiser* (New York), 22 Sept. 1800; *Daily Advertiser* (New York), 22 Sept. 1800; *Gazette of the United States and Daily Advertiser* (Philadelphia), 23 Sept. 1800. Samuel H. Olney and 126 others, petition to the Overseers of the Poor of the Town of Providence, 4 Oct. 1806, Providence Town Papers 60:142 008724, RIHS; copy signed by Thomas Sessions and 53 others, Providence Town Papers 60:433 008725, RIHS; copy signed by Philip Allen and 32 others, Providence Town Papers 60:144 008727, RIHS.

53. Pemberton to Belknap, Boston, 12 Mar. 1795, in "Slavery in Massachusetts," 393. Eliot to Belknap, [Boston, 1795], in "Slavery in Massachusetts," 383. Holyoke to Belknap, in "Slavery in Massachusetts," 401.

54. George Frederickson, *The Black Image in the White Mind: The Debate on Afro-American Character and Destiny, 1817–1914* (New York, 1971), ch. 1. Brissot de Warville, *New Travels* (1964 ed.), 232–33.

55. Samuel Eliot Morrison, "A Poem on Election Day in Massachusetts about 1760," *Publications of the Colonial Society of Massachusetts* 18 (1917): 54–62. C. Dallett Hemphill, *Bowing to Necessities: A History of Manners in America, 1620–1860* (New York, 1999).

56. James Forten, *Letters from a man of colour on a late bill before the Senate of* Pennsylvania (Philadelphia, 1813), 8. Susan G. Davis, *Parades and Power: Street Theatre in Nineteenth-Century Philadelphia* (Philadelphia, 1986), 38–48. Nash, *Forging Freedom*, 177, dates the incident at 1805.

57. On 30 Dec. 1782, a newspaper account facetiously referred to the Mason's annual feast of Saint John as the feast of "St. Blacks," which prompted a letter from Hall to Mr. Willis, 31 Dec. 1782: Harry E. Davis, "Documents Relating to Negro Masonry in America," *Journal of Negro History* 21, no. 4 (Oct. 1936): 412–13.

58. Nash, *Forging Freedom*, 176, quoting *New York Evening Post*, 10 July and 12 July 1804. Jack Tager, *Boston Riots: Three Centuries of Social Violence* (Boston, 2001).

59. Susan Juster, *Disorderly Women: Sexual Politics and Evangelicalism in Revolutionary*

New England (Ithaca, N.Y., 1994), 1–45. Dell Upton, "White and Black Landscapes in Eighteenth-Century Virginia," in *Material Life in America, 1600–1860,* ed. Robert Blair St. George (Boston, 1988), 357–69. George C. Mason, *Annals of Trinity Church, Newport, Rhode Island, 1698–1821* (Newport, 1890), 1:155 (19 Apr. 1772). Stephen Gould to Brown, Newport, 8 Aug. 1822, MBP. About 1800 the Presbyterian meetinghouse in Southington, Connecticut, had "a large square pew . . . over each stairway for the negroes, and the younger took the stairs for seats"; "Early Recollections of Mrs. Nancy Roys, Born in 1792," *Connecticut Magazine* 10, no. 1 (1906): 77–79.

60. Robert J. Dinkin, "Seating in the Meetinghouse in Early Massachusetts," in *Material Life in America,* 407–18.

61. Henry R. Stevenson, receipt for part of a pew by Dinah Roberts, 29 July 1806, Jeremy Belknap Papers, MHS. Mason, *Annals of Trinity Church,* 1:324 (2 Sept. 1818). Harvey Newcomb, *The "Negro Pew": Being an Inquiry Concerning the Propriety of Distinctions in the House of God on Account of Color* (Boston, 1837). Litwack, *North of Slavery,* 196–97.

62. Gordon Wood, *The Radicalism of the American Revolution* (New York, 1992).

63. David Waldstreicher, *In the Midst of Perpetual Fetes: The Making of American Nationalism, 1776–1820* (Chapel Hill, N.C., 1997), 306–8.

64. Frederickson, *Black Image in the White Mind,* ch. 1. Lamont D. Thomas, *Rise to be a People: A Biography of Paul Cuffe* (Chicago, 1986), 111, 114–15. Henry: Winthrop D. Jordan, *White over Black: American Attitudes toward the Negro, 1550–1812* (Chapel Hill, N.C., 1968), 544.

65. Thomas, *Rise to be a People,* 107–12. Forten quote: Julie Winch, *A Gentleman of Color: The Life of James Forten* (New York, 2002), 193. Cuffe quote: [Unknown] to John Parrish, New Bedford, 9 Aug. 1807, Cox, Parrish, Wharton Papers 5:85, HSP.

66. Arthur O. White, "Prince Saunders: An Instance of Social Mobility among Antebellum New England Blacks," *Journal of Negro History* 60, no. 4 (1975): 531. Nash, *Forging Freedom,* 184–85, 237–38. White, "'It Was a Proud Day,'" 41–43.

Nine ||| *Hard Scrabble*

1. *Hard-Scrabble Calendar: Report of the Trials of Oliver Cummins, Nathaniel G. Metcalf, Gilbert Hines and Arthur Farrier; who were indicted with six others for a Riot, and for aiding in the pulling down a Dwelling-House, on the 18th of October, at Hard-Scrabble* (Providence, 1824), 3.

2. C. Dallett Hemphill, *Bowing to Necessities: A History of Manners in America, 1620–1860* (New York, 1999), pt. 3.

3. Jesse Sweet testimony, in *Hard-Scrabble Calendar,* 7–8; see also 10–12, 26, 23.

4. Samuel V. Allen testimony, in ibid., 12. Newell Stone testimony, in ibid., 12–13. Hiram Davis also heard the same account the night after the riot, ibid., 13.

5. Alexander Saxton, *The Rise and Fall of the White Republic: Class Politics and Mass Culture in Nineteenth-Century America* (New York, 1990); David R. Roediger, *The Wages of Whiteness: Race and the Making of the American Working Class* (New York, 1991). See also Eric Lott, *Love and Theft: Blackface Minstrelsy and the American Working Class* (New York, 1993).

6. James Oliver Horton and Lois E. Horton, *In Hope of Liberty: Culture, Community, and Protest among Northern Free Blacks, 1700–1860* (New York, 1997).

7. John S. Gilkeson Jr., *Middle-Class Providence, 1820–1940* (Princeton, N.J., 1986), 20–21.

8. *The Providence Directory; Containing Names of the Inhabitants, Their Occupations, Places of Business, and Dwelling-Houses* . . . (Providence, 1824).

9. *The Providence Directory* (Providence, 1826), 87–88.

10. *Rhode Island American,* 5 Oct. 1824, 2.

11. William J. Brown, *The Life of William J. Brown* (Providence, 1883), 6, 18, 29–31. Robert J. Cottrol, *The Afro-Yankees: Providence's Black Community in the Antebellum Era* (Westport, Conn., 1982), 41–66. On New York City: Shane White, *Somewhat More Independent: The End of Slavery in New York City, 1770–1810* (Athens, Ga., 1991), 150–84.

12. Cottrol, *Afro-Yankees,* 48. Elizabeth Blackmar, *Manhattan for Rent, 1785–1850* (Ithaca, N.Y., 1989). See also Paul E. Johnson, *A Shopkeeper's Millennium: Society and Revivals in Rochester, New York, 1815–1837* (New York, 1978), 48–55.

13. Leonard P. Curry, *The Free Black in Urban America, 1800–1850: The Shadow of a Dream* (Chicago, 1981): 49–81. *Cottrol, Afro-Yankees,* 47–52. *Providence Directory* . . . (Providence, 1830), 141–44. Irving H. Bartlett, *From Slave to Citizen: The Story of the Negro in Rhode Island* (Providence, 1954), 27.

14. *Hard-Scrabble Calendar,* 14, 23. Bartlett, *Slave to Citizen,* 30–31.

15. Brown, *Life of William J. Brown,* 89–90.

16. William G. McLoughlin, *Rhode Island: A History* (1978), 128. Patrick T. Conley, *Democracy in Decline: Rhode Island's Constitutional Development, 1776–1841* (Providence, 1977), 233–37.

17. Gordon Wood, *Radicalism of the American Revolution* (New York, 1992). Alan Taylor, "From Father to Friends of the People: Political Personas in the Early Republic," *Journal of the Early Republic* 11 (1991): 465–91.

18. Stanley J. Lemons and Michael A. McKenna, "The Re-enfranchisement of Rhode Island Negroes," *RIH* 30, no. 1 (1971): 3–13.

19. Anthony Kinnicutt, petition for right to vote, 1780, PTP 1520. In Connecticut, similar petitions were presented in the early nineteenth century, after the state explicitly disfranchised nonwhites in 1814. Two "men of color" from New Haven objected to taxation without representation; Public Records of the State of Connecticut, RG 2 (General Assembly Papers, Rejected Bills), box 2, docs. 45, 46, CSA. Similar petitions came from several free persons of color in Norwich and New London (RG 2, box 4, doc. 5) and in Hartford (RG 2, box 35, docs. 93a, b, c).

20. *Rhode Island American,* 5 Oct. 1824: 2. Conley, *Democracy in Decline,* 184–216.

21. *Providence Patriot,* 9 Oct. 1824, 2.

22. Cottrol, *Afro-Yankees,* 58: most of the founders had independent households, two notable exceptions being recent arrivals to town.

23. Gary B. Nash, *Forging Freedom: The Formation of Philadelphia's Black Community, 1720–1840* (Cambridge, 1988). David Waldstreicher, *In the Midst of Perpetual Fetes: The Making of American Nationalism, 1766–1820* (Chapel Hill, 1997), 325–48. Joanne P. Melish, *Disowning Slavery: Gradual Emancipation and "Race" in New England, 1780–1860* (Ithaca, N.Y., 1998), 163–209.

24. Brown, *Life of William J. Brown,* 88.

25. *Dreadful Riot on Negro Hill* (Boston, 1827), text reprinted in David Grimsted, ed., *Notions of the Americans* (New York, 1970). Town Council Minutes, 28 Feb. 1820, PTP 167:37. See also the petition: PTP 103:81. On efforts to suppress "noise and tumult" in Market Square and "to preserve the passage way upon the side Walks, unobstructed," see Town Council Minute Book, 30 Apr. 1826, 11:472, Providence City Archives.

26. Brown, *Life of William J. Brown*, 83–85.

27. *Hard-Scrabble Calendar*, 5–6, 8–9.

28. Ibid., 23 (Sweet); 12 (Allen); 17–18.

29. Ibid., 6, 19–21.

30. *Providence Gazette*, 23 Oct. 1824.

31. Town Council Minute Book, Providence City Archives: (patrols) 18 Mar. 1823, 11:83–84; (lamps) 27 Apr. 1823, 11:86; (patrols) 27 Apr. 1823, 11:86. Also, 7 Mar. 1823, PTP 170:39 A, RIHS.

32. Stephen Tillinghast, Samuel Carlisle, Moses Brown Ives, Report of the Nuisances Committee to the Providence Town Council, 9 Sept. 1822, PTP 111:60 00386961. Town Council Minutes, 13 Feb. 1826, PTP 172:234. Petition of complaint of several shops that should not be allowed to sell liquors, 7 Oct. 1822, PTP 111:54. Liquor license, June 1822, PTP 111 0038860.

33. John Lasell and sixteen others, petition to the Providence Town Council re: James Lee, 8 Sept. 1817, PTP 93:15 0027955, RIHS. Town Council Minutes, 19 June 1820, PTP 176:135. Thomas Hull, complaint re: Judith Maxwell and Rachel Smith, 25 Feb. 1822, PTP 169:1 E. Town Council Minutes, 5 Jan. 1829, PTP 176:80 E. Re: complaint against Noel Collins, 16 Aug. 1804, PTP 153:70 005791. For example, in 1804 a group of neighbors wrote to defend Noel Collins against the accusation of Comfort Wheaton that he was keeping a disorderly house; they asserted that they were neighbors who had never been disturbed by him or his family and believed him to be honest and industrious and approved his continued residence "during good behavior." The neighbors include Richard Olney, Nathaniel Metcalf, and Pero Brown.

34. Town Council Minutes, 20 Mar. 1820, PTP 167:52.

35. Ibid., [June 1820], 175:211 A.

36. Complaint of Moses Staunton against Mary Cooper, 27 Apr. 1816, PTP 87 0024971. Of the fifteen witness, those who can be identified in the 1824 directory are heavily concentrated in point of land south of Wickenden Street, many of them on Hill Street. In 1822 Moses Staunton appears on a list of "colored" boarders (PTP 112:118 0039155), which places him in a boardinghouse near Fox Point at the southern end of the East Side—apparently along with Mary Wamsley and her five children.

37. Walter R. Danforth, order to Henry Alexander and Thomas Cooke, 27 Aug. 1821, PTP 168:157 D. "List of all the Coloured people in this town who are Housekeepers," 1822, PTP 112:118 0039155. "Names of the Heads of Families, Owners of the Houses & Tenements where they reside," PTP 112:118 0039156. Thirty-four were husbands living with wives alone or with children; 4 were men living with children; 14 were women living with children; 20 were single men; 36 were single women. Town Council Minute Book, 14 Mar. 1823, 11:78, Providence City Archives. Town Council Minutes, 26 Dec. 1822, PTP 169:243. James

Thurber, notice to Town Council re: William Apes, 25 Mar. 1825, PTP 127:26 004197. The 1824 directory listed Thurber at 221 North Main Street—near the Hard Scrabble neighborhood.

38. *Hard-Scrabble Calendar,* 16 (Tillinghast).

39. On Boston: Jeremy Belknap, "Answers to queries Respecting the Slavery and Emancipation of Negroes in Massachusetts," *MHS Collections* 4 (1795): 209–10. On Philadelphia: Richard Godbeer, *Sexual Revolution in Early America* (Baltimore, 2002), 299–334. On New York: Timothy J. Gilfoyle, *City of Eros: New York City, Prostitution, and the Commercialization of Sex, 1790–1920* (New York, 1992), 17–22. Providence in the 1790s: complaint about notorious women infesting the neighborhood around old Baptist Meetinghouse, 26 Aug. 1794, PTP, 20:95, 8863; petition, 2 Aug. 1802, PTP 53:73. On one alleged "bawdy woman" in Providence in the 1790s: Ruth Wallis Herndon, *Unwelcome Americans: Living on the Margin in Early New England* (Philadelphia, 2001), 145–48. On the political dynamics of "sex panics": Gayle S. Rubin, "Thinking Sex: Notes for a Radical Theory of the Politics of Sexuality" (1984), reprinted in *The Lesbian and Gay Studies Reader,* edited by Henry Abelove, Michele Aina Barale, and David M. Halperin (New York, 1993), 3–44.

40. Moses Brown and sixty-two others to the Providence Town Council, complaint re: women corrupting youths, 25 July 1817, PTP 93:13 0027950. Petition of a large number of "respectable inhabitants," 25 July 1817, PTP 165:37.

41. Caleb Eldredge, 9 Jan. 1823, RI Petitions 51:23. Carol Pateman, *The Sexual Contract* (Stanford, 1988). Marybeth Hamilton Arnold, "'The Life of a Citizen in the Hands of a Woman': Sexual Assault in New York City, 1790–1820," in *Passion and Power: Sexuality in History,* ed. Kathy Peiss and Christina Simmons (Philadelphia, 1989), 35–56. Sharon Block, "Coerced Sex in British North America, 1700–1820" (Ph.D. diss., Princeton University, 1995). The great example of a "bad woman" who made good was from Providence: a courtesan daughter of a prostitute who ended up doing well, marrying well and becoming unexpectedly respectable: Gilfoyle, *City of Eros,* 55–75.

42. Thomas Hudson, complaint re: Thankful Sharpe, 30 Nov. [1821], PTP 168:8 B. Samuel Thurber et al., complaint re: Calvin Hill, 21 May 1821, PTP 168:81 D and F. Petition of John Waterman et al., 1 July 1822, PTP 111:51. George Olney and fifteen others, Oct. 1825, RI Petitions 54:26.

43. George Olney and fifteen others, Oct. 1825, RI Petitions 54:26.

44. *Hard-Scrabble Calendar.* The trial records at the Rhode Island Judicial Records Center contain only the indictments, lists of witnesses, and other technical documents but none of the depositions or examinations: CCP PC Minute Book, 1824–28, Nov. 1824, CCP PC Docket Book 7, Nov. 1824, and file papers.

45. "Oh Dear, What Can the Matter Be?" (ca. 1795), in Theodore Ralph, *The American Song Treasury: One Hundred Favorites* (New York, 1986), 40–44. *Hard Scrabble, or Miss Philises Bobalition* (Boston, [1825]), John Hay Library, Brown University.

46. Phillis Wheatley, *Poems on Various Subjects, Religious and Moral . . .* (n.p., 1816). Phillip Lapsansky, "Phillis Wheatley, Derision, and Celebration," in *The Annual Report of the Library Company of Philadelphia for the Year 2000* (Philadelphia, 2001), 47–51. The two variant editions of *Dreadful Riot on Negro Hill!* (Boston, 1816) are at the LCP. *Dreadful Riot on Negro*

Hill! (Boston, 1827), Library of Congress. *Copy of a Letter from Phillis, to her Sister in the Country, describing The Riot on Negro Hill, Bosson, Ulie, 47th 1800028* (Boston, 1828), Boston Public Library. *Dreadful Riot on Negro Hill! Copy of a letter . . .* (New York, 1832). *Grand Bobalition of Slavery. Grand and most helligunt Selebrashum of de Bobalition of Slabery in de Nited Tate ob Neu Englunt, and commonwet of Bosson in de country of Massa-chuse-it* ([Boston, 1819?]), John Hay Library.

47. Waldsreicher, *In the Midst of Perpetual Fetes*, 328–44. *Invitation, Addressed to the Marshals of the "Africum Shocietee," at the Commemoration of the "Abolition of the Slave Trade"* (Salem, Mass., 1816), Boston Public Library. *Grand Celebrashun ob de Bobalition ob African Slavery!!!* (Boston, 1825), Library of Congress. *Reply to Bobalition of Slavery. Dialogue between Scipio and Cato, and Sambo and Phillis, occasioned by reading the account of Bobalition proceedings* (Boston, 1819), Library of Congress.

48. *A Treatise on the Intellectual Character, and Civil and Political Condition of the Colored People of the U[nited]. States; and the Prejudice Exercised Towards Them: With a Sermon on the Duty of the Church to Them. By Rev. H. Easton, A Colored Man* (Boston, 1837), 41–42.

49. See, for example, *Dreadful Riot on Negro Hill* (Boston, 1827), LCP.

50. Sylvia Wallace Holton, *Down Home and Uptown: Representations of Black Speech in American Fiction* (Madison, Wisc., 1984). For a range of examples from the 1780s to 1820, see the letters of Jenny, Cesar, Bonno, Elizabeth, Margaret and Peggy Harrison in the papers of their former master Moses Brown, RIHS. On the language of these letters: Melish, *Disowning Slavery*, 170–71.

51. *Reply to Bobalition of Slavery* (Boston, 1819) at the Library of Congress is purportedly written in the dramatic style of "Massa Shakespole." Jill Lepore, *A Is for America: Letters and Other Characters in the Newly United States* (New York, 2002), 15–41. David Stimpson, *The Politics of American English, 1776–1850* (New York, 1986), 3–18.

52. *Grand Bobalition, or "Great Annivversary Fussible"* ([Boston], 1821), Library of Congress.

53. On Phillis Wheatley: Henry Louis Gates Jr., "Editor's Introduction: Writing 'Race' and the Difference It Makes," in *"Race," Writing, and Difference*, ed. Gates (Chicago, 1986), 7–9. *An Oration on the Abolition of the Slave Trade; Delivered in the African Church in the City of New York, January 1, 1808 . . . by Peter Williams, Jun., a descendant of Africa* (New York, 1808), in Dorothy Porter, *Early Negro Writing, 1760–1837* (Boston, 1971), 343–54.

54. The main variant between the two copies at the LCP is that one says "Bossun or Providencee," the other only "Bossun." See Lapsansky, "Phillis Wheatley, Derision, and Celebration," 49.

55. *New-Years address, by the carriers of the Providence Patriot, to its Patrons* (Providence, 1825). Jane Lancaster, "Encouraging Faithful Domestic Servants: Race, Deviance, and Social Control in Providence, 1820–1850," *RIH* 51, no. 4 (1993): 76–82. Edward Williams Clay, *Life in Philadelphia*, pl. 4 (Philadelphia, 1828), LCP.

56. *Reply to Bobalition of Slavery* (Boston, 1819), Library of Congress.

57. Maria W. Stewart, *Religion and the Pure Principles of Morality* in Porter, *Early Negro Writing*, 461–63. James Forten Jr., "An Address Delivered before the American Moral Reform Society, by James Forten, Jr., Philadelphia, August 17th, 1837," in Porter, *Early Negro*

Writing, 232. Maria W. Stewart, *An Address Delivered at the African Masonic Hall, Boston, February 27, 1833*, in Porter, *Early Negro Writing*, 132–33.

58. *Grand Celebration! Of the Abolition of the Slave Trade* (Boston, 1817), BPL. *The Reply to Bobalition of Slavery* (Boston, 1819), Library of Congress.

59. *Bosson Artillerum Election, or the African's Reply To the Burlesque on the late Celebration of the Abolition of the Slave Trade* (Boston, 1817), BPL.

60. *Bobolition of Slavery!!!! Grand Celebrashum By de Africum Shocietee!!!!!!* (Boston, 1818), BPL. *Grand Celebrashun od de Bobalition ob African Slavery!!!* (Boston, 1825), Library of Congress. *Grand Celebration! Of the Abolition of the Slave Trade* (Boston, 1817). Text reprinted in Joshua Sharp, *Country Almanack, for 1820* (Charlestown, S.C., [1819]). Shane White, "'It Was a Proud Day': African Americans, Festivals, and Parades in the North, 1741– 1834," *JAH* 81, no. 1 (1994): 35–38.

61. *Grand Celebration! Of the Abolition of the Slave Trade* (Boston, 1817). *Grand Jubelum!!! Order 12f Annebersary of Affricum Bobalition* (Boston, 1827), John Hay Library.

62. *Grand Celebrashun od de Bobalition ob African Slavery!!!* (Boston, 1825), Library of Congress. *Bobalition of Slavery!!!!* (Boston, 1818). *Grand Bobalition of Slavery! By de Africum Shocietee* (Boston, 1820), LCP.

63. *A Discourse Delivered in St. Philip's Church, for the Benefit of the Coloured Community of Wilberforce, in Upper Canada, on the Fourth of July, 1830, by the Rev. Peter Williams, Rector of St. Phillip's Church* (New York, 1830), in Porter, *Early Negro Writing*, 294–302 (quote 295–96). William Whipper, "To the American People," "Minutes and Proceedings of the First Annual Meeting of the American Moral Reform Society Held at Philadelphia . . . 1837," in Porter, *Early Negro Writing*, 204. Stewart, *Religion and the Pure Principles of Morality*, 469.

64. *Hard Scrabble, or Miss Philises Bobalition* (Boston, [1825]), John Hay Library.

65. Peter P. Hinks, *To Awaken My Afflicted Brethren: David Walker and the Problem of Antebellum Slave Resistance* (University Park, Pa., 1997), 91–115. Stewart, *Religion and the Pure Principles of Morality*, 461.

66. *An Address, Delivered on the Celebration of the Abolition of Slavery, in the State of New-York, July 5, 1827. By Nathaniel Paul, Pastor of the First African Baptist Society in the City of Albany* (Albany, 1827), 19–20.

67. Stewart, *Religion and the Pure Principles of Morality*, 465, 469–70.

68. Hosea Easton, *A Treatise on the . . . Colored People* (Boston, 1837), 43.

69. On Hall: Brown, *Life of William J. Brown*, 89–90.

70. On Gardiner: Edwards, "Memoir," *The Works of Samuel Hopkins*, ed. Sewall Harding, 3 vols. (Boston, 1865), 1:154–56. *Providence Gazette*, undated clipping, ca. 1825, Rhode Island Black Heritage Society, Providence.

71. Complaint of George Olney and others re: Peter Brown and Thankful Sharpe, 14 Oct. 1825, PTP 172:111 A and B. Town Council Minutes, 17 Oct. 1825, PTP 172:114 C, RIHS. Jones report: unidentified clipping, ca. 1825, Rhode Island Black Heritage Society. George Olney and others, petition complaining of the evil coming from disorderly houses in Olney Lane, 31 Oct. 1825, PTP 172:141 A. Another similar complaint: *Literary Cadet and Saturday Evening Bulletin* (Providence), 26 Nov. 1826.

72. Introduction, *Hard-Scrabble Calendar*, 3.

73. Howard P. Chudacoff and Theodore C. Hirt, "Social Turmoil and Governmental Reform in Providence, 1820–1832," *RIH* 31, no. 1 (1972): 21–31, quote 28.

74. Jill Lepore, *The Name of War: King Philip's War and the Origins of American Identity* (New York, 1998).

Epilogue ‖ *Democracy in America*

1. Susan Scheckel, *The Insistence of the Indian: Race and Nationalism in Nineteenth-Century American Culture* (Princeton, N.J., 1998).

2. Alexis de Tocqueville to his father, Washington, 28 Jan. 1832, in George Wilson Pierson, *Tocqueville and Beaumont in America* (New York, 1938), 667.

3. Alexis de Tocqueville, introduction to *Democracy in America,* trans. George Lawrence, ed. J. P. Mayer (New York, 1988), 18, 25–26, 39, 50.

4. Alexis de Tocqueville, "Some Considerations Concerning the Present State and Probable Future of the Three Races that Inhabit the Territory of the United States," in *Democracy in America,* 316.

5. Tocqueville, *Democracy in America,* 317–24.

6. Ibid.

7. "Stockbridge petition," *Columbian Orator* (Boston, 1795), 46–47.

8. William Apess, "Eulogy on King Philip: As pronounced at the Odeon, in Federal Street, Boston" (Boston, 1836), in *On Our Own Ground: The Complete Writings of William Apess, a Pequot,* ed. Barry O'Connell (Amherst, Mass., 1992), 280–81, 286.

9. William Apess, "An Indian's Looking-Glass for the White Man" (1833), in O'Connell, *On Our Own Ground,* 157–60.

10. *Liberator,* 25 Jan. 1834; William Apess, "Indian Nullification of the Unconstitutional Laws of Massachusetts, Relative to the Marshpee tribe, or, The Pretended Riot Explained" (Boston, 1835), in O'Connell, *On Our Own Ground,* 221–22.

11. Apess, "Indian Nullification," 205.

12. Apess, "Eulogy on King Philip," 305.

13. Apess, "An Indian's Looking-Glass for the White Man," 157–58.

14. Apess, "Eulogy on King Philip," 230.

15. William Hamilton, *An Oration on the Abolition of the Slave Trade, delivered in the Episcopal Asbury African Church in Elizabeth-St.* (New York, 1815), in Dorothy Porter, *Early Negro Writing, 1760–1837* (Boston, 1971), 391–99. Russell Parrott, *An Oration on the Abolition of the Slave Trade . . . at the African Church of St. Thomas* (Philadelphia, 1814), in Porter, *Early Negro Writing,* 383–90.

16. James Mars, *Life of James Mars, A Slave Born and Sold in Connecticut. Written by Himself,* 8th ed. (Hartford, 1869), 2.

17. Frederick Douglass, "The Meaning of July Fourth for the Negro" (5 July 1852), in *The Life and Writings of Frederick Douglass,* ed. Philip S. Foner, vol. 2 (New York, 1950).

18. James Forten Jr., "An Address Delivered before the American Moral Reform Society" (231) and unattributed "Declaration of Sentiment" (200–202), both from *Minutes and*

Proceedings of the First Annual Meeting of the American Moral Reform Society (Philadelphia, 1837), in Porter, *Early Negro Writing.*

19. Apess, "Eulogy on King Philip," 306, 310.

20. "Declaration of Sentiment," 201.

21. Tocqueville, *Democracy in America,* 316, 343–44.

22. Ibid., 316–17. Carroll Smith-Rosenberg, "Davy Crockett as Trickster: Pornography, Liminality, and Symbolic Inversion in Victorian America," *Journal of Contemporary History* 17 (1982): 325–50. Eric Lott, *Love and Theft: Blackface Minstrelsy and the American Working Class* (New York, 1993).

23. Maria W. Stewart, *Religion and the Pure Principles of Morality,* in Porter, *Early Negro Writing,* 469–70.

24. Malcolm X, "The Ballot or the Bullet" (3 Apr. 1964), in *Malcolm X Speaks,* ed. G. Breitman (New York, 1965), 23–44.

A   N O T E   O N   S O U R C E S

When I began this project, I was aware that the past is a foreign country, but I had no idea that it would turn out to be so many different foreign countries. In the past several decades, historians have greatly expanded their view of who was involved in early American history, what is important about their experiences, and how their experiences can be studied most fruitfully. A narrow strip of English settlement has become a wide-ranging Atlantic world— and a vast continent inhabited by diverse native peoples, by French and Spanish as well as British colonists, and by a massive migration of enslaved West Africans. Meanwhile, historians have sought to explore the work of scholars in literary studies, anthropology, and cultural criticism and have engaged in ongoing dialogues about how to frame questions, use evidence, and communicate with one another. The notes that follow outline some of the secondary literature that turned out to be most influential and inspiring.

A generation ago, New England, long given pride of place in the national historiography, was in danger of being dismissed as deviant, unimportant, indeed irrelevant—and only in the past few years has the region begun to rejoin a newly understood colonial world. Daniel Boorstin's survey of the principal regions of English settlement on the mainland— *The Americans: The Colonial Experience* (New York, 1958)—showed little deference to the Puritans and vaunted instead what he saw as Virginia's pragmatism, individualism, and capitalist vigor. This tendency was encouraged by subsequent social and cultural histories of the Mid-Atlantic colonies, the Chesapeake region, the Deep South, and the West Indies. Much of this work was brilliantly synthesized by Jack P. Greene in *Pursuits of Happiness: The Social Development of Early Modern British Colonies and the Formation of American Culture* (Chapel Hill, N.C., 1988). Only disreputable little Rhode Island, with its religious tolerance and ethnic diversity, approximated the dominant and enduring trends established in the Mid-Atlantic colonies: ethnic heterogeneity, individualism, and economic competition. It was not until the nineteenth century—when orthodox New England abolished established churches, attracted a more heterogeneous population, and developed an economy based on manufacturing and commercial farming—that the North really came into being as a region. On nineteenth-century New Englanders' efforts to convince themselves and the nation that they were in fact the center of the nation, a useful introduction is Stephen Nissenbaum, "New England as Region and Nation," in *All over the Map: Rethinking American Regions,* edited by Edward L. Ayers, 38–61 (Baltimore, 1996).

At the same time, ongoing work on the history of Native Americans and Africans in the Atlantic world suggested new ways of thinking about the "colonial" aspect of the colonial period. Historians have never been entirely unaware of the presence of Indians and Africans in New England's past, but not until recently have historians begun to try to integrate them into the region's broader history. Among the earliest contributions to the *Massachusetts Historical Society Collections,* published in the 1790s, were an essay arguing that the Natick Indians were disappearing in the face of English settlement and a report on the abolition of slavery in the region. In the nineteenth century, Francis Parkman's masterful narratives of the colonial wars between Indians, the French, and the English told the story of an epic clash of races that Anglo-Saxons were destined to win. In contrast, William DeLoss Love's still useful *Samson Occom and the Christian Indians of New England* (Boston, 1899) focused on the political strategies pursued by Indian peoples long after the English conquered the region. Meanwhile, the sectional crisis over slavery inspired new attention to the role of Africans in New England's past. The *Life of James Mars, A Slave, Born and Sold in Connecticut. Written by Himself* (Hartford, 1864) was explicitly intended to remind northerners that the South was not alone in its history of slavery. After the Civil War, a number of popular writers and genealogists produced nostalgic histories of colonial slavery, and professionally trained historians traced institutional and legal developments—such as William Dawson Johnston, *Slavery in Rhode Island, 1755–1776* (Providence, 1894). In the early twentieth century, African American scholars—such as Lorenzo Johnston Greene in *The Negro in Colonial New England* (New York, 1942)—emphasized the agency of enslaved and free blacks in shaping their own lives.

Nevertheless, the work of these scholars remained largely outside the "mainstream" of New England history. Even now, histories of Indians in early America tend to focus disproportionately on the earliest moments of encounter and conflict, despite important work on ongoing negotiations with European colonists, such as Daniel K. Richter's *Looking East from Indian Country* (Cambridge, Mass., 2001). Meanwhile, studies of black northerners—such as Gary B. Nash's *Forging Freedom: The Formation of Philadelphia's Black Community, 1720–1840* (Cambridge, Mass., 1988)—tend to begin with the abolition of slavery in the late eighteenth century. Finally, histories of "race" in the North—such as David R. Roediger's *The Wages of Whiteness: Race and the Making of the American Working Class* (New York, 1991)—tend to focus on the mid-nineteenth century. It was as part of an attempt to bring these stories together that I set out to write this book: to reconnect New England with the rest of American history, to bring the history of Indians forward in time and the history of Africans back in time, and to appreciate how members of all three groups were influenced and defined by their interactions with one another.

As I began to think about colonialism and culture, my thought was influenced by the insights of literary scholars, anthropologists, and postcolonial theorists. At the heart of much current debate about history and culture lies the legacy of nineteenth-century folk-nationalist ideology. Nineteenth-century exponents of America as a white republic argued that peoples of color could never be fully integrated into the national body politic in large part because Indian culture was dying out and black culture had been enervated by slavery. In opposition, a number of scholars set out to emphasize instead the cultural continuity and coherence of both Indian peoples and African Americans; most influential was Melville J. Hershkovits, *The Myth of the Negro Past* (1941; Boston, 1990), which offered a transnational perspective on West Africa, the Caribbean, and Latin America as well as the United States.

An attempt to apply this approach to New England is William D. Piersen, *Black Yankees: The Development of an Afro-American Subculture in Eighteenth-Century New England* (Amherst, Mass., 1988). Over the past generation, the quest for authentic "survivals" in African American and Native American culture was reframed by historically minded anthropologists who suggested more dynamic ways of modeling cultural change and exchange. Particularly useful for me were Anthony F. C. Wallace, "Revitalization Movements: Some Theoretical Considerations for Their Comparative Study," *American Anthropologist* 58 (1956): 264–81; Sidney W. Mintz and Richard Price, *An Anthropological Approach to the Afro-American Past,* (Philadelphia, 1976); and Clifford Geertz, *Available Light: Anthropological Reflections on Philosophical Topics* (Princeton, N.J., 2000).

Several broad trends of the past generation have helped shaped my thinking. First, ongoing work has produced more detailed and sophisticated understandings of African American and Native American cultures in the colonial period. Particularly compelling examples are John R. Thornton's "African Dimensions of the Stono Rebellion," *AHR* 96 (1991): 1101–13, and James Hart Merrell's *The Indians' New World: Catawbas and Their Neighbors from European Contact through the Era of Removal* (Chapel Hill, N.C., 1989). Second, historians have sought to emphasize not merely the influence of colonists on the colonized but also the influence of the colonized on the colonizers. Especially useful to me were historian Mechal Sobel's *The World They Made Together: Black and White in Eighteenth-Century Virginia* (Princeton, N.J., 1988) and critical theorist Paul Gilroy's *The Black Atlantic: Modernity and Double Consciousness* (Cambridge, Mass., 1993). Finally, Gilroy's work on race and nation, and those of a number of postcolonial critics, have challenged many of the assumptions that undergirded the more romantic strains of modern multiculturalism. See, for instance, K. Anthony Appiah, "The Multiculturalist Misunderstanding," *New York Review of Books,* 9 Oct. 1997, 30–36. Almost a century ago, W. E. B. DuBois, in *The Souls of Black Folk: Essays and Sketches* (Chicago, 1903), emphasized themes that have been more recently elaborated by scholars such as Homi K. Bhabha, "Of Mimicry and Men: The Ambivalence of Colonial Discourse," *October* 28 (1984): 125–33. An inspiring combination of deep, broadranging research and conceptual sophistication was Richard White's *The Middle Ground: Indians, Empires, and Republics in the Great Lakes Region, 1650–1815* (New York, 1991), which complicated the classic problem of cross-cultural communication by emphasizing the role of strategic misunderstandings and loose analogies in the protean politics of culture and identity.

In seeking to understand slavery in eighteenth-century New England, the rich recent literatures on the antebellum South, the early British colonies, and West Africa provided useful models and instructive points of contrast. A wealth of new research has allowed broad syntheses such as Ira Berlin's *Many Thousands Gone: The First Two Centuries of Slavery in North America* (Cambridge, Mass., 1998), which emphasizes regional differences and change over time. Until recently, work on slavery in the North, such as Edgar J. McManus's *Black Bondage in the North* (Syracuse, N.Y., 1973), was largely restricted to chronicling legal and demographic developments. Just how broad a framework is now possible was made clear by John Thornton in *Africa and Africans in the Making of the Atlantic World, 1400–1680* (New York, 1992). Much work on slavery in the past generation has sought to champion the agency of enslaved people by emphasizing overt modes of resistance. A helpful caution is Michael F. Brown, "On Resisting Resistance," *American Anthropologist* 98, no. 4 (1996): 729–35. Also useful for their analyses of both practical and symbolic negotiations of power are James Scott, *Domination and the Arts of Resistance* (New Haven, 1992), and E. P. Thompson, *Customs in Common* (New York, 1991). Meanwhile, a number of scholars have attempted to draw attention to the lives of women as well as men and to bring together often separate studies of masters and slaves. An notable example of both efforts is Elizabeth Fox-Genovese's *Within the Plantation Household: Black and White Women of the Old South* (Chapel Hill, N.C., 1988). Walter Johnson's eloquent *Soul by Soul: Life inside the Antebellum Slave Market* (Cambridge, Mass., 1999) usefully emphasizes the interrelated identities of slaves, masters, and traders. An insightful legal analysis is Ariela Julie Gross, *Double Character: Slavery and Mastery in the Antebellum Southern Courtroom* (Princeton, N.J., 2000). This work helped suggest to me the importance of relationships in New England not only between masters and slaves but also among members of both groups and the larger community. Particularly influential was Orlando Patterson's *Slavery and Social Death: A Comparative Study* (Cambridge, Mass., 1982). My work on slavery in New England has sought to explore the triangular negotiations over power and identity: to understand how the struggles of masters and slaves to define themselves and each other were shaped by the responses of family members, neighbors, and members of broader civic communities.

Until recently, the history of abolition in New England was told as a simple story of triumphant national progress. Arthur Zilversmit, *The First Abolition: The Abolition of Slavery in the North* (Chicago, 1967), saw the process as a basic conflict between liberal political theory and glaring injustice which northerners virtuously resolved by validating the ideals of 1776. David Brion Davis's brilliant *The Problem of Slavery in the Age of Revolution, 1770–1823* (Ithaca, N.Y., 1975) took a more complex look at the relationship between ideology, self-interest, and power. One of his paradoxical conclusions was that modern essentialist ideas about race developed out of Enlightenment debates about racial equality. The most recent study, Joanne P. Melish, *Disowning Slavery: Gradual Emancipation and "Race" in New England, 1780–1860* (Ithaca, N.Y., 1998), emphasizes the racism of abolitionists but largely ignores the role of black New Englanders in their own emancipation and their subsequent efforts to shape public debates about race and the republican body politic. A more comprehensive approach to the social dynamics of this transformation has been recently produced by Gary B. Nash and Jean R. Soderlund, *Freedom by Degrees: Emancipation in Pennsylvania and Its Aftermath* (New York, 1991). But how was slavery abolished without establishing racial equality? My thinking was influenced by recent work on sensibility and the relationship between "natural rights" and "natural affections." Particularly useful in this regard were Karen Halttunen, "Humanitarianism and the Pornography of Pain in Anglo-American Culture," *AHR* 100 (1995): 303–34, and Julie K. Ellison, *Cato's Tears and the Making of Anglo-American Emotion* (Chicago, 1999). Larry E. Tise, *Proslavery: A History of the Defense of Slavery in America, 1701–1840* (Athens, Ga., 1987), provocatively argues that northerners played an important role in the development of antebellum pro-slavery ideology. This work helped me explore the nature and limits of antislavery ideology while also emphasizing the triangular negotiations between slaves, masters, and the public.

At the time I began this project, there was a fierce and wide-ranging debate within the academy about the notion that identities of gender, race, and to some extent class have an "essential" basis in the physical body. Early works tended to focus on the ideas of white people about people of color. The long-running debate over the origins of modern racism—was it the cause of slavery? or the product of slavery?—culminated in Winthrop D. Jordan's classic *White over Black: American Attitudes toward the Negro, 1550–1812* (Chapel Hill, N.C., 1968). Studies of Indians in American literature worked from similar assumptions. Richard Slotkin's *Regeneration through Violence: The Mythology of the American Frontier, 1600–1860* (Middletown, Conn., 1973) helped spark interest in how early Americans' racial attitudes shaped their self-perceptions and affected important political developments. Other influential examples are F. Nwabueze Okoye, "Chattel Slavery as the Nightmare of the American Revolutionaries," *WMQ* 37, no. 1 (1980): 5–28; Carroll Smith-Rosenberg's essays, including "Dis-Covering the Subject of the 'Great Constitutional Discussion,' 1786–1789," *Journal of American History* 79, no. 3 (1992): 841–73; and Jill Lepore, *The Name of War: King Philip's War and the Origins of American Identity* (New York, 1998). This line of inquiry helped me think about race as involving all members of the society and as closely connected to notions of nationhood and citizenship.

During the 1980s, a number of scholars in literary studies and critical theory began to argue that racial categories—and not just attitudes about them—were, at root, products of history. This debate and parallel discussions about women, gender, and sexuality as categories of historical analysis helped suggest new ways of framing long-running debates about identity and power in history. Particularly useful for me was Barbara Jeanne Fields, who, in "Ideology and Race in American History," in *Region, Race, and Reconstruction*, edited by J. Morgan Kousser and James M. McPherson (New York, 1982), emphasizes that race is constantly performed and reproduced, not an essence but a set of practices that are both contingent and constantly reinvented. One imaginative study is Philip J. Deloria, *Playing Indian* (New Haven, 1998). In some ways, this recent emphasis on performed, rather than essential, identities harkens back to classic sociological studies such as Erving Goffman's *The Presentation of Self in Everyday Life*, revised edition (Garden City, N.Y., 1959), which focuses on class and subject positions. Emphasis on the social construction of identities has allowed scholars to explore the difficult questions of how particular "discourses" of race and gender come into being historically and how disembodied cultural "forces" influence individuals. For me, a particularly useful analysis of gender was Carol F. Karlsen, *The Devil in the Shape of a Woman: Witchcraft in Colonial New England* (New York, 1987). Meanwhile, a burgeoning number of separate studies of women, blacks, Indians, and people of different social classes have prompted ambitious efforts to create a more integrated framework of analysis. A particularly influential example has been Kathleen M. Brown, *Good Wives, Nasty Wenches, and Anxious Patriarchs: Gender, Race, and Power in Colonial Virginia* (Chapel Hill, N.C., 1996). This work has helped me think about the interrelationships of race, gender, and social rank in colonial society. I've been especially interested in ways in which individuals define group boundaries and affinities in relationship to others.

Throughout this project, I have been fascinated by the ways in which racial identities seem to extend, exaggerate, or overlap with other kinds of identities. An important body of work has recently explored the relationships between citizenship, family life, and sexuality. Herbert Gutman, *The Black Family in Slavery and Freedom, 1750–1925* (New York, 1976), effectively rebutted the longstanding argument that slavery had destroyed patriarchal, nuclear families—and helped fuel a debate over whether middle-class Euro-American definitions of family really ought to be held up as a universal standard. In my thinking about the status of slave "marriages," a useful perspective was offered by Michael Warner, *The Trouble with Normal: Sex, Politics, and the Ethics of Queer Life* (New York, 1999). The best recent studies of gender and sexual regulation in New England also consider racial dynamics: Cornelia Hughes Dayton, *Women before the Bar: Gender, Law, and Society in Connecticut, 1639–1798* (Chapel Hill, N.C., 1995), and Sharon Block, *He Said I Must: Coerced Sex in Early America* (Chapel Hill, N.C., forthcoming). Richard Godbeer, *Sexual Revolution in Early America* (Baltimore, 2002), is a useful survey. Recent studies of marriage and the family among New England Indians include Ann Marie Plane's recent *Colonial Intimacies: Indian Marriage in Early New England* (Ithaca, N.Y., 2000) and Daniel Mandell's insightful "Shifting Boundaries of Race and Ethnicity: Indian-Black Intermarriage in Southern New England, 1760–1880," *JAH* 85, no. 2 (1998): 466–501. Meanwhile, Christine Stansell's *City of Women: Sex and Class in New York, 1789–1860* (New York, 1986) exemplified a new interest in multiple class-oriented sexual cultures. For my purposes, Michel Foucault's *The History of Sexuality*, Vol. 1, *An Introduction* (New York, 1978), remains useful for its emphasis on the power dynamics of long-term changes in the meanings of sexual acts and the boundaries of sexual identities—and for his central preoccupation with the modern emergence of sex at the heart of individual and social identity. Gayle S. Rubin, "Thinking Sex: Notes for a Radical Theory of the Politics of Sexuality" (1984), reprinted in *The Lesbian and Gay Studies Reader*, edited by Henry Abelove, Michele Aina Barale, and David M. Halperin (New York, 1993), 3–44, helped me think about early-nineteenth-century associations between racial and sexual disorder.

Military service also played an important role in defining and performing membership in the body politic. Written as part of an intervention in national debates over slavery and black equality, William C. Nell's *The Colored Patriots of the American Revolution* (Boston, 1855) celebrated the contribution of black men in that struggle—a claim that Sidney S. Rider sought to rebut in his *Historical Inquiry Concerning the Attempt to Raise a Regiment of Slaves by Rhode Island during the War of the Revolution* (Providence, 1880). Recently, Sylvia R. Frey, *Water from the Rock: Black Resistance in a Revolutionary Age* (Princeton, N.J., 1991), demonstrated the central role of slaves and free blacks during the war in the Chesapeake region and the Deep South. Benjamin Quarles's *The Negro in the American Revolution* (Chapel Hill, N.C., 1961) remains useful for the northern states. The role of black and Indian soldiers in the war has become easier to reconstruct thanks in part to efforts of local historians and of the Daughters of the American Revolution to identify individual servicemen. Meanwhile, new works have emphasized the process of mobilization, the experience of soldiers, and life on the home front: John Shy, *A People Numerous and Armed: Reflections on the Military Struggle for American Independence*, revised edition (Ann Arbor, Mich., 1990); Robert A. Gross, *The Minutemen and Their World* (New York, 1976); Richard Buel Jr., *Dear Liberty: Connecticut's Mobilization for the Revolutionary War* (Middletown, Conn., 1980). These studies helped me think about the meaning of military service in the context of broader negotiations over manpower and citizenship.

As I worked on this project, I became more interested in the relationship between new ideas of citizenship after the Revolution and contemporary efforts to understand human nature, the body, and racial difference. A classic starting point for exploring the world of eighteenth-century natural history is Antonello Gerbi's *The Dispute of the New World: The History of a Polemic, 1750–1900* (1955), revised edition, translated by Jeremy Moyle (Pittsburgh, 1973). Useful in different ways were Stephen Jay Gould, *The Mismeasure of Man* (New York, 1981), and Nancy Shoemaker, "How Indians Got to Be Red," *AHR* 102, no. 3 (1997): 625–44. Bruce Dain, *A Hideous Monster of the Mind: American Race Theory in the Early Republic* (Cambridge, Mass., 2003), emphasizes that black thinkers were also part of the debate over race and human nature. Another useful analytical model was Thomas Laqueur, *Making Sex: Body and Gender from the Greeks to Freud* (Cambridge, Mass., 1990), which describes a roughly contemporary turn to the body as a source of essential difference between men and women. Carole Pateman's *The Sexual Contract* (Stanford, 1988) is one of many useful works on theories of citizenship and gender in the eighteenth century. My approach has been to focus on specific cases that created crises of interpretation in the early Republic in order to explore the boundaries between emerging scientific discourses and popular knowledge.

These issues lead to the question of the relationship between democracy and white supremacy in America. Over the past generation, political historians have reshaped our understanding of the emergence of a recognizably democratic political culture in the United States. Gordon Wood, *The Radicalism of the American Revolution* (New York, 1992), persuasively argued that the revolution in American politics and society was a much longer and more difficult process than we previously thought. At the same time that political historians argue for an "opening" of American political culture in the early nineteenth century, social historians—such as Paul E. Johnson, *A Shopkeeper's Millennium: Society and Revivals in Rochester, New York, 1815–1837* (New York, 1978)—have documented growing economic stratification, declining opportunities for most northerners, and increasingly self-conscious class divisions. Some of the political tensions that resulted are chronicled in Patrick T. Conley, *Democracy in Decline: Rhode Island's Constitutional Development, 1776–1841* (Providence, 1977). Meanwhile, a third body of scholarship has documented the development of free black communities in the nineteenth-century North. For example, Leonard P. Curry, *The Free Black in Urban America, 1800–1850: The Shadow of a Dream* (Chicago, 1981), documents declining job opportunities for free blacks, increasing geographic segregation, and more explicit political disfranchisement. As C. Vann Woodward argued long ago in *The Strange Career of Jim Crow*, 3d revised edition (New York, 1974), the familiar patterns of American white supremacy were first established in the antebellum North.

Only recently, however, have historians attempted to bring together our understanding of broad changes in political culture and society with new work on free black communities to produce a more dynamic understanding of the relationship between democracy and race in the antebellum North. An ambitious, broad-ranging effort to consider the place of race in the national political culture was Alexander Saxton, *The Rise and Fall of the White Re-*

public: Class Politics and Mass Culture in Nineteenth-Century America (New York, 1990). Most recent studies, such as Roediger's influential *Wages of Whiteness,* have focused more narrowly on the working class and on European immigrants in the antebellum period. Eric Lott, *Love and Theft: Blackface Minstrelsy and the American Working Class* (New York, 1993), usefully focuses on the interplay between fear and fantasy, domination and desire. This body of scholarship on antebellum "whiteness," however, has not fully considered either the role of blacks and Indians in shaping debates about citizenship or connections between longstanding racial hierarchies and broader changes in political culture. Two useful attempts to relate black and white political culture in the early Republic are David Waldstreicher, *In the Midst of Perpetual Fetes: The Making of American Nationalism, 1776–1820* (Chapel Hill, N.C., 1997), and Shane White, "'It was a Proud Day': African Americans, Festivals, and Parades in the North, 1741–1834," *JAH* 81, no. 1 (1994): 13–50. Thinking about these works led me to focus on the case of the Hard Scrabble riot of 1824 as an opportunity to explore changes in political culture and economic possibilities, the development of urban free black communities, and public debates between black, Indian, and white leaders over the nature of the American body politic.

In the end, this book returns to some of the basic questions that inspired Edmund S. Morgan's classic *American Slavery, American Freedom: The Ordeal of Colonial Virginia* (New York, 1975). Morgan provocatively argued that slavery and racism did not *contradict* the lofty principles of the Revolution but instead helped to make the American experiment with republican governance possible. As I have attempted to think about American history in terms of the interactions of Indians and Africans as well as Europeans, I have been struck by the similarities, as well as differences, between the early histories of the North and the South. And, as I continually rediscovered in so many ways, the legacy of the colonial past remains an important part of our increasingly global future.

INDEX

Page numbers in *italics* indicate illustrations and charts.